*Praise for*
# OTHER POWERS

"Once again, Barbara Goldsmith, one of our foremost social historians, has brilliantly woven together a scrupulously documented, vividly written tapestry of an era. She illuminates the years around the Civil War—with incisive new light—with her striking portraits of some of its most dramatic figures."

—ROBERT CARO

"More memorable than a dozen histories, this important book sheds light not only on the past but on the present."  —GLORIA STEINEM

"This fascinating story of a remarkable woman wonderfully illuminates the vagaries of religion, sex, finance, feminism, and publicity in Victorian America."

—ARTHUR SCHLESINGER, JR.

"Engrossing! A beautifully written biography about a remarkable woman who would remain relatively unknown if it weren't for Barbara Goldsmith's resolute and rewarding research."  —GEORGE PLIMPTON

"Wonderfully researched and elegantly written."  —DOMINICK DUNNE

"Barbara Goldsmith's Victoria Woodhull is irresistible. Goldsmith brilliantly and amply explores Woodhull's involvement in the politics of the woman's rights movement, the widespread fad of Spiritualism, the struggle to 'purify' the American soul, and the sensational Beecher-Tilton case, without ever losing track of her heroine. Scrupulously researched and well told, this is a biography guaranteed to keep the reader reading."  —PETER GAY

"An important slice of social history and a mirror held up to the America of our own time. . . . At once a fascinating tale [and] an intimate portrait of a glittering cast of characters."  —MICHAEL BESCHLOSS

"Goldsmith has produced that rarest of books: a scholarly biography that reads like a page-turning novel. . . . The first historically reliable life of one of American history's most unusual and compelling women."  —ELLEN CAROL DUBOIS

"Barbara Goldsmith has pierced the nineteenth century with a golden hatpin. *Other Powers* will change not only the way we look at women's history but the way we look at history, period."  —JANE STANTON HITCHCOCK

"What a great work! I think what Barbara Goldsmith has done is extraordinary—all those layers and the interweaving of politics, spiritualism and suffrage. She has captured the most fascinating period of our history—The American Century—The Woman's Century. A remarkable accomplishment."　　—LYNN SHERR, correspondent, *20/20, ABC News*

"This thoughtful and painstakingly researched account of Woodhull's life will pose a challenge to all of us who take inspiration from U.S. feminist and antislavery traditions. Like Woodhull, this book will be controversial. Like Woodhull, this book will challenge our sense of what it means to live freely, morally, without hypocrisy, and against constraints of class and gender."
　　—PEGGY COOPER DAVIS, author of *Neglected Stories: The Constitution and Family Values*

"Anyone interested in the metaphysical sciences will embrace this compelling account of how women found solace from their earthly struggle through spirit communication. *Other Powers* is a masterfully woven historical record of the passionate fight for political, personal, and spiritual freedom."
　　—MARY T. BROWNE, author of *Love in Action* and *Life After Death*

"Victoria Woodhull has long been a heroine of mine, not least because her life evokes so many of the strange mysteries of the old America. And Barbara Goldsmith has written the first study that is truly worthy of Woodhull—sharp and seductive, yet utterly honest. You will find yourself aroused and instructed by every page of this fascinating book."　　—SEAN WILENTZ, Princeton University

"Thoroughly researched and beautifully written, *Other Powers* is a riveting narrative of the fraud, lust, mortality, and political intrigue of the Civil War and Reconstruction era. Through apt context and intersecting stories, Goldsmith explains how the mid-nineteenth-century American culture produced Victoria Woodhull, Free Love, Spiritualism, and the soap opera of the Beecher-Tilton adultery trial. This is a brilliant synthesis and masterful biographical writing. . . . A wonderful book."　　—JOAN HENDRICK, Trinity College

"Barbara Goldsmith carries us into a remarkable moment of history, when spiritualism, investment, avarice, and women's rights converged, when the futures of the Erie Railroad and the institution of marriage seemed equally vital. With the peerless Victoria Woodhull at the center of her story, she plunges us into a group of men and women who shared little more than their willingness to risk everything to refashion fundamental institutions. Their friendships precipitated crises in the history of sexuality and capitalism. Thoroughly familiar with the written record that her characters left behind, the author writes history with the immediacy of journalism."　　—ANN D. GORDON, editor of *Selected Papers of Elizabeth Cady Stanton and Susan B. Anthony*

# OTHER POWERS

*Victoria Woodhull, 1868. At thirty, she was sent by her spirit guide on a great mission.*

# OTHER POWERS

*The Age of Suffrage,
Spiritualism, and the Scandalous
Victoria Woodhull*

# BARBARA
# GOLDSMITH

**HarperPerennial**
*A Division of HarperCollinsPublishers*

First HarperPerennial edition published 1999.

Designed by Virginia Tan

Library of Congress Cataloging-in-Publication Data
Goldsmith, Barbara.
Other powers : the age of suffrage, spiritualism, and the
scandalous Victoria Woodhull / by Barbara Goldsmith. — 1st ed.
p.    cm.
Originally published: A.A. Knopf, 1998.
Includes bibliographical references and index.
ISBN 0-06-095332-2
1. Woodhull, Victoria C. (Victoria Claflin), 1838–1927.
2. Feminists—United States—Biography.
3. Women—Suffrage—United States—History.
4. Suffragists—United States—History.  I. Title.
[HQ1413.W66G65  1999]
305.42'092—dc21
[B]       97-49464

99 00 01 02 03 ❖/RRD 10 9 8 7 6 5 4 3 2 1

*To my dearest friend*

To preach the doctrine you must live the life.

—VICTORIA WOODHULL

Do as I do. Consult the Spirits.

—COMMODORE CORNELIUS VANDERBILT

Orthodoxy is *my* doxy and heterodoxy is *your* doxy. . . .

—THE REVEREND HENRY WARD BEECHER

# Contents

|  |  |  |
|---|---|---|
| | *Introduction* | XI |
| PROLOGUE | *A Page of History* | 3 |
| ONE | *Born Again in the Lamb's Blood* | 8 |
| TWO | *A Child Without a Childhood* | 18 |
| THREE | *The Spiritual Telegraph* | 28 |
| FOUR | *My Long-Accumulating Discontent* | 38 |
| FIVE | *You Ugly Creature* | 50 |
| SIX | *True Wife* | 63 |
| SEVEN | *Willfully Did Kill* | 72 |
| EIGHT | *God Bless This Trinity* | 84 |
| NINE | *An Accident of Fate* | 96 |
| TEN | *Draw Its Fangs* | 110 |
| ELEVEN | *A Dangerous Man* | 122 |
| TWELVE | *Written in Fire* | 132 |
| THIRTEEN | *To Equal Account* | 142 |
| FOURTEEN | *Consult the Spirits* | 156 |
| FIFTEEN | *We Are Ready. We Are Prepared.* | 172 |
| SIXTEEN | *Soup for Three* | 187 |
| SEVENTEEN | *A Hard Place* | 196 |
| EIGHTEEN | *The Evangel* | 209 |

x           *Contents*

| NINETEEN | *Your Child Is Not My Child* | 219 |
| TWENTY | *The Yawning Edge of Hell* | 232 |
| TWENTY-ONE | *The Woodhull Memorial* | 246 |
| TWENTY-TWO | *Silence, Time, and Patience* | 258 |
| TWENTY-THREE | *The Worst Gang* | 272 |
| TWENTY-FOUR | *This Girl Is a Tramp* | 287 |
| TWENTY-FIVE | *Yes! I Am a Free Lover!* | 298 |
| TWENTY-SIX | *A Heavy Load* | 310 |
| TWENTY-SEVEN | *Mrs. Satan* | 324 |
| TWENTY-EIGHT | *Burst Like a Bombshell* | 337 |
| TWENTY-NINE | *I Can Endure No Longer* | 349 |
| THIRTY | *What Have We Done Now?* | 360 |
| THIRTY-ONE | *A Monstrous Conspiracy* | 374 |
| THIRTY-TWO | *Human Hyenas* | 389 |
| THIRTY-THREE | *Daniel in the Lion's Den* | 405 |
| THIRTY-FOUR | *A Meteor's Dash* | 419 |
| THIRTY-FIVE | *The Last Enemy* | 432 |
| | *Abbreviations* | 449 |
| | *Notes* | 451 |
| | *Bibliography* | 495 |
| | *Acknowledgments* | 515 |
| | *Index* | 517 |

# Introduction

"DO AS I DO. Consult the Spirits!" Commodore Vanderbilt told a *Tribune* reporter in 1870, when asked how he'd made his millions. Then he added, concerning the stock of the Central Pacific Railroad, "It's bound to go up. . . . Mrs. Woodhull said so in a trance."

Two decades ago I came across this exchange in connection with a book I was writing on the Vanderbilt family. I had no idea what it meant, though it piqued my curiosity. Soon afterward I discovered that the Commodore was a dedicated Spiritualist, one of an estimated 10 million or so in the United States in the post–Civil War decade. Also, I learned that "Mrs. Woodhull," another dedicated Spiritualist, was the notorious Victoria Woodhull, whom a tabloid referred to in 1872 as "The Prostitute Who Ran for President."

These fragmentary details led me to look further into the connection between Vanderbilt and Woodhull and especially into Spiritualism. From the study of Spiritualism, I was inevitably led to the woman's rights movement, both before and after the Civil War, for one of the many ways women managed to relieve the burdens imposed upon their gender was by seeking empowerment through the spirits. Not all members of the woman's rights movement were Spiritualists, but woman's rights were inseparable from Spiritualism.

What interested me most was how the social and sexual mores, the pressures and events of that time, affected these people, particularly women. I have relied mainly on such primary sources as letters, diaries, conversations recorded in shorthand, the public and private writings of the principals concerned, trial transcripts, and, of course, the newspapers of the day. In 1870, there were thirty-five daily newspapers in New York and another eighteen in Brooklyn. The papers of those icons of the woman's movement, Elizabeth Cady Stanton and Susan B. Anthony, are contained in 110 reels of microfilm that I have been fortunate enough to live with for the past few years. Much of the research for this book has been culled from the thousands upon thou-

*Victoria presents* The Woodhull Memorial *to Congress, January 11, 1871.*

sands of pages of brittle, yellowing trial transcripts: the Great Vanderbilt Will Contest; the case brought by Roxanna Hummel Claflin, Victoria Woodhull's vengeful mother, against Victoria's second husband, Colonel James Blood; the murder trials of Daniel McFarland, Hester Vaughn, Edward (Ned) Stiles Stokes; and, especially, the trial involving the distinguished journalist Theodore Tilton, who sued the leading churchman of his day, Henry Ward Beecher, for having seduced his wife.

The Beecher-Tilton Scandal Trial, as it came to be known, captured the imagination of the American public much as the O. J. Simpson trial has in our time. For two years, it dominated headlines and was exhaustively analyzed in private homes, public auditoriums, and pulpits throughout the nation, as well as in several books. Although the trial seemingly revolved around an alleged seduction, it also raised in the most vivid way the issue of sexual relations at that time and the role of church and state in defining and regulating these relations.

As I was led deeper and deeper into the world of Victorian America, I was surprised to find that many of the books I read, especially the biographies, had little to say about the larger historical context surrounding their subjects. To see how the people and events associated with Victoria Woodhull interacted, I created, with the help of a computer, a chronology that eventually extended to four hundred pages. From this I was able to see what the various characters, whose lives intersected with Victoria's, were doing and often thinking at specific times. People who seemed in the books I'd read to dwell in separate worlds could now be seen as parts of a larger drama. This inevitably led to a better understanding of the texture of the age and the lives of women than I had previously encountered.

Major events in this book have, of course, been previously recorded. The Civil War draft riots, the collapse of the gold market on Black Friday, September 24, 1869, the impeachment proceedings against President Andrew Johnson, have been treated in numerous books. My contribution, I believe, was to look at these and similar events through the lives of some of the people involved, a process that was both enlightening and arduous because the relevant materials were not easily found.

Some of the documents that proved most valuable to me have only recently become of interest to historians. Lists of household furnishings, descriptions of food, the wardrobe of a "woman of society," helped me grasp the quality of these lives. Such details as Catharine Beecher's numbingly precise instructions on how to press a shirt, involving the use of some twenty items, brought the ritualistic drudgery of domestic existence into sharp relief.

In many of the books I read, particularly those of the period, important material that revealed the actual character of these people had been expurgated. For example, the letters of Susan B. Anthony were altered by her official biographer, Ida Husted Harper, to make her seem decorous and pure, rather than the direct, insightful person she undoubtedly was. Pages from Anthony's diary relating to the sexual excesses and blackmail schemes of Victoria Woodhull and her sister, Tennessee Claflin, were ripped out and destroyed by Harper, as were the pages relating to the crucial controversy of this book. Harper boasted that she kept a bonfire going for a week with just such unacceptable material. Fortunately, from the letters of Anthony's colleagues and friends that refer to these missing pages, I was able to reconstruct much of what Harper suppressed. Again and again, in the letters I quote, one finds the directive "Burn this!" Fortunately, we are the beneficiaries of the repeated failure to obey this command.

Perhaps the most startling discovery was the extent to which Spiritualism and the inception of woman's rights were intertwined. At a time when women had no power to achieve equal rights, they relied on the "other powers" provided by Spiritualism to sustain their efforts. Through the mouths of trance speakers came words of wisdom from long-dead seers, and from the spirits came the courage to go forward. The rise of Spiritualism coincided with Samuel B. Morse's invention of the telegraph, an invisible means of communication, and expanded at a time when a devastating war had imposed the unbearable loss of husbands, sons, and lovers.

The Spiritualist influence on Victoria Woodhull has in most accounts of her life been largely dismissed or ignored. But as Victoria herself said, to tell her life without her spirits would be "as if you were writing *Hamlet* and decided to leave out his father's ghost." I can unequivocally say that Victoria Woodhull's belief in the spirits and their great powers was genuine. This belief shaped her life and informed her existence. The title bestowed on her in her heyday, the "Joan of Arc of the Woman's Movement," was apt, for there is no doubt that she too heard the voices that defined her mission.

My research on Victoria Woodhull was complicated by the fact that after she was forced to flee to England in 1877, she forged many documents in order to obscure her past. In some of these bogus documents she changed her own name as well as the names of her relatives and assigned them reputable occupations and royal ancestry. More reliable are the materials available in this country. In newspaper, family, and court archives, I have been able to obtain such rare documents as the original indictment brought against Tennessee Claflin for manslaughter and the papers of Victoria's second husband, Colonel James Blood, relating his service in the Sixth Missouri Regiment during the Civil War.

It has been deeply rewarding to come to know Victoria Woodhull, and I am grateful for the opportunity to share this knowledge with my readers. I have endeavored to supply some of the historical context in which Victoria and the women of her era struggled, for without this setting, her career, indeed her entire life, would seem merely eccentric or even aberrant. The religious ferment that accompanied the so-called second Great Awakening and the movements it spawned—temperance, abolition, and the struggle for woman's equality with man—is at the heart of this story.

Victoria Woodhull achieved her brief renown in a world where the most famous preacher in America, Henry Ward Beecher, was said to preach to "at least twenty of his mistresses every Sunday" but a woman wore a "scarlet letter" for the act of adultery. This was a world where prostitution was a widely accepted social custom, wives were considered property, unwanted infants were wrapped in rags and deposited on doorsteps or in the river, and working women made barely enough to keep themselves alive. In this world Hester Vaughn lay in a pool of blood next to the frozen corpse of her newborn child, and Abby Sage McFarland saw her former husband murder her fiancé and be acquitted by an all-male jury.

In this society, Victoria Woodhull pictured herself as "the evangel," but she was, in fact, a woman before her time. Her views on marriage and divorce and the sexual equality she called "free love" are relevant today. Her spirit is with us still.

# OTHER POWERS

# A PAGE OF HISTORY

MAY 5, 1892: As the delegates to the National American Woman Suffrage Association convention filed into the Auditorium Theatre in Chicago, they found on the seats a leather-bound pamphlet titled "A Page of History." On the first page was an announcement that Victoria Woodhull would run for president of the United States against Grover Cleveland and Benjamin Harrison. The rest was a compendium of extravagant praise from such leaders of the woman's rights movement as Susan B. Anthony, who called Victoria a "bright, glorious, young and strong spirit"; Elizabeth Cady Stanton, who predicted, "In the annals of emancipation the name [Victoria Woodhull] will have its own high place as a deliverer"; and Paulina Wright Davis, who said, "I believe you were raised up of God to do wonderful work and I believe you will unmask the hypocrisy of a class that none others dare touch." Isabella Beecher Hooker lent the religiosity for which her family was famous by stating that Victoria was "Heaven sent for the rescue of woman from the pit of subjection." What the pamphlet did not say was that this praise had been written a quarter of a century earlier.

The following day, about a dozen reporters waited impatiently in Parlor K of the Wellington Hotel for Victoria Woodhull's press conference to begin. It had been scheduled for ten, but by eleven she still had not appeared. In order to placate the newsmen who were threatening to leave, her husband, John Biddulph Martin, the wealthy head of a family-owned bank in London, ordered the waiters to serve whiskey and ham sandwiches. Thus they were standing about eating and drinking when Victoria swept into the room holding the arm of her sister, Tennessee, now Lady Cook, Viscountess of Montserrat. They were dressed identically, in blue velvet gowns trimmed with Venetian lace. Victoria wore her trademark white rose at her throat, just as she had done twenty years earlier, when she had first run for the United States presidency. The sisters made a stunning pair: At fifty-four Victoria retained the fine, chiseled features and ramrod posture that reminded some of her admirers of Queen Victoria. At forty-six, Tennessee was still an ivory-skinned beauty with red hair and a delicate cleft chin.

Victoria Woodhull Martin greeted each of the reporters and then announced that her nomination was sponsored by the NAWSA. She said she had composed a letter of acceptance that would be distributed at the end of the conference and added, "If my political campaign for the Presidency is not successful, in fact, it will be educational for women."

Actually, both Martin and his wife knew that this was a costly but hopeless campaign, but they didn't care. They were interested not in American politics but in British society. John Martin was convinced, even if his British friends were skeptical, that his wife had once been the respected leader of the woman's rights movement in America. If she could recapture that position now and prove it, with scrapbooks full of praise from the American press, then Martin might be able to convince his social peers, who had long shunned and reviled his American wife, that the scandalous rumors surrounding her were merely the spiteful gossip of misinformed bigots.

Though few Americans any longer remembered who Victoria Woodhull was, her old antagonist Lucy Stone, the Boston woman's rights leader who was in Chicago for the convention, could never forget. She felt that two decades earlier, Victoria had almost wrecked the movement. The following day, when Lucy read of Victoria's press conference, she called one of her own and told the reporters, "The statement that Mrs. Biddulph Martin is our candidate for president is wholly without foundation. We have no presidential candidate, and we do not even know the persons who are said to have nominated her."

After Stone's statement, the younger members of the NAWSA ridiculed Victoria's claim. Many of them denounced her as a self-aggrandizing charlatan who had long since been abandoned by the movement. These women assumed the endorsements were bogus, and one representative, Mary Frost Ormsby, sent her copy to Susan B. Anthony and wrote, "Knowing your love of *truth* and *justice* . . . I take the liberty of sending this out to you. . . . I was deceived by Mrs. Martin into the belief she was a philanthropist and an honest woman. My eyes are now opened, I know to the contrary." There is no record that the seventy-two-year-old Anthony replied to Mrs. Ormsby, but she carefully pasted Ormsby's letter in her scrapbook. It would have been difficult for Anthony to explain to someone of Mrs. Ormsby's generation that the praise of Victoria Woodhull, attributed to her and the others, was genuine.

In his effort to influence the NAWSA delegates, John Martin suggested contacting Isabella Beecher Hooker, the eminent Spiritualist, woman's rights advocate, and member of the prestigious Beecher family, who had written Victoria that she would be in Chicago for the convention. To her husband's surprise, Victoria said she wanted nothing to do with Mrs. Hooker. Martin protested. Hadn't she told him that Isabella was her closest American friend, the one who had supported her in what she referred to as her "Gethsemane"? Still Victoria was adamant.

Two days later, hoping to find a strong ally, John Martin, without his wife's knowledge, arranged to meet Isabella Beecher Hooker in a parlor off the main lobby of the Sherman House. He was accompanied by a male secretary who recorded the ensuing conversation in shorthand, and later typed it. At seventy, Isabella was frail, suffered from arthritis and had trouble hearing, but she was still prominent in the movement. After a brief exchange of pleasantries, Martin said, "Mrs. Hooker, I am glad Mrs. Martin is not here. Some things are easier to say outside of her presence. My wife does not seem to recollect why it is that her work of twenty years ago on the suffrage movement has been forgotten while her attack on your brother Henry Ward Beecher is not forgotten."

Of course Isabella knew the answer to John Martin's question, but she would not tell him about his wife's catastrophic involvement with her brother, the great Brooklyn preacher, which had led to Victoria's imprisonment and exile. Instead she changed the subject and recalled a happier time a quarter of a century earlier when Isabella first saw Victoria Woodhull standing against a corridor wall of the Capitol building in Washington, nervously waiting to address a joint session of Congress, an honor that had been awarded to no other woman.

"Her dress was peculiar," commented Isabella.

"How so?" asked Martin.

"She wore a felt hat such as men wear. When she rose to speak I thought she would have fainted. Her face flushed in patches. I was fascinated by Mrs. Woodhull."

How could John Martin understand that fascination and all that had happened as a result? And who would have thought that what started with Victoria's assertion of equal rights for women would eventually cause them both to become reviled outcasts? "You know Mrs. Henry Ward Beecher is writing recollections of my brother in a Philadelphia paper in which I am treated unkindly," she said.

"I know this is a painful subject," replied Martin, who seemed concerned only for Victoria. "But you know that my wife was attacked in Henry Ward Beecher's biography. I tell you plainly we will have it all out, come what may to any of his family."

Turning his threat aside, Isabella continued to recall the tangled past. "My brother Henry called on me to denounce Victoria. I refused. I said that I knew nothing against her and all that I knew of my own knowledge was in her favor. Then my friends began to fall away. I was estranged from my family. My daughter, now in Heaven, told me I had no right to imperil my husband's life for the sake of Mrs. Woodhull. Because I would not denounce her they tried to make me out insane. I was left alone. Quite alone. No one can tell what I suffered." The secretary's notes of the conversation are so precise that one almost hears her despairing voice.

John Martin replied, "You forget, Mrs. Hooker, what my wife suffered."

Isabella chose not to answer this accusation, but said wearily, "All this is an old story. Mrs. Martin forgets how long she has been away from America. If she wants supporters for her campaign she should spend ten thousand dollars and put out a special edition of *The Arrow,* the great organ of the Spiritualists. They will support her."

Abandoning his efforts to win Isabella over, Martin replied with evident annoyance, "I will tell her what you say, but after this interview it is hardly necessary that you should meet with her." With this he dismissed Isabella, the loyal friend who had once stood with Victoria on what appeared to be the brink of a new world.

Despite his failure to recruit Mrs. Hooker, John Martin persisted. He arranged to meet with Joseph R. Dunlop, the publisher of the *Chicago Mail,* and asked him to run an article in his newspaper about Victoria Woodhull and what she had done for women. Dunlop obliged. On May 8, 1892, an article appeared, "Tennie and Her Vickie," which began mildly enough, "The Woodhull and Claflin campaign for the presidency is being launched and delegates have arrived in Chicago to participate in the convention in which the gentle Victoria is to be nominated." But the *Mail* added that when Victoria and her sister, Tennessee, lived in Chicago they operated "a *house* in a grand and peculiar style" and practiced spurious fortune-telling and healing techniques. Their mother, Roxanna (Roxy) Claflin, was described as a bogus fortune-teller. Their father, Reuben (Buck) Claflin, was a charlatan and a thief. The article concluded, "And all America knows that Victoria Woodhull was solely responsible for the greatest scandal of the century."

Victoria told her husband that these "lies" were ruining her health and threatening her life. Would she never be free of her malicious enemies? The day after the *Mail* printed its story, John Martin appeared, over his wife's objections, at the Cook County Circuit Court and lodged a suit against Dunlop and the *Mail* for $100,000 in damages.

Undaunted, on May 10, Dunlop ran another article stating that Tennessee Celeste Claflin, though now a titled English lady, was still under indictment in Ottawa, Illinois, on a charge of manslaughter dating back to 1863. "It was so long ago. It was another world," Tennessee told John Martin by way of explanation. Evidently, all of this proved too much for the conservative banker. He dropped the case against Dunlop and the *Mail* and took Victoria and Tennessee back to New York, where they boarded the *Persian Monarch* to Southampton.

But who was Victoria Woodhull? John Martin knew her in only one of her many roles, as the adored wife who shared his life. But she was also the Spiritualist, the "high priestess" of free love, the crusading editor, the San Francisco actress and part-time prostitute, the founder of the first stock brokerage firm for women, the disciple of Karl Marx, the blackmailer, the presidential candidate, the sinner, the saint.

She had been all of these and more, for in her many aspects she combined in abundance many of the influences that shaped the women of her world. Her compassion for their suffering was the most persistent and most genuine of her feelings, and Victoria never stopped believing that the spirits had brought her into the world to lead a "social revolution." She said that from her birth, and even before, she had been marked for this fate. As a Spiritualist and a clairvoyant, she claimed to remember every event in her life, even to the moment of her conception, even to her birth when her mother clasped her to her breast and "the look of pain and anguish . . . was burnt into my plastic brain as she suckled me."

# CHAPTER ONE

# BORN AGAIN IN THE LAMB'S BLOOD

Roxy Claflin stood on the frozen, rutted road, shivering in her threadbare calico dress as the late December winds lashed the frosted fields of Homer, Ohio, and resolutely awaited the messenger of God. When at last the black-cloaked rider, whom she had seen in one of her visions, thundered past on his mud-spattered black horse, she felt the beginning of exaltation. She would be reborn as fresh to creation as Eve.

In 1837, in the farm towns of Ohio, most religious revivals occurred in the long, dormant period from winter to spring. As if summoned by an unseen force, the isolated farmers, storekeepers, and laborers assembled in remote barns and churches to yield themselves up in pain and ecstasy, to obliterate themselves, to emerge, born again, from a crucible of fire. This young nation was ruled externally by its government but internally by rigorous Calvinist doctrine. Those who denied God's power were no more free of His iron hand than those who affirmed it. In these years heaven and hell were awesomely present, and revivals swept the nation. But the old Puritan faith that prescribed harsh laws of predestination and infant damnation had begun to yield to the less stringent "new Calvinism" of the kind preached by the great Lyman Beecher, who proclaimed that, through conversion, one could forge one's own destiny. If men and women chose a life of virtue, both they and their offspring might be spared damnation. Beecher's new, gentler Calvinism was intended to save souls for his church, for he knew that the world was changing, and no longer were people content to be consigned to an immutable place in society or in the hereafter over which they had no control. In nearby Cincinnati, Beecher preached this doctrine at revivals over the objections of the Presbyterian Church Synod.

In October 1835, the synod charged Lyman Beecher with heresy. At his trial, Beecher's twenty-two-year-old son, Henry Ward, stood by his side, handing him the books and other documents to which he referred in his defense. According to contemporary accounts, Lyman Beecher's defense was so equivocal and protracted that the weary church synod disbanded before it got around to asking his opinion on predestination. Later, when he too began to preach, Henry Ward Beecher would learn to follow his father's example of shading the truth to save his popularity, if not his soul.

Henry Ward Beecher was the fourth and dullest of Lyman's six sons. His mother, the former Roxanna Foote, was a brilliant, lighthearted woman who died when Henry was three. In a sermon, he would recall that as a child he had not even one toy. In school, Henry's slow wits and his stammer brought punishment. Often he was confined to the girls' corner, where he sat on a stool for hours at a time wearing a peaked paper dunce cap. Yet he laughed easily and knew how to flatter and charm.

At fourteen, Henry was sent to the Mount Pleasant Classical Institution in Amherst, Massachusetts, where he met Constantine Fondolaik, whose parents had been killed by the Turks in the massacre of 1822. Henry saw Constantine as "a young Greek God" and wrote, "We are connected by a love which *cannot* be broken." At nineteen, both young men were sent to Amherst College, and Henry declared, "We will love and watch over one another, seeking by all means in our power to aid and make each other happy." Throughout his life Henry Ward was able to feel such love for both the men and women who attracted him. As for Constantine, he died fifteen years later of cholera. Henry named his third son in memory of his dear companion.

In May of his freshman year at Amherst, Henry met Eunice Bullard, the daughter of a stern doctor who lived near Worcester, Massachusetts. Dr. Bullard discouraged his daughter's high spirits and gave her a strict Puritan upbringing. Once, when she appeared at the dining room table in a low-cut silk dress, her enraged father remarked that she must be cold, then picked up a tureen of soup and flung it at her. After a two-year sporadic courtship, Henry bought Eunice an engagement ring for which he paid 85 cents. That done, for the next three years he saw Eunice only twice. His constant companion, however, was Constantine, and on school vacations they traveled around the country demonstrating phrenology, the new so-called science that showed how the size and shape of the skull defined character and intelligence. At last, after a six-year, on-and-off-again courtship, Henry and Eunice were married.

Twenty-six-year-old Henry Ward Beecher secured his first pastorate as minister of the Second Presbyterian Church in Indianapolis in May 1839. It was a poor congregation, and the parish house was only ten feet wide. Eunice said the bedroom was so small that she was "obliged to make the bed

*Eunice Bullard, 1837. Henry bought her
an engagement ring for 85 cents.*

*Henry Ward Beecher, the fiery young
preacher at twenty-six*

on one side first, then go out on the veranda, raise a window, reach in and make the bed on the other side." They had arrived in the midst of a malaria epidemic, which Henry knew about but had not disclosed to his pregnant wife for fear she would not agree to the move. Soon Eunice came down with the disease and gave birth to a stillborn child. Her next child died at fifteen months.

In the five years that followed this death, Eunice aged prematurely from the effects of her repeated pregnancies but produced three living children. By then her husband had become a fiery revivalist preacher and had discovered that he could reach souls through raw emotion in a way that he never could do through intellect alone. He conducted revivals throughout Ohio and Indiana. In the woods near Terre Haute he whipped his audience into such a frenzy that he was able to bring a thousand men, women, and children into the fold in a single day. This burgeoning new country provided fertile ground for the second wave of what was known as the Great Awakening. So fiery was the spirit of revival that upstate New York and New England, where it was strongest, came to be called the Burned-Over District.

Beecher preached to a country on the brink of a dramatic change, both economic and ideological. John Deere had just invented the steel plow. The Pitts brothers had patented the first steam-powered threshing machine. The first transatlantic crossing by steamship was about to take place. Yet the "peculiar institution" of slavery still fueled the economy of the South, and even in the North abolitionism was not yet popular or safe. In 1837, Elijah Lovejoy, an Illinois editor who attacked slavery, was met by an enraged mob who smashed his presses. As he tried to prevent them from setting fire to his warehouse, Lovejoy was shot dead. Wendell Phillips, the twenty-six-year-old scion of a wealthy and prestigious Boston family, had been drifting through life as a dilettante lawyer. He was so affected by Lovejoy's death that he decided to dedicate himself to continuing this man's mission to free the slaves.

In Abolition Hall on Sixth Street in Philadelphia, Angelina Grimké spoke of the senseless death of Lovejoy and urged the immediate emancipation of the slaves. She condemned "a respectable woman of Charleston" who, during recent revivals, held thrice-daily devotions in the same room that only hours before had been filled with the screams of her slaves as she lashed them with cowhide. Grimké stood her ground while the audience smashed every window in the hall. The next day the mob returned to the hall and burned it down. They then proceeded to Thirteenth Street and set fire to African Hall, a Negro orphanage.

*Henry and Eunice with two sons. Eunice aged prematurely,
as she had nine children and five miscarriages.*

This was an age in which men were free to treat women with the same detached cruelty as they did their slaves. For women, regardless of class, marriage meant the surrender of every right to property and person. A woman's wages were given directly to her husband. If she sought a divorce her husband was legally entitled to sole custody of the children. Women had no legal rights to the disposition of their personal possessions upon death. Women could not testify in court or serve on a jury and were barred from universities, law schools, and medical schools. Women could not vote.

No laws protected a woman from physical abuse at the hands of her husband or father unless such abuse resulted in death, though a few states stipulated the size of the instruments that might be used to inflict punishment. One judge upheld the right of a husband to beat his wife, writing that to do otherwise would "disrupt domestic harmony." A wife's body was to be used at her husband's will; she could not deny him sexual access. If she ran away, the law of the nation supported her recapture and return. The United States followed Sir William Blackstone, the authority on English common law, who held that "the husband and wife are one, and that one is the husband."

Women's lives were an endless round of pregnancy, childbearing, and domestic duties. They worked hard and died young. In the East in the year 1837, women worked in more than one hundred low-paying industrial occupations. The recently invented spinning jenny and the power loom provided employment in factories where women worked for fifteen or sixteen hours a day, for which the wage was $3 a week. In the West, in addition to their domestic duties, women often worked beside their men at hard manual labor. The other occupations that yielded money to women were severely limited: teaching, midwifery, prostitution, and, for the select few, writing.

The church supported this repression. The doctrine of John Calvin preached that Eve had caused the expulsion from Eden, that women brought sin into the world and thus condemned all "mankind" thereafter to toil and suffering. The marriage ceremony, a sacrament of the church, specified the word *obey.* From the pulpit, male ministers laid down the laws of personal conduct for women and declared themselves the sole intermediary between God and human beings.

But by the late 1830s the old Calvinist belief that one's fate was predestined and the doctrine of infant damnation were becoming increasingly intolerable, particularly to women of all classes. At a time when one in every two babies died, women were sorely in need of solace, the promise of salvation, and a better world beyond. The loosening of the old Calvinist grip on the American religious psyche was typified by Henry Ward Beecher, who took the more permissive doctrine of his father, Lyman, to an extreme. Henry Ward's revivalist preaching was a cauldron of emotionalism compared to the steely Puritanism it was displacing. To Victoria Woodhull's mother—the ignorant, deprived Roxy Claflin—revival offered up the hope that if only she could yield her soul up to God, she would, by her own will, be saved.

The life of Roxy Claflin, born Roxanna Hummel, was crude and harsh. Illegitimate, poor, uneducated, brutalized, she enjoyed the unintended benefit of being free of the constraints of respectable society, free to find her own lonely, superstitious way. Years later, the proper ladies of the East and the titled ladies of Europe would inquire of Roxy Claflin's daughters, Victoria and Tennessee, about their antecedents, and over the years the family history grew more illustrious: Roxanna was the daughter of a wealthy Dutchman. Roxanna was a descendant of Pocahontas. In Roxanna's veins flowed "the royal blood of Germany." Eventually, Victoria Woodhull proclaimed that the family was descended from Alexander Hamilton and George Washington.

What was the truth? A *Hartford Courant* reporter once asked Roxy where she came from, and she replied, "Nowhere." She was squat and fat, with stubby legs, and spoke with a thick German accent. She could neither read nor write. A common rumor was that Roxy was the illegitimate daughter of Captain Jake Hummel, a German immigrant who owned a tavern, The Rising Sun, in Hummel's Wharf, Pennsylvania. But it was also said that Captain Jake had simply taken the name Hummel from the town itself, which had been named for much older settlers. Another tale was that Roxy was the illegitimate daughter of "a real Hummel" mother and that her father was Simon Snyder, a three-term governor of Pennsylvania, who had farmed her out to the local tavern keeper.

It is known that at thirteen Roxy Hummel was working as a maid in Selinsgrove, Pennsylvania, in the home of Governor Simon Snyder's son John, a rich rake with a love of horseflesh and women. Once, John had served as best man at a friend's wedding, and when the ceremony was over he plunked the new bride in his carriage and sped off with her to Utica, New York. Several months later he brought her back, but when her husband refused to accept his belated and pregnant bride, John installed her in his own household, where she lived with her illegitimate daughter, whom John named Utica. John Snyder remained a bachelor all his life. Their status brought no stigma in this free-wheeling town with twenty taverns to every church, where stolid middle-class Methodists rubbed elbows with roisterers and gamblers.

On a June morning in 1824, Reuben Buckman "Buck" Claflin galloped into Selinsgrove with a string of jet-black horses that, after several scrubbings, turned out not to be black at all. No one doubted that Buck was a horse thief who had hastily disguised his booty, but this only enhanced his reputation. Buck was callous, cold, cruel, and smart, all traits that John Snyder found handy. He promptly hired this horse thief to run his private racing stable. Together, they gambled and drank and visited brothels. The pounding of hooves at dawn often marked the reckless riders' passage home.

Buck came from East Troy, Pennsylvania, where the fractious Claflin brood, who were famous for their strength and cunning, had built a timber cabin and carved out a crude farm in the dense pine wilderness. This was cruel country where hard work yielded a meager existence. Buck's brother

Carrington could shoulder a 283-pound barrel of salt from the Eagle Hotel to the Sugar Creek Bridge, a quarter mile away, and back again. But the brilliant, erratic Buck had little use for manual labor. He taught himself to read and write and had a natural aptitude for mathematics. As an adult, he read law with a local attorney but was too restless to stick to a desk job. He traveled from one settlement to another, playing cards, betting on horse races, and trading horses. When Buck arrived in Selinsgrove with his string of stolen horses, he was twenty-eight, tall and lanky, with an unkempt beard and a prominent nose already covered with a red web of broken capillaries. He wore a black patch over his right eye. Some said he lost his eye in a childhood accident; others that it had been poked out in retribution for an unpaid gambling debt.

The towns along the Susquehanna River swarmed with rough raftsmen. Buck thrived in this atmosphere, taking the suckers for their cash with a crafty cut of the cards (it was said that he could remember the order of every card in the deck) or some other confidence scam. When he lost at the races, sometimes he paid his debts with counterfeit money. One sheriff caught him holding a counterfeit $20 bill, but Buck stuffed the evidence in his mouth and swallowed it.

At John Snyder's, Buck was given a room next to Roxy Hummel's. In December 1825 they were married. Four months later Margaret Ann was born. John Snyder said Margaret Ann might be his daughter, since Roxy had served both his own and Buck's sexual needs. If indeed both Roxy and John were the issue of Governor Simon Snyder, the incestual implications of impregnating her seemed not to trouble him. Such was the casualness with which these matters were treated.

During the day in these river towns, men congregated in the carnival atmosphere of horse races and horse sales. At night they crowded the taverns to drink, gamble, and brawl till dawn. As the men amused themselves, their women, whom they liked to call their "chore horses," would spend what little money they had to buy a bit of hope. Buck put Roxy to work telling fortunes in temporary tents where the ground was covered with sawdust, damp from tobacco juice. When the women crossed Roxy's palm with their pennies, she would comfort them with her visions. She assured bereft mothers that their dead infants were happy in the bosom of the Lord.

Roxy's nervous energy and superstitious nature assisted her. She would fall into a trance, and with the help of the spirit of the Virgin Mary, whom in her broken English she called "the holy mudder in Israel," would speak of what had been and what was to come. On days when the force seized her, Roxy would run to a hilltop and shout to God to forgive her sins and those of her neighbors, which she would then reveal at the top of her lungs. Buck was said to make use of these revelations in his blackmail schemes.

As Buck traveled from one Pennsylvania river town to another, his wife and family trailed along. They moved to Troy, to Beech Creek, to Glen Union, to Sinnemahoning (which local folk said should simply be called Sin, since there wasn't much else there). Buck ran a tavern and worked on riverboats. Usually he stayed in one place just long enough to clean up and clear out.

In eleven years of wandering, Roxanna Claflin gave birth to six children. Two girls, Delia and Odessa, died in infancy. The surviving girls were Margaret Ann and Polly; the boys, Maldon and Hebern. In 1837, Buck and Roxanna arrived in Homer, Ohio, their pockets bulging with cash from Buck's various scams. They put all their money down on a ramshackle one-bedroom frame house with wild bittersweet vines climbing over the broken-down porch. Behind the house was an untended apple orchard and, across the field, a gristmill with a flowing millrace. Roxanna, with no friends and no company except her children and her spirit visions, waited as she did each year for the revivalist preacher to come and set up his tent for what would be a winter-long series of ecstatic meetings.

To women repressed in every way, the release provided by a revival was intense. The line between religious and sexual ecstasy was often crossed in the excitement. The Reverend John Humphrey Noyes, a New England preacher, was among the first to recognize this phenomenon, especially among women. "Religious love is a very near neighbor to sexual love and they always get mixed in the intimacies and social excitements of revivals," he wrote. "Hence these wild experiments and terrible disasters."

Noyes first encountered this unacknowledged sexuality in the revival experience as a young minister. In February 1837, he preached at a revival in Brimfield, Massachusetts, and watched with chagrin as the power of his words loosed a flood of emotion. Prim young maidens in the congregation fell "into a state of frenzy over which I could exercise no control," he wrote. That night Noyes, sensing that he had triggered a dangerous force, fled Brimfield and trudged through the snow until he reached his father's house, sixty miles away in Putney, Vermont.

After his departure, two of the young women, Mary Lincoln and Maria Brown, found their way to the bed of the Reverend Simon Lovett "and suffered themselves to be taken in the act." When Mary's father, a respected physician, heard of her sin he cast her out of his house and she fled to the home of her friend Flavilla Howard. Within hours, many other young women flocked to Flavilla's home "to praise the Lord, to sing and dance and kiss each other in a frantic way." Dr. Lincoln arrived to reclaim his daughter, but Mary would not go with him. She cried out that her father was possessed by a devil and "smote him on the face in order to cast it out."

The following day, after prophesying that Brimfield was to be burned to the ground in a great conflagration as described in Genesis, Mary and Flavilla fled the anticipated "fiery hail." It was past midnight when these two stumbled into an isolated farmhouse begging shelter. They were barefoot and naked. Mary's toes were so frozen that several had to be amputated. For over a week it was thought that the girls would die of exposure but they survived and, with the revival spirit gone out of them, meekly returned to Brimfield.

Seven hundred miles from Brimfield, on Christmas Eve of the same year, 1837, Roxy Claflin was caught up in the third night of a turbulent Methodist revival. Outside the night was frigid, but inside the hastily constructed tent it was warm with the heat of bodies as they swayed and prayed and called out to the preacher, who conjured up visions of souls writhing in hell. The Calvinist conversion in Brimfield and this Methodist revival in Ohio provided an identical ritualistic transformation. First came the proclamation of sin—the filth and evil clinging to the human soul. Then the mounting fear and terror—the look into the abyss. Then the casting of oneself upon God's mercy—the throwing off of all personality in abject surrender of self. Finally, in heightened consciousness and new understanding, the cleansed soul emerged.

Driven by the preacher's fiery words, Roxy rose from the bench, her face damp with sweat. She swayed in place, then moved into the aisle and, clasping her hands together in front of her face, began to spin round and round, twisting and turning in torment until the bonnet tumbled from her head and, held by its strings, bounced along behind her. "Glory hallelujah," she shouted, and, as her frenzy grew, "Clasp me to you," "Save me," and "I am coming to you." Her eyes glazed over, and she began to babble in tongues. A staccato cacophony of unintelligible syllables spilled from her lips amid a white foam of spittle until she fell to the ground and cried out, "I am born again in the Lamb's blood!"

Buck pulled his wife to her feet and dragged her to the back of the tent, where he threw her down behind a sturdy bench, pulled her skirt over her head, and forced himself into her. All around them people were falling to the ground, groaning, crawling, barking like dogs. Religious ecstasy and sexual fervor became as a single flame, sweeping the revival. And thus, according to her own account, was Victoria Woodhull conceived.

CHAPTER TWO

# A CHILD WITHOUT
# A CHILDHOOD

As the nineteen-year-old Queen Victoria read *Oliver Twist,* thereby learning for the first time of the "squalid vice" and "starvation in the workhouses and schools" of her own realm, far away in Homer, Ohio, on September 23, 1838, Roxanna Claflin gave birth to her seventh child and named her for the queen, whose coronation had taken place that year. Three more children followed: Utica in 1841 (named for the illegitimate daughter of Roxy's former employer and perhaps half-brother, John Snyder); a nameless son who died; and, in 1846, Tennessee Celeste. After ten births and three deaths, the family was complete.

The Claflin children lived in squalor under their parents' chaotic rule. Buck's only money came from odd jobs and various deceptive schemes. Homer, Ohio, was a town of about four hundred inhabitants. Middle-class Methodists ran the local stores and grew wheat and corn. Day after day, eight distilleries produced boatloads of corn whiskey. Excessive drinking—a disease masked as a social pleasure—was a part of life: an anodyne, a means of controlling slaves or blighting Indians, an excuse to beat one's wife and children. The dirt roads in Homer were pockmarked by tree stumps, and wagons often sank into the deep mud. Ditches, dug along the sides to contain the spring rains that flooded roads and fields, were clogged with refuse. Malaria, cholera, and typhus regularly swept the town. People still believed that maggots spawned inside the bellies of dead animals. The sources of infection were a mystery.

Bands of pigs roamed the streets and nosed into outhouses. The Claflins, who had no outhouse, dug holes in the backyard. In the spring they retrieved the human excrement to nourish their garden. Like others in the town, they drew their water from a backyard well. Traditionally, wash day was on Monday, the day after dressing up for church. The rest of the week people worked and slept in their everyday clothes. Wood was chopped and carried into the house to a cookstove. The ashes were emptied into barrels and used to absorb the pools of water that gathered around the steps. Smoke from lard-oil lamps darkened the rough wood walls of their house.

For a time Buck's twin brother, Robert, his wife, and their nine children lived with them. Regardless of sex, they slept three or four to a bed or sprawled on the floor in the bedroom, kitchen, and cellar. The children had no regular routine or chores. They distressed the neighbors by using the same unwashed green flask to fetch both beer and milk. At mealtimes they often begged at back doors. The Scribners next door could hear Roxy screaming at the squabbling children. Fierce quarrels were followed by equally fierce reconciliations. Roxy had a crude, mystic sense of family unity and insisted that no one go to bed angry.

Victoria would later say that her mother was a Spiritualist before such a movement existed. Roxy told her children of her visions, of how she had seen Jesus extend his bloody hands toward her and how she had recognized the devil because he had a small red tail and a cloven hoof. Victoria's biographer, Theodore Tilton, later wrote that Mama Roxy "tormented and harried her children until they would be thrown into spasms, whereat she would hysterically laugh, clap her hands, and look as fiercely delighted as a cat in playing with a mouse. . . . This lady, compounded in equal parts of Heaven and Hell will pray till her eyes are full of tears and in the same hour curse till her lips are white with foam."

As for Buck Claflin, he ruled absolutely over his family. His children were his property, and near-worthless property at that, to be broken like wild horses. He beat them for no reason at all. After a particularly brutal beating, Victoria's favorite brother, Maldon, ran away and was never heard from again. Roxy said that he was working on a railroad somewhere— maybe in heaven. Theodore Tilton wrote that Victoria "was worked like a slave—whipped like a convict. Her father was impartial in his cruelty to all his children; her mother, with a fickleness of spirit that renders her one of the most erratic of mortals, sometimes abetted him in his scourgings and at other times shielded the little ones from his blows."

After Roxy lost a child to typhus, she began to doctor her children with something new on the American scene—mesmerism. Roxy saw her first demonstration of mesmerism at a local fair where Buck had set her up as a fortune-teller alongside the two-headed cow and the snake charmer. Mesmerism emerged in the late 1700s, after the Viennese physician Franz Anton Mesmer treated a female patient suffering some fifteen ailments, including blindness and paralysis of her left hand. Mesmer decided that these symptoms were hysterical in origin, somehow relating to this woman's

*Roxy (Roxanna) Hummel Claflin and Buck (Reuben Buckman) Claflin.*
*She was an illegitimate, illiterate fortune-teller.*
*He was a con man and a thief.*

highly restricted life. Mesmer instructed his patient to swallow a solution containing traces of iron and then he attached magnets to her legs and stomach. Instantly, she felt tumultuous waves of energy and fell into a crisis state similar to a seizure. After several such treatments, the woman was totally cured.

Therapeutic magnets dated back to the ancient Greeks, who used them to halt bleeding, soothe inflammation, purge infection, and promote general healing. Magnets themselves, according to the theory, did not heal but induced the body to heal itself. Mesmer said that the curative power of magnets derived from their stimulation of an invisible electrical energy or a fluid in the body. He named this process "animal magnetism."

To apply this animal magnetism for curative purposes, Mesmer ordered the construction of a *baquet,* an oak tub twenty feet in diameter, outfitted with a series of iron rods connected to "magnetized" jars of water. As many as two dozen patients could occupy the tub at one time, and as they did so Mesmer wrapped his small frame in a voluminous, lilac-colored cape and pranced about waving a metal wand. He also played a glass harmonica to stimulate more vibrations. During the treatment some patients would be seized by an uncontrollable force as in the revival experience. Mesmer's patients often emerged "cured" of insomnia, Saint Vitus' dance, rheumatism, blindness, stammering, and other ailments.

It was Mesmer's disciple the Marquis de Puységur, however, who developed what came to be known as mesmerism. Puységur professed to cure ailments by controlling the flow of electrical energy throughout the body but as a side effect, he sometimes awakened in his subjects supernormal powers. Puységur's magnetized patients would fall into deep sleeplike trances in which they frequently could perform extraordinary feats of clairvoyance, telepathy, and precognition. Once awakened, his patients had no memory of these accomplishments, but often their former ills had vanished. Mesmerism had reached the previously undiscovered unconscious.

Both mesmerism and revivalism seemed to demonstrate that by abandoning oneself to a powerful force, one could effect immediate renewal of body and spirit. From earliest childhood both Victoria and her sister Tennessee remembered their mother going into a trancelike state and transmitting electrical energy to their bodies through her hands to cure them when they were ill. Roxy said she used her "other eyes" to read their minds. Mesmer's animal magnetism frequently was identified by its proponents as "the power of the soul," and when Roxy doctored her children with mesmerism she pronounced them "sanctified."

No one has yet fully explained the extraordinary feats mesmerized subjects could perform, feats achieved by Mama Roxy and some of her children. From childhood Victoria, Tennessee, and their brother Hebern said they experienced clairvoyant visions and healing powers. Of these powers, Tennessee seemed to have the largest share, but Victoria also apparently possessed skills demonstrated by mesmerized subjects, such as mind reading, finding lost objects, and describing events taking place where she had never been or before they occurred.

When mesmerism crossed from Europe to America, it found no medical auspices under which to establish its claims, and so the emphasis on healing gave way to sensational demonstrations at fairs and carnivals. Most often the chosen subject was a young woman. At the Homer, Ohio, fair of 1845, Rose Scott, an attractive girl of fifteen, was put into a trancelike state by a male mesmerist. According to a newspaper report, a bottle containing ammonia was then passed under her nose with no visible effect. Her finger was pricked with a hat pin, but there was no reaction and, mysteriously, no blood. The mesmerist then produced a red handkerchief and announced it was a snake. Rose recoiled in terror. When he suggested that she was covered with vermin, she frantically clawed at her bodice. Here was a passive, compliant female with no will of her own; the sexual implications were obvious.

Experiments in mesmerism took place throughout the country. In 1843, Henry Ward Beecher, having polished his skills as a revivalist, began practicing mesmerism as well. He mesmerized his sister Harriet Beecher Stowe with repeated success. During the first session she noted, "He succeeded in almost throwing me into convulsions—spasms and shocks of heat and prickly sensation ran all over me. . . . This strange tempestuous effect was occasioned simply by our sitting opposite to each other with our eyes fixed and our thumbs in contact for about thirty minutes and it was dissipated by making reverse passes which relieved first my head, then my lungs, then my lower limbs and lastly my arms."

A new age was dawning, one of electrical impulses, invisible energy, and other unseen, unexplained phenomena. In 1842, Samuel F. B. Morse petitioned Congress for $30,000 to construct a telegraph line between Washington and Baltimore. In the debate that followed, the representative from Tennessee suggested an amendment mandating that half the appropriation go to experiments in mesmerism. The chairman of the congressional committee noted that the suggestion was not out of order, because "it would require a scientific analysis to determine how far the magnetism of mesmerism was analogous to the magnetism employed in telegraphs." Thus faith in invisible powers, mediated not by preachers in their Calvinist pulpits, but accessible to all believers, was becoming a feature of everyday life. And for women, revivalism and mesmerism presented heretofore unimagined opportunities to exert personal power.

BEYOND A THICK hedge that separated them from the Claflins lived the Scribners, a respectable Methodist family. In their bright kitchen, red-and-white gingham curtains framed the windows, and gleaming copper pots hung above the woodstove. Victoria would later describe this kitchen as typical of those she saw "in Heaven." What a different world was this cozy household from the chaos and instability next door. Vickie, the interloper, longed to be a part of the Scribners' world, but her disreputable background shut her out. In adulthood she would come to despise the word *antecedents*.

Mrs. Scribner forbade her daughter Laurie to play with the shiftless Claflins, and one day when the child returned from the Claflins' orchard carrying a basket of green apples, her mother beat her with a willow switch. Stable and secure, the world of the Scribners was bound by conformity to a set of rigid principles. Catharine Beecher, the eldest child in the famous family of preachers, wrote a *Treatise on Domestic Economy* in 1841 and dedi-

*Catharine Beecher.*
*She was unmarried and a virgin but was*
*considered America's prime expert on child-*
*rearing and "domestic economy."*

cated it "To American Mothers." Her book dictated the rules for house-
holds like the Scribners', where a woman's proper role was to make a man's
home his castle. In her widely accepted view, a woman must sublimate all
personal ambition and desire, which were evil, and devote herself to per-
fecting the hearth and home. This was "woman's sphere."

Catharine Beecher preached a gospel of perfect domesticity elevated to
godliness. Throughout the nation, middle-class white women deferred to
her rules. System and order were Miss Beecher's holy creed, accompanied
by specific instructions on laundering, housekeeping, cooking, personal
hygiene, and female education. With absolute clarity and conviction, this
unmarried virgin of forty-one, who had no home of her own, prescribed
how to raise a generation of women.

> The physical and domestic education of daughters should occupy
> the principal attention of mothers . . . and the stimulation of the
> intellect should be very much reduced. . . . Much less time should
> be given to school and much more to domestic employments, espe-
> cially in the wealthier classes. . . .
>
> Needle-work, drawing, and music, should alternate with domes-

tic pursuits. One hour a day devoted to some study, in addition to the above employments, would be all that would be needful to prepare for a thorough female education. . . . Those who have the most important duties of society to perform—men—should have well-disciplined and well-informed minds.

When Victoria's brothers and sisters begged at the Scribners' back door, these righteous Christians sometimes handed them a plate of scraps or, on rare occasions, milk and johnnycake. But Victoria wouldn't beg. It was Mr. Scribner's sister, twenty-one-year-old Rachel, who answered the door on the day when five-year-old Vickie inquired if there were any chores she could do. Rachel saw that under the grime the child was beautiful: brown ringlets, arresting blue-gray eyes, and a quiet pride that made her different from the rest of the raucous clan next door.

Rachel Scribner took Vickie into her warm kitchen and into her heart. For a year Vickie visited almost daily, and Rachel taught her to read and write and saw that the child never went hungry. She washed her hair and praised Vickie's quick intelligence. One morning Vickie arrived at the Scribners' home to find the draperies drawn and a pine coffin in the parlor. Rachel Scribner had been stricken with cholera and died, all within twelve hours.

Years later, Victoria recounted her first spiritual vision—her first escape from an intolerable world. She was standing in the apple orchard, unable to cry, when the spirit of Rachel Scribner, a few hours dead, came to her. The spirit took Victoria by the hand, and she "felt herself gliding through the air." They traveled on a spiral path, engulfed in an intense white light, until they arrived at the spirit world. Heaven appeared to this small, perplexed child to be like the ordered world in which the Scribners lived, a world of well-kept homes, well-dressed men and women, of laughing and singing children, of peace and love. She later wrote,

I saw the spirits descending to earth and mortals ascending to the Spirit World and mingling in common unity. The people seemed to be much engaged as people are. They were coming and going as if they were very busy, and the scenery of that world was a counterpart of this.

I met some spirits who I since know to be Demosthenes, Bonaparte and Josephine. They told me that I was to be in their charge, and that they were to constantly guard, guide, instruct and care for me so that I should be, when grown, fitted to do their work on earth.

Towards the close of the visit, for such it really was, I was shown what I now know to have been a panoramic view of the future. The mountains and valleys changed places with the seas, the entire face of the nation underwent a transformation. Cities sank and people fled before appalling disasters in dismay. Then a wondrous calm settled over everything. Confusion, anarchy and destruction were replaced with a scene of beauty and glory which is beyond the power of language to describe. The earth had been changed into a paradise and had become the common abode of people of both spheres. The spirits said that all this would be realized during my life and that in making it possible I would bear a prominent part.

When I returned to physical consciousness, I told my mother, as well as I could in my childish way, all that had happened to me. My body had been unconscious for two hours. I had been among the angels.

By her own account Victoria was "a child without a childhood." From the time she could remember she had been farmed out as "a household drudge" to begin at dawn on endless rounds of washing and ironing, running errands, spading gardens, chopping wood, laying fires, tending infants. Buck collected her meager wages. Retreating perhaps from the cruelty and preternatural excitement of her surroundings, Vickie turned to the spirits. She later told Theodore Tilton that since childhood she had been aided by them. He wrote, "She has been lifted over the ground by angelic helpers lest she should dash her feet against a stone. When she had too heavy a basket to carry, an unseen hand would sometimes carry it for her. Digging in the garden as if her back would break, occasionally a strange restfulness would refresh her and she knew the spirits were toiling in her stead."

Victoria believed that the spirits guarded and sustained her. "I often performed the most laborious tasks without fatigue and mastered studies only by magic. Another more singular experience was when walking it seemed to me my feet did not touch the ground. While I saw my body going along, I was two or three feet above in the air. This phenomenon has followed me all my life."

It was Roxy herself who set her daughters on the road to the spirit world. She predicted that there would be better days for them. She had seen it in a vision: One day they would be rich and would "ride around in their own carriages." When they were shunned by their more respectable neighbors, she told her girls that they were "different" and what she did, or they did, was right simply because they did it. She told them that God was within them, and so any action they took could not be wrong. This feeling of entitlement was to persist throughout Vickie's long life.

When Roxy took her to the log schoolhouse, Vickie would ignore the children who laughed at her tattered clothes and the teacher who clipped a clothespin on her nose to discipline her. She would console herself with what her mother had told her. Vickie was a quiet child, unlike the other Claflins, and she absorbed knowledge effortlessly. She could look at a page once or twice and know it by heart, an ability that would serve her well in later life.

Buck's main occupation at this time was the sale, for $1 a bottle, of a "Life Elixir," which contained alcohol and laudanum, an opiate, mixed with herbs and molasses. Roxy brewed it and began using it herself. Once while Roxy was mixing a batch of elixir in a kettle strung up in the fireplace, Vickie saw the door open to admit a tall, lean man. "A red silk handkerchief concealed his face," but she knew he was the devil because "I saw not a booted foot but a cloven hoof." The devil stared into her eyes, Vickie later recounted, but it was he who flinched and abruptly left the house.

When she was ten, she also recalled, her two-year-old sister, Tennessee, lay in her cradle unable to move, near death from pneumonia. As Vickie sat rocking her sister, two angels appeared and pushed her away from the cradle. They fanned the baby's face with "pale white hands and blew sweet breath upon her." When Roxy entered the room, Vickie lay on the floor in a trance while Tennessee lay rosy and healthy in the crib.

Buck Claflin was never a man to ignore an opportunity to make money. As the revival fires raged throughout Ohio, child preachers became a popular attraction. A girl of seven preached hellfire and damnation while perched on her father's shoulder. A towheaded boy of five stood on a crate, and at the end of his sermon cast a black handkerchief to the ground and shouted, "So shall sinners fall in Hell." From the time Vickie was eight, Buck Claflin took her around Ohio to preach, and the child captivated audiences with her magnetism and ecstatic fervor. Vickie would stand on two crates, one on top of the other, and stare down at the faces in the crowd. "I am the Word. . . . Sinners, repent," she commanded. "Listen to me, for I know things you do not know. I can cure or I can smite!" No doubt she had heard this admonition from revivalist preachers and she repeated it with such passion that her listeners cringed. Even in her youth she was a consummate showman, addicted at an early age to the attention she received.

After nine years in Homer, Buck began long treks; sometimes he'd walk twenty miles and return home with "bleeding feet and haggard face." In the fall of 1847, he insured his gristmill against fire for $4,000, which seemed odd because he never operated it. One Saturday night he set out on one of his walks and spent the night in a town ten miles away. The following morning he headed home, but in the late afternoon stopped at the Brandon Tavern, only two miles from his house. He was still there at eleven that night when he walked to the window and said to the landlord, "There is a red glow in the sky to the south. I have a presentiment that's my gristmill on fire." Buck borrowed a horse and galloped into Homer to find a heap of smoldering ashes where his mill had been.

When Buck went to collect the insurance, the people of Homer began to wonder about the unused gristmill. Soon there was talk of arson and even more talk of tar and feathers and cleansing the town of this primitive, cheating clan. Roxy was suspected of torching the mill, and so was ten-year-old Vickie. Buck disappeared, leaving Roxy and her brood without food or money.

The previous year, Buck had worked for a few months as a postmaster. After he disappeared, a trunk filled with empty envelopes addressed to Homer residents was found in the post office, Buck having pocketed the money and whatever else of value he found in them. In January 1848, the upstanding Christian women of Homer organized a bazaar, and the proceeds were given to Roxy Claflin on the condition that she leave town and rejoin her husband, wherever he might be. Meanwhile, far away in the heart of the Burned-Over District near Rochester, New York, the powers that had been nurtured in Victoria were about to be given a name, and that name would soon identify a new religious movement dominated by women: Spiritualism.

# CHAPTER THREE

# THE SPIRITUAL
# TELEGRAPH

Aт six o'clock on the night of March 31, 1848, John and Margaret
Fox shooed their daughters, eleven-year-old Catherine, called Kate,
and thirteen-year-old Margaretta, called Maggie, upstairs to the
bedroom in their tiny saltbox house with two windows in front and three
on each side, in Hydesville, New York. All week strange nocturnal noises
had disturbed them—mysterious raps and bumps that could not be
explained. Tonight they were determined to put the girls to bed early to
make up for lost sleep. No sooner had the Fox sisters gone upstairs than the
banging began again, this time with great force and rapidity, resounding
throughout the house. John and Margaret rushed upstairs, entered the
room, and stood transfixed. The children were in bed, but the raps were
now louder than ever.

Kate Fox was a year older than Victoria Claflin and gave off the same
aura of intense energy. As her parents stared, she jumped out of bed and
began talking to an unseen presence. "Follow me," Kate commanded, snap-
ping her fingers as she paraded around the room. A steady progression of
raps seemed to follow her. "Now, do as I do," she said, and clapped her
hands three times. Three distinct raps answered her. "Three raps mean yes,"
Kate announced to her astonished parents. Her mother then asked, "Are
you a disembodied spirit?" Three rapid raps followed.

Within the week, twelve people had squeezed into the Foxes' bedroom.
William Duesler, a neighbor, sat on the bed next to Mrs. Fox, whose questions were answered with such distinct raps that Duesler felt the bedstead
shiver. Then Duesler began pointing to various people in the room; he
asked how many children they had, how many sons, how many daughters,
how many children had died. Each time the number of raps was correct.
Duesler asked the ages of different people in the room and finally asked his

own age. Thirty-one raps was the answer. He was confounded: "I did not think anyone about here knew my age except myself and my family."

By May 1848, so many people had made pilgrimages to the Fox home— peeking in the windows, camping in the yard, lighting bonfires at night— that Maggie and Kate fled. Maggie went to the nearby house of her married brother, David, and Kate to her thirty-three-year-old married sister, Ann Fish (known by her middle name, Leah), who lived in Rochester.

Rochester, in the heart of the territory that had been burned over by the fiery streak of the second Great Awakening, was known for its freethinking atmosphere, and many of its inhabitants supported abolition, including a group of Quakers who believed that the enslavement of body or soul was degrading and unjust. Of the six hundred Quakers in the Rochester area, Amy and Isaac Post were among the most prominent. Isaac was a prosperous druggist, and he and his wife met and entertained other abolitionists in the parlor of their comfortable home at 36 Sophia Street. Their cellar was a station on the Underground Railroad that transported runaway slaves to Canada.

William Lloyd Garrison, publisher of *The Liberator,* who had been dragged half-naked through the streets of Boston for his antislavery views, and Wendell Phillips, now a dedicated abolitionist, frequently stayed with the Posts. So did Frederick Douglass, an escaped slave who had become an eloquent abolitionist lecturer and with help from the Posts and others had started his own newspaper, *The North Star.* Douglass so cherished the Posts' friendship that while away on a lecture tour he wrote, "I should love much to look into your home . . . about once in [every] twenty-four hours."

The Posts' radicalism came gradually. At their Quaker meetings, Isaac and Amy said they were "moved by the spirit" to speak out against slavery, but they were forbidden to do so by the strictures of these gatherings. Therefore, they and several other antislavery Quakers withdrew from this traditional group and became followers of Amy Post's cousin, Elias Hicks. But prejudice followed them, and within the year the "Hicksites" had censured Isaac and Amy Post for participating in antislavery societies with non-Quakers. Once again the Posts withdrew, and with a small group of liberal followers founded the Waterloo Congregational Friends.

One of their group was Daniel Anthony. Once the well-to-do owner of a cotton mill, Anthony had lost his savings in the financial panic of 1837, and retreated to a "six-penny farm" in Rochester, where he scratched out a laborious living. To supplement his meager income he'd secured a job as Rochester district salesman for the newly formed New York Life Insurance

*Maggie (Margaretta) Fox, Kate (Catharine)
Fox, and Leah (Ann Leah) Fox Fish.
They penetrated the barrier to communicate
with the dead.*

*Amy Post. She concluded that "an unbroken
chain of communication [exists] between the
Infinite and all beings."*

Company and traveled extensively throughout the area soliciting customers. The second of his seven children, his twenty-eight-year-old daughter, Susan B. Anthony (in her teens she abbreviated her middle name, Brownell), had secured a position as headmistress of the Female Department at the Canajoharie Academy and was self-supporting. Daniel Anthony greatly influenced his daughter's thinking. In a typical letter he wrote Susan, "Of what use is preaching and all this pretended and blind devotion so long as this horrible business of trafficking in the bodies of men, women and children is sanctioned and actually carried on by those making the highest pretensions to goodness . . . sanctioned by both the Civil and Religious Institutions of this Republican and Christianized land."

Six miles from the Posts' Rochester home was that of Thomas and Mary Ann McClintock, and it was there that in June 1848 the Posts and several other members of the Waterloo Congregational Friends gathered around a mahogany tea table in the parlor to draw up an agenda for their group. The tilt-top table with three legs was a common fixture in many parlors but now, according to those present, a remarkable occurrence took place. As members of the group presented their ideas, the table began to vibrate with raps of approval from the spirits. As word of this phenomenon spread, the McClintocks' table became famous as the first "spirit table." Soon it was believed that certain tables served as catalysts to transmit the thoughts of the spirits.

In the Rochester area rappings began to be heard in many homes. Rapidly the methods of spirit communication became increasingly sophisticated. At first, spirit messages were spelled out by a series of raps, from one to twenty-six, corresponding to the letters of the alphabet. Then people began speaking the letters of the alphabet, and the spirits rapped at the appropriate letter. Spirit messages were further speeded up when it was discovered that both Kate Fox and her sister Leah's daughter, Lizzie Fish, could fall into trances and directly communicate with those who had "passed over."

Kate Fox, then living at Leah's house, sent a note to Amy Post that she had contacted the spirit of the Posts' five-year-old daughter, Matilda, who had died the previous year. The respected Posts promptly appeared at the Fish residence and became enthusiastic participants in these new discoveries. Acts of mediumship and clairvoyance quickly became the order of the day.

At Leah Fish's house, family and visitors felt the cool touch of invisible spirit hands. As Leah played the piano, she later wrote, those present said they felt "the deep throbbing of the dull accompaniment of the invisibles, keeping time to the music as I played." At dinner, with guests present, loud raps would often be heard, and one end of the table would rise up and thump down, sending plates and glasses flying. Isaac Post discovered that the spirits could take over his hand and produce "automatic writing." In this manner, he insisted, he wrote *Voices from the Spirit World,* a book with an introduction by Benjamin Franklin and containing messages from Washington, Jefferson, and Voltaire, all long dead.

The following November, Amy Post accompanied Maggie Fox and Leah Fox Fish to Corinthian Hall, the largest auditorium in Rochester, where they were to undergo the first of three arduous public tests of their strange powers. People began lining up at dawn, and by nine o'clock, when the box office opened, more than seven hundred had gathered. There were four hundred tickets, and at 75 cents each they went as fast as the cashier could hand them over. By six in the evening some tickets were being scalped for as much as $10. When Maggie and Leah arrived, they were taken to a back room to face a committee of sour-faced ladies who instructed them to strip off all their clothing. Amy Post, who was shocked at this demand, stood guard over them and draped their naked bodies in borrowed shawls while their garments were minutely examined. Once this procedure was completed, they were taken to the stage to face a committee of men chosen for their skill at exposing frauds.

As the inquisition began, Maggie and Leah's skirts were twisted around their ankles and tied securely in place with handkerchiefs. Then a member of the committee moved forward and placed his right hand on Maggie's feet, anchoring them in place. He put his left hand on the floor. Though Maggie could not move, raps came from the floor. The procedure was repeated with Leah, with similar results. Several other tests were conducted, but no one could locate the source of the raps.

On the second day of tests no further progress was made. Some members of the committee postulated that ventriloquism or some such device was causing the raps. Handkerchiefs were tied around the sisters' mouths, but the rapping continued. On the third and final night, the committee decided to test for electrical energy. Almost a century before, Benjamin Franklin had said that electricity represented the force of "disembodied spirits." An early Spiritualist described electricity as "the God principles at work." Hoping to demonstrate that these so-called spiritual phenomena were caused by the sisters directing electrical energy, it was advertised that they would be examined while standing on materials that did not conduct electricity.

Anticipation was keen. The audience packed the auditorium, anxiously awaiting the tests that would finally expose Maggie and Leah. So sure was a reporter from the *Rochester Democrat* that a fraud would be revealed that he had written an article to that effect, which already was set in type. One member of the examining committee vowed he would throw himself over Genesee Falls if he could not discover some trick. Another said he would forfeit his new beaver hat.

The sisters were once again examined by the ladies' committee before appearing onstage, where the spirits rapped answers to a number of questions, each time correctly. Next, they were asked to stand on a mound of pillows to halt the transmission of electrical impulses. But when they called upon the spirits, time and again the raps were heard. No trick was exposed, but no man committed suicide or lost a hat. The reporter rewrote his article. And a new religious movement was under way.

Members of the Posts' immediate group of Waterloo Congregational Friends were among the first converts to Spiritualism. These liberal, antislavery freethinkers had carried to an extreme the Quaker principle that God's laws were written in every human soul. Their declaration of principles maintained that "an unbroken chain of communication exists between the Infinite and all beings." This conviction seemed to be confirmed in the year 1848, when telegraph lines finally reached the Rochester area, making it possible to send messages by means of a little understood electrical force. The concept formulated by Isaac Post that one could utilize a "Spiritual Telegraph" to establish a line of communication with those who had "passed over" was no more difficult for these people to accept than the telegraph itself. Thus the barrier between the mortal and the spirit worlds had been penetrated.

The rise of Spiritualism came at a time of rapid territorial and economic expansion. Not only Morse's telegraph but other technological advances—canals, railroads, and steamships—led to a new America whose boundaries seemed both limitless and God-given. In 1845, when Texas joined the Union as the twenty-eighth state, Congress affirmed the "right of our Manifest Destiny to overspread and to possess the whole of the continent." But as the country grew, Ralph Waldo Emerson spoke for a lost security when he wrote, "Instead of the social existence which all shared, now there was separation." The Calvinist ethic that once had held everyone in place was fading, and the search for alternative meaning in a transformed world had begun.

Many Spiritualists turned to the teachings of Emanuel Swedenborg, a highly influential Swedish philosopher. In 1750, while in a trance, Swedenborg claimed to have seen the spirit world and recorded what he saw there. In the heavenly society, all goods and services were shared, and men were permitted both wives and concubines. Swedenborg's vision not only fulfilled male fantasies but also exploited the nascent interest in science. He wrote that "the Spirit World is derived from atoms . . . the disintegrating chemical action of electricity and magnetism which throws out ethereal particles into the great ocean of unindividualized spirit." In a like manner, in the 1840s a French disciple of Swedenborg, Charles Fourier, propounded "a common system of movement for the material and the spiritual world." Fourier's theory of "passional attraction" advocated free sexual relationships based on "elective affinities."

Religion, sex, and the role of women were being reshaped by forces and theories that seemed mysterious and difficult to comprehend. Perhaps the strangest synthesis of these elements was to be found in a so-called machine built in 1853 by a Spiritualist and trance medium, John Murray Spear. With "spirit guidance," Spear constructed a contraption of zinc batteries, metal balls, and thousands of copper wires, encased in a wooden frame. He named it the New Motor. The purpose of this machine was as vague as the man himself, but he claimed that it not only harnessed spiritual electricity but also housed an as-yet-unborn soul.

With the Virgin Mary in mind, Spear declared that this new force was to be given life through a woman. Soon after, a Boston Spiritualist said that she had experienced an immaculate conception and bore in her womb the "living principle" of Spear's machine. The woman, large of stomach, prostrated herself before the machine, and, having undergone labor pains, she reached "a crisis," and her stomach flattened. Then Spear announced that "at precisely the time designated and at the point expected, motion appeared in the New Motor corresponding to embryonic life."

This announcement was met with skepticism and fear. The New Motor, or the Wonderful Infant, as Spear now referred to it, was called the work of the devil. When Spear moved his creation to Randolph, New York, because of its "lofty electrical position," panic spread throughout New England. Within the week, a mob broke into the shed that housed the Wonderful Infant and smashed it to bits. Spear related how the frenzied group "tore out the heart of the mechanism, trampled it beneath their feet, and scattered it to the four winds."

Spear's bizarre experiment acknowledged the life-giving force of women. And it was to women that the appeal of Spiritualism was especially potent. Louise Chandler Moulton, an early convert to Spiritualism, was typical— born to strict Calvinist parents who banned the reading of romances, dancing, and playing games of chance, including backgammon. Throughout her childhood she was plagued by "an awful foreboding of doom and despair." She would wake "in the depth of the night, cold with horror" and think, "Why, if I'm not among the elect I *can't* be saved, no matter *how* hard I try." Through Spiritualism her fate was now in her own hands.

Death too inspired Spiritualism. "Woman's sphere" was confined to the home, where death was an all too frequent visitor. In New York State, as the first spirit rappings were being heard, half of the deaths were of children under five. Beloved relatives died at home, most often attended by women. Beyond loneliness and grief, women, particularly middle-class Christian women who had been plagued by doubt as to the fate of the departed, could now see these dear souls safely nestled in the hand of God. Spiritualists responded to death as a transforming event: Rather than mourn, they wore white at funerals, where mediums delivered messages from the newly arrived spirits in Summerland (the Spiritualist name for heaven).

The attribution of purity and passivity to the female nature made women ideal vehicles to channel messages. By the 1850s, a group of female trance speakers were among the first women permitted to speak in "promiscuous assemblies," which meant gatherings of both sexes. Speaking with the authority of the spirits but without personal responsibility for what they said, these women could not be censored for their statements. Since the spirits were guiding them, they had courage, for they spoke the truths of a greater power. Women, no matter how ill-educated, could now transmit the wisdom of spirits as diverse as Socrates and Benjamin Franklin: Not surprisingly, the rights of women were very much on the minds of these great thinkers.

Spiritualism was dominated by women, and its manifestations most frequently occurred in places within their control. "Not in Church, not in Capitol, but in the family came the first demonstrable recognition of immortal life and immortal love—the holiest truth to the holiest place," wrote Andrew Davis, an early convert to Spiritualism. And the preacher Charles Beecher observed, "It is not in its published literature, its periodicals, its lectures, and its public mediums that the strength of the movement lies. It is in its family or home circles." Séances were conducted around parlor tables where men and women held hands to form Spirit Circles. Ouija boards with planchettes were common accessories. (The planchette was a heart-shaped piece of wood mounted on three gliders. It was said to respond to magnetic forces passing through the fingers, which guided the point of the instrument to a letter of the alphabet. In this manner spirit messages were spelled out.)

*A spiritscope. In 1855 Dr. Robert Hare invented this machine
to prove that spirits exist.*

Revivalists and even traditional preachers described the beauties of
heaven and the torments of hell so vividly that they seemed very real places.
A Spiritualist named William Hayden noted that the very ministers who
comforted parishioners by assuring them that the deceased "are not gone
but are often with you, watching over you, loving you" were shocked when
he told them that he had verified this statement by communicating with
the dead. These thoughts were echoed by Warren Felt Evans, the Spiritualist minister and author of *The New Age and Its Messenger:* "If a person
becomes sufficiently spiritual before his departure to a higher realm, to see,
hear and even converse with those who walk the velvety soils of the land of
perpetual spring . . . his sanity is seriously called into question."

After the death of his wife, Roxanna, Lyman Beecher impressed upon
his children that she was still with them. Although she had died when
Henry Ward Beecher was a child of three, he would later say his mother was
the guiding influence and inspiration of his life. Because of her, he professed to see God not as a strict father but as a loving, nurturing, and for-
giving mother. In Roxanna's spirit, Henry Ward Beecher would conceive his
*Gospel of Love,* which two decades later would make him the most popular
preacher in the nation.

This new Calvinism, with its revival ritual, the powers released by mesmerism, and puzzling unseen electrical forces, had pointed the way to Spir-

itualism. Twenty years later, Theodore Tilton's wife, Elizabeth, called Lib, who was to play a pivotal role in the life of Victoria Woodhull, said that as she knelt by the corpse of her dead son, Paul, she saw two angels descend through the stained-glass dome of her Brooklyn Heights home and in a blaze of white light carry his spirit up into the realm of heaven. And the "Spiritual Telegraph" hummed with the words of comfort, reassurance, and power that women, even the strongest, so desperately needed.

# MY
# LONG-ACCUMULATING
# DISCONTENT

I N 1848, as spirit raps swept the Rochester area, they served not only to communicate with the dead but to give courage to the living. Just one month after the three-legged spirit table in the McClintocks' parlor reverberated with raps as the Waterloo Congregational Friends were formulating their declaration of principles, Elizabeth Cady Stanton and four other women assembled in the same parlor to discuss the plight of women. Three of these women—Mary Ann McClintock, Lucretia Mott, and Jane Hunt—were Waterloo Congregational Friends. The fourth, Mott's youngest sister, Martha Coffin Wright, had been expelled by the Quakers for marrying "out of meeting." To these women Elizabeth Cady Stanton, a frustrated thirty-three-year-old mother of three sons, "poured out . . . the torrent of my long-accumulating discontent with such vehemence and indignation that I stirred myself, as well as the rest of the party, to do or dare anything." Stanton wrote that she and the other women were determined to call a "convention to discuss the social, civil, and religious condition and rights of women," to be held July 19 and 20 in the Wesleyan Chapel in Seneca Falls, New York.

It was essential that they prepare a statement of their beliefs, but Stanton said she and her companions "felt as helpless and hopeless as if they had been suddenly asked to construct a steam engine." Lucretia Mott, a well-known Quaker preacher and abolitionist, was the only one who had any experience as an organizer. The rest of the women were occupied solely as wives and mothers. Reports from antislavery and temperance conventions were suggested as models for their declaration, but these documents seemed dull and imprecise. Time grew short until only five days remained before the convention, and still no paper had been written. Stanton, desperately seeking inspiration, sat down at the McClintocks' spirit table, picked up the Declaration of Independence, and began reading it aloud. At once the women decided to use it as the basis for their own Declaration of Rights and Sentiments. "We hold these truths to be self-evident, that all men *and women* are created equal. . . ." Miraculously, the ideas began to flow as Elizabeth Cady Stanton placed her paper on the spirit table and wrote the declaration for "the first organized protest against the injustice which has brooded for ages over the character and destiny of one-half the race."

Stanton wrote from experience, for she knew full well the oppression of women. After nine years of marriage she had found herself isolated on the outskirts of Seneca Falls, suffering from "mental hunger." Her husband, Henry Stanton, had wanted to move there to relieve his lung congestion, but he was gone most of the time, pursuing his legal and political career and organizing New York's Free Soil Party. In fact, he had been absent for the birth of each of their three sons. Elizabeth was now occupied with household chores and the time-consuming homeopathic cures she administered to her three boys—five, three, and almost two—all of whom had contracted malaria. She had learned this method from her brother-in-law, Edward Bayard, who had left a promising law practice to become a homeopathic physician. Elizabeth approved of his career, although her sister Tryphena, Edward's wife, who was active in homeopathic medicine herself, felt he was giving up all chance of wealth. Edward longed for understanding and affection, but Tryphena thought his ideas and aspirations impractical.

Homeopathy was practiced as a more benign alternative to morphine and alcohol, the most common medications, and to the purging, bloodletting, blistering, and cutting administered with dubious results by practitioners of the "heroic medicine" of the day. According to the first homeopathic physician, Dr. Samuel Hahnemann, a minuscule amount of a disease-causing agent could be diluted with liquid, creating a "spiritlike" essence. If this substance was then introduced into the body, the patient could be cured of that disease.

In accepting homeopathy, as in other aspects of her life, Elizabeth Cady Stanton chose to think for herself. She gave birth to each of her children attended by a midwife rather than a doctor. The morning after her fourth son was born, she wrote, "I got up, bathed myself in cold water and have sat by the table writing several letters." She noted with some humor that others were waiting for her to die to prove her theories wrong. In a time when the infant mortality rate in America was 50 percent, Stanton bore seven healthy children, whom she raised to adulthood. In a world of seven-course meals she was to declare, "We know what not one woman in ten thousand does

LEFT: *Lucretia Coffin Mott—the Quaker pioneer of woman's rights*
RIGHT: *Martha Coffin Wright. She joined her older sister, Lucretia, in rebelling against the subjection of women.*

*Elizabeth Cady Stanton. Her rage against the male establishment fueled her fight for woman's rights.*

know—how to take care of a child, make good bread, and keep a home clean. . . . Our children . . . are healthy, rosy, happy and well-fed. Pork, salt, meat, mackerel, rancid butter, heavy bread, lard, cream of tartar and soda, or any other culinary abominations are never found on our table." Stanton's thoughts on sewing were equally unconventional: "As an amusement it is contemptible; as an education of head or heart, worthless . . . as a support the most miserable of trades."

Although she asserted her independence by adamantly refusing to be addressed as Mrs. Henry Stanton, Elizabeth felt keenly her subordinate role as a woman. She recalled the moment when this feeling of inferiority had begun: In July 1826, the eleven-year-old Elizabeth Cady tiptoed into her parents' parlor to find it a "silent chamber of death." The drapes were drawn, the darkened room lit only by two sputtering candles. The mirrors and pictures were draped in white linen. Beside the open casket of her brother Eleazer sat her father. The eminent judge Daniel Cady was pale and immobile. "As he took no notice of me, after standing a long while, I climbed upon his knee. . . . He mechanically put his arm around me and, with my head resting against his beating heart, we both sat in silence, he thinking of the wreck of all his hopes in the loss of a dear son, and I wondering what could be said or done to fill the void in his breast. At length he heaved a deep sigh and said, 'Oh, my daughter, I wish you were a boy!' Throwing my arms about his neck, I replied, 'I will try to be all my brother was.' "

And she did. Elizabeth learned to ride a horse with great skill and daring. At Johnstown Academy she excelled in Latin, Greek, and mathematics. "I resolved . . . to be at the head of all my classes and thus delight my father's heart. . . . I surprised even my teacher, who thought me capable of doing anything. I learned to drive and to leap the fence and the ditch on horseback. I taxed every power, hoping some day to hear my father say, 'Well, a girl is as good as a boy, after all.' But he never said it." Elizabeth became keenly aware that no matter how she tried, "father . . . prefers boys." She suffered from what William Blackstone had referred to in his *Commentaries* as "the defect of sex."

There were to be no Cady men. Of Margaret and Daniel Cady's eleven children, all five boys died, while five of the six daughters lived to adulthood. Elizabeth was the seventh child born into this socially prominent and affluent family in Johnstown, New York, forty miles northwest of Albany. Her father became a congressman in 1815, the year of her birth, and subsequently a New York Supreme Court judge. Her mother was the daughter of

Colonel James Livingston, who had fought under Washington in the Revolution. Margaret Cady was almost six feet tall, an imposing, cool woman whose energies went to producing children and to overseeing a supremely well-organized household. Elizabeth usually saw her mother at teatime and dinner; she thought of her as a distant queen.

As a child Elizabeth would sometimes sit unnoticed in a corner of her father's office in her red flannel dress, the stiff linen collar scratching her neck while she listened to women pleading with Judge Cady to right the wrongs against them. She heard about the husband who took his wife's hard-earned wages to buy liquor while their children starved; about unremitting beatings; about children taken away by husbands, their mothers forbidden ever to see them again. Old Mrs. Brown came to Judge Cady to help her keep the farm that her grandfather and father had owned before her, one that had been willed by her late husband to a stepson. And Flora Campbell came crying to Judge Cady because her husband had mortgaged her farm, over her objections, and now creditors were taking it away.

Under the law there was nothing Judge Cady could do. He would take down his heavy law books and read the statutes aloud. Later, unobserved, Elizabeth would mark the pages he'd read and replace the books in the bookcase upside down so she could find them again. She planned one night to tiptoe into her father's office with a scissors and cut out all the bad laws that made women cry. She told this to Flora Campbell, and soon her father was explaining that cutting the laws from his books would do nothing to change them.

When Elizabeth was ten, Edward and Henry Bayard, the sons of Delaware senator James A. Bayard, came to read law in Judge Cady's office. A few months after her brother Eleazer's death, Elizabeth's eldest sister, Tryphena, eleven years her senior, married Edward Bayard. Edward loved to tease Elizabeth by reading her the most vexing laws relating to women (glass, eggs, and women could not be insured), passages from the Bible ("But I suffer not a woman to teach, nor to usurp authority over the man, but to be in silence"), and *The Taming of the Shrew* (Elizabeth hated Petruchio and sympathized with Kate). Elizabeth's anger smoldered, but "I soon noticed that, after losing a few games of chess, my opponent talked less of masculine superiority," she later wrote. A particularly arrogant student in Judge Cady's office was taken by Elizabeth on a ten-mile gallop. "I left him . . . half dead at his hotel, where he will be laid out, with all his marvelous masculine virtues, for a week at least," she exulted.

Elizabeth's mother, Margaret, was forty-one when Eleazer died, but her husband still demanded a son. In the next five years she suffered seven miscarriages. At last she gave birth to another son, also christened Eleazer. The child died at four months. Margaret, physically and emotionally exhausted after eleven births, retreated to her bed in her darkened bedroom. Escaping into illness, she determined to remain in a condition where her husband could not impregnate her again. (When she ceased menstruating, Margaret recovered her health.) As she languished, Tryphena and Edward took over as surrogate parents to Elizabeth and her two younger sisters, Margaret and Catherine.

At fifteen Elizabeth graduated with highest honors from Johnstown Academy and hoped to go to Union College in Schenectady with the boys. Her ambivalent father, at once proud of her accomplishments but feeling that they were not befitting a girl, who should be trained for the role of mother and housekeeper, forbade his daughter any more formal education. As she was to complain sometime later, "To think that all in me of which my father would have felt a proper pride had I been a man, is deeply mortifying to him because I am a woman." When her brother-in-law Edward Bayard interceded for Elizabeth, the judge agreed to send her to Emma Willard's Female Seminary in Troy, New York, where she spent two years studying the essential female graces: music, dancing, and French. The academic courses were at a level far below what she had already mastered. At Emma Willard she felt purposeless, bored, and full of vague longings.

The revival season began that spring in Troy, and the great reverend Charles Grandison Finney arrived to bring souls to salvation. Finney was considered a leader of the new Calvinists, a man so persuasive and feared by the more restrained clergy that Lyman Beecher had tried to keep him from bringing his "streak of fire" into Beecher's own pastorate in Litchfield, Connecticut. The rebellious Elizabeth easily came under Finney's sway:

> I can see him now, his great eyes rolling around the congregation and his arms flying about in the air like those of a windmill. . . . He described Hell and the Devil and the long procession of sinners being swept down the rapids about to make the awful plunge into the burning depths of liquid fire below and the rejoicing hosts in the Inferno coming up to meet them with the shouts of the Devil echoing through the vaulted arches. He suddenly halted and pointing his index finger at the supposed procession, he exclaimed:
> "There, do you not see them?"
> I was brought up to such a pitch that I actually jumped up and gazed in the direction to which he pointed, while the picture glowed before my eyes and remained with me for months afterwards.

Yet Elizabeth could not achieve conversion, an essential step in finding salvation, because she was unable to follow the revivalist ritual that demanded she expunge her entire personality and feel herself "a monster of iniquity." She found the process "puzzling and harrowing to the young mind." She sought out Finney and confided, "I cannot understand what I am to do. If you should tell me to go to the top of the church steeple and jump off, I would readily do it, if thereby I could save my soul, but I do not know how to go to Jesus."

Finney's answer didn't help. "Repent and believe. That is all you have to do to be happy here and hereafter." Later Elizabeth was to say, "Such preaching worked incalculable harm to the very souls he sought to save. Fear of the Judgment seized my soul. Visions of the lost, haunted my dreams. Mental anguish prostrated my health. . . . Returning home, I often at night roused my father from his slumbers to pray for me, lest I should be cast into the bottomless pit before morning."

Alarmed by his daughter's condition and shocked by what he considered Finney's vulgar camp-meeting conversions, Judge Cady took his daughter to Niagara Falls to regain her health, accompanied by Tryphena and Edward Bayard. Edward explained to Elizabeth "the nature of the delusion" she had experienced in the revival process, "the physical conditions, the mental processes, the church machinery by which such excitements are worked up and the impositions to which credulous minds are necessarily subjected." The new Calvinism, he told her, was as hypocritical as the old, and he encouraged her to pursue truth in her own way. Edward took her for long walks. At night, his face illuminated by the campfire, he read to her from Scott and Dickens. He delighted in Elizabeth's fine intellect and found her beautiful. Soon she forgot about the fires of hell. Two months later, Elizabeth visited the Edward Bayards. The walks began again, the teasing, the frolicking. One day, caught off guard, Edward told Elizabeth the secret burning in his breast—he loved her. Elizabeth in return admitted what she had previously not admitted even to herself—she was in love with her brother-in-law.

He begged her to run away with him. She resisted. On several occasions Edward, to promote his secret suit, cast himself as chaperone when Elizabeth and her sister Margaret went to New York to visit another sister, Harriet. One moonlit night Elizabeth and Edward strolled along the Battery as he spoke openly of his love. New York was far from Johnstown, and walking with this handsome, attentive man—her friend, her soul mate, her love—she realized that with him she might have the adventurous life she wanted. Seeing the ships glittering in the harbor, he begged her to sail away with him. She was tempted, but she realized that to be with Edward she would have to betray her sister Tryphena, and they would both become outcasts. There was no way for them to have a life together.

To escape this clandestine romance Elizabeth fled to Peterboro, New York, to visit her cousin Gerrit Smith. There she met a lawyer and fellow houseguest, Henry Stanton. Like Edward Bayard, he was ten years her senior; like Gerrit Smith, he was a famous abolitionist. On bright fall mornings two carriages would start off from the Smiths' house for antislavery meetings. They would return at midnight, their passengers tired but exhilarated by what they had heard. Henry Stanton was a clear thinker and a forceful speaker. On a crystalline October day, Henry and Elizabeth went riding through a blaze of autumn colors. As the horses walked "slowly through a beautiful grove, he laid his hand on the horn of the saddle and, to my . . . pleasure and astonishment," proposed marriage. Elizabeth, by now twenty-four, accepted.

Edward Bayard was infuriated by this turn of events and used his influence with Judge Cady, who was not an abolitionist, to discredit Stanton. The judge threatened to disinherit Elizabeth if she married him. The pressure was relentless, and after a visit to the Bayards in February 1840, Elizabeth broke off her engagement. Henry Stanton told Gerrit Smith he "dreaded the influence of Mr. Bayard," but he would not abandon his suit and continued to write to Elizabeth. In May 1840, Henry told Elizabeth that he would be abroad for eight months, working for the American Anti-Slavery Society. As his departure approached, she saw herself being drawn back into the untenable situation with her brother-in-law, Edward.

Elizabeth made up her mind. There was no time for a trousseau; on Friday, May 10, 1840, she and Henry Stanton were married. She wore a simple white gown and insisted the word *obey* be stricken from the ceremony. The following day they sailed for England and the World Anti-Slavery Convention. It was said that after her marriage Edward Bayard never allowed himself to be in a room alone with Elizabeth and that he never stopped loving her. As for Elizabeth, thirty-one years later, on a moonlit walk with Isabella Beecher Hooker, she "in an unguarded moment unveiled . . . as never to mortal eyes before" that even after all the years of marriage and seven children, she was still in love with Edward Bayard and to him went "the steadfastness of my affection." Elizabeth was to say that instead of "seeking solace elsewhere" she had channeled her energies into the fight for woman's rights.

. . .

ON THE MORNING of July 19, 1848, the first woman's rights convention was called to order in the Wesleyan Chapel in Seneca Falls. Although the first day was reserved for women, men came and were allowed to stay. As Elizabeth watched the chapel fill, she became fearful. In addition to writing the Declaration of Rights and Sentiments, she had drafted resolutions for the convention. On her own initiative she wrote, "RESOLVED—That it is the duty of the women of this country to secure to themselves their sacred right to the elective franchise."

For Henry Stanton this was too much. He opposed his wife's revolutionary claim to the ballot. He told her that she would turn the proceedings into a farce and that he wanted no part of it. He would leave town rather than attend her meeting. She refused to budge, and he left. Elizabeth Cady Stanton later maintained that her husband had supported her resolution, but her letters and diary show that friction between them grew in proportion to her independence. Judge Daniel Cady came to Seneca Falls and questioned his daughter's sanity, once again threatening to disinherit her if she did not withdraw her outrageous demand for suffrage. Even the ardent woman's rights advocate Lucretia Mott opposed Stanton's resolution, telling her, "Oh, Lizzie! If thou demands that, thou will make us ridiculous! We must go slowly."

Elizabeth, resolution in hand, turned to Frederick Douglass, who was attending the meeting. She had met him four years earlier at a meeting of the American Anti-Slavery Society and had written of him at that time, "He stood there like an African Prince, conscious of his dignity and power, grand in his physical proportions, majestic in his wrath, as with keen wit, satire, and indignation he portrayed the bitterness of slavery, the humiliation of subjection to those who in all human virtues and capacities were inferior to himself."

Stanton asked Douglass what single act would most benefit his own people. "The ballot," he replied. "Yes," said Stanton, "I see that the ballot is exactly what we women need!" Emboldened by Douglass's response, Elizabeth presented her resolution to give women the vote. Amy Post, who had arrived at the Seneca Falls convention directly after a séance with Leah Fox Fish, forcefully endorsed the resolution, as did Mary Ann McClintock. Frederick Douglass too supported the resolution, stating, "Our doctrine is that right is of no sex." After a heated debate at the third and final session of the convention, Elizabeth's resolution passed—barely.

When the convention adjourned, the participants agreed to reconvene at the Unitarian church in Rochester two weeks later. This time the convention was organized by Amy Post. Empowered by Spiritualism, Post was even

*Susan B. Anthony at twenty-eight.*
*She rejected the "draining trap" of marriage.*

bolder than the Seneca Falls women. Lucretia Mott's husband, James, had chaired the first convention, but Amy Post persuaded the women to elect a female president, a move so unprecedented that even Elizabeth opposed it. Nevertheless, Abigail Bush (who had become a Spiritualist after witnessing the Fox sisters' powers at the Posts' home) became president. And Elizabeth apologized for her "foolish conduct."

With a Quaker sense of obligation, Daniel Anthony attended the Rochester convention and signed the Declaration of Rights and Sentiments, as did his wife, Lucy, and youngest daughter, Mary. His daughter Susan B. Anthony would return from the Canajoharie Female Academy the following year and shortly thereafter join Elizabeth Cady Stanton in the battle for woman's rights, one that would last until their deaths and beyond. When their relationship began in May 1851, Susan was thirty-one, almost five years younger than Elizabeth. Susan B. Anthony liked to dress in fashionable plaid and had a number of suitors. However, she suffered from a wandering right eye (and therefore preferred to be photographed in profile). This self-consciousness about her condition contributed to her later image as an "old maid," but it was a conscious choice on her part to avoid the draining trap of marriage. Susan had intense feelings for her female friends and loved them with a passion that others reserved for the men in their lives.

In the next few years, what had begun at Seneca Falls became a powerful movement. First came word from Ohio that a woman's rights convention was being planned there as well. Then Lucy Stone, one of the first women to attend Oberlin College and one who had refused to take the name of her husband, allied herself with Paulina Wright Davis, who lectured on anatomy to women, whose own bodies were often as foreign to them as the moon. These two planned yet another woman's rights convention, to be held the next fall in Worcester, Massachusetts.

In those early years, Stanton often called upon Anthony to come and "make the puddings and carry the baby while I ply the pen." Stanton most often stayed at home to raise her family while Anthony presented her friend's position papers at conventions. Anthony was not a natural public speaker, and even she sought help from spiritual sources. While on the road she wrote to Stanton, "Oh dear, dear! If the *spirits* would only just make me a *trance medium* and put the *rights* into my mouth. You can't think how earnestly I have prayed to be made a speaking medium for a whole week. If they would only come to me thus, I'd give them a hearty welcome."

Spiritualism and the inception of woman's rights were inextricably intertwined. Elizabeth Cady Stanton heard spirit raps in her home. And when Gerrit Smith's daughter Elizabeth (Libby) Smith came for a visit, she too heard them. (Three years later Libby Smith would introduce "bloomers"— the Turkish pantaloons and short skirt named for the newspaper editor Amelia Bloomer—as a protest against clothes that constricted a woman's movement and impaired her health.) In a letter to his cousin Isaac Post, George Willets chronicled how belief in the spirits had become widespread among the first woman's rights advocates. He wrote,

> As to the rapping heard at Rochester and which I heard when then away from the [Fox] girls . . . I hear it very frequently, and much more now than then. . . . Thomas McClintock's folks are very sure that they have heard the same. Also Elisabeth Stanton. Gerrit Smith's daughter was on a visit to E. Stanton and heard about it. She went home and told her mother who had full faith in it and the daughter wrote to E. Stanton, a day or two since, that her mother had heard it several times so if it is Humbug it seems to spread fast.

Spiritualism and woman's rights drew from the same well: Both were responses to the control, subjugation, and repression of women by church and state. Both believed in universal suffrage—the equality of all human beings. For women—sheltered, repressed, powerless—the line between divine inspiration, the courage of one's convictions, and spirit guidance became blurred. Not all woman's rights advocates became Spiritualists, but Spiritualism embraced woman's rights.

CHAPTER FIVE

# YOU UGLY CREATURE

**B**UCK CLAFLIN saw money in the tremendous success of the Fox sisters and the swift spread of Spiritualism. In 1848, after Buck's flight from Homer, he rejoined his family in nearby Mount Gilead, Ohio. The Claflins moved in with Vickie's older sister Margaret Ann, who had married Enos Miles, the town druggist. The Claflin clan descended on Mr. Miles, fighting and squabbling as always. As for Margaret Ann, she had never been exposed to proper middle-class living and was not about to change her ways. Her marriage ended soon after her family arrived, when Enos caught his wife in a local hotel room with a man. The usually mild-mannered druggist pursued Margaret Ann down Mount Gilead's main street brandishing a butcher knife.

A penchant for unrestricted sex seems to have been a family trait. Polly Claflin too had married respectably. Her husband, Ross Burns, was a lawyer who later became lieutenant governor of Kansas. But Polly, a true Claflin, sent notes to admirers via boys in the town. When Ross Burns found out, he divorced her. Polly claimed that Burns had walked out on her while her baby was dying, and after her son's death, for two days she followed Burns everywhere, carrying the corpse in her arms.

Five-year-old Tennessee, who had been farmed out to relatives near Williamsport, Pennsylvania, was soon reading the thoughts of her neighbors. She told a farmer who had lost his calf exactly where to find it. When a Mrs. McDonell offered the child some fruit, Tennessee inquired, "But where is the best fruit?"

"What fruit?" asked Mrs. McDonell.

"The fruit you put away," answered Tennessee.

It was true. Mrs. McDonell had hidden the best fruit before the child's arrival.

All of this skeptics might explain away, but there was more: Newspaper accounts at the time relate how Tennessee awoke one night screaming in

terror. She had seen a vision of a building in flames. She described the fire
to her relatives and then to reporters in minute detail, including what the
firemen were wearing and how they had been unable to reach the blaze. A
month later, just such a fire took place at the Dickinson Seminary in nearby
Williamsport. So precise was the child's description that she was accused of
starting the fire. A subsequent investigation proved her innocence.

When Buck heard of the ruckus his child had caused and how her fame
was spreading and people were flocking to her for advice, he bought himself a wagon with a bright red canopy trimmed with bouncing blue cotton
balls, picked up Tennessee, and took her on the road, billing her as the
"Wonderful Child." Tennessee told fortunes, located objects, predicted the
future, and delivered spirit messages. After a time, he took her back to
Mount Gilead and teamed her up with Victoria in imitation of the Fox sisters. Buck moved his daughters into Mrs. Webb's boardinghouse, where they
conducted séances at tables that resounded with raps, channeled spirit messages, and produced spirit music—for a price. Buck collected the money.

Utica was of little use to her father. Although she was very pretty, she
was slow, self-occupied, and could not convince an audience that she was in
touch with the spirit world. She was consigned to help her mother brew
Buck's "Life Elixir." Utica was soon addicted to corn whiskey and opium.

While Tennessee accepted her powers with a light heart, often resorting
to generalities about love and money when no spirit inspired her, Victoria
was intense and erratic. Buck, expecting only a performance, was dismayed
when Vickie lost herself in deep trances. She would emerge from this state
debilitated and unaware of what had happened. Many years later she wrote
that in one such trance she had told a man, on his way to New York to meet
his family, that his wife's spirit said that three hours previously their ship had
foundered in a storm and both she and the children had drowned. The man
was alarmed but continued on his way only to find that the ship had sunk at
the precise time Vickie had specified. On another occasion she announced
that she'd encountered the spirit of a young girl who said she had come for
her brother. Only one man at the séance table had a deceased sister, but he
was discounted because he was only twenty-eight. The following morning
he was found dead in his bed.

In order to intensify his daughters' performances, Buck starved them
for days at a time. Victoria would later tell her biographer, Theodore Tilton,
that "in my own home I was treated with a cruelty that still beclouds the
memory of my early days." Buck brutally beat her with braided willow
withes or a stick of firewood, and Vickie often intimated that he sexually

abused her as well. Years later, Vickie would say that Buck made her "a woman before my time." And she would tell Lucretia Mott and her sister Martha Coffin Wright, "All that I am I have become through sorrow."

By her own account, after a particularly "savage" episode, Victoria went down to the stream behind their house and began to wash herself clean when she saw a phosphorescent sparkling in the water that materialized into a powerful spirit, "a majestic guardian" next to whom Buck Claflin was but a puny toy. She saw the spirit clearly—a stalwart young man wearing a white toga and a laurel wreath in his tightly curled brown hair. He spoke to her with words of comfort, telling her that she would "rise to a great distinction, that she would emerge from her poverty and live in a stately house, that she would win great wealth in a city crowded with ships, that she would become the ruler of her people."

At fourteen, finding no way out of an intolerable situation, Victoria manifested the behavior that would typify the rest of her life. Unable to protect herself from the parents who enslaved her emotionally, abused and exhausted, this child-woman retreated to a safe world. Wracked with rheumatism, shaking with fever, and unable to leave her bed, she conversed daily with her two dead sisters, Delia and Odessa. "I would talk to them as a girl tattles to her dolls." Angels also came and went, and these "gracious guests" became her "constant companions."

When Buck began losing money because of Victoria's illness he consulted a local physician, Dr. Canning Woodhull, who, at twenty-eight, had a reputation for being a rake and too fond of alcohol. Woodhull visited Victoria and was taken with the beautiful, fragile young girl. He prescribed a nourishing diet, regular school lessons, and walks in the fresh air to revive her spirit.

Victoria later told Tilton that when she recovered, Canning Woodhull asked her to the Fourth of July picnic, and upon returning her to her door said, "My little puss, tell your father and mother that I want you for a wife." Roxy, like many wives of child abusers, had closed her eyes to her husband's worst offenses but instinctively saw in Woodhull's proposal a way to end an unexpressed problem. Victoria, with unusual delicacy, later wrote that her mother was "not unwilling to be rid of a daughter whose sorrow was ripening her into a woman." Buck, however, was determined to hold on to his daughter and told Dr. Woodhull to stay away. Four months later, in November 1853, fifteen-year-old Victoria Claflin eloped with Canning Woodhull. "My marriage was an escape."

.  .  .

WHILE VICTORIA WOODHULL embarked on a traditional marriage, a radical fringe seeking political, religious, and personal equality was pursuing alternative ways of life. Inspired by European thinkers, so-called utopian communities began to proliferate in the United States. After his New Motor was trampled by the mob in Randolph, John Murray Spear founded a commune at Kinatone, New York, where children were raised in a common house and marriage was abolished in favor of complete sexual freedom. Three decades after the Reverend John Humphrey Noyes had incited the sexual frenzy at Brimfield, he founded the community of Oneida in upstate New York. In 1869, Noyes wrote, "Since all the saints are on a par together in equal dedication to faith, communism among them in a sex relation as in all others is the only logical arrangement." Therefore, "sexual intercourse should be no more restrained by law than eating and drinking." Other such communities included Brook Farm in Massachusetts, New Harmony in Indiana, Memonia and Berlin Heights in Ohio, and Modern Times, founded by Stephen Pearl Andrews in the pine barrens of Long Island, forty miles east of New York City.

The brilliant Stephen Pearl Andrews had mastered thirty-two languages. At thirty-one, on a trip to England in 1843, he became interested in the phonetic shorthand system of Isaac Pitman and subsequently introduced it to America. In 1849, Andrews became a correspondent for the *New York Tribune,* owned and edited by Horace Greeley, for which he recorded congressional debates in his loops and dashes. Stephen Pearl Andrews wanted to reform all aspects of society and in 1851, founded the community of Modern Times as a model to demonstrate what he termed his "New Age" philosophy. Andrews proposed a new domestic arrangement in which sexual relations were based solely on "spiritual affinities." The cofounder of Modern Times, Josiah Warren, thought Andrews's free love views were "more troublesome than a crown of thorns," but Andrews insisted that they were nothing more than the affirmation that free love was "the antithesis of enslaved love."

For Andrews, a cool intellectual, the idea that no government, church, or law should encroach upon an individual's freedom to choose a mate seemed logical, but in practice his experiment led his followers into a thicket of sexual aberration. Modern Times's colonists tied a red thread to their index fingers to announce that they were married and untied it when they decided not to be. No one questioned a child's paternity. In time this community became the refuge of fanatics and faddists. Men and women paraded about naked. One woman lived solely on beans until she died.

Andrews, undaunted, then founded the New York Free Love League and held twice-weekly meetings to propound his philosophy. Horace Gree-

*Stephen Pearl Andrews. He believed in the
"science of Spiritualism" and in free love.*

ley, appalled by these liberal sexual views, attacked the league in his newspaper. Shortly thereafter Andrews's clubhouse was raided, and four people
were arrested for disorderly conduct. Greeley then carried on a written
debate with Andrews in the *Tribune* on the subject of the relationship
between the sexes. Greeley wrote that no matter what the feelings or circumstances, the marriage bond was indissoluble. Andrews argued the
utopian view that the only relationships that should endure were those
based on love. Andrews's further statements about sex were so inflammatory that Greeley refused to print them, so Andrews published his side of
the debate in a book, *Love, Marriage, and Divorce, and the Sovereignty of the
Individual,* a virtual textbook on free love.

The overwhelming majority of Americans favored Greeley's view that
traditional marriage, sanctioned by church and state, was the only proper
arrangement. For women, a middle-class marriage was depicted in books
and sermons as an entry into a safe world of hearth and home. Married
women were taught to be the power behind the throne, responsible for
men's moral conscience, raising sons to run the world. Horace Greeley, in
the debate with Andrews, wrote that sexual relations should be for the pur-

pose of procreation only and declared, "All sexual relations that do not contemplate this end are sinful." He believed that divorce, or even remarriage while a former spouse was alive, was "adultery" and that "every form of sexual relationship except the union for life of one man with one woman" was a sin. Greeley practiced what he preached, but his own marriage was far from a typical, traditional union, for his unfeeling adherence to the conventions of the day tipped his wife's fragile constitution into madness. And the life they lived represented, in a monstrous fashion, the dark side of the celebrated American dream of "woman's sphere."

IN AUGUST 1849, Horace Greeley arrived in Rochester, and Elizabeth Cady Stanton took advantage of his visit to invite him to meet with her to discuss coeducation. The conversation was inconclusive, but Greeley's real purpose lay elsewhere: His wife, Mary Cheney Greeley, had instructed him to fetch Kate Fox. Mary was convinced that this remarkable eleven-year-old was the person she needed to contact her recently deceased child, Arthur, whom the Greeleys had called Pickie.

Horace Greeley met Kate, persuaded her to accompany him to New York, and escorted her to his ugly, barren Turtle Bay farm on the East River. Kate was to provide the means by which the inconsolable Mary could keep her child with her in death as in life. In return, Greeley promised Kate that the *Tribune* would support her. Greeley was "convinced beyond the shadow of a doubt of the [Foxes'] perfect integrity and good faith" and assured his readers that the sisters themselves did not cause the rappings to occur.

The first séance Kate Fox conducted at the Greeleys' farm was attended by Jenny Lind, "The Swedish Nightingale," the operatic soprano whom P. T. Barnum had imported to New York. As raps began to shake the Greeleys' table, Lind demanded of Horace, "Take your hands from under the table!" Greeley obliged by clasping his hands on top of his head, but the raps did not stop. Within minutes, Kate Fox fell into a trance and summoned the spirit of Pickie.

With Kate Fox as the trance medium, Mrs. Greeley and her deceased five-year-old "dream boy," Pickie, were soon communicating daily. However, in transmitting messages between Pickie and his mother, Kate sensed something ominous. Like others who had come to live under Mary Cheney Greeley's roof, Kate felt contaminated by this woman's bizarre behavior, a mania that demanded obedience to her intractable whim. The Greeleys' dark and unfurnished home was oppressive. The food, through slavish devotion to the regimen of Dr. Sylvester Graham, was confined to bran bread, overcooked rice and beans, porridge (often rancid), and puddings. Kate Fox, undoubtedly aware that the mighty *Tribune* could make or break her career, knew she must remain until winter, but she wrote to Amy Post in Rochester, "I am very lonely. Oh, how I miss you." To her brother David she lamented, "Why did I leave my mother? . . . My head aches so I can hardly write." Perhaps Kate's powers revealed to her the truth of Pickie's nightmare life and violent death and that of the four Greeley infants who had died before him. For this was no average grieving mother and no loving, protective father. In fact, Mary Cheney Greeley and her husband, despite their public image of marital harmony and rectitude, played out a vicious drama of domestic derangement.

Mary Cheney had met Horace Greeley in 1834, when she was twenty-two—a thin, nervous girl with prominent, hyperthyroid dark-brown eyes and rapid speech in which the words tumbled out. Bright and well educated, she had left the boredom of her Cornwall, Connecticut, home to teach at a girls' school in New York City. Mary boarded at a "Graham House" on Barclay Street. Sylvester Graham, the founder of these houses, had been a sickly orphan child. As an adult he'd studied physiology and diet, cured himself, became a popular lecturer, and established boardinghouses that adhered to his principles: no alcohol, caffeine, meat, or butter or other shortening. Dr. Graham was particularly known for his tasty, ginger-colored rectangular crackers. Emerson called him "the poet of bran bread and muffins." He believed in exercise, loose clothing, drinking lots of water, and confining sexual intercourse to twelve times a year. The diet at Graham House featured bread, rice, molasses, milk, vegetables, and pies made with fruit juice as a sweetener. Mary Cheney was Dr. Graham's dedicated disciple. At Graham House the food was excellent, but it was often gray and nearly inedible when Mary cooked it.

Horace Greeley, then twenty-three, was a fellow boarder. The son of impoverished, alcoholic parents who owned a small farm near Amherst, New Hampshire, Greeley had escaped to New York and the world of the intellect, starting his own small weekly publication, *The New Yorker.* They seemed a good match: Horace Greeley was lost in a world of ideas, and Mary was "crazy for learning." They were married in July 1836. Mary came into the marriage with savings of $5,000, but in the first year of their marriage *The New Yorker* nearly foundered in the great financial crisis that gripped the country. In 1837, one out of seven people in New York City was receiving alms. The city was filled with beggars and homeless people who slept in the streets. By the following Christmas, Mary's money was gone, and she resumed teaching to help support them both.

LEFT: *Horace Greeley. He was admired by the public but despised by his wife.* RIGHT: *Mary Cheney Greeley, 1834. At twenty-two she was "crazy for learning" but was cast into a domestic hell.*

In the winter of 1838, Mary's firstborn son died at three months, and five months later she suffered a miscarriage. At the time, Horace Greeley was in Albany and wrote a friend, "My wife is in bad health and is left utterly alone in New York through the worst part of the year—a circumstance which pleases neither of us." For Mary the horror had begun: She felt herself trapped in a world from which she was desperate to escape. When Horace returned from Albany that winter, he found a note from Mary awaiting him at his *New Yorker* office, informing him that she had abandoned wedded life "because her fire would not burn." But she did not run away, or perhaps she left and then came back. Her husband found her at home.

Six months later Mary suffered another miscarriage. This woman who had been "crazy for learning" now entered a nightmare world of medical quackery. For the sake of propriety, female bodies were not examined by male doctors, who prescribed treatments nonetheless. Mary was bled and purged and given calomel and so much morphine that the world became a blur. At this time Horace wrote to Margaret Fuller, a famous writer and woman's rights activist whom Mary Greeley greatly admired, "Mary is terribly ill and downhearted—a miscarriage of the worst kind and a great danger of the loss of her eyesight. She is now unable to bear the light and must be kept so all winter, without reading or doing anything, but I think she will ultimately recover."

The following year another son was born to this distracted, apathetic woman whose fragile psyche and body were being torn apart by a sexual routine she loathed and over which she had no control. Day after day, Mary sat listlessly on a bare mattress in a darkened room, unable to attend to herself, much less her infant. The baby lay in a crib in that bleak room and soon died. A pattern had been established: "Mrs. Greeley is in her usual bad health," wrote her husband in the winter of 1841. In the same year Greeley launched his penny daily, the *New York Tribune,* which was housed in a second-floor attic at 30 Ann Street in lower Manhattan, some three-and-a-half miles south of the Turtle Bay farm. Often Greeley slept there at night. On Christmas, he stayed all day in his office. He became increasingly obsessed with work.

When he was at home Horace referred to his wife as "Mother" and slavishly waited on her, ignoring her deep depression, her tantrums. An accommodation was made: Mary Greeley, though confused and demented, was left to be supreme ruler of a nightmare realm in which her husband cast himself as an ineffectual observer. Being impotent in this domestic world, Greeley asserted the one aspect of virility remaining to him by regularly impregnating his wife.

For Mary Greeley sexual intercourse with her husband led to disastrous results. One morning after she had submitted to an unwanted conjugal visit, she informed Horace that she was leaving. That same afternoon she sailed for Europe and did not return for five months. "Mrs. Greeley's life is all absorbed in the pettiest, meanest cares—and going off for months," wrote Horace. When she returned, her husband again impregnated her in what was now a pattern of creating children to be neglected and ignored by his distracted wife. A public that was to find Horace Greeley's eccentricities amusing—his absentmindedness, his one blue sock and one brown, the way he sometimes mistakenly sent *The New Yorker* to *Tribune* subscribers—could not know that these traits extended to an increasing diminution of awareness of the environment in which he lived, a blunting of his own responsibility for the horrendous acts that took place in his home.

The Greeleys' Turtle Bay farm was nicknamed "Castle Doleful" by Horace. Here a desperate Mary, seeking a way out of her domestic hell, abandoned the medical doctors who had damaged her mind and body and turned to phrenology, symbols, omens, and finally to the spirit world. Mary began conversing with the spirits that she said inhabited the house and banned almost all visitors, saying that they created "bad magnetism." She sent people away if they failed to acknowledge the spirit raps that she heard.

Servants invariably quit after a few days, no matter how much they needed the money. She would let no light into certain rooms, no fire could be lit on certain days, no tree was to be cut down because it might harbor spirits, no animal was to be slaughtered—old cows fell down and died in her over-grown pasture.

On the rare occasions that Horace Greeley was at home, it was he who built the morning fire, milked the cows, and cleaned the house. Greeley wrote that Mary kept house in a "Castle Rackrent" fashion. The house remained bare save for beds and chairs—there were no curtains, no rugs, no pictures. Meals were sparse, erratic, dismal.

Mary would observe laundry day by washing a single garment over and over perhaps a dozen times, after which, hands red and raw, she would fly into a screaming fit. Catharine Beecher's *Treatise on Domestic Economy*, which had become the bible of domesticity, included twelve pages "On Washing," eleven pages "On Whitening, Cleansing, And Dyeing," and seven pages on preparing to iron a garment. Her list of some twenty items required for doing laundry was so demanding and detailed that it took mas-sive concentration just to read it. In addition to the ironing board itself, she specified

*A séance in 1871. Thousands of Americans gathered around parlor tables to experience spirit manifestations.*

a woolen ironing-blanket, and a linen or cotton one, to put over it;
a large fire, of solid wood and charcoal, (Unless stoves or furnaces
are used); a hearth, free from cinders and ashes, and a piece of
sheet-iron, in front of the fire, on which to set the irons; . . . three
or four old holders, made of woolen, and covered with old silk, as
these do not take fire like cotton or linen; a ring, or iron-stand, on
which to set the irons, and a piece of board to put under it, to prevent very hot irons from scorching the sheet; a linen or cotton
wiper, one for each ironer, and a piece of beeswax, to rub on the
irons when smoked. There should be, at least, three irons for each
person ironing. There should also be one or two large clothes-
frames, on which to hang the clothes, when ironed; and a small one
for the smaller articles. . . .

Mary Greeley had neither time nor patience for Catharine Beecher's
idealized, endless list. She would thrust her iron into a fireplace full of ashes
and vigorously press soot into a garment. Then, observing her work, often
she would hurl the iron across the room. Her husband found that laundry
day was a good time to steer clear of Mary and remarked on her "inability
to accomplish anything." Often Horace would return home on the eleven
o'clock Harlem stagecoach, arriving at midnight to find his wife crouched
in a corner, obsessively scrubbing the floor. Sometimes she would scrub the
same spot till dawn, before falling into an exhausted sleep on the floor.
    It was in 1844 that their blond, blue-eyed son, "Pickie," had been born.
Mary determined to keep this child far from the world. When Pickie began
to walk, she locked the gates of the farm so no visitor could arrive unan-
nounced. No children were permitted to play with Pickie. He was kept on
a strict Graham diet and allowed no "dirty food"—meat or sweets or condi-
ments. Mary insisted that he see her visions, hear the spirit raps she heard,
and talk to angels as she did. Eventually, the child complied.
    To keep Pickie to herself and presumably to avoid sexual intercourse,
Mary insisted that her husband stay away much of the time. He began lecturing throughout the Midwest, often sleeping in his red-and-blue blanket
roll on the floor of railroad stations. When Pickie was two, Greeley
addressed a letter to his son, "Your sore, sick father will return home this
week to his own crazy house and his boy's bright smiles." Then, addressing
his wife, he wrote, "My piles are ugly, especially a great new one, and my
general health is not good. . . . I hear nothing to interest you." Under such
circumstances, their reunions could hardly have been joyful or sexually
pleasurable.

But return he did, and nine months later Mary gave birth to another child—a girl. But she wanted only Pickie and the hermetic world they shared. In a series of letters to Margaret Fuller, Horace Greeley chronicled the horrors in his own home as if he were a detached observer. He made no effort to correct the situation or to find help for his wife's mental condition. In these letters he observed that his life had become so bleak that he had taken to boarding in the city. The little girl lay in her basket, "while Mother often said she wished her dead on account of the labor and anxiety she caused." The baby became so weak from hunger that she could barely cry but lay staring with eyes exaggerated by her gaunt countenance. "Pickie regarded her as a rival and an obstacle to his enjoyments, urging that she should be given away." No one lifted her from her basket for days at a time as she lay in her own excrement. She died on May 6, 1847. Wrote her father, "I never saw a creature so patient under suffering and so grateful for kindness, and her love for me was a precious wonder. . . . It is awful to think how friendless and often, I fear, consciously so, our blessing was. . . . With proper treatment and care, I am sure my darling would have survived. . . . A week after the funeral Mother said to [Pickie], 'Are you not sorry for the death of little sister?' 'Yes,' he replied, and after an instant's thought added, 'but you couldn't take care of us both.' "

Pickie dictated a letter to Margaret Fuller: "I had a pretty little sister. We called her Dotty. She was so little. She had very bright eyes. She looked at me so still. I did not like her eyes. She has gone to another world and I am very sorry."

Pickie was then three and a half, but Mary, in her effort to keep him as her own, still dressed him in a long white linen shift and diapers. His blond curls remained uncut. But Pickie had begun to assert himself. When he showed the least tendency to disobey, his mother whipped him, sometimes several times a day. Wrote Greeley, "When I came home at 10½ p.m. he had been hours in bed but was still broad awake (his mother had whipped him twice). His mother whips him often but never rules him, and I have no voice in his management and never can have." Greeley added the observation that Pickie was "sick of hope deferred."

The child eked out his lonely existence playing with blocks or pebbles. Increasingly he came to resent his mother. He fantasized that he had been adopted and that his real mother was a kindly Dutch woman who had been too poor to keep him. As Pickie's temper grew more erratic, the beatings grew more savage. Mary took to threatening him with spiritual terrors: phantoms that would plunge him in boiling oil, invisible devils that lived in their upper chamber. Horace wrote, "He is governed and restricted and cramped till he hates all law and all authority. . . . When beaten, as he was when we rode out last Saturday, he looks her in the eye with an aspect of indignation and grief, yelling, 'O you ugly creature!' He does not get whipped so often as he did, for his Mother has adopted the plan of shutting him up in the upper chamber, which speedily brings him to subjection."

When Pickie was five, Mary Greeley encouraged her husband to spend the winter in Washington. But before departing, once again he impregnated her, and once again a daughter was born. Within the first eight months of her life baby Ida suffered "malaria, diarrhea, sprue and cholera." Miraculously she survived, but Pickie too contracted cholera, and he died within twelve hours.

Pickie had been swept away, but even then Mary refused to loosen her iron grip. It was at this time that she conceived the idea of summoning the eleven-year-old Spiritualist Kate Fox to establish communication with her son. In the four months that Kate lived with the Greeleys, every day Mary spoke to her "angel" Pickie through Kate. Spirits occupied the house. Kate wrote a letter to Amy Post describing one séance: "The piano was sweetly played upon by spirit fingers and the guitar was played, then taken up and carried above our heads. Each person in the circle was touched." She related how the spirits "ring bells and move tables all when our feet are held. We have convinced many skeptical people." But of Mary Cheney Greeley, Kate Fox wrote, "How I hate her!"

# CHAPTER SIX

# TRUE WIFE

B Y THE time Victoria Woodhull became a famous woman's rights advocate, she would use the example of her own first marriage to condemn all oppression in marriage. Her detractors would object that, just as her many spiritual "predictions" were revealed in retrospect and could not be proved, so she had invented incidents in her own marriage simply to illustrate the subjection of women. Her critics claimed that Dr. Canning Woodhull was a gentleman who had taught this wild child manners and the ways of polite society. That was true. But it was also true that he was an alcoholic and a morphine addict.

According to Victoria Woodhull's highly colored account, Canning had not shared her bed since the third night of their marriage. He slept at the local brothel. She knew that because when the money ran out and she went to look for him, following his trail from tavern to tavern, she finally found him eating pigeon pie and drinking champagne, surrounded by whores.

At night she would stand by the window, waiting. Sometimes in the early morning hours she would hear the faltering steps of her husband as he stumbled along the cobblestones. One night she saw Canning Woodhull in a vision, "walking unsteadily across a road that I instinctively knew was on the outskirts of the city. With my soul I watched over him as he went into the Freemont Hotel and lay down on a sofa. As he lay down, his billfold fell on the floor." A clerk moved quickly, picked up the billfold, and furtively stuffed it behind the sofa cushion. When Dr. Woodhull returned home the following morning, he could not remember where he had been. Vickie went to the Freemont Hotel, identified the clerk, and retrieved her husband's money.

After only six weeks of marriage she discovered a letter in her husband's jacket pocket. "Did you marry that child because she too was *en famille?*" the writer asked. Reading further, Vickie realized that this letter was from her husband's former mistress, whom he had sent to Terre Haute, where she gave birth to a boy. Woodhull was also sending her money. Although Vickie

was married to a man "mostly with his cups and his mistresses," she still
sought his love. When he was sober Canning Woodhull had a certain sweet
passivity and he was attentive to her. She called him "Doc" and marveled at
how much he knew. He was less harsh than her father.

Winter of 1854 found the Woodhulls living in a tenement in Chicago.
Just after Christmas, Vickie, attended by her "half-drunken" husband, gave
birth to a son. For years thereafter, she dwelt on her "mortal agony" and
insisted that she remembered "icicles clinging to her bed post." After the
delivery, Dr. Woodhull promptly left. A next-door neighbor miraculously
appeared to wash and feed the new mother. When Vickie produced no
milk, the neighbor wrapped the baby in a blanket and carried him to
another woman with a newborn son who nursed both babies. On the third
day after her son's birth, Vickie became delirious. Childbed fever raged
through her body. Three days later Mama Roxy appeared, declaring that
she had been summoned by the spirits. Victoria remembered nothing of her
mother's arrival. That same evening Woodhull returned from a drunken
bender and both husband and mother—one employing medicine, the
other the spirits—snatched Vickie back from "the iron door."

The son, Byron (named for the poet, who had died thirty years earlier),
was an imbecile who never developed teeth and whose speech was never
more than a series of grunts. Sometimes Victoria said Byron was an idiot
because Doc had kicked her in the stomach while she was pregnant. At
other times she said that, as an infant, Byron had fallen from a second-story
window. Sometimes, she blamed herself.

Victoria still believed that marriage was a sacred institution, and she
"wrestled with God" to find a way to live with this arrangement. The next
winter, when Doc once again deserted her, Vickie left Byron with her
mother and set out in search of her husband. Melodramatically, she later
described herself as wearing a thin calico dress, no underwear, and only
India rubbers on her feet as she ran through the frozen streets of Chicago.
In that condition, she burst into the dining room of the boardinghouse
where Doc sat at dinner with his fellow boarders and the mistress whom he
called his wife. When she saw her husband so comfortable, so warm in the
light of the fire, her rage exploded. She was lonely and hungry, she said, and
she was his "true wife." She told of all that had befallen her, until there were
tears in the eyes of the boarders and the mistress's face turned scarlet. Then
and there the listeners forced "the harlot to pack her trunk." Vickie's
shamed husband took her by the hand, and together they returned to their
rented hovel.

They needed money and a new life. "Go West, young men, and grow up with the country!" Horace Greeley commanded in the *Tribune*. In 1849, gold was discovered in California, which a year later became the thirty-first state. In the next seven years the population of California grew from fifteen thousand to three hundred thousand as prospectors mined $450 million worth of gold. Commodore Cornelius Vanderbilt, seeing a way to increase his shipping fortune, provided a quick route to the goldfields across the isthmus of Nicaragua. When his crew found the San Juan River too dangerous and threatened mutiny, the Commodore took the wheel, tied down the safety valve, and ran his boat up the river to its destination. In 1858, with gold still attracting people from across the nation, Vickie and Doc set out for San Francisco with four-year-old Byron.

This was a place of wealth, teeming with men as rough and raw as the roustabouts of Buck Claflin's youth. But soon Victoria found herself and her family "beggars in a land of plenty." No one had time to listen to her visions and predictions unless they concerned the location of the precious ore they were seeking. Men outnumbered women twenty to one and found their pleasures in taverns and brothels. Desperate for money, Victoria answered an ad to become a "cigar girl" in a tavern. After one day of crude remarks, undisguised groping, and bold sexual propositions, she was fired by the owner, who told Vickie that her reticence was bad for business and that he needed to have "somebody who can rough it." But he walked her home, and on meeting Doc Woodhull, discovered that he was a fellow Freemason. He gave Vickie a $20 gold piece and wished her good luck.

Day after day Vickie sat sewing, the only work she could find. Her average wage was 38 cents a day. Anna Cogswell, an actress, hired Vickie to alter her costumes, and they became friends. When Vickie confessed, "It is no use. I am running behind, and I must do something," Anna suggested that she appear onstage. Vickie's unusual facility for instantly memorizing a text served her well here, as it would later in her career. She said that she could be given a new part in the morning, rehearse it by day, and be letter-perfect by night. She also boasted that overnight her wages jumped from $3 to $52 a week, but that was quite a different matter.

To be a so-called "actress" was not as difficult or degrading as being a "cigar girl," but it was an entry into the world of the demimonde. In theaters, in America and abroad, from across the gas footlights affluent men chose the women who would later occupy their beds. The ballet and opera choruses also provided such opportunities for sexual selection. The tutus of the ballerina fully exposed the leg, while in the theater, low décolletage and tightly laced bodices emphasized breasts that were semi-exposed, elevated, and served up like ripe melons. Victoria wore such costumes for her part in *The Country Cousin* and in *New York by Gaslight*. When the evening's performance finished, the revels began.

It was at one of these so-called parties that Anna Cogswell introduced Victoria Woodhull to another destitute "actress," Helen Josephine Mansfield, called Josie. The daughter of a reporter for a Boston newspaper, Josie had come with her parents in 1852 to Stockton, California, where her father was killed in a duel. Her mother then moved to San Francisco and married a professional gambler named Richard Warren. Josie would later say that her stepfather sexually molested her when she was twelve and continued to do so for three years, threatening to maim her if she ever spoke of it. Josie did not tell her mother, who by this time was drinking heavily. By the time Josie was fifteen, her stepfather was selling her to other men. Once he forced her to have intercourse with a wealthy attorney named D. W. Perley, after which he popped out from under the bed, pointed a loaded pistol at Perley's head, and demanded $500.

To escape her stepfather's blackmail schemes, Josie eloped with a strolling actor named Frank Lawlor, who often performed onstage with Anna Cogswell. Victoria Woodhull's and Josie Mansfield's paths would cross again, a decade later and three thousand miles away, in New York. By then, neither would be an actress and neither would be destitute.

Soon Vickie came to hate what she euphemistically referred to as "the stage." At twenty, she was supporting a feebleminded son and a husband who, now lost in a fog of drugs and alcohol, had become equally dependent on her. After two years of acting and casual prostitution Vickie was becoming increasingly desperate. "I am meant for some other fate," she told herself. She later wrote that one evening while performing in the ballroom scene of *The Corsican Brothers,* suddenly she heard her sister Tennessee's voice calling out, "Victoria, come home," and saw a vision of Tennie beautifully dressed in a striped red-and-white French silk frock, standing beside Mama Roxy. "Come home!" her sister called out again, beckoning her. Vickie bolted from the stage and, still wearing her pink silk ball gown and silver slippers, ran through the night to her lodgings and threw her few belongings into a bag. The next morning Vickie, Doc, and Byron, then six, boarded a steamer heading for New York.

Whether Victoria was a reliable witness to the events of her own life is debatable. She was never to explain why the spirits summoned her or why she fled, but abrupt escapes "guided by the spirits" were to become a pattern. On the voyage she recalled that she was "thrown into such vivid spiritual states" that she "produced a profound excitement among the passengers" with her trance speaking and her visions. Victoria claimed that when at last she landed in New York and took the train to Columbus, Ohio, Tennessee greeted her at the door wearing the frock Vickie had seen in her vision. Mama Roxy said that she had instructed Tennie to use her powers to "send the spirits . . . to bring her [Vickie] home."

The Claflins were prospering: By 1860, Tennessee had become her father's golden goose. He would ride into town in his bright wagon with his daughter seated at his side, take rooms at a boardinghouse or hotel, and place an ad in the local paper:

## A WONDERFUL CHILD!
### Miss Tennessee Claflin
### Who is only fourteen years of age!!

This young lady . . . has been endowed from her birth with a super-natural gift to such an astonishing degree that she convinces the most skeptical of her wonderful powers. She gives information of absent friends, whether living or dead, together with all the past, present and future events of life.

She can see and point out the medicine to cure the most obstinate diseases—even those that for years baffled our best physicians—and can direct salves and liniment to be made and used that will cure old sores, fever sores, cancers, sprains, weakness in the back and limbs and other complaints. . . .

She will point out to ladies and gentlemen their former, present and future partners . . . and when required will go into an unconscious state and travel to any part of the world, hunt up absent friends, whether dead or alive, and through her they will tell the inquiring friend their situation and whereabouts, with all the events of life since they last met. . . .

She may be consulted at her room [address inserted] from the hours of eight o'clock a.m. to nine o'clock p.m. Price of consultation, $1.00.

Tennessee worked thirteen hours a day while Buck collected the money and sold his alcohol- and opium-laden cure-all, now renamed "Miss Tennessee's Magnetic Life Elixir," at $2 a bottle, double the old price. "It was a hard life," Tennie would later declare. "I was forced to humbug people for the money."

When Victoria rejoined the family, she found that her father had amplified his daughter's real powers with his own chicanery. When Buck arrived in town, he would visit the local cemetery and copy information from the tombstones. Also, there was a lively black market in what came to be known as the "Blue Book," which listed the local people most likely to attend séances and gave their family histories, including the names and dates of those who had died, as well as information on present romantic or domestic attachments and personal habits.

Fortune-tellers and thought-readers were known to use a technique called "muscle-reading": If a member of the audience called out the alphabet, the mind reader could guess the correct letter by watching his expression. In another trick, if a person was asked to write six names on a slip of paper, one of which was that of a dead relative, the writer usually did not hesitate on the correct name and thus revealed which one to choose.

Then there was "one ahead," which made it possible for fraudulent mediums to read messages written inside tightly folded pieces of paper. The medium drew a folded piece of paper from a bowl and, with a look of intense concentration, pressed it against her forehead and read the message "through the power of her mind." The medium then unfolded the paper and supposedly read the message aloud. The trick lay in staying one message ahead of the audience. The first message was made up by the medium, then confirmed by an accomplice planted in the audience. What the medium had in fact unfolded and memorized was the next message she was to recite.

Aside from Buck's tricks, real powers manifested themselves in the twenty-two-year-old Victoria as they did in the fourteen-year-old Tennie. In a state of almost ecstatic excitement, Victoria would see auras around her clients and know immediately when someone was sick. Once she told a judge, the father of a seemingly healthy fifteen-year-old daughter, that the girl would die within the year and her prediction came true.

The first records of Victoria's magnetic healing go back to this time. She derived her techniques from her mother's early doctoring, which Roxy in turn had learned from observing carnival demonstrations of Franz Anton Mesmer's animal magnetism. The right hand was thought to contain positive magnetic energy, the left negative. Between the two hands a current was generated similar to that observed by Mesmer and the Marquis de Puységur. By passing one's hands along the body without actually touching it, healing magnetic fluid was said to be stimulated. If one believed.

By 1860, magnetic healing had become a popular alternative medical treatment. In Elmira, New York, sixteen-year-old Olivia Langdon (called

Livy) was returning home on a winter's day when she slipped on the ice. She was carried to her bed. By morning she was paralyzed. For two years Livy Langdon remained in this condition, lying flat on her back in a darkened room. A parade of physicians visited her, but all hope of recovery slipped away until, as a desperate measure, a Spiritualist healer, Dr. Jarvis Rogers Newton, was called in. He marched into Livy's bedroom, pulled back the heavy draperies, and flung the windows open. He said a brisk prayer, then put both of his arms around Livy's shoulders and announced, "Now we will sit up, my child." Livy sat up. Newton then declared, "Now we will walk a few steps, my child." And she did.

Years later Livy's husband, the author Samuel Clemens, known as Mark Twain, asked Dr. Newton the secret of his success. Newton replied that he wasn't sure himself, but he suspected that some form of electricity passed from his body into that of the patient. After this explanation, Clemens began to recommend faith healing, although he was aware of the frauds perpetrated by many so-called healers. In *Huckleberry Finn* the king, a charlatan, declares, "I've done considerable in the doctoring way. . . . Layin' on o' hands is my best holt—for cancer and paralysis, and sich things and I k'n tell a fortune pretty good when I've got somebody along to find out the facts for me."

One thing was sure: Faith in the healer was essential to the cure. And Victoria inspired faith. Women came to her to cure their diseases, but just as often, to unburden themselves of their deepest secrets with tales of sexual abuse and perversion, of sickness induced by maltreatment and neglect, of poverty and oppression. Women confided their cares, their hopes, their fears and longings, and Victoria tried to help them with clairvoyant advice and predictions. All her life she would carry with her the memory of the miseries of the "thousands of women" who came to her for hope.

Victoria believed in her own power to transmit magnetic energy that would put the person she touched under her control. When she greeted people, she took both of their hands in hers. It was often reported that in her grasp one felt a current of energy, a remarkable warmth and light flowing throughout one's body. Victoria also believed that the animal magnetism she generated could disable her enemies. She had learned this early on, when people mocked her preaching and she would stare at them, unblinking, until they turned away. One woman was so affected by her gaze that, in front of a crowd, her false teeth popped out of her mouth.

Victoria would tell fellow Spiritualists that on the periphery of her vision she could see objects—eggs, small bottles, lorgnettes with metal frames—that tumbled and turned slowly in space before alighting at her feet. She maintained that suddenly her water glass would fly out of her hand, her pot of lip rouge would whirl away and plop down in the middle of her wineglass. She said that before her concentrated gaze rings cracked open and forks bent out of shape, their prongs twisting and braiding.

Victoria's boasts concerning her powers extended far beyond those of most Spiritualists. She wrote in several documents that on one occasion when she returned home, Roxy told her that Byron had been seized by a fit and had died two hours earlier. "No. I will not permit his death," Victoria exclaimed, and ran to him. Tearing her dress open to the waist, she clasped her son's cold body and concentrated all her energy on generating heat. She "glided insensibly into a trance. . . . I beheld Jesus standing in the doorway. His arms were outstretched showing me His hands and feet. I saw the scars of His crucifixion. . . . My whole future was foreshadowed in that time." When Victoria regained consciousness, she reported, the boy, soaked with perspiration, was alive in her arms.

Victoria, who by now had learned from her father's showmanship, decided to strike out on her own. Leaving her family in Ohio she set out for Indianapolis, Indiana, with her husband and son, where she rented rooms at the Bates House and placed an announcement, or "card," in the local newspaper advertising herself as a "Clairvoyant Medium and Magnetic Healer." But these powers alone did not provide sufficient income: After two months in which "servant girls" patronized Mrs. Woodhull, she was accused of using the extra rooms she had rented for assignations and was ejected from the Bates House for "disorderly conduct."

Now seven months pregnant and once again destitute, Vickie begged her husband to borrow money from his father. She later claimed that she and Canning visited Dr. Woodhull's father, a judge in Rochester, but he refused to help them. (However, there is no record of a Judge Woodhull in or around the Rochester area at this time.) In April 1861, in yet another rented room, Vickie gave birth to her second child. After a protracted labor the baby was delivered at four a.m. by the shaking hands of Doc Woodhull, who, totally inebriated, half-severed the umbilical cord without tying it off, placed the baby girl on the pillow next to Vickie's head, and left the house. Vickie lapsed into an exhausted sleep from which she awoke to find her hair and the pillow soaked with blood. Drop by bloody drop, her baby's life was oozing away. With the last of her strength she bit through the cord and tied it herself.

Unable to move from the bed, she reached out, found a broken chair rung that lay nearby, and banged on the wall, calling for help. She repeated this again and again until a woman who lived in the next house heard the rapping through the wall. The front door was locked, but the woman removed a grate in the basement and climbed the stairs to rescue the new mother.

Three days later, while Vickie sat in bed holding little Zulu Maud in her arms, she looked out the window and caught sight of her husband "staggering up the steps of a house across the street, mistaking it for his own." It was then that she finally asked herself, "Why should I any longer live with this man?"

# CHAPTER SEVEN

# WILLFULLY DID KILL

s Victoria lay in the tenement room holding her newborn daughter, at four-thirty a.m. on April 12, 1861, Confederate shore batteries under the command of Brigadier General Pierre G. T. Beauregard opened fire on South Carolina's Fort Sumter. After a thirty-four-hour bloodless bombardment, Major Robert Anderson instructed Private Hart to lower the Union flag, which was then carefully pointed, put in a mailbag marked "Major Anderson, Fort Sumter, April 14, 1861," and dispatched to the Bank of Commerce vault in Washington for storage. Anderson then surrendered to Confederate troops.

For many the Great Rebellion came as a surprise: Only the previous month in his inaugural address Lincoln had declared, "I have no purpose, directly or indirectly, to interfere with the institution of slavery in the States where it exists." But the cauldron of controversy concerning several issues had boiled over—states' rights against federal authority, the expanding industrial North against the agrarian South, slaveholders against those who had no need for slave labor. As the country mobilized, Northern experts predicted victory within ninety days. Lincoln issued a call to arms, and seventy-five thousand volunteers responded.

Women quickly stepped out of their traditional roles. For the past decade many women had fought for their rights, but now they tacitly agreed to postpone equality and enfranchisement for the war effort. Lucy Stone gave up the income from her woman's rights lectures and made shirts for Union soldiers. Mary Livermore, a Chicago woman's rights advocate, began what was to become four years of visiting camps and hospitals, organizing sanitary aid societies, and meeting countless times with President Lincoln. She overcame the opposition to women nurses at the front and raised more than $100,000 for medical supplies. She was responsible for wiping out scurvy by bullying farmers into donating fresh fruit, which was then rushed by rail to the troops. Traveling through Illinois, Livermore saw "women in the fields everywhere, driving the reapers, binding and shucking

*Mary Livermore was a heroine
of the Civil War who fought on for
woman suffrage.*

and loading the grain." Susan B. Anthony returned to her father's New England farm and did hard manual labor so her brothers could be released for the fight.

In Brooklyn, the Plymouth Church Ladies Guild provided clothing and food packages for Union soldiers. Largely because of its flamboyant and charismatic preacher, Henry Ward Beecher, Plymouth Church was the most prominent of the scores of churches in this, the third-largest city in the country. Beecher's patron was Henry Bowen, the owner and publisher of the *Independent,* a popular religious newspaper. His wife, Lucy, had organized the Ladies Guild but shortly thereafter fell mysteriously ill. On a fall day in 1862, Lucy Bowen—thirty-eight, the mother of ten, still a beauty—lay on her deathbed. She spoke in a whisper as her husband bent over her, "I cannot meet my Maker unless you know," she breathed. She told her husband how her preacher had seduced and abandoned her. For more than a year Lucy Bowen had gone to Beecher's private study at Plymouth Church, and he had called her his love. He had given her a key to the door so that she could enter, lock the door behind her, and wait for his triple rap.

*Henry Ward Beecher's Plymouth Church (and below) during a Sunday sermon*

*The church is located on Orange Street, between Hicks and Henry Streets in Brooklyn.*

One day when Beecher was not expecting her, Lucy approached the door and saw another woman insert a key in the lock and move quickly inside. Lucy heard the bolt snap into place. The realization that she was not the only woman with whom Henry Ward Beecher was consorting broke her heart. But for Henry Bowen the worst of his wife's confession was that she vowed she loved Beecher still.

Bowen swore himself to silence, for to expose Beecher was also to expose the fact that he had been cuckolded. Furthermore, Bowen had an enormous stake in the financial stability of Plymouth Church. He was a founding member and owner of the land on which the church stood. Plymouth Church bonds yielded him 7 percent interest, and he received part of the revenues from the pew auctions. Knowing of Beecher's power, he allowed his wife's seducer to officiate at her funeral. In reprisal, however, Bowen used his wife's confession to force Beecher to become his puppet by endorsing all manner of merchandise advertised in the *Independent,* from Chickering pianos, to Waltham watches, to the indignity of trusses. As Bowen's demands escalated, Beecher sought escape. Abruptly, he left his pulpit, wife, and children, and embarked for England to lecture for the Union cause.

In Beecher's absence, Henry Bowen's fortunes began to rise, and to a great extent he had Theodore Tilton to thank for it. Tilton, a gifted writer of twenty-eight, was Beecher's protégé. Henry Ward Beecher had thought Lincoln an unfit candidate who would be defeated for the presidency in 1860 and had criticized him from the Plymouth Church pulpit in August 1861, flatly declaring the war "a failure." For the first time, however, Tilton disagreed with Beecher, and he unequivocally supported the president in Bowen's *Independent.* As a result, Bowen was appointed collector of the Port of Brooklyn and became a powerful political figure, the king of local patronage, devoting himself to licensing ships and collecting duties on their cargo. It was up to Bowen to determine if such cargo was legal or illegal. If illegal, he confiscated the goods, which were stored in warehouses owned by himself and other prominent political figures.

As the war progressed and the harbor filled with supply ships, Bowen and his cronies had an unlimited opportunity to collect kickbacks and bribes. His greed even extended to the insignificant: He hired a gang of Irish street urchins to peddle, on Chatham Street, the groceries and clothes that had been confiscated. In one year, Bowen's income reportedly increased from $23,000 to $183,000. In the second year of the war, Bowen built the largest and most imposing house in Brooklyn on the corner of Willow and

*Henry Bowen was said to be the richest and most
treacherous man in Brooklyn.*

Clark Streets, a huge white colonial mansion with terraced Italianate gardens, wide lawns, and a magnificent view of the river and the bay. He had the faces of each of his ten children carved into the frames of his mahogany armchairs.

From England came word that Henry Ward Beecher had taken the country by storm. As he toured Liverpool, Birmingham, and Manchester, even before he spoke a word he was greeted with enthusiasm. This was a happy time for him, for he received the "soul-food"—the unconditional approbation—he craved. And at home Tilton published article after article on Beecher's success, though Bowen tried to shake his confidence in his mentor. One day as the two men stood at the rail of the Fulton Street ferry, Bowen told Tilton of Lucy's deathbed confession. Soon after, from his summer home in Woodstock, New York, he wrote Tilton, "I sometimes feel that I must break silence. . . . One word from me would make a revolution throughout Christendom . . . and Beecher would be driven from his pulpit and from Brooklyn in twelve hours."

On July 21, 1861, soldiers both blue and gray carried their dead and dying from a battlefield in Virginia: The Union soldiers called it Bull Run; the Confederates, Manassas. In Philadelphia, a nineteen-year-old Quaker girl, Anna Dickinson, speaking at the Academy of Music, accused General George B. McClellan, commander of the Union forces, of "cowardice and treason" for having delayed so long in engaging the enemy. As a result she was fired from her position at the United States Mint in Philadelphia, where she had worked as an adjustor six days a week, eleven hours a day, for $28 a month. But the fervor of her speech so inspired the famous abolitionist publisher William Lloyd Garrison that he hired Anna to speak for his cause. Thus Dickinson's brilliant career was launched, one that would meaningfully affect both the woman's rights movement and the life of Victoria Woodhull.

By early 1862, President Lincoln was convinced that if he issued an emancipation proclamation freeing the slaves, he could create economic and social chaos in the Southern states, but he hesitated to do so until the Union won a decisive battle. During the darkest days of the war, the president made a trip to Brooklyn to consult with Theodore Tilton, whose opinion he had come to value, though Tilton was neither a politician nor a soldier. The president intended his visit to be secret, but soon all Brooklyn knew that he had come to Lib and Theodore Tilton's Livingston Street home and that, when their daughter Florry presented Lincoln with a bouquet of flowers, he bent down and kissed her on the cheek. It was said the president left Brooklyn more determined than ever that the issuance of an emancipation proclamation was necessary.

At Antietam in Sharpsburg, Maryland, the North won a battle, but at a terrible price: Seven thousand of General Joseph Hooker's men were killed in fourteen minutes. Nevertheless, this Pyrrhic victory gave the president the confidence to draft an emancipation proclamation to take effect on January 1, 1863. Many doubted that Lincoln had the courage to fulfill his promise, but on December 31, Frederick Douglass was among the hopeful who attended a midnight freedom-watch service at Tremont Temple in Boston. When a telegraph messenger arrived with the news that Lincoln had indeed issued the Emancipation Proclamation, there was cheering and then absolute silence. Then Douglass raised his voice in song, and the crowd followed: "Sound the loud timbrel o'er Egypt's dark sea. Jehovah hath triumphed, his people are free."

Lincoln was a reluctant emancipator. Though the proclamation technically freed 3 million blacks, it excluded slaves in Union-occupied territories and in the four border states that had remained loyal to the Union. A London newspaper observed that "a human being cannot justly own another . . . unless he is loyal to the United States."

A Spiritualist medium, Mrs. Nettie Colburn Maynard, who had conducted séances in the White House at which Lincoln was present, claimed that the president had been moved to emancipate the slaves through a spirit message she had transmitted to him. Mary Todd Lincoln, a devoted Spiritualist, declared that she had been present when the message was transmitted. Their son Robert later denied that his father was in any way affected by such communications. As death on the battlefield became an ever-present reality, Spiritualism grew stronger. Its adherents, according to several contemporary sources, swelled from about 2 million in 1850 to about 7 million by 1863.

In that same year, with the Union army depleted, Congress passed a conscription act. But a rich man need not go to war; he was allowed to buy a substitute to serve in his place for $300. In the heat of July, in New York City, a protest against America's first forced draft, led by impoverished Irish immigrants—who did not want to die for the sake of freeing black men to compete with them for jobs—soon expanded into a riot. Elizabeth Cady Stanton, who was now living in New York, where her husband, Henry, was deputy custom collector for the Port of New York, witnessed the riot. Her eldest son, Daniel (called Neil), who worked as a clerk in his father's office, was standing in front of their house on the night of July 13 when a "brutal mob" of Irish ruffians strode down the street and seized him. "Here's one of those three-hundred-dollar fellows!" one shouted. Elizabeth thought her son was about to "be torn limb from limb." But as she later wrote, "Neil with great presence of mind, as they passed a saloon said, 'Let's go in, fellows, and take a drink.' He treated the whole band. . . . 'Oh,' they said, 'he seems a good fellow, let him go.' "

That night, Elizabeth, thinking that the rioters might attack her for her antislavery views, sent her "servants and the children to the fourth story . . . opened the skylight and told them, in case of attack, to run out on the roof into some neighboring house." The sky turned red as the Colored Orphan Asylum at Fifth Avenue and Forty-third Street, less than two blocks from her house, was burned to the ground by the rioters. A bystander saw a black child "three years of age thrown from a fourth-story window and instantly killed. A woman one hour after her confinement was set upon and beaten with her tender babe in her arms. . . . Children were torn from their mother's embrace and their brains blown out in the very face of these afflicted women. Men were burnt by slow fires." It took four days for soldiers and the police to disperse the mob. More than one hundred black people had been killed and scores more were maimed.

*On the night of July 13, 1863, an enraged Irish mob looted and destroyed
the Colored Orphan Asylum.*

Henry Stanton returned from Albany the following day. Although his
job at the Custom House was a powerful one, his superior wrote to the secretary of the Treasury, Salmon P. Chase, that his work was lackadaisical, and
that "his mind is more absent than his body." He was referring to Stanton's
careless supervision of Custom House bonds. In wartime, every ship that
entered New York harbor was required to secure its cargo with a bond filed
at the Custom House. Once it was determined that the ship's cargo was not
contraband, the bond was returned. Cargoes without bonds were seized by
the government. By the spring of 1863, it was discovered that bonds being
held for certain shipments had disappeared. The Treasury Department
investigated, and by fall Henry Stanton was implicated. He questioned his
son Neil, who confessed to taking the bonds and selling them.

Because Henry Stanton refused to speak about his son's crime, he was
accused of complicity and even of allowing munitions to reach enemy lines.
Henry insisted that he was innocent and that his son had been the "weak
victim of wily scoundrels." He placed much of the blame for the public
scrutiny he had received on his wife's increasingly visible radicalism. She in

turn became more determined than ever to become an individual in her own right.

IN THE midst of the war, the Claflin family arrived in Ottawa, Illinois. Eight years later, Victoria was to write that the war had come as no surprise to her. "For years before the Rebellion, I frequently saw armies marching in the air, heard the roar of cannon and the rattle of musketry, and the negroes fleeing before them." Of her sister Tennie's powers she wrote,

> When Lincoln was on his way to Washington, to be inaugurated President, my sister Tennie was with father and mother at a promi-nent hotel in Pittsburgh. Thousands of the inhabitants had assem-bled in the street. . . . As the carriage . . . came in sister's sight, she . . . exclaimed, "He will never leave the White House alive. I heard a pistol shot and saw the blood running from his head, and his coffin in the carriage with him."

While others were swept up by the war, Buck Claflin thought only of profit based on human need. What disease most plagued mankind? Cancer! He decided that a cancer cure would make him a fortune. Within six months of his arrival in Ottawa, "Doctor" Reuben B. Claflin and his fam-ily were doing well enough to rent the entire Fox River House, the town's oldest hotel. Here, on the second floor, Buck Claflin set up an infirmary. He advertised himself as the "AMERICAN KING OF CANCERS . . . Dr. Claflin guarantees a cure in all cases where patients live up to directions. . . . Cancers killed and extracted, root and branch, in from 10 to 48 hours with-out instruments, pain or use of chloroform, simply by applying a salve of the doctor's own make." The salve that purportedly cured cancer was a home brew. In an iron vat in the backyard, the coarse Roxy, assisted by the comely Utica, could be seen stirring a mixture that contained scent, sheep's fat, and lye.

The Fox River House overflowed with Claflins. After ten years of mar-riage, Victoria had divorced Canning Woodhull and returned to her family with her two children, the idiot Byron and the thriving Zulu Maud. Mar-garet Ann, divorced from Enos Miles, was there with her four children. So was Polly Burns and her daughter, Rosa, as well as Utica and brother Hebern, who now called himself Dr. Hebern Claflin.

All the Claflin girls were beautiful, especially the three youngest—Vic-toria, Utica, and Tennessee. To Roxy it seemed a miracle that so plain a woman should be the mother of such daughters. To Buck, their beauty was yet another opportunity to make money. He advertised in the *Ottawa Free Trader* that on the first floor of the Fox River House lessons in the "cult of love" were to be taught. In the summer of 1863, there were several complaints that the extra rooms at the Fox River House were being used for assignations and that Buck's daughters were prostitutes. The charges were never proved.

In addition to whatever sexual services were offered, Tennessee's clairvoyant powers were becoming well known. Three weeks after the battle of Gettysburg, a local newspaper carried an account of a soldier with a bullet still embedded in his foot who "hobbled in on crutches" to the Claflin infirmary. As Tennie felt his toes she exclaimed, "Why, Captain, you were not wounded in battle!"

"How then did I receive my wound?" he challenged her.

"When the rebels evacuated and the federal army moved forward in pursuit, you lingered behind and were shot by a rebel concealed in a tree."

The soldier was "thunderstruck," for, by his account, this event was known only to himself.

Since Tennie was the most famous of the family, her name was used in Buck's advertisements. They specified that she alone would apply her father's cancer treatment. Buck's salve was so strong that it could strip paint from the side of a barn. After the treatment, the screams of the patients sometimes could be heard throughout the neighborhood. Victoria wrote that once she looked under the bedclothes and saw the damage: ragged, livid areas, pus, blood, and exposed cartilage. She was reminded of a slaughtered animal. One evening, risking her father's anger, she asked Buck why he used this treatment, and he answered, "There are only three cures for cancer—cut it out, poison it with arsenic, or burn it out. I burn it!"

Buck's testimonials appeared in local newspapers, luring more sufferers. One read, "Mrs. Rebecca Howe, recovering from a dangerous situation after treatment by MISS TENNESSEE CLAFLIN wishes to thank this remarkable child and recommends [she] be consulted for cancer treatment." The canny Buck had used Mrs. Howe's name because he knew she had breast cancer. In these strict times, women rarely spoke of their bodies. At dinner parties hostesses sometimes referred delicately to the "bosom" of the turkey. But Rebecca Howe read the testimony and, knowing she was dying, wanted to tell the truth. She wrote to the *Ottawa Republican* that in fact, her breast had been "wholly eaten away" by the lye salve applied by Tennie. She was racked with unbearable pain and prayed only for a quick death. She concluded that "Miss Claflin is . . . an imposter, and one wholly unfit for the confidence of the community." Two local doctors attested to the truth of Rebecca Howe's statement and to the hideous pain she had endured.

Four days later, the cancer infirmary was raided by a local marshal and two doctors. Buck Claflin was not present when they pushed past Utica and Mama Roxy and charged up the staircase. Private rooms on the second floor housed new patients undergoing treatment. At the end of the hall was the infirmary ward. The door was open, and there, on rows of unmade cots, were found dying, unfed wrecks of humanity lying in their own excrement. Dr. Joseph Stout stated that not even in the newly opened infamous Andersonville prison camp in Georgia, where one out of every three Union prisoners died, had there been such neglect. Rebecca Howe died that same day.

Within a fortnight, nine separate complaints of disorderly conduct, blackmail, and medical quackery had been lodged against the Claflins, but all these paled beside the charges against Tennessee Claflin: She was indicted for manslaughter. The indictment read, in part:

> On the first day of November in the year of our Lord one thousand, eight hundred and sixty-three, in the county of La Salle, and on divers other days and times . . . one Tennessee Claflin did feloniously and willfully place upon the right side of the breast of one Rebecca Howe divers quantities of deleterious and caustic drugs by means of which a large amount of flesh was . . . consumed and destroyed . . . and that Rebecca Howe then and there became mortally sick, sore and distempered in her body and the aforesaid did languish in mortal sickness and thereby died on the seventh day of June, eighteen hundred and sixty-four. . . . We say that Tennessee Claflin in the manner aforesaid feloniously and willfully did kill and slay contrary to the statutes . . . one Rebecca Howe.

It was thought that a local lawyer who fancied Tennessee had warned her when he was commissioned to draw up the indictment. In any case, by the time an arrest warrant was issued, the Claflins had disappeared, and the matter soon vanished in the chaos of war. On March 4, 1865, Lincoln was inaugurated for the second time, and by the first week in April, Robert E. Lee's army had dwindled to fewer than thirty thousand men. Grant requested a surrender. Lee asked for terms. On Palm Sunday, April 9, 1865, on the Appomattox road in Virginia, the firing stopped as out of the Confederate line rode a lone soldier, a white flag fluttering from the end of his staff. As Generals Grant, Schuster, and Ord trotted down the road to meet General Lee at the courthouse, the two armies waited in silence. It was over.

The Fort Sumter flag that had been lowered four years before was taken from the Bank of Commerce vault in Washington, D.C., and shipped in its original mailbag to the government transport *Arago,* docked at the foot of Beach Street in Brooklyn, New York.

# CHAPTER EIGHT

# GOD BLESS THIS TRINITY

THE POST Office van, covered with red, white, and blue bunting, its horses' collars decorated with gold stars, came hurtling at full gallop down Brooklyn's Beach Street pier, lined on both sides by a crowd estimated at two thousand. After an abrupt halt, two blue-coated soldiers jumped down, unloaded a mailbag inscribed "Major Robert Anderson, Fort Sumter, April 14, 1861," and presented it to the now general Robert Anderson, as his wife, son, and three daughters looked on with pride. From the bag, Anderson withdrew the American flag and gave it to Sergeant Hart, the soldier who had lowered it during the evacuation of Fort Sumter.

Henry Ward Beecher stood on the pier arm in arm with Theodore Tilton, once his protégé and now the editor in chief of the *Independent*. Standing there in the bright April sunlight, they seemed the most successful of men—men in whom reposed the American future. Beecher had not thought to include his wife, Eunice, in the trip to Fort Sumter, but Tilton had invited his wife, Lib, who refused. Though Tilton never asked her reason, she volunteered that she was not well enough to attend. Most likely she was intimidated by so auspicious a gathering. "I could never be a lady of fashion," she had once admitted.

Henry Bowen, though publisher of the *Independent,* had not officially been invited to the ceremonies, but he had chartered a boat and arranged his own party to follow the government transport *Arago* on which Sergeant Hart, bearing the flag, and sixty-one dignitaries and their families were to set sail from Brooklyn. One by one the governors of Maine, New Hampshire, Vermont, Rhode Island, Connecticut, and Massachusetts came aboard to be joined by members of Lincoln's cabinet when the ship docked at Fortress Monroe, Virginia.

Good Friday, April 14, 1865: At Fort Sumter the day was clear and cool, the sky a brilliant blue. Henry Ward Beecher stood upon a heap of stones, the wind ruffling his long, graying hair as he gave the keynote speech to an assemblage that included some of the most prominent men in the nation. After the flag was raised to the accompaniment of a single bugler, Beecher said, "My friends, fellow citizens, and brother soldiers, I am here to fulfill the cherished wish of my heart through four long, long years of bloody war, to restore to its proper place this dear flag. . . . I thank God that I have lived to see this day. 'Glory to God in the highest.' "

In the hourlong address that followed, Beecher referred several times to his "brother soldiers," but in fact he had been absent for eighteen months during the "Great Rebellion," in luxurious exile in England, where he had fled after Henry Bowen's late wife, Lucy, confessed to the affair with him. Members of Plymouth Church, reading in the *Independent* of Beecher's great success abroad and seeing that in his absence their membership had fallen off and the price of pews had dropped precipitously, pressured Henry Bowen to bring him back. The greedy Bowen, though busy accumulating graft from his position as collector of the port, still missed his share of the pew auction funds. And so Beecher returned—triumphant.

Henry Ward Beecher was now the most famous preacher in America. The special ferries that ran from New York to Brooklyn every Sunday were known as "Beecher's Boats." When the original Plymouth Church burned down in 1849, two years after Beecher's arrival, the new church on Orange Street in Brooklyn Heights was designed according to his specifications. Here Beecher stood, not behind an altar, but on a rectangular platform jutting out into the audience, surrounded by his parishioners. Beecher was a consummate showman; he could imitate any dialect, impersonate men or women, make his audience laugh or cry or feel the fire of God. But above all, it was *what* he said that was particularly suited to these uncertain times. Gone were the Calvinist tenets of his father, Lyman Beecher. In their place was the warm, self-indulgent "Gospel of Love." Beecher declared that to be truly religious, one must sin: "Christ can save you, because you *are a sinner,* not because you aren't one." He preached, "What is terribly and dangerously heterodox this year may be accepted as the very essence of orthodoxy next year. What is orthodoxy? Orthodoxy is *my* doxy and heterodoxy is *your* doxy, if *your* doxy is not like *my* doxy."

Although his mother had died when he was a toddler, he credited her with his moral teachings. Beecher called himself "wife and mother" to his parishioners. He referred to God as the "Mother of the Church." This feminized, romantic conception was a part of his custard-cream vision, as he told a gathering, "When questions of justice and humanity are blended, woman's instinct is better than man's judgment. From the moment a woman takes the child into her arms, God makes her the love-magistrate of the family, and her instincts and moral nature fit her to adjudicate questions of weakness and want."

And above all there was love—unquestioning, abounding love. The permissiveness of his pulpit utterances, the lavish decoration of his home, his fine silk handkerchiefs, square-toed gleaming leather shoes, his expanding waistline, the unpolished gems in his pocket, were all of a piece. Pleasure, comfort, wealth, were what God had willed for Henry Ward Beecher and for his parishioners. To a new group of capitalists, who had thrown morality to the winds during the war, this was a self-justifying doctrine. From his pulpit Beecher roared, "Ye are Gods. Your faces are crystalline." An entire flock followed Beecher's teachings and none more faithfully than Theodore Tilton's tiny, impressionable wife, Lib, who said of herself, "I cannot think, only feel."

Victoria Woodhull's ragtag existence and her quest for bare survival were far removed from the concerns of the ordered society in which Lib Tilton lived. Here was a life as circumscribed as that of a perfectly executed needlepoint. At the beginning of the war, Brooklyn had been a city of one hundred thousand people and fifty churches. It had five banks, a public library, a city hall, and a police force fifty strong. This city provided a refuge for substantial, white, middle-class families bent on escaping New York's increasing congestion, rising costs, pollution, and influx of immigrants. "Cool, fragrantly airy and no mobs," proclaimed a real estate advertisement. New York City was only a penny ferry ride away.

In this valentine of a world, appearance was all important. For the women there were fashionable clothes, perfectly appointed homes, seven-course dinners, church every Sunday. These women played Chopin, embroidered, darned socks, washed clothes, became pregnant yearly. Lib (Elizabeth) Richards Tilton was a woman of her time and environment: a woman of malleable clay in a world where men did the molding.

On October 2, 1855, in Brooklyn's Plymouth Church, Theodore Tilton and Lib Richards had been joined in holy matrimony by the Reverend Henry Ward Beecher. They were a striking couple—the bride scarcely five feet tall, with jet-black hair and intense, luminous dark-brown eyes; and towering over her, the groom in the traditional morning coat and top hat, six-foot-three, with a mane of blond curls, clear blue eyes, and an abstracted air that masked a fierce intelligence. Lib was engulfed in a sea of white peau-de-soie with a bertha of Brussels lace. At her throat was a gold and pearl heart, a gift from her late father, who had been a jeweler. The groom

*The Beecher home on Columbia Heights in Brooklyn*

later stated that he had chosen the "most ideal woman in the world." The bride brought to the altar the desire "to fulfill his every need and dedicate my life to being worthy of his love. We will be as one," she declared fervently.

Lib was two years older than her groom, who had chosen this, his twentieth birthday, as their wedding day. Although Lib's mother would have liked a more ambitious match, she thought her only daughter was growing rather "long in the tooth," and Tilton was said to be a man with a future. The son of a Monmouth County, New Jersey, shoe manufacturer with a comfortable business, at only sixteen he had secured a job as a reporter on Greeley's *Tribune,* but in 1853 had transferred to the *New York Observer,* a religious newspaper. There, his major assignment was to report stenographically (using the new system introduced by Stephen Pearl Andrews) the sermons of Henry

Ward Beecher. Tilton crossed the river to the city of Brooklyn, joined Plymouth Church, and moved into Mrs. Richards's stolidly middle-class Harrison Avenue boardinghouse.

It was generally acknowledged that Lib and Theodore were well suited. Both were devout. Theodore wrote that he had been brought up "in the old school Presbyterian Church. . . . My earliest religious bent was toward extreme Calvinism." Tilton admired Beecher for the unbridled emotionalism of his sermons—passages of which he committed to memory. Since childhood, Lib had found in Beecher's Plymouth Church "a home," a place of friendship and warmth. She attended Sunday school, then became a teacher there, and every Sunday she listened to her preacher. And what a preacher he was. Henry Ward Beecher presented a God and a Christ as he envisioned himself—unconditionally loving, caring, understanding. Hearing his words Lib often felt a "kind of ecstasy," which lifted her out of the strict discipline and stubborn grind of her boardinghouse existence.

To the Tiltons, Plymouth Church was more than a place of worship; it defined one's social standing and business opportunities in the Brooklyn community. While at a Plymouth Church service, Joseph Richards, Lib's only brother, had met Henry Bowen, who hired him as assistant publisher of the *Independent*. Directly after the Tiltons' marriage, Joe Richards persuaded Bowen to hire Tilton, who was pleased to leave the *Observer* because that newspaper would not endorse the abolition of slavery.

Beecher rarely wrote out a sermon and indeed usually began his preparations only two hours before he spoke. He liked the thrill of the extemporaneous and said that he would rather "serve my sermons hot." Tilton recorded Beecher's words as he spoke them and, after editing, printed them in the *Independent*, thereby providing Beecher with a new source of revenue and increasing the preacher's audience by some four hundred thousand readers. Many people bought the paper solely for Beecher's sermons, articles, and columns, but often he was lax about deadlines and failed to deliver. These lapses were legendary. When Beecher had written for *Bonner's Weekly*, Robert Bonner had posted boys in shifts outside his door, twenty-four hours a day, until they returned with his copy.

Robert Bonner, who had spent years coddling Beecher, knew how hard it was to get him to produce. In order to win his star contributor's gratitude, Bonner gave him a set of matched bays worth $3,500. Within hours of their arrival, Beecher, with a child's glee, hitched them to a carriage, and with his wife, Eunice, at his side galloped in record time to his Peekskill home. Two hours later, one of the horses dropped dead. The other, lame for life, was given as a work horse to a local farmer.

LEFT: *Lib (Elizabeth) Richards Tilton, 1863. At thirty, Mrs. Tilton was docile and domestic.* RIGHT: *Theodore Tilton, 1863. At twenty-eight, Tilton was the powerful editor of the* Independent.

Beecher's gestures were frequently more theatrical than brave. As a young revivalist in the Midwest, he had not come forward against slavery. But the men who brought him to Plymouth Church, financier John Tasker Howard and Henry Bowen, who was the son-in-law of Lewis Tappan, a leader of the abolitionist movement, were militant antislavery advocates. In May 1854, when the Kansas-Nebraska Act became law, Beecher pledged that Plymouth Church would supply twenty-five Sharps rifles to Northern settlers heading for Kansas. These rifles became known as "Beecher's Bibles." Lucy Tappan Bowen had, in her intimate relationship with Beecher, goaded him to write antislavery articles in the *Independent,* and Tilton had been happy to ghostwrite them for him.

One Sunday, while the Reverend Richard Salter Storrs's neighboring Church of the Pilgrims was mounting a quiet campaign for funds to buy slaves and give them their freedom, Henry Ward Beecher produced on the platform of Plymouth Church a beautiful mulatto girl of twenty and told his congregation she was "to be sold by her own white father . . . for what purpose you can imagine." Beecher held up iron shackles and cast them to the floor, trampling them underfoot. He ordered the girl to take down her hair and, as it streamed about her shoulders, called out like an auctioneer,

"How much for her?" Women began throwing their jewelry onto the platform. Men emptied their pockets and unfastened their watches, tossing the contents into the ushers' baskets until they overflowed, were emptied, and overflowed once again.

Realizing Beecher's stunning appeal, in 1858 Bowen offered him the editorship of the *Independent* and assured him that young Theodore Tilton would, in Beecher's words, "relieve me wholly from routine office work." Tilton continued to ghostwrite for Beecher, but he was allowed to have his own byline on his other articles and was promoted to assistant editor. Not only Beecher's words and style but also his ideas deeply influenced Tilton. He was "dazzled" by Beecher and later said, "I came to love him as I had no other man."

In the *Independent* offices at 5 Beekman Street in New York City, Beecher would stretch out on a couch, rattling off his ideas while Tilton feverishly took the notes he would later shape into articles. Then the two would stroll arm in arm down the cobblestone streets, heady with idealistic conversation. They would drop in at art galleries, antiques shops, rug dealers. (Beecher purchased so many Oriental rugs that he would pile them one on top of another, often four deep, in the various rooms of his house.) Beecher admitted that if he saw something he desired, he had to possess it. Often he went on spending sprees, bringing home paintings, bric-a-brac, leather-bound books with uncut pages, and bolts of silk, all of which he would smuggle past his disapproving wife, Eunice. At dusk, Beecher and Tilton would often find a restaurant and the conversation would continue over quail and claret. Finally, like father and son, they would board the ferry for the trip home to Brooklyn. Beecher basked in Tilton's idolatry, saying, "His mind was opening freshly and with enthusiasm upon all questions. I used to pour out my ideas of civil affairs, public policy, religion and philanthropy. Of this he often spoke with grateful appreciation."

In the first six years of their marriage the world expanded for Theodore Tilton, but for Lib Richards Tilton little changed, save for the shattering of her hopes that she and Theodore would "be as one." Even by the standards of the day their life was not that of a normal married couple. As newlyweds, Lib and Theodore lived at Mrs. Richards's boardinghouse, where Lib's widowed mother had married one of the boarders, Nathaniel B. Morse, a respected Brooklyn judge. In this full house the young couple were never alone. Theodore, enthralled by words and the prospect of moving ahead, worked day and night, churning out articles and columns with amazing facility. Lib relied on her mother and the chatter of the boarders for company.

Then came the children, three in four years, and Lib took to her bed for months at a time, debilitated by the seemingly unending cycle of birth and nursing, depressed and in pain from a prolapsed uterus. She later said, "At the birth of my second little girl I was sick in bed from the middle of April until September, when I sat up for the first time. My husband never gave me any sympathy at all." After the birth of the third child, she recalled, "I had a very severe and prolonged sickness but when he saw me he never felt that I was sick because I always tried to seem well, I felt so desirous of his presence. I had no attention whatsoever from him. I do not think it was from neglect so much as from an inability on his part to understand that I was sick and suffering. My doctor, Dr. Portman, said, 'There is care and trouble in that woman's mind and I cannot help it with medicine.'" The following year, Lib was delivered of a fourth child, Matilda, "beautiful Mattie," who wasted away—no one knew why—and was dead at six months. In all that time her husband expressed no word of sympathy and no regret. The gulf between them grew wider.

There is every indication that the root of the Tiltons' discontent was their disappointing sexual relationship. Whatever her dreams of romantic love, the sexual act itself was for Lib, as she was later to explain, one of dutiful submission. She feared the pregnancies that resulted from their infrequent couplings. Theodore found Lib "cold" and "inadequate." He was irritable and critical of her. She "scolded and chided" him. Lib lamented that "he spent a great deal of his time at home in moods of dissatisfaction with the surroundings, yearning and wanting other ministrations. There was nothing in our home that satisfied him."

With each rebuff and imagined inadequacy, Lib Tilton's religious fervor grew until she was spending hours each day on her knees, praying beside the green damask chaise longue in her bedroom. Mrs. Morse, Lib's mother, was a termagant who lost no opportunity to berate her son-in-law for his neglect of Lib. She would work herself into "manias and frenzies," said Theodore. Her marriage to Judge Morse soon became unhappy, and he too came under fire. One evening she was so enraged that she beat the venerable judge on the chest and began to strangle him until his face turned blue. Theodore and two other boarders were able to free the judge only after one of them clasped a chloroform-soaked handkerchief over Mrs. Morse's face.

Shortly after Beecher fled to England, Bowen gave Tilton a raise and appointed him editor in chief of the *Independent*. Unlike his employer, Tilton was naive about business and was delighted and grateful when Bowen doubled his salary to $6,000. But he preferred not to introduce the new people he met in his more exalted position to the "mildew," as he called it, of the boardinghouse. He thought a man determined to "make a name for himself" needed a proper setting.

Theodore insisted the family move from Harrison Avenue to the more fashionable Brooklyn Heights, where he purchased a house at 174 Livingston Street. To Lib, the three-story white clapboard house with its broad steps was too large. There was a front parlor with an organ and a melodeon for herself and daughters Florry and Alice, and a back parlor with a stone fireplace that warmed the entire downstairs. The most unusual feature of the house was a stained-glass dome over the third-floor sitting room. Around the arch surrounding the dome was the inscription, "And into whatsoever house ye shall enter, first say peace be unto this house."

Beecher had taught his protégé well. Tilton wanted nothing but the best. He bought expensive furnishings and decorated the house, as a local newspaper noted, with "luxurious carelessness; the wallpaper was of a dainty cream color, picked out with gold. . . . The carpets were of the finest, hanging baskets at the windows were replenished every day with the choicest of flowers." The library was furnished with a red velvet chaise longue and matching tufted club chairs. Scattered about the living room were damask sofas and heavy walnut chairs carved with cherubs' faces. On the walls hung dozens of etchings, including a copy of Theodore Tilton's favorite painting, Jacques Louis David's *Oath of the Horatii,* a parable of war and love in which three brothers are about to fight to the death three adversaries with no regard for the fact that one of them is betrothed to their sister, seen weeping in the background. A scene of Sixtus returning home from war to find his wife dead also appealed to Tilton's taste for melodrama. Despite the extravagant luxury Theodore permitted himself, he frequently berated his wife for overspending on the children's clothes and household management. Having come from a boardinghouse, Lib had no experience running a home of her own and often vexed her husband by her inability to cope with her newly acquired servants and possessions.

In the houses Theodore Tilton now visited, the linen and silver were always just so, the meals perfectly and silently served. He chastised Lib in front of the butcher for not knowing which cut of meat to order. When she begged him to help her with the niceties of domestic life he saw in other homes, saying, "Alone I can do no better, but with you I think I can," he replied angrily, "I do not call upon you to go to the office to do my work. This is yours."

There was no doubt that Theodore found Lib inferior and woefully inadequate. He corrected her grammar. He told her that she did not dress with sophistication. He confided to his closest friend, Francis De Pau

Moulton, known as Frank, that his wife was a "small woman, without presence, not a woman of society, not a woman of culture." He regretted that "he had married her young and that he had grown and developed and that she had not." Frank Moulton and his wife, Emma, spent a great deal of time with the Tiltons. Although Frank belonged to no church and believed in no religion, Emma had been brought up in Plymouth Church and taught in the Sunday school with Lib Tilton. Later Frank was to observe of the Tiltons' marriage, "Here is Theodore marrying at twenty a woman like a Spanish nun. He is a bold, frowning, gifted man, a product of Plymouth Church. She is the female product, an idealist, interesting by fervent sincerity, but she made religion a bore and became irksome to her husband."

Frank Moulton's own marriage was a happy one. Unlike Theodore and most men of his day, Frank treated his wife as an equal and even held that she more than earned half his wages, which he gave her for the long hours she spent keeping house. He often said that he had married Emma for her honesty and that they were good friends. Frank Moulton was employed at the dry goods firm of Woodruff & Robinson, which had prospered during the war selling cloth to the Union Army. Perhaps chosen for his imposing presence—as tall as Tilton and with flaming red hair and beard—Moulton had been put in charge of the firm's warehouses and frequently was seen striding along the waterfront with a gun tucked prominently in his belt. When he was not on tour in dangerous areas, the gun was hidden in a shoulder holster under his jacket. Moulton possessed an air of authority even without a firearm. It was this quality no doubt that made Theodore trust and confide in him as he had in his mentor, Henry Ward Beecher.

When Beecher returned from England in the winter of 1863, he found Tilton in the editorial chair of the *Independent* and Bowen surrounded by a powerful clique of Plymouth Church members who were in charge of Brooklyn's political patronage. Beecher's flock, especially the ladies, looked upon him with adoration, but he needed to carve out a niche for himself. It had been a year and a half since his sermons had appeared in the *Independent,* a considerable financial loss. Beecher went to Robert Bonner, who gave him the extravagant sum of $24,000 to write a novel, *Norwood or Village Life in New England,* to run in fifty installments in *Bonner's Weekly.* But Beecher could not pull himself away from the lively life with his parishioners to get down to work. He tried writing a chapter or two but threw them away, despairing of his own wooden prose.

In Beecher's absence, the Tiltons' home had become a gathering place for the great political and intellectual minds of the day. Mary Cheney Greeley spent so much time in Europe that, at Theodore's invitation, Horace began to stay with them. Lib set aside a room for him, and Theodore designed a desk two feet higher than normal, because Greeley liked to raise his arms up and write at chin level. Horace Greeley had purchased a farm in Chappaqua in 1853, but he was so comfortable that even when Mary and their daughters, Ida and Gabrielle, the only two children who had survived, returned from Europe, he continued to live at the Tiltons' during the week.

Theodore Tilton had flourished in Beecher's absence, and he was eager to repay his dear mentor. He advised Beecher to mend his fences with Lincoln, which the preacher did, praising from his pulpit Lincoln's courage in having issued the Emancipation Proclamation and calling him "a great statesman." Once again, Tilton recorded Beecher's sermons and printed them in the *Independent*. With $500 of his own money, Tilton commissioned a portrait of Beecher by William Page of the National Academy. Beecher posed fifty times and Page's studio became another pulpit for him. Sitting in a yellow velvet chair on a raised platform, his gray Puritan cloak tossed rakishly over his shoulders, he reigned as king-prophet over an assembly that included such visitors as Horace Greeley, Wendell Phillips, General Benjamin Butler, and Frank Moulton.

When Beecher had finished a session posing for William Page, he would try to induce Tilton to stay out as late as possible. Beecher confided that he dreaded "going back to my own house," saying that his life with Eunice was a "hell on earth" and that their conversation at the breakfast table was "the vainest, the most vapid, the most juiceless, the most unsaccharine of all things." Theodore, proud of his new home and the people who visited there, urged his mentor to drop in. At first, Beecher found Lib Tilton all but speechless in his presence. Though she was now thirty-one and the mother of three living and one dead child, Beecher described her as "childlike in appearance . . . she was a child in nature, delicate in health, with a self-cheerful air." Plymouth's pastor was given the sitting room with the spectacular dome in which to work, and Lib faithfully checked his ink and other supplies and hushed the children when he was writing. After an afternoon at the Tiltons', Beecher exclaimed, "Oh, Theodore, God might strip all other gifts from me if he would only give me a wife and a home like yours."

Beecher had been severely blocked and unable to proceed with his novel. "I was almost in despair," he later confessed. "My team would not pull. . . . I needed something that would give me the courage to go on with it." He masked his apprehension with humor, telling Elizabeth Cady Stanton that he was considering a train wreck to end the whole thing. And when he spoke to Lib about the two chapters he had written, he said jovially,

"People have said that I, not sister Harriet, wrote *Uncle Tom's Cabin,* but they will never say it again after reading *Norwood.*"

One day Theodore Tilton mentioned that his wife had "a remarkable gift as a critic" and that he took everything he wrote to her. He urged Beecher to do the same. Beecher read Lib a part of a chapter and she began to comment on his work. He noted that she could "tell whether a speech put into [his heroine] Rose Wentworth's mouth was one a woman would be likely to say." Soon Beecher was writing with ease.

Even in recommending his wife as a critic, Tilton had been grudging. Lib was, he said, "so domestic a woman that this talent was concealed." As for Lib herself—whose husband made her feel so inadequate that she could barely function, who had taken to her bed for months at a time with a malady "in her soul"—the gratitude of the exalted Reverend Beecher gave her the confidence she had lacked. "I never felt a bit of embarrassment with Mr. Beecher, but to this day I never could sit down with Theodore without being self-conscious and feeling his sense of my inequality with him," she later said.

In the final months of the war, Theodore Tilton went to Washington to help plan the peace that now seemed certain. Lib wrote him there of Beecher's salutary effect on her health. "I took my first walk to the Court Street cars without much difficulty so that I feel free again and will walk out every day." And Theodore replied, "I am glad Mr. Beecher called on you. I will write to thank him." Lib regarded the relationship between her preacher, her husband, and herself as a religious entity, and she wrote, "God bless this Trinity."

At ten-fifteen p.m. on Good Friday, April 14, 1865, Henry Ward Beecher, Theodore Tilton, and a host of other dignitaries boarded the steamer *Quaker City* to return from the flag-raising ceremony at Fort Sumter. At about the same time, in Brooklyn, Lib Tilton knelt in prayer beside her bed. Passing through Philadelphia that evening, Tennessee Claflin, by her own account, was seized by a vision and blurted out, "Tomorrow the whole nation will drape itself in mourning."

And in Washington, D.C., John Wilkes Booth—a derringer in his right hand, a dagger in his left—entered the president's box at Ford's Theatre and pumped a bullet into Abraham Lincoln's skull. The following morning Vice President Andrew Johnson took the oath of office as president of the United States.

# CHAPTER NINE

# AN ACCIDENT OF FATE

B Y AN ACCIDENT of fate, the control of the executive branch of the government, with all its patronage and the extended powers granted during the war, now fell into the hands of a Southerner, a former Democrat and a strong supporter of states' rights. "I had thought that states' rights, which interfere with Congress enforcing the rights of citizens of the United States, were buried forever in the red sea of blood that has flowed south of the Potomac!" bellowed Senator Benjamin Butler. He was wrong. Whether the individual states could choose their own governance, superseding federal law, was to become one of the major issues of this Reconstruction period.

During the recent war, Butler had been the occupying general of New Orleans. "Beast Butler" he was called for hanging a rebel who tore down the Union flag and for issuing an order that women who treated his troops disrespectfully should be regarded as prostitutes. His most ingenious edict declared that every escaped slave under his jurisdiction was to be considered the "contraband of war" and therefore free.

On the morning after Lincoln's assassination, Benjamin Butler organized a meeting of radical Republican senators and congressmen to make sure that Andrew Johnson would not lose all they had fought for by negotiating a "soft peace." Johnson, a self-made man who had risen from poverty to the governorship of Tennessee and the United States Senate, had not been opposed to slavery and had owned five slaves himself, but in 1864 Lincoln chose him as his running mate on the Union Party ticket, hoping to unify the nation at the war's end.

The radical Republicans stood on the party's left and had shared the common goal of freeing the slaves. In reality, this freedom came not through the Emancipation Proclamation but through the Thirteenth Amendment to the Constitution, which had been proposed in February 1865, but had yet to be ratified. The amendment specified,

*General Benjamin Butler, 1862. In New Orleans, they called him "Beast Butler."*

1. Neither slavery nor involuntary servitude, except as a punishment for crime, whereof the party shall have been duly convicted, shall exist within the United States, or any place subject to their jurisdiction.

2. Congress shall have power to enforce this article by appropriate legislation.

But the question of the black people still stuck like a bone in the throat of a shattered society. The problem was how to integrate into this new nation "property" that had been kept ignorant, poor, and governed by the lash. As early as 1863, Lincoln had made it known that he would accept from the South "temporary arrangements for the freed people." He felt that black men who had fought in the war should be enfranchised but hoped that at the war's end the whole problem could be solved by persuading black people to emigrate to other countries. The previous year, through an agreement with the Republic of Haiti, two American promoters had settled a group of Negroes off the Haitian coast on Ile à Vache. Within a year, half the settlers were dead of forced labor and starvation, and Lincoln brought the survivors back to the United States. Radical Republican George W. Julian of Indiana declared in a burst of frankness to his fellow congressmen, "The real trouble is that *we hate the negro*. It is not his ignorance that offends us, but his color."

Although Andrew Johnson supported the Thirteenth Amendment, and initially the radical Republicans were optimistic about Reconstruction, by late summer Johnson's Southern sympathies became apparent. The president's Reconstruction plan (he preferred the term "Restoration") for the South was to form loyal state governments under provisional governors. His only demands were that government officials take a loyalty oath, repudiate Confederate debt, and ratify the Thirteenth Amendment. Johnson granted mass pardons to former Confederates (twenty thousand within two years). He announced that as soon as the Southern state governments were formed, he would revoke martial law and withdraw federal troops. Reconstruction, he declared, would then be completed.

Not yet begun! responded the appalled radical Republicans in Congress. This was no Reconstruction but a virtual return to prewar conditions. Johnson's policies confined the Negro to a permanent underclass and a cheap source of labor. The charismatic champion of Negro rights Wendell Phillips declared that if Johnson prevailed, then the Union had fought a "murderous and wasteful war . . . for no purpose at all." Just as the Republicans feared, eight Southern states quickly established "Black Codes" specifying, among other provisions, that black children could be "bound out" as apprentices for no wages. Blacks who were not employed could be arrested and then hired out to pay their prison fines. If such a hired hand left his job, he forfeited his wages and was rearrested. Though they were now emancipated, black people had no civil rights.

Theodore Tilton and Henry Ward Beecher took opposite positions in regard to the legal protection of black people. Tilton allied himself and the *Independent* with the radical Republicans in Congress. He wrote a series of unsigned articles attacking Johnson for his indulgence of the South and his "wretched treatment of black people." Tilton perceived that only if the federal government acted with all due speed "while the defeated South lies supine at the feet of the North" could equal rights be secured.

Beecher, however, wholeheartedly endorsed Johnson and his policies. Now it was Beecher, not Tilton, who had the ear of a president, and there were rumors that he would assume a Cabinet post. Indeed, one Sunday he ended the morning sermon dramatically with, "And may I not be seduced away from this pulpit!" On Sunday night, October 22, 1865, with three thousand people filling the pews and overflowing into the aisles of Plymouth Church, the Reverend Beecher delivered what the *Times* called "A Great Political Sermon." Although he did not mention Theodore Tilton by name, Beecher began by saying that articles defamatory to President Johnson had appeared in the *Independent*. He wanted it clearly understood that someone else wrote those unsigned critical articles, and he wished it known that he felt Andrew Johnson should have "unstinting praise" as a "great American president."

Beecher said Johnson's plan for state governments was enlightened and he pleaded for "love and good will" toward the defeated South. He said, "I hold that it is not possible for us in the North, except in a remote way, to affect the condition of the black man in the South," and suggested that America rely upon "the kindness of the white man in the South, which is more important to the blacks than all the policies of the nation put together. . . . The laws and intents of the government and of ourselves will prove to no avail if they are unpleasant to the white people of the South."

Tilton was angered to the very marrow and retaliated with an essay in the *Independent*, objecting to Beecher's reference to reliance on the "kindness" of Southern white men. "There is no such kindness," he wrote. "Does any man suppose that the Southern states of their own kindness will ordain equal rights? Why is the South annulling her ordinances of secession? Because she is coerced. Why is she abolishing slavery? Because she is coerced. And when will she ordain equal suffrage? Only when she is coerced." Tilton also took exception to the statement that the North was "remote" and powerless to change the situation. "On the contrary we hold that the power of the North in a direct way, may not only greatly affect but entirely revolutionize the condition of the black man in the South, that is, by the intervention of Congress to secure equal suffrage." Tilton wrote that the consensus of Congress was that if Johnson had, during the first months of his presidency, declared to the South, " 'I want the negroes to vote,' the South would have acquiesced without a murmur because it was expecting such a policy to be enforced."

Lib Tilton was dismayed by the conflict between her husband and her preacher. She wrote to Theodore, who was in Washington working with the radical Republicans, expressing her concern. He replied, "I have not seen Mr. Beecher and I suppose his difference is a difference only of opinion and not good will. But I am right and can't be driven from the rock under my feet." The first crack in Tilton's idolatry of Beecher had appeared.

Tilton vowed to keep his personal and political relationship with Beecher separate. But he was clearly torn. In November, returning home for a brief visit, he wrote to Beecher, "My friend, from my boyhood up you have been to me what no other man has been—what no other man can be. While I was a student the influence of your mind on mine was greater than all the books and all the teachings. By you I was baptized—by you married. You have been my minister, teacher, father, brother, friend, companion." At the same time, however, he warned his wife to be careful of her preacher's visits and told Lib about Beecher's alleged affair with Lucy Tappan Bowen and certain other loose conduct with women. Lib had observed how the women of Plymouth Church flung themselves at their preacher when, she said, what this lonely man needed was "soul-food." She was determined, her husband later noted, "to demonstrate that there was a woman who was superior to the silly flatteries with which many ladies in his congregation had courted his society—to demonstrate the honor and dignity of her sex."

For four long years, woman's rights advocates had put their own dream of equal rights aside and had worked ceaselessly for the Union cause. With victory, once again they were ready to fight for their rights. Many of their friends from abolitionist days supported them. Among these was Henry Ward Beecher, who wrote an editorial, "Woman's Influence in Politics," recommending that women be given the vote. One rainy afternoon he saw Susan B. Anthony wearily walking along Columbia Heights. He clapped his hand on her shoulder and asked, "Well, old girl, what do you want now?" When she told him she was on her way to a woman suffrage meeting he volunteered to take up a collection for her. The following Sunday he raised $200 for her cause. Theodore Tilton, although deeply dedicated to Negro enfranchisement, also championed the cause of woman's rights. He wrote in the *Independent* that both groups were entitled to the rights and privileges of white males because a "re-examination of the Declaration of Independence has powerfully suggested the equality of all human beings."

Elizabeth Cady Stanton, however, while she believed that the climate was now excellent for woman's enfranchisement, felt that little could be done for the Negro. In January 1866 she wrote, "When Andrew Johnson began the work of reconstruction, the negro's opportunity was lost. Politicians will wrangle over that question for a generation. Our time is now." Many, however, took the opposite view, contending that there was little practical chance that the complex issue of woman's rights, which cut deep into the social, religious, and economic structure of the nation, could be dealt with at this time. Right now the needs of the Negro were pressing; still more important: If the Republicans were to secure a majority in Congress, they needed black votes.

*Henry Ward Beecher preaching to the adoring women*

Though she believed in the primacy of woman's rights, the practical Stanton, realizing that the force of Congress was behind the Negro, decided that it would be politic to strive for the enfranchisement of Negroes and women simultaneously. Stanton and Anthony sought the advice of Theodore Tilton: Was there no way to grant suffrage to, as Stanton phrased it, "both classes of disenfranchised citizens"?

Tilton studied the question and came up with the idea of combining the Anti-Slavery Society and the Woman's Rights Society into a powerful coalition to espouse both causes, to be called the American Equal Rights Association. He diplomatically suggested that Wendell Phillips, who believed in the primacy of Negro rights and therefore might be a potential adversary, act as president of the new organization and that Frederick Douglass serve as a member of the coalition. Douglass accepted in good humor, writing to Stanton, "I have about made up my mind that if you can forgive me for being a negro, I cannot do less than to forgive you for being a woman." Phillips was less obliging and wrote, "While I could continue arguing for woman's rights, just as I do for temperance every day, still I would not mix the movements. That in my view is where . . . you and I differ. I think such a mixture would lose for the negro far more than we should gain for the woman."

Stanton was appalled by this response and wrote,

> We have fairly boosted the negro over our heads, and now we had better begin to remember that self-preservation is the first law of nature. Some say, "Be still, wait, this is the negro's hour." But I believe this is the hour for everybody to do the best thing for reconstruction. A vote based on intelligence and education for black and white man and woman—that is what we need . . . and press in through the constitutional door the moment it is open for the admission of Sambo.

"Sambo"! With this bigoted rhetoric, Stanton had unknowingly taken the first step toward alienating the very people she most needed as allies.

Just as Amy and Isaac Post's home had been a center for abolitionists, the Tiltons' home was now a center for woman's rights advocates. At first, Lib Tilton had little to say to the "strong women" who gathered at her home, but later she recalled, "It mattered very little to me who they were— I took an interest—the house was open and I really feel that you should give me credit for that one gift of mine, if it is a gift, of seeing something in almost every one to be interested in—even those women who have troubled me so much."

Theodore Tilton, now the powerful editor of the *Independent,* found himself in a world of ideas that Lib had difficulty comprehending, and her husband consistently made her inadequacies painfully clear to her. One night he took her from what she termed her "sick-bed" to a woman's rights gathering. When Lib hesitated in the doorway, clutching her husband's arm, he admonished her gruffly, "Don't come near me tonight." Once before at a similar function, she said that he told her, " 'I would give five hundred dollars if you were not by my side,' meaning that I was so insignificant that he was ashamed of me."

Among these women, Lib was comfortable at first only with Susan B. Anthony, in whose quiet strength she found reassurance. She admired Stanton but initially was cowed by her intellect. Often at night Lib would leave her husband alone at the chessboard only to wake in the morning to find

*Tennessee Claflin, 1869. She was forced to prostitute her "other powers" for financial gain.*

him in the same position. Lib could not grasp the game but when Mrs. Stanton came to stay, she played chess with Theodore till three in the morning and bested him more often than not. Stanton enjoyed chess but said of it, "You seldom meet a woman who knows the game. They all say it's too hard work, as if thinking were not one of the pleasures of life." In time, Lib would become close to Mrs. Stanton, Paulina Wright Davis, and especially Laura Curtis Bullard, but that would come later, when she was "a changed woman."

IN JANUARY 1864, when the Claflins fled Ottawa to avoid the manslaughter charge against Tennessee, Victoria decided to take her children, ten-
year-old Byron and three-year-old Zulu, to Chicago. Within the week an
advertisement appeared in the *Chicago Mail* announcing the opening of an
establishment for magnetic healing at 265 Wabash Avenue, Chicago, proprietress Victoria Woodhull. Along with the treatments, Victoria dispensed
advice on health, love, and money—everything she was asked came down
to these three subjects. She became unusually keen in anticipating questions and in establishing an invisible bond with her clients. At about the
same time in Cincinnati, the rest of the Claflins moved into a boardinghouse on Mound Street at the corner of Sixth and placed a sign in that window advertising Tennessee Claflin—Fortune-Teller and Magnetic Healer.
Two months later, when they'd made a little money, the family rented a
two-story house. As usual there was trouble with the law. A police officer
followed the spouse of a prominent lumber merchant to the Claflin house,
where he found the merchant's wife in an upstairs bedroom in the company of a gentleman not her husband. She was arrested and charged with
adultery.

Four complaints were lodged against the Claflin family for running
a house of prostitution but they managed to stay put until they met one
Dr. James Kerr, who manufactured a cure-all tonic called "Kerr's System Renovator." Kerr, a frequent visitor at the Claflins' establishment,
would later say that Tennessee had tried to blackmail him with evidence
of his sexual escapades. He said that she had him "dead to rights" but that
he told her, "Not me. I'm just like you!" Kerr lived openly with a
Madame English, "the most notorious woman in Cincinnati." Together
they turned the tables on the Claflins, obtaining depositions from the servants that revealed much of what went on in their bedrooms, naming the
women who occupied the rooms but not the men. Kerr presented this evidence to the chief of police, James L. Ruffin. Overnight, the Claflins disappeared. Three weeks later they turned up in Chicago and moved in with
Vickie.

In the summer of 1865, Victoria, Tennessee, and the self-proclaimed
doctor Hebern Claflin took to the road with their traveling medicine show,
driving Buck's wagon through Missouri, Arkansas, and Tennessee. For Victoria Woodhull it was business as usual and if she took notice of a society
that was irrevocably being transformed, there is no record of it. The black
population of Memphis, Tennessee, had been 3,882 in 1862. In 1865, the

*Victoria Woodhull, 1871. Her mission was to create a social revolution.*

16,509 blacks outnumbered the 11,194 white residents. The Spiritualist Elizabeth Meriwether, who had fled in 1862, returned to find that

> Negro squatters were everywhere. As we drew near Memphis the farm houses on the road side had been either deserted or burned to the ground. Some of the troops were black. They spoke no word to me, I spoke no word to them; their black faces and blue uniforms frightened me. In those days, just after the war, we did not know what the Yankees meant to do to the crushed and conquered Confederate soldiers. Those negroes were armed; they would get leaves of absences; they could walk from Fort Pickering to Ridgeway in half an hour; no friends or neighbors were near me. Can you wonder, my children, that I was uneasy?

A new group of politicians was taking over in Memphis. They frequented the local taverns, where Vickie and Tennie read their palms and occasionally left to spend the night with one or another of them. One evening Tennessee spotted a young gambler, John Bartels, who had just won a fistful of gold pieces in a faro game. She married him the next week. Scarcely a month later, on the way back to Chicago, Bartels asked his wife about a ten-dollar bill she had mysteriously acquired after disappearing for several hours. "Where'd you get it?" he demanded. Tennie wouldn't tell him. This led to a bitter quarrel, after which she agreed to give him her share of the proceeds from the trip on the condition that he go away and divorce her.

Their return to Chicago was flamboyant; if Victoria could not be accepted by society she was nevertheless determined to be noticed. Even as a child when she had preached on The Mount of Olive, her longing for recognition was evident. The wagon rolled into Chicago accompanied by a four-piece brass band and outriders who, to the consternation of the neighbors, galloped up to the door whooping Indian war calls.

By the fall of 1865, the Chicago house was teeming with Claflins. Victoria told them that the spirits had commanded her to go to St. Louis, and she left her own house and her family behind. She used the alias Madame Holland and once again advertised herself as a magnetic healer and clairvoyant fortune-teller. It was in St. Louis that Colonel James Harvey Blood entered the life of twenty-eight-year-old Victoria Woodhull.

At the start of the war, Blood had been a city auditor and president of the St. Louis Railroad Company; a conservative, prosperous man of impeccable reputation who lived in a whitewashed house with his wife, Isabel, and two daughters. Then Blood saw Missouri ripped apart over the question of slavery. Three-quarters of the white men fought for the North, one-quarter fought for the South—brother against brother, friend against friend.

Blood was one of the first to enlist for the Union in the Sixth Missouri. At Sink Pole Woods in March 1862, Colonel Blood received a bullet in his right shoulder. In May, he fought in Corinth, Mississippi, and received another bullet in the right arm. In December, he was wounded in the left hand at Chickasaw Bluff and took two bullets in the left thigh during the assault on Vicksburg. As he waited his turn in the surgeon's tent, he saw limbs being hacked off and bullets pried out with no anesthetic. He returned to his own tent, doused his thigh with whiskey, and with a hunting knife cut the two bullets out and bound the wounds. Unable to fight further, Blood returned to St. Louis a hero. Although he appeared untroubled, his soul had been as ravaged as his body. In 1864, he became the president of the St. Louis Society of Spiritualists. Blood claimed to be in constant communication with his brave companions who had died in the war.

Victoria Woodhull's version of her first encounter with Colonel Blood is romantic: The tall stranger strode into her darkened chamber and sat before her in a low chair. Immediately, she fell into a trance and announced, "I see our futures linked. Our destinies are bound together." When she emerged from her trance, these two were united "on the spot by the powers of the air." In fact, Blood's wife had asked him to accompany her to the Washington Avenue office of one "Madame Holland," who advertised "wonderful cures of female complaints by means of clairvoyance." Soon it was James Blood, not his wife, who frequented Madame Holland's establishment.

That summer Colonel Blood and Vickie fled. Blood left everything behind—wife, children, job, reputation, and a debt of $3,700. He bought a brightly colored wagon with a ball-fringed top like Buck Claflin's, and he and Vickie set out on the road through Missouri and the Ozarks, calling themselves Dr. and Mrs. James Harvey. They repeated a familiar routine: The colonel became the advance man and manager; Vickie read the past and future, gave advice, and provided treatment for physical and emotional problems. When they had made enough money they returned to St. Louis just long enough for Blood to obtain a divorce, give his wife all his possessions, and pay off his debt. Then they moved on.

Meanwhile, the Claflin family in the Wabash Avenue house in Chicago were up to their old tricks amid an atmosphere of illicit sex and blackmail. Young women, many of whom were servant girls, came to have their for-

*Colonel James Harvey Blood, 1868. Victoria told
him, "Our destinies are bound together."*

tunes told. Some stayed late and along with the four unattached Claflin
girls—Tennessee, Margaret Ann, Polly, and Utica—entertained men.

Blackmail had always been Buck's most lucrative sideline. Five years
later, Victoria described how her father blackmailed more than one man
who visited his daughters by pretending to be the distraught father of a
ruined virgin.

> Father, at times a Mephistopheles, waits till the inspiration of cun-
> ning overmasters his parental instinct . . . and lodges an indictment
> against his own flesh and blood, takes out his handkerchief to hide
> a few well-feigned tears, clasps his hands with an unfelt agony and
> money in hand hobbles off smiling sardonically at the mischief he
> has done.

Tennessee, at twenty, was still the star of the show. Since the age of
eleven she had been the main support of her disreputable relatives. Victoria
said that the family was united only in their determination that Tennie

"should earn all the money." Utica was jealous of her younger sister, which may be why she provided—or created—this description of her activities at this time: "Tennie has had ten men visit her in one night and after each, I've bathed her, given her a new night-robe, and perfumed her for the next."

Once again, neighbors complained that the Claflins were running a house of prostitution, but as usual the charge was difficult to prove. Instead, the neighbors lodged two suits for fraudulent fortune-telling. The landlord, eager for an excuse, canceled the Claflins' lease and evicted them. It was then that Tennessee rebelled. She packed a small suitcase, found Victoria and Colonel Blood, and, with tears in her eyes, asked her elder sister, "My God, have I got to live this life always?"

Victoria could no longer suppress her anger. Because of their father, Tennessee had been branded as a prostitute and still faced a charge of manslaughter. Victoria, in times of pain and terror, had been able to retreat into the world of the spirits. They permeated her soul and comforted her and she believed in them the way others believed in the mercy of Christ. But for Tennessee there was only the reality of her squalid life. "I was almost lost," she was later to admit.

Victoria provided for her younger sister the protection she had been unable to provide for herself. Under Blood's aegis, for the first time, both women were treated decently and allowed to think for themselves. Tennessee admired the colonel and was grateful to him for his part in rescuing her. But Roxy Claflin hated James Harvey Blood for the influence he had over her daughters and Buck hated him for taking away his source of income.

# CHAPTER TEN

# DRAW ITS FANGS

A S THE YEAR 1866 began, the radical Republicans were still a minority in the Thirty-ninth Congress; nonetheless they were determined to diminish the president's power and defeat his so-called Restoration. In February, Congress passed an act to extend the duration and grant additional federal enforcement powers to the Freedmen's Bureau, which had been established to help the emancipated slaves. Johnson vetoed the act. Although the Thirteenth Amendment freed the slaves, it did not give them the right to vote or protect them from abridgements of their civil rights by state governments. In April, Congress passed a sweeping civil rights act that specifically empowered all native-born persons over the age of twenty-one (except for "Indians," who were not considered citizens) to enter into contracts, sue, testify in court, and serve on juries. It granted federal jurisdiction over state courts and invalidated discriminatory state laws. Maine senator Lot M. Morrill, a supporter of the act, said, "This species of legislation is absolutely revolutionary. But are we not in the midst of a revolution?" Johnson vetoed this act too.

Theodore Tilton, who had been in Washington to help draft this legislation, was enraged by Johnson's veto and in the *Independent* declared that if President Johnson recklessly continued to usurp Congress's function, he should be impeached. Tilton was the first to suggest impeachment in an American newspaper, a suggestion praised by Republican newspapers across the country and endorsed by such politicians as William Lloyd Garrison, Thaddeus Stevens, Wendell Phillips, and Benjamin Butler. The *Argus* called Tilton "the rising young star of America."

Asserting the power of the federal government, the moderate Republicans, the largest group in Congress, banded with the radical Republicans and passed the Civil Rights Act over Johnson's veto. On April 30, the Fourteenth Amendment, intended to bolster this legislation, was introduced into Congress. The first and second sections of the amendment granted the freedmen citizenship and, while not specifically mandating the vote, severely reduced the representation in Congress of any state that denied any *male* citizen this privilege. The third section, written under the guidance of Stevens and Butler, was added to curb Johnson's presidential pardoning power. It specified that a two-thirds vote of Congress was required before any former Confederate could hold public office.

Stanton, Anthony, and President Johnson opposed the Fourteenth Amendment for very different reasons. The previous summer, as the amendment was being drafted, Stanton had written Anthony, "I have argued constantly with Phillips and the whole fraternity but I fear one and all will favor enfranchising the negro without us. Woman's cause is in deep water." For the first time the word *male* had been introduced into an amendment to the American Constitution. President Johnson for his part objected to the amendment because the first section, designed to protect the newly emancipated Negro from any abridgement of his rights by the states, implicitly asserted the power of the federal government over states' rights. But his fury was aimed at section three, which transferred his pardoning power to Congress. Although it did not require his signature, Johnson denounced the Fourteenth Amendment and urged the Southern states not to ratify it. Ten of the eleven sided with him in rejecting the amendment.

The Republicans were now convinced that the Southern states had not accepted defeat, while the Democrats felt that the Republicans were ready to use any means to control the federal government "even if it meant to Africanize the South." The Civil Rights Act had gone into immediate effect and "Black Codes" were being voided throughout the South. The Southern state governments, subject to federal military authority, were powerless. In Pulaski, Tennessee, six former Confederate soldiers banded together to take matters into their own hands and formed a secret society. Corrupting the Greek word *kyklos,* meaning circle, they added Klan for alliteration: the Ku Klux Klan. Throughout the South, white men governed by pistol and rifle.

Bitter in defeat, militant Southerners afflicted the Negro with the hatred they felt for the mighty Yankee. During the war, Memphis had been the headquarters of the Third United States Colored Heavy Artillery at Fort Pickering and became a haven for the black "contrabands" who lived in a ghetto in South Memphis known as Licksville. By 1866, the emancipated Negroes had set up twenty-two schools in this vicinity and farmed land that had been leased to them with the promise that one day they would be permitted to buy these properties. It was soon rumored that these blacks planned "to take control of the city," a belief strengthened by the crowds of tattered but neat Negroes who, having earned their first wages, spent them in Memphis shops where no black people had previously dared to venture.

On April 30, 1866, by order of the War Department, the remaining black regiments in Tennessee were mustered out and ordered to turn in their arms. With these troops officially disarmed, what happened next, although later said to be "spontaneous," was in fact a planned exercise in terror. By Tuesday, May 1, 1866, only 150 black soldiers remained at Fort Pickering when members of the largely Irish police force began a race riot. Many of these men had been Confederate soldiers in the Third Calvary Regiment and had taken part in the massacre at Fort Pillow, where every black Union soldier taken prisoner was shot.

Special targets of violence were the hospitals and schools operated by the Freedmen's Bureau, where the rioters taunted their victims as they beat them, telling them to ask their friends at the bureau for help. More than $100,000 in black property was destroyed. Four schools were burned and a black student, Rachael Hatcher, was shot and then set afire by John Pendergast and his sons Pat and Mike. After two days, federal troops finally arrived and ended the violence. No white person had been killed or injured by a black person. Forty-six black men, women, and children lay dead, and 285 more were maimed. Although there were hundreds of witnesses, no white man was arrested. And Elizabeth Meriwether observed, "One good result of the Memphis riot and massacres was the improved behavior of the negroes."

The horror of the Memphis riot strengthened the position of the radical Republicans in Congress. It also made the enfranchisement of the Negro a question of life and death. An exasperated Theodore Tilton recommended in the *Independent* that Negro troops be reactivated and used to occupy the South. "They are the natural terriers to watch such rats. They know every trick of the rattlesnake. Therefore, let them be the chief charmers to tame it and draw its fangs."

The following week, on May 10, 1866, a joint meeting of the Anti-Slavery Society and the Woman's Rights Society convened at the Church of the Puritans in Union Square, New York. Although the atmosphere was one of hope and cordiality, there was a division over the primacy of Negro rights. Equally divisive was the mounting political and personal rivalry between Beecher and Tilton.

The Anti-Slavery Society met first. Susan B. Anthony pointed out that the membership of the two organizations was virtually identical and, following Tilton's advice, put forth a resolution that the groups amalgamate.

Wendell Phillips vigorously opposed the resolution and it was voted down. However, at the Woman's Rights Society meeting that followed, with Stanton presiding, Wendell Phillips spoke in favor of woman suffrage with the caveat that it would be pursued *after* Negro rights were secured. Anthony, still hoping to align the groups, now proposed that the Woman's Rights Society change its name anyway, calling itself the American Equal Rights Association (AERA), to emphasize the goal of universal suffrage for Negroes and women alike. The resolution passed.

Late in the day Tilton mounted the platform. This strikingly handsome man was at the height of his powers: "Mrs. President, this convention is called to consider the most beautiful and humane idea which has ever entered into American politics—the right of woman to that ballot which belongs equally to all citizens." Then with a jab at Johnson, he continued, "At least one President is right—I mean *this* President," and he pointed to Stanton. "She does not claim the ballot for women as women, but for women as citizens. One asks, shall we have a woman for President? I would thank God if today we had a *man* for President."

When he concluded, Tilton turned his attention to Beecher, his ridicule masked as humor. "According to the programme, it is now my friend Mr. Beecher's turn to speak, but I observe that this gentleman, like some of the rest of the President's friends, occupies a back seat. While, therefore, he is sitting under the gallery, I will occupy your attention just long enough to give that *modest man* a chance to muster nerve enough to make his appearance in public." Laughter erupted throughout the hall at this absurd vision of Beecher as a shrinking violet.

Beecher rose from his seat, walked the length of the hall, and mounted the platform. Greatly animated, his face aglow with perspiration, he spoke for an hour to a rapt audience of women that included Lib Tilton. Beecher spoke of woman being in every way man's equal and even his superior. He preached a gushing gospel of loving words but they contained little practical advice.

> You may . . . ask me, "What is the use of preaching to us that we *ought* to [vote] when we are not permitted to do it?" . . . But the reason you have not voted is because you have not wanted to. It is because you have not felt that it was your duty to vote.
>
> I stand on far higher ground in arguing this question than the Right of Woman. I go to the Supreme bench and argue it on the ground that the nation needs woman, and that woman needs the nation, and that woman can never become what she should be,

and the nation can never become what it should be, until there is no distinction made between the sexes as regards the rights and duties of citizenship—until we come to the twenty-eighth verse of the third chapter of Galatians.

Beecher, carried away by his own rhetoric, faltered. Turning to Tilton, he asked, "Galatians—what is it?"

"I don't know," replied Tilton icily, refusing to help the preacher. The insults began. During Tilton's opening speech he had mentioned Lucy Aikin's *Life of Addison* but inadvertently had referred to the author as Lucy Western, a well-known actress of scandalous reputation.

"If it was Lucille Western, you would," Beecher said jovially, and, extracting a small white Bible from his pocket, he read from Galatians, "There is neither Jew nor Greek, there is neither bond nor free, there is neither male nor female; for ye are all one in Christ Jesus. . . ."

Once again Beecher turned to Tilton and with a flourish handed him the Bible. "Theodore was a most excellent young man when he used to go to my church. But he has escaped from my care lately and now I don't know what he does."

Tilton spoke over the chuckling:

In the midst of the general hilarity produced throughout the house by my friend's speech, I myself have been greatly solemnized by being made, as you have witnessed, the public custodian of his New Testament. At first I shared in your gratification at seeing that he carried so much of the Scripture with him. But I found, on looking at the fly-leaf, that the book after all was not his own, but the property of a lady—I will not mention her name. I have, therefore, no right to accept my friend's gift of what is not his own.

With that Tilton handed the Bible back to Beecher. Warming to the audience, he continued:

I remember that when he came home from England, he told me a story of a company of ten ministers who sat down to dine together. A dispute arose among them as to the meaning of a certain passage of Scripture—for aught I know the very passage in Galatians which he just now tried to quote, but couldn't. Some one said, "Who has a New Testament?" It was found that no one had a copy. Pretty soon, however, when the dinner reached the point of champagne,

*Wendell Phillips. This aristocratic
abolitionist had a secret lover.*

some one exclaimed, "Who has a corkscrew?" And it was found
that the whole ten had, every man, a corkscrew in his pocket!

Beecher interrupted with equally false joviality, "Now I know enough
about champagne to know that it don't need any corkscrew!"

"How is it that you know so much more about corkscrews than about
Galatians?" Tilton replied.

The mutual antagonism was apparent despite the laughter.

THE FOLLOWING DAY Anthony and Stanton met with Tilton and Phillips.
Anthony resented Wendell Phillips's public objection to amalgamating the
Anti-Slavery and Woman's Rights societies. But Phillips, more than anyone
else, could be credited with awakening the nation to the evils of slavery and
he was not about to jeopardize the black vote by joining forces with these
women. The discussion concerned the women's campaign to strike the
word *male* from both the Fourteenth Amendment and the proposed revision of the New York State Constitution. Phillips emphasized that the New
York State Constitution also included the word *white* and argued that that
was the sole word which must be eliminated. Phillips—so magnetic that a

close friend observed, "Whoever came into personal relationship with him felt the charm and spell of his power"—managed to convince Tilton that he was right. Theodore then recommended that the newly renamed American Equal Rights Association circulate petitions throughout the state "praying for the enfranchisement of the negro and postponing [women's] demands until the next revision of the New York State Constitution." Tilton added that "the question of striking out the word *male* shall of course be presented as an intellectual theory but not as a practical thing to be accomplished at this convention."

To Anthony's dismay, Stanton did not object. Anthony was staggered and exclaimed, "I would rather cut off my right hand than ask for the ballot for the black man and not for women!" As she turned to leave the meeting, she overheard Tilton whisper to Stanton, "What does ail Susan?" Elizabeth replied, "I cannot imagine. I never before saw her so unreasonable and absolutely rude."

Anthony was convinced that Phillips had triumphed over Stanton's reason. She had succumbed to the charisma of this aristocrat whose family had arrived aboard the *Arbella,* and in 1630 had been among the Puritan founders of the Massachusetts Bay Colony. That evening a hurt and outraged Anthony, ready to do battle, arrived at Stanton's house only to find her friend pacing up and down. "Oh, Susan," she berated herself, "do tell me what is the matter with me!" Elizabeth said that Phillips had publicly betrayed them, had treated her like a manipulable child, and she had gone along with it. She vowed that this would never happen again.

Anthony too had become wary of Phillips. His actions at the convention had been a political betrayal, but another factor influenced her as well: Anthony's attachment—later called "the most passionate affection of her life"—to Anna Dickinson, the fiery Quaker orator. Twenty-four years younger than Anthony, Anna was the child of an abolitionist father who, when she was four, suffered a fatal heart attack while giving an antislavery speech. At fourteen, she began to teach school to aid her impoverished, widowed mother, and four siblings. She was nineteen in 1862 when she made her official debut at the Boston Music Hall. Both Anthony and Phillips had attended and were entranced by Dickinson. Anna Dickinson had long worshiped Wendell Phillips. When she was fifteen, she spent one afternoon on her knees scrubbing the sidewalk in front of the Philadelphia Academy of Music in exchange for free admission to hear Phillips speak. After her Music Hall speech, the usually restrained Phillips came forward, grasped both of Anna's hands in his, and said, "My dear Anna, you brought tears to my eyes—they had almost forgotten the sensation."

*Anna Dickinson—the Quaker girl who became America's most
persuasive speaker for woman suffrage*

In Boston, Phillips saw Dickinson "almost every day." Anthony, also
smitten, soon became convinced that of all "our girls" Anna Dickinson
would be her successor in the leadership of the movement. Anna was
thought to be a great beauty, plump and rosy, with an hourglass figure, dark
eyes, dark hair, a youthful glow. Whether she was truly beautiful is debatable: Some pointed to her hatchet chin, her flat nose, and deep-set eyes. But
when she spoke, Wendell Phillips said, it was with a "demoniac-like elo-
quence." Mark Twain wrote that "her vim, her energy, her tremendous
earnestness, could compel the respect and attention of an audience, even if
she spoke in Chinese." Phillips tried to enlist Anna solely in the cause of
Negro suffrage, but she also supported woman suffrage. And so a powerful
emotional and political triangle began to form, as Anthony and Phillips
contended for "the possession of her soul."

In the congressional election year of 1866, Elizabeth Cady Stanton
declared herself an independent candidate from the Eighth District of New
York. Although women could not vote, if elected by male voters, they could
serve. Stanton found the campaign a "merciless duty," for she also had the

responsibility for a full domestic household. "I must buy butter and meat, hear youngsters spell and multiply, coax parted threads in stocking heels and toes to meet again . . . and smooth down the ruffled feathers of imperious men or cross chambermaids and cook," wrote Stanton. "Then comes Susan, with the nation on her soul, asking for speeches, resolutions, calls, attendance at conventions."

This, of course, was a reference to the unmarried Anthony's ceaseless campaigning while Stanton was more or less housebound. Susan looked on with dismay as Elizabeth's family increased, and disapproved of her failure to use abstention as a means of birth control. Unlike other women of her day, Anthony did not think that only the man enjoyed sexual intercourse. When Stanton became pregnant with her seventh child, Anthony wrote a friend, "I only *scold now* that for a *moment's pleasure* to herself or her husband, she should thus increase the *load of care* under which she already groans." In November, after months of campaigning in an election where women could not cast their ballots, Stanton received only twenty-four votes.

Meanwhile, President Johnson toured the country carrying a message of his own to "the people." In New Orleans a "much excited" Johnson told a reporter he was certain "the people of the South . . . were to be trodden underfoot to protect niggers." He hinted that Northern radicals meant to assassinate him and called them traitors. When asked to name these men he cried out, "I say Thaddeus Stevens of Pennsylvania is one. I say Mr. Sumner of the Senate is another, and Wendell Phillips is another!" The *Times* called Johnson's speeches "vulgar, vindictive and loaded with self-pity," and Tilton wrote in the *Independent,* "The people have been witness to the mortifying spectacle of the President going about from town to town, accompanied by the prominent members of the Cabinet on an electioneering raid, denouncing his opponents, bandying epithets with men in the crowd, and praising himself and his policies. Such a humiliating exhibition has never before been seen, nor anything even approaching to it."

In July a riot broke out in New Orleans that took place during a political gathering for universal suffrage attended by black and white men and women. Forty-eight black men, women, and children were killed, and 250 more were injured. Against the background of this struggle for the future of the nation, Beecher and Tilton found themselves in a major political fight of their own. Johnson was scheduled to appear in Cleveland at the Soldiers and Sailors Convention, which enthusiastically supported Johnson's allies in this congressional election year. Beecher, who was invited to attend as chaplain, received the invitation at his farm in Peekskill, New York, where he had taken his family to avoid the cholera epidemic sweeping New York and other cities. Fearful of making the trip to Cleveland, he begged off, saying that it was mowing time and his hay fever had been acting up. But he wrote a letter, which was reprinted in newspapers throughout the country, endorsing the convention's recommendation that the South be allowed to rely on state governments with regard to their treatment of the Negro. "If they [the Negroes] have the stamina to undergo the hardships which every uncivilized people has undergone in its upward progress, they will in due time take their place among us," wrote Beecher. "That place cannot be bought, nor bequeathed . . . it will come to sobriety, virtue, industry and frugality."

"The Cleveland Letter," as it came to be known, met with a storm of criticism both for urging postponement of Negro enfranchisement to some hazy future and for what the *Times* called Beecher's "unqualified endorsement" of the faltering President Johnson. Beecher's letter infuriated many radical Republicans and clergymen but most of all Theodore Tilton. The intensity of Tilton's anger was, no doubt, influenced by his personal feelings about his wife's growing attachment to Beecher. Tilton excoriated his former idol in the *Independent,* attacking him for having misused the great power of the church for base political ambition. "He has done more harm to the American Republic than has . . . any other citizen except Andrew Johnson," Tilton wrote.

The power of Tilton's fiery rhetoric threatened Beecher in a manner he had not thought possible. Horace Greeley, and even Henry's brother, the preacher Edward Beecher, attacked him for his intimations of white supremacy and his support of Johnson. Henry Ward Beecher called a meeting at the vast Brooklyn Academy of Music. Abandoning his usual extemporaneous style, he read a carefully prepared statement disassociating himself from the Democratic Party. "During the first three weary, dark and disastrous years there was an utter want of outspoken sympathy with our Government on the part of the Democratic Party. I cannot belong to that party."

But Tilton would not let the public forget that Beecher's words had a hollow ring, for during that time he had constantly attacked the government and called Lincoln "the worst candidate possible." Tilton wrote, "The spectacle at the Academy of Music had in it a touch of humiliation which even the noblest passages of the address did not redeem. . . . Something of true moral grandeur is wanting in the position of a veteran who, after twenty-five years of service as a pioneer of political opinion, has nothing nobler to say than simply, 'I am not a Democrat.' "

Tilton's blistering criticism bewildered Beecher, but nothing disturbed him so much as the committee formed within Plymouth Church itself to consider his dismissal. Beecher had been sure of the personal loyalty of his parishioners and considered Plymouth Church his own property. The committee was organized by Henry Bowen, and his son Henry Jr. was appointed chairman. The group included several church members who had benefited from Bowen's patronage during the war. Bowen at last saw an opportunity to avenge himself for Beecher's affair with his late wife. More important—for this was a game of wealth and power—if Beecher were forced to resign, Bowen could put a pawn in his place, and the political patronage emanating from Plymouth Church would be his.

Henry Ward Beecher reeled under the shock of this blow and went for advice to John Tasker Howard, one of the investors in the J. B. Ford publishing syndicate and a founder of Plymouth Church. Howard owed Beecher a considerable debt. During the war his son Joseph had been a *Times* correspondent known for such antics as filing his story then tying up the wire for hours so his rivals could not reach their newspapers with their own accounts. For Joe Howard, an unprincipled rapscallion, the war had held unlimited possibilities for gain. On the night of May 17, 1864, he and a friend had filched Associated Press memo paper, envelopes, and a stylus and delivered to several New York newspapers the news that General Grant's Virginia campaign was faltering and that Lincoln had issued an order to draft four hundred thousand men.

Howard knew that when this grim news was circulated, the price of gold was bound to rise. Indeed, the following morning, after several newspapers printed the bogus dispatch, the gold market jumped eight points, yielding Joe Howard a $40,000 profit. By afternoon, however, the hoax had been discovered and soldiers with drawn bayonets arrived in the editorial rooms of the participating newspapers and demanded that they issue retractions. It was not long before Howard was found out and dispatched to Fort Lafayette prison.

John Tasker Howard pleaded with Beecher to secure his son's release. Without changing his clothes, Beecher left for Washington and returned the following afternoon with a full pardon. By evening Joe Howard was once again in what Beecher was later to call "the weeping bosom of his family."

Now, on John Howard's advice, Beecher wrote a letter disclaiming any attachment to Johnson. Howard then carried Beecher's letter to the uncommitted committee members and lobbied on the preacher's behalf. In a powerful act of persuasion, Howard caused the committee to disband. Bowen's coup had failed, but had left opposing political factions within Plymouth Church.

Beecher vowed to let Bowen know the price of disloyalty. He withdrew his sermons from the *Independent,* and local advertising dropped precipitously. But this was a small gesture compared to what happened next: Within three weeks President Johnson had removed Henry Bowen from his newest political appointment as tax collector for the Third Ward, which encompassed the greater part of the city of Brooklyn. He dismissed Bowen's staff and canceled contracts with Bowen's cronies. As this vast political patronage was snatched from his grasp, Bowen, who had so far unstintingly supported Tilton and the popular forces behind him, began to reassess the situation. What should he do to recapture position and power?

# CHAPTER ELEVEN

# A DANGEROUS MAN

IN SEPTEMBER 1866, Theodore Tilton was once again on the road as a delegate to the Loyalist convention in Philadelphia, organized to combat Johnson's congressional electioneering. (This convention was composed of delegates from both Northern and Southern states who had remained loyal to the Union during the recent war.) The choice of five women delegates seemed radical enough, but when Frederick Douglass was appointed from Rochester, several radical Republicans found themselves in a precarious political position. Facing a congressional election in only two months, they needed support in the Southern and border states that opposed black enfranchisement. Many Republicans feared that the presence of a black delegate would cost them this support and possibly the election.

Douglass had made headlines when he'd visited the White House to remind President Johnson that empowering his people to vote would give them the means "with which to save ourselves. . . . The fact that we are . . . subject to taxation, to volunteer in the service of the country, subject to being drafted, subject to bear the burdens of the State, makes it not improper that we should ask to share in the privileges of this condition." According to his private secretary, Johnson answered "in a manner which indicated repressed anger," saying that giving Negroes the vote might lead to "a conflict of races" and he suggested emigration as a solution to the problem. "The President no more expected that darkey delegation yesterday than he did the cholera," the secretary told a *World* reporter, and he added that Johnson had remarked when they left, "Those damned sons of bitches. . . . I know that damned Douglass. He's just like any nigger and he would sooner cut a white man's throat than not."

Douglass would find himself and his cause equally unwelcome at the convention in Philadelphia. Ironically, even some of the delegates who had been steadfast abolitionists feared that the very success of their crusade to end slavery might grant too large a measure of power to the newly freed slaves, a view typified by Henry Blackwell, who, with his wife, Lucy Stone, led the powerful New England woman suffrage contingent. Returning from a recent visit to the South, Blackwell said that he was willing for the Negro to have suffrage, "but not under such conditions that he should rule the South."

On the train to Philadelphia, a group of delegates to the Loyalist convention banded together to ask Douglass to resign his appointment in the interest of granting Congress control over Johnson. Douglass answered, "Gentlemen, with all respect, you might as well ask me to put a loaded pistol to my head and blow my brains out."

Theodore Tilton and Anna Dickinson, a Philadelphia delegate, were warned by Thaddeus Stevens not to ally themselves with Douglass. The capitulation to political expediency was clear: As a young man, Stevens had given his life's savings of $300 to buy the freedom of a slave who was being sold away from his family. He had been among the first to endorse Negro suffrage. Now ill and close to death, he had instructed that he be buried in a nonsegregated graveyard. Yet the pragmatic Stevens was willing to do whatever was necessary to elect a Republican majority in Congress.

The following morning, Philadelphia newspaper headlines declared of the convention, "Philadelphia Full of Miscegenists." "Negro Insurrection To Be Incited." "First Grand National Convention of Spiritualists, Woman's Rights, and Negro Worshipers." Douglass strode through the crowd of delegates in front of Philadelphia's Independence Hall amid tense silence. He observed that the other delegates seemed "ashamed and afraid" of him, turning away as if repelled by a negative magnet. Among the few who greeted him, he recognized only Benjamin Butler.

Douglass realized that the delegates were lining up two by two for a march through the city but no one approached him. "I was the ugly and deformed child of the family." He stood in increasing isolation as the line of pairs grew longer. "Who of my brother members would consent to walk with me?" he asked himself. None seemed willing. He would have to walk alone—a pariah. But as the line began to move out, a tall, lanky man with blond curls cascading to his shoulders appeared at Douglass's side. "He came to me in my isolation, seized me by the hand in a most brotherly way, and proposed to walk with me in the procession. I have been in many awkward and disagreeable positions in my life, when the presence of a friend would have been highly valued, but I think I never appreciated an act of courage and generous sentiment more highly than I did that of this brave young man." This man was Theodore Tilton.

Tilton, who had not been able to amend his humanity for political

*Frederick Douglass. As an escaped slave he lectured for abolition
but was reprimanded for sounding like a refined white man.*

expediency, came in for sharp criticism. An angry Thaddeus Stevens wrote,
"A good many people here are disturbed by the practical exhibition of social
equality in the arm-in-arm performance of Douglass and Tilton. It does not
become radicals like us particularly to object but it was certainly unfortunate at this time. The old prejudice now revived will lose us some votes.
Why it was done I cannot see except as foolish bravado."

Because of its incendiary nature, discussion of the Negro vote had been
excluded from the convention. But as Frederick Douglass noted, "Miss
Dickinson, Mr. Tilton and myself felt that any reconstruction of the South
leaving the freedmen without the ballot would leave them in the absolute
power of the old master class." On the final day, through Anna Dickinson's

urging, Tilton introduced the subject, which, according to Douglass, caused "tumult and confusion in the midst of which the president . . . and other officers left their places on the platform, declaring the convention adjourned." When Tilton called out at the top of his lungs, "This convention is *not* adjourned, as the majority remains in this hall," the delegates from the border states also stood up and stormed out. Even so, a majority remained.

Once calm had been restored, Tilton and the remaining delegates nominated a new president, and Anna Dickinson made a forceful plea for a constitutional amendment that would, once and for all, guarantee Negroes the vote against any restrictions that might be imposed by the individual states. Then Tilton formally put forth resolutions that would become the basis of the Fifteenth Amendment:

> The right of citizens of the United States to vote shall not be denied or abridged by the United States, or by any State, on account of race, color, or previous condition of servitude.
>
> The Congress shall have power to enforce this article by appropriate legislation.

In the absence of the hostile delegates, the resolutions passed with little opposition, marking Theodore Tilton as a hero to some and a dangerous man to others.

In November 1866, a Republican Congress swept into power, its cause aided by the atrocities in the South and the seemingly out-of-control bigotry of Andrew Johnson. With more than enough votes to override every presidential veto, the plans for Reconstruction could at last be implemented. Theodore Tilton's dream of a new society of equality and justice appeared within reach, but the problems in the way of this goal were massive and required more selflessness than those in power possessed. By law, December 18, 1866, marked the deadline for freeing the slaves. On that evening, thousands of bewildered black people were turned out by their former owners onto the roads of the South. The plight of these abandoned souls weighed heavily on Theodore Tilton's mind.

Tilton was dismayed at politicians who had little regard for the equality of black people or of women. As his disillusionment grew he cut himself adrift to explore new possibilities and new ways of looking at the world. From his writings at this time we know that he felt "alone and despairing," but also that he was "striving to tear off, little by little—since I cannot do it at a stroke—some of the bandages that have hitherto bound me blind."

As if trying to find a touchstone, after a lecture in Springfield, Illinois, he visited Abraham Lincoln's grave. Chilled to the bone, he bent down and scooped up an oak leaf that lay near the headstone. Later that night he put the leaf in an envelope and wrote to his wife,

> I never thought that Abraham Lincoln was one of the great men of the world but I had always a tender feeling towards him, akin to personal affection. The great fault of our American statesmen and public leaders is a lack of that moral courage which, of all endowments, makes men most truly great. More and more I believe in absolute fidelity to Liberty, Justice, and Equality. Every public man who compromises these great principles retards the progress of his country.
>
> Mr. Lincoln's fame rests on his Proclamation—a measure to which he was driven somewhat against his will. He was willing to save slavery if he could thereby save the Union. This willingness to compromise with wrong showed a mind not great in the highest sense. But he was a noble, grand, and illustrious man after all . . . death canonizes a great character! The world magnifies its favorite names into colossal fame. Abraham Lincoln's name and fame will probably overtop the records of all other men of the nineteenth century.

Among the beliefs that Theodore Tilton had begun to question was the traditional religion that previously had sustained him. He wrote to Lib,

> The more I think of the whole subject of religion, of theology, of the church, of doctrines, of creeds, I am inclined to undervalue or rather see little value in everything but the Christian character. . . . I see so much in my travels that goes to show how men content themselves with low lives instead of the high . . . with selfish greed instead of generous self-sacrifice. . . . Hereafter I mean to take pattern, not after men, but after the Great Teacher.

The sexual conventions of the day also came under Tilton's scrutiny. In Beecher's church he had been taught that the highest love transcended passion. (This, of course, implied that wives were chosen for their purity and high-mindedness, while sexual pleasure was to be found in the company of "vile women," the common term for prostitutes and other women of easy virtue.) As Tilton had explained to Lib, "Men and women who have the mere natural *instinct* for loving, love with the heart, but they who have a true *genius* for loving, love with the soul." In his novel *Norwood,* Beecher wrote that sexual passion needs "rein and curb." But in practice both Tilton and Beecher struggled with the sacred and the profane. Beecher, by way of justifying his own licentious behavior, later explained to Frank Moulton, "If love was proper and not wrong therefore it followed that any expression of that love, whether by a shake of the hand or a kiss of the lips or even bodily intercourse was not wrong." Yet despite this endorsement of "free love," the self-indulgent Beecher deplored his own sexual excesses, and his sexual gratification was followed with the bathos of guilt.

This pattern was not unlike Tilton's own and typified the dilemma of many religious men of the day. Tilton too found himself in a constant spiral of sin and repentance, and he confided to his wife,

> I believe that I have less self respect than in former days. . . . I find myself a constant sinner. Lately I have many times bowed my head like a bulrush. I have once or twice done right under strong provocation to do wrong, and I have several times done wrong under a mere gossamer of temptation.

Like her husband, Lib Tilton was caught in the vise of sexual hypocrisy: Women of her class were trained to transcend carnal desire, thereby fulfilling the religious ideal of spiritual superiority. Catharine Beecher's guide to behavior specified,

> Do not suffer your hand to be held or squeezed, without showing that it displeases you by instantly withdrawing it. If a finger is put out to touch a chain that is round your neck, or a breast-pin that you are wearing, draw back, and take it off for inspection. Accept no unnecessary assistance in putting on cloaks, shawls, overshoes, or anything of the sort.

When Theodore was leaving for a lecture in Altoona, Pennsylvania, Lib stood on the train platform and asked plaintively if her love had "totally and thoroughly" satisfied him. Tilton replied in writing, "I believe that my love . . . is as much as it is possible for a man to bear toward a woman. . . . Do you still chide yourself for a fancied failure in filling your husband's ideal of a wife?"

Indeed she did. For Tilton, in trying to justify his promiscuity, blamed Lib for his "falling into sin" and finally told her that because of her coldness, he was not above "taking a woman while on the road." For her part, Lib meekly accepted his judgment. She later wrote, "I understood very well that I was not to have the attention many wives have. I gave him to understand that what might be regarded as neglect under other circumstances would not be so regarded by me. I realized that his talent and genius must not be narrowed down to myself. To a very large extent I attribute to that the later sorrows of my life."

But slowly Lib too began to change, for while her husband was away, she found herself increasingly attracted to her preacher. Early on, undoubtedly sensitive to the extent of Mrs. Tilton's repressed sexuality, Beecher emphasized the purity of their relationship. He told her of Fourier's view that an affinity of souls marked the genuine love that was available only to those of the highest nature. True marriage was one in which a man selected his spiritual wife. Lib wrote her husband, "I live in profound wonder and hushed solemnity at this great mystery of soul loving to which I have awakened." For the present, Mrs. Tilton controlled her powerful sexual attraction to Beecher by praying for hours at a time. Yet a part of her recognized the impending danger of her relationship with Beecher, for she also wrote her husband, "No temptation or fascination could cause me to yield my womanhood." And the words, "I am afraid!"

Lib gradually came to see that she became more attractive to her husband because of her relationship with Beecher. And, although he denied it, Theodore was becoming increasingly jealous. In November 1866, from Washington, Tilton wrote his wife, "I think any man is a fool to be jealous. If he is jealous *without cause* he is foolish, if *with* cause more foolish." But he showed his true colors when he ended the letter with, "Up till midnight after my lecture last evening talking with Edward Beecher about his backsliding Brooklyn brother."

When Tilton returned home between lecture tours, he spoke incessantly to Lib of Beecher's misguided politics and profligate ways, and he accused her of enticing Beecher with her sensuality. Lib was horrified at the thought and denied it, but she spent hours locked in her bedroom examining her face and body for telltale evidence that she was a wanton. She later reflected,

> When Theodore said I had a sensual influence, I used to become impregnated with this idea of his myself. I wondered if it was so and would think it over and over.
>
> He would often talk to me that way by the hour and try to persuade me it was true, but then when I used to get from under his

*Theodore and Lib Tilton—the picture of
domestic bliss*

influence I was perfectly sure that no man ever felt that way toward
me. Hearing that, day after day, week after week, it made me sick
and caused me to distress myself. It kept me in embarrassment. It
was a hard thing to live under.

Now Tilton questioned his wife after every pastoral visit. Later she said,
"I tried to give him a full accounting. . . . I would throw out a remark
which Mr. Beecher had made and Theodore would say, 'You didn't tell me
that.'

" 'Oh yes, I did mean to tell you, but I forgot,' I'd say.

"And he'd say, 'You lie!' "

At Christmas, feeling the need of his wife's affection in a world that seemed increasingly hostile, Theodore asked Lib to meet him in Chicago and chided her about her growing attachment to Beecher.

Now that the other man has gone off lecturing you can come to me, leave home, children, kith and kin, and cleave to whom you originally promised to cleave. Oh, frailty, thy name is woman. . . . If you can get anybody to pour tea for you, and to take sauce from the servants, and to receive pastoral visits, I shall expect to meet you. . . . I don't expect to be lonesome much longer.

But even this domestic anchor had pulled free. Lib refused to come, giving their daughter Alice's illness as the reason. In fact, under Beecher's influence, Lib had begun to feel herself a "full woman" and therefore to question the passionless role thrust upon her by Theodore. When they were apart, the concept of her pure spiritual nature was bearable, but when they were together the role became troubling. Theodore addressed her as "My espoused saint" and wrote her, "If you should ever appear to me anything less than the ideal woman, the Christian saint I know you to be, I shall not care to live a day longer." She answered,

During the early part of your absence it was well enough to suffer you to believe in my perfection, but as you near home, it is wise to dispel the infatuation little by little, and convince you of the humanity and frailty of your loving

Wife

On Christmas Eve, when Tilton returned home, his wife lavished on him the newly found sexuality that her preacher had awakened in her. This sudden passion in an eleven-year marriage perplexed Tilton. Three days later, when Theodore left to resume his lecture tour, Lib wrote him in the revealing terms one might use to describe one's first orgasm and made a tortured effort to justify her relationship with her husband and her preacher.

My Own True Mate:
      . . . I have been thinking of my love for Mr. B. considerably of late and those thoughts you shall have. Remember, "My heart in this new sympathy for one abounds towards all." Now, I think I have lived a richer, happier life since I have *known* him. And have you not loved me more ardently since you saw that another high

nature appreciated me? Certain it is, I never in all my life had such rapture of enthusiasm in my love for you—something akin to the birth of another babe—a new fountain opened enriching all. . . . For many years, I did not realize the blessing. What remorse it brings to me! Memories bitter, awful!

But to return to Mr. B. He has been the guide of our youth, and, until the three last dreadful years when our confidence was shaken in him, we trusted him as no other human being. . . . It is not strange then, darling, that on a more intimate acquaintance my delight and pleasure should increase. Of course, I realize what attracts you both to me is a supposed purity of soul you find in me. Therefore, it is that never before have I had such wrestlings with God that He would reveal Himself to me. . . . I live in an agony of soul daily.

And Tilton replied,

I like Mr. Beecher in many aspects as well as I ever did but he has ceased to be my soul's prop—ceased to inspire me to my best life. I believe he is not as morally great as he once was. . . . There was an older virtue which has gone out of him—an influence which used to brighten my life when I came under its ray; an influence, however, which became gradually quenched like a vanishing sunbeam.

# CHAPTER TWELVE

# WRITTEN IN FIRE

IN MAY 1867, as the Tiltons were wrestling with the question of marriage in a modern world, Mary Cheney Greeley returned from a seven-month sojourn in Europe. In fact, between 1858 and 1866, she had spent the equivalent of four years abroad. Only with an ocean separating Mary from her husband did she gradually regain her equilibrium and overcome the paranoia that had been induced by the opiates and other harsh treatments administered to her by eminent doctors. At fifty-five, Mary had passed the age of childbearing and, no longer a recluse, she now directed her febrile energy to the cause of woman's rights. Mary had allied herself with Stanton and Anthony in combating the male domination that she felt had ruined her life. Though she despised her husband as much as ever, she enjoyed the company of their daughters, Ida and Gabrielle. Rather than give Horace Greeley any kind of comfort, the women in his family seemed to have an unspoken pact that his home should be as unwelcoming as possible. After fourteen years, the Chappaqua farmhouse remained almost as bare as the day Horace had acquired it. In Paris, Mary had purchased crates full of embroidered Belgian linen, Limoges china, and weighty silver, but stored them unopened in the basement.

Mary Greeley soon learned that her husband had been appointed chairman of the suffrage subcommittee of the New York State Constitutional Convention to take place in Albany in June. Stanton and Anthony, she also discovered, had been conducting a massive campaign to collect thousands of signatures to amend the Constitution, which presently granted the vote solely to *male* and *white* citizens. Mary arranged a formal meeting with her husband in the offices of the *Tribune* and arrived with Elizabeth and Susan. When Greeley heard of their campaign, he squinted through his wire glasses and cautioned, "This is a critical period for the Republican party and the life of the nation. The word *white* in our Constitution at this hour has a significance which *male* has not. Your turn will come next." When they protested, Greeley threatened, "If you persevere in your present plan, you need depend on no further help from me or the *Tribune*."

That June, Stanton and Anthony were nevertheless granted a hearing before Greeley's suffrage subcommittee in Albany. When Stanton gave her testimony asserting the right of women to vote, Greeley interrupted her: "The ballot and the bullet go together. If you vote, are you ready to fight?" She replied, "Yes, we are ready to fight, sir, just as you did in the late war, by sending our substitutes."

Petitions signed by twenty-eight thousand men and women advocating woman suffrage were then presented. The galleries were crowded awaiting the chairman's report. Stanton and Anthony, knowing of Greeley's animosity, held one petition to be presented last, but they informed the press of its contents in advance. As Greeley stood to address the convention, a delegate called out, "Mr. Chairman, I hold in my hand a petition signed by Mrs. Horace Greeley and three hundred other women of Westchester asking that the word *male* be stricken from the Constitution." Mary Cheney Greeley had openly defied her husband.

Over shouts and female cheers, an angry and obviously embarrassed Greeley read his report, his hand shaking as he held the papers: "Your Committee does not recommend an extension of the elective franchise to women. However defensible in theory, we are satisfied that public sentiment does not demand and would not sustain an innovation so revolutionary and sweeping, so openly at war with a distribution of duties and functions between the sexes as venerable and pervading as government itself, and involving transformations so radical in social and domestic life."

The next time Horace Greeley saw Stanton and Anthony was at a Sunday night reception at the Tiltons' home in Brooklyn. Stanton watched Greeley making his way across the room and whispered to Anthony, "Prepare for a storm."

"Good evening, Mr. Greeley," she said, and extended her hand.

Greeley did not take her hand. He told her, "I saw the reporters prick up their ears and knew that my report and Mrs. Greeley's petition would come out together with large headings in the city papers and probably be called out by the newsboys in the street. You are always so desirous in public to appear under your own name, why did you in this case substitute 'Mrs. Horace Greeley' for 'Mary Cheney Greeley,' which was really on the petition?"

"Because I wanted all the world to know that it was the wife of Horace Greeley who protested against her husband's report," Stanton replied.

"Well, I understand the animus of that whole proceeding. . . . You two ladies are the most maneuvering politicians in the state of New York. . . . Now let me tell you what I intend to do. I have given positive instructions that no word of praise shall ever again be awarded you in the *Tribune* and that if your name is ever necessarily mentioned, it shall be as Mrs. Henry B. Stanton." Abruptly, he turned away. Greeley's *Tribune*, a newspaper that supported woman suffrage, was now closed to Stanton and Anthony. They had made a formidable enemy.

Other powerful allies and friends were also alienated by the aggressive way these two women furthered their cause. Anticipating that the final wording of the Fifteenth Amendment would include the word *male*, they drew up a petition to the House of Representatives stating that they would oppose any amendment "to extend or regulate suffrage" unless it made "no distinctions . . . between men and women." But when they solicited signatures from their former supporters, they were rebuffed. Stanton's cousin Gerrit Smith, for whom she had named her third son, wrote, "I can not sign the petition you send me. Cheerfully, gladly, can I sign a petition for the enfranchisement of women. But I can not sign a paper against the enfranchisement of the negro man unless at the same time woman shall be enfranchised. The removal of the political disabilities of race is my first desire—of sex my second."

At meetings and conventions Stanton and Anthony were asked by former allies to change their position that unless the Fifteenth Amendment included women they would oppose it, but they refused. In her frustration, Stanton once again descended to racism.

> Would Horace Greeley, Wendell Phillips, Gerrit Smith, or Theodore Tilton be willing to stand aside and trust their individual interests, and the whole welfare of the nation, to the lowest strata of manhood? If not, why ask educated women, who love their country . . . who feel that their enfranchisement is of vital importance . . . to stand aside while 2,000,000 ignorant men are ushered into the halls of legislation?

Stanton's superior attitude toward those she termed "Sambo," coupled with her criticism of the church, the laws governing marriage and divorce, and the male establishment in general, severely damaged her political effectiveness. She was conflicted. She knew that she needed men to further her cause and to provide the money to go forward, but she resented their domination. Three years previously she had written Anthony, "I am not alone,

*A woman's rights convention, 1850s. Strong women felt they could change their "social, civil, and religious condition."*

as my niece is with me. She is a beautiful woman. I wish you and I had been beautiful; then we could have carried all men with us to heights divine and entrenched them on principle." Still, Stanton realized as well that a society that forced women to manipulate men degraded both sexes. "Man has been molding woman to his ideas by direct and positive influences, while she, if not a negation, has used indirect means to control him and thus in most cases developed the very characteristics both in him and herself that most needed repression."

Stanton smarted over the wounds inflicted by the men of her class who had kept her an outsider and betrayed her. "I wish you were a boy!" had been her father's dictum. Elizabeth Cady Stanton appeared a capable housewife and mother; benign, becurled, fashionably dressed. Her appearance and manner posed no threat, and yet her internal rage at being sealed out of the "halls of legislation" by men fueled her continuing fight for woman's rights.

The next battlefield was Kansas, where separate amendments to the state Constitution had been proposed to enfranchise women and Negroes.

Stanton and Anthony arrived in late August 1867. An endless expanse of prairie rolled out in front of them, accented by sparse clusters of sod shanties. This was the land where John Brown and his sons had spilled their blood. Anthony set up headquarters near her brother's home in Leavenworth. Stanton, campaigning separately, was warmly accepted by the pioneer women, who gave her what they had—a place in an unkempt bed shared with several children, cold water, bacon floating in grease, coffee sweetened with sorghum, biscuits green with mold, dried fruit. Much of the state was inaccessible by rail, so day after day she rode to remote prairie towns in a carriage drawn by two mules.

Yet with all the physical discomforts, the open spaces of Kansas and the welcoming, honest people invigorated Stanton, and she came to envision a life for herself and Henry where they might be together in a way that had not previously been possible. Stanton's marriage had deteriorated. Henry Stanton was now an editor of the *New York Sun,* but he resented the fact that his wife's increasing fame eclipsed his own. Here, she thought, was a place where they might reconcile and not compete. She wrote to Henry, "This is the country for us to move to. . . . We could build [a house] for $3,000. . . . You would feel like a new being here. You could be a leader here, as there is not a man in the state that can make a really good speech."

In the Kansas campaign, both Stanton and Anthony were becoming emotionally and financially drained. Greeley's *Tribune* and Tilton's *Independent,* Stanton noted, were "*the* papers out here." Stanton knew that Greeley would oppose her, but she wrote to Tilton for help. He wrote a single editorial advocating the passage of both amendments. In October the flamboyant George Francis Train arrived in Kansas to campaign with Anthony. Train was a showman in the P. T. Barnum mode. He dressed in a purple brocade jacket with a lime-green satin vest and red boots, and people stared at him wherever he went. Train had already achieved fame by traveling around the world in eighty days—a record—thereby inspiring the novel by Jules Verne. Train was the owner of New York's most successful horse-car line but he had made most of his fortune as the prime organizer of the Credit Mobilier, a holding company for the stock of the Union Pacific Railroad. It was into this entity that profits flowed at the rate of almost $20 million a year, as the government ceded more than 450 million acres for settlement and underwrote the westward expansion of the railroads with tax dollars: $16,000 a mile through the plains, $32,000 a mile through the desert, and $48,000 a mile through the Rocky Mountains. The previous inhabitants, the Indians, were driven off their land or killed as the West became the land of the future.

*George Francis Train.*
*Was he a visionary or a madman?*

Train's speeches advocating the vote for women but not for "low-down nigger men" won the votes of the Irish and other Democrats. But his blatant racism soon alienated many woman's rights advocates. Lucy Stone termed Train "a charlatan" and "a lunatic." William Lloyd Garrison, editor of *The Liberator,* wrote that he was "mortified and astonished beyond measure in seeing Elizabeth Cady Stanton and Susan B. Anthony traveling about the country with that crack-brained harlequin." Anthony was also criticized for using $1,000 of the American Equal Rights Association's funds to cover Train's speaking expenses when he could easily have afforded to pay for himself. Finally, both amendments were defeated by a two-thirds majority in Kansas, leaving blacks and women equally disfranchised.

After the Kansas campaign, Anthony wrote to Anna Dickinson, "Not one leading politician stood by us in the deadly breach. They all mean to delude us into silence and use us to serve party ends." And she confided to her diary, "All the old friends, with scarce an exception, are sure we are wrong. Only time can tell but I believe we are right."

One day Train asked Anthony why she did not start her own publication. "Not lack of brains, but money," Anthony told him.

"I will give you the money," volunteered Train.

Desperate for support, Stanton defended the alliance with Train. "Mr. Train . . . has some extravagances and idiosyncrasies but he is willing to devote energy and money to our cause when no other man is," she wrote. "It seems to me it would be right and wise to accept aid even from the devil himself, provided he did not tempt us to lower our standard." Stanton's words were to prove prophetic, for in the not too distant future her association would be with the woman soon to be known as "Mrs. Satan"—Victoria Woodhull.


THEODORE TILTON TOO was coming to distrust the politics of Reconstruction. His utopian dream of a new society was fast vanishing as he became increasingly disillusioned with politics and public life. Determined to find his own way, he fancied himself a brave explorer taking nothing for granted, no cant, no fixed dogma. "The old religious teachings, the orthodox view, the dread of punishment, the atonement, have less and less power over my mind," he wrote. Ironically, at the very time Tilton turned from conventional religion, his immense power emanated from his editorship of the *Independent,* a newspaper that influenced a nation of churchgoers. Wary of Henry Bowen's growing use of the power of his paper for personal and political gain, and perhaps also concerned by his own descent from orthodoxy, Tilton confided to Lib that he no longer knew if he wished to make the *Independent* his life's work. There even had been a groundswell to nominate him for lieutenant governor of New York State, but Tilton refused to run. He wrote Lib, "I have no ambition to be rich—I never have, none to be in political office, none for social or fashionable preeminence, none that I can detect for oratorical distinction and not a great deal for literary reputation."

To fill the gap left by the increasing cynicism he saw about him and his alienation from Beecher's church, he began to turn to Spiritualism. After reading the biography of Mrs. Pomeroy, a dedicated Spiritualist and clairvoyant, he wrote to Lib,

> I was struck with a little passage as follows: "It was," said she [of a near-death experience], "a prophetic state. I have looked into the

future. I know of things that are to be hereafter." Such experiences are not uncommon with good men and women near death. I never can read of such an experience except with a thrill. The future is not so far from us. The Kingdom of God is around us. The veil is thin which divides our eyes from the vision of Jordan. Sometimes in sleep, sometimes in wakefulness, there comes to us a glimpse "of the glory that is to be revealed." Our customary notions of the other life are distorted, misshapen, and deformed. Our prevailing theologies have covered our eyes with stained windows.

Theodore Tilton was among the millions who found comfort in Spiritualism in the postwar society. The movement that had begun with the spirit-rapping of the Fox sisters three decades before was at its zenith at the end of the Civil War. The unbearable death of a generation of young men—the hope of America—encouraged the belief that these souls had simply "passed over." They were reachable in a land just beyond the living where they could be called upon to comfort and support the bereft they had left behind. Spiritualist publications flourished and one of them, *The Banner of Light,* optimistically estimated that Spiritualism had gained a million adherents a year for the previous three years and they now numbered ten million.

Victoria Woodhull and Colonel Blood combined their belief in Spiritualism with a doctrine equally at odds with conventional religion: free love. Utopian communities and other attempts to reform the sexual customs of society had met with little success but still many Spiritualists held free love as a panacea. Of all the radical ideas then current, free love was the most controversial. It represented the ultimate expression of female liberation and profoundly threatened a male-dominated society.

For Blood and Woodhull, Spiritualism and free love provided a rationale for the way they lived. Blood, having seen the horrors of war, knew the fragility of life. He believed that those who had died so wastefully were hovering near. What he did not believe was that sexual exclusivity was a matter of concern and he accepted with equanimity the exchange of sexual favors for politics, pleasure, or profit. Both Tennessee and Victoria were later to say that they had received money for sex. And though it was said that Victoria once threw her shears at Blood when she found him with another woman, on most occasions she was not given to jealousy.

Victoria Woodhull and James Harvey Blood were married in 1866, but they obtained a divorce two years later to protest the confinement of the marriage laws. Five years after the divorce, when Blood was asked, "How long have you and Mrs. Woodhull been separated?" he replied, "We were never separated. . . ." Colonel Blood arrived at his theories intellectually, while Victoria Woodhull led life as she must. But both philosophies, the theoretical and the empirical, were identical.

When, in order to survive, Victoria read fortunes and performed magnetic healing and occasionally sold her body to keep her soul intact, there were two Victorias: one protected and empowered by the spirits and one who experienced the world's cruelty. Therefore, it is not surprising that there are two accounts of her life at this time: the one that Theodore Tilton would later include in his biography of her, and the actual life recorded in newspapers, court records, and other documents. Tilton's flattering portrait represented Victoria's dream of empowerment and her escape from the oppressive life of an exploited and exploiting woman. According to Tilton, when people came to Victoria,

> By divine inspiration, she would instantly know the names, residences, and maladies of these strangers. . . . Her purse grew fat. She reaped a golden harvest.
>
> First at Indianapolis and afterward at Terre Haute, she wrought apparently miraculous cures. She straightened the feet of the lame, she opened the ears of the deaf, she detected the robbers of a bank, she brought to light hidden crimes, she solved psychological problems, she unveiled business secrets, she prophesied future events. . . . Benedictions . . . were lavished upon her; money flowed in a stream toward her. . . . The sum total of the receipts of her practice . . . to the time of its discontinuance by direction of the spirits, was $700,000. The age of wonders has not ceased!

In the real world Victoria achieved few such wonders. With Tennessee and Colonel Blood, she moved constantly from town to town, scrambling for a living. The sum of $700,000 would not come her way for another three years, and then it would be the largesse of one of the most powerful men in America. As she grew older, Victoria had, by her own account, become discouraged, although she clung to her belief that everything she suffered was preparation for a mission for which the spirits had selected her above all others.

Victoria later said that on a "temporary sojourn" to Pittsburgh, she was sitting in the parlor of yet another boardinghouse when the spirit in the white toga once again came to her. "Your work is about to begin," he said. "All these years we have been preparing you for a great mission. . . . Go to

New York City, to 17 Great Jones Street. There you will find a house ready and waiting for you and yours." Then a vision of a house filled with comfortable furniture floated before her eyes. She saw the bedrooms, the parlor, the stairs, and a front entry hall, where a large black book rested on a mahogany table. Because the book lay flat upon the table, she could not read the title. Gradually, the picture blurred and vanished.

Then the spirit reappeared before her. "Who are you?" Victoria asked. "All these years you have never said. Tell me now."

The spirit pointed to a white marble-topped table that stood nearby and with his index finger traced letters across its surface. At first the letters were invisible, then faint; then they became brighter and brighter until they burst into flame. Victoria read the name written in fire—Demosthenes.

# CHAPTER THIRTEEN

# TO EQUAL ACCOUNT

THE DARK BLUE railroad car with New York & Harlem—Albany RR emblazoned in gold on its side rolled through the green fields of the village of Harlem, burrowed through the deep Mount Prospect tunnel from Ninety-sixth to Ninety-second Street, and emerged on Fourth Avenue. From the train Victoria and Tennessee could see shanties, herds of goats grazing near the dusty tracks, occasionally a factory or brewery, its chimneys belching black smoke against the blue sky.

Pollution and noise threatened to ruin the city. To protect the fashionable downtown areas, citizen pressure for a clean environment had forced through a city ordinance in 1850 banning street-level steam locomotives below Forty-second Street. Thus Forty-second Street became the transfer point for railroad passengers. Here the train halted abruptly and the steam locomotive was detached. The cars were uncoupled and hitched one by one to teams of four horses for the journey to the Twenty-seventh Street terminus. Though this process took some forty minutes, few passengers left their seats to descend into the sea of mud in which pigs, goats, and chickens roamed free and climbed onto the steps of the nearby newly constructed hospital of the Society for the Relief of the Ruptured and Crippled.

In the previous six years the population of the city had doubled. Now, in 1868, it was nearing 1 million inhabitants. The train yard at Fourth Avenue and Forty-second Street bisected the city, providing an invisible wall behind which poverty, filth, and pollution were confined to the east while the affluent new city expanded to the west. On the east were factories and at least a dozen breweries, including Gillig's, Ahle's, Neidlenger, and Schmidt. Immigrants—German, English, Irish—crowded the four- and five-story tenements lining Third and Second Avenues. Along the East River were the slaughterhouses to which cattle were driven across the length of Forty-second Street from the Hudson River docks. And on the rocks above the river was a gang-ridden slum called Dutch Hill.

A different city lay to the west: On Fifth Avenue from Thirty-fourth to Forty-second Street stood the high-stooped brownstone houses of New York's wealthy. On Sundays, fashionable couples would stroll on the elevated walkway of the Reservoir at Fifth and Forty-second Street. Real estate experts who had predicted that the rich would never live farther uptown than Forty-second Street were being proved wrong. The brutal but convenient destruction of the Colored Orphan Asylum at Forty-third and Fifth by Irish protesters during the 1863 draft riots had left the avenue wide open to the postwar expansion.

Seeing it before others, Commodore Cornelius Vanderbilt, on whose line Victoria and Tennessee arrived in New York, had purchased large tracts of land around his Forty-second Street train yard as far uptown as Forty-eighth Street, as well as various parcels on Madison and Fifth to Fifty-second Street. Vanderbilt was said to be the richest man in America. Now seventy-four, the Commodore had bought his first share of railroad stock in 1862, only six years before, to show his superiority to his eldest son, William Henry, who had also purchased railroad stock. But almost immediately the Commodore, who had risen from being the impoverished captain of a Staten Island ferryboat to owning the largest fleet of ships in America, saw that steamboats and railroads were about to change places in the future of transportation in America. Eighteen sixty-eight was the year that railroads finally webbed the nation from coast to coast, and by that time Vanderbilt owned the New York & Harlem, the Hudson River, the Albany, the New Haven, the New York Central, and seven other railroad lines.

Of the many entrepreneurs who saw the future, Vanderbilt was perhaps the most visionary. And literally so. He said the glittering new city of New York had come to him in a vision and that he had purchased land because he had seen that eventually the city would extend uptown along Fifth, Madison, and Fourth Avenues to Ninety-sixth Street. With remarkable foresight, Vanderbilt eventually buried the tracks to the north of his depot under Fourth Avenue (now called Park Avenue), all the way uptown to the Mount Prospect tunnel, so that his trains would not disturb the affluent residents who he said would one day live there.

The Commodore devised a plan to bring together his railroad lines and build a central terminal at Forty-second Street. He planned a magnificent facade for this terminal facing in a westerly direction, and although he hired civil engineer Isaac C. Buckhout and architect John B. Snook to carry out his wishes, the Commodore said his vision had revealed exactly what Grand Central Station would look like.

*Commodore Cornelius Vanderbilt. Known for his business acumen, he also experienced visions and believed in Spiritualism.*

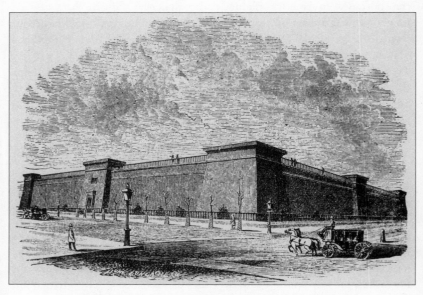

*The Reservoir at Forty-second Street and Fifth Avenue. Fashionable couples paraded around the elevated walkway.*

## NATIONAL POLICE GAZETTE.

Vol. 2. No. 27—$2 A YEAR.          NEW-YORK, SATURDAY, MARCH 13, 1847.          FOUR CENTS A NUMBER.

THE FEMALE ABORTIONIST.

*Ann Lohman, alias Madame Restell,*
*"The wickedest woman in New York"*

Another investor who believed that upper Fifth Avenue inevitably would be the place to live was Charles Lohman. Although he did not believe in visions, he saw signs that this neighborhood would become fashionable: A magnificent new Central Park was emerging from 59th to 106th Street with a new northern extension to 110th Street. Work on the park had proceeded even during the Rebellion, with miles of lanes set aside for trotters and carriages.

Lohman heard that John Hughes, the first Catholic archbishop of New York, planned to buy ten lots on the northeast corner of Fifth Avenue and Fifty-second Street for his official residence. A decade earlier the block from Fiftieth to Fifty-first Streets had been purchased for the construction of Saint Patrick's Cathedral. Work had been suspended because of the war and lack of funds, but now construction was about to resume. Lohman, who hated the archbishop because he had denounced his wife for her popular surgical practice, quickly purchased the lots himself for the grand sum of

$36,500. Virtually next door to Saint Patrick's, the Lohman mansion arose, an imposing four-story brownstone with stables and a walled garden, and every window decorated identically with window shades in a gaudy floral print. In May 1867, a discreet silver plaque engraved Office Female Physician appeared on the low iron railing in front of the basement door to One East Fifty-second Street. Ann Lohman, better known as Madame Restell, "the wickedest woman in New York . . . the infamous abortionist," was open for business.

The horse-drawn railroad car bearing Victoria and Tennessee proceeded briskly down Park Avenue through the prosperous Murray Hill district. As they passed Thirty-eighth Street, Victoria, had she glanced to the right, would have seen the forty-foot-wide brownstone mansion that, two years later, would become her residence. Four blocks to the south, at Thirty-fourth Street, also just off Fifth Avenue, was Annie Wood's discreet brownstone, the fanciest house of prostitution in the city.

It was late in the afternoon when the sisters piled into a carriage for the final leg of their journey. The gaslights were already lit in the Women's Bureau at 49 East Twenty-third Street, where Susan B. Anthony and Elizabeth Cady Stanton were closing an issue of *The Revolution*. Both women were known to work until dawn, delighted to be able at last to fight for woman's rights in their own publication. At Fourteenth Street and Union Square the carriage turned onto the great thoroughfare of Broadway. Lining both sides of the street were magnificent marble, brownstone, and cast-iron buildings. Here the rich in top hats and ermine-trimmed capes mingled with ragged beggars. The division between the haves and the have-nots was becoming increasingly evident. The carriage almost slowed to a halt. The sixty-foot-wide street was crowded with vehicles of every description—carriages and pushcarts, buses drawn by teams of eight horses, lone riders—all desperately trying to maneuver though the jam.

At the Bowery the carriage rolled by the Cooper Institute, where the previous week Anna Dickinson had made an impassioned speech on the subject of equal wages for women. The great star of abolition and woman suffrage, wearing a rich, pearl-gray silk dress trimmed with cherry satin and a necklace with a magnificent ruby "fit for an Empress's crown," had been escorted to the stage by Peter Cooper himself and introduced by Henry Ward Beecher. At last the sisters' carriage turned off Broadway and into the quiet charm of Lafayette Place, graced by a colonnade of ancient elms, then made another turn into Great Jones Street.

Victoria wrote her remarkable accounts of her fulfilled visions well after they occurred. Thus it was many years later that she described that when, as

*Broadway, 1868—looking north from just below Fulton Street*

weary travelers, they arrived at 17 Great Jones Street, it was nearly dusk. Victoria's hand trembled, she later wrote, as she banged the knocker on that darkened door. She saw a light in an upstairs window and heard someone on the stairs. Then the door opened to reveal a woman who smiled and exclaimed, "Oh, you've come about the rooms." Then the woman instructed them to wait in the entrance hall while she readied their beds. The house was identical to the one in Victoria's vision. On the table rested the same book but this time she could read the title: Impressed in gold letters on the black leather cover was "The Orations of Demosthenes."

VICTORIA WOODHULL ARRIVED in Manhattan in 1868 at a watershed moment in the history of America: Many people had lost belief in the capacity to control their own lives, while others, who only a decade earlier had been hod-carriers, stevedores, and red-necked farmers, were today's millionaires. This was the New York of Boss William Marcy Tweed, the grand sachem of Tammany Hall, who came to power by naturalizing 41,112 Irish immigrants in one year on the proviso that they vote for his candidates. On a salary of $10,000 annually, the boss had purchased a Fifth

Avenue mansion worth $2 million. Though barely begun, his courthouse—promised to the people early in 1867 for $250,000—was rumored to have cost millions already.

From the crucible of war a ruthless new society was emerging, one in which the delicate question of civic virtue was overwhelmed in the grab for money and power. A society in flux had slipped over the line until excess and corruption were accepted and their practitioners revered and exempt from judgment. The institutions of so-called morality—the law, the church, the government—were easily bent to serve these powerful newcomers. "What do I care for law, hain't I got the power," bellowed Commodore Vanderbilt.

For upper- and middle-class women, the war had expanded life's horizons. During this period many of them had functioned as individuals, often brilliantly. But while men returned from the war to careers and travel and the exhilaration of power, these women were once again relegated to "woman's sphere," idled by their affluent husbands who thought of them as ornaments or servants. Many women reacted strongly against these constraints. The birthrate in New York City fell precipitously. Infanticide was common, abortion rampant. Newspapers carried advertisements for "female physicians" like Madame Restell, who guaranteed to alleviate "disturbing problems," a euphemism for unwanted pregnancies.

For both women and men, the hypocritical illusion of domestic bliss was challenged by women's new awareness. The male establishment resisted accordingly: The homeopathy practiced by Edward Bayard and his sister-in-law Elizabeth Cady Stanton came under attack by members of the New York Academy of Medicine, who called it "quackery and charlatanry." Their own "heroic medicine," they said, was the only legitimate practice. Male doctors attacked midwives and drove many of them from the profession.

With little to occupy their time except mindless pursuits, women of means often became languid, pale, and subject to a condition that had not previously existed: neurasthenia, defined as a hysterical weakening of the constitution. Medical doctors often dealt with nervous or rebellious women by administering a "rest cure," isolating women patients for months at a time and forcing them to remain in bed with no distractions on a diet consisting solely of liquids. Supervised by a male doctor, the patient once more became docile and compliant, her body, as one physician explained, "recycled and taught to make the will of the male her own."

Female neurasthenia was found to be "allied to the sexual organs." A woman's sexual drive was perceived as a danger both to men and also to herself, since the capacity to "over-excite the sexual appetites" could bring about male violence. It was believed by many members of the male medical establishment that women were unclean and infectious. Dr. Augustus Kinsley Gardner, a leading gynecologist of the day, warned that women communicated venereal disease to men who had intercourse with them "in close proximity to the period of their monthly courses. . . . I do not believe that a man often communicates disease to a woman," he wrote.

In 1868, American gynecological surgeons began performing clitoridectomies to quell sexual desire in women, which was considered a form of derangement. Upper- and middle-class white women who had been taught that any sexual urges were sinful, willingly surrendered their bodies to these male doctors, who tested them for this abnormal arousal by stimulating the breast and clitoris; if there was a response, they surgically removed the clitoris. Bearing the guilt of the victim, some women who had felt desire became complicitous in their own bodily mutilation. One observed that her clitoridectomy scar was "as pretty as the dimple in the cheek of sweet sixteen."

The idea that men had strong sexual urges, whose gratification was socially acceptable, while women were pure and passionless seemed absurd to Victoria Woodhull. She advocated the same sexual standards for both men and women. It would take two more years before she publicly proclaimed a hidden truth that few women of the day would admit or even imagine.

Some women seem to glory over the fact that they never had any sexual desire and to think that desire is vulgar. What! Vulgar! The instinct that creates immortal souls vulgar? Who dares stand up amid Nature, all prolific and beautiful, where pulses are ever bounding with the creative desire, and utter such sacrilege. Vulgar rather must be the mind that can conceive such blasphemy. No sexual passion, say you. Say, rather, a sexual idiot, and confess that your life is a failure . . . and no longer bind your shame upon your brow or herald it as purity. Bah! Be honest, rather, and say it is depravity. It is not the possession of strong sexual powers that is to be deprecated. They are that necessary part of human character . . . they are the foundation upon which civilization rests.

Shortly after their arrival at Great Jones Street, Victoria and Tennessee were joined by Colonel Blood, who began working for his brother George on a small New Jersey newspaper. Soon Buck Claflin appeared, for their father was not about to lose a good source of income. Victoria and Tennie already had begun visiting the houses of prostitution and assignation on

Fifth Avenue and in Murray Hill, and Buck was soon accompanying them, selling Miss Tennessee's laudanum-laden "Magnetic Life Elixir." Laudanum, an opium derivative, was popular with prostitutes, some of whom consumed as much as fifteen grams a day. Those who preferred not to deal with Buck and were able to venture outside their establishments could go to the drugstores on Mercer, Greene, Wooster, Laurens, and Thompson Streets where large quantities of opium were sold without a prescription and buyers were not asked to register by name.

Victoria and Tennie were medical practitioners of a different sort from their father. Sharing the knowledge they had learned under Buck's aegis, they sold prostitutes such medications as sponges soaked in vinegar that, inserted in the vagina, absorbed a man's discharge and helped to destroy it; sweet-scented water that cleaned the area; and a clove anesthetic that prevented pain and made the women seem warm and eager. These products made life easier for the women and provided the sisters with much-needed cash.

In 1868, New York City alone was estimated to have more than twenty thousand prostitutes. Two blocks from Victoria's house was the Midnight Mission for the Rescue of Fallen Women. Nightly, Christian ladies served soup, read Scripture to these women, and advised them where to obtain respectable jobs that provided a bare subsistence. The mission drew its women mostly from the infamous houses of prostitution on Greene Street, where half-clad women displayed themselves in the open windows.

No effort was made to conceal the city's many houses of prostitution. In fact, *A Gentleman's Guide,* a popular book, listed the various houses and the services they made available. Some houses sent business cards to men registering at hotels. The police commissioner reported that there were more than six hundred houses of prostitution, another hundred assignation houses for illicit trysts, and thousands of available women who worked as cigar girls and waitresses in saloons and dance halls. Prostitution was an integral part of society. An evening's entertainment for men often included a fine dinner at Delmonico's, a vintage brandy, and a visit to a house of prostitution.

During the war the women who had followed General Joe Hooker's troops were nicknamed Hooker's girls or simply *hookers.* As families in the South disintegrated, many women migrated to Northern cities and supported themselves through prostitution. By the last year of the war, half the prostitutes in New York City were said to be from the South. The social observer George Templeton Strong noted in his diary, "According to the talk of the New York Club the harlotry of the city is largely reinforced by

Southern refugee women who were of good social standing at home but find themselves here without means of support and forced to choose between starving and whoring." He added a commonly held view that allowed these victimized women no sympathy: "It seems a just retribution of the Southern slaveholding chivalry who have been forcing their female slaves—black, mulatto, and quadroon—to minister to their pleasures that their rebellion should drive their wives and daughters to flee northward and prostitute themselves to Northern 'mudsills' and plebeian 'Yankees.' "

Men acted out their sexual fantasies and desires with prostitutes on the assumption that their wives were too pure for such actions, and men justified their conduct by condemning these women as "vile," blaming them for the base passions they aroused. To most men and many women as well, these prostitutes deserved their destruction. By enticing men they had committed a sin that would lead down the steep path to ruin, disease, and death. George Ellington, a social chronicler of the day, wrote,

> The fashionable *demi-monde* soon lose conscience and are as dead to its value as to the value of virtue. Let them lead gay lives while they may, they will go down. Their beauty will fade . . . before many months you may see them in a den in Greene or Mercer Street . . . a year will not pass before they may want for a crust of bread. Today, they ride in a gilded coach to Central Park, the time may not be far distant when they will ride to Blackwell's Island in the "Black Maria."

Victoria Woodhull would later write in a speech (that she gave on 150 consecutive nights) that in her career she had met "hundreds upon hundreds" of prostitutes and that the common wisdom of the day was wrong.

> There are many popular fallacies about prostitution . . . that the average life of prostitutes is about four years . . . but it is caused by dissolute living, and drinking, and by the diseases which usually accompany promiscuous intercourse.
>
> The real truth about this is that those prostitutes who never drink, who never permit themselves to become diseased are among the healthiest of women and hold their beauty and vigor to an advanced age.
>
> I know hundreds of wives who confess privately that they would not live another day with their husbands if they had any other method of support and yet pass the poor prostitute as though

*A visit to a first-class house. In 1868 there were more*
*than twenty thousand prostitutes in New York City.*

her touch were leprous. . . . There may be prostitution in marriage
and proper commerce in the bawdy house. It depends upon the
specific conditions attending the act itself and not where or how it
is obtained.

Victoria was welcome in the netherworld of prostitutes and it is
through her that we are able to gain a realistic picture of their lives. To Victoria, prostitution was a business. She would later write an analysis of the
day-to-day finances of these women. A first-class prostitute paid her
madam $40 a week for the use of her room and gave her 20 percent of her
profits. Towels were extra. The madam paid politicians from the district

about $100 a week for protection. Once a month police officers arrested a few prostitutes who were released the same day after paying a fine of $100. Each prostitute paid the patrolman "$3 to $10 a week and granted him the privilege of visiting her gratis." Police captains and sergeants were also "accorded the privilege of frequenting without charge such inmates as they may select." Victoria commented, "The amount of degradation and bodily injury to which [these women] must daily submit to meet these combined charges and demands may be imagined." Some of these women found permanent or semi-permanent arrangements with their wealthy and influential clients and graduated from prostitute to mistress.

Once Victoria Woodhull became a popular figure, she decried the corruption of a society that sanctioned this double standard:

> We are told that prostitution is a "necessary evil." . . . Necessary indeed! Isn't it rather your shame and my shame and the dishonor of womanhood and the disgrace of manhood that should make the stones weep to contemplate—innocent, virgin girls from twelve to sixteen years of age—your daughters, mine perhaps—sacrificed to this "necessary evil."
>
> Statistics inform us that there are two hundred and fifty thousand professional prostitutes in the country, one-tenth of whom are in New York City, and that these are visited and supported by not less than two and a half millions of men—one-third of the voting population of the country. Think of it! A quarter of a million professional female prostitutes and two and a half millions of professional male prostitutes, ten men to one woman. . . . When you condemn the poor women, whom you have helped to drive to such a life, remember to visit your wrath upon the best men of the country as well. . . .
>
> Until women come to hold men to equal account as they do the women with whom they consort, or until they regard these women as just as respectable as the men who support them, society will remain in its present state of moral excellence. A man who is well known to have been the constant visitor to these women is accepted into society, and if he be *rich* is eagerly *sought* both by mothers having marriageable daughters and by the daughters themselves. But the women with whom they have consorted are *too vile* to be even acknowledged as worthy of Christian burial, to say nothing of common Christian treatment.

Two months after her arrival in New York, Victoria received a visit from a young actress she had known in California. The actress had arrived in the city penniless and asked Victoria to introduce her to a house of prostitution. Together they went to Annie Wood's "house," where an assignation was arranged with a prominent judge, a deacon of his church. When the judge gave the girl half the usual fee, Victoria intervened, demanding the full fee, and the judge paid the rest. Annie Wood was impressed with Victoria's management of the situation.

From the outside, Annie Wood's house was similar to other Murray Hill brownstones, except for its drawn curtains. Inside, however, according to *A Gentleman's Guide,* the house was furnished like a Southern mansion, and served French and New Orleans cuisine. The service was said to be perfection. Copies of Rembrandt, Van Dyke, Hogarth, and Reynolds hung on the walls. The bedrooms featured four-posters draped in Brussels lace, and the ceilings were mirrored.

Since Annie Wood admitted that she used an alias, the account of her past that she provided in a sworn affidavit cannot be verified. However, if true, it would explain the taste and luxury displayed in her establishment. Annie claimed to have been born into the family of a wealthy plantation owner in Savannah, Georgia. She said she had lost her entire family and fortune in the war. Like so many other Southern women, she migrated to New York and, after a brief career on the stage, purchased her present establishment with the help of an unnamed investor. She described her house as a kind of club frequented by "only the best gentlemen." As an example, she said that during the evening's entertainment, matters of political and financial importance could be discussed in a discreet atmosphere.

Although the men who visited her house undoubtedly were unaware of it, Annie recorded, in two big black books, their names, professions, and pertinent information about their sexual preferences. Annie was to prove herself a good friend to Victoria and Tennessee, for as a later letter reveals, she would make these books available to them to do with what they might.

According to *A Gentleman's Guide,* Annie specialized in mulatto women. (In the census of 1860, five hundred and eighty-eight thousand mulatto women were counted in what were then the slave states, a clear demonstration of the white man's mastery over his property.) In addition to these women, Annie provided a parody of what she herself might once have been. She dressed her most special whores as Southern belles who seemed aristocratic and virginal. They wore white silk gowns decorated only with thick yellow, blue, or pink satin sashes and received visitors in a conservatory with white latticework covering the windows and forming a cathedral dome.

Annie Wood would later tell Victoria Woodhull that the way she felt about her own life was expressed in the copy of Bernini's statue of Daphne and Apollo, which she placed in the fountain in the center of this room. The white marble statue was of a nude Daphne in flight, writhing in fear and stretching her slim arms upward. Apollo's muscular arms grasp the nymph in the moment of capture. One can see the roots springing from Daphne's toes as, desperately seeking escape, she transforms herself into a laurel tree.

# CHAPTER FOURTEEN

# CONSULT THE SPIRITS

I N THE world of the demimondaine the most open of secrets was Commodore Vanderbilt's insatiable sexual appetite. In the world of the Spiritualists the most open of secrets was the Commodore's support of any medium, fortune-teller, or healer who could aid him in his insatiable search for riches and immortality. He paid Mrs. Tufts, a medium from Staten Island, enough money to retire to Vermont when she rid him of two spirits: a boy of seven who had been crushed under the hooves of Vanderbilt's four white-footed trotters as they sped around the reservoir in Central Park, and a railroad worker who had been mangled under the wheels of the Commodore's *Flying Devil* and appeared before him in a bloody, shredded, and oil-stained condition.

Vanderbilt instructed his barber to collect his hair and burn it, for fear that someone who secured a lock would have power over him. He believed that through portraits one could communicate with those who had "passed over," and kept a miniature of his late mother in his breast pocket above his heart. He despised doctors and followed the advice of Spiritualist healers, one of whom had instructed that saltcellars be placed under each leg of his bed to ward off evil spirits.

It was common knowledge that Commodore Vanderbilt saw all callers at his town house at 10 Washington Place, no matter who they were. He usually dispatched them promptly and rudely, but said he never knew where a good idea might come from. Within a month of his arrival, the ever alert Buck Claflin arranged a meeting between his Spiritualist daughters and the Commodore. When the crusty Vanderbilt peered over the balcony of his Greek revival mansion and saw the two women standing below, he could not have failed to be impressed: There stood Victoria with her delicate cameo features and Tennessee with her overblown figure. Vanderbilt had an eye for women, so much so that the housemaids frequently quit to escape his prurient advances.

The Commodore, for all his bluster, was old and lonely. Despite his fortune he was not welcome in society. He swore like a stevedore and spat tobacco juice onto his hostesses' Persian carpets. He was nearly illiterate. His home life was bleak; he and his wife, Sophia, had barely spoken for a decade. Sophia had borne the Commodore twelve children, and when they were young and poor she worked at Bellona Hall, their Staten Island boardinghouse, with one child at her breast and several others trailing behind.

Two decades earlier, when Sophia mustered the courage to object to his pursuit of the children's governess and refused to go along with his plan to move to a New York City town house, the Commodore established complete domination over her by having her committed to Dr. McDonald's insane asylum in Flushing. His eldest son, the obese William Henry, arranged for his mother's internment, and when the governess fled after being driven frantic by the Commodore's sexual advances, William Henry found another young girl "to content" his father, saying, "The old man is bound to have his way and it is useless to oppose him."

If not for the intercession of Vanderbilt's mother, Sophia would have remained in the insane asylum while the Commodore played his beloved whist, raced his magnificent trotters, conducted business, and pursued women. Phebe Hand Van der Bilt summoned her son to Staten Island and told him he'd better fetch his wife back if he knew what was good for him. (Sophia was not only his wife but his first cousin, the daughter of his father's sister, Eleanor.) "I would never cross that woman," he said of his mother. From that time on, Sophia had been compliant, uncomplaining, and aloof.

The summer after the Commodore met Victoria and Tennessee, following his usual routine, he repaired to Saratoga for the racing season and to take the spa water. Sophia, having little place in her husband's life, remained behind and moved into the home of her daughter and son-in-law, Mary Louise and Horace Clark. On August 17, 1868, Commodore Vanderbilt was sitting on the porch of the United States Hotel, drinking beer and smoking a black cigar when word came that Sophia had died of an apoplectic attack. Six hours later, he arrived in New York in his private railroad car, *Duchess*. Two days after that, Sophia was interred in the Vanderbilt Mausoleum at the Moravian Cemetery on Staten Island. Horace Greeley, who had been one of the pallbearers, wrote in the *Tribune* that Mrs. Vanderbilt had "lived nearly seventy-four years without incurring a reproach or provoking an enmity."

Soon Victoria and Tennessee became daily fixtures in the Commodore's household, for they answered his considerable needs: Although he was still slim and spry enough to race his horses and spend hours at his one-desk, one-secretary office on Fourth Street near Broadway, he was slowing down. His hearing was failing, and he suffered from heart trouble, a hernia, kidney stones, constipation, and an enlarged prostate. At meals he had been known to consume pâté de foie gras, woodcock, Spanish mackerel, and saddle of venison, accompanied by Burgundy or Veuve Clicquot or beer. Tennessee took over: She babied, cajoled, and disciplined Vanderbilt, removing the rich foods from his diet and insisting that he walk as well as drive his horses. She tried to get him to stop smoking, but he said, "When I have to give up smoking, you may give *me* up." Tennessee's treatments consisted of clystering (a high enema), manipulating the prostate, and magnetic healing. With her left hand acting as a negative magnet, the right as a positive, she claimed to reverse the polarity of his body and to expel negative energy.

Almost everyone was terrified of the Commodore, but not Tennessee. Their relationship was light and affectionate. She called him "old boy" and "the old goat." He called her "my little sparrow." Four servants were later to recall that they often found her occupying the Commodore's bed in the morning. "Ample"—that was Vanderbilt's word for Tennessee—ample breasts, ample hips, inviting. She was what she was and didn't care what anyone thought. Her jealous sister Utica said that when Tennessee asked the Commodore how many women he'd had, he replied, "A thousand," to which Tennessee laughingly responded, "Then I am only half as bad as you are, for I have had but five hundred." Within a few months of Sophia's death, in the fall of 1868, the "old goat" asked Tennessee to become the next Mrs. Vanderbilt.

If Tennessee ministered to the Commodore's body, Victoria ministered to his soul and eventually to his purse as well. Sitting in the darkened parlor under Phebe Hand Van der Bilt's portrait, Victoria transmitted messages to him from his mother, who had died fifteen years earlier. When Victoria was in the room, the Commodore said he could even smell his mother's presence—a combination of strong soap and lavender. His mother was the only woman he had truly loved. He liked his eight daughters well enough but told people, "After all, they're not Vanderbilts." His two living sons, William Henry and Cornelius Jeremiah, he called a "blatherskite" and a "sucker," respectively. William Henry was hardworking and dull and, what was more irritating to the Commodore, prudent and obedient: He'd bring round his sons, Willie K. and Cornelius, for hymn singing and money-grubbing, but the Commodore said there was no life in any of them. The Commodore refused to see Cornelius Jeremiah, an epileptic, because he was unable to admit that he could produce a less-than-perfect human being. He also felt that Cornelius Jeremiah was God's reprimand to him for having married his first cousin. This poor son nevertheless loved his father deeply and would stand for hours on the back porch hoping to catch a glimpse of the Commodore. Horace Greeley occasionally lent Cornelius Jeremiah money. The Commodore told Greeley that he would never pay him back for the loans to his son. "Who the devil asked you?" Greeley shot back.

The Commodore had once despised his father as well, but he softened his attitude in his old age. Convinced that Victoria Woodhull truly was able to relay messages from his beloved mother, Vanderbilt offered her $100,000 if she would go into a trance and conjure up his father, then describe the old man well enough for an artist to paint a portrait. Prudently, she declined, but soon Victoria was to make a great deal more money than that by conjuring up some numbers for the Commodore.

In February 1868, Commodore Vanderbilt engaged in a battle with Jim Fisk and Fisk's partner, Jay Gould, for control of the Erie Railroad. Fisk and Gould had won because at a secret meeting in a suite at the American Club Hotel at Broadway and Seventeenth Street, the Erie directors decided to print more than one hundred fifty thousand new shares of Erie stock. The suite was the residence of Josie Mansfield, Fisk's newly acquired mistress and a friend of Victoria Woodhull's from their acting days in San Francisco. As Fisk remarked, "If this printing press don't break down, I'll be damned if I don't give the old hog all he wants of Erie." Finally, on March 10, having bought the one hundred fifty thousand shares without gaining control of the Erie, the Commodore caught on. The humiliation was as painful as the swindle. With Victoria Woodhull's help, it would not happen again.

The world of high finance and the low life of prostitutes seemed totally separate, but in fact they converged in the elegant brothels Victoria visited. At these establishments, women entertained the richest and most powerful men of the day in their beds, and yet they were considered insensate and invisible. Some madams, including Annie Wood, undoubtedly made the most of the opportunity this provided. As Wall Street traders, city officials, businessmen, and politicians gathered in her parlor, Annie listened carefully to what they said. She also trained her "girls" to encourage the men to boast of their financial maneuverings, instructing these women both in the art of extracting information and in seeming ignorant of what they had heard.

Victoria was an intimate of Annie Wood and knew many of the prostitutes who worked in her house. It was there that Vicky became reacquainted with her friend from San Francisco, Josie Mansfield. Josie and her husband, Frank Lawlor, had come to the city in 1864 in the hope of finding employment in the theater. They were unsuccessful and soon Lawlor, who admitted that Josie had married him only to escape the sexual abuse inflicted upon her by her stepfather, found that his wife was "going astray" and divorced her. According to Annie Wood, Josie became so impoverished that she had but one dress and could not pay her rent. It was then that she began to frequent Annie Wood's house on Thirty-fourth Street, where she set her sights on the overblown Jim Fisk, a regular patron.

Josie knew of Fisk's wild behavior, his quiet wife in Boston, and his free spending: He would give $100 bills to any pretty prostitute who caught his eye. In November 1867, Fisk arrived at the bordello for an evening's entertainment and was immediately taken with the buxom Miss Mansfield. Although Josie professed to find Fisk intelligent and manly, she refused his money and rebuffed his advances. For three months Josie skillfully withheld her favors, thereby inflating her worth. Then she allowed Fisk to pay the overdue rent on her tiny room on Lexington Avenue, after which he installed her in the American Club Hotel suite. Fisk underwent a remarkable change: He trimmed his unkempt red mustache and waxed the ends to handlebar perfection, he wore French cologne and kept his boots shined. This besotted lover bought Josie a roomful of dresses and gave her $50,000 in cash and about five times that in Tiffany emeralds.

Josie became a lady of fashion. Daily the hairdresser called, teasing her hair into a variety of puffs, curls, and frizzes. Once every two weeks the enamelist painted her face, shoulders, neck, and arms with a compound of bismuth and arsenic that gave her skin a much-desired deathlike pallor. To be a woman of fashion was a full-time occupation carried to an absurd degree. George Ellington described the requirements:

> The *elite* do not wear the same dress twice . . . she has two new dresses of some sort for every day in the year, or seven hundred and twenty. . . . She must have one or two velvet dresses which cannot cost less than five hundred dollars each; she must possess thousands of dollars' worth of laces, in the shape of flounces, to loop up over the skirts of dresses as occasion shall require. Walking-dresses cost from fifty to three hundred dollars; ball-dresses are frequently imported from Paris at a cost of from five hundred to a thousand dollars. . . . Nice white llama jackets can be had for sixty dollars; *robes princesse,* or overskirts of lace, are worth from sixty to two hundred dollars. Then there are . . . dresses for all possible occasions. A lady going to the Springs takes from twenty to sixty dresses and fills an enormous number of Saratoga trunks.

*Josie (Helen Josephine)*
*Mansfield, 1871*

*Jim Fisk.*
*Hoping for money, the*
*impoverished Ninth*
*Regiment of the New York*
*State National Guard*
*elected him colonel.*

Fisk complained that in one year he spent $30,000 to equip Josie ($5,000 more, he noted, than the president's salary). Her casket of jewels contained her fabulous emeralds, a set (necklace, earrings, tiara) of diamonds, a set of pearls, a set of corals, a medallion set, and twenty-five finger rings. Within the year Fisk had given Josie a house in her own name at 359 West Twenty-third Street, only half a block west of Fisk's Opera House. He also supplied her with several maids, a cook, butler, and coachman. Yet Josie's demands on Fisk escalated: He said that she was more temperamental than an opera diva. Once when she asked Fisk for an extra $30,000, he sent Boss Tweed himself to mediate. Tweed asked her what it was she really wanted. "I want more," she replied.

One of Fisk's business associates was a startlingly handsome playboy with jet-black hair and classic features named Edward (Ned) Stiles Stokes. Stokes was married to the daughter of a furniture tycoon, and both his father and father-in-law paid his debts and supplied him with cash to disport himself at well-known restaurants and Broadway gambling houses. Fisk, taking a liking to Stokes, lent him some money for an oil venture, named one of his 125 canaries after him, and introduced him to Josie.

Several times a day, Fisk sent a messenger to Josie's house with notes outlining his plans. Woodhull was to observe of Mansfield that "she obtained not only Fisk's money but she also participated in his business secrets. He concealed nothing . . . of his business plans and aspirations from her." Although both women denied any business association, there is little doubt that, for a price, Josie Mansfield shared these plans with Victoria Woodhull. And on the client register of Woodhull, Claflin & Co. (a Wall Street investment firm formed in the winter of 1869) there was listed an H. J. Mansfield. Josie Mansfield's given name was Helen Josephine.

By the end of 1868, Vanderbilt was giving Victoria and Tennessee a percentage of the profits from his business transactions. In a trance state, Victoria offered him uncannily accurate financial advice, and the Commodore was shrewd enough not to question whether her sources were from this world or another. In December, Vanderbilt made the boldest move of his career. He declared an 80 percent stock dividend on the Central Pacific Railroad (issuing four extra shares for every five now owned). On Christmas Day, Victoria visited the Commodore and offered advice from the spirits. That evening, he told a young widow to place all her savings in Central stock. "It's bound to go up. . . . Mrs. Woodhull said so in a trance," he declared. On the Monday after Christmas, the Central stock opened at $134. By the time the exchange closed, it had bounded up to $165. It was rumored that the Commodore had allocated the profits on three thousand shares, or $93,000, to Victoria and Tennessee. When the Commodore was asked how he made such astute financial decisions, he laughed and replied, "Do as I do. Consult the spirits."

THROUGH THE COMMODORE, Victoria and Tennessee were gaining money and influence. Victoria would later say that this was part of the spirits' preparation for a great mission. But for now, the nature of her work was yet to be revealed and seemed confined to self-aggrandizement. Meanwhile, across the river in Brooklyn, seemingly unrelated events were about to bring into sharp relief the issues with which the new society struggled, ones that would eventually clarify for Victoria that her spirit-guided mission would be to launch "a social revolution."

The relationship between Lib Tilton, her husband, Theodore, and

Henry Ward Beecher was becoming increasingly complex. Like Victoria Woodhull and Josie Mansfield, Theodore Tilton had also entered a privileged world of great wealth. Women of all classes had joined the woman's rights movement and the previous summer there had been a convention in one of America's most fashionable resorts, Newport, Rhode Island. The exquisite Paulina Wright Davis invited Tilton to stay at her mansion. Mrs. Davis had been involved in woman's rights since 1850. Widowed at thirty-two, she married Thomas Davis three years later. Davis, a man of wealth and social position, served in the Rhode Island legislature and for two decades had unstintingly supported his wife's efforts.

Never had Tilton seen such "great luxury" and display as in Newport. "Here one sees at the same glance the ocean and its waves, and silk dresses and scented handkerchiefs. I don't relish the comparison . . . I am more than ever content with my own moderate resources," he wrote Lib. Paulina was comfortable in this opulent milieu, though Lucy Stone criticized her for wearing magnificent French dresses, made on a mannequin in Paris. Stone called Davis "fickle," but Paulina defended herself, saying that she was "determined to do my utmost to remove the idea that all woman's rights women are horrid old frights with beards and mustaches who want to smoke and swear."

Davis knew that many women did not understand their own bodies, and she determined to do something about it. Her own couture mannequin inspired her to have an anatomically correct *femme modele* constructed, which she imported to America and used in demonstrations before women's groups. Paulina had been a Calvinist until the church's indifference to slavery and its repression of women drove her from the church and into abolition and woman's rights. "I was not a happy woman until in mature life I outgrew my early religious faith and felt free to think and act from my own convictions," she asserted. As early as 1848, Davis had been instrumental in the drafting of the Woman's Property Act, which enabled Stanton and other women to own houses in their own names. Ironically, this act was sponsored by rich men who did not wish their sons-in-law to inherit property they had left to their daughters.

At dinner one night in Newport, Tilton was seated next to Laura Curtis Bullard, an heiress whose considerable fortune derived from a patent medicine, Winslow's Soothing Syrup, created by her father. Frank Curtis had this one child only, and he doted on her, educating her in Switzerland and supporting her lavish lifestyle in Paris. For the past two years she had been a widow. Having spent much time in Europe, she had adopted the French upper-class morality and the free love views of Charles Fourier, John

Humphrey Noyes, and Stephen Pearl Andrews. Bullard was attracted to Tilton and suggested that an "affinity" could be pursued as long as it didn't interfere with their lives. Soon, she was to envision herself as Theodore Tilton's "Spiritual Wife." Soon, he was to embark on what he termed "a great friendship" with Mrs. Bullard.

While Tilton was away from Brooklyn, Beecher spent more and more time at the Tiltons' home, where, seated at Greeley's desk, he worked on the final installments of *Norwood.* As a token of his growing affection, he gave Lib a small watercolor of a trailing arbutus and symbolically wrote of it in his novel: "It is like the breath of love. The pure white and pink blossoms in sweet clusters lie hidden under leaves or grass, and often under untimely snows. Blessings on thee! Thou art the fairest, most modest, and sweetest-breathed of all our flowers!" When Susan B. Anthony visited, Lib showed her the painting. "My pastor brought that to me," she said with pride.

In *Norwood* the love remained secret: Beecher called it "nest hiding." He wrote of Rose Wentworth, his heroine: "It would seem as if, while her whole life centered upon his love, she would hide the precious secret by flinging over it vines and flowers, by mirth and raillery, as a bird hides its nest under tufts of grass, and behind leaves and vines, as a fence against prying eyes." Seven years later, Lib wrote Beecher of her efforts to protect him from scandal: "My endeavor was entirely to help you, keep you from all suffering, to bear myself alone. My weapons were love, a large untiring generosity, and *nest hiding!*"

With the end of his novel in sight, Beecher once again went to see his friend John Tasker Howard, the influential publisher. Howard, in turn, approached a Jay Cooke employee, Samuel Wilkeson (who happened to be Elizabeth Cady Stanton's brother-in-law). Wilkeson was known for bringing excellent manuscripts to the J. B. Ford syndicate. During the recent war he had been both a correspondent for the *New York Times* and a promoter of the bonds that Cooke was selling to help finance the Union armies. Wilkeson arranged for the J. B. Ford syndicate to advance Beecher $20,000 for a new book, a two-volume life of Christ. Wilkeson himself was so enthusiastic about its potential profits that he invested $10,000 of his own money in the project. Beecher began work immediately on *The Life of Jesus the Christ,* and when he finished the first chapter he read it privately to Mrs. Tilton. Lib was pregnant once again, which no doubt kept carnal thoughts at bay. When Beecher asked how the Virgin Mary might have felt with the Christ child in her womb, Lib described her own feelings as she touched her swelling stomach. Then, she later recalled, she went upstairs and returned with "a little sketch of one of my Bethel lessons on 'Mary, the Mother of Jesus,' as an example of a woman's faith."

In Henry Ward Beecher, Lib Tilton found the affection she had so long craved. One Saturday he arrived at Livingston Street with his arms so full of yellow chrysanthemums that he had to pound on the door with his foot. "I am hungry to see your children," he declared.

"Are you really? Then come up directly and see them," she answered. That day Lib had laid out on the bed of Florry's room a profusion of white lace, dimity, and calico dolls' dresses. Lib and Beecher sat on the floor with the three children, laughing and chatting as they dressed each doll. Six-year-old Alice carried her doll to him. "What will you name her?" Beecher asked. When Alice did not reply, he suggested, "Rose Wentworth," the heroine of *Norwood*. "Yes, yes, Rose," agreed Alice, and clapped her hands in delight.

As Lib's confidence grew, the woman's rights people who congregated about her husband and who met at her house no longer seemed intimidating. She became corresponding secretary of the New York branch of the American Equal Rights Association and informed Theodore after a meeting, "You will be amused to know that Susan [B. Anthony] made me Chairman and said afterwards that 'I did as well as Theodore himself.' I always want to represent you well." For the first time she felt herself competent; when Anthony began to publish *The Revolution*, Lib became its poetry editor.

Paul Tilton was born at the end of January 1868, and the following week, when Theodore returned home, Lib presented him with his new son. On the night his son was born, Tilton had been lecturing in Akron, Ohio, after which he retired to the Empire House for a passionate encounter, presumably with Laura Curtis Bullard. The next morning he experienced "a terrible wrestling with my soul" and decided that his own heart was "a dark place to look into." Tilton vowed that for Paul and for his own soul, he would try to make a "rebeginning." In an agony of self-flagellation he told his wife that he was prepared to break off his "great friendship" with Mrs. Bullard. He vowed to be a "better man," a "faithful husband," and swore that if Lib would help him, they would form a unit against the world. They fell on their knees and prayed to God "to perfect our union."

For her part, Lib Tilton, having fallen in love with her preacher, had struggled to keep that love "pure." She no longer had the protection of an advanced pregnancy, and Beecher was becoming more explicit in his sexual advances. He kissed her on the lips in what he later termed "a paroxysmal kiss." He told her, "I have a greater love for you than any woman in my life and wish to find in you the solace of life which had been denied to me by an unaffectionate marriage at home."

Pressured by both her ardent preacher and her repentant husband, an experiment in faithfulness seemed a safe choice. And so the Tiltons embarked on this quest, at first with high hopes. He wrote, "I regard my last evening spent with you at home as the most memorable point in my whole life. You opened for me, that night, the gate of Heaven, which had so long seemed shut." She wrote, "I am so safe and strong and glad in your love that I am conscious of an entire change toward every one, an independence like maidens feel when they decide upon one of their choice. . . . I am waking to a new life."

But, in Theodore's absence, high hopes gradually turned to grim determination. The pressure began to build as Lib came to question her husband's faithfulness and her own ability to resist her preacher. Two months later, Theodore again declared his fidelity: "My vows I shall keep, and not break. With God's help, and with yours, I shall be the faithfulest man in the world." Lib answered, "Theodore, do you *know* what you have written? . . . That it might be so, I earnestly wish. That it is so, *I cannot believe.*" His waffling reply was, "Innocence or guilt, in most of us, depends more on the measure of our temptation than on the measure of our virtue. . . . How morally sublime was Christ's word to the woman, 'Neither do I condemn thee.' "

Finally, in despair, Lib wrote to her husband complaining of his protracted absences and neglect of her. And, as if warning him, she ended the letter with, "My brain has run wild since 4 o'clock—sleep forsook me. The love of man or two men is not restful, while the love given to God is peaceful beyond expression." Theodore, otherwise occupied, replied,

> Your last note reminded me that I had not written you from Washington as warmly as I wrote from the West. I felt that you wronged me by not reflecting on the difference between my situation here and my situation there. Here every minute of my day is busy, there I did nothing all day but sit in a car or a hotel and wait for the evening.

In Washington, Theodore Tilton was indeed involved in momentous events. Even after the Republicans gained control of Congress in 1866, President Johnson continued to oppose them. Throughout the year 1867 a series of Reconstruction acts had been passed by Congress over Johnson's repeated vetoes. The president cut back on the military and fired more than sixteen hundred officeholders he deemed sympathetic to the radical Republicans and replaced them with men who would strengthen the local civil governments he had previously installed. On March 2, 1867, Congress retaliated by passing an act restricting his authority as commander in chief of the armed forces. The Tenure of Office Act, passed the same day, prohibited the president from removing any civil officeholder until his successor had been approved by the Senate.

That summer, when Congress was not in session, Johnson removed his bitter enemy, Edwin M. Stanton, as secretary of war. When Congress reconvened, Stanton was reinstated, and in December furious radical Republican members of the House introduced a resolution to impeach the president. The resolution was rejected 108 to 57. Two months later, Johnson declared the Tenure of Office Act unconstitutional and once again dismissed Stanton. On February 21, 1868, two years after Theodore Tilton had first called for Andrew Johnson's impeachment in the *Independent,* public and political opinion had become so negative that the House by a vote of 126 to 47 resolved that the president "be impeached of high crimes and misdemeanors in office." Congress was now compelled to find evidence to justify its action. A seven-man committee was appointed to prepare the articles of impeachment.

During this period, Theodore Tilton spent many months in Washington writing article after article for the *Independent* supporting Radical Reconstruction and criticizing Johnson for his "vulgarity and traitorous behavior." Tilton was among the most influential writers in America in turning the public against Johnson, but it was Johnson himself who, by opposing the Republicans and Radical Reconstruction, had lost all chance of being nominated for president. Even Tilton quickly saw that the real reason for removing the president—his bigotry and pro-South sympathies—could not be grounds for impeachment. Benjamin Butler, newly elected to the House of Representatives, and a member of the seven-man committee, was carried away with anger and wanted to charge Johnson with numerous crimes. Although Tilton knew that these charges were false, he objected only to Butler's accusation that Johnson had been complicitous in the assassination of Lincoln. As Tilton yielded to political expedience, he began to question his own character. "I have less faith in my moral integrity now than at any former period in my life," he wrote Lib. "I feel myself scarred, spotted, miserable."

Finally, on March 3, eleven articles of impeachment were adopted. The first eight related to Johnson's attempt to remove Stanton; the others related to his "attempt to bring into disgrace, ridicule, hatred, contempt, and reproach the Congress of the United States." On the instructions of his defense counsel, William Evarts, the president did not appear before the Senate. Evarts, a member of Plymouth Church, hated Theodore Tilton for first suggesting that Johnson should be impeached. He vowed that one day he would destroy Tilton as Johnson was now being destroyed. When the trial began, Evarts cleverly steered the testimony to the narrow legal issue of the meaning of the Tenure of Office Act. Within two weeks Tilton wrote that in his view the president would be acquitted, and even Butler admitted to Evarts that he wished he were on the other side.

Behind the scenes, President Johnson and Evarts maneuvered to compromise with the moderates in the Senate. When the Senate voted on May 16, the vote fell one short of the required two-thirds majority needed to impeach Johnson. Amid the pandemonium that ensued, a dying Thaddeus Stevens, who had spent his life fighting against slavery, was carried into the chamber by two attendants. He called out, "What was the verdict?" When he heard it, Stevens threw his arms into the air and shouted, "The country is going to the devil." Benjamin Butler called a press conference to announce that he was launching an investigation of certain senators who had taken bribes.

The next day, Tilton rode the cars to Chicago for the Republican National Convention where General U. S. Grant (his given name was Hiram Ulysses Grant, but U. S. Grant had a ring to it) received the presidential nomination. The Democratic National Convention followed two months later. On the twenty-second ballot, Horatio Seymour was chosen to run against Grant. Susan B. Anthony had applied to be a delegate to the convention and to present a petition that woman suffrage be made a plank of the Democratic platform. Although too ill to attend the convention, Mary Cheney Greeley was one of the four signers of this petition, once again lending her support in a manner guaranteed to antagonize her husband. Anthony was rejected as a delegate, but a clerk duly read her demand on the floor of the convention, at the conclusion of which the women in the gallery cheered and then the delegates returned to business as usual. The woman suffrage issue was not dealt with during the campaign.

In August 1868, while Theodore Tilton was once again in Newport, his eight-month-old son, Paul, whom Tilton hardly knew, died of cholera. A distraught Lib was on her knees, praying in the sitting room in which Paul's body lay when, according to her account, the stained-glass dome overhead became suffused with light. The room glowed as two angels descended and, each taking a hand, flew with Paul through the dome and disappeared into the clouds.

*The committee that drafted the Articles of Impeachment against President Andrew Johnson. Benjamin Butler appears at the lower left.*

Beecher came down from Peekskill to officiate at the funeral. And a most unusual funeral it was: With the death of her baby, a dramatic new system of belief entered Lib Tilton's life. Like her husband before her, Lib Tilton now turned to Spiritualism. Susan B. Anthony, who attended the funeral, was surprised to find the house "filled with sunshine" and Lib not in the traditional black of mourning but dressed all in white in the Spiritualist tradition. To Anthony, Lib seemed gladdened by the thought that her "babe" was safe in heaven.

Theodore Tilton quickly returned home, but his reserved nature made it impossible for him to say anything that would comfort his wife and she was later to say that she resented him for this. He did, however, have sexual intercourse with her, and when he left in September she once again found herself pregnant. She also said that her heart yearned for her lost baby and she felt guilty about his death. Lib asked Beecher if perhaps she could have done something to save Paul. He reassured her that there was nothing. Her preacher comforted her and filled the void. Almost a decade later, Theodore

Tilton was asked in civil court, "Do you believe that your wife loved Beecher more than you?" To which he replied,

> No, but he was the sympathetic, ever-present friend. In my family life I could not give her the novelty of sympathy. Our loss was common. . . . Beecher was her God. I was her husband.
>
> Beecher was all self love. She was merely convenable. In one of Mrs. Beecher Stowe's novels the remark is made that a seduced woman thinks herself purest when she is nearest to the point of being debauched. Had the date of this novel, "The Minister's Wooing," been nearer our time I should have thought Mrs. Stowe drew that point from my wife.

On October 9, 1868, the Brooklyn Academy of Music was filled to overflowing for an election rally for U. S. Grant. On a curtain behind Henry Ward Beecher there appeared a greatly enlarged Thomas Nast cartoon showing Grant being welcomed at the front door of the White House by Miss Columbia, Nast's symbol for America. Nast had included in the cartoon a dejected Horatio Seymour who crouched next to a lamppost from which hung the corpse of a lynched Negro.

Lib Tilton, in the tenth row, was enthralled. Beecher's endorsement of Grant was unqualified and addressed the issues that troubled voters the most.

> It is said that General Grant is a drunkard. I do not believe a word of it. But I had rather have General Grant a drunkard than Horatio Seymour sober! It is said that General Grant knows nothing of civil affairs. Certainly Seymour knows nothing of military affairs. It is said that Grant is not a statesman. I have always said that what we meant to make a President of, was a great deal of common sense.

The applause was thunderous. Lib later said that she tried to fight her way down the aisle to congratulate her preacher but the crowd was too dense. Therefore, on the following afternoon, October 10, 1868, she went to Beecher's house in Columbia Heights. Beecher's family was still in Peekskill. Lib found him in his writing room on the second floor at the rear of the house, with an unparalleled view of New York Bay, the southern tip of Manhattan, and the East River. That evening a glowing Lib wrote in her diary, "A Day Memorable."

*Henry Ward Beecher's writing room: "A Day Memorable"*

Henry Ward Beecher had a way of speaking of his personal concerns through his sermons. A few weeks later from the Plymouth Church pulpit he intoned,

> The man who has been wallowing in lust, the man who has been on fire in his passions, and who by God's great goodness has been brought to an hour and a moment when . . . his monstrous wickedness stands disclosed in him—that man ought not to wait so long as the drawing of his breath. . . . He will stand up and say, "Here I am, a sinner, and I confess my sin and I call on God to witness my determination from this hour to turn away from it." That is the wise course, and you would think so, if it was anybody but yourself.

# CHAPTER FIFTEEN

# WE ARE READY.
# WE ARE PREPARED.

O N CHRISTMAS Day 1868, as Victoria Woodhull advised the Commodore that his Central Pacific Railroad stock was "bound to go up," in a Philadelphia garret an incident was about to take place that would bring into sharp focus the injustice toward women in the post-war society.

The German immigrant landlady spoke little English. She held up two fingers to indicate $2 and said the word "Now." Twenty-year-old Hester Vaughn, desperate for a place to stay, reached into the pocket of her loose calico dress and put the money in her palm. The third-story garret was unheated and as a blizzard raged, Hester, who had been without food for three days, began a violent labor. She crawled to the door to call for help. Twenty-four hours passed before the landlady heard Hester's low moans. When she opened the door, Hester lay semiconscious on the rough wood floor in a pool of blood. Her dead baby was still attached to a crudely tied umbilical cord. The constables arrived an hour later and, since she could not walk, they carried her to prison. The newborn's body was so frozen that a portion of the skin stuck to the floor and was torn away as the corpse was lifted. Hester Vaughn was charged with infanticide. She was tried without a lawyer and convicted.

To bring Hester into the courtroom, where she would be sentenced to the gallows, required the services of a Philadelphia physician, Dr. Susan A. Smith. She found Vaughn lying on a bare cot in Moyamensing prison, staring blankly at a rat crouched in the corner. As she examined the prisoner, she elicited her story: Hester Vaughn had come from Gloucestershire to marry her fiancé, only to find him already married to another. Alone and deserted, she became a scullery maid in Jenkintown, then a dairymaid at a nearby farm. One night as she lay in bed, her employer raped her. She was too dispirited to run away. Four months later when her pregnancy began to show, this man gave her $40 and told her to clear out by dusk. She went to Philadelphia, worked as a seamstress, slept in doorways and in an alms-house, and finally rented the garret where, alone and unassisted, she had given birth. She told Dr. Smith that she had knotted the cord in an effort to save herself and her child from bleeding to death. Susan Smith left the prison and contacted Anna Dickinson, who lived a few houses away from Dr. Smith on Locust Street.

Anna was a natural choice to intercede on Hester's behalf, for she had become one of the most famous women in America, "the Queen of the Lyceum." Across the nation, she had wooed her audiences to the cause of abolition, and when the war ended, lectured on woman's rights so passion-ately that she was often referred to as the "Joan of Arc" of the movement. With few professions open to women, the Lyceum lecture circuit provided a desirable way of life—a means to earn money and fame, to travel, to have one's opinions heard. Agencies such as Redpath's, Fall's, the Boston Lyceum Bureau, and the American Literary Bureau in New York arranged these tours. Though not as successful as Anna Dickinson, Anthony, Stanton, and other woman's rights advocates also traversed the country, lecturing in town after town and resting only on Sundays. On one such tour, Anthony noted in her diary, "The year's work full 13,000 miles travel—170 meetings."

Other speakers on the Lyceum circuit included Spiritualists, trance mediums, political orators, and medical practitioners. In the quiet world of provincial America, their appearance was eagerly anticipated. From Octo-ber to May thousands of people across the country were willing to pay from 50 cents to $5 for the privilege of listening to these visitors, who earned any-where from $75 to $1,000 a night (less expenses and agents' fees).

These lecturers adopted unique mannerisms, presentation, and dress, to distinguish them from all the rest. Dickinson, who had once worn a plain gray Quaker dress, now wore a Paris gown and expensive jewelry. She bobbed her curly brown hair and wore a jaunty Alpine cap. Anna became the idol of repressed women: She earned her own money; she dressed beau-tifully; she traveled wherever she wished; she owned a horse and scandalized people when she raced the animal astride.

Dickinson's popularity and political power were especially appealing to three influential men. Although an aura of intimacy pervaded these rela-tionships, had it been publicly perceived that she was actually sexually involved with any of the three, it would have been her ruin. The first two were married, and adultery brought ostracism from traditional society and, in several states, a prison sentence. The third, a bachelor, had vowed he would marry a virgin.

Wendell Phillips was Anna's first mentor. At fifty-seven, he retained his wiry energy and craggy good looks; a full head of dark hair, close-cropped burnsides, a pronounced cleft in his chin. His aristocratic mien and devotion to Radical Reconstruction seemed to put him above all personal concerns. By 1868, this great orator had been married for thirty-three years to an invalid who was confined to her room and often to her bed. They had no children.

The second of Anna's admirers was Benjamin Butler. He was physically unattractive, small and plump, with a disproportionately large head and sunken eyes engulfed in bags of flesh. A drooping eyelid added to his sinister appearance. Yet Butler had such vitality and power that many women were attracted to him. His wife, Sarah, a former actress, was ill with thyroid cancer, but she joined her husband and their only daughter, Blanche, in the campaign for woman's rights.

Butler was drawn to Anna and gave her political advice. It was rumored that he also wrote many of her speeches. He became close to Anna's entire family and secured a job for her brother Edwin in the Washington pensions bureau. From there Edwin wrote to his sister that Butler had dropped in and asked for her address, "So I suppose thee'll have a love letter the day before or after this reaches thee."

And finally, there was Whitelaw Reid, who came to interview Anna in 1863, when he was a correspondent for the *Cincinnati Gazette*. He was then twenty-six, and she twenty-one. Reid was immediately taken with her. Although from a humble background, Reid envisioned for himself the life of an aristocrat. In 1864, Reid became the London correspondent for Horace Greeley's *Tribune* and lived in splendor on Chester Square, giving dinners that reportedly "outshone those at the American Embassy." When peace came the following year, he tried his hand at plantation farming but soon returned to the editorial staff of the *Tribune*.

Of Anna's three devotees, Whitelaw Reid was the only bachelor and newspapers frequently carried the rumor that he and Anna would marry. Reid wrote Anna's sister Susan that he'd received a letter from Schuyler Colfax congratulating him on "my impending marriage to 'that brilliant girl, Miss D.,' besides any number of other letters and newspaper paragraphs without number." He ended the letter by praising Anna's courage in bearing "it as stoically as I do."

Anna, when she learned of Hester Vaughn's plight from Dr. Smith, left

*Whitelaw Reid, 1863. At twenty-six he was a correspondent for the* Cincinnati Gazette.

immediately for New York, where she went at once to the offices of *The Revolution*. As always, Susan B. Anthony was delighted to see "her love," "her darling," "her chick a dee dee." Anna had totally captured Susan's heart. Anthony wrote to her on tear-stained paper, "My soul goes out to you in real mother yearnings—I don't believe you have believed the depths thereof." Susan yearned to give Anna "one awful long squeeze," and no matter how busy she was, she would travel anywhere to see her. "I do so long for the scolding and pinched ears and everything I know awaits. . . . What worlds of experience since I last snuggled the wee child in my long arms."

Anthony was horrified, but not surprised, to hear of Hester Vaughn's death sentence. But times were changing: Now she had her own journal, and article after article appeared in *The Revolution* condemning the injustice done to Hester. The Workingwomen's Association organized a protest at Apollo Hall, where Anna Dickinson brought tears to the eyes of hardened reporters. The association demanded a new trial or an unconditional pardon. Elizabeth Cady Stanton visited Governor John W. Geary of Pennsylvania to ask for the pardon. She argued that Vaughn was a victim of a cruel male society and that Hester's seducer was the one who should be tried for this crime. Geary refused to help, explaining to Stanton, "You have no idea how rapidly the crime of infanticide is increasing. Some women must be made an example of. It is for the establishment of a principle, Ma'am."

"Establishment of a principle, indeed! Yes, I suggest you inaugurate this good rule by hanging a few women," Stanton replied.

For a year *The Revolution* continued to pursue Vaughn's story, running many articles on Hester's failing health. Stanton wrote that women should be judged by a jury that included women and that capital punishment was cruel and useless and should be abolished. The New York branch of the American Equal Rights Association circulated petitions throughout the country protesting Vaughn's imprisonment. Members of Congress were solicited, and George W. Julian and Samuel C. Pomeroy wrote letters to Governor Geary. After a year of mounting protest, Vaughn was pardoned. The first branch of the Workingwomen's Association, whose members earned scarcely enough to feed and clothe themselves, helped raise $300 to send Hester Vaughn back to England.

The Workingwomen's Association had been Susan B. Anthony's idea; she believed that women should be self-supporting and must organize to achieve this goal. With this in mind she set up New York's Number One Branch of the Workingwomen's Association to benefit female typesetters and clerks, and a few weeks later created a second branch in a boarding-house tenement housing factory girls, most of whom were seamstresses. These young girls worked from ten to fourteen hours a day and generally earned $4 to $8 a week. Jammed into the boardinghouse dining room for the initial meeting were more than a hundred weary women in plain calico dresses. When the chairs ran out they sat or sprawled on the floor. Anthony told them she wanted to know about their working conditions so that she might help them. At first the women remained silent but then one spoke up: "I get two dollars apiece for making ladies cloth cloaks."

"How long does it take to make one?" asked Anthony.

"Less than a day. It's partly machine and partly handwork."

There was a ripple of dissent in the room—this seemed far too easy. One chalk-faced girl said, "Me—I make lace collars for twenty-two cents a dozen. In a day, twelve hours work, that's sixty-six cents."

A woman held up her raw, blistered hands. "I am a carpet-sewer. I work nearly three days and sew fifty yards of carpet, and when I asked the boss to pay me for sewing the borders, which is additional work, he laughed and said it was 'chucked in.'"

Another woman explained that after she had made a coat she was required to dampen it in starch water and iron it without extra pay. No coat that was not glossy and well pressed was accepted. "I took in two dozen last Tuesday," said the bleary-eyed woman, "and had a neighbor in to help. But both of us working steady all day and half the night, just as hard as we could, finished the lot by Friday evening. It was a hard earning of a dollar and a half, Ma'am, to divide between two, and both of us widders, but we're thankful to get it for all that. There's many a one wanting work that can't get any."

Susan told these dispirited women, "You must not work for these stingy prices any longer. Have a spirit of independence . . . and you will get better wages for yourself. Get together and discuss, and meet again and again. I will come and talk to you."

At this point talk was all Anthony had to offer but she inspired women with her quiet determination not to accept oppression. And there was no doubt that *The Revolution* bolstered her effectiveness. Its columns advocated such measures as fair wages, an eight-hour workday, and a tax on foreign products. Its Wall Street news revealed the manipulations of Fisk and Gould and their fellow schemers. Accounts of their misconduct were often picked up by the popular press. Elizabeth Cady Stanton used *The Revolution* to attack preachers, politicians, and the insensitive wealthy.

> Women are starving today and every day in the streets of New York but what cares the pulpit about it? Such a question need not be asked the politician. Still less need we stop the gilded coaches in Central Park to ask of beauty, wealth and fashion a question so impolite, so impertinent. And yet . . . these three classes . . . enact every civil statute, establish and regulate every civil law and custom, frame fashion and enforce all the religious faiths. The statute book benefits the rich only.

Stanton's position, however radical, was understandable, but her blind rage against the male establishment, combined with her feelings of class superiority, weakened her argument and further alienated those she most needed to accomplish her purpose. "The male element is a destructive force, stern, selfish, aggrandizing, loving war, violence, conquest, acquisition, breeding in the material and moral world alike discord, disorder, disease, and death. . . . The idea strengthens at every step, that woman was created for no higher purpose than to gratify the lust of man. . . . Society as organized today," she concluded, "is one grand rape of womanhood under the man power."

Members of the conservative Boston branch of the American Equal

Rights Association were appalled by this increasing radicalism. The New England society tried to distinguish itself from the New York society by drawing up its own agenda, emphasizing that woman suffrage was to be "a clear cut separate single question," not mixed with "side issues" such as the problems of working women, the present laws of marriage and divorce, and the protest against the male establishment. As a practical matter, Lucy Stone on behalf of the New England society encouraged the support of men, which she considered essential to the cause. This group voted unanimously that "prominent and able men, particularly ministers" should join with them. Henry Ward Beecher promptly became a member.

The New England group made it clear that there would be no reconciliation with New York until all connection was severed with the intolerant George Francis Train, financier of *The Revolution,* who used its pages to attack "niggers" and "that infamous Fifteenth Amendment." The most vocal adversary of Train was Mary Livermore, who decided that Train must be wiped out of the picture as effectively as she had wiped out the disease of scurvy in the Union troops during the Civil War. "We are now in the midst of a serious quarrel with Miss Anthony and Mrs. Stanton and the Train admixture," wrote Lucy Stone.

Anthony knew that a fractured woman's movement would have little power, and so she acceded to Stone and Livermore's demand to drop Train's name before the next American Equal Rights Association convention. Train, realizing that he could no longer use *The Revolution* to promote his views, told Anthony, "Omit my name from your journal—and let me work out my destiny alone." He withdrew not only his writing but his monetary support, and on May 10, 1869, Train left New York on the first trip by rail to California and then attended the ceremony where the Union Pacific and the Central Pacific Railroads were connected at Promontory Point near Ogden in Utah Territory. Here spikes of gold and silver were driven into the tracks that now extended from the Atlantic to the Pacific oceans.

A reconciliation between the two groups seemed possible. Mary Livermore, seemingly placated, wrote Anthony, "I have written to the New England friends to let bygones be bygones and come to the May meeting. It seems to me personal feelings should be laid aside and women should all pull together." On the morning of May 9, the American Equal Rights Association convention met in the handsome Steinway Hall on Fourteenth Street between Union Square and Irving Place. On the platform sat Vice Presidents Elizabeth Cady Stanton, Frederick Douglass, and Henry Ward Beecher. Lib Tilton, with the secret flowering of her relationship with

*A Union Pacific train in rugged Utah territory in 1869, when the Union and Central Pacific Railroads finally connected*

Beecher and her new feelings of confidence, had joined the Executive Committee. She stood at the rear of the hall with her daughter Florry, collecting tickets.

Lucretia Mott, the association's president, was home with a spring flu. In her place Stanton, as first vice president, assumed the chair. The Reverend O. B. Frothingham stood and, as if trying to head off trouble, announced that he was sure a "generous, sweet atmosphere will prevail" at this meeting. No sooner had he finished speaking than Stephen Foster, a New England farmer who had been an early abolitionist, sprang to his feet and declared, "I object to certain persons who have prevented harmony and destroyed the efficiency of this organization." Then looking at Stanton he announced, "One of these is our presiding officer."

Stanton answered, "I would like you to state in what respect." In reply, Foster mentioned Train and his ridicule of the Negro and opposition to the Fifteenth Amendment. Foster demanded that *The Revolution* repudiate Train "because of his course in respect to the negro's right." When Anthony declined, Foster insisted that both Stanton and Anthony "retire and leave us to nominate officers who can receive the respect of both parties." His ultimatum drew applause, after which there was a heated exchange concerning Anthony's bookkeeping and renewed charges that she had misused $1,000 of American Equal Rights Association funds to cover the cost of Train's speaking tour in Kansas the previous year.

"She never kept any books or account of the expenditures," declared Foster.

"That is false!" Anthony exclaimed. "Every dollar ever received by me and every dollar expended, item by item, was presented to the trust fund committee of Boston, of which this gentleman is a member." Then, in a desperate effort to justify herself, Anthony added, "They voted me a check of $1,000 to balance the account."

This in fact was not true, for Anthony had received no such check, and Stephen Foster, hoping to discredit her by making more of this minor distortion than was warranted, replied, "I would be glad to believe Miss Anthony, but her statement is not reliable."

Stanton rapped down her gavel. "You are out of order, Mr. Foster," she declared. Stanton was indignant that this matter was being publicly aired to humiliate Anthony before so large an audience. Lucy Stone's husband, Henry Blackwell, interceded.

> The facts of the case are these. . . . Miss Anthony brought in a statement of her expenditures to the society. No one doubts that all the expenditures were actually made as she reported. Her statement made due to herself from the society $1,000. Miss Anthony, for the sake of harmony and the good of the cause has given up her claim for this $1,000. In regard to this we have to say that we are entirely satisfied with the settlement thus made. I think this question might well have been kept back.

Then Stanton called for a vote of confidence from the convention, which was carried, but the atmosphere had turned adversarial. The tension increased when Stanton proceeded to attack the male establishment and the Negro. Bringing up the same old threats and playing on the same old fears used time and again, she warned,

> The Republican Party today congratulates itself on having carried the Fifteenth Amendment of the Constitution, thus securing "manhood suffrage" and establishing an aristocracy of sex on this continent. . . . The lower orders of men . . . the slaves of yesterday are the law-

makers of today. . . . The legislation of the ignorant African . . . in whose eyes woman is simply the being of man's lust . . . must culminate in fearful outrages on womanhood, especially in the Southern states.

Think of Patrick and Sambo and Hans and Yung Tung, who do not know the difference between a monarchy and a republic, who cannot read the Declaration of Independence or Webster's spelling book, making laws for . . . the daughters of Adams and Jefferson . . . women of wealth and education. . . . Shall American statesmen, claiming to be liberal, so amend their constitutions as to make their wives and mothers the political inferiors of unlettered and unwashed ditch-diggers, bootblacks, butchers and barbers, fresh from the slave plantations of the South . . . to establish an aristocracy based on sex alone?

As soon as Stanton finished, Frederick Douglass rose and moved toward the lectern. He had come to the convention to observe, not to speak, but now he could not contain himself. In the past he had declared his loyalty to Stanton, recalling, "When there were few houses in which the black man could have put his head, this woolly head of mine found refuge in the house of Mrs. Elizabeth Cady Stanton, and if I had been blacker than sixteen midnights without a single star, it would have been the same." But Stanton's speech had deeply wounded him. She had joined the horde of oppressors. Controlling his emotions, he told the convention:

There is no name greater than that of Elizabeth Cady Stanton in the matter of woman's rights and equal rights, but . . . the employment of certain names, such as Sambo, and the gardener, and the bootblack, and the daughters of Jefferson and Adams and all the rest that I cannot coincide with. . . .

Douglass's own cause burned with a white-hot flame.

I must say that I do not see how anyone can pretend that there is the same urgency in giving the ballot to woman as to the negro. With us, the matter is a question of life and death, at least in fifteen states of the Union. When women, because they are women, are hunted down through the cities of New York and New Orleans; when they are dragged from their houses and hung upon lampposts; when their children are torn from their arms and their brains dashed out upon the pavement; when they are objects of insult and outrage at every turn; when they are in danger of having their homes burnt down over their heads; when their children are not allowed to enter schools, then they will have an urgency to obtain the ballot equal to our own.

Lucy Stone also felt that Stanton's bigoted arguments were holding women back. If women lent their support to powerful men and to the cause of Negro enfranchisement, the favor, she believed, would soon be returned. In this she represented the vast majority of woman suffragists. The audience was quiet as Stone spoke. Even Anthony conceded that Stone "made *the speech* of *all the women*—and quite outdid her old self."

The gentleman who addressed you claimed that the negroes had the first right to the suffrage. . . . But I want to remind the audience that when he says what the Ku-Kluxes did all over the South, the Ku-Kluxes here in the North in the shape of men, take away the children from the mother and separate them as completely as if done on the block of the auctioneer. Over in New Jersey they have a law which says that *any* father—he might be the most brutal man that ever existed—may by his last will and testament dispose of the custody of his child, born or to be born, and that the mother may not recover her child. And that law modified in form exists over every state in the Union, except in Kansas.

Woman has an ocean of wrongs too deep for any plummet, and the negro, too, has an ocean of wrongs that can not be fathomed. There are two great oceans; in the one is the black man, and in the other is the woman. But I thank God for that Fifteenth Amendment, and hope that it will be adopted in every state. I will be thankful in my soul if *anybody* can get out of the terrible pit.

At the evening session, the Stanton and Anthony faction were overwhelmed by the powerful men and New England women who dominated the convention. A series of resolutions supporting the ratification of the Fifteenth Amendment and urging a separate amendment for woman suffrage was presented and passed over the objections of the New York group. Henry Blackwell then read out a resolution clearly aimed at disavowing their association with Stanton's more radical views.

*Resolved:* That in seeking to remove the legal disabilities which now oppress woman as wife and mother, the friends of woman suffrage are not seeking to undermine or destroy the sanctity of the marriage relation, but to ennoble marriage, making the obligations and responsibilities of the contract mutual and equal for husband and wife.

No sooner had Blackwell read the resolution than Mary Livermore stepped forward. This forty-eight-year-old woman who weighed nearly two hundred pounds was as commanding as she was direct and blunt. She said that originally she had submitted a stronger resolution, and although she'd agreed to the Stone-Blackwell version, having slept on it, she had changed her mind. Then she read,

*Resolved:* That while we recognize the disabilities which the legal marriage imposes upon woman as wife and mother, and while we pledge ourselves to seek their removal by putting her on equal terms with man, we abhorrently repudiate Free Loveism as horrible and mischievous to society, and disown any sympathy with it.

There it was—*free love*—an epithet hurled straight at Mrs. Stanton and members of the New York branch of the American Equal Rights Association. Anthony was the first to respond, saying, "This howl comes from those men who know that when women get their rights they will be able to live honestly and no longer be compelled to sell themselves for bread, either in or out of marriage." Free love was an easy target for opponents of the New York group. In fact, they did not advocate free love; their agenda was ambiguous on this issue. But Mary Livermore seized upon free love to denounce their radicalism in general and reduced Stanton's entire effort to reform the laws of marriage and divorce to this simple assault.

At this point, Victoria Woodhull seemed to have no common ground with the New York women who sought suffrage. But the concept of free love was broad and murky, and could encompass everything from amending the Constitution of the nation regarding women's enfranchisement to allowing one to indulge in sexual relations with whomever one chose for however long one chose. Free love meant different things to different people.

Lucy Stone was outraged by her friend Mary Livermore, because they had thoroughly discussed keeping the explosive issue of free love out of the convention. Stone declared,

I am unwilling that it should be suggested that this great, sacred cause of ours means anything but what we have said it does. If anyone says to me, "Oh, I know what you mean, you mean Free Love by this agitation," let the lie stick in his throat. You may talk about Free Love, if you please, but we are to have the right to vote. Today we are fined, imprisoned, and hanged without a jury trial by our peers. You shall not cheat us by getting us off to talk about something else.

Lucy Stone had a powerful personal reason for avoiding the subject of free love. It was common knowledge that her husband and fellow equal rights advocate Henry Blackwell was passionately pursuing Abby Hutchinson Patton, the wife of a prominent stockbroker, Ludlow Patton. Abby was also a member of "The Hutchinson Family," a singing group that campaigned for woman's rights. She had been on the campaign trail with Blackwell, three years earlier, at a time when he had felt jealous of his wife's burgeoning career and fame. Abby Patton fed Henry's ego and called him a "grand and secret love."

Henry's sister, the physician Elizabeth Blackwell, wrote of his infatuation, "I can say nothing about Harry [as the family called Henry]. The *thing* grieves and disgusts me. Poor fellow!" and added the directive so frequently seen in such letters, "Burn this at once!" Indicating that this subject was bandied about, Emily Blackwell, another sister, wrote that she'd heard through a third party that "Mrs. P." might wish to break off her "relations" with Henry and she hoped that he did too, but "I shall not feel sure . . . how their good resolutions hold out . . . nor do I know what the result will be between H & L for I have not seen them."

Like Lib Tilton, Lucy Stone blamed her husband's straying on her own sexual inadequacies. His sisters agreed, pointing out that in her devotion to woman's rights Lucy had neglected her husband. At this very meeting Abby Patton sat scarcely ten feet from Lucy Stone, and few could miss the difference between the two. Abby Patton—petite, dimpled, with a voice "like a songbird"—wore a lavender velvet dress with a large garnet breast-pin and green satin ribbons in her hair. Lucy Stone—small, plain, and plump, a dark mole prominent above her upper lip—wore a black silk dress with a delicate white lace collar; her hair, parted in the middle, was severely pulled back and unadorned. The tension in the air was palpable.

Month after month Henry had vacillated between his wife and Mrs. Patton. A brother-in-law noted that he had a strong "butterfly streak." Lucy, who had begun to suffer from blinding headaches, wrote Henry, angrily demanding the income from her own properties, which she wanted to separate from his. Lucy wanted her husband back but could not bear the humiliation of demanding his return. Shortly before this convention she gave him an ultimatum: She was putting their daughter Alice in boarding school and moving to Boston. She would try to finance a newspaper that they could edit together if he wished. He could follow or not. As she prepared to move to Boston she wrote, "I feel crushed, and torn, and homeless. . . . I shall try and work through the paper for the future and quit this lecturing field altogether . . . and shall certainly not continue my mode of work—tho it is my natural way."

By the final day, the convention had clearly split apart on the issues. Ernestine Rose, a member of the New York group, pointed to the powerful men who offered no help. She said that when Horace Greeley was asked what "impartial suffrage" meant, he replied, "Why man, of course. The man and the brother." "They do not speak of women and sisters," said Rose. A frustrated Stanton's form of address indicated to the gathering just who had the power: "*Gentlemen* and Ladies, I take this as quite an insult to me. It is as if you were invited to dine with me and you turned up your nose at everything that was set on the table."

The imposing Mary Livermore answered, "It certainly requires a great amount of nerve to talk before you, for you have such a frankness in expressing yourself that I am afraid of you." The audience laughed at this, for Livermore had her own sharp claws. "If you do not like the dish, you turn up your nose at it and say, 'Take it away, take it away.'" She made a dismissive gesture with her left hand. "Throughout the day the men who have attended our convention have been turbulent. . . . I say it frankly, that the behavior of the majority of men has not been sympathetic to you!" There were cheers in the hall.

On leaving Steinway Hall, Livermore halted in front of Susan B. Anthony. "The American Equal Rights Association is an awful humbug. I would not have come . . . nor would any of us, if we had known what it was. We supposed we were coming to a woman suffrage convention."

The following night at a meeting of the Brooklyn branch of the AERA, Stone and Blackwell heard a rumor that Stanton and Anthony were so upset that they were about to form a national society of their own. On Saturday morning, Livermore asked Anthony if there was any such plan. She denied it. That night, after Stone, Blackwell, and Livermore had left the city, Stanton and Anthony called a meeting at the Women's Bureau. As soon as the parlors, halls, stairway, and offices were filled, Elizabeth Cady Stanton announced a so-called impromptu business meeting. That night a new group was formed—the National Woman Suffrage Association. Stanton wanted only women to join the new organization, a proposition her husband Henry Stanton heartily endorsed: "Having been drilled for twenty years privately, I am convinced that women could do it better alone." But Tilton and Anthony disagreed, and an all-female organization was voted down. New goals were set forth: to oppose the Fifteenth Amendment because it did not include women (an almost hopeless task, since the amendment already had been ratified by twenty of the thirty-six states); to secure a Sixteenth Amendment specifically enfranchising women; to fight for every aspect of woman suffrage, including women's right to an eight-hour workday and pay comparable to men; and to demand more rights in marriage and more lenient divorce laws so that women would not be regarded as their husbands' "property." Declared Elizabeth Cady Stanton, "We are ready. We are prepared."

# CHAPTER SIXTEEN

# SOUP FOR THREE

VICTORIA WOODHULL was about to fulfill the prediction that one day she would possess $700,000. Her good fortune would come about through the worst financial debacle in the history of America: the collapse of the gold market, September 24, 1869—Black Friday.

At the end of the Civil War, American paper currency had become so weak that it took $241 of paper "greenbacks" to buy $100 worth of gold. Four years later, as prosperity returned, $100 in gold could be bought for $135 in greenbacks, but the price was unstable, and the gamblers on Wall Street speculated in currency as they did in stocks. In the spring of 1869, gold fell to $131, and Jim Fisk and Jay Gould bought $7 million worth. For bold operators such as these it seemed possible to manipulate the price of gold and even corner the market. But the U.S. Treasury had nearly $100 million in gold in its vaults and would, on occasion, sell a few million dollars' worth when it was needed for trade. Only if these vast reserves were kept off the market could the price of gold be manipulated.

The previous year, directly after Abel Rathbone Corbin had married President Grant's middle-aged sister Jenny, Jim Fisk and Jay Gould began to cultivate Corbin as a friend. In the summer of 1869, Gould bought $1.5 million in gold and earmarked it for the Corbins. He told them that if the price of gold rose, the profits would be theirs. Gould then offered a similar arrangement to Assistant U.S. Treasurer Daniel Butterfield and to General Horace Porter, Grant's personal secretary and trusted friend. Though Butterfield accepted the bribe, Porter sent Gould's offer back with a sharp note: "I have not authorized any purchase of gold and request that none be made on my account. I am unable to enter into any speculation whatever." Finally, in a bold stroke, Gould purchased $1.5 million in gold earmarked for President Grant's wife, Julia. Within the week Gould forwarded to Abel Corbin two checks for $25,000 each, representing profits, made out to Jenny Grant Corbin and to her sister-in-law, the first lady of the nation.

On September 2, 1869, the president arrived in New York on his way to

Saratoga and had breakfast with the Corbins. Abel Corbin somehow persuaded Grant to write a secret letter instructing Treasury Secretary George Boutwell not to sell gold until he personally gave the order. When Boutwell came to New York from Washington two weeks later, several prominent businessmen told him how the gold market was being manipulated. Fisk, worried that Boutwell might crack under the pressure, arranged to have William O. Chapin, his trusted employee, deliver a letter to the White House urging the president to stand fast on his decision not to sell gold.

On September 18, 1869, Chapin took the eight a.m. Pennsylvania Central train and arrived in Baltimore that evening. He hired a horse at a local stable and rode all night, forty-one miles at a breakneck pace, arriving at the White House the morning of September 19 to find President Ulysses S. Grant and General Horace Porter playing croquet on the lawn. Chapin dismounted and gave the president Fisk's letter. Grant opened the envelope, read the message, put it in his pocket, and said, "There will be no reply." Chapin proceeded to the nearest telegraph office and wired his employer, "Letter delivered all right." The telegraph clerk tapped out the message, which arrived at Fisk's office. But it read, "Letter delivered. All right." One tiny dot, one tiny error—but when Fisk received the reply that seemed to say "All right," he believed that the corner on the gold market was safe.

The week after Grant wrote Boutwell the secret letter advising him not to sell gold, Victoria Woodhull visited Commodore Vanderbilt and in a trance advised him to buy gold at $132. Vanderbilt committed his entire reserves and, using several brokers, acquired $9.5 million at that price. The sale of gold was not conducted in the stock exchange itself but in an adjacent Gold Room on Broad Street and Exchange Place. The Gold Room resembled a Greek amphitheater, in the center of which was a fountain decorated with a bronze cupid and dolphins spouting water. Two mechanical indicators, one inside, another outside the building, told the current price of gold. On Wednesday, September 22, gold rose to $137 and then to $141.

At lunchtime, Jenny Corbin received a letter from her sister-in-law, Julia Dent Grant. The final line read, "Tell Mr. Corbin that the President is very much distressed by your speculations and you must close them as quick as you can." Abel Corbin summoned Jay Gould. Both men were in a panic. Corbin insisted Gould buy him out. Gould refused but said he would guarantee that the price of gold held. Early Thursday morning Gould met with Fisk at the home of Josie Mansfield to plan a strategy. They decided to drive the price of gold up to $150 and then, with others still eager to buy, they would sell out their holdings. To effect this plan, they placed anonymous sell orders with several brokers. Then Fisk returned to the Gold

Room and bought up all the gold in sight, thereby stimulating others to do the same. When the exchange closed, gold stood at $144.

That evening, Victoria Woodhull once again visited the Commodore and advised him to sell his gold at exactly $150. She said that she had seen a vision of a gold bubble bursting and the number 151. Perhaps the figure of $150, the price at which Fisk and Gould planned to unload their gold, came from the spirits, though it is more likely that Victoria had heard what the plans were from Josie Mansfield. In any case, the Commodore promised Victoria that if her prophecy came true, she would receive half of his profits.

Friday morning, September 24, was cloudless and temperate. When trading opened at ten o'clock the indicator read $150, and the Commodore, heeding Vickie's advice, sold his $9.5 million worth of gold. By eleven-thirty gold was worth $160. As the price rose further, hundreds of screaming brokers and speculators crowded the floor of the Gold Room, waving scraps of paper. Men rushed to the fountain in the center of the room and splashed their fevered faces; some thrust their heads under the spouting dolphins. The National Guard was sent from Brooklyn to keep order in the street. The outdoor indicator steadily rose up and up. By noon gold stood at $162.

On the corner of Broad Street and Exchange Place, Jim Fisk, accompanied by Josie Mansfield, watched from his carriage as the outside monitor touched $163. Close by in her own carriage, Victoria Woodhull sat next to Colonel Blood. None of the parties seemed perturbed that gold had risen past $150. The *Sun* later noted that "amid the pandemonium Mrs. Woodhull sat unmoving, a half-smile on her lips." There is no doubt that once the indicator moved past $150, Victoria knew that she had fulfilled her mother's prophecy that evermore she would ride around in her own carriage.

For days brokers had been pleading with the president to avert a national collapse by selling gold. At his New York office, Assistant Treasurer Daniel Butterfield, who had been counting the profits on the $500,000 in gold Fisk and Gould had bought for him, understood that he could delay no longer. He sent a wire to Treasury Secretary George Boutwell in Washington which read, "Much feeling and accusation of government complicity."

Boutwell and Grant conferred. At one o'clock, Boutwell wired Butterfield, "Sell four million gold tomorrow and buy four million bonds." Butterfield secretly sent a messenger to Fisk and Gould informing them of what was about to happen. Then he publicly announced the government's plan to sell gold the following day. The impact was instantaneous; within thirty minutes gold plummeted from $164 to $132.

Investment houses that had been the bulwarks of Wall Street went

*The panic in the Gold Room on Black Friday, September 24, 1869*

bankrupt in the riptide. By midnight twenty-five people had committed suicide. It took months to straighten out the debacle of Black Friday. Dozens of clerks spent eight days simply compiling the flood of transactions. A congressional committee eventually established that Fisk and Gould had indeed sent the first lady $25,000 in profits, but Abel Corbin had cashed the check, so there was no way to verify that the money had reached Mrs. Grant. The committee decided that the president himself probably knew nothing of the scheme. Daniel Butterfield was asked to resign but was not further penalized. Commodore Vanderbilt made a profit of $1.3 million, of which he was said to have given Victoria Woodhull half. That, added to her earlier profit on the Central Pacific, made her a very rich woman.

SOME SAID IT had started as the Commodore's joke: He'd boasted that he could set up a monkey on Wall Street, and when the public heard he was behind the critter, it would make millions. Two beautiful female stockbrokers would be sure to attract attention in a world geared to celebrity. In the welter of publicity that followed, no one mentioned Vanderbilt's bold acumen in backing an enterprise that attracted more than four thousand visitors on opening day and found an untapped source of female money, to say nothing of information, unavailable to other Wall Street firms.

In the winter of 1869, Victoria and Tennessee rented two parlors at the genteel Hoffman House and set up the brokerage firm of Woodhull, Claflin & Co. On January 19, 1870, calling cards were sent from the firm. "Mrs. Victoria C. Woodhull," read one; the other, "Mrs. Tennie C. Claflin" (she no longer wished to be called Tennessee). Each parlor was decorated with oil paintings, statuary, green velvet sofas, and a piano, making it look, as a reporter observed, like "a ladies' drawing room." A portrait of their patron, Commodore Vanderbilt, was displayed next to a painting of two plump angels, their pink arms wrapped around a gold cross, under the inscription Simply to Thy Cross I Cling.

The trial balloon floated giddily away: Within a month Woodhull, Claflin & Co. had become so successful that Victoria and Tennie C. were forced to move to larger quarters at 44 Broad Street. The desks in the new offices were carved with a Greek scroll-and-key design in honor of Victoria's spiritual guide, Demosthenes. In the front office a telegraphic stock indicator clattered steadily. Facing the indicator, with a Marvin safe at his back, Colonel Blood sat at a massive desk. Blood had demonstrated his business acumen in St. Louis and now took the lead in running the firm. The colonel enlisted his brother George, a former newspaperman, as chief bookkeeper. The records were meticulously kept.

The crowd attending the official February 14 opening included Commodore Vanderbilt, Boss Tweed, and Jim Fisk accompanied by the elegantly dressed Josie Mansfield. By noon so many people crowded Broad Street that policemen, one hundred strong, were sent in to keep order. Thereafter, they all came—celebrities, customers, other brokers, the curious, and, of course, women. Woodhull, Claflin & Co. differed from other Wall Street firms in that there was a spacious private back office, completely cut off from the front offices by a richly carved walnut partition topped with ornamental glass. This office, accessible by a rear entrance, was restricted to women.

Society women and heiresses, small-business owners, writers, teachers, and housewives who had saved modest amounts hidden from allowances supplied by their husbands flocked to the rear entrance. So did women like Josie Mansfield, to invest the money they had earned as actresses or at houses like Annie Wood's and Molly de Ford's. (Indeed, Madame de Ford later said that the firm had earned her a profit of $30,000 in one year.) These women brought information and money to Victoria, who knew what to do with both.

*A cartoon of Victoria and Tennessee driving the bulls and the bears of Wall Street, in the* Evening Telegraph, *February 18, 1870*

The press welcomed the flashy novelty of Victoria and Tennie C., two beautiful women who made good copy and courted publicity, riding to work in their open chariot, tucking solid-gold pens behind their ears, wearing identical empress-blue velvet gowns. So many men crowded the offices that they were forced to put a sign in the window: "All gentlemen will state their business and then retire at once." The press called them "The Bewitching Brokers," "The Queens of Finance," "The Sensation of New York." Many afternoons the sisters could be found in the women's office, where they offered female clients champagne and strawberries dipped in chocolate as they sat behind their massive desks. They left the actual work of the brokerage to the men up front while they entertained clients or stuffed their scrapbooks with clippings.

Commodore Vanderbilt appeared at the Woodhull, Claflin & Co. offices almost daily, and he once remarked to a *Sun* reporter that many women were buying the Central certificates sold through the firm because they had his picture on them. The renamed Tennie C. remained close to the Commodore even though six months previously he had reneged on his offer of marriage. It seems that William Henry, the Commodore's canny son, aware that he and his wife, Maria, would never be accepted into society if his crude father married a Spiritualist fortune-teller, had arranged for the visit of a distant cousin from Mobile, Alabama, a nurse who was widowed during the war. Mrs. Crawford arrived with her nineteen-year-old daughter, Frank. On August 21, 1869, the Commodore eloped to Canada with Miss Frank Crawford. Later, when he was asked why he had married the daughter instead of her more suitable mother, he replied, "If I'da married her, Frank would have gone off and married someone else. Now I have them both."

In any case, the Commodore's marriage had no effect on his appetites, and his young wife offered no visible objection when on Tennie C.'s next visit to Washington Place he kissed her full on the mouth and exclaimed, "You might have been Mrs. Vanderbilt."

"Didn't you say you'd marry me?" asked Tennie.

"I intended to have done so, but the family made other plans."

The rumor persisted that Tennie C. was still sexually intimate with the Commodore. When asked by a reporter from the *Brooklyn Eagle* if she found the role of Vanderbilt's "protégée" awkward, she replied, "Were I to notice what is said by what they call society, I could never leave my apartment except in fantastic walking-dress and ballroom costume. I despise what those squealing, crying girls or powdered, counter-jumping dandies say of me."

Susan B. Anthony, intrigued by these sisters, visited them. As she made her way down Broad Street, she lifted the skirt of her black silk dress to avoid the mud, garbage, and tobacco juice. When Anthony arrived at Woodhull, Claflin & Co., she was directed to the rear women's entrance, where Victoria welcomed her enthusiastically and praised her for her work. Although this was their first meeting, Anthony, always on the lookout for people to aid her cause, asked Victoria if she would join the suffrage movement. Victoria replied, "Just wait until we get ourselves firmly established in our business and we will show you what we will do for the rights of our sex." At this point, a waiter entered with a lunch tray, which he placed on an empty desk. In an article she wrote for *The Revolution,* Anthony expressed her pleasure that these businesswomen were waited upon just like men. She ended the article with, "I found two bright, vivacious creatures, full of energy, perseverance, intellect, and pluck, and I said to myself, here are the elements of success."

Although the sisters' escapades undoubtedly were designed to attract publicity, they also violated the feminine taboos. Tennie C. once called a reporter into her office to show him the man's banking suit she was wearing. The reporter gaped at the trousers that ended three inches above her ankle and said, "If you wear that out on the street, there'll be a riot worse than the draft riot." Tennie C. nevertheless wore the man's jacket and waistcoat but added a long black broadcloth skirt, and Victoria soon joined her in wearing this attire.

Clothes were a political statement. Women who dressed like men threatened the entire structure of male domination. An eminent physician, reinforcing this belief, stated that women who wore men's clothes manifested an aggressiveness unbecoming to their sex. Earlier when Elizabeth Cady Stanton's cousin Elizabeth (Libby) Smith Miller first wore the "bloomers" that she had designed, woman's rights advocates, including Stanton herself, recommended this as an unconstricting, healthful costume. However, Stanton was so criticized for this mode of dress that after several months she abandoned it, feeling that women were spending too much time defending their attire and not enough on the issues.

During the war, women such as Mary Livermore and other members of the Woman's Sanitary Commission wore bloomers as they nursed the wounded and waded through the muck and gore of the battlefield. But with the war over, women were pressured into wearing whalebone fashions that squeezed their waists so tightly that they were often short of breath, their internal organs were displaced, and the pressure on their kidneys and bladder increased. Skirts used twenty yards of material, and bustles of iron wire often weighed as much as twenty pounds. Fashionable women went through life like hobbled horses.

The fashions of the day also reflected the current sexual standards. Pure, passionless wives were prized, but to procreate, a man must be sexually aroused, and therein lay the dilemma. Women solved this problem by concealing themselves from head to toe but with breasts upthrust and buttocks padded. Tennie C. and Victoria chose men's attire not only for publicity but also to protest the fact that women were kept in their place by clothes.

The sisters conspicuously flouted the accepted conventions of the day in other ways as well. It was an unwritten rule that women were not permitted in restaurants in the evening unless accompanied by a man. Delmonico's, at the corner of Broadway and Chambers Street, was among the grandest of these establishments. One night at seven, when Victoria and Tennie C. arrived at Delmonico's and ordered tomato soup for two, the startled waiter ran to fetch the owner. Lorenzo Delmonico leaned over the table and explained, with seeming solicitude, the error that had been made in seating the ladies: "We assumed a gentleman was joining you. Just pretend to be talking to me and I'll walk out the door with you. Then people will think you just came to speak to me. That will make it look all right."

"Make what look all right?" Victoria asked.

*Tennie C. Claflin, in men's clothing, c. 1870*

"I can't let you eat here without a man. It would start an awful precedent," Delmonico said nervously.

"Don't let us embarrass you," Tennie C. remarked, then stood and left the restaurant only to return a moment later with their coachman in scarlet coat and leather boots. She sat him uncomfortably between herself and Victoria. "Now, waiter," directed Victoria, "you may bring us tomato soup for three."

# CHAPTER SEVENTEEN

# A HARD PLACE

BY THE fall of 1869, Victoria Woodhull was flourishing, but Elizabeth Cady Stanton was foundering. Her personal life had broken apart. With her father's legacy, Stanton bought a house in Tenafly, New Jersey. Her husband, Henry, remained in New York, concentrating on his newspaper career and the company of his political cronies. Except for the youngest, the children were away at college. Though Henry visited from time to time, the marriage was in effect over. To soothe her shattered ego, she joined the Lyceum circuit and traveled throughout the West. She told Anthony that her views on marriage and divorce were warmly received and that women flocked to her "with their sorrows."

As Stanton retired from the fray, Lyman Beecher's youngest daughter, Isabella Beecher Hooker, was making herself known within the woman's rights movement. Mrs. Hooker lived with her husband, John, at Nook Farm, a prosperous community just outside Hartford, Connecticut. Her distinguished neighbors included Isabella's half-sister, the author Harriet Beecher Stowe, and her husband, Calvin; the Charles Dudley Warners (Warner was the editor of the highly respected *Hartford Courant*); and new arrivals Samuel Clemens and his wife, the former Olivia Langdon. Livy was the girl who in 1860 had slipped on the ice and lay paralyzed until a Spiritualist healer cured her. Clemens, using the name Mark Twain, had just published *Innocents Abroad,* whose great success launched him on his illustrious career. Of the inhabitants of Nook Farm, Isabella, with her Beecher assurance and preacher predilections, was clearly the social leader, and invitations to her Sunday night dinners were coveted.

For years Isabella had tried to "measure up" to the rest of the Beechers, especially Harriet and Catharine, and to her famous preacher brothers, especially Henry. She wondered when she would find something for herself, something that would bring her the recognition they had achieved. Belle, as she was called, was seventeen when she met John Hooker, a law clerk in her brother-in-law's office. When he proposed, she looked at the women around her, at their repeated pregnancies and domestic servitude, and observed that the role of wife might mark an end to her life before it began. "I do regret that so many fine women are made unhappy by firstly, being petted and spoiled by attention and admiration while young ladies and then learning all at once . . . they are to have *no* will of their own except so far as it coincides with their husband's." After two years of vacillation, however, Isabella married John and fell into the life she had feared, isolated domesticity and quiet anger.

Of her four children, one died in infancy. In her diary she wrote, "I should enjoy reading [a scientific book] through, but it requires close attention and this it is almost impossible for me to give with Mary at my elbow and with my brain half asleep from want of fresh air and company and exercise." Isabella blamed her inadequacies on her unequal schooling. "At sixteen and a half, just when my brothers began their mental education, mine was finished. . . . Father, poor minister as he was, could send them to College and Seminary, all *six*—cost what it might—but never a daughter cost him a hundred dollars a year, after she was sixteen."

In 1852, when she was thirty, Isabella visited Harriet, a few months after the publication of *Uncle Tom's Cabin,* to find her sister celebrated throughout the land. If only Isabella too could become successful. "Oh my *soul*—if you would only teach me how to earn money," she mused, "but there's no use in hoping—I can't write a book nor draw pictures—nor do any other productive work." To her children, Isabella was as stern a disciplinarian as her mother had been. Once, when eight-year-old Mary annoyed her, she talked to her "gently and persuasively," but when the child ignored her, Isabella flew into a rage, grabbed a long-handled brush, and savagely beat her daughter, who struggled violently. "She was frightened horribly and tho half choked" looked over at her little sister and shouted, " 'I want Alice to go out.' " Although Mary behaved after this beating, her mother was mortified at her own loss of control.

Undeniably, Isabella was a woman of passions, some uncontrollable. Later she admitted that her first feelings of power developed during a secret flirtation in the early years of her marriage. "You *can have* no idea of the pleasure of being admired and loved after having been shut out from the world as I have been . . . and filled with care and anxiety and labor. . . . The fact is I was engaged so young that I had little time to know my power until after my destiny was sealed."

In 1860, Isabella wrote her first article for publication, a timid essay called "Shall Women Vote? A Matrimonial Dialogue." It concluded, "If absolute power were in my hands, I would not open the polls to women today—no, nor next year, nor ever, unless public opinion demanded it." She signed herself Mrs. John Hooker. But by 1868 forty-six-year-old Isabella, still energetic and unfocused, found herself at Nook Farm with a near-empty nest. Only her fourteen-year-old son, Ned, was still at home. It was then that she turned to the woman suffrage movement. In the November and December issues of *Putnam's Magazine,* she published a second literary effort, printed anonymously, "A Mother's Letters to a Daughter on Woman Suffrage." She wrote that the woman's movement should address itself to prostitution, divorce, education, "and the whole system of insane asylums, poor houses, jails and many other institutions of modern civilization." Shortly thereafter she became president of the Connecticut Woman Suffrage Association.

In the summer of 1869, Isabella spent convention week in Newport with Paulina Wright Davis—a week that would change her life. There she met many members of the newly formed National Woman Suffrage Association, including Anthony and Stanton. For three days, Isabella literally sat at the feet of these two women and became convinced of their sincerity. She wrote, "Mrs. Stanton . . . is a noble woman, a magnificent woman . . . my prejudices against her . . . certainly go down under the influence of her presence and conversation. . . . I love her as well as I do Miss Anthony. . . . Sometimes she fails in judgment . . . but in right intentions never."

After leaving Newport, Isabella was summoned by Harriet, who wanted her editorial help. For Stowe, accustomed to adulation, criticism was something new, but then she had never before written about sex. In the *Atlantic Monthly,* she had published "The True Story of Lady Byron's Life" in response to a recent biography of Byron that portrayed his wife as a harridan whose frigid nature had driven the poet to despair and death. Harriet, a friend of Lady Byron's, refuted this, writing that Byron had banished his wife and infant daughter for the sake of an incestuous relationship with his half-sister, Augusta Leigh.

Stowe's article was denounced by a public that refused to acknowledge the possibility of incest. The *Independent* found the article "revolting, obscene garbage . . . barren in proof, inaccurate in dates, infelicitous in style and altogether ill advised." With Isabella's help, Stowe boldly turned her article into a book. It was ignored by the press, however, and became her only literary failure. Thereafter, she observed that public censure was something to be avoided.

While helping Harriet to edit her Lady Byron book, Isabella took it upon herself to organize a woman's rights convention to take place in Hartford. Her husband, John, sisters Harriet and Catharine, and brother Henry

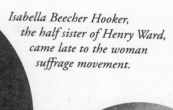

*Isabella Beecher Hooker,
the half sister of Henry Ward,
came late to the woman
suffrage movement.*

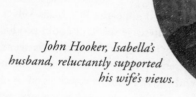

*John Hooker, Isabella's
husband, reluctantly supported
his wife's views.*

*Paulina Wright Davis. She taught women
to understand their own bodies.*

agreed to attend. Imperiously, she advised the New York delegation on "dress, manners, and . . . all the Christian graces." She instructed them to moderate their militant rhetoric in the cause of unity. Stanton replied in a letter to Hooker that the instructions amused her, but she indicated that she was annoyed at Isabella's officiousness. She promised to wear a dress "worthy of a place in the opera house of Hartford . . . give my hair an extra curl and wreath my face in its sweetest smile," but she added that when she had "demanded my right of suffrage twenty-five years ago, all my friends were shocked and grieved. . . . Your anxiety reminds me of the unhappy hen that butchered a bunch of ducks that danced in the waves and flapped their wings, and seemed to enjoy an element where the good hen feared to go."

Stanton accommodated Mrs. Hooker, against her better judgment but the Hartford convention did little to unify the New England and New York groups. One month later Stanton wrote,

> I did my best to obey orders, and appeared in a black velvet dress with real lace and the most inoffensive speech I could produce. All those passages that would shock the most conservative were ruled out, while pathetic and aesthetic passages were substituted in their place. From what my friends said, I believe I succeeded in charming everyone but myself and Susan who said it was the weakest speech I ever made. I told her that was what it was intended to be.

Lucy Stone, who led the New England delegation at the Hartford convention, was under great stress. Newly settled in Boston, she was trying to cope with her husband's affair with Abby Patton while simultaneously raising money for a newspaper. In October 1869, Emily Blackwell reported that her brother was once again with Mrs. Patton and that he "injuriously and foolishly keeps up Lucy's discomfort and distress by refusing utterly to terminate" the affair. Stone also brooded that Stanton and Anthony had formed the National Woman Suffrage Association without her knowledge. "Underhanded," she called it, and concluded that the solution was to turn the New England society into a national association to be called the American Woman Suffrage Association. Henry Ward Beecher agreed to be president, and the first AWSA convention was scheduled for late November 1869, in Cleveland.

Lucy Stone rationalized that the new organization was based on different convictions, not rivalry, and mailed a copy of the "call" to Anthony at *The Revolution* with a cordial note: "I *hope* that you will see it as I do that with two societies . . . we shall secure the hearty active cooperation of *all* the friends of the cause better than either could do alone. . . . So far as I have influence this society shall never be an enemy or antagonist of yours in any way." But when Stone heard that Stanton and Anthony had been invited to the AWSA Cleveland convention, she wrote a friend that she hoped they would stay away, since it would be "so dreadful an incubus to take them up again!" And Henry Blackwell made a special trip to New York to ask Theodore Tilton to dissuade them from attending.

When Stanton heard of this, she responded by writing in *The Revolution* that the Boston group were "hypocrites" and that "the names of persons are appended [to the call] who have been sedulously and malignantly working for two years to undermine certain officers in the National Association." Stanton refused to attend the convention, but Anthony, putting personal feelings aside, went, hoping to gain support for a Sixteenth Amendment granting the vote to women. She was not invited to sit on the podium and was appalled to find that the delegates, rather than supporting a Sixteenth Amendment, merely criticized the direction in which the assertive National Woman Suffrage Association was leading the movement and attacked Stanton's views on marriage and divorce. Finally, Anthony felt impelled to speak:

> So help me, Heaven! I care not what may come out of this convention, so that this great cause shall go forward to its consummation! And though this convention by its action shall nullify the [NWSA] of which I am a member, and though it shall tread its heel upon *The Revolution,* to carry on which I have struggled as never mortal woman or mortal man struggled for any cause . . . still, if you will do the work in Washington so that this [Sixteenth] Amendment will be proposed, and will go with me to the several legislatures and *compel* them to adopt it, I will thank God for this convention as long as I have the breath of life.

On the day after the Cleveland convention, Horace Greeley attacked Stanton and Anthony's NWSA, writing in the *Tribune* that it mistook "rashness for courage, folly for smartness, cunning for sagacity, badinage for wit, unscrupulousness for fidelity, extravagance for devotion. effrontery for heroism, lunacy for genius, or an incongruous mélange for a simple palatable dish." But an even larger controversy had arisen in New York, one that was about to rip asunder the last shred of unity in the woman's movement.

·  ·  ·

*Lucy Stone—the eloquent New England
woman's rights champion*

*Henry Blackwell—Lucy's straying husband, who
blamed his sexual infidelity on his wife's career*

AT 5:30 IN the afternoon on Wednesday, November 25, 1869, the famous journalist Albert Richardson entered the *Tribune* offices, strode across the newsroom, and stopped to read his mail. From behind a pillar Daniel McFarland took aim and fired. The ball, discharged from scarcely three feet away, entered Richardson's abdomen an inch below the navel. McFarland took off at a run, turning up Printing House Square and running down William Street. He was apprehended a few hours later in his room at the Westmoreland Hotel.

Albert Richardson had returned from the war a broken man. The horrors he had seen as correspondent for Greeley's *Tribune* had been followed by two years in the hands of the rebels in Salisbury prison, where he learned that his wife and child had died of cholera. Devastated, he returned to the *Tribune* and wrote a successful book on the generals of the Union army but until he met Abby Sage McFarland he felt that life was merely to be endured until death came as the rescuer.

Abby Sage had been living in Madison, Wisconsin, when she met Daniel McFarland at a reading she was giving for the benefit of the local hospital. She was seventeen when she married McFarland, who, impressed by her sweet voice, trained her to be an actress. Convinced that Abby could support him, he sold their furnishings, pawned her jewelry, and moved to New York City. When Abby could not find employment, McFarland began to drink heavily. He beat his wife when she became pregnant, then abandoned her. Abby's parents, asking no questions, welcomed her back to their small farm in Manchester, Vermont. Eighteen months later McFarland begged for a reconciliation. Abby returned, but so did Daniel's drinking and abuse. Abby was later to say,

> He would lock himself in the room with me and give way to such terrible furies that only extreme pride and self-control prevented me from making my misery known. He brought home what he professed was prussic acid and threatened to force me to take it. He would snatch my scissors from my workbasket and bearing open his breast he would brandish them about, swearing he would let out his heart's blood before me. He told me that he kept loaded pistols with which he would at any moment shoot me.

In the winter of 1866, Lucia P. Calhoun, the *Tribune's* society editor, for whom Abby had written a few theater notes, told two friends of her impoverished state. The first, Horace Greeley's sister, Mrs. Sinclair, befriended Abby and gave her money to buy clothes for herself and her son, Percy. The second, Albert Richardson, also tried to help her by prevailing upon Greeley to recommend Daniel McFarland for a patronage job at the Custom House. McFarland, often too drunk to perform his duties, was fired. Richardson intervened again and secured a position for him with the Internal Revenue Service.

One morning Abby arrived at the *Tribune* offices with her face swollen and a black eye concealed with makeup. Richardson took her to lunch, and she told him that her husband had savagely beaten her over the years but there was nowhere to turn, no one to help. The next day Richardson rented a room next to the McFarlands' at a boardinghouse at 72 Amity Street. He pushed his bed against the wall between his bedroom and theirs and vowed that if he heard one blow or one cry, he would enter the room and rescue Abby. Although he had never spoken of it, he had fallen in love with her.

At 11:30 p.m. on Wednesday, March 14, 1867, Albert met Abby at the stage door of the Winter Garden theater, where she was playing the small role of Nerissa in *The Merchant of Venice*. As they walked arm in arm, Daniel McFarland emerged from a dark side street carrying a fourteen-inch four-barreled revolver. Richardson felt the gun at his back and instinctively spun round, striking McFarland. The gun discharged three times, wounding Richardson in the hip, but he held McFarland until two policemen arrested him. In the presence of witnesses, Daniel McFarland agreed to a separation. Some three weeks later, however, he intercepted a letter from Richardson in which he addressed Abby as "My Dearest Wife" and said that, should she become legally free, he wanted her to be just that. He declared his love and wrote that he would do whatever he could to make her life rich and beautiful.

With money from Richardson, Abby went to Indiana to establish the year's residency required for a divorce. (Indiana had the most liberal divorce laws in the country except for Wisconsin, where incompatibility was grounds for divorce.) She returned to New York the week of November 20, 1869. Daniel McFarland learned that Richardson had purchased a farm in New Jersey and after his marriage expected to live there with Abby. Live there with *his property*! Five days later, McFarland shot Richardson.

When he was shot, Richardson slowly pulled himself up the narrow stairs of the *Tribune* to the office of Whitelaw Reid, where he collapsed into a chair and announced, "I am in need of a surgeon." He was so calm that Reid didn't realize that Richardson was wounded, but when he saw blood seeping through his waistcoat, Reid quickly summoned a doctor. Richardson was carried to the Astor House. He asked the doctor, "Do you think I will live?" The doctor answered, "If you live forty-eight hours you will be out of danger, but your life is in extreme peril."

When it became increasingly obvious that Richardson would die, as a last wish he requested that Henry Ward Beecher marry him to Abby. The preacher, caught up in the ecstasy of his own relationship with Lib Tilton, was only too happy to comply. He performed the ceremony with Horace Greeley as witness. Richardson died the following morning.

Almost immediately the news circulated that Abby was still legally married to Daniel McFarland—an Indiana divorce was not recognized in New York. Beecher was severely criticized for performing the wedding ceremony. The press took up the attack. William A. Bartlett, a prominent lawyer, wrote in the *Sun,*

> Consider, married men of New York! Husbands and fathers! By what
> frail and brittle tenure your homes . . . your wife . . . are yours. . . .
> Reverend Henry Ward Beecher stands ready to marry her to the first
> libertine . . . who comes boldly and even proudly forward, holding
> by the hand and leading Lust to her in triumph over religion.

*The deathbed marriage of Abby Sage McFarland and Albert Richardson.*
*The Reverend Henry Ward Beecher officiates.*

Members of the clergy also joined in the criticism of Beecher. The Reverend George B. Cheever wrote, "The tendency of these times towards excessive self-enjoyment and loose views of religion and the marital bonds led to this tragedy as a natural result." The Reverend W. A. Scott added, "The deathbed marriage was a blasphemous act and was more sensational than the tragedy itself."

Henry Ward Beecher found himself more and more threatened. In the *Sun,* he defended himself: "I took every statement of every kind respecting the affair . . . without time to investigate. The man was dying. Was that a time for sifting evidence?"

Unlike Beecher, members of the National Woman Suffrage Association did not run for cover. To a crowded audience at Steinway Hall, Anna Dickinson said of Richardson, "Once in a while God blesses the world with a great lover. This man was such a one." When she heard hisses from the gallery, she addressed the men in the audience directly: "Love signifies companionship, friendship, understanding, some similarity of sentiment, of pursuits, of interests. . . . I stand here to warn you, sirs, that the woman of the present is not the woman of the past, that she will mete to you as you mete to her."

Stanton's response was still more radical. On behalf of the NWSA, she called for a revision of the divorce laws and wrote,

> Marriage today is in no way viewed as an equal partnership, intended for the equal advantage and happiness of both parties. Nearly every man feels that his wife is his property, whose first duty, under all circumstances, is to gratify his passions, without the least reference to her own health and happiness, or the welfare of their offspring; and so enfeebled is woman's judgment and moral sense from long abuse that she believes so too and quotes from the Bible to prove her own degradation.

Lucy Stone alleged that members of the NWSA, through their stand on the McFarland-Richardson case, wished to undermine the laws of marriage. She accused them of being infiltrated with "loose women" and "free lovers" who intended to make "easy divorce" a part of their platform. She appealed to Beecher, as president of the AWSA, to persuade the women of Plymouth Church to join her organization, not Stanton's. Perhaps in her effort to preserve her own precarious marriage Stone feared anyone who would make the laws of divorce more lenient. Lucy was trying desperately to keep her husband. Stoic but anguished, she begged her sister-in-law Emily to influence her brother to give up Mrs. Patton. "It is not good for him to . . . take up the old snare," she wrote.

On January 8, 1870, the second anniversary of *The Revolution,* the first issue of Stone's *Woman's Journal* appeared. The pointedness of the date was, of course, intentional. *Woman's Journal,* an immediate success, was backed by six prominent Boston businessmen who invested $10,000 each. Mary Livermore, a powerful adversary of the NWSA, was appointed editor. Harriet Beecher Stowe, Catharine Beecher, and Henry Ward Beecher became contributors.

Susan Howard—the wife of Beecher's friend and benefactor John Tasker Howard, and the mother of *Sun* editor Joe Howard—was perplexed by the controversy. She wrote Isabella Beecher Hooker that Lucy Stone had accused members of the NWSA, including Mrs. Stanton, "of holding free love doctrines." Isabella replied that she could not understand why Lucy was now making such a fuss over Stanton's views, since "it is certain that Mrs. S. entertains no new views, none that Mrs. Lucy has not heard from her years ago." Isabella explained that Stanton "has come to look upon easy divorce as a blessing and a necessity. But to say that she ever advocated this as a means of *personal gratification* to woman or man is simply to insult her."

To reassure Mrs. Howard that the goal of the NWSA was "purely suffrage," Isabella enclosed a copy of its constitution but then, in an odd gesture, checked off the names of the women who might be pointed out by adversaries as "loose women or free lovers." Isabella wrote that Lucy Stone had made the same free love accusations to her brother Henry and ended her letter with an appeal to her friend to think for herself.

Susie, you are in a hard place and I am not urging you to try to defend anybody. . . . I only wish my dear brother [Henry] could be persuaded to hear some of these things and not because I wish to wean him from his new alliance or friendships but because he could be much more useful to them and to the whole cause by understanding the countercurrents . . . if he does not allow himself to be warped and set against other workers. . . . Oh Susie, *few men* know what this battle means—but many women, wives and mothers, know and feel it all, feel it for their sisters if not for themselves. I am one of these and I stagger under the weight of my load.

Evidently, Susie Howard was not allowed the privilege of thinking for herself. Isabella's letter was answered by Mrs. Howard's son Joe, who wrote not to Isabella but to her husband, John Hooker, stating that Lucy Stone's allegations were widely accepted in Brooklyn. John Hooker, who had unwillingly been dragged into the controversy, replied of Mrs. Stanton, "From what little I have seen of her I do not fancy her at all. . . . She is a bold and strong thinker but she has not a refined nature. She is however a pure woman, and seeking to promote purity in others. There is not a particle of the sensuality that we generally regard as incident to 'free-loveism' about her. Her notions are very far from pleasing me, but they are notions, not feelings, a groping mind, not a wantoning heart."

Lucy Stone and her compatriots could level their accusations at Mrs. Stanton because the doctrine of free love and woman's rights had much in common: The concept of equal relations between the sexes was identical and led to the fight for many reforms, including the vote and the liberalization of marriage and divorce laws. But free love was abhorrent to many women as well as men because it openly acknowledged equal female sexuality. Free love presupposed female sexual satisfaction, which was scorned as "personal gratification" and therefore "vile." It granted women the right to refuse sexual intercourse, freeing them from male sexual coercion. In this it violated both legal strictures and the teachings of the church, which mandated sexual submission. Also, while free love did not advocate promiscuity, its tenets were liberal enough to encompass flagrant sexual behavior that shocked many open-minded women. It was one thing to believe in the theory of free love and quite another to practice it.

# CHAPTER EIGHTEEN

# THE EVANGEL

Rich at last! Scarcely four months after Black Friday, in January 1870, Victoria and Tennie C. leased an elegant brownstone at 15 East Thirty-eighth Street, just off Fifth Avenue in Murray Hill. After a lifetime of wandering, of rented dwellings and few personal possessions, the sisters could finally achieve their fantasy of success and luxury. The next weeks were filled with shopping sprees for Oriental rugs, oil paintings, and Venetian glass chandeliers. The downstairs rooms were hung throughout with purple velvet. And everywhere there were mirrors, even on the ceiling of the mahogany-paneled library. In the main salon, incense burners hung from the gilded ceiling. According to the *Sun,* this room featured a "wondrous dome . . . a flood of light beaming through a circular sheet of glass painted in the most exquisite colors [depicting] the loves of Venus in delicate lines." Victoria's bedroom was lined in green velvet with a matching green velvet and gold fringed bedspread and gilt chairs, while Tennie C.'s bedroom was draped in deep purple velvet and lilac-patterned silk imported from France. The *Star* called their house a "Modern Palace Beautiful."

Even before the house was furnished fifteen family members had moved in. In addition to Victoria, Tennie C., and Colonel Blood, there was Victoria's son, Byron, a gangly sixteen-year-old with the mind of an infant, and her devoted nine-year-old daughter, Zulu Maud. Buck and Roxy arrived, followed by Utica, Margaret Ann and her three children, and Polly and her daughter, Rosa Burns, as well as Polly's new husband, Dr. Sparr, a magnetic healer. Many afternoons Roxy and Utica raided Tennie C.'s and Victoria's closets, playing dress-up like two children; then they would sit in the parlor drinking together. When there was no other alcohol Utica drank drugstore bay rum. Mama Roxy took to pawning Tennie C.'s jewelry, which led to screaming arguments ending with Mama's tears and promises to reform. Buck charged a new wardrobe to his daughters and, decked out like a proper Wall Street broker, began visiting the offices of Woodhull, Claflin & Co., offering advice to Colonel Blood. When a runner arrived with $3,000 worth of bearer bonds, Buck cashed them and pocketed the proceeds.

One evening there was a knock on the door, and on the doorstep stood Dr. Canning Woodhull, stick-thin and shaking like a wet spaniel from delirium tremens. "Oh, Doc, you poor fellow!" exclaimed Victoria. Dr. Woodhull joined the Claflin ménage and, when he was not fogged with morphine and alcohol, helped look after his son, Byron. Victoria told a *Herald* reporter that with her staff of twelve and all her family, "it costs us over twenty-five thousand dollars a month to live."

At this rate, within a short time Victoria's funds would be exhausted, but for the moment she was free of debt and ready to make her mark. Later she claimed that in February, Demosthenes came to her and told her, "Your work is about to begin." That work, she said, was to lead a domestic and social revolution to rectify the injustices toward women. Although the transformation from self-aggrandizement to selflessness would take some time, it had begun. Colonel Blood, who had read Karl Marx and believed in a world free of cruelty and corruption, was undoubtedly a major influence. The greatest influence on Victoria Woodhull, however, was the "New Age" philosopher Stephen Pearl Andrews, who sought her out the month she moved into 15 East Thirty-eighth Street.

With his flowing gray hair and beard and his abstracted air, Andrews cut a striking figure. For the past four years he had lived with his second wife, Esther, a Spiritualist, magnetic healer, and trance speaker. Their boarding-house on the corner of Fourteenth Street near the Academy of Music had become the center for a group of radical Spiritualists who believed in his vision of a utopian society, which he called the Pantarchy. Andrews, as leader, called himself the Pantarch. He declared that the Pantarchy would "replace the corrupt system that was evolving to afford plunderers' profits to the few, while demeaning the dignity of labor" and predicted "a grand domestic revolution" whose keystone was his long-held belief in free love.

Andrews's problem was money. He and his group were just scraping along until he met Victoria Woodhull. So impressed was Victoria with his ideas, which coincided with some of her own practices, that she immediately backed him. Her spacious parlors were put at Andrews's disposal for meeting rooms and he filled them with members of the Pantarchy and other radical Spiritualists. His wife had just completed a course at the Eclectic Medical College of the City of New York, "for the free and untrammeled investigation and practice of medicine" and had become an expert at herbal healing as well as magnetic healing. Esther Andrews and Victoria became friends at once. In a trance, Esther reportedly suggested successful cures for maladies that had eluded doctors. To cure Colonel Blood's arthritis, she warned him to avoid nightshade vegetables. "Abandon your carriage and walk. . . . Eat what flies or grows above the earth, and you will improve," she instructed. At the séance table, Esther warned Victoria that a spirit had said, "Beware the Judas kiss," and told her that she would be betrayed by a member of her own family.

Despite the presence of her crude kin, Victoria soon established herself as a notable hostess, and her house attracted not only members of the Pantarchy but also advanced thinkers and celebrities of the day, including the famous Spiritualist Laura De Force Gordon, a trance medium and defender of woman's rights who was greatly admired by Susan B. Anthony. Among Victoria's other guests was Elizabeth Stuart Phelps, author of the Spiritualist book *The Gates Ajar,* in which she assured her readers that the living would be reunited with the dead once one passed through "the gates" separating this world from heaven. Reflecting one of the main appeals of Spiritualism, she maintained that she had written *The Gates Ajar* to comfort "the bereaved wife, mother, sister, and widowed girl." Though vigorously attacked by the clergy as "heresy," it sold eighty-one thousand copies in the United States and one hundred thousand copies abroad in less than a year.

Victoria also attracted powerful business, political, and military figures, mostly of a freethinking kind, among them Benjamin Butler, who was intrigued by the beautiful Victoria and her unconventional entourage. When Butler first met Victoria in 1870, his wife, Sarah, was in Germany, seeking a cure for her thyroid cancer. The rumor was afloat that Anna Dickinson would not marry Whitelaw Reid, as predicted, but would marry Butler as soon as Sarah died. Butler was indeed pursuing Dickinson and writing her passionate love letters while she herself seemed to be making plans for married life with a secret lover. Anna announced that this would be her last lecture season and that a personal involvement would cause her to retire from public life. The *Cincinnati Enquirer* noted, "The name of the gentleman was not ascertained nor when it is to come off." Reid enclosed the clipping and wrote defensively, "Are my congratulations in order? And shall I send congratulation or condolence to the gentleman from Boston? Have you seen the latest about *me*? My physicians have forbidden me to marry and so I am making the Tribune my bride!" Whitelaw Reid's and Dickinson's biographers both assumed Butler was "the gentleman from Boston," but as future events were to reveal, they were mistaken as to the identity of Anna's secret lover.

In any case, by the summer of 1870, Butler had become a frequent visitor at Woodhull's house, and their relationship was close. Victoria spoke of

Butler's intimate habits, his compulsive snacks of doughnuts washed down with whiskey, the way his unlit cigar traveled round and round in his mouth when he tried to stop smoking. Whether Butler's relationship with Victoria was sexual as well as political is unclear, although she readily admitted that she visited Butler "at night" to ask him if he would open the Judiciary Committee's mind to a Sixteenth Amendment to give women the vote. There was even a published rumor that Butler had offered to help Victoria Woodhull in the cause of woman suffrage if she would allow him "an opportunity to feast his eyes upon her naked person." When Butler was confronted with this report he remarked coyly, "Half-truths kill."

Benjamin Butler was a strong supporter of woman's rights and was known to encourage controversy in Congress. In Victoria Woodhull he undoubtedly saw a way to further his ideas. Thus far Woodhull had limited knowledge about either of the woman's rights organizations and was unaware of the split between the New York and Boston groups or of the opprobrium heaped on Henry Ward Beecher for the deathbed marriage of Albert Richardson and Abby Sage McFarland, but now she was rich and longed for a mission. The canny Butler decided to exploit this ambition, and he was supported by Andrews and Blood, who also saw the political use to which this beautiful, charismatic woman could be put. While Stanton and Stone were squabbling, and Henry Ward Beecher was defending himself against accusations of free love, Victoria Woodhull, propelled by the men behind her, boldly asserted herself. In April 1870, a notice was placed in the *Herald*:

> While others of my sex devoted themselves to a crusade against the laws that shackle the women of the country, I asserted my individual independence. . . . While others sought to show that there was no valid reason why woman should be treated . . . as a being inferior to man, I boldly entered the arena of politics and business and exercised the rights I already possessed. I therefore claim the right to speak for the unenfranchised woman of the country and . . . I now announce myself as a candidate for the Presidency.

Since the presidential election was still two years away, Victoria's announcement belonged more to the world of publicity than to politics. But Butler, Blood, and Andrews even then were building a constituency and a platform for their ideas of social reform. They made their first substantial move the following month, on May 14, 1870, with the first issue of *Woodhull & Claflin's Weekly*. Victoria Woodhull and Tennie C. Claflin were

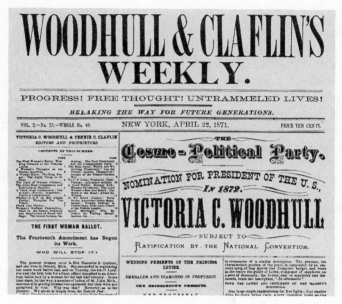

*The first page of the* Weekly *endorsing Victoria's bid
for the presidency*

listed as editors and proprietors and J. H. Blood as managing editor. Ten cents bought a single copy and four dollars a year's subscription. The first issue contained a mélange of radical theorizing, fashion, sports, a serial by the female author Amandine Dupin Dudevant (who had adopted the nom de plume George Sand), and several columns on Spiritualism, trance speakers, and magnetic healing, prompting one observer to say that the journal was "edited in one world and published in another." The *Weekly* was as eccentric and eclectic as Victoria herself, but its purpose was straightforward: to promote Victoria Woodhull as a leading advocate of the political reforms of the day.

Victoria and Tennie C. used their celebrity status and the interest in Spiritualism to draw attention to themselves. In the third issue, Victoria published the first of a series of political writings under her own signature. She explained that they were written on the two or three evenings a week when, in a trance state, she sat either in her upstairs parlor in winter or on the roof in summer. As Victoria spoke, Colonel Blood, sitting nearby with pen and paper, took down her words. Then a few hours later, when she emerged from her trance, Blood would read back what she had said, and these thoughts would become her articles. Victoria declared that she did not recall what she had said in her trances.

It is unlikely that the intricate political arguments and legal knowledge that marked these articles originated with her. They echo the writings of Andrews, Blood, and Butler. Interspersed with these technical arguments, however, were illustrations drawn from Victoria's own life. What Victoria Woodhull declared in her various trances, what was her personal inspiration, and what was written for her, no one can say. Some said Victoria was the instrument of powerful men; she herself contended she was the instrument of the spirits. While others no doubt used her as a flamboyant parrot, she herself came increasingly to believe that the spirits had chosen her to become "the ruler of the whole world." And she went still further to declare, "I am the evangel."

AT THE DISASTROUS American Equal Rights Association convention in May 1869, when the woman's movement split apart, Elizabeth Cady Stanton ended her final speech by declaring, "The need of this hour is not territory, gold mines, railroads or specie payments, but a new evangel of womanhood, to exalt power, virtue, morality, true religion, to lift man up into the higher realms of love, purity and thought." But as yet she had no idea where that "evangel of womanhood" might be, and meanwhile her organization was in desperate trouble. The delegates who were about to meet at the National Woman Suffrage Association convention in Washington in January 1870 were a considerably weakened group. Lucy Stone's rival American Woman Suffrage Association had attracted many powerful women and men, including Henry Ward Beecher, Wendell Phillips, and William Lloyd Garrison. Stanton and Anthony's ranks, on the other hand, were filled with inexperienced young women venturing out on their own for the first time. Most had to "beg at the pockets" of husbands or fathers for the money to go to Washington to protest male domination. The NWSA delegation was received by members of Congress in a committee room of the Capitol. The most prominent women sat at a table in the center while behind them the new members settled into their seats like a covey of doves. The world of politics was strange and incomprehensible to most of them. Instead, there was much talk of dress and proper deportment, intermingled with a giddy feeling of escape. Amid this chatter, Stanton called the meeting to order.

The portly Reverend Samuel May opened with a prayer and then called for every woman in the room who desired the ballot to raise her hand. Only

*William Lloyd Garrison with his daughter Fanny.*
*The great abolitionist favored the vote*
*for black men before women.*

a few timid hands rose, accompanied by much giggling. Stanton was astounded by the reaction of her raw recruits. "The Reverend May has adopted a very bad manner in submitting the question," she said. Then Stanton directed any woman opposed to a Sixteenth Amendment to enfranchise women to stand. "Those in favor are to remain seated," she said emphatically. To Stanton's dismay, as the laughter continued, an overwhelming majority of women from her delegation rose to their feet.

Stanton and Anthony were paying a heavy price for their opposition to enfranchising black men unless women also got the vote. At an antislavery festival in New York two weeks later, Stanton approached Wendell Phillips, but he turned on her "like a shark with sarcasm and ridicule." Stanton took this as another demonstration of male oppression and wrote,

To have Wendell Phillips withdraw his velvet paw as if one were unworthy to touch the hem of his garment—this is enough to rouse one's blood to the white heat of rebellion against every "white male" on the continent. When I think of all the wrongs that have been heaped upon womankind, I am ashamed that I am not forever in a condition of chronic wrath, stark mad, skin and bone, my eyes a fountain of tears, my lips overflowing with curses, and my hand against every man and brother! Ah, how I do repent me of the male faces I have washed, the mittens I have knit, the trousers mended, the cut fingers and broken toes I have bound up!

It was in this atmosphere of animosity that Daniel McFarland was brought to trial for the murder of Albert Richardson. He sat in the courtroom in a tattered black frock coat, conversing earnestly with the palm of his hand, held in front of his face. The all-male jury found McFarland not guilty by virtue of insanity. But the "insane" Daniel McFarland—not Abby, the child's mother—was granted sole custody of their son, Percy. He walked from the courtroom holding the weeping boy's hand.

On May 17, 1870, the National Woman Suffrage Association organized a protest against the McFarland verdict, to be attended by women only. Three thousand assembled at Apollo Hall, where Stanton argued that "the husband's right of property in his wife" was the central problem in marriage. She said the jury had found McFarland not guilty because "neither woman nor slave can testify against their supposed masters." By declaring Abby's divorce illegal, the court permitted any "bloated drunkard or diseased libertine" to possess and coerce a woman sexually. It was time therefore for "an entire revision of the laws of New York on marriage and divorce." Marriage as it existed, said Stanton, was "nothing more or less than legalized prostitution. . . . I rejoice over every slave that escapes from a discordant marriage."

On the same day as the NWSA protest, the opposite view of marriage and divorce appeared in the *World* and the *Tribune* written by the mighty Catharine Beecher, the domestic high priestess of family life. Addressing the case of Abby McFarland, she wrote, "A woman may separate from her husband for abuse or drunkenness and not violate law, but neither party can marry again without practically saying, 'I do not recognize Jesus Christ as the true teacher of morals and religion.' " In this she represented the popular view that marriage was a sacred institution, entered into for life, no matter what the consequences. In fact, remarriage for widows was widely considered immoral as well. Even Anthony herself said, "I hate the whole doctrine of 'variety,' of 'promiscuity.' I am not even a believer in second marriages after one of the parties is dead, so sacred and binding do I consider the marriage relation." But Anthony was able to separate her beliefs from what she felt was the greater good of womankind.

Lib Tilton was distressed by the friction between the NWSA, in which her husband was so active, and the rival AWSA, headed by her beloved preacher. As she saw her friends at Plymouth Church joining Beecher's organization she asked her husband to intervene and unite the two associations, saying that the chance for enfranchisement would fall by the wayside unless they could reconcile their differences. Theodore agreed and advised Anthony that, in spite of all that had happened, reconciliation would be a wise course of action. "No, no," Anthony replied, "self-respect, self-justice forbid it. I stand plaintiff, not defendant, before that woman [Lucy Stone] and the Boston clique." Nonetheless, Tilton determined to try for an amalgamation of the two organizations. Lucy Stone was as opposed as Susan B. Anthony, but she agreed to a meeting. When they met and Tilton failed to persuade Stone to unite with her rivals, he lost his temper and threatened, "I will form a new society. . . . I can carry it, for I have a paper, I have the platform, and I have a pen."

The parent American Equal Rights Association, whose membership was now split between the rival organizations, had virtually ceased to function, but some branches still had not affiliated with either of the two new organizations. In a clever but deceptive maneuver, Tilton plotted with Stanton to change the name of the NWSA to the Union Society and thus absorb as many branches of the old AERA as possible. Stanton admitted that she had "grand times" doing this but wrote, "Boston is *awful* sore." Having grabbed off whatever AERA membership it could, the Union Society then dissolved and resumed its old name. Lucy Stone's group called this action "unconstitutional" and retaliated by announcing that the AWSA would hold its 1870 convention in New York City. The abyss yawned wide. There was no way left to bridge it.

And so, as the NWSA held its convention at Apollo Hall in New York early in May, the AWSA held a simultaneous meeting in the same city at Steinway Hall. The New England visitors attracted large audiences and a favorable press; the New York group was ill attended and largely ignored. The NWSA meeting had barely convened on the second day when a resolution was put forth that, since the AWSA had chosen Beecher as president, Stanton and Anthony should resign their offices and a "popular man" should lead them. The two women had no choice but to agree. Stanton, who blamed men for her subjection, yielded control to a man. Theodore Tilton was elected president. Henry Ward Beecher and Theodore Tilton were now presidents of rival organizations. Tilton wrote Beecher a congratulatory letter and requested "mutual co-operation in the cause of woman's enfranchisement." Beecher responded with a cordial but noncommittal note. Both letters were a sham.

*The Revolution* too had lost ground to *Woman's Journal* and was beset by financial problems. Anthony spent much of her time trying to raise money, but she was overwhelmed. She hoped that Anna Dickinson, whose huge lecture fees had made her rich, would take over the editorship of *The Revolution.* "If Anna Dickinson will be sole editor, I say Glory to God! . . . Tell our glorious little Anna if she only will nail her colors to that mast and make the dear old proprietor free once more, I will sing her praises till the end of time." But Anna, on the road lecturing with Wendell Phillips, declined. Finally, Theodore Tilton arranged for *The Revolution* to be sold for a token payment of $1 to the heiress Laura Curtis Bullard, with whom he had carried on a long-term love affair and who remained completely under his spell. Anthony wrote in her diary that giving up her paper "was like signing my own death-warrant" and added, "I feel a great calm sadness like that of a mother binding out a dear child that she could not support." Laura Curtis Bullard inaugurated her editorship with a lavish reception at the Brooklyn house she had purchased to be near Tilton. And Tilton wrote to Anna Dickinson, "The Revolution is (as perhaps you have heard) in what is equivalent to my own hands, 'To have and to hold.' "

Although Stanton railed against the AWSA, calling its members "sick unto death with propriety," and Anthony declared, "What an iceberg is that Boston, God help them to their live senses—nothing human can," there was no doubt that the AWSA was triumphant. It now signed up men and women in twenty-two states and territories. In the first six months of 1870, thirteen state suffrage associations affiliated themselves with the AWSA, and only a branch in Wisconsin went to the NWSA.

William Lloyd Garrison went so far as to write that Stanton had become a "female demagogue" and that she and Anthony were both "untruthful, unscrupulous and selfishly ambitious." Their "old friends" had deserted them. Years later, Stanton was to write that only a few "stood firmly together under a steady fire of ridicule and reproach even from their lifelong friends . . . and most of the liberals in the press. The position of the women seemed so untenable to the majority that at times a sense of utter loneliness and desertion made the bravest doubt the possibility of maintaining the struggle of making themselves fairly understood." But Stanton had said what was needed in these desperate times was "a new evangel of womanhood" and, as if the spirits themselves had intervened, Victoria Woodhull had announced, "I am the evangel."

# CHAPTER NINETEEN

# YOUR CHILD IS NOT MY CHILD

JULY 4, 1870: The wiry Bowen and the plump Beecher were encased to the waist in the burlap potato sack. "One, two, three—jump," shouted Beecher as the two former adversaries hopped across the Woodstock Common. The crowd cheered as the mismatched pair crossed the chalk line to win the sack race. John Tasker Howard ran up to hug both men. These new allies were warmed by the sun, by the adulation of the crowd, and by the presence of their illustrious guest, President Ulysses S. Grant—in short, by their burgeoning power.

EVER SINCE HENRY Bowen had tried to drive Henry Ward Beecher from Plymouth Church four years earlier and Beecher had retaliated by cutting off Bowen's political patronage, they had been bitter enemies. Though Bowen missed no opportunity to slander Beecher, he had done little to hurt him. Six months before this Independence Day celebration, Bowen had tried to strengthen his hand by buying control of the *Brooklyn Daily Union,* a small-circulation Republican newspaper, and appointing Tilton editor. With this paper added to the popular *Independent,* Bowen hoped not only to influence the people of Brooklyn, but to enrich himself further by supporting candidates who could repay him with patronage. But in a surprise move Samuel Wilkeson, on behalf of Jay Cooke, teamed up with John Tasker Howard, and purchased a newspaper for Henry Ward Beecher. The paper, named the *Church Union,* was promptly renamed the *Christian Union* to broaden its scope. Henry enlisted his famous sisters, Harriet and Catharine, as well as his brothers, Edward and William, to write for his paper and began successfully competing with Bowen and Tilton for subscribers.

Beecher was clearly regaining his power, and it was his Republican faction, not Bowen's, that was fast becoming Brooklyn's dominant political force. Until 1868, the federal government and the state legislature had controlled the patronage in the city of Brooklyn. The latter had passed a bill to transform Fourth Avenue into a boulevard and another to improve Third Street, work that had cost $600,000 in taxpayer money over the previous eight years and was still far from finished. In the election of 1868, by campaigning against the corrupt state legislature, the Democrats won every office by a vast majority—in fact, 110 percent of the registered voters. District Attorney Morris, a Democrat, was called in to conduct an investigation into illegal voting. Though few anticipated that he would find wrongdoing in his own party, Morris obtained sixty indictments. The Democratic Party then released papers showing that Morris himself was drawing the salary of a nonexistent clerk in his office. The indictments were dropped, but the people of Brooklyn had become disillusioned with Democratic rule. The Brooklyn Republicans won the next election by a wide margin, and Plymouth Church provided a powerful political base for them.

In the previous three years, a group of Republicans had joined Plymouth Church and were now so close to their preacher that they were known as "Beecher's boys." These were not religious parishioners but ambitious politicians. They had been able to join the church because Beecher had nullified the requirement that applicants must subscribe to the Articles of Faith. Newcomers merely had to express a "desire" to become a "Christian" for admission to his flock. Among this group was Benjamin Tracy, a pugnacious lawyer who was appointed United States district attorney in 1870, as a reward for his loyalty to the Republican machine. Tracy was well suited to replace Tilton as Beecher's acolyte. He believed that personal loyalty and friendship superseded all moral principles and declared, "Lying in defense of a good friend is justified." Tracy organized the Republican members of Plymouth Church into a tight, effective group.

While the Beecher-Tracy contingent was popular with the federal government, Bowen was not. The problem was Theodore Tilton. Bowen had promised Grant his full cooperation and yet, under Tilton's leadership, his newspapers had become hostile to the president. Tilton had praised Grant's inaugural address but soon began to sour on the new administration, attacking its corruption both in the *Independent* and the *Brooklyn Daily Union*. He wrote that Grant dispensed his vast political patronage to "second rate people" and accepted money and favors in return. Tilton also censured the president for failing to bring peace to the South and for his tardiness in suppressing the activities of the Ku Klux Klan. He wrote that the Republican Party was indifferent to the Negro question. "If we do not educate the Negro into the fabric of our society, we will be paying the penalty for generations to come," Tilton warned. In December 1869, he even went so far as to recommend impeaching the Supreme Court for failing to uphold the Civil Rights Act.

Henry Bowen suffered on another front as well: Samuel Wilkeson was not only Henry Ward Beecher's friend and supporter but also the chief agent for Jay Cooke's Northern Pacific Railroad. In 1869, with the granting of the railroad's charter, 47 million acres of land had fallen into Cooke's hands. Wilkeson, sent on a reconnaissance trip to the West, had written Cooke, "There is no end to the possibilities of wealth here. . . . Jay, we have got the biggest thing on Earth. Our enterprise is an inexhaustible gold mine." With the generous government grants and subsidies, and the army taking care of the "Indian question," the Northern Pacific promised vast rewards.

Wilkeson understood that the merits of the great railroad must be sold to the American people for the government grants to continue. Cooke gave Wilkeson virtual carte blanche to bribe influential members of the press with free Northern Pacific stock. Beecher was given $15,000 worth of stock for the purpose of "influencing the public mind to favor the new railroad" in his newspaper, and Horace Greeley received $20,000 worth on the same premise. However, when Wilkeson approached Theodore Tilton, he flatly refused the gift, saying, "I am a poor man, but my principles are not for sale." When Bowen made an appointment to see Sam Wilkeson and asked that he too be given Northern Pacific stock, Wilkeson answered that Tilton had refused to promote Northern Pacific stock in the *Independent* and had said he might even investigate whether the railroad bonds were worth the price they were selling for. Since Bowen could not control his own editor, said Wilkeson, how could he expect to be given stock?

Adding to his dilemma, Bowen had married a young woman who complained bitterly that her social life had been ruined because Henry Ward Beecher clearly avoided the Bowens and other church members had followed suit. Without the benevolence of Plymouth's pastor, the Bowens had become political and social pariahs.

It was then that Bowen saw a way to weaken Tilton's position. He volunteered to pay all of Tilton's expenses as long as he remained on the road, lecturing or writing for Bowen's newspapers. Then, with Tilton sidetracked, Bowen made a bold move to recapture the patronage that had once enriched him. He sent his nephew Henry A. Bowen, a major Grant supporter, to Washington to see the president and tell him that his uncle was now in complete control of both the *Independent* and the *Brooklyn Daily Union,* and that

Theodore Tilton was merely an employee. Young Bowen told the president that both newspapers would fully support him, and he invited Grant to spend the Fourth of July weekend at his uncle's estate in Woodstock, New York. Grant accepted.

Once this was accomplished, Bowen sent a message to Beecher and his backers, Sam Wilkeson and John Howard, saying that they were all men of influence and adding that the president was shortly to arrive as his guest. If they could be reunited, he would be pleased to invite them as guests as well. A meeting followed, and when Bowen entered, he walked over to Beecher and embraced him, saying, "My friend, the time has come for us to forget all our differences." "Yes," Beecher replied, his eyes misting with tears, "we must be friends. There must be no break between us. It would kill me." Bowen then declared that if the breach caused by Tilton could be mended, together they might control the entire Republican Party in Brooklyn. After the meeting Bowen, Beecher, and Howard walked the streets of Brooklyn, their arms linked as they recalled how twenty-three years before they had conceived the blessed Plymouth Church.

And so by noon on July 4, 1870, as the threatening skies cleared, thousands gathered on the Woodstock Common awaiting a glimpse of Ulysses S. Grant, the first presidential visitor since George Washington. One by one the dignitaries took their places on a platform wrapped with red, white, and blue bunting. One speaker followed another, and it was almost two o'clock when General Stewart L. Woodford began to speak. By this time, no matter how momentous the occasion, the crowd was hungry and restless. Woodford's voice was so low that few could hear him, and most only saw him wildly waving his arms. Occasionally a shrill phrase, "on this our glorious anniversary," "the dear old flag," or "Fathers of the Republic," would float forward. President Grant, the *Times* noted, sat "like a mummy in a little chair and seemed in profound thought." The crowd began talking and jeering and kept it up until Woodford sat down. Beecher stood and called out, "Hey. See here. I want you boys to quiet down. It isn't a square thing to make all that noise." The audience fell silent and then began to chant, "Beecher, Beecher, Beecher." When the preacher spoke, there was no movement in the crowd, and when Beecher referred to Grant as "our greatest warrior, our greatest president," Grant "brightened and smiled."

The Russian minister Baron De Catacazy spoke last, after which Henry Bowen called for three cheers for the emperor of Imperial Russia. The ceremony concluded with the singing of "The Star Spangled Banner." Then four hundred dignitaries and their wives repaired to Bowen's mansion for a late lunch, after which the ladies played croquet and the men conducted various competitions, including the sack race. United with Beecher, Bowen had won not only the sack race but also a prominent position in the race for political power and patronage.

THE MATCHED GRAY horses charged through the black night, but no night was as black as the darkness in Lib Tilton's soul. When the carriage stopped at 174 Livingston Street, Brooklyn, she alighted and stood for a minute clutching her silk shawl about her shoulders and gazing up at the room on the second floor in which baby Paul had died. Perhaps if he had lived she would not be facing this night and the darkness within her. Another son, Ralph, had his first birthday on June 20, just two weeks before, but even this baby had not erased the pain of Paul's loss.

With a heavy tread, she mounted the stairs to the room where her husband sat at his desk under the gaslight, absorbed in his writing. Theodore Tilton, whose controversial views were well known, had not been invited to Woodstock. He imagined Lib to be, as usual, in Schoharie with the children to avoid the July heat. What impelled her sudden return was not immediately apparent. Lib bent forward to kiss his cheek. Noting her husband's surprise, she explained, "I have come to tell you a secret I have long kept in my heart, a secret I resolved to tell you but lacked the courage."

Then sinking to her knees before her husband she implored, "Before I speak I wish your solemn word to do no harm to the person concerning whom this secret is to be told." Bewildered, Theodore Tilton agreed. Lib wrapped her arms around her knees and, swaying back and forth, told the details of "a passionate fondness" for Henry Ward Beecher that had become a full-blown sexual affair. Theodore questioned his wife closely: Why had she never told him of this affair? Why was she telling him now? Lib replied that she was consumed with guilt and remorse and that in the past few weeks the burden had become too much to bear. What she did not mention was that she was pregnant again and that her husband would realize that this time the child could not be his. Theodore Tilton had been away on a four-month Lyceum tour when her "love babe," as she called it, was conceived.

When Lib's confession was over, Tilton grabbed his hat and coat and stormed out of the house feeling "just blasted." He went to his office at the *Brooklyn Daily Union* and remained there for three days of soul-searching. He was later to say that after that "purging" he emerged "light-headed— ready to forgive." Unable to change his vision of his wife as pure, Tilton rationalized that her affair must have been prompted by "high religious love. I think she sinned as one in a trance. I don't think she was a free agent." He determined to make only one demand: that Lib tell her seducer that her husband knew about the affair but would keep it secret. Tilton was so struck by his own "magnanimity" that later he said, "For the following two weeks I lived a kind of ecstasy."

After those two weeks, Tilton decided that the open marriage he enjoyed should extend to his wife as well. They would be "loving friends," both free to pursue their "affinities" should any arise. With that Theodore piled his wife into a carriage and took her around to meet Laura Curtis Bullard, so that Laura could hear of the new arrangement from Lib's own lips. Soon after, Mrs. Bullard became a frequent visitor to the Tilton household and Lib's closest friend. Theodore told associates that his wife was "as advanced in her social theories as myself."

Even though Tilton and Beecher were presidents of rival woman suffrage organizations and politically at odds, their personal relationship seemed restored. Once again the Reverend Beecher was welcomed into the Tiltons' household. Theodore encouraged his wife to take an "affinity . . . to save her health and life." One day when Beecher visited, after a few minutes of conversation he asked Lib to accompany him on a carriage ride. When she declined, her husband "playfully reproached her," declaring that she should go, that the air would do her good and certainly she was entitled to some "private time." And so she went. But this exercise in free love lasted only three months. One evening in October, as Lib ascended the staircase her husband looked at her thickening body with a sudden realization. "It is his!" he shouted. His wife trembled but did not reply.

The next day Stanton and Anthony came to Brooklyn to meet with Tilton. In the afternoon Stanton accompanied him to the new offices of *The Revolution,* which he and Laura Curtis Bullard now edited, and then to Mrs. Bullard's house for dinner. As the meal progressed, Tilton, wineglass in hand, became increasingly agitated and finally exploded: "Henry Ward Beecher, that abominable man, has ruined my life. Oh, that the damned lecherous scoundrel should have defiled my bed and at the same time professed to be my best friend." Tilton said that he could accept free love, that he had confessed his own infidelities to his wife and there was no jealousy. Was not Mrs. Bullard now his wife's best friend? Under these circumstances he expected that Lib would confess her infidelities to him. But her unexpected pregnancy struck him with full force. "Had he come to me like a man and confessed his guilt, I could perhaps have ignored it, but to have him creep like a snake into my house and I so blind as not to see. . . . Oh, it is too much." Stanton recalled that she had never seen "such a manifestation of mental agony. He seemed upon the very verge of insanity."

It was eleven-thirty when Tilton returned home to find his wife and Susan B. Anthony waiting for him in the parlor. Lib jumped to her feet and dashed across the room, planting her scant five feet before his six-foot-three-inch frame, as if to block his entrance. She berated him for not picking them up for dinner as he had promised. Tilton looked genuinely surprised. "Was I to take you?" he asked.

"Liar!" screamed Lib.

"Your child is not my child. I don't know who my children belong to," Tilton cried out in an anguished reply. Then with a swift gesture he struck Lib full across the face.

Lib dashed up the stairs and into her bedroom with Anthony following behind. No sooner had Anthony locked the door than Tilton turned the knob, pounding and shouting, "Let me in, let me in."

"You're insane!" screamed Lib.

"Open up, or I'll break it down."

Anthony moved toward the door. "I will not turn this key," she announced. At that moment she felt that Tilton might kill his wife.

"No woman shall stand between me and my wife," yelled Tilton.

"If you enter this room it will be over my dead body!" Anthony shouted back.

There was silence, and then they heard Theodore's footsteps retreating. Frightened by what might happen next, Lib and Susan pushed the bed against the door in case he tried to break in. After an hour or so the two women were so tired that they climbed into bed together and Lib, snuggling close to Susan, poured out the details of her love affair with her "God and preacher," Henry Ward Beecher. She said it was her husband who had set her on the path to free love. Theodore had promised to forgive and forget, but her pregnancy had shattered that hope. He'd taken money from the mouths of their children to pay for an abortion at Madame Restell's for some girl he'd gotten pregnant. Now he wanted her to abort Beecher's baby. She knew that her "love babe" was in danger.

"Did the Reverend Beecher use force in having you yield to his advances?" asked Susan, trying to comfort this distraught and fragile woman.

"No. He treated me with the kindness one would a child. I resolved many times to yield no more, but as often my good resolutions failed."

"Is Beecher aware that your husband knows of this affair?"

"No," replied Lib. She told Anthony that her husband's one request was that she tell Beecher but that she couldn't bring herself to do it. She admitted that she had invented excuses because it was "so difficult to say." First he had been away on vacation and then when he came back Theodore had welcomed him into the household, and things seemed calm once again. But now she could not hide her pregnancy and she did not know what to do. She told Susan that were it not for the children and the fact that she had no means to support herself, she would leave Theodore forever. She wanted to run away, but where could she go? Then, abruptly, as if she realized there was no escape, she sat up and reached for her robe. "I think I'd better go to him and apply cool water to his head," she said. "It will soothe him."

"No," directed Anthony, "you are not to leave this room. It is not safe."

In the morning, the three assembled for breakfast. Theodore spoke not a word through the entire meal. When it was over, he looked at Anthony and said in a voice brimming with hatred, "Never enter my house again."

"I shall enter whenever I choose," Anthony shot back. But she never came again. And, she confided to her diary: "It is almost an impossibility for a man and a woman to have a close, sympathetic friendship without the tendrils of one soul being fastened around the other, with the result of infinite pain and anguish."

Elizabeth Cady Stanton had spent the night at Laura Bullard's. When she returned to her home in Tenafly, New Jersey, Stanton found Anthony sitting on her doorstep. Susan scolded her for forgetting that Mrs. Bullard's dinner invitation had included herself and Mrs. Tilton and then told her about the terrible events of the previous night. "Fresh with astonishment," they compared notes. Stanton said, "Theodore related a very strange story to Mrs. Bullard and me last evening." After she had heard the details, Anthony replied, "Mrs. Tilton told essentially the same thing to me."

Under the circumstances, it was no wonder that the Tiltons wanted privacy, but it was just at this time that Lib's mother, the volatile Mrs. Morse, asked to live with them. The Honorable Nathaniel B. Morse had withstood his wife's violent temper long enough. After she came at him one night brandishing a carving knife, he determined to divorce her. When Tilton told Mrs. Morse that she could not live with them, she turned on her son-in-law with rage, calling him "a scoundrel" and saying that his debts piled up while her poor daughter, humiliated by her "skinflint of a husband," scrimped along mending clothes.

As Mrs. Morse's fury mounted, she mentioned what Tilton later described as "my liaison with Mrs. Tilton's most intimate and honored friend," and accused him of spending time with that "vile woman" and of helping her with *The Revolution,* which paid him not a penny. "All these woman's rights people, these free lovers, you put upon my child."

"Madam," warned Tilton, "speak respectfully of the master of this house and of his guests or leave now. As for good behavior, in this respect I hold your daughter responsible."

An incredulous Mrs. Morse turned to Lib. "Why? What have *you* done, my child? Have *you* been doing wrong?"

The abruptness of the question rendered Lib mute. Without answering, she left the room. Mrs. Morse ran after her, shouting, "Is it Beecher? Is it Beecher? Is it Beecher?" over and over. Lib stopped still, then slowly turned toward her mother, hung her head, and nodded.

"Oh, my God!" cried Mrs. Morse. Flying to her daughter's defense, she turned on Tilton: "If you had gone for your family instead of looking after woman's rights meetings, you would not be obliged to look up your lost trunk!"

"Leave my house!" bellowed Tilton in return.

Mrs. Morse then struck him repeatedly with her parasol, shouting, "Woman's rights have killed you!"

The following morning, Lib Tilton packed her bags and without a word fled to Marietta, Ohio, to the home of friends. From there she wrote,

Oh Theodore, Theodore!

What shall I say to you? My tongue and pen are dumb and powerless but I must force my aching heart to protest against your cruelty. . . . Do you not know that you are fulfilling your threat that "I shall no longer be considered the saint"? Do you not know, also, that when in any circle you blacken Mr. B's name—and soon after couple mine with it—you blacken mine as well?

Theodore, *your past* is safe with me, rolled up, put away never to be opened—though it is big with stains of various hue—unless you force me for the sake of my children and friends to discover it, in self-defense or their defense. . . . Would *you* suffer were I to cast a shadow on any lady whom you love? . . . . Once again I implore you for your children's sake, to whom you have a duty in this matter, that *my past* be buried—left with me and my God. He is merciful. Will you, His son, be like Him?

I feel that you are not in the condition of mind to lead the woman suffrage movement, and I implore you to break away from it and from your friends Susan, Mrs. Stanton and every one and every thing that helps to make a conflict with your responsibilities as husband and father.

Tilton was at his office at the *Brooklyn Daily Union* when his wife's letter arrived. He read it twice over and then burned it. It did not occur to him that she had made a copy and had sent it to her mother. Lib returned to 174 Livingston Street on November 9, to find that Theodore's rage had not abated. When she entered the library, he said, "So the harlot has returned!" Pointing to the red velvet chaise longue by the fireplace, he exclaimed, "This has been consecrated to sexual intercourse between you and Reverend Beecher. Our daughter Florry knows. She asked me about it. I can stay here no longer." He promptly left for Frank Moulton's house.

Tilton next resigned from Plymouth Church. Jealousy aside, his views had become too radical for Beecher's church. He now espoused Stanton's views of marriage and carried them one better. In view of his own experience, he wrote an article in the *Independent* titled "Love, Marriage and Divorce."

> Marriage without love is a sin against God—a sin which, like other sins, is to be repented of, ceased from and put away. No matter with what solemn ceremony the twain may have been made one, yet, when love departs, then marriage ceases and divorce begins. This is the essence of Christ's idea. To say that He granted divorce only for a gross and fleshly crime is to forget that He called the eye a paramour and the heart of wanton's bed.

On December 3, 1870, Laura Curtis Bullard put her pen to paper as well and asserted that woman suffrage was dead as a political movement and that the right to divorce was much more important.

> Women know their own wants, and they know that they do not want suffrage a thousandth part as keenly as they want a reform of the marriage and divorce laws, and a general readjustment of the family relations. . . . What a woman wants is freedom to marry and to be mistress of herself after marriage; freedom to freely sunder a yoke she has freely bound.

Lucy Stone and many other women were shocked that Tilton and Bullard, in their espousal of free love, had abandoned the cause of woman's rights. Moreover, Mrs. Morse was now convinced that Tilton planned to divorce her daughter and elope to Europe with Mrs. Bullard. Without her daughter's knowledge she consulted her own divorce lawyer to see what settlement could be made in such an event. She reasoned that Henry Ward Beecher was the most powerful of men, and if he was as truly devoted to her daughter as he professed, could he not become her discreet companion and give her "the comfort of a paramour"?

Bessie Turner, a fifteen-year-old who had come to the Tiltons as a servant but had become Lib's ward, was dispatched to the Beechers' home to implore the preacher to visit Mrs. Tilton. As instructed by Mrs. Morse, Bessie recited a litany of Theodore Tilton's cruelties toward his wife and added that when Lib was gone, Theodore had tried to seduce her but that Bessie had rebuffed him.

Beecher appeared the next morning. He sat next to Lib. Mrs. Morse, who did most of the talking, sat facing them. "You are about to hear of cruelties beyond imagining," she began and then matter-of-factly told Beecher that Tilton came home drunk at night and frequently knocked his wife to the floor with his fist and kicked her. He was subject to uncontrollable rages. When on the road he held orgies with "strange women." "My daughter has lived a life of great unhappiness and has been subject to great cruelty and deprivation. Her life with Mr. Tilton has become intolerable."

What Beecher said next filled Lib with dread: "This is a case in which I feel a man cannot give the best counsel. It is a case, it seems to me, where a woman is needed. If you will allow me, I shall be glad to bring my wife and let her hear, for I think much of her judgment about such things."

Mrs. Morse sprang to her feet. "I will bless her if she will come. Bless her as long as I live."

As Beecher was leaving, Mrs. Morse explained in a hurried whisper Lib's so-called embarrassing condition. In an odd turnabout reflecting the morality of the day, she blamed her daughter for Beecher's having seduced her. "She is mourning for *her sin*," Mrs. Morse intoned. The preacher put his arm around Mrs. Morse's shoulder and said, "You must call me 'Son,' and I will call you 'Mother.'" And then he confirmed Lib's fear that her baby might be snatched from her by assuring Mrs. Morse that he personally would provide the money to see that her "darling" received the proper medical attention.

Beecher returned the next day with his wife, Eunice, who listened to Mrs. Morse's complaints of Theodore's inhumanity to his wife. Of course, there was no mention that Lib was pregnant with the child of Eunice's husband and that this was the reason for Theodore Tilton's behavior. When

Mrs. Morse was through, Eunice, who was greatly touched, turned to her and said of Lib, "I shall adopt your poor daughter." The following morning, as the Beechers sat across from each other at the breakfast table, Eunice told her husband that she had been up most of the night thinking about poor Mrs. Tilton's suffering. She must separate herself from that irresponsible villain.

Hardly looking up from his newspaper, Henry commented, "It is a drastic step."

"Were she my daughter, I would say, 'Separate,' " insisted Eunice. "He will drag her down and disgrace her." Then Henry casually reached for a scrap of paper, scribbled some words, and pushed them across the table to his wife. The note read, "I incline to think that your view is right and that a separation and settlement of support will be wisest—Henry Ward Beecher."

"Is this all right?" he asked. And when Eunice said yes, he instructed, "Bring it round for me then."

NOW BEGAN Lib Tilton's bleak December days, liquid gray days that ran together with no beginning or end. She was more than five months pregnant and it was becoming more difficult to conceal the life within her. She sent Florry, Alice, Carroll, and baby Ralph to her mother's. She sent the servants away. The house fell silent. There was no fire in the grate, no food in the larder. Her unborn child, the proof of her infidelity, had caused "all this torture and embarrassment and humiliation," yet she wanted this "love babe." At night when no one could see her shame, Lib, feeling "that there was no place for my head in that doomed house," would wander the streets of Brooklyn wearing a hooded cloak. She returned at dawn "to creep into the basement and lie down anywhere, feeling utterly wretched."

When Mrs. Beecher brought the note from her husband, Lib Tilton knew full well that the life she carried within her was about to be expunged. No one wanted it—not her husband, or her preacher, or his wife, that beetle-browed woman who called her "daughter." One morning she felt an uncontrollable urge to flee. She dressed quickly and ran down the steep steps of the Livingston Street house, turning her back on that place with its memories of infidelity and death. For hours Lib Tilton wandered the streets. How could she run away? Where would she go? Later, in a stumbling, lame explanation she would say, "I thought I would never come back, but then, you see, I found that I had left my purse at home and so of course I had to return. You see I had to."

On the eighth, or perhaps the tenth day of her isolation, for she had lost track of the days, she saw that the sky was clear and a light snow had descended. Once more she donned her cloak and pulled the hood over her head to conceal her face. Now Lib knew where she was going. A man driving a wagonload of wood saw her trudging along the muddy road. She shook her head "no" to his offer of a ride. At noon she arrived at the Greenwood Cemetery and made her way to the place where her children, Paul and Mattie, were buried in the frozen earth. "Such tiny graves," she thought, and sank to her knees, then spread her body across the cold earth as if to warm the graves of her children. She lay there "and felt peace." She knew not how long it was before she felt a rough hand grasp her shoulder. "Get up, girl," commanded the groundskeeper. "There's no place for you here." Lib did not move. "Get up, do you hear me!" he said, and began to shake her.

Lib Tilton stood. "If there is one spot on earth that is mine, it is these two graves," she said. The groundskeeper regarded her soberly, then removed his hat and bowed his head. "I did not know they were yours," he said. He turned and left. Lib recalled, "I stayed there lying on the little graves all the rest of the day."

*The entrance to Greenwood Cemetery*

# CHAPTER TWENTY

# THE YAWNING
# EDGE OF HELL

Henry Bowen threw a copy of the *Brooklyn Daily Union* on the desk and demanded of his editor, "What is the meaning of this?"

"Of what?" Tilton asked.

"Of this line, 'Let General Grant when he is smoking his cigar think over this matter.' I never smoked a cigar in my life, sir, and if any one of my sons were to smoke I would disown him."

"Everybody knows that General Grant smokes," replied Tilton wearily.

"That may be," shouted Bowen, "but I will not have them know it through the *Union!*"

Bowen was furious with Tilton. Ever since the Fourth of July celebration when he had entertained Grant, Bowen had tried to no avail to persuade Tilton to support the president in the *Brooklyn Daily Union.* Making him the editor had been a miscalculation. "If anybody in King's County expects to see the *Union* consenting to be chained like a coach dog to the Republican or any other party, he is woefully mistaken," Tilton wrote, and pledged himself to expose corruption at all levels of government. His paper advocated the nomination in both parties of more able men who would not tolerate such scandals as Black Friday and the Tweed ring, which he called "the curse of two great cities."

Bowen was a partner in several warehousing operations with Erastus D. Webster, who was in charge of the Brooklyn Navy Yard and its various activities. When Webster received the regular Republican nomination to fill a vacant seat in Congress in an interim election for the Third District of Brooklyn, Bowen promised him the support of his two newspapers. However, in a meeting in Bowen's office, Tilton told Webster that he had no intention of supporting him. Webster turned to Bowen: "I understand what Mr. Tilton is saying, but with your assistance I think . . ."

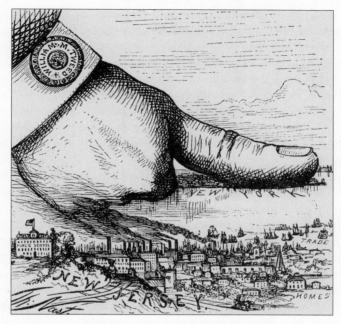

*Boss Tweed's New York by Thomas Nast*

"Address yourself to me, sir," Tilton interrupted. "Mr. Bowen has no more charge over this newspaper's opinions than you have."

Tilton attacked Webster in print as "a corrupt dispenser of federal patronage." Across the East River, New York City seethed with corruption, and Tilton, fearing that the same thing was about to happen in Brooklyn, joined with a group of young idealists who called themselves liberal Republicans. They nominated their own candidate, W. A. Fowler, to oppose Webster, and Tilton agreed to support Fowler in the pages of the *Brooklyn Daily Union.* For Bowen this was the last straw. He called Tilton into his office and told him, "I will not mince words. In the future the *Independent* and the *Brooklyn Daily Union* must support my candidate."

"I will not agree to that," Tilton replied.

"Then I surmise the only way for me to obtain the backing I want would be to dismiss my editor."

"Yes, but that is the only way," said Tilton.

That would not be easy: In the nine years since Tilton had taken over as editor of the *Independent,* the annual revenues from subscriptions and advertising had almost tripled, from $91,733 to $300,305. It had become the most popular and influential religious weekly in the nation, claiming more than half a million readers. On December 19, 1870, Henry Bowen found a way around the problem: He told Tilton that he was taking over the editorship of the *Independent* himself but would pay Tilton $5,000 a year as a contributor. Tilton would continue as editor of the *Brooklyn Daily Union* at a yearly salary of $7,000. Tilton also was guaranteed a minimum of $3,000 a year in bonuses. Tilton's former annual salary of $10,000 would now be increased by half. Implicit in this new contract, at least in Bowen's mind, was that the increase would buy loyalty.

A meeting of the Republican general committee was scheduled for the evening of December 21. That morning the *Independent* carried two notices: one that Henry Bowen had become its editor and another stating that the *Independent* was endorsing Erastus D. Webster for Congress. At seven o'clock that evening Bowen marched into the meeting confident that he would recapture his former patronage. But as the meeting progressed, Bowen was astounded to find that the Beecher contingent, headed by United States District Attorney Benjamin Tracy, would not support him and instead had allied themselves with Tilton's liberal Republicans and the Democrats. Together they were supporting Fowler to crush Webster and gain control of Brooklyn.

A motion was put before the general committee to endorse Fowler. When Bowen objected, he was shouted down. Then Benjamin Tracy read a report he had prepared asserting that when Henry Bowen was tax collector, he had placed Brooklyn's funds in a personal bank account for months at a time, defrauding the city of the interest. Colonel Morton, another member of Plymouth Church, moved that Bowen be brought up on charges of tax fraud.

A furious Bowen countercharged that Tracy was making this accusation so that his own group would "control patronage," thereby admitting that he himself sought that control. Oliver Worth, a blacksmith on Bowen's payroll, argued with Colonel Morton, who suddenly "bolted across the room and struck Worth a tremendous blow in the face." A melee ensued—chairs were thrown into the crowd, and four enraged men seized Bowen and began beating him. "Fists flew and heavy knocks fell thick and fast. . . . Men struggled and clenched and confusion prevailed until the lights were put out and the whole business brought to a close by the intervention of the police," read a report in the *Brooklyn Eagle*. A bruised Bowen went home to bed. The following day he received written notification from the general committee that it had expelled him. Once again, Henry Bowen had tumbled from power.

ON THE MORNING of December 23, according to a later account in the *Sun,* Mrs. Theodore Tilton, escorted by her mother and Bessie Turner, was seen entering and leaving the Fifth Avenue office of the abortionist Madame Restell. The article further alleged that money for an abortion had been provided by Henry Ward Beecher. When Emma Moulton arrived that afternoon to drop off some Christmas presents for the children, she found her friend Lib lying in bed, the sheets red with blood. Lib told her that she'd had a miscarriage as a result of the "anxiety night and day" created by her mother.

In the next room, Mrs. Morse sat at Greeley's desk, her fury flowing out through her pen. To Tilton she wrote,

> You infernal villain! This night you should be in jail. Your slimy, polluted, brawny hand curses everything you touch. . . . I will publish you from Dan to Beersheba. . . . I can with one stroke of my pen bring you to your knees and brand you for life. The world will be better for the riddance of such a villain and think no more of putting you aside than killing the meanest cur which runs in the street.

Next she wrote to Henry Ward Beecher, whom she addressed as "My Dear Son," reminding him that he had told her to call him by that name. "I told *darling* [Lib] I felt if you could, in safety to yourself and all concerned, you would be to me all this endearing name. Am I mistaken? Mother."

Her last letter was to her son-in-law's employer, Henry Bowen. In it she accused Theodore of being a free lover and informed Bowen that he was about to divorce her daughter and move to Europe with Mrs. Bullard. She concluded, "Of Theodore Tilton's infidelities Mrs. Beecher can enumerate them far better than I."

Bowen received Mrs. Morse's letter the day after Christmas. It gave him the excuse he had been seeking to get rid of Tilton. He summoned Theodore to his home on Willow Street and began to dress him down as a heathen, libertine, and drunkard. Bowen referred to the essay Tilton had written on "Love, Marriage and Divorce," saying that such blasphemy had no place in a religious publication. Bowen was clearly preparing to dismiss his editor. "I note, sir," he said, "that you have not attended church much lately."

Tilton replied, "Never again will I cross the threshold of Plymouth Church. And *you* better than any man living know why." Then he told Bowen how the Reverend Beecher had seduced Lib just as he had seduced Bowen's late wife, Lucy. Both men had been cuckolded.

Bowen once had hoped his knowledge of Beecher's adultery would give him power over the preacher, but then he saw that there was no way to destroy Beecher without injuring himself, his ten children, and their mother's memory. For eight long years he had watched helplessly as Beecher's wealth and popularity grew. In an instant Bowen changed direction: Perhaps Theodore Tilton would be the God-given instrument that finally would destroy Beecher, or failing that, these men might destroy each other, thus ridding him of two problems. "I cannot stand it any longer," Bowen declared. "You and I owe a duty to society in this matter. That man ought not to stay another week in his pulpit. It is not safe for our families to have him in this city. I challenge you as a matter of public duty to write an open letter."

Tilton agreed, and the two began to draw up a statement. "Sir, I demand you immediately cease from the ministry of Plymouth Church," Tilton wrote.

"And that he leave Brooklyn and his influence here behind," Bowen said.

"And that you quit the city of Brooklyn as a residence," Tilton wrote.

"Good, good," said Bowen. Then, pressing his advantage, he dictated, "And that you withdraw from the *Christian Union* and never again write for that publication nor have your sermons printed."

Tilton paused for a moment. He sensed something wrong. "No," he said, "I won't write that."

Bowen backed off, but suggested, "We must add the phrase 'for reasons which you explicitly understand.'" Tilton added that phrase and wrote the note anew.

> Sir,
>     I demand that for reasons which you explicitly understand you immediately cease from the ministry of Plymouth Church and that you quit the city of Brooklyn as a residence.

When it came to signing the letter, Bowen told Tilton that it should bear his signature alone. Again Tilton felt uneasy. Would such a demand be honored with only his signature? Bowen reassured him by saying that he would personally carry the letter to Beecher, sustain the charges, and produce the necessary documentation if called upon. And so Theodore Tilton signed the letter and gave it to Henry Bowen.

When Tilton returned home, he was surprised to find Frank Moulton, whose wife had come to relieve Lib's nurse, in the parlor. When Tilton told his friend what had just occurred, Moulton instantly understood that Bowen was using Tilton to accomplish his own ends. "You made your demand all alone?" he asked incredulously.

"Bowen gave me his word he would sustain my charges."

"Oh, Theodore, you have left him a chance to play you a trick. You are a ruined man!"

Lib Tilton lay in bed, listlessly watching as her husband paced up and down, but she sat up abruptly when he told her of his ultimatum to Beecher. "If Mr. Bowen makes war on Mr. Beecher and if you join in it and if Mr. Beecher retires from his pulpit, as he must under such an attack, sooner or later everybody will know the reason why and that will be to my shame and to the children's shame. I cannot endure it!" To these men, infidelity was a pawn in the game of power and wealth but to Lib it was her life. "I have always been treated as a nonentity—a plaything—to be used or let alone at will. But it has always seemed to me I was a party not a little concerned," she later reflected. "Make peace," she implored her husband, "if not for me then for the love of your children."

Seeing her so desperate and knowing he had blundered, Theodore softened toward his wife: "Then you must write him telling him I know everything." Elizabeth propped herself up in bed and, calling for pen and paper, wrote Beecher what she had never been able to tell him, that her husband knew everything about their relationship. She ended her letter with a prayer for reconciliation between her preacher and her husband.

BOWEN HAD GONE immediately to Beecher's study at Plymouth Church with Tilton's letter demanding the preacher's resignation. Beecher read the demand and then sat silently, drumming his fingers on the arm of his chair. Finally, he looked at Bowen and said, "This is sheer insanity. The man is crazy." The demand did not refer to Beecher's affair with Mrs. Tilton, and Bowen realized that Beecher had no inkling Tilton knew of it.

"Have you any answer?" inquired Bowen.

Once again there was a long silence; then Beecher asked, "Where do you stand in this?"

*Frank (Francis De Pau) Moulton—*
*the mediator in this matter*

Knowing that his ploy to remove Beecher had failed, Bowen said, "Mr. Tilton has become your enemy, but I will be your friend."

"You are friendly toward me?" asked a skeptical Beecher.

"We have settled our differences," replied Bowen.

Bowen was ready to join the powers he could not defeat but wanted as much as possible in return. In a veiled manner, the negotiations began. Bowen assured Beecher that he had already removed Tilton as editor of the *Independent* and was ready to dismiss him altogether. "In my opinion you are correct," said Beecher. "A man as tainted as Tilton cannot properly be retained on the *Independent* without doing it damage." Beecher, whose own newspaper was threatened by Tilton's success, went even further: "With respect to Mr. Tilton's continued employment on the *Union*, I think that as the editor of the Republican organ in Brooklyn he will get the paper into trouble." Bowen nodded in assent.

The bargaining continued. On a small note card Bowen mapped out the price of his "friendship": His *Independent* would once again have the right to publish Beecher's sermons and lecture-room talks. Beecher would publicly announce at a Friday-night prayer meeting what an excellent man Bowen was, thereby restoring his social status. He would express his friendship to Bowen in a letter, which could be shown to President Grant if necessary. Beecher would retract what he had said to injure Bowen politically, and the tax fraud charge would be dropped. He would instruct Wilkeson and Howard to grant Bowen a free interest in the J. B. Ford syndicate, which owned Beecher's two-volume *The Life of Jesus the Christ* as well as a new edition of his sermons and hymns, thereby giving Bowen a financial incentive to protect Beecher's reputation.

And finally came the big reward: Beecher would have Wilkeson arrange to retain Bowen as an agent to sell Jay Cooke's new issue of Northern Pacific railroad bonds. That night Bowen left with his note card initialed by Beecher. There had been no mention of Beecher's affair with Mrs. Tilton. The interview had been "strictly business."

On December 29, 1870, Bowen received the following letter:

Dear Mr. Bowen,

The understanding between us whereby you fully and permanently identify yourself, your paper . . . and your nephew with the interest of the Northern Pacific Railroad Company is as follows: On your part you give . . . the exclusive interest and influence of your money columns and your editorial columns to the enterprise and bonds of the Northern Pacific Railroad Company. . . . On our part . . . we will advance you on January 2, 1871, $15,000 on the Northern Pacific bonds . . . and each month thereafter a sum of $10,000 is to be credited until the sum of $60,000 is thus earned.

Jay Cooke & Company

Tilton was at his desk at the *Brooklyn Daily Union* when he looked up to see Bowen. "I have determined to meet Mr. Beecher face to face—," he began.

With the passion of a man caught out, Bowen interrupted. "If you should inform Mr. Beecher of the allegations I have made concerning his adultery . . . or tell him I had anything to do with that letter, you will be cashiered from both my papers."

"I'll do just as I think best," Tilton answered coldly.

"Then you are finished," bellowed Bowen. "If you intimate I had any connection with this, I shall have you ejected from these offices by force. I shall cast you into the street."

Scarcely an hour later, a letter was delivered to Tilton's home canceling his contract both as a contributor to the *Independent* and as editor of the *Brooklyn Daily Union*.

FRIDAY, DECEMBER 30, 1870: The wind howled across Columbia Heights as parishioners alighted from their carriages and hurried into Plymouth Church for the weekly prayer meeting. Once inside, top hats and bonnets were removed and shaken; boots were stamped free of snow. Women's coats with ermine or fox trim were hung next to men's lined with beaver. Skates were hung on pegs by parishioners who had come from a nearby pond. Despite the weather the crowd was more than a hundred strong, for these Friday-night meetings were popular events. Henry Ward Beecher would sit in a commodious green-velvet armchair in the downstairs lecture room and converse with his parishioners about matters of the heart and soul. He improvised as he spoke, intoxicated by his own rhetoric, and he encouraged others to cross-examine him on any subject. The pastor cherished these meetings, for it was here that he came in personal contact with members of his flock. One of them described Beecher as "a sort of evangelical Bacchus."

Beecher had started down the stairs to the lecture room when Frank Moulton stepped forward and grasped his arm. "Mr. Beecher, Theodore Tilton is at my house and wishes to see you immediately."

Beecher pulled away, shaking off Moulton's hand. "This is Friday night. This is a prayer meeting night. Tell him I cannot go."

"He wants to see you in regard to a letter he sent you through Mr. Bowen."

Beecher seemed unimpressed. "Not now."

Moulton persisted. "There is a letter written by Mrs. Tilton in regard to your relations with her. Mr. Tilton, I believe, has his wife's full confession. I think you had better go."

Moulton watched Beecher's face flush. As Benjamin Tracy passed the two men on the stairs, the preacher called out to him, "Take the prayer meeting for me please, Ben," and silently followed Moulton from the church. Whirling snow surrounded them as they trudged, heads bent low, fighting the wind. "This is a terrible night. There is an appropriateness in this storm," muttered Beecher. "Has he truly got that confession?"

"He has, for I have seen it," answered Moulton.

"Oh, my God," said Beecher. "Where can I go? What can I do?"

"I don't know. I am not a Christian, I am a heathen, but I will try to help you."

Together they moved silently through the snow to Moulton's house. Tilton was waiting for Beecher in the upstairs parlor. As Beecher entered, Tilton locked the door, put the key in his pocket, and gestured to Beecher to sit down. Tilton remained standing. "I presume, sir, that you received from me, through Mr. Bowen, a letter demanding your retirement from your pulpit and from the city of Brooklyn," he said formally.

"Yes, I have received it," Beecher answered with equal formality.

"I called you here tonight in order to say you may consider that letter unwritten, unsent, blotted out!"

A look of relief passed over Beecher's face. "Thank you. Thank you, dear Theodore."

"Your thanks should not go to me but to Elizabeth. This meeting is not for your sake, nor for my sake, but for her sake. We must protect one another and make peace. But you must know that as for me not only have you injured me in my business relations but you have corrupted my wife, teaching her to lie, to deceive." He withdrew from his pocket Elizabeth's confession and began reading it aloud. Beecher's face and neck turned bloodred. "Theodore, I am in a dream—this is Dante's Inferno," he blurted out. "You have a right to kill me. I have forfeited my life to you. Take it."

"No," answered Tilton, "but you shall not walk serenely over this town while I go to work with sorrow and a sore heart every day. . . . Know that you are discovered."

Henry implored Theodore to give him permission to see Lib "for the last time," and Tilton acquiesced, telling him to come to his house later that evening but warning him, "See to it, sir, that you do not chide her for the confession she has made. For if you smite her with a word, I will smite you in ten-fold degree." With that, Tilton unlocked the door.

As Beecher staggered down the stairs clutching the banister, Frank Moulton, who was standing below, heard him mutter to himself, "This will kill me." When the dazed preacher walked through the front door without his coat, Moulton dashed out and covered him. Beecher was later to say that the news of Lib's confession "fell like a thunderbolt on me . . . I went forth like a sleepwalker while clouds were flying in the sky. The winds were out and whistling through the leafless trees, but all this was peace compared to my mood within."

When Beecher arrived at the Tiltons' house at eleven that evening, Bessie Turner led him to Lib's bedroom, where he found her lying "white as marble with closed eyes as in a trance, her hands upon her bosom, palm to palm as one in prayer." He pulled up a chair next to her bedside, reached out and took her hand in his, and then began to cry. Through his tears he observed the faintest quiver run through Lib's body. It seemed "as if she was going to die," he later said, yet his first thought was that he might be found responsible and "left by her death with this terrible assertion hanging over me."

"You have slain me. You have ended my usefulness," Beecher whispered in her ear.

Lib, who had been unable to resist her preacher while strong, was now without will. His words of persuasion took but little time. Then he gave her pen and paper, and as he held the inkwell for her, she wrote what he dictated. When Beecher left her chamber, the note was tucked firmly in his breast pocket:

> December 30, 1870
> Wearied with importunity and weakened by sickness I gave a letter implicating my friend Henry Ward Beecher under the assurances that that would remove all difficulties between me and my husband. That letter I now revoke. I was persuaded to it—almost forced—when I was in a weakened state of mind. I regret it and recall all its statements.
>
> E. R. Tilton

At midnight, the embers in the fireplace still glowed. The nurse, Lucy Mitchell, finally satisfied to hear Mrs. Tilton's even breathing, dozed off. She was awakened by a "buzzing sound." As Lib Tilton cowered in a corner of the bed, a frightened bird in a nest of rumpled sheets, her husband loomed above her. "This will never do, Mr. Tilton," said Lucy, rousing herself. "Mrs. Tilton is very ill, seriously ill, and must not be disturbed."

"Get out!" commanded Tilton. Lucy, seeing the look in his eyes, scrambled to obey. Outside the door she was unable to hear the exact words, but later said that Mr. Tilton was shouting and his wife was answering in a tone of entreaty. After some time, Theodore jerked open the door, and Lucy almost fell inside as he stormed past her. Lib Tilton was shaking uncontrollably. Lucy put a pillow under her to elevate her hips. She stroked her patient's head and repeated again and again, "There, there, dear!"

> December 30, 1870—Midnight
> My Dear Husband,
> I desire to leave with you, before going to bed, a statement that Mr. Henry Ward Beecher called upon me this evening, and asked me if

*Beecher directs Lib Tilton to write a letter retracting her confession of adultery.*

I would defend him against any accusation in a *Council of Ministers* and I replied solemnly that I would in case the accuser was any other person than my husband. He dictated a letter, which I copied as my own . . . designed to vindicate Mr. Beecher against all other persons save only yourself. . . . You and I are pledged to do our best to avoid publicity. God grant a speedy end to all further anxieties.

Affectionately, Elizabeth

The following day Mrs. Tilton summoned Frank Moulton to her bedside. She implored him to retrieve the letters she had written under duress the previous night, first for Beecher and then for her husband. "Burn them!" she begged.

ON NEW YEAR'S EVE, a gun tucked under his jacket for protection, Frank Moulton checked the warehouses of Woodruff & Robinson to make sure they were secured against holiday revelers. He then proceeded to Beecher's home to retrieve Mrs. Tilton's letter vindicating the preacher. He found him in his bedroom, staring out of the window at the river view. A weary Moulton removed his overcoat and placed his gun on a nearby bureau. Moulton explained that Theodore Tilton had given him a letter from Mrs. Tilton renouncing the letter Beecher had dictated to her. The only way this matter could be kept quiet was if all the letters were destroyed. He must hand over Mrs. Tilton's letter of retraction. Beecher later said he agreed to comply because he felt both endangered and conscience-stricken: "The case was strongly against me. My old fellow worker Tilton had been deprived of his eminent place and influence, and I had counseled it. His family had well nigh been broken up, and I had advised it. His wife had long been sick and broken in health and body, and I had been the cause of all this wreck." With the usual flood of tears, the preacher turned to Moulton: "I call upon you to save me. My life is ended." Then he walked to his desk, opened the drawer, and handed Moulton Lib's letter.

Beecher and Moulton had identical recollections of this conversation, but Beecher denied that he had also justified his behavior by saying to Moulton, "The red lounge on which we consummated our love was to me an almost sacred object. . . . My acts of intercourse with that woman were as natural and sincere an expression of my love for her as the words of endearment which I addressed to her. There seemed to be nothing in what we did together that I could not justify to myself on the ground of our love for each other and I think God will not blame me for my acts with her. I know that at present it would be utterly impossible for me to justify myself before man."

Moulton was to say that "this was impressed upon my mind because it was the first annunciation of the justification of the doctrine of free love that I had ever heard."

WITH A CLEAR SKY and the Brooklyn temperature at forty degrees, the year 1871 began. As Tilton sat at his desk writing a letter to Bowen denouncing his treachery, a few blocks away at 124 Columbia Heights, Henry Ward Beecher stood before a ten-foot Christmas tree. The Sunday-school children had decorated it with garlands of pine cones and holly and swags of brightly colored crocheted balls studded with cloves. The white lace table-cloths were heaped with pies, cookies, cakes iced in red and green, preserved fruits, and other sweetmeats. The piano tinkled out a series of hymns and popular tunes. For the first time in seven years, Henry Bowen and his young wife were invited to the reception. While his wife mingled happily with her friends as they compared Christmas gifts, Bowen drew Beecher aside and proudly told him he had followed the preacher's advice and fired Tilton from both of his newspapers. Beecher felt "a sudden stab." Events were becoming more and more complicated. Only two days before, this action would have been welcomed, but now it might precipitate a crisis.

Beecher hastily wrote a note to Frank Moulton asking him to come by as soon as possible. When Moulton arrived at seven, Beecher excused himself from the festivities and the two men went upstairs. What would happen now that Bowen had fired Tilton? Beecher asked. Would an enraged Theodore tell all? According to Moulton, he "buried his face in his hands and wept," saying "he had meditated suicide and could not live to face exposure. . . . He had wakened as from a sleep and likened himself to one sitting dizzy and distracted on the yawning edge of Hell." Beecher told Moulton that if the affair were to be revealed, he wanted "notice in advance so that he might take some measure, either by death or flight, to hide himself from the world's gaze." For the first time Beecher shifted the blame for all that had happened. "I don't understand how *she* could have done this to me," he complained.

"To avert the storm," Moulton suggested that Beecher write him a letter saying that he would resign as president of the AWSA, thereby eliminating one area of friction with Tilton, president of the NWSA. He told Beecher, "I know that Theodore loves his wife and will hesitate to bring his own family down." If Beecher apologized for his conduct, Moulton would carry his letter to Tilton, whose pride would be saved, and everything might be set aright. Too agitated to write, Beecher dictated the letter to Moulton and then signed it.

Brooklyn, January 1, 1871

My Dear Friend Moulton,

I ask through you Theodore Tilton's forgiveness, and I humble myself before him as I do before my God. He would have been a better man in my circumstances than I have been. I can ask nothing except that he will remember all the other breasts that would ache. I will not plead for myself. *I even wish that I were dead. . . .*

H. W. Beecher

# CHAPTER TWENTY-ONE

# THE WOODHULL
# MEMORIAL

"I SHALL GO TO the Washington convention to work, not to speak. Tilton should be secured by all means—his wife too. Our parlor needs her demure, motherly, angelic sweetness as much as our platform needs him. These little, quiet, domestic women are trump cards nowadays. I wish I had a whole pack of them," wrote Isabella Beecher Hooker to Susan B. Anthony in December 1870. Isabella, like almost all the Beechers, was an expert at telling other people how to behave. She was convinced that she could do a better job of running the National Woman Suffrage Association convention, scheduled for January 1871, than Stanton and Anthony, who she felt had become too controversial. When Isabella first proposed "taking the Washington convention into my own hands," a dispirited Stanton wrote to Anthony that she was ready to let Isabella do just that. "Let us exalt Mrs. Hooker, who thinks she could manage the cause more discreetly and more genteelly than we do. . . . I am ready to rest and see the salvation of the Lord."

In the preceding few months Stanton had withdrawn. "You know when I drop anything, I drop it absolutely," she wrote to Anthony. "You cannot imagine what a deep gulf lies between me and the past." She refused to cancel her lecture engagements in order to attend the Washington convention, but she did send Isabella $100 as a substitute for her presence. Mrs. Hooker was delighted, but Anthony "looked disgusted" and told her that Stanton "must appear before the congressional committees, at any rate." Isabella tactlessly wrote back to Stanton, "I don't know what to say. You will talk more forcibly than any one else and in committee you are invaluable. Still, I want your money, and I could do without you on the platform."

Isabella's letter was "a slap in the face . . . quite blunt and egotistic and somehow it hurts my self-respect," Stanton wrote. She decided to boycott

Hooker's convention and wrote Anthony urging her to do the same, but Anthony replied,

> Mrs. Hooker's attitude is not in the least surprising. She is precisely like every new convert in every reform. . . . The only thing surprising in this case is that you, the pioneer, should say to each of these converts, "Yes, you may manage. I grant your knowledge, judgment, taste, culture, are all superior to mine. I resign the good old craft to you altogether."
>
> To my mind there never was such suicidal letting go as has been yours these last two years. I am now tee-totally discouraged. . . . How you can excuse yourself is more than I can understand.

When the women Hooker had assembled gathered for a preliminary meeting in a committee room of the Capitol, Anthony congratulated George Julian of Indiana for introducing a Sixteenth Amendment to grant women the vote, but she pressed the congressmen to move the stalled bill out of the House Judiciary Committee. When she finished, one of the senators scolded her as if she were a schoolchild. "Miss Anthony," he said, "Congress has no time to attend to such questions, even if they were worthy of consideration." Anthony answered, "*If* we had the *votes,* gentlemen, the time would be forthcoming and even at hand."

After the meeting, Hooker and Anthony returned to the home of Senator Samuel Pomeroy, with whom they had been staying. Picking up the *Daily Patriot,* Isabella read an announcement that one Victoria Woodhull, a self-proclaimed candidate for president, had been granted a hearing before the Judiciary Committee of the Joint Houses of Congress, to present a memorial on the question of woman suffrage. This unprecedented honor was to occur on the same morning that the NWSA convention was officially scheduled to open.

Isabella expressed her astonishment to Senator Pomeroy and his wife. How did this Victoria Woodhull secure a hearing? Who was she? Who were her antecedents? Pomeroy chastised her: "She is for your cause, is she not? . . . Men never could work in a political party if they stopped to investigate each member's antecedents and associates. If you are going into a fight, you must accept every help that offers."

Susan then told Isabella about a document known as *The Woodhull Memorial,* which Benjamin Butler was said to have written. She had procured a copy and felt that it might provide the argument they needed for women to achieve enfranchisement. The Washington press had been alerted to the hearing and Anthony was sure that Victoria Woodhull would make news. She had met Woodhull briefly when she interviewed her for *The Revolution* and was impressed both with her beauty and her wealth. Their own delegation had received scant attention and only one newspaper notice, which said the delegates were "beautiful enough to win the hearts of Congress," hardly a recommendation for political action. What they must do, Susan insisted, was to postpone the opening session of their own convention and appear the following morning in the committee room in a show of solidarity before Congress and the press.

ALL THIS HAD come to pass through Benjamin Butler's efforts. During the winter of 1870, the pragmatic Butler had informed Victoria that a Sixteenth Amendment to give women the vote would go no further than the Judiciary Committee. To put a bill in committee was a classic way to kill it with study or neglect. It was a common political practice that would never change, he told her. On November 19, 1870, under Victoria's signature, *Woodhull & Claflin's Weekly* published an article asserting that the Sixteenth Amendment was dead in committee but that this was irrelevant because the Constitution of the United States defined women as "citizens," and citizens were entitled to vote. This was followed two weeks later by an erudite document, complete with legal and constitutional precedents. Victoria would later say that when she awakened from a trance one winter afternoon, Colonel Blood gave her this document, which had been dictated through her but conceived by the spirits. Skeptics noted, however, that it featured the blunt language and piercing arguments for which Butler was known.

In December, at Butler's behest, Woodhull appeared in Washington with *The Memorial of Victoria C. Woodhull* in hand and petitioned Congress to pass a declaratory act asserting women's right to vote. Two days later, she delivered a copy of the *Memorial* to the Senate, and George Julian requested that it be presented to the Judiciary Committee. Woodhull spent Christmas at Butler's house in Washington while his family was away. No sooner had Victoria returned to New York than she received a message from him: She had been invited, on Thursday, January 11, 1871, to present *The Woodhull Memorial* to the combined Judiciary Committee of both houses of Congress—in person.

The woman who went to Washington was actually an amalgam of others—her views of enfranchisement, marriage, divorce, and the relations between the sexes were largely Elizabeth Cady Stanton's. She wore the same stylish black velvet dress and Alpine hat as Anna Dickinson. She pulled her hair back in a bun like Lucy Stone, and her only adornment was a single white rose at her throat. Yet there was one trait that was truly her own—her passion.

Because of her stage training and her extraordinary visual memory, Victoria could render the most complicated legal arguments convincingly, without notes. She needed these skills to keep her composure, for she was later to admit that, although she knew the spirits were her allies, she was terrified. In the corridor of the Capitol building, Benjamin Butler stood next to the trembling newcomer. The meeting was to be held in a spacious marble-walled conference room, but smoke from a malfunctioning stove forced its occupants to leave. As they waited for a new room, Butler grasped Victoria's arm and whispered, "Be strong." Her defense of free love, he knew, made her the radical of radicals, but he told her to ignore any slights or snubs from the other suffragists, especially from their leader, Isabella Beecher Hooker. A congressman standing nearby overheard Butler and remarked, "It would ill become these women, especially a Beecher, to talk of antecedents or cast any smirch upon Mrs. Woodhull, for I am reliably assured that Henry Ward Beecher preaches to at least twenty of his mistresses every Sunday." The nervous Victoria was only dimly aware of the remark. It was the first she had heard of the rumor, but she noted that it seemed "to have a subduing effect instead of arousing indignation" among those standing nearby.

A few minutes later, Butler left to inspect the new room. He seemed completely in charge of the proceedings, ordering the windows opened to ventilate the cramped quarters. A large rectangular mahogany table dominated the room. Chairs were carried in and placed around this table and in rows on both sides. Isabella Beecher Hooker and Susan B. Anthony sat in the second row of chairs, side by side. Newspaper reporters leaned against the bookshelves lining the back wall. Butler checked to make sure that all the committee members were seated around the table, disappeared, and reentered leading Victoria Woodhull into the room. She held tightly to Butler with one hand while with the other she clutched Tennie C., who was engulfed in a ruffled green taffeta shawl that set off her copper hair. As she was about to sit down, Victoria turned and stared Isabella full in the face, and Isabella felt herself mesmerized by those blue-gray eyes.

It was ten in the morning when Butler called the meeting to order. John A. Bingham of Ohio, the chairman, introduced Victoria Woodhull. As she stood, her face drained of color; she leaned forward and grasped the edge of the table. Isabella was sure she was about to faint. She began in an almost inaudible whisper with long pauses between words. Then she stopped. Her lips moved silently as if in prayer. Suddenly, a change came over Victoria: Red patches glowed on her cheeks as she began reading her *Memorial* in a mellifluous, low voice that gained authority with every phrase. Isabella noted that her voice had become infused with "fire and freedom."

Woodhull maintained that women already had the right to vote and proposed that Congress merely pass a declaratory act to that effect. She noted that the first section of the Fourteenth Amendment states, "All persons born or naturalized in the United States and subject to the jurisdiction thereof, are citizens of the United States and of the state wherein they reside." Furthermore, though the Constitution gave the states the right to "regulate suffrage," the wording did not grant them the right or power to prohibit it.

The women of the Wyoming territory had been granted the vote the previous year, and Woodhull asserted that they, and every other woman in the nation, were entitled to vote under Article Four, Section Two of the Constitution, which states, "The citizens of each state shall be entitled to the privileges and immunities of citizens in the several states." She pointed out that the Founding Fathers had used the word "persons," specifying neither male nor female, but that

> after the adoption of the Fourteenth Amendment, it was found that still more legislation was required to secure the right to vote to all who were declared to be citizens. And the Fifteenth Amendment was passed by Congress and ratified by the states. . . . We must regard this amendment as though there had been no negroes requiring enfranchisement. We must divorce our minds from the negro and look at the Constitution *as it is* . . . the basis of equality is constructed *by all* and *for all* and from which all partake of *equal* rights, privileges and immunities.
>
> The sovereign will of the people is expressed in our written Constitution, which is the supreme law of the land. The Constitution makes no distinction of sex. The Constitution defines a woman born or naturalized in the United States, and subject to the jurisdiction thereof, to be a citizen. It recognizes the right of citizens to vote. . . . All people of both sexes have the right to vote, unless prohibited by special limiting terms. . . . No such limiting terms exist in the Constitution.

Isabella was fascinated by Woodhull and could see that for the first time men were listening to "the sheer logic of a woman's argument." And there was more: This woman had succeeded in a man's world. She had the power to change things. When Woodhull ended her speech, she sat down abruptly, limp as a rag doll. The physical transformation was noticeable to the reporters who recorded the scene. Tennie C. reached over and held her sister's hand. Mrs. Hooker observed that she regarded her sister "with a look of prayerful sympathy . . . one of the most beautiful expressions I have ever seen."

After the meeting Anthony and Hooker followed Julian to his office, where they found Victoria and Tennie already seated on his couch. When Woodhull was introduced to Mrs. Hooker, she sprang to her feet, clasped both of Isabella's hands in her own, looked at her intently, and remarked, "We have met before." And Isabella knew it was true. She felt the intense current of Woodhull's personal magnetism. Here at last was the evangel they had so long awaited. To Isabella this woman was the instrument of "the Heavenly Father. . . . It impressed me profoundly and in a manner I could never describe with the conviction that she was Heaven sent for the rescue of woman from the pit of subjection."

Victoria later told Isabella that in a trance she had seen "a great vision. . . . I see the near approach of the grandest revolution the world has yet known and for the part you shall play in it, thousands will rise up and call you blessed. It was not for nothing that you and I met so singularly."

A few days after Woodhull presented her *Memorial,* as Mrs. Hooker passed Charles Sumner, the senior Republican senator from Massachusetts, he drew her aside and said, "I was at a dinner party of twenty senators and each was asked in turn whether Woodhull's arguments could be answered, and not one suggested an answer. . . . Mrs. Hooker, this is the first time in my life that I realized that disenfranchisement means the same to you that it would to me."

Isabella believed that women would soon have their freedom. The previous year they had faced a "dead Congress." Now they were being noticed, talked about, helped. Four committee rooms at the Capitol were made available to them. Congressman Albert Gallatin Riddle arranged for *The Memorial of Victoria C. Woodhull* to be set in electrotype. Thousands of copies were sent out, as well as five thousand letters asking for petition signatures from women demanding the vote. Instead of the usual mailing costs of 25 cents for a single sheet and 50 cents for a double one, these materials were sent free of charge, saving thousands of dollars, because of congressional franking privileges supplied by Benjamin Butler.

*Isabella Beecher Hooker. Now a complete convert to Spiritualism, she felt Victoria Woodhull was "Heaven sent for the rescue of women."*

The second week in February, Victoria Woodhull received an invitation to visit President Grant at the White House. He greeted her warmly and then gestured to the presidential chair. "Someday you will occupy that chair," he said, according to her recollection of the event. No doubt this was flattery, but the impressionable Woodhull believed him. She also believed that President Grant had been directed by a higher power to deliver this message to her. In fact, he may have been directed by his wife, Julia, who had been impressed by *The Woodhull Memorial* and had written Victoria indicating her support.

Woodhull was bringing a new strength and optimism to the movement. Stanton and Anthony—desperate to further their cause—embraced her eagerly and asked no questions about her "antecedents," following Senator Pomeroy's suggestion not to pry into her past. Whatever she had done or been was none of their business. Stanton declared that Woodhull's arguments constituted a "new departure," and as a result the entire "manner of agitation is radically changed." She wrote to Victoria,

> In declaring that women are already citizens and pointing the short way to freedom, you have inspired the strongest of us with new hope and enthusiasm. In securing a hearing before the Judiciary Committee of Congress . . . you have lifted the debate on woman suffrage from the low ground of expediency, where ordinary men insist on holding it, into the higher realm of constitutional law. You have attacked too the last stronghold of the enemy—the social subordination of women.

And Anthony wrote,

> Bravo! My Dear Woodhull!
> I feel new life—new hope that our battle is to be short, sharp and decisive. . . . I have never in the whole twenty years' *good fight* felt so full of life and hope. Go ahead! bright, glorious, young and strong spirit, and believe in the best love and hope and faith of
> Susan B. Anthony

Anthony knew that in addition to leadership Woodhull had enough money to subsidize a small delegation of women to remain in Washington until spring. One of those who stayed was Isabella Beecher Hooker, who within three months had compiled the names of eighty thousand women who demanded the vote through a declaratory act. This list was presented to Congress, and a buoyant Isabella wrote, "Early next winter we *shall* be declared voting citizens."

Only Stanton seemed discouraged when the Majority Report on the Memorial denied the "petitioner's prayer" for a declarative act that women as citizens could vote. She wrote to Anthony that it was "the crowning insult to us from the Republican party." Benjamin Butler and William Loughridge wrote a favorable Minority Report and copies were sent out to twenty thousand influential individuals.

Isabella began to believe that Victoria might be "His [God's] own instrument for working out the deliverance from bondage. . . . He has opened the Red Sea before us who were willing to pass through under her leadership."

Seeing Victoria day after day, Isabella felt it her duty to groom this unconventional woman for the exalted position she was to hold. As she had once instructed Mrs. Stanton on proper deportment and behavior, she now set about molding Mrs. Woodhull into an upper-middle-class matron. On receiving a letter from Victoria scrawled on four sheets of wrapping paper, Isabella responded:

> Burn this as soon as sent! I want you to use nice notepaper hereafter—and send in envelopes. These are too rough . . . a dreadful eyesore to me. Now if you are to be our accepted standard bearer—be perfect, be exquisite in neatness, elegance and decorousness.

But as Isabella was trying to impose her vision on Victoria, the latter in turn was imposing her own ecstatic spiritual vision on Mrs. Hooker's mind and heart. "I have seldom been so drawn to any woman," wrote Isabella. "I know she has visions and is inspired by *spiritual* influences but her inspiration seems very like my own, a simple reliance on a Heavenly Father."

When Victoria confided to Isabella her conviction that she was "to be President next time and thus *ruler of the whole world*—our country being destined to rule all others," Isabella cautioned her never to disclose this. But she wrote her husband, John, of it and added, "I dare not tell you all I see in the future. . . . God knows it and that is enough."

On Thursday, February 16, 1871, Victoria Woodhull, Isabella Beecher Hooker, and Benjamin Butler were asked to lecture at Lincoln Hall in Washington on the subject of constitutional equality. An elated Isabella wrote to Victoria, "I have this moment read your letter of acceptance *My Darling Queen,* and it is all I could ask. You are fitted for political strife and a pure leadership. . . . I give you my blessing and deepest sympathy and warmest prayers."

When Isabella confessed that she had never spoken to such an audience and "did not dare see that I could," Victoria told her to draw upon her other powers. With the help of the spirits Isabella would not speak for herself but would transmit words of immortal truth. "As I am about to speak, I call upon the spirits. They surround me and protect me. I sense them hovering about me in the air . . . and the light beaming through. I am doing their bidding." This convinced Isabella that the spirits were inspiring and protecting her as well. When Isabella rose to speak, she, who had so long ago written to her husband, "I can't write a book nor draw pictures—nor do any other productive work," found a rapt audience being influenced by her. Isabella later wrote that she had given a powerful speech, "The finest address I ever delivered. . . . It flowed out of my inner consciousness as if it were part of my very being." Long after, that speech seemed to her a "veritable inspiration," and from that moment on she felt that evermore, "my strength shall be equal to the day."

Woodhull's own speech, which followed, incorporated passages from the Butler and Loughridge Minority Report. A newspaper report called it "a triumph," and Hooker noted, "I verily believe not one who heard her great speech (for it is truly great—I never saw an audience of 1400, many standing, listen as this did to a bare legal argument in my life) has wished to utter a word against her or has been able to do it."

But Isabella had not counted on the American Woman Suffrage Association and its *Woman's Journal,* which stated that the alliance of the National Woman Suffrage Association with a woman like Victoria Woodhull was far worse than its association with the bigoted George Francis Train. Rumors of Victoria's past had begun to catch up with her. Mary Livermore was a Chicago resident, and she recalled that there had been unsavory newspaper stories about the Claflin clan. Livermore was quoted as saying that Woodhull was unfit to be involved in woman's rights: "Her hands are unclean." And once again members of the AWSA accused the women of the NWSA of embracing free love. Anthony had her fill of these accusations. She wrote to the Spiritualist Laura De Force Gordon,

> If I had time or space I could tell you . . . the lie to it. . . . Our fastidious Boston friends can't *see nor* hear the roar of the Woodhull shot . . . because it isn't of the *true blue Boston ring*—I verily believe those *men* and their *echoes,* the women—would rather women should grovel in the mire of disfranchisement another whole century than that they shall be lifted out by what they term *"unclean hands."*

At Harriet Beecher Stowe's behest, Henry Ward Beecher wrote a letter to their sister Isabella asking her to drop her association with this "pseudo-banker" whose opinions were "unusual and dangerous." Catharine Beecher and Mary Perkins also reacted violently to their sister's association with this creature of dubious reputation. Finally, Harriet wrote Isabella at length that a parishioner of Plymouth Church had observed Mrs. Woodhull in the company of a "certain senator" while traveling at night on the train to Washington. The parishioner related how Woodhull had invited him to visit her hotel room later that night, but he declined. In the morning, he met the senator and told him that Woodhull was "not a proper woman for you to be with," to which the senator replied that he needed her because she had promised to "bring over" a congressional opponent.

Much disturbed, Isabella wrote to this member of her brother's church to confirm Harriet's account. But even when he replied that those indeed "were the facts," Isabella concluded that the facts were not damning, only the inferences drawn from them. It had become impossible for Isabella to envision Victoria Woodhull, this woman whom she had quickly come to love, as anything but pure. "It is a great comfort to me thus to believe in her innocence," she confessed.

However, as more rumors of Victoria and Tennie C.'s exploits drifted back to Isabella, she wrote to Anthony for advice.

> Dear Friend Susan,
>
> Now as to Mrs. Woodhull—we are in a quandary . . . my sisters, all three . . . have nearly crazed me with letters imploring me to have nothing to do with her. . . . I was never so perplexed to form a judgment in my life and my prevailing belief is in her innocence and purity. . . . I shall always love her and in private shall work for her redemption if she is ensnared. . . . I can't guess who is really behind her nor what will become of herself and paper and party if she has any. You will send this I hope to Mrs. Stanton and . . . she will be able to  make some examination of this mysterious family.
>
> Of Tennie C. I hear the most dreadful stories—yet she has the face of a sweet innocent child.

Undoubtedly, Isabella thought that women who had led the life attributed to Tennie would appear dissolute. The idea that sin was reflected in one's countenance was a common misconception. After Victoria visited Lucretia Mott and her sister, Martha Coffin Wright, in Philadelphia, the latter wrote to Anthony: "No one can be with her [Woodhull] without believing in her goodness and her purity but with her past we have nothing to do. She said to me, 'All that I am I have become through sorrow' and I had no desire to lift the veil from that." Anthony answered Isabella's query about looking into Woodhull's background in an irate, direct manner.

> When we begin to search *records, past* or *present*—of those who bring brains or cash to our work for enfranchising women—it shall be with those of *the men—not the women,* and *not a woman— not Mrs. Woodhull*—until every insinuation of gossip of Beecher,

Pomeroy, Butler, Carpenter shall be *fully investigated*—and each of them shall have proven to *your* and our satisfaction—that he never flirted, trifled with, or desecrated any specimen of Womanhood.

No! No!! Mrs. Hooker—it won't do to begin that—*are we more than Christ himself*—that we shall thrust from us the *woman accused*—Christ repeats to you and to me and to all women—"*Let her who never sinned in spirit* or in act cast the first stone"—not until we *chastise and refuse men* will I consent to *question women*—and it is *only that Mrs. Woodhull is a woman*—and that *we are women*—*all of an enslaved class*—that we ever *dream* of such a thing. . . .

You see the *theory* you propose for the *Woodhull Scandal* applied to *men*, living or dead is simply ridiculous. . . . I know you will see at once that the moment we begin the work of making *one woman account to us*—*our turn* may come next and no end to the *persecution* that would follow.

Anthony's admonition was exactly what Isabella needed to hear. When next Mary Livermore wrote her, disparaging Woodhull's antecedents and accusing her of "licentiousness," Isabella replied,

Woman cannot be injured by woman—only men are in danger— to them a vile woman is indeed the spark to a tinder, to us she is a sister for whom God has made us accountable. . . . Indeed the reason this is any campaign at all is that men perceive at last that the little white symbol of power is coming into our hands and begin to realize what we shall do with it. . . . The lips of women are being unsealed . . . and the day of judgment and purity draws nigh.

# CHAPTER TWENTY-TWO

# SILENCE, TIME, AND PATIENCE

A BITTERLY cold winter had settled over Brooklyn. "There came scarcely one human being of all the church people and not a friend to call on me," lamented Lib Tilton. So quickly had the rumors spread across Brooklyn and into the heart of Plymouth Church that all shunned her. She lived, she said, in "a marked house"—marked with the sign of Cain, for had Theodore Tilton, her husband, and Henry Ward Beecher, her God, not been as brothers?

On January 11, 1871, in a snowstorm, Lib heard a knocking at her door. It was the elegantly dressed Paulina Wright Davis. "Oh, you have come to see me! For weeks I have been shut up from the world. I thought no one ever would come," Lib said, and burst into tears. Paulina entered the house to find it freezing. No fire had been lit in the hearth. At once, Lib obsessively related the events of the past months, starting with her husband's rage, triggered by the confession that she was enceinte by Mr. Beecher. Lib seemed surprised that Mrs. Davis had no knowledge of her affair and told her that the facts were "known and discussed in a considerable circle" and were "impossible to conceal."

Mrs. Davis was struck by Lib's desperation. She seemed pathetic, even deranged. Paulina left that evening for Washington, where she was introduced to Victoria Woodhull. Like Isabella, Paulina was much taken with the fiery Spiritualist. One evening she told Victoria about Mrs. Tilton's affair and the abortion, and said with passion, "I came away from that house, my soul bowed down with grief at the heart-broken condition of that poor woman, and I felt that I ought not to leave Brooklyn until I had stripped the mask from that infamous, hypocritical scoundrel Beecher."

For all his protestations of forgiveness Theodore Tilton too thought of Beecher as a villain who had cost him his marriage, his profession, and his power. As he brooded on this, he drank heavily and contemplated suicide.

He could hardly look at his wife and took most of his meals with the Moultons. One afternoon Theodore unexpectedly returned home at four o'clock and found his wife on her knees in prayer beside the red velvet chaise longue, the scene of her infidelity. He pulled Lib to her feet, wrenched the wedding ring from her finger, and forced her to accompany him to Greenwood Cemetery. There he ground the ring beneath his heel into the dirt that covered their children's graves.

The enraged Tilton did not keep his promise of silence about his wife's affair. Lib's mother, Mrs. Morse, wrote to Beecher, "I know of twelve persons he has told and they in turn have told others. . . . He swears as soon as the breath leaves her body, he will make the whole thing public and this prospect is the one thing which keeps her alive."

Frank Moulton had not destroyed Lib's incriminating letters as he had promised. He was later to say that he had kept them in case Beecher once again damaged Tilton. In any case, Tilton wrote out several copies of Beecher's letter of apology and distributed them at whim. On her next visit he gave a copy to Elizabeth Cady Stanton. He pointed to the phrase in the letter of apology that read, "I humble myself before him," and boasted, "We have Plymouth Church at our feet."

Stanton tried to restore calm. Having been tempted to run away with Edward Bayard, she understood Beecher's dilemma. She urged Theodore to build a house for the family near her in New Jersey, where they could "enjoy a new peace and happiness." She wrote, "Let the dead past go, waste no energies in regret, but garner up the wisdom that comes from experience for future worth. You do not know how much interest and sympathy I feel for you and your little wife."

It did not take long for Sam Wilkeson to discover that his sister-in-law had a copy of Beecher's self-incriminating letter, and he arranged a meeting with her. She arrived with Susan B. Anthony, and both women related all that Lib and Theodore had told them separately that evening in Brooklyn. Stanton then told Wilkeson that women in her organization as well as many men "heard and repeated the scandal." (She was later to write, "That Henry Ward Beecher was deeply infected with these [free love] doctrines was no secret at all. . . . Mr. Beecher held a sexual theory which he believed to be in advance of the present constitution of society.") Wilkeson mopped his ample brow and said, "If this gets out, it will knock *The Life of Christ* higher than a kite!"

Wilkeson beseeched these women not to make their discoveries public. He explained that Henry Ward Beecher must be supported at all costs: The *Christian Union,* Plymouth Church, and the J. P. Ford syndicate, pub-

*Samuel Wilkeson, who tried to suppress the*
*scandal. Portrait by Mathew Brady, 1863*

lishers of *The Life of Jesus the Christ,* had too much at stake to see Beecher
sacrificed. Stanton realized that "the destruction of Mr. Beecher would be
the destruction of all these." As Beecher himself was later to say, "I have
been the centre of three distinct circles . . . the *great* church . . . the *news-*
*paper* . . . the *book.* . . . The *sensitiveness* of so many of my people would
have made any appearance of trouble . . . an occasion of alarm and notice,
and have excited, when it was important that rumors should die and everything be quieted."

Stanton put it more bluntly: "It was a matter of money. The church
property is not taxed, its bonds in the hands of the wealthy men of that
organization are valuable, and the bondholders, alive to their financial
interests, stand around Mr. Beecher, a faithful, protecting band—not loving truth and justice less, but their own pockets more." Though Elizabeth
Cady Stanton was his wife's sister, Wilkeson threatened her. He said that
with all this money at stake the "lie," as he called it, would be "saddled
upon us women," wrote Stanton. Beecher must not fall. Sam Wilkeson
assumed that most problems could be solved with money. Using his position as chief representative of Jay Cooke's Northern Pacific bond syndicate,

Wilkeson wrote Tilton that he was prepared to send him, as he had Henry Bowen, an immediate payment of $15,000 and added,

> You are in trouble. I come to you with a letter just mailed to Jay Cooke, advising him to secure your services as a platform speaker to turn New England, old England, or the great West upside down about our Northern Pacific.
>
> Pluck up heart! You shan't be trampled down. Keep quiet. Don't talk. *Don't publish.* Abide your time and it will be a very good time. Take my word for it.
>
> Sam Wilkeson

Tilton was hard up for cash but, unlike Bowen, he was not a man to take a bribe. He did not reply to Wilkeson's letter.

It fell to Frank Moulton to suppress the scandal and make peace among the parties. With Beecher's encouragement he went to Tilton and offered him a trip abroad with his family to be financed by Wilkeson and his associates. As Moulton might have predicted, Tilton angrily refused. This was not the way to placate an honorable man. Moulton knew that much of Tilton's bitterness came from the loss of his job and thus his public platform. Laura Curtis Bullard's ownership of *The Revolution* had in effect made it Theodore Tilton's publication, but Laura had tired of the financial and emotional drain. Anthony wrote to her beloved Anna that Mrs. Bullard wanted her to "*take back The Revolution*—she is sick & tired of the work & the new Co. of sinking the cash—& they have spent it *so foolishly.*" Anthony worried that her rivals in Boston would acquire the paper, "*thus putting* in Lucy Stone's hands *the prestige,* the results of all *my hardest 20 years.*" But after owning *The Revolution* for eighteen months, Mrs. Bullard simply abandoned it.

Moulton told Tilton that he would be able to secure funds from people who admired him to finance a new publication, the *Golden Age,* which would be solely owned and edited by Tilton. What Moulton did not tell Tilton was that Henry Ward Beecher would be his major financial backer. To raise his share of the money, Beecher persuaded his wife, Eunice, to sign a mortgage for $5,000 on their Columbia Heights home. Also, unbeknownst to Tilton, Moulton arranged for Beecher to pay the tuition at a private boarding school in the West for Bessie Turner, Lib's ward, who had been privy to the entire scandal.

But no sooner had one problem been solved than another arose. Mrs. Morse had counted on Beecher's becoming her "Son"—in other words, on his supporting Lib as his permanent mistress. But Beecher, in her eyes, had simply abandoned them. She wrote to the preacher asking him for money. "Can you help? . . . With a rent of $1,500 and an income of $1,000 the consequence is with other expenses I shall be by the first of the month terribly behind." When Beecher ignored her letter she wrote again: "You have not seen fit to pay any attention to the request I left at your house now over two weeks since. . . . Do you know when I hear you cracking your jokes from Sunday to Sunday and I think of the misery you have brought us, I think with the Psalmist there is no God." Finally, she threatened to reveal "the secret of her [daughter's] life."

Beecher prevailed upon Moulton to win Lib Tilton's confidence and urge her to stop her mother's threats. He assured Moulton that his love affair with Mrs. Tilton was ended forever and he "would do all he could to restore her love" to her husband. But all communication between Beecher and Lib had been forbidden by Tilton. Frank Moulton suggested that the preacher write to Mrs. Tilton to convince her to trust Moulton as the peacemaker while Frank himself would secure Theodore's permission to deliver the letter. Beecher wrote,

> When I saw you last I did not expect ever to see you again or to be alive many days. God was kinder to me than were my own thoughts. Mr. Moulton the friend whom God sent to me has proved above all friends that ever I had, able and willing to help me in this terrible emergency of my life. His hand tied up the storm that was ready to burst upon our head. May not this friend stand as a priest in the new sanctuary of reconciliation, and mediate and bless you, Theodore, and my most unhappy self? He will be a true friend to your honor and happiness. In him we have a common ground.

With Moulton as go-between, Mrs. Tilton stopped her mother's threats, and the Tilton household once again took on a semblance of normality. Feeling that at last all was well, Lib wrote Laura Curtis Bullard about the events of the past months. Only Laura could fully understand the great social experiment on which they had embarked, an experiment that had so disastrously failed.

> Dear Friend and Sister:
>     You, like me, have loved and been loved. . . . I find in you an element to which I respond . . . I cannot reason—only feel. Memo-

ries of you fill me with admiration and delight. I have caught up your card picture and kissed it again and again, praying with tears for God's blessing to follow you and to perfect in us three the beautiful promise of our nature. But my sweet and dear I realize in these months of our acquaintance . . . how almost impossible it is to *bring out* these blossoms of our heart's growth—God's gifts to us—to human eyes. Our pearls and flowers are caught up literally by vulgar and base minds that surround us on every side, and so destroyed or abused that we know them no longer as our own, and thus God is made our only hope.

My husband has suffered much with me in a cruel conspiracy made by my poor suffering mother, with an energy worthy of a better cause, to divorce us by saying that I was seeking it because of Theodore's infidelity, making *her* feeling *mine*. . . .

All might have been well had not Theodore decided to summon Beecher to his house to determine the paternity of Ralph, who had been born on June 20, 1869. Beecher arrived while the Tiltons were finishing breakfast, and Lib was asked to confirm the date that their affair began. She checked her diary and said it was on October 10, 1868, that she had made the entry "A Day Memorable." After making a quick calculation, Tilton, satisfied that Ralph was his child, announced that he would change the boy's name to Frank, in honor of Frank Moulton. But Lib, having seen her preacher again, could not resist the urge to correspond with him clandestinely. "My future either for life or death would be happier could I but feel you *forgive* while you forget me," she wrote. And a week later: "Does your heart bound *towards all* as it used? So does mine! I am myself again . . . of course I should like to share with you my joy but I can wait for the Beyond!" To which Beecher replied, "Your note broke like spring upon winter and gave me an inward rebound to life. No one can ever know, none but God, through what a dreary wilderness I have passed."

VICTORIA WOODHULL HAD gone to Washington to find fame but stayed to work for woman's rights and soon came to believe she possessed the power to alleviate the burdens of women like herself who had been abused and exploited and had been powerless in a man's world. She often heard spirit voices telling her what she must do. She vowed that no longer would she use her powers frivolously or for personal gain but to transform society and lead women to the millennium.

On the night she returned from Washington, Victoria, "as a talisman against any temptation toward untruthfulness," stitched into the sleeve of each of her dresses the second verse of the 120th Psalm: "Deliver my soul Oh Lord from lying lips and from a deceitful tongue." To Isabella Beecher Hooker she poured out her innermost thoughts.

My Dear, dear friend,

I am often compelled to do things from which my sensitive soul shrinks and for which I endure the censure of most of my friends. But I obey a Power which knows better than they or I can know and which has never left me stranded and without hope. I should be a faithless servant indeed were I to falter now when required to do what I cannot fully understand, yet in the issue of which I have full faith.

None of the scenes in which I have enacted a part were what I would have selfishly chosen for my own happiness. I love my home, my children, my husband, and could live a sanctified life with them and never desire contact with the wide world. But such is not to be my mission. I know what is to come, though I cannot yet divulge it. My daily prayer is that Heaven may vouchsafe me strength to meet everything which I know must be encountered and overcome. . . .

On March 28, 1871, the very day that Victoria Woodhull returned from Washington, Paris workers supported by elements of the bourgeoisie, who were embittered by France's loss to Prussia in the War of 1870, and offended by the new laws to protect creditors and landowners, rebelled. They formed their own municipal council and issued the proclamation of the Paris Commune. Two days later the national government and the communards were at war. Immediately, Stephen Pearl Andrews became a supporter of the Paris Commune and convinced Victoria Woodhull that the communards were honoring the rights of women by guaranteeing them economic, social, and political equality with men. In Paris, he said, women were living her dream of breaking away from their traditional roles.

Victoria Woodhull, following Andrews's lead, was determined to follow in the footsteps of her French sisters and allied herself with radical elements who hoped to transform American society. The American Labor Reform League, a group composed of anarchists, socialists, and other freethinkers, had scheduled its first meeting for May 8 at Cooper Institute, and at Andrews's suggestion, Woodhull presented the keynote speech. It had been composed by Andrews, although at the time she claimed to have written it. She read "The Great Social Problem of Labor and Capital" without passion and stumbled over a few of the longer words, nonetheless she added the support of radical labor reformers to the Spiritualist and woman's rights groups who endorsed her for the presidency.

For the first time Victoria took an active part in the editorial policies of *Woodhull & Claflin's Weekly.* She changed the motto from "Onward and Upward" to "Progress! Free Thought! Untrammeled Lives." Early in 1871, while she was in Washington, articles appeared in the publication favoring the legalization of prostitution. Now editorials by Woodhull herself explained that those articles, written in her absence, were contrary to the actual views of the *Weekly.*

WHEN ISABELLA BEECHER Hooker returned to her Nook Farm home in Connecticut, she set about changing the minds of her sisters about Victoria Woodhull, particularly Catharine, who had been living nearby with their sister Harriet Beecher Stowe, with whom she had co-authored *The American Woman's Home,* a guide to proper deportment, domestic duties, and child care. Catharine had recently completed *Woman Suffrage and Woman's Profession,* in which she praised domesticity as woman's total fulfillment and insisted that women had no place in politics. For thousands of women Catharine Beecher spoke with authority on maternal and marital felicity, neither of which she had experienced.

Catharine was the eldest of Lyman Beecher's eleven surviving children, born at a time when her father, a great Calvinist preacher, was young and full of fire. Catharine was the center of his attention until she was two and his first son was born. She had been a rambunctious girl whose father was constantly trying to control her, both mind and body. When she was eight, Lyman Beecher held her head in a bucket of water until, sputtering, drowning, her willfulness gone, she acquiesced to his complete authority. Equality vanished in the water that swept into her mouth and nose. Fourteen years later, sexuality vanished in the water that swept her fiancé to a fate where her father insisted he had gone unredeemed. At twenty-two, Catharine had met Alexander Fisher, an acclaimed mathematician and, by several accounts, a gentle soul. "I could not ask for more delicacy and tenderness," she wrote a friend. Shortly after their engagement, Fisher sailed for Europe to study advanced mathematics but his ship foundered and he was lost at sea.

At the time of Fisher's death, Lyman Beecher was forcing upon his daughter the act of conversion, the complete submission and obliteration of self in the name of his Calvinist faith. Before Fisher's departure Catharine had attempted to achieve conversion, but with his death she refused her father's harsh religion with its commitment to predestination, which allowed the possibility that Alexander might burn in hell. Yet in her dreams she saw the water engulf him and heard her father's voice call out the dread phrase, "No salvation!"

Catharine rejected Calvinism and chose a life whose rules she created for herself. Teaching would be her religion, and guiding a generation of women, her mission. She believed women should use gentle wiles to persuade the men who dominated them, on the theory that they would not deny their dutiful wives and children. Women might thus gain power by influencing husbands and sons toward greater benevolence. She feared men for their abstract power, but most of all Catharine feared sex, equating it with violent possession. "As things now are, men have the physical power that can force obedience; in most cases they have the power of the purse and in all cases they have civil power." "Force obedience" the way her father, Lyman Beecher, had when he held her head in that bucket of water.

Catharine was particularly fond of her half-sister, Isabella, who had been born just two months before Fisher was lost at sea. At fourteen, Isabella was taken into the school Catharine had founded, the Western Female Institute in Cincinnati, Ohio, and given the only education she was to receive. Catharine tried to keep an open mind concerning her sister's attachment to Mrs. Woodhull but she strongly believed that Victoria and women like her were introducing an explosive element into politics, demonstrating a power that they should not possess, much less wield. She wrote, "Many intelligent and benevolent persons imagine that the grand remedy for the heavy evils that oppress our sex is to introduce woman to political power and office, to make her a party . . . in the scramble and fight for political offices, thus bringing into this dangerous melee the distinctive tempting power of her sex. Who can look at this new danger without dismay?"

If only her sisters could meet Victoria Woodhull, thought Isabella, they would be "just as much in love with her as the rest of us." She explained to Harriet and Catharine that Woodhull had been selected as God's instrument for righting social injustice. Although she did not understand all of Woodhull's theories, Isabella told Catharine that she was convinced that this woman was a visionary and that Isabella herself was destined to play a great part in her divine plan. Woodhull had at her command spirit forces that would bolster her. She had penetrated the curtain between heaven and earth so that the spirits could cross over. As Victoria had demonstrated to her, Isabella made a ladder with her fingers showing her sisters the way one climbed to higher and higher planes until they passed over effortlessly from earthly life to another world.

Though Catharine was disparaging, Harriet Beecher Stowe was sympathetic to Spiritualism. After her son, Henry, drowned while swimming in the Connecticut River in New Hampshire, Harriet turned to Spiritualism to make contact with him. She said she could see her dead son's spirit and other spirits hovering nearby. Her husband, Calvin, also had visions. Once Calvin left their house to catch a train but, remembering he had forgotten his hat, returned to get it. Harriet was sitting at the desk writing. He passed her by without a word. Finally, she asked, "Why will you not speak to me?" Calvin replied, "Oh, I thought you were one of my visions."

Harriet believed that Spiritualism was "a reaction from the intense materialism of the present age"; nonetheless she told Isabella that she disapproved of any of the Beechers associating with this "vile woman." Perhaps because Harriet so disapproved, Catharine gave in to Isabella's persuasion and agreed to meet with her sister's "Darling Queen." Catharine felt that "Mrs. Woodhull is a pure woman holding a wrong social theory and ought to be treated with kindness if we wish to win her to the truth."

As Catharine stood under the immense crystal chandelier in the Woodhull living room, Victoria greeted her cordially, extending both her hands so that Catharine could feel her magnetism. Since it was a mild spring day Victoria suggested a ride in Central Park. At three o'clock carriages arrived for their afternoon promenade. Victoria and Catharine settled into the crimson velvet seat of Woodhull's brougham, which was equipped with parasol holders, a small vanity, and a call bell for summoning the driver. Catharine Beecher felt obligated to show this uneducated woman how misguided she was: No doubt Woodhull's feelings for woman's oppression were sincere but her methods were destroying any hope of progress. Catharine opposed almost everything Victoria was for. "Disastrous influences—the teachings of Free Love, the baneful influence of Spiritualism . . . the fascinations of the *demimonde,* the poverty of thousands of women who, but for desperate temptations, would be pure—all these malign influences are sapping the foundations of the family state," she had written.

Catharine, accustomed to the deference of other women, began in her didactic way to lecture Victoria who, once or twice, tried to answer but found it impossible to interrupt this determined woman. Catharine explained that it was terribly dangerous for a woman to try to establish herself as the equal of man. Only at great peril did she try to challenge man's power

*Harriet Beecher Stowe and her husband, Calvin Stowe.*
*President Lincoln said to Harriet, "So you're the little woman who*
*started this great war."*

directly. She told Victoria that a woman of breeding—one with proper antecedents—could gently persuade men and that this moral power was the only proper one to wield.

*"Antecedents!"* Would Victoria never escape these women who felt superior to her, who regarded her simply as one of the shiftless Claflins? *Antecedents*—how dare she!

Catharine droned on, preaching her domestic gospel: A woman's sexual acquiescence was a gentle gift that found its proper place in procreation. Any other manifestation was evil. Marriage was a sacred, lifelong bond. Easy divorce and free love were "the same as asking civilized human beings to return to the lustful instinctiveness of animals." If Victoria adhered to this dangerous doctrine she would soon be alone in her satanic beliefs, which, Catharine cautioned, "must come from a misunderstanding of women's role or else you are in the possession of some powerful, malignant spirits."

Anger welled up in Victoria; suddenly around Catharine's head she saw a band of devils with rat-tails. Later Victoria wrote of this occasion, "Catharine Beecher imagined the malignant spirits manifested by herself were mine instead of hers. She was drunk of them and as drunkards invariably do, thought that they were confronting instead of being possessed by her."

"You are misguided," Victoria finally said. "Many great people have already accepted and are living my theories of social freedom though they are not ready to become its avowed advocates, as I am. You speak of Free Love with derision while your own brother, Henry Ward Beecher, the most powerful preacher in America, openly practices it. I do not condemn him, I applaud him. Would that he had the courage to join me in preaching what he practices."

"Evil!" Catharine exclaimed. It seemed to Victoria that Catharine suddenly wilted, drawing herself into the corner of the carriage. "I know my brother is unhappy but he is a true husband. I will vouch for my brother's faithfulness to his marriage vows as though he were myself."

"But you have no positive knowledge that would justify your doing so," said Woodhull.

"No . . . no positive—," stammered Catharine. "I know he is unhappy. Mrs. Beecher is a virago, a constitutional liar and a terrible woman altogether, so terrible his friends and family seldom visit. But unfaithful—no. I will hear no more of it."

"You will hear," said Victoria. "In concubinage with his parishioner's wife—it is common knowledge. And if you were a proper person to judge, which I grant you are not, you should see that the facts are fatal to your theories."

Catharine was now livid. Wisps of hair as gray as her complexion shook as if on tiny springs. "Victoria Woodhull, I will strike you for this. I will strike you dead!" she cried out.

"Strike as much and as hard as you please. Only don't do it in the dark so I cannot know who is my enemy."

"Stop!" commanded Catharine, who then clambered out of the carriage, and holding her voluminous skirt moved rapidly across the Greensward of Central Park. Victoria watched her go, the devils with rat-tails sailing off through the sky, a fluttering covey of malignancy like a dark cloud above her head.

From Hartford, Isabella noted, "Sister Catharine returned last night. Saw Victoria and attacked her on the marriage question, got such a black eye as filled her with horror and amazement. I had to laugh inwardly at her relation of the interview and am now waiting for her to cool down!" Catharine Beecher never denied Woodhull's account of what had passed between them during their Central Park carriage ride, but she did not tell Harriet or Isabella the specifics of their conversation or mention their brother Henry. From then on, however, Isabella was under increased pressure from her sisters to abandon her new friend. Catharine referred to Victoria and Tennie C. as "those two prostitutes." Harriet Beecher Stowe and Mary Beecher Perkins wrote a joint letter to John Hooker, imploring him to bring Isabella "back to God and away from that harlot."

Isabella fought back. "Do you believe I could have taken her to my heart as I have done, if I did not believe her true and pure?" she wrote her sisters, and reminded Harriet how she had stood by her during the Lady Byron affair. Isabella bluntly added, "You and Mrs. Perkins each have a drinking, licentious son, and yet you know that you would be glad for them to marry the purest young girl and have tried every means to effect it hoping it might redeem them, and yet you judge Mrs. Woodhull."

When Susan B. Anthony was asked by a *Tribune* editor if she knew about "Mrs. Woodhull's antecedents," she answered that she "did not care any more for them than I do about those of the members of Congress." Victoria Woodhull, though she professed indifference, was stung by the accusations against her. It was at this point that she began what was to become a lifelong attempt to manufacture an idealized genteel background for herself. Eventually, this was to extend to her changing the names and professions of various members of her family. She offered one such sanitized history to Martha Coffin Wright, one of the most powerful members of the woman suffrage movement, who then relayed it to her daughter, Eliza: "She and her five sisters, all married but one, have always lived together in their father's house—one of the largest on Fifth Avenue. . . . She scorns the innuendoes against her character and challenges any one to point to a single act in her life that would not bear scrutiny. She says 'let them float,' they do not hurt her and she has not time for any notice of them." But, in truth, notice them Victoria Woodhull did. And how they rankled. Victoria wrote Isabella,

> Under all the curses and imprecations which are being heaped upon me, strong though I feel, I need some little sustaining presence from those who I believe comprehend me. . . . I must confess to not a little surprise that whatever I have done or may do is at once denounced as imprudent, unwise and the endeavor made to stigmatize me as a very improper person.
>
> I shall not change my course because those who assume to be better than I desire it. . . . It grieves me that there should be anything to interfere with obtaining justice at the earliest possible moment. Some say they would rather never obtain it than that it should come from such a source. Why should the . . . *Woman's Journal insinuate* without stating. I thought that it was a question of *Right* under the *Constitution,* I did not know that it was a question of *Antecedents!*

# CHAPTER TWENTY-THREE

# THE WORST GANG

TWENTY-THREE years had passed since Seneca Falls and the first glimmering of woman's rights. To celebrate that anniversary, the National Woman Suffrage Association scheduled a weeklong convention to begin at New York's Apollo Hall on May 11, 1871. And once again the American Woman Suffrage Association announced a simultaneous convention at Steinway Hall. The previous year, the NWSA had been virtually ignored or dismissed while the AWSA received glowing press coverage. This time, however, their organization would not be overlooked, for Anthony, Stanton, and Hooker had aligned themselves with Victoria Woodhull, a woman no one could ignore.

For the forces behind Victoria Woodhull, the NWSA convention provided an opportunity to promulgate their views and develop a greater constituency for her bid for the presidency. Stephen Pearl Andrews drew up twenty-five articles to be presented to the convention, representing his own vision of a utopian world. The first article dealt with woman's rights, but the rest advocated such wide-sweeping reforms as a revised civil and criminal code, government control of public enterprises, public ownership of mines and waterways, distribution of public land to settlers, high taxes on income and property. As Andrews was completing this list, his wife, Esther, died. Stricken, he locked himself in an upstairs bedroom of Woodhull's house and said he would remain there until Esther informed him that she had "safely made the journey to Summerland." Elizabeth Cady Stanton stepped into the breach and stayed at Victoria's house to help complete the final arrangements for the convention.

Ever since her arrival in New York, Mama Roxy had been openly hostile to visitors and "that damn scoundrel Blood," who had stolen the daughters who were her livelihood. Her daughter Polly's husband, Dr. Benjamin Sparr, had moved into the house and soon became Roxy's ally in trying to extort money from her daughters' acquaintances. The final rift came when

Roxy confided to Tennie that, just as they used to do, a letter had been written to "a certain gentleman" that should yield them lots of money. When it arrived they could go back to Ohio to begin life anew. Tennie bristled. "What have you done?" she demanded of her mother. "Never, never will I go back to that life." It was one of those blackmail letters—she knew it. And worse, she made her mother admit that it had gone to Commodore Vanderbilt. Then and there Tennie knew that she had lost the Commodore as a patron. Vanderbilt didn't care what people said about him, but he had trusted Victoria and Tennie. Now that trust had been irrevocably broken and Tennie knew that no matter what she did or said he would never forgive them.

Tennie, as always, was unable to cope with this woman who had emotionally enslaved her. Instead, she turned her rage on Dr. Sparr. This was his doing. Three days before the convention, Roxy and Buck Claflin and the Sparrs were banished from the house on East Thirty-eighth Street, but Tennie paid the rent for her parents at a comfortable boardinghouse. As Tennie had predicted, the Commodore severed all connection with them. Soon after, when a reporter asked Vanderbilt how his Wall Street protégées were faring, he answered, "They hain't no friends of mine. From what I hear, you shouldn't be associating with such folks."

There was not a vacant seat in Apollo Hall: Members of the NWSA, Spiritualists, working women, businessmen, politicians, and members of Section 12 of the International Workingmen's Association—a socialist organization that represented labor in its Marxian opposition to capitalism—were in attendance. In 1869, Stephen Pearl Andrews had received permission from the General Council of the International in London to form two American branches. Victoria was named honorary president of Section 12, the more visible of the two. Some NWSA members refused to sit next to Victoria, lest the contagion of her reputation infect them. Susan B. Anthony noted, "great trouble allowing Mrs. Woodhull on our platform." Stanton insisted that Woodhull be placed between herself and the venerable Lucretia Mott "to give her respectability." When Mott hesitated, Stanton told her that Victoria had the courage to advocate openly what people like Henry Ward Beecher practiced secretly. Woodhull was duly seated.

A reporter noted that Victoria sat perfectly still: ". . . a small splinter of the indestructible. . . . If her veins were opened they would be found to contain ice." But her keynote address was electrifying. She was obviously in the grip of an ecstatic vision: Women could change the world if only they dared change it. Her rhetoric was now militant.

Why do I war upon marriage . . . because it is, I verily believe, the most terrible curse from which humanity now suffers, entailing more misery, sickness, and premature death than all other causes combined. . . . Sanctioned and defended by marriage, night after night there are thousands of rapes committed, under cover of this accursed license. I know where of I speak—millions of poor, heartbroken, suffering wives are compelled to minister to the lechery of insatiable husbands when every instinct of body and sentiment of soul revolt in loathing and disgust. . . . Prate of the abolition of slavery, there was never servitude in the world like this one of marriage.

I have asked for equality nothing more. . . . Sexual freedom means the abolition of prostitution both in and out of marriage, means the emancipation of woman from sexual slavery and her coming into ownership and control of her own body, means the end of her pecuniary dependence upon man . . . means the abrogation of forced pregnancy, of antenatal murder of undesired children and the birth of love children only.

Woodhull preached a new gospel. She directed women to

rise and declare . . . yourself free. Women are entirely unaware of their power. Like an elephant led by a string they are subordinated by . . . just those who are most interested in holding them in slavery. If the very next Congress refuses women all the legitimate results of citizenship . . . we shall proceed to call another convention expressly to frame a new constitution and to erect a new government. . . . We mean treason, we mean secession, and on a thousand times grander scale than was that of the South. We are plotting revolution! We will overthrow this bogus Republic and plant a government of righteousness in its stead. . . .

Cheers filled the hall, and women waved their handkerchiefs to show approval. When Woodhull returned to her seat, Lucretia Mott, tears rolling down her cheeks, reached over and clasped Victoria to her breast.

The applause had scarcely quieted when Paulina Wright Davis came forward and read out a series of resolutions that had been written by Stephen Pearl Andrews the previous month. One of them, though it did not mention Victoria Woodhull by name, was clearly written with her in mind:

The inquisitional impertinence of an investigation into the personal characters of women who are able and willing to cooperate in the movement . . . shall be completely and definitely set aside and ended. All laws shall be repealed which are made use of by Government to interfere with the rights of adult individuals to pursue happiness as they may choose. . . . This will place the intercourse of persons with each other upon their individual honor.

This resolution was, of course, an endorsement of free love. The women of the rival AWSA were shocked, and Mary Livermore countered with opposing resolutions. Anthony wrote in her diary, "AWSA meeting passed resolutions saying that they were not Free Lovers. Why not one saying that men are not thieves and murderers?"

Martha Coffin Wright felt that the press, and especially Horace Greeley's *Tribune,* had falsely reported that the NWSA had adopted Stephen Pearl Andrews's "ridiculous string of resolutions," which Mrs. Davis had read "in the innocence of her heart." In fact, she noted, "they fell deader than Casca, and no action at all was taken on them." Then, reflecting her reservations about Andrews's influence, Wright wrote to Anthony, "It seems to me we have pretty squally times ahead. I wish there was an oyster big enough to hold that *Pearl* of great price, or that he might share the fate of his namesake *Stephen*. His foolish mistimed resolutions have done harm in giving the philistines a chance to rejoice." Anthony agreed: "*Professor Purlo's hypotheses* are too ridiculous—his moonshine impracticalities—oh dear dear what terribly *rough seas* we do have—but the *calm* must be near." The worst, however, was yet to come.

On the morning that Victoria Woodhull left for Apollo Hall to make her revolutionary speech, Colonel Blood had hidden the *Times,* which carried the news that Roxanna Claflin, the mother of the self-appointed presidential candidate Victoria Woodhull, had appeared before one Justice Ledwith and sworn out a warrant for the arrest of "James H. Blood, alias Dr. J. Harvey," on charges that he "had succeeded in corrupting her daughters Victoria and Tennessee" and had "entirely weaned them from their affectionate and never to be consoled mother." Mrs. Claflin also charged that she had "often heard Blood insist that Tennessee should make efforts to secure the attentions of different married gentlemen of wealth in order that they might make money out of them. Such men as were secured, she charged, were blackmailed by Blood." Mrs. Claflin alleged that the house on Thirty-eighth Street was overrun with woman's rights people, communists, and free lovers brought into the household by Blood and Andrews.

On the afternoon of May 15, 1871, the Essex Market police court was jammed with spectators. Roxy Claflin, wizened in a worn black silk-faille dress and a black Spanish-fringed shawl, told the judge, "My daughters were good daughters until they got in with that man Blood. He threatened my life several times. . . . He said he would not go to bed until he had washed his hands in my blood. He is one of those who has no bottoms in his pockets. You can keep stuffing in all the money in New York but they never fill up. If my daughters would just send this man away, as I have told them to do, they might be millionairesses."

Roxanna Claflin drew a breath and then clasped a Bible to her breast. "I say here and I call heaven to witness that there is the worst gang of communists and free lovers in that house that ever lived—Stephen Pearl Andrews and Dr. Woodhull and lots more such trash and—"

Roxy's own lawyer, Steven Townsend, interrupted. "Keep quiet, old lady," he commanded. But she continued. "I want to tell the judge what these people are—they're trash. . . . I was threatened in that house. If it had not been for my son-in-law Dr. Sparr they would have put me on Blackwell's Island—so help me God. They would have driven me to an insane asylum. They've got Stephen Pearl Andrews, that old free lover who is the worst man on earth. Until that free love and communist business came into my family there was peace and quietness. Stephen Pearl Andrews, that old free lover who asked, 'What is Jesus Christ more than any other man?' " In the course of her testimony Roxy Claflin spoke of communism and free love over and over again. After Roxy was excused, Polly Sparr took the stand and stated that she had not seen Blood use violence toward her mother but she had seen Tennie and Vickie invoke the spirit of Demosthenes, who, "speaking through Vickie, threatened my mother that she would be taken to an insane asylum."

Victoria was the next witness. She testified that she had married Dr. Woodhull at fifteen years of age and had subsequently divorced him. She said she had married, divorced, and remarried Colonel Blood and had lived with him for eleven years. Victoria added that the proceeds from her brokerage house supported as many as twenty family members. At various times, there had been ten children residing at Thirty-eighth Street. She asserted that her mother had "abused Colonel Blood without any cause whatsoever. The whole trouble was that my mother wanted to get Tennie back, wanted her going around the country telling fortunes. That is the cause of this action."

Then Colonel Blood testified. Townsend questioned him on his marital status. Colonel Blood was evasive. He said he had married Mrs. Woodhull in 1866.

"Was Mrs. Woodhull divorced when you married her?" asked Mr. Townsend.

"I don't know."

"Were you not afterwards divorced from Mrs. Woodhull?"

"Yes, in Chicago in 1868."

"How long were you separated from her?"

"We were never separated. We continued to live together."

"When did you remarry?"

"I'm not sure."

"Have you seen Dr. Woodhull?"

"I see him every day. We are living in the same house."

"Do you and Mrs. Woodhull and Dr. Woodhull occupy the same room?"

Colonel Blood glared at Roxy's lawyer but made no reply. His own lawyer, John Reymert, said, "Please tell the court that Dr. Woodhull lives in the same house and who supports him."

"The firm of Woodhull, Claflin and Company has supported the whole of them," Colonel Blood shot back. "Mrs. Woodhull's boy received a fall when he was young. He needs his father's medical care and treatment."

There was a stir in the courtroom as these irregular arrangements came to light. Blood had couched his explanation in conventional terms, for he was not about to testify to his true belief in "the abolishment of the marriage statute as it is now constituted." Both Blood and Woodhull openly espoused free love theoretically but maintained that their personal conduct was a strictly private matter. They were aware that throughout history, sexual promiscuity had been used as a weapon against those one wished to destroy.

Tennessee Celeste Claflin followed Blood to the stand. She turned to smile at the reporters in the front row, looked up imploringly at the judge, turned to stare at Townsend, and then kissed the Bible. She began to testify as if she were speaking to friends. "Mr. and Mrs. Sparr, they lived with me until I had to dump them out. I have always supported that man and his wife." Not waiting for a question from Townsend, she added, "I never knew Colonel Blood to use violence toward my mother. He only treated her too kind. In fact, I don't see how he stood it. My mother and I always got along together until Sparr came into the house. Benjamin Sparr has been trying to blackmail people through my mother."

Judge Ledwith interrupted: "This is altogether irrelevant, if it is objected to, I will rule it out."

Townsend said, "I have objected, but I can't stop her from talking." From her purse Tennie removed a sheaf of letters and began waving them.

"I have been accused of being a blackmailer. The *Tribune* said that I humbugged Commodore Vanderbilt. Other papers have said that I blackmail men for money. I want it ventilated. I have a lot of letters here supposed to be written by my mother for the purpose of blackmailing different persons in this city. My mother can't read or write. They were written by this man Sparr."

Again Judge Ledwith cut in, "Those letters are ruled out."

Tennie disregarded him. "I came here to sustain my character and I'm going to sustain it. Mrs. Woodhull has a protector but it's been announced to the world that I am a blackmailer. They're trying to make me out a bad woman."

Townsend tried to clarify the matter. "What was the reason that your mother quarreled with Colonel Blood?" he asked.

"My mother was against my sister Vickie and Colonel Blood because they have taken me from the life of a traveling clairvoyant and fortune-teller. They are the best friends I ever had outside of my mother, and they rescued me. I am a Spiritualist, and I have great power, but it was a hard life, and I could not endure it. My mother has said that she would ruin me and bring me back to my old life. But she was influenced by this man Sparr and his wife."

Reymert leaned forward and said softly, "Madam, just try to answer the questions." But Tennie was overwrought. "I have always been the martyr of this family. Yes, since I was eleven years old I used to tell fortunes with her, and since I was fourteen years old I have kept thirty or thirty-five deadheads. I am a clairvoyant. I am a Spiritualist. I know my power!

"Many of the best men in the street know it too. Commodore Vanderbilt knows my power. I have humbugged a great many rich people, I admit it. But I did it to make money to keep all these deadheads. I have led a terrible life, and because I will not return to it and leave my present position, I am persecuted."

The judge turned to Reymert and asked, "Can't you keep her from this irrelevant testimony?" Then he directed both lawyers to approach the bench. While they conversed, Tennie sprang from the witness chair, ran to the mother who had caused all this damage and trouble, and clasped her in her arms. "Come with me, come with me, let us leave here," Tennie implored. Polly Sparr pulled at her mother, trying to separate the two women. Colonel Blood moved forward, patted Tennie on the cheek, and whispered softly, "Retire, my dear. Do retire. You are only making yourself conspicuous." Reymert then asked for a recess while Tennie was led into an inner chamber. Shortly thereafter, it was announced that Tennie C. Claflin would not resume the stand.

At last reporters began to look carefully into the history of Victoria's family. All during anniversary week, accounts of "the Woodhull Convention" were accompanied by scandalous revelations. The *St. Louis Times* divulged much of the Claflins' tawdry background, including Buck's pilfering of the post office mail in Homer, Ohio, and the suspicion that he had burned down his own gristmill to collect the insurance. The paper then turned to Victoria herself, stating that she had a scandalous "antecedent history." After she had operated "a *house* in Chicago in a grand and *peculiar* style," it reported, "she removed to the sedate city of St. Louis . . . where she appeared as the proprietress of an eclectic institution located on Sixth Street next door to the present City Dispensary."

The *Cleveland Leader* reported, "One unfortunate fact . . . is that Mrs. Woodhull has made herself a prominent figure in the Woman Suffrage Movement . . . and now her shameful life has been exposed, it will follow that the enemies of female suffrage will point to her as a fair representative of the movement. . . . In Cincinnati years ago, she was the same brazen, snaky adventuress that she now is."

Henry Bowen in the *Independent* excoriated both Woodhull and her publication.

> No subject discussed during anniversary week excited so much attention as the question of suffrage for women. . . . The excitement was not a little fanned by the sudden revelation of facts in the private life of Mrs. Woodhull. . . . Mrs. Stanton, Miss Anthony and Mrs. Hooker had been foolish to have given a prominent place to Mrs. Woodhull. . . . *Woodhull & Claflin's Weekly* with its coarse treatment of all the sacred things of human life is enough to condemn anyone whose name is associated with it.

In a letter to Mrs. Stanton written during anniversary week, Martha Coffin Wright complained about Horace Greeley's "persistent determination to fasten the Free Love question" on the NWSA. Now Greeley attacked with even more ferocity. The *Tribune* headline read, "Free Love Is Free Lust." Of Woodhull, Greeley wrote that she was "one who has two husbands after a sort, and lives in the same house with them both, sharing the couch of one, but bearing the name of the other (to indicate her impartiality perhaps)." He demanded that the NWSA explain why it had made a leader of someone who followed this doctrine.

Horace Greeley might be a popular hero, but to Victoria Woodhull he was a villain. She had met Mrs. Greeley through Stanton and knew that Mary's rage against her husband was the only thing that kept her going. Here was a man who had destroyed his wife's physical health with repeated pregnancies and her mental condition with his gross insensitivity. She struck back in *Woodhull & Claflin's Weekly.* Victoria wrote what no one else was willing to say aloud.

> Mr. Greeley's home has always been a sort of domestic hell. I do not mean that Mr. Greeley has proved an unfaithful husband. . . . On the contrary he has been held up . . . as a model husband in that particular and for that reason the fault and opprobrium of domestic discord has been heaped on Mrs. Greeley. Who has ever troubled himself to inquire how much . . . Greeley has had to do with

*A portrait used during Greeley's presidential campaign, 1872.* LEFT TO RIGHT: *Horace Greeley, daughters, Gabrielle and Ida, Mary Cheney Greeley*

souring the temper, unstringing the nerves, and completely disorganizing the machinery of a delicate woman's organization.

Free love, two husbands, the destruction of marriage laws—even some of the most forward-thinking members of the woman's movement balked at having Woodhull associated with their cause. Sara Burger Stearns expressed the opinion of the majority: "I would like to have the name of Victoria C. Woodhull as connected with Woman Suffrage as soon *forgotten* as possible. We can better afford to wait for years . . . than to attempt the question of 'free love'. . . . The woman who declares 'marriage' the 'greatest evil of the Age' must not be the principal one to be heard."

But Isabella Beecher Hooker refused to denounce her beloved Victoria "at the bidding of a hostile press." She admitted, "I do not understand all her views—and I have had no time to ask her concerning them—nor to study these new social theories." In answer to Sara Burger Stearns's critical letter, Isabella explained that she was sure that Victoria Woodhull used the term *free love*

> with a meaning of her own different from this hateful one, as she will someday explain, I hope. . . . I know that she is striving to put down lust and exalt love, that her motives are exalted and her life pure and her whole nature spiritual in an uncommon degree. . . . The *Tribune* knows and so does every editor and reporter and reader, that neither you nor I, nor anyone of the prominent workers for suffrage believes in Free Love, according to the popular meaning of that word, which is free lust . . . but they know as well that if they can frighten us into disavowing any sympathy with such a powerful woman as Mrs. W. is proving, both because of her own brain and heart and because of her command of money (a thing we never had in our ranks before) and because of the influence of her paper among *Spiritualists* (a very large and increasingly influential class) and among businessmen and politicians, then they have dealt a severe blow at the whole suffrage movement and set it back years.

Elizabeth Cady Stanton was infuriated by the press and the women of the AWSA, who eagerly joined in the attack on Woodhull. How dare these women accuse Woodhull when their own lives were rife with scandal! And so it began, the rending and tearing of all they had accomplished. Stanton told Woodhull about such matters as Henry Blackwell's affair with Abby Patton. There had been talk about other leaders of the AWSA: The Reverend Phebe Hanaford had just moved to New Haven without her husband and had declared that she intended to separate from him, and there was some question whether Mary Livermore would follow her example. Furthermore, Stanton told Victoria the names of two "kept women" who sat on the Boston platform. Finally, in her fury she disclosed the reason that Henry Ward Beecher had resigned as president of the AWSA and described the behind-the-scenes efforts to quell the scandal.

Neither Stanton nor Anthony had any illusions about Woodhull's personal conduct, nor did they feel the need to justify it. Their relationship was strictly for the sake of a greater purpose. Anthony wrote, "I will take by the hand every prostitute I can find who seeks to escape the inequalities of that law which places all womanhood at the mercy of manhood." Stanton too dealt with the larger issue:

> In regard to the gossip about Mrs. Woodhull I have one answer to give all my gentlemen friends. When the men who make laws for us in Washington can stand forth and declare themselves pure and unspotted from all the sins mentioned in the Decalogue then we will demand that every woman who makes a constitutional argument on our platform shall be as chaste as Diana. . . .
>
> We have had women enough sacrificed to this sentimental, hypocritical prating about purity. This is one of man's most effective engines for our division and subjugation. He creates the public sentiment, builds the gallows, and then makes us hangmen for our sex. . . . If Victoria Woodhull must be crucified, let men drive the spikes and plait the crown of thorns.

It was in a mood of indignation over Woodhull's persecution by hypocrites who in truth were practicing free lovers that Stanton left to meet Anthony on a western tour. Amelia Bloomer, president of the Iowa Woman Suffrage Society, was later to say, "Mrs. Stanton whispered the scandal to [me] and said 'the Woodhull knows all about it.' " As Stanton and Anthony traveled across the West, the story of the Beecher-Tilton affair spread in woman suffrage circles. A miasma of scandal engulfed the cause.

Had the woman suffrage movement been a cohesive force, undoubtedly it would have had a strong voice in American politics. This was a time when the radical Republicans were sympathetic to the rights of women. They needed women's support, as they did that of black men. But the woman's movement was now shattered by personal attacks and counter-attacks, while the greater issue of enfranchisement languished amid gossip and recrimination. The window of opportunity was closing, and almost fifty years would pass before women were granted the vote.

On the day Victoria's trial ended in the Essex Market courthouse, France's government forces and the Paris communards clashed in a bloody battle. Victoria said later that upon returning from the courtroom she fell into an exhausted sleep only to be awakened by two of her spirit guides, Bonaparte and Josephine. At their behest, Victoria left her body and journeyed to a hill high above the Town Hall of Paris, where she could see that the Palais-Royal, the Ministry of Finance, the Rue de Rivoli, and the Rue Royale were all aflame. As the fire spread, the Porte Saint-Martin, the Hotel de Ville, the Bastille, and Bercy "were belching forth blood-red columns of fire."

As a final act of defiance, the communards set fire to the Tuileries Palace and, on the Left Bank, the government buildings of the Quai d'Orsay. When the last barricades fell on May 28, 1871, much of Paris lay in ruins. The government forces lost one thousand men and the communards twenty thousand. Forty thousand communards were arrested during the next month.

Mama Roxy's accusations of communism and the destruction of the Paris Commune coincided. The threat of communism haunted the United States. Though only two of the ninety seats in the Paris Commune had been occupied by Marxist communists—the commune consisted largely of working-class socialists—the American press ignored the distinction. The *Telegram* stated that the New York "communists . . . given the opportunity of the Parisians would be the same repulsive monsters," and the *World* called Section 12 of the International Workingmen's Association and its honorary president, Victoria Woodhull, "a menace" and "a foul contagion." In St. Louis, the liberal reformer Carl Schurz wrote that the International had originated in Sicily and was linked to the Mafia.

On the morning that the revolt of the Paris Commune reached its climax, Colonel Blood staggered out of Victoria's house, blood streaming down his face. Utica had struck him on the head with a chair. Twenty minutes later, Mama Roxy appeared at the police station and lodged yet another complaint against Blood. When reporters arrived at the Thirty-eighth Street house, Mama Roxy was sitting on the stoop awaiting them. "You know what a hell-hound that Blood is," she protested. At that moment Tennie walked up and surveyed the scene. "Come on, come on," she said to the reporters with resignation, and beckoned them inside, where she sank into a chair and began a tirade of her own. "All these people," she gestured wildly. "Leeches! For years they have lived this contemptible life and now useless like so many bloated corpses they utter the screams of the infirm."

Victoria, hearing the commotion, descended the stairs and said quietly, "I believe Tennie ought to use the gift God has given her not in the mercenary way. She was forced . . . to prostitute her powers. . . . We don't want any scandal."

But scandal there was, and it followed them everywhere. One Miss Achsah Truman, known as "a woman of the town," lodged a suit against Victoria saying that she had given her $800 to invest and that was the last she had seen of the money. Utica Brooker was arrested three times on charges of drunkenness and soliciting men. At the end of May, Dr. Benjamin Sparr's naked body was discovered slumped over a desk in a room at French's Hotel. He had died of an apoplectic attack. Clutched in his hand was an unfinished letter beginning, "Vickie, Colonel and Tennie included . . ."

As further scandals surfaced, the women of the AWSA tried to disassociate their organization from any views expressed by "the Woodhull." Mary Livermore accused Victoria of falsely claiming "to lead the movement"

*Paris burns: The communards set fire to the Tuileries Palace and, on the opposite bank, the government buildings on the Quai d'Orsay.*

while "advocating and practicing . . . lawless licentiousness." Lucy Stone's daughter wrote, "No woman is regarded with so much abhorrence by almost all decent people."

Anthony wrote of the AWSA, "What effort more than Herculean to save themselves from contamination from the touch even from the hem of the Woodhull garments. It is too sick! When will they begin the *washing* of their men champions and workers? It is high time." And Martha Coffin Wright, who had seen the ups and downs of the movement since its inception at Seneca Falls, deplored the situation: "The division is so senseless . . . that I have no patience with it."

Victoria Woodhull retaliated in the way she knew best—the Claflin way. In the *Weekly* appeared an editorial:

> Without pretending to a perfect knowledge of, or caring a fig about, the history of the *personnel* of either branch of the woman movement, we are led to suspect that this over-pious, over sensitive, Boston wing have much more to conceal than their more outspoken sisters of Apollo Hall. . . . Mrs. Livermore, it is a rather delicate thing for . . . those "who live in glass houses to throw stones," and you very well know that most people do live in these brittle tenements.

Anthony knew the risks that members of the American Woman Suffrage Association were taking by provoking Victoria Woodhull, who was privy to scandal concerning Livermore and other people in this group. Anthony commented,

> This fresh howl will soon be over—I learn the Boston folks begin to feel the kick of their Free Love gun firing quite painfully—they must be awfully ashamed of themselves—if there be any such possibilities left unto them.
>
> Mrs. Hooker is in Boston today preaching . . . Christ and the Woman at the Well—"Thou hast had five husbands and the one thou now livest with is *not* thy husband—go preach my gospel"— has Woodhull a more *numerous* record of husbands that are *not* husbands? Well, we are fallen upon strange times but there is no way but to live them . . . judging not, lest we be also judged.

Woodhull needed support and needed it quickly. On May 22, 1871, she wrote a "card" to the editors of the *World* and the *Times*.

Because I am a woman and because I conscientiously hold opinions somewhat different from the self-elected orthodoxy which men find their profit in supporting . . . self-elected orthodoxy assails me, vilifies me and endeavors to cover my life with ridicule and dishonor. . . .

One of the charges made against me is that I live in the same house with my former husband, Dr. Woodhull, and my present husband, Colonel Blood. The fact is a fact. Dr. Woodhull, being sick, ailing and incapable of self-support, I felt it my duty to myself and to human nature that he should be cared for. . . . My present husband, Colonel Blood, not only approves of this charity but co-operates in it. I esteem it one of the most virtuous acts of my life.

Victoria issued a warning:

I do not intend to be made the scapegoat of sacrifice to be offered up as a victim to society by those who cover over the foulness of their lives and the feculence of their thoughts with a hypocritical mantle of fair professions, and by diverting public attention from their own iniquity in pointing the finger at me. . . . I believe in Spiritualism. I advocate Free Love in its highest, purest sense, as the only cure for the immorality . . . by which men corrupt and disfigure God's most holy institution of sexual relation.

Then in a thinly disguised reference to the Beecher-Tilton affair she added,

My judges preach against Free Love openly, practice it secretly. For example, I know of one man in a neighboring city, a public teacher of eminence, who lives in concubinage with the wife of another public teacher of almost equal eminence. All three concur in denouncing offenses against morality. "Hypocrisy is the tribute paid by vice to virtue." So be it. But I decline to stand up as the "frightful example." I shall make it my business to analyze some of these lives and will take my chance in the matter of libel suits.

# CHAPTER TWENTY-FOUR

# THIS GIRL IS A TRAMP

THEODORE TILTON appeared at the Woodhull residence the following morning, the *World* tucked under his arm. "Who do you mean in this card?" he asked with feigned innocence.

"I mean you and Mr. Beecher," Victoria replied. Tilton, of course, already knew that. The previous evening, in a three-hour conference with Moulton and Beecher, he had been designated to endear himself to Woodhull so that "some influence might be brought to bear to induce this sudden enemy to suppress the dangerous tale." Tilton implored Victoria, "Don't take any steps now. . . . I can be of service to you. . . . Let me take you over to Mrs. Tilton's, and you will find her in no condition to be dragged before the public."

Victoria agreed. Lib greeted her cordially and asked her to sit and talk while she sewed a checked-silk dress for Florry. They spoke quietly about the joys and burdens of motherhood. When Victoria was about to leave, Mrs. Tilton rose and presented her with a book of poetry, which she inscribed, "To my friend Victoria Woodhull."

Woodhull soon became a frequent visitor in the Tilton home, where the conversation revolved around woman's rights, Spiritualism, and free love. According to Victoria, she told Theodore that the trouble was not his wife's affair but "the false social institutions under which we still live." She ridiculed the "dreadful suzz, maudlin sentiment, and mock heroics" he was exhibiting over a matter she found to be "the most natural in the world" and commented that "our sickly religious literature, Sunday school morality, and pulpit phariseeism humbugged him into the belief he ought to feel and act in this harlequin and absurd way." And she told Lib, "Be kind to and sympathize with the new attraction rather than be waspish and indignant. . . . I have learned that the first great error most married people commit is in endeavoring to hide from each other the little irregularities into which all are liable to fall. Nothing is so conducive to continuing happiness as mutual confidence."

Frank Moulton also was enlisted to befriend Mrs. Woodhull. He was struck both by Victoria's intelligence and her "unexpected modesty." Because he considered his wife his full partner in life, he said to Emma, "I want you to take a look at that woman and tell me what you think of her." Emma, as described by her husband, was "a broad-minded, self-possessed woman able to take care of herself," one who accepted "life on the theory of human imperfection." She found Victoria to be high-strung, magnetic, and dedicated to the idea that she had the power to eliminate women's suffering. Emma too opened her home to Victoria.

To ingratiate himself further, Tilton offered to put his pen at Woodhull's service to legitimize her and her theories. Anna Dickinson was then the most sought-after woman lecturer in America, and Victoria was determined to outdo her. In the *Golden Age,* Tilton bestowed Anna's title upon Victoria, writing, "If the woman's movement has a Joan of Arc, it is this gentle but fiery genius. . . . Little understood by the public, she is denounced in the most outrageous manner by people who do not appreciate her moral worth." Because Dickinson was admired for the physical freedom that few women were able to enjoy, Tilton wrote of Woodhull, "She can ride a horse like an Indian, and climb a tree like an athlete; she can swim, row a boat, play billiards, and dance. Moreover, as the crown of her physical virtues, she can walk all day like an Englishwoman."

Tilton rewrote *The Woodhull Memorial* so that it would have a more popular ring when she presented it on the Lyceum circuit. But his most ambitious task was a biography that Woodhull insisted he write based on rough notes from Colonel Blood. Woodhull and Tilton were in the difficult position of having to explain how her mother had turned on her and accused her of scandalous acts in the recent court action. In fact, it was hard to describe to an outsider the tremendous hold both parents had established through their psychological and physical domination of their children. Tilton's explanation was clever if convoluted. Describing the Claflin family, he wrote,

> Such another family-circle of cats and kits, with soft fur and sharp claws, purring at one moment and fighting the next, never before filled one house with their clamors since Babel began. They love and hate—they do good and evil—they bless and smite each other.
>
> Being daughters of the horse-leech, they cry "give." The whole brood are of the same feather—except Victoria and Tennie. . . . Victoria is a green leaf, and her legion of relatives are caterpillars

who devour her. Their sin is that they return no thanks after meat; they curse the hand that feeds them. They are what my friend Mr. Greeley calls "a bad crowd."

But it was Victoria's other powers that proved the most thorny: In the first draft, Tilton made no mention of her spiritual gifts. Victoria objected. "You have left out the most important parts!" she admonished him. Spiritualists were among her strongest supporters, and it was vital to Woodhull that she prove herself to this group. Tilton was told to include her communication with the other world, her success as a clairvoyant and trance speaker, and even the incident where, like Christ himself raising Lazarus, she had brought her son, Byron, back from death.

"You want me to say that you have called a dead child to life?" Tilton asked incredulously.

"Yes, to do otherwise would be as if you were writing Hamlet and decided to leave out his father's ghost." So Tilton wrote,

I must now let out a secret. She acquired her studies, performed her work, and lived her life by the help (as she believes) of heavenly spirits. From her childhood till now (having reached her thirty-third year) her anticipation of the other world has been more vivid than her realizations of this. She has entertained angels, and not unawares. These gracious guests have been her constant companions. They abide with her night and day. They dictate her life with daily revelations and like St. Paul, she is "not disobedient to the heavenly vision." . . . Every characteristic utterance which she gives to the world is dictated while under spirit influence, and most often in a totally unconscious state. The words that fall from her lips are garnered by the swift pen of her husband and published almost verbatim.

Tilton went all out in his service to Mrs. Woodhull. His biography was so florid that *Harper's Weekly* wrote of it, "If apples are wormy this year, and grapes mildew, and ducks' eggs addle, and bladed corn be lodged, it may all be ascribed to the unhallowed influence of Mr. Tilton's life of Victoria Woodhull." Lucretia Mott's niece Marianna wrote of the biography, "Can anything but infatuation or aberration explain its absurdities?" And Julia Ward Howe, author of the "Battle Hymn of the Republic," made the dire prediction, "Such a book is a tomb from which no author again rises. . . . It would have sunk any man's reputation anywhere for common sense."

Tilton, however, seemed unembarrassed and believed what he had written. When interviewed by a reporter from the *Sun,* he said of Victoria, "Her sincerity, truthfulness, nobility and uprightness of character rank her in my mind, as a pious Catholic would rank Saint Teresa."

"You astonish me," said the reporter.

"Not more than I myself was astonished at the singular revelation of her character to me, as one of the most upright, truthful, religious, unsullied souls I have ever met."

There is no doubt that Tilton's involvement with Woodhull, which began for practical purposes, had now become infatuation. During the summer of 1871 he spent many nights at the Woodhull house and often slept with her on the cool rooftop. They swam at Coney Island and rowed in Central Park. Woodhull inculcated Tilton with her free love doctrine, which he was more than ready to assimilate. She told him, "A popular objection against Free Love is that it breaks up families. My answer to this indictment is that a family which falls in pieces when Free Love strikes it is already broken up and waiting for a loophole out of which to escape."

While appearances suggest that they were lovers, Tilton never commented on the subject. Three years later, however, after Tilton had disassociated himself both from free love and from Victoria herself, she told a reporter from the *Chicago Times,* "Mr. Tilton was my devoted lover for more than half a year. . . . He slept every night for three months, in my arms." But when a New York journalist later asked her to verify this statement, she replied, "I am not a fool. A woman who is before the world as I am would not make such a flagrant statement, even if it were true." Perhaps she had never said it. Perhaps it was said by a Victoria possessed by the spirits, who was another woman altogether.

Of all the allies Woodhull sought, Henry Ward Beecher was the most valuable. She insisted on meeting him to woo him to her cause. Although Moulton and Tilton prevailed upon Beecher to accede to Woodhull's wishes, he flatly refused. Three weeks after her "card" the following statement appeared in *Woodhull & Claflin's Weekly*:

Civilization is festering to the bursting point in our great cities and notably in Brooklyn. . . . At this very moment, awful and herculean efforts are being made to suppress the most terrific scandal which has ever astounded and convulsed any community. . . . We have the inventory of discarded husbands and wives and lovers, with dates, circumstances and establishments. . . . Confidences which are no confidences abound.

Beecher changed his mind.

> My Dear Victoria,
>     I have arranged with Frank that you will see Mr. Beecher at my house on Friday night. He will attend a meeting at the church till ten o'clock and we will give you the rest of the evening as late as you desire. You may consider this fixed. Meanwhile on the sunshiny day I salute you with a good morning—peace be with you.
>
>                                                 Yours, Theodore Tilton

They met in the late evening, these two charismatic people who had much in common: Both could persuade and provoke, both were inspired by the adulation of their followers, both derived their strength from higher powers. In an effort to exert his considerable charm, Beecher, according to Woodhull, confided that he kept a spirit table at Plymouth Church and informed her of his early use of mesmerism. In this and in two subsequent meetings, Beecher convinced her that they thought alike. He told her that he too advocated a reform of the marriage laws. "Marriage is the grave of love," Beecher avowed. "I have never married a couple that I did not feel condemned."

"Why then do you not preach that conviction?" asked Woodhull.

"If I were to do so I should preach to empty seats." Beecher said he preached the truth as fast as he thought people could accept it. "Milk for babies, meat for strong men."

Victoria "held society to be upside down." She felt she could persuade Beecher to join her in her holy quest to achieve the idyllic world that the spirits had revealed to her. "Beecher's life was Woodhull's faith," Frank Moulton was to observe. "She hoped from hearing him talk in his lofty way . . . that she might wheedle or compel him to come forward and thus make her theory of the reconstruction of society respectable."

Convinced that her new allies would stand by her, Victoria wrote Isabella that she was sure her brother Henry would provide the introduction for a speech she was to present at Steinway Hall in November on "The Principles of Social Freedom." Isabella well remembered the letter she had received from her brother criticizing Woodhull, so she questioned the truth of Victoria's assertion and wrote her "a most indignant and rebuking letter" saying that her brother would never become involved. Woodhull's reply astonished Isabella "by its calm assertion that she considered [Henry] as true a friend to her as I myself." She wondered what hold her friend Victoria had over her brother and sent her letter to Theodore Tilton, asking him to "write me what it all meant." Tilton did not reply.

Isabella was totally dedicated to Victoria—a disciple of this "strange prophet." Nothing could sway her. When a friend, Anna Savery, sent her Woodhull's "card" and the threatening statement that had appeared in the *Weekly* mentioning "the inventory of discarded husbands and wives and lovers" and asked her for an explanation, Isabella replied:

As to what Mrs. Woodhull means by that threat I do not know and I have no time to ask. I have never talked with her on the social question fifteen minutes and I will not. My ground is that she alone of all the women in the U. States succeeded in getting a hearing and a report out of a dead Congress. . . . She has . . . appeared to me as . . . a prophetess full of visions and messages to the people which it would be woe unto her to refrain from proclaiming even though martyrdom was sure to follow. . . .

She is a mystery to me but so is every *forerunner* to the people of his or her day and for one I am determined to keep my eyes and ears and heart open to any woman who thinks she has a word from above to deliver unto the nations. . . . I verily believe that the *hour* of woman approaches and is even upon us. . . . If the spirit world is what she conceives it to be and is eagerly waiting to pour down upon us in a purifying flood—let it come . . . my heart will exult with joy. . . .

The feeling on this Woodhull matter has nearly killed me. . . . I am driven to death. . . . Just now my sister Catharine is attacking Mrs. W's private character *infamously* so as to keep people from going out to hear her. The result is she will have a jam next time and last week had a good house on a stormy night. It is dreadful having foes in your own household.

When Catharine Beecher heard that Victoria Woodhull was to lecture in Hartford she attacked her in the *Courant*. Under the pseudonym of "a Lady of Connecticut," she asked, "Can anyone support a woman who maintained that when a wife and mother loved elsewhere, she should forsake her family for that love, who maintained also that a woman who fulfilled conjugal duties after that specific love was gone was guilty of prostitution?" Catharine then went on to conclude that only Victoria's sister Tennie C. "exceeds her in indecencies."

Stephen Pearl Andrews countered with an article for the *Weekly* reminding the readers of the *Courant* that Mrs. Woodhull had spoken to an audience of four thousand in Cleveland and had said nothing offensive. To bolster Woodhull's reputation, he published the letter from Isabella Beecher Hooker in which she had addressed Victoria as "My Darling Queen." As a result of all this publicity, as Isabella had predicted, the Hartford Opera House was filled to capacity.

This brought on another barrage of criticism. The Reverend Phebe Hanaford rescinded her invitation to Isabella to speak at her First Universalist Church of New Haven because of her "unholy alliance" with "the notorious mistress of Colonel Blood's affection." Referring to the "Darling Queen" letter, she wrote to Isabella, "Every drop of Beecher blood in your veins ought to cry out against her life of shameful disregard of propriety. . . . A repentant Magdalen I can accept as a co-laborer—but a woman who 'glories in her shame' never!"

Hard put to defend herself, Isabella blamed Andrews in her reply: "That private note of mine was the outpouring of an admiration I could no longer repress. . . . I said this woman is a Born Queen and I owe her the allegiance of my heart—so I wrote just as I felt and it was printed by a *man* without her knowledge."

While Isabella had become Woodhull's greatest defender, Horace Greeley and his editor Whitelaw Reid, who was in charge of the day-to-day operations of the *Tribune,* led the attacks on Mrs. Woodhull. Presumably, Isabella felt that Anna Dickinson could influence Reid, for she repeatedly wrote to her complaining of his treatment of Woodhull. The previous spring, when Woodhull first threatened to expose the private lives of those who opposed her, she wanted to use the *Tribune* as an outlet. Greeley was away on a lecture tour so Woodhull sent an urgent message to Whitelaw Reid asking him to visit her. According to his account, when he arrived he found Victoria and Theodore together. "Mrs. Woodhull received me cordially and at once began detailing her stories about Mr. Beecher to the effect that he was a practical free lover who ought to be honored in his practice but denounced for his hypocritical professions—who kept a regular harem in Brooklyn and had more illegitimate children than any other man in town— with much more equally revolting and incredible." She then went on to denounce other prominent people in Brooklyn, New York, and Boston. When she had finished, Tilton begged Reid to dissuade Mrs. Woodhull from trying to publish her accusations in his or any other newspaper.

After a second visit, when Reid was chastised by Victoria both for failing to publish her story and for not trying to stop the critical coverage of her in the *Tribune,* she warned him that she possessed certain information about Anna Dickinson that would prove disastrous were it made public. Less than a fortnight after Reid's second visit to Woodhull, he received a frantic summons from Anna that implied that she was being threatened. He answered, "I shall break all engagements, and go over Saturday night— leaving here at midnight, and reaching the Continental about five in the morning. I'll go up to your house immediately after breakfast—say by nine to ten o'clock." After Reid's visit he wrote to Anna, consoling her and advising her how to handle threats and gossip. "Take Beecher for a model," he instructed. "He works with ease to himself and bears the misfortunes that harrow the minds of all . . . in a way that strengthens rather than weakens him."

As Isabella continued to write to Reid complaining about the *Tribune*'s treatment of Mrs. Woodhull, he began to weary of the situation. He visited Isabella at Nook Farm in August hoping to placate her, but to no avail. Finally, an exasperated Reid wrote to her explaining that neither he nor Horace Greeley had written anything about Victoria Woodhull that was not true. He added with sarcasm, "I must and do always treat her as I treat all women, demi-rep, slanderers or ladies, with needful courtesy where I meet them."

Harriet Beecher Stowe, no longer able to ignore the situation, visited Henry at Twin Mountain House in New Hampshire and confronted him with the rumors. He vigorously denied them, after which she announced that Woodhull was "a snake and should be given a good clip with a shovel." Using the powerful weapon of her pen Harriet began a serial, "My Wife and I," which appeared in installments in the *Christian Union*. Stowe felt that humor would accomplish what a diatribe might fail to do. Victoria Woodhull appeared in a thinly veiled portrait as the shameless adventuress and newspaper owner Audacia Dangyereyes. The scenes depicted were perilously close to those that had recently occurred.

"I have just come from the Police Court, where there's a precious row. Our friend 'Dacia Dangyereyes is up for blackmailing and swindling and there's a terrible wash of dirty linen going on."

"How horribly disagreeable," said Eva, "to have such women around. It makes one ashamed of one's sex."

In a play on words, Isabella appeared as Mrs. Cerulean, since "her head was in the blue." Pointing to the scandal in the courtroom and all that had followed, Harriet hit upon Isabella's trait of loyalty to the underdog. As Isabella had admitted, "The truth is, the more people are mistaken and going in a wrong way . . . the more I am inclined to keep company with them in the hope of using with them what influence I may have, toward a right way." Now Harriet wrote of her sister's loyalty to Victoria Woodhull, "You will see, Mrs. Cerulean will adhere all the closer for this. It's persecu-

*Victoria Woodhull as the seductress Audacia Dangyereyes,*
*in Harriet Beecher Stowe's "My Wife and I"*

tion, and virtue in all ages has been persecuted. Therefore, all who are persecuted are virtuous. Don't you see the logical consistency? And then, don't
the Bible say, 'Blessed are ye when men persecute you, and say all manner
of evil against you'?"

Harriet also satirized Isabella's spiritual vision and painted her sister as
a gullible fool.

'Dacia . . . conducted herself in a most sweet and winning manner
and cast herself at her feet for patronage; and Mrs. Cerulean,
regarding her through those glory spectacles which she usually
wears, took her up immediately as a promising candidate for the
latter day. Mrs. Cerulean don't see anything in 'Dacia's paper that,

properly interpreted, need make any trouble; because, you see, as she says, *everything ought to be love.* . . . Then the infinite will come down into the finite, and the finite will overflow into the infinite, and in short, Miss 'Dacia's cock's-feathers will sail right straight up into Heaven, and we shall see her cheek by jowl with the angel Gabriel, promenading the streets of the new Jerusalem. That's the programme.

Meanwhile, 'Dacia's delighted. She hadn't the remotest idea of being an angel, or anything of the sort, but since good judges have told her she is, she takes it all very contentedly. Mrs. Cerulean is a respectable woman, of respectable family, and this girl is a tramp, that's what she is, and it is absolutely impossible that Mrs. Cerulean can know what she is about.

The final draft of Woodhull's speech, "The Principles of Social Freedom," to be presented at Steinway Hall on November 20, was carefully crafted by Stephen Pearl Andrews to be "as soft" as possible so that Henry Ward Beecher could introduce Victoria without embarrassment. The bulk of the speech traced the changing attitudes toward social freedom from the sixteenth century to the present. Victoria herself carried it to Brooklyn, met Beecher in his study at Plymouth Church, and presented him with the document. She asked that he read it carefully and suggest revisions before introducing her at Steinway Hall. But as the days grew short, she had no word from Beecher, and Tilton told her that Beecher was afraid that if he introduced her he might be "tarred and feathered" with her belief in free love. On the day before she was to speak, the following letter was delivered to Beecher.

Dear Sir:

For reasons in which you are deeply interested as well as myself and the cause of truth, I desire to have an interview with you, without fail, at some hour tomorrow. Two of your sisters have gone out of their way to assail my character and purposes . . . and thus to defeat the political ends at which I aim.

You doubtless know that it is in my power to strike back and in ways more disastrous than anything that can come to me but I do not desire to do this. I simply desire justice from those from whom I have a right to expect it and a reasonable course on your part will assist me to it. I speak guardedly, but I think you will understand me.

I repeat that I must have an interview tomorrow, since I am to speak tomorrow evening at Steinway Hall and what I shall or shall not say will depend largely on the result of the interview. . . .

They met at the Moultons' house, in the fading afternoon light. Beecher was fully aware of the Damoclean sword Woodhull held over his head, but still he resisted. When all of her arguments seemed to fail she told Beecher that his attachment to Mrs. Tilton would surely be revealed to the public. "The only safety you have is in coming out as soon as possible as an advocate of social freedom and thus palliate, if you cannot completely justify your practices, by founding them at least on principle. Your introduction of me would bridge the way."

"I cannot. I cannot!" Beecher cried out. "I should sink through the floor. I'm a moral coward on this subject and you know it. I am not fit to stand by you, who go there to speak what you know to be the truth. I should stand there a living lie."

Beecher knelt on the sofa beside her and clasped her face between his hands. He began to weep and to beg her, "Oh, let me off. Let me off."

These histrionics had no doubt been effective in the past, for Beecher had used them often, but Victoria was not impressed with this "maudlin display." "Mr. Beecher, if I am compelled to go upon that platform alone, I shall begin by telling the audience why I am alone and why you are not with me."

Beecher replied, "I cannot face this thing! I can never endure such a terror. Oh! if it must come, let me know of it . . . in advance that I may take my own life."

# CHAPTER TWENTY-FIVE

# YES!
# I AM A FREE LOVER!

I N FRONT of Steinway Hall, ten-foot-long streamers, bright red with gold letters, read Freedom! Freedom! Freedom! They were drenched with rain, and several had whipped free and twisted in the wild wind. At the entry door, seven-foot-high posters proclaimed Victoria C. Woodhull . . . The Principles of Sexual Freedom . . . Free Love, Marriage, Divorce and Prostitution.

At seven o'clock, a full hour before the lecture, three thousand people, a capacity audience, jammed into the hall and crowded the stairs and corridors. The raffish and the respectable jostled each other in eager anticipation. On the street, a "lady of the evening," her hair a bright hennaed red, called out to no one, "I hope by God I haven't come here in all this rain for nothing!" Nearby, as hundreds of people were turned away, fistfights broke out.

In a small anteroom behind the stage, Victoria and Tennie C. found themselves surrounded by reporters. Victoria wore a black silk dress with her signature white rose at her throat. She whispered to a *Herald* reporter, "Your paper has never misrepresented me, I know it won't now," then reached into a vase nearby and handed him a white rose. Tennie, who was talking animatedly to the reporters, suddenly lifted her skirt to reveal her ankles encased in gaiters.

From time to time Victoria glanced toward the entrance to the anteroom. At seven forty-five Tilton and Moulton elbowed their way through the crowd to her side. After Woodhull left Brooklyn that afternoon, they had tried to persuade Beecher to introduce her. Tilton suggested that Beecher say he disagreed with her views but that she had a right to express them. Finally, Beecher said he would be there, though he was not sure if he "could bear the ordeal." But at ten minutes after eight Henry Ward Beecher still had not appeared. An impatient audience began to clap and pound their feet. Then a chant began: "Woodhull, Woodhull, Woodhull!"

Victoria, close to tears, clutched Theodore's arm. "There isn't one brave man in the circle of two cities to preside at my meeting." Then resolutely she walked down the long dim corridor toward the stage. When she was about ten paces ahead of him, Tilton moved quickly after her. "Are you going to introduce her?" Moulton called out.

"Yes, by Heaven, since no one else has the pluck to do it."

Victoria paused in the wings as the clapping and stomping roared in her ears. Tennie, noting her sister's pallor and glazed eyes, saw the danger that might lie ahead if the spirits intervened. If that happened Vickie would become another person—ecstatic, swept away, engulfed by her visions—and who knew what she might say or do? "Vickie, be calm," Tennie cautioned. As Victoria moved reluctantly onto the stage, the audience rose as one. People ran forward to crowd around the platform, leaning perilously close to the gas footlights. Utica—still beautiful and sweet-faced but in her usual state of partial inebriation—adjusted the panniers of her pink *peau de soie* skirt and settled next to a group of her friends in a front box that partially jutted out onto the stage. Tennie repaired to an identical box opposite.

Amid the uproar, Victoria stood frozen in place, blinking rapidly and staring out at the audience. At that moment Tilton strode on stage. Taking Victoria by the arm, he led her forward and raised his arms to silence the crowd.

Ladies and gentlemen, happening to have an unoccupied night, which is an unusual thing for me in the lecture season, I came to this meeting actuated by curiosity to know what my friend would have to say in regard to the great question which has occupied her so many years of her life. Five minutes ago, I did not expect to appear here, but several gentlemen have declined to introduce our speaker, one after another for various reasons, chief among them being objections to this lady's character. I know it, and I believe in it, and I vouch for it. As to her views, she will give them to you herself and you may judge for yourself.

Tilton's voice became infused with passion. "It may be that she is a fanatic. It may be that I am a fool. But before high Heaven I would rather be both fanatic and fool in one, than be such a coward as would deny this woman the sacred right of free speech."

From her perch in the stage box Utica Brooker leaned forward to study her sister as Vickie began reading her speech. In the wings, Stephen Pearl Andrews ran his finger across the page, following the words in his copy as she spoke them. In the context of a historical review of social freedom, Woodhull examined male and female relationships in several societies. The audience sat quietly but this was not what they had come to hear. It was not until she reached the present day that Victoria Woodhull turned to the controversial issue of woman's rights.

> The basis of society is the relation of the sexes. . . . There is no escaping the fact that the principle by which the *male* citizens of these United States assume to rule the *female* citizens is *not* that of self-government but that of despotism. . . . Our government is based upon the proposition that all men and women are born free and equal and entitled to certain inalienable rights, among which are life, liberty, and the *pursuit* of happiness. What we, who demand social freedom ask is simply that the government of this country shall be administered in accordance with the spirit of this proposition. *Nothing more, nothing less.*

Warming to the subject of sexual equality and free love, she looked out at an audience who now eagerly awaited her words. A flush colored Victoria's pale cheeks as once again she created an invisible connection with the audience. Abandoning Andrews's written text, she now peppered her speech with language of her own.

> The wiseacres stop and tell us that *everybody* must *not* pursue happiness in his or her own way. . . . I say they're wrong. They're just humbugging you. What I believe to be the truth I endeavor to practice and in advocating it permit me to say I shall *speak* so *plainly* that *none* may complain that I did not make myself understood.
>
> Marriages have endeavored to . . . hold the people in subjection to what has been considered a standard of moral purity. . . . But let us inquire into this matter. . . . Is marriage where two meet and realize that the love elements of their natures are harmonious . . . or is it where a *soulless form* is pronounced over two who know *no* commingling of life's hopes? . . . The courts hold if the law solemnly pronounce two married that *they are married,* whether

love is present or not. . . . It is a stupid law which can find no analogies in nature.

Marriage must consist of love or of law. . . . People may be married by *law* . . . and they may also be married by *love* and lack all sanction of law. . . . Law cannot compel two to love. . . . This is a matter that concerns *these two* and *no* other living soul has *any human* right to say aye, yes or no, since it is a matter which is none of their business. . . . Where there is *no* love as a basis of marriage there should be *no* marriage!

Victoria could feel the spirits all about her. It was these spirits for whom she spoke, all those suffering souls whose burden she carried on her frail shoulders. As she continued to depart from Stephen Pearl Andrews's speech, she seemed unaware of the rapt audience drinking in her radical doctrine or of the force of her words.

I do not care where it is that sexual commerce results from the dominant power of *one sex* over *the other,* compelling him or her to submission against the *instincts of love.* And where hate or disgust is present, whether it be in the gilded palaces of Fifth Avenue or in the lowliest purlieus of Greene Street, *there* is prostitution, and *all* the law that a *thousand* State assemblies may pass cannot make it otherwise.

Victoria's passion lifted the audience to a spiritual frenzy as an almost sexual ecstasy gripped the crowd. Caught in her spell, they burst into wild applause and cries of "Hurrah!" But as the roar subsided, from the stage box where Utica sat came the sound of hissing, which led to more applause and still more hissing. Then the jealous Utica stood. Like her mother, she was determined to bring her sister down. Her envy, fueled by laudanum and alcohol, knew no bounds. At thirty, Utica had been drinking steadily for half her life. A beatific smile lit her face as she called out to her sister, "How would you like to come into this world without knowing who your father was?"

Utica instinctively knew that the philosophical doctrine of free love collapsed in the real world. The theories of the desiccated old Stephen Pearl Andrews had little emotional power, but Victoria was a desirable, magnetic woman, and from her, free love became explicitly sexual. And if one actually practiced free love, the result would be illegitimate children, often with no one to raise them. Victoria stumbled as she attempted to answer her sister. "There are thousands of noble men and women in the world today who never knew who their fathers were," she replied. "Every person is . . . entitled to pursue *happiness* in whatever direction he or she may choose."

But Victoria's spirit spell had been shattered. She had lost control of her audience. The hissing escalated. Utica sat down with a smile of victory as Victoria tried to continue: "In all contracts, people have the protection of the government to contract for an hour, a day, a week . . . least of all does the government require that any of these contracts be entered into for life. Why should the social relations of the sexes be made subject to a different theory?" Without specifically mentioning Beecher she said, "When Christian ministers are no longer afraid or ashamed to be Christians they will embrace this doctrine. Free Love will be an integral part of the religion of the future."

From Utica's box a woman's voice screamed out, "Yah, yah, yah—we've had enough of you." Once again, Vickie struggled on.

They assert that the murder of Richardson by McFarland was the legitimate result of *Free Love,* but I deny it. McFarland murdered Richardson because he believed that the law had sold Abby Sage's *soul* and *body* to him, and, consequently, that *he owned her* and that no other person had any right to her favor and that she had no right to bestow her love upon any other person. . . . The murder of Richardson, then, is not chargeable to his love or her love, but to the fact of the supposed ownership, which the law of marriage conferred on McFarland.

I have a better right to speak, as one having authority in this matter, than most of you have, since it has been my province to study *Free Love* in all its various lights and shades. When I practiced clairvoyance, hundreds, aye thousands, of desolate, heart-broken men, as well as women, came to me for advice. . . . The tales of horror, of wrongs inflicted and endured, which were poured into my ears, first awakened me to a realization of the hollowness and the *rottenness of society* and compelled me . . . to ask the question whether it were not better to let the bound go free. In time, I was fully convinced that marriage laws were productive of precisely the reverse of that for which they are supposed to have been framed.

If our sisters who inhabit Greene Street and other filthy localities choose to remain in debauch, and if our brothers choose to visit them there, they are only exercising the same right that we exercise in remaining away. . . . I can see no moral difference between a woman who marries and lives with a man because he can provide for her wants and the woman who is not married but who is provided for at the same price. . . . The sexual relation must be rescued from this *insidious* form of *slavery*. Women must rise from their position as *ministers* to the *passions of men* to be their equals. Their entire system of education must be changed. They must be trained like men, [to be] independent individuals, and not mere appendages or adjuncts of men, forming but one member of society. They must be the companions of men from choice, never from necessity.

Again, Utica stood and waved her white silk handkerchief rapidly to attract attention. She knew her sister was now totally in the thrall of the spirits. Cheers and hisses filled the hall. "Sit down," yelled a voice. "It's her sister," screamed out another. Vickie could no longer be heard above the tumult. She walked to the right side of the stage, leaned over the rail of Tennie's box, and asked her sister, "Can't you get Utie to go out?" At that moment a policeman appeared in the box on the opposite side of the stage, but as he caught hold of Utica's arm people cried out, "Leave her alone." The policeman sheepishly left the box. Tilton walked forward and shouted, "This meeting was called for the lady who was speaking when this interruption occurred. . . ."

"I am her sister," Utica called out.

"I am in the chair," responded Tilton.

"Mrs. Woodhull, are *you* a free lover?" a voice shouted.

"The love I cannot command is not mine," she replied. "Let me not disturb myself about it nor attempt to filch it from its rightful owner—"

"You have not answered the question," interrupted Utica.

Victoria flung her speech to the floor. She tore the white rose from the neck of her dress, and her words tumbled out: "*Yes! I am a free lover!* I have an inalienable, constitutional, and natural right to love whom I may, to love for as long or as short a period as I can, to change that love every day if I please! And with that right neither you nor any law have any right to interfere. I mean just that and—"

But the noise was deafening, and few heard the end of Victoria's speech. What Utica had sought to do, she had done. Victoria's opponents were now in the ascendancy. The newspapers reported the most inflammatory aspects of her Steinway Hall speech. "Free Lover Lectures on Free Love," announced the *Argus* headline. "Died of Free Love . . . The Woman

Suffrage Movement," proclaimed the *Gazette*. Even Tilton ran from the scandal. The *Tribune* quoted him as saying, "It was not the printed speech that did the damage, it was the interjected remarks. . . . She said violent things!"

Victoria Woodhull's problem was passion. When she openly admitted, "To preach the doctrine you must live the life!" she was censured as "a vile woman," one who possessed the carnal power to captivate and destroy men.

Martha Coffin Wright said that all over the nation women lined up against Woodhull and joined "the Free Love panic." She wrote,

> I cannot understand the nice distinctions on the Free Love question and I don't mean to try. . . . It is hardly worthwhile to ostracize those who believe they have found a remedy for it all in some refined and incomprehensible idea of Free Love. The outcry, in most cases, proceeds I think, either from the timid, who are afraid of their own, or other people's shadow, or from the hypocritical, who join in the cry of "stop thief!" or from those who have always held aloof, as an excuse for their indifference, people who cannot trust in the eventual victory of truth over error.

Woodhull's supporters were now limited to members of the NWSA, who saw in her beliefs their last chance for enfranchisement; to Spiritualists, who accepted her as one of their own and had elected her president of their national association; to members of Section 12 of the International Workingmen's Association, of which she was honorary president.

To solidify the support of labor, Woodhull spoke at a meeting of the Reform Labor League on "The Impending Revolution." The content was vintage Andrews: a condemnation of the railroad barons, of corporate monopolies and of the great land grab that had appropriated property belonging to the Indians. After Roxy's clumsy attempt to blackmail Commodore Vanderbilt, Victoria and Tennie C. no longer had access to his world of money and power. With nothing left to lose, Victoria read Andrews's attack on the Commodore and his son William Henry.

> A *Vanderbilt* may sit in his office and manipulate stocks or make dividends by which in a few years he amasses fifty million dollars from the industries of the country and he is one of the remarkable men of the age. But if a poor, half-starved child were to take a loaf of bread from his cupboard to prevent starvation, she would be sent

first to the Tombs and thence to Blackwell's Island. . . . . It is a crime
for a single person to steal a dollar, but a corporation may steal millions of dollars and be canonized as saints.

The *Times* ridiculed the speech saying that Woodhull was "capable of
mischief in inflaming the unthinking hostility of the poor to the rich."
Undeterred, Andrews published the *Communist Manifesto* in the *Weekly,*
the first appearance in America of Marx and Engels's 1848 document that
called for the abolition of private property, child labor, and all rights of
inheritance as well as calling for free education and a heavy progressive
income tax.

On Sunday, December 17, 1871, a parade was organized to protest the
French government's execution of Louis-Nathaniel Rossel the previous
month for his participation in the Paris Commune. (Ironically, Rossel had
been a member of the commune for only nine days, after which he'd
resigned in protest over its military inefficiency.) Andrews selected Victoria
to lead the parade. On the appointed day, approximately ten thousand people assembled at Cooper Institute and marched to the muffled beat of a
drum corps composed of black Civil War veterans. First there was a
catafalque drawn by six gray horses draped in black, behind which walked
Tennie C. and Victoria carrying the flag of the Paris Commune. They were
followed by members of Section 12 of the International, holding a banner
that proclaimed, "Honor to the Martyrs of the Universal Republic." Cuban
revolutionists marched with flags of blue and white, French refugees with
red banners. Irish, German, and Italian groups were joined by members of
the Printer's Society and the Workingwomen's Association. The procession
moved like a funeral cortege down the Bowery. Police guarded their way as
crowds gathered to mock and jeer the marchers.

Five years later, when criticism of her radicalism had reached its height,
Victoria explained that she had reluctantly agreed to Andrews's request
because the spirit of Napoleon Bonaparte had appeared before her and had
warned her that "there would be a riot of the most fearful character" if she
did not appear at the head of the procession. After Napoleon left Victoria
said that she had experienced a vision in which she saw herself leading the
parade past the door of her former residence, 17 Great Jones Street. Victoria then described how Bonaparte's prophecy had proved true: As the
parade moved down the Bowery it was blocked by a wagon upset by a runaway team. The marchers were unable to move and the crowd moved menacingly toward them. Victoria, noticing that they were at the intersection of

Great Jones Street, turned east on to the nearly empty street and led the parade directly past her old house. The police told her afterward that her quick action was what had saved the crowd "from being massacred."

This explanation was typical of the convoluted manner in which Woodhull used her clairvoyance to justify her actions. By the time she gave this explanation in 1876, Victoria realized that her support of the Marxist International had been misguided. To justify her error she claimed that the decision had not been hers but the spirits'. In retrospect, she wrote that although this parade "was the beginning of our financial ruin (as those who were supporting us could not understand why we should connect ourselves with the parties of whom that movement was made up) we never faltered in our allegiance to the spirits whom we served, but literally obeyed their every command."

The Rossel demonstration, which was meant to coalesce Woodhull's supporters, did just the opposite. Not only were conservatives offended but hard-line trade unionists and Marxists denounced it as a shameless public-ity stunt. A German branch of the International noted that the Americans were more interested in Woodhull's "dazzling eyes and free love" than in establishing an eight-hour workday. After reading a subcommittee report that free love had "perverted the aims of the Association," Karl Marx him-self suspended Section 12 until the next General Congress, scheduled for the following spring, with a strong recommendation that it be expelled at that time.

It was becoming increasingly risky for the women of the NWSA to place their hopes on Victoria Woodhull, but Elizabeth Cady Stanton saw no other way to achieve their goal. She wrote,

> Some people carp at the "National" organization because it endorses Mrs. Woodhull. . . . Those of us who were convinced by her unan-swerable arguments that her positions were sound had no choice but to follow. What if foul-mouthed scandal, with its many tongues, seeks to defile her? Shall we ignore a champion like this? . . . Admit for the sake of argument that . . . she has been or is a courtesan in sentiment and practice. When a woman of this class shall suddenly devote herself to the study of the grave problems of life . . . shall we not welcome her to the better place she desires to hold? Victoria C. Woodhull stands before us today a grand, brave woman, radical alike in political, religious, and social principles. Her face and form indicate the complete triumph in her nature of the spiritual over the

sensuous. The processes of her education are little to us, the grand result is everything.

ON JANUARY 8, 18_ Victoria Woodhull and Colonel Blood took a train to Brattleboro, Verm___ attend the funeral of Jim Fisk, who had died violently two days earlie__ ___andalous death was attributable to his mistress, Josie Mansfield. Josie ___ grown discontented with Fisk and decided to leave him for Ned Stokes, t__ __ried dandy who had caught her eye. To support Stokes, Josie tried to __ __mail Fisk for $200,000. Unless the money was forthcoming, Josie thre___ __d to tell how he had bilked the public through the Erie Railway Com__ "It is only four years ago since you revealed to me your scheme for steal__ __ Erie books," she wrote. She also threatened to reveal how he had rigge__ __e gold market. "You surely recollect the fated Black Friday," she wrote w__ __ sarcasm, and asserted that he was mistaken in his assumption that th__ __d been "no witnesses" to his "transactions." She said that she knew the __ __e of this information, and it could be measured in dollars. Finally, __ said that unless money was promptly paid, she was prepared to m__ __heir affair public by giving the *Herald* some thirty-nine letters Fisk ha__ __itten to her.

But Fisk was not a man to be bla__ __ailed. He told his wife about his relationship wit__ __ __ come to terms with her errant husband and w__ no__ __armed. Fisk had bought her a house in Boston, where she live__ __ quiet life with a female friend, attended church, played the piano, tended her garden. He lavished on her every luxury and seldom bothered her with his presence. She regarded him more as an attentive son than as a husband. Lucy had all the material possessions she wanted, a life with no cigar smoke, no alcohol, no sexual demands—a more felicitous arrangement than was the lot of many of her sex.

Josie also had misjudged the reaction of the public. Fisk was an acknowledged knave and buffoon, but in these rapacious times, success counted more than virtue. When he was not forthcoming with the cash, Stokes removed $200,000 from an oil account that, unbeknownst to Fisk, still bore Stokes's name as a cosigner. Fisk retaliated by filing an embezzlement suit against Stokes, after which Josie filed what was perhaps the first palimony suit in America.

Fisk marshaled his forces against his former mistress and her lover. Madame Annie Wood, in a sworn affidavit, asserted that shortly after the affair with Stokes began, Josie had asked Annie to provide a room at her

*Ned (Edward Stiles) Stokes—*
*Josie Mansfield's vain, playboy lover*

*Ned Stokes shoots Jim Fisk.*

Thirty-fourth Street "house" for trysts with him. Josie's servants also testified about her several lovers, including Stokes. Then on November 28, 1871, Ned Stokes was indicted for embezzlement. He was taken to the Ludlow Street jail, where he was allowed to bring his Oriental carpet, whiskey, and bottled water, and to have his dinner sent in from Delmonico's. On Saturday, January 6, 1872, Stokes was released on bail. He proceeded to the Yorkville police court to attend the second hearing of Mansfield v. Fisk. Throughout the morning session, Stokes heard himself depicted as a dissolute wastrel and a thief. That afternoon he hailed a carriage and arrived at the Grand Opera House just in time to see Fisk getting into his carriage and overheard him direct his driver to the Grand Central Hotel. Stokes took a shortcut through the ladies' entrance of the hotel and stationed himself at the top of the stairs. Fisk was on the fourth step when Stokes produced a pistol from under his double-breasted gray overcoat and fired twice. His porcine target was impossible to miss. A doctor probed for the bullets, but they were deep in Fisk's bowels. "When you were a boy did you ever run away from school and fill yourself with green apples?" Fisk asked the doctor. "I feel just as I used to. . . . I've got a bellyache." He died the following morning.

After Fisk's death, Josie Mansfield enjoyed a certain celebrity. She sued his widow for the $200,000 she claimed Fisk owed her, but lost the case. Subsequently, she married an alcoholic playboy and moved to Paris. Stokes, who was tried three times for Fisk's murder, spent a scant six months in Sing Sing. Commodore Vanderbilt said that after Jim Fisk's death he was able to elicit his late rival's financial advice through a trance speaker, Mrs. Harris. He said that Fisk was now both truthful and helpful.

# CHAPTER TWENTY-SIX

# A HEAVY LOAD

December 29, 1871

Dear Mrs. Woodhull,

Will you ask Demosthenes if there is any new argument not yet made on the 14th and 15th Amendments that he will bring out through some of us at the coming convention. . . . I want Frank Moulton to make a speech and his pretty wife to be there to adorn the platform. *I have written T.T. and will never forgive him if he fails us at this time.* We must not please Boston by having our convention a failure. Could we get *Beecher to speak one evening all by himself*? He ought to do that much for us having spoken and presided for Boston. Try and bring that to pass. I think Moulton and Theodore could. See them about it.

Ask the spirits of Rachel, Elizabeth Barrett Browning, Malibran and Hemans to send down some fine woman's suffrage songs. I know they are all interested in our struggle and see as clearly as I do that we must sing as well as argue ourselves into the political kingdom. Can you manage to get our *call* in all the New York papers? It should be flying all over the country by this time. . . . Have you invited some of the best Labor Reform speakers and some of the best Spiritualists? Let us have a real old fashioned protracted meeting full of enthusiasm. I would rather make a few blunders from a superabundance of life, than to have all the proprieties of a well embalmed mummy. Let me hear from you.

With Kind Regards, Elizabeth Cady Stanton

In this remarkable letter Stanton, with no discernible hesitation, asks Woodhull to contact some of the most famous women of the ages, all dead: the biblical Rachel; the poet Elizabeth Barrett Browning; Maria Felicita Malibran, a world-renowned singer who died in 1836, at the age of twenty-eight; and Felicia Dorothea Hemans, a Welsh poet whose body lay in a crypt beneath St. Anne's church in Dublin.

The second week in January 1872, Woodhull appeared on the platform of Lincoln Hall in Washington bracketed by Stanton and Anthony, who had traveled from Nevada without breaking her journey. After Woodhull's admission that she was a practicing free lover, further attempts to defend her personal conduct were abandoned. Even Isabella had changed tactics: She read a poem to the convention whose meaning was clear. It was about a stained little hand that might save all of mankind and womankind because it did not fear to work where a pure white hand would never venture.

At Stanton's request, Woodhull had written Beecher asking him to speak at the convention. He answered that his lecture schedule did not permit him to come, but before mailing the letter sent it to Moulton for approval and noted, "I do not mean to speak on the platform of *either* of the two suffrage societies."

Moulton and Tilton had taken all responsibility for placating Woodhull. Prudently, Beecher, whose career was now at its zenith, had kept his distance. The first volume of *The Life of Jesus the Christ* brought Beecher accolades, and a series of lectures delivered at Yale, published as *The New Haven Lectures,* confirmed him as America's leading liturgical thinker. Tilton, on the other hand, thanks to his radicalism and his public alliance with Woodhull, found himself sinking—lectures canceled, money scarce, fame extinguished. Moulton asked Beecher to put a good word in the *Christian Union* about Tilton's publication, the *Golden Age,* but Beecher wrote merely that the *Golden Age* was a small publication unattached to any church views. A dismayed Moulton wrote, "I am ashamed of it and would rather you had written nothing."

Tilton was stung by this latest insult, and when he drank he told anyone who would listen that Beecher had seduced his wife. Sam Wilkeson said of it, "This whole affair [is] the subject of conversation in the clubs." Lib Tilton, continuing her forbidden correspondence with Beecher, warned him of her husband's rage. A fearful Beecher turned Lib's letter over to Moulton and wrote to him,

> It seems that a change has come to T. . . . Ever since he has felt more intensely the force of feeling in society and the humiliations which environ his enterprise, he has growingly felt that I had a power to help which I did not develop. . . .

Nothing can possibly be so bad as the horror of great darkness in which I spend much of my life. I look upon death as sweeter-faced than any friend I have in the world. . . . To live on the sharp and *ragged edge* of anxiety, remorse, fear, despair, and yet put on all the appearance of serenity and happiness, cannot be endured much longer.

The pressure on Beecher was unrelenting. At this time the Northern Pacific syndicate was so short of cash that workers were being paid in scrip, but when Sam Wilkeson told Henry Bowen that he would not be able to continue his commission payments, Bowen too threatened to expose Beecher. Frank Moulton decided it was time to settle matters once and for all. He went to Wilkeson and pointed out how much money would be lost if Beecher's reputation was destroyed. An enlightened Wilkeson agreed to bribe Tilton and Bowen into silence. Bowen was given a year's commission from the strapped Cooke syndicate and an extra $7,000, with which he paid off Tilton, who had lodged a suit against Bowen for violating his newspaper contracts. Subsequently, Tilton wrote Anna Dickinson that with this payment, "The whole case has terminated most happily."

Having made a major investment, Sam Wilkeson insisted that a written document, a "tripartite agreement," be executed in which Bowen, Tilton, and Beecher agreed to put aside all their past grievances and accusations "real or imagined" and make no further threats. When the agreement was signed, Wilkeson wrote to Moulton and advised, as a "closing act of justice and duty," that he place all the damaging correspondence in "the flames of the friendly fire in your room of reconciliation." Frank Moulton did not burn the correspondence.

In the coming presidential election, Tilton saw a chance to regain his power. Grant's first term had been so corrupt that the word "Grantism" became a synonym for graft, greed, and nepotism. The laissez-faire president had surrounded himself with relatives and politicians who dispensed patronage for gargantuan personal gain. Disaffected Republicans, including Theodore Tilton and many other newspapermen, calling themselves liberal Republicans, advocated "an uprising of honest citizens."

Since the night at Steinway Hall when Victoria had admitted to practicing free love, Tilton had seen that Beecher was right in distancing himself from her, and he had begun to do the same. Now came the final break. Tilton told Victoria that he was going to the liberal Republican convention with Whitelaw Reid and would report it for the *Tribune*. Since that paper had been particularly critical of Woodhull, clearly he could no longer be associated with her politically. "You are a liar!" Woodhull told him. "Why not be truth-ful and admit you are going to Cincinnati to nominate Mr. Greeley for pres-ident?" Later Victoria was to say that at that moment she experienced a vision of Tilton walking along, followed by a coffin containing the body of Horace Greeley. She mentioned this vision to Tilton and cautioned, "You will be responsible for putting him in that coffin . . . responsible for his death."

In her otherworldly way, Woodhull had sensed the change in Tilton. His own abject failure and Beecher's success had made a cynic of this once-idealistic firebrand. Now, through the liberal Republican Party, Tilton saw a chance to become more powerful than Beecher, and he was about to sac-rifice his principles for personal gain.

On May 1, 1872, the liberal Republican convention convened. Whitelaw Reid and Theodore Tilton lobbied to put Greeley's name among the presi-dential candidates. On the sixth ballot, the convention nominated Greeley for president and chose Governor Benjamin Gratz Brown of Missouri for vice president. Many newspapermen supported the nomination of a fellow journalist. (One exception was E. L. Godkin, the editor of *The Nation*, who wrote that this was the biggest disaster since the news of the first battle of Bull Run.) The majority of experienced political reformers, however, were disappointed to have a candidate with no previous political experience.

Susan B. Anthony attended the convention hoping to gain support for woman's enfranchisement, but was shocked to hear Tilton declare that woman's rights was not to be an issue in the campaign. An irate Anthony observed, "None but the liberals deride us now and Theodore Tilton stands at their head in light and scurrilous treatment." At the regular Republican convention in Philadelphia a month later, Grant was nominated by accla-mation for a second term. Three weeks after that, the Democrats in Balti-more joined the Liberal Republicans in nominating Horace Greeley, an odd marriage to say the least: Men who had spent their lives as Republicans were now allied with Democrats who urged a "soft peace" and an end to Radical Reconstruction.

When Susan B. Anthony arrived at the Democratic convention she stated her position in the *World*: "Baltimore Warned—Anthony says the Democrats Must Endorse Woman Suffrage or the Strong Minded Will Work for U. S. Grant." The warning did little good. At none of the con-ventions had Anthony been able to obtain support for women. Finally, Henry Blackwell managed to persuade the regular Republicans to issue a statement that "the honest demands of any class of citizens for equal rights should be treated with respectful consideration." Stanton called this weak statement the "Philadelphia splinter" in the party's platform and said that the Republicans would soon cut it down to a "toothpick." But Anthony felt that this was their only alternative. "Baltimore will not recognize our claim so of course we must make as *big a noise* over the 'splinter' . . . as possible."

In the coming election, women faced a dilemma, for it was obvious that both parties intended to give only token support to woman's enfranchisement. Only Victoria Woodhull unequivocally supported women. Martha Coffin Wright wrote her daughter Ellen Garrison that Woodhull maintained that "both parties were utterly corrupt and a new one, labor and woman suffrage, should be formed. She was full of enthusiasm and faith in the coalition." By early spring Hooker and Stanton had become so convinced that Woodhull alone represented their needs that they seriously considered creating this political party to endorse her for president. Anthony, who knew that this would amount to a mere political protest with no chance of convincing either Republicans or Democrats, was becoming increasingly wary of lending her name in support of a woman who was controlled by men like Blood and Andrews. She wrote,

> We have no element out of which to make a political party, because there is not a man who would vote a woman suffrage ticket . . . and all our time and words in that direction are simply thrown away. My name must not be used to call any such meeting. . . .
>
> I tell you I feel utterly disheartened. . . . Mrs. Woodhull has the advantage of us because she has the newspaper and she persistently means to run our craft into her port and none other. If she were influenced by *women* spirits, either in the body or out of it, in the direction she steers, I might consent to be a mere sail-hoister for her. But as it is, she is wholly owned and dominated by *men* spirits.

The 1872 National Woman Suffrage Association convention was scheduled for the first week in May at Steinway Hall. Isabella Beecher Hooker was now a complete convert to Victoria's belief in spirit guidance. She wrote, "Oh, if I were only *omnipresent* wouldn't I do this business up handsomely. It makes me frantic, if I would allow myself to be anything but calm and hopeful, to think how much I could do if *my soul could work outside my body.*"

By now Isabella was also convinced that her brother was guilty of adultery. Victoria had been the first to tell her of her brother's free love practices and assured Isabella that they would soon be revealed and that she would become a heroine if she could persuade Henry to come forward with his views on the subject. Victoria told Isabella, "I know that Mr.

Beecher . . . need not stand alone for an hour, but that an army of glorious and emancipated spirits will gather spontaneously and instantaneously around him and that the new social republic will have been forever established." Stanton and Anthony also confirmed that the story was true, although Anthony would provide no details.

Isabella later wrote Henry,

> Mrs. Stanton told me precisely what Mr. Tilton had said to her when in the rage of discovery he fled to the house of Mrs. B. [Bullard] and before them both narrated the story of his own infidelities as confessed to his wife and hers as confessed to him. . . . The only reply I made to Mrs. Stanton was that if true you had a philosophy of the relation of the sexes so far ahead of the times that you dared not announce it, though you consented to live by it.

Isabella now asked Henry if there was anything she could say at the next NWSA convention that would pave the way for more liberal sexual attitudes. Henry was appalled by the letter and decided to play on his sister's emotions.

April 25, 1872

My Dear Belle,

I do not intend to make *any* speeches on any topic during Anniversary Week. Indeed, I shall be out of town. I do not want you to *take any ground this year except upon suffrage.* You know my sympathy with you. Probably you and I are nearer together than any of our family. I cannot give reason now. . . . Of some things *I neither talk nor will I be talked with.* For love and sympathy I am deeply thankful. The only help that can be grateful to me or useful is *silence* and a silencing influence on all others. A day may come for converse. It is not now. *Living or dead, my dear sister Belle, love me.* . . .

Isabella's immediate reaction was fear that her brother would kill himself once the truth came out. She later recalled, "My mind flew back to the sentence which suggested suicide to me the moment I read it. . . . And I believed even that." Her fears seemed to be confirmed when Stanton showed her the copy she had been given of Beecher's letter of apology in which he'd written, "I even wish I were dead." An overwrought Isabella determined that she must find a way to save her brother's life.

Isabella warned her husband, John, that it was only a question of time until the scandal became public, and that Henry might end his life. John reacted by telling his wife that his own nervous condition was such he was sure he would die from this added strain. Sensing catastrophe, Isabella arranged for her husband to go to Europe. He begged her to come with him, but, worried about Henry, she sent her daughter Mary in her place. A trip to the Alps did not improve John's health as Isabella had hoped, but at least at this distance the anxieties of one did not exacerbate those of the other.

With her husband abroad, Isabella occupied herself by taking control of the arrangements for the NWSA meeting in May. Both Stanton and Anthony were away on Lyceum lecture tours and knew little of the plans. In early May, a weary Susan B. Anthony was sitting in a railroad station in Illinois, waiting for the train that would take her to her next speaking engagement, when she saw a man reading *Woodhull & Claflin's Weekly.* When he left she picked up the discarded paper and, leafing through it, saw that a "People's Party" was to be inaugurated at the NWSA convention to support Victoria Woodhull for president. The "call" read in part, "We believe the time has come for the formation of a new political party whose principles shall meet the issues of the hour and represent equal rights for all." The sponsors of this new party were listed as "Isabella Beecher Hooker, Elizabeth Cady Stanton . . . Susan B. Anthony." Anthony jumped to her feet, dashed to the wireless office, and sent sharp messages to Stanton and Hooker demanding the withdrawal of her name. "I do not believe in any of us women, the majority of whom do not even own our bodies to say nothing of our purses—forming a *political party—slaves* and paupers—do we see the farce."

Three days before the start of the convention, Anthony returned to New York and called on her friend Elizabeth Phelps of the Women's Bureau. Mrs. Phelps was well known for her involvement in woman's rights and was frequently featured in the popular press. She was said to be an heiress, yet no one could determine where her money came from or if indeed she had any. There was said to be a mysterious benefactor but again no one could be sure. To the tabloids' delight, in the spring of 1871 this so-called "millionairess" was arrested for shoplifting 22 cents' worth of sweet sticks at Macy's. She was released the same afternoon, but this notoriety exposed Elizabeth Phelps to gossip, speculation, and blackmail.

Victoria Woodhull seemingly had come to Mrs. Phelps's defense in the *Weekly,* where she described how Mr. Macy's underpaid waiter-girls were known to pocket the money for an item that had been legitimately sold to a customer. Victoria suggested that merchants such as Macy and A. T.

Stewart could stop the stealing by paying their employees a livable wage. But was Victoria Woodhull really Elizabeth Phelps's defender? Soon after Anthony's arrival at the Women's Bureau, a much disturbed Mrs. Phelps confided to her that Victoria had visited the previous week and demanded $500 or her name would be included in an article describing "the sexual liaisons and free love practices of some of the best-known women in the reformatory movement." Mrs. Woodhull, said Phelps, not only specifically accused her but also Laura Curtis Bullard, Mary Livermore, and Phebe Hanaford among others, and remarked, "If these women practice what I preach and yet play the hypocrite, I am prepared to broadcast this news all over New York City." Mrs. Phelps said she had not given Victoria any money because she didn't have it to give. Anthony wrote in her diary, "Called on Mrs. Phelps. Heard Woodhull's move to blackmail the women."

Desperate to recruit support for her presidential bid, Victoria had indeed compiled a set of "slips" detailing the sexual behavior of various individuals in the suffrage movement who she felt were maligning her. Much of this information came from Stanton, Hooker, and from the more scandalous daily tabloids. These "slips" were sent out to the women named, accompanied by a note stating that unless the accusations against her ceased and a payment to support her campaign was forthcoming they would see themselves in an article on free love in the *Weekly* titled "Tit for Tat." When Tilton heard this, he told Victoria that if she destroyed the "slip" on Laura Curtis Bullard he would help her "kill the rest." Sometime later, when what she had done came to light, Woodhull tried to justify her actions by writing,

> I concluded to shut the mouths of a clique of loose and loud-tongued women who were continually stabbing me . . . and making me a fiend incarnate in the eyes of the people. I grouped the clique together in an article of which I sent each member a printed *slip*. . . . The filthy fountains suddenly ceased to vomit forth their slime and I have had no occasion to publish the article but if it still arise I shall not hesitate to do so.

Paulina Wright Davis, who had retreated to Europe for her health, received a letter from Victoria enclosing a proof of "Tit for Tat." Mistakenly thinking it had been published, Mrs. Davis wrote,

> My Dear Victoria,
> Driven to bay at last you have turned, poor hunted child, and dealt a cruel blow. . . . Every one of these women you name has

been hounded by men and now it suits them to make cat's-paws of them to hunt you. . . . Dear child, I wish you had let them pass and had taken hold of these men whose souls are black with crimes and who set up to be the censors of morality. . . . The first time I ever saw Mrs. Phelps, I was told by a *man* that she was a woman of damaged reputation. Men are the chief scandalmongers of the age. It is they who report all the vile scandals of New York here and so make society detestable. You are not fooled by them, hence you must be crucified.

Anthony had no such sympathy for Victoria and was outraged by her blackmail schemes. After leaving Mrs. Phelps she traveled to Tenafly to confront Stanton about Woodhull and the People's Party. Anthony said that she had paid for Steinway Hall to be used by the NWSA, and she insisted that any other group could rent its own hall and meet somewhere else. Stanton replied that Anthony was being "narrow minded and domineering."

At a business committee meeting of the NWSA, held the day before the convention was to begin, Victoria Woodhull announced that this was to be a joint convention of her People's Party and the NWSA. Anthony responded that her group alone could use Steinway Hall. Stanton was now so angry with Anthony that she resigned as president and refused to preside at the convention. Anthony was elected in her place. However, Stanton did attend the first session and, defying Anthony, asserted in the keynote speech that women should vote in the coming election as members of Woodhull's People's Party. Then, according to Anthony's diary, Woodhull's supporters "claimed right to possess the meeting. Evident they were bound to try their strength and strategy." Anthony controlled the situation by refusing to recognize Mrs. Woodhull, but later wrote, "There was never such a foolish *muddle* all come of Mrs. S. [Stanton] consulting *with* and conceding *to* Woodhull."

On the following evening, however, as the meeting was about to end, Victoria Woodhull stepped forward and announced in a clear voice, "I move that this convention adjourn and meet jointly with the People's Party tomorrow morning at Apollo Hall!" Anthony, sensing the audience was with Victoria, refused to put the motion. But Victoria once again called out the motion, and a majority of voices cried, "Aye, aye, aye." In a desperate effort to stanch the flow to Woodhull, Anthony announced, "You are not members of our organization. You cannot vote. This meeting is adjourned. We will meet in this same place tomorrow." She was ignored. Victoria Woodhull stood before the audience and spoke as if possessed by the spirits. She told them of her vision of a world free of corruption and oppression. But as the words tumbled out, Anthony left the platform, located the janitor, and ordered him to extinguish the footlights and then every other gaslight in the hall. In the darkness, bewildered women groped their way to the exits.

May 10, 1872: "Friday—National Convention . . . small audience. The fiasco's perfect—from calling People's Convention—never did Mrs. Stanton do as foolish a thing—all cause near being lost," Anthony wrote in her diary. "Saturday: I was never so hurt with this folly of Mrs. Stanton. Sunday: Pleasant day—but sad to me. Our movement as such is so demoralized by the letting go of the helm of the ship to Woodhull—though we rescued it—it was by a hair breadth escape."

Anthony waited apprehensively to see how the *Weekly* would depict the newest schism in the woman's movement. "I never before came so near to losing all knowledge of myself as at New York those days—the Woodhull paper is not yet here." Days later, she wrote in her diary with some relief, "Woodhull paper comes freighted with glorious triumph. She subsumes

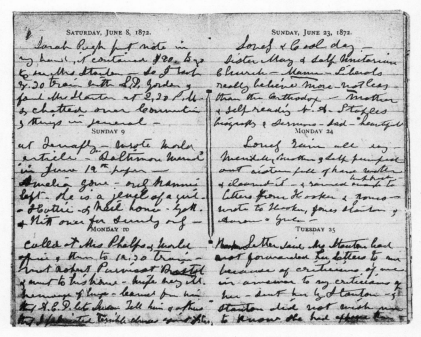

*Susan B. Anthony's diary. The entries from June 11 to June 22 have been ripped out.*

everything into service, no denunciating, simply calls too slow. But the job
a tee-total failure . . ."


AT THIS MOMENT Victoria Woodhull was in her glory. At the Saturday
Apollo Hall meeting the name People's Party was quickly changed to the
Equal Rights Party and Victoria Woodhull was officially nominated as its
candidate for president of the United States. She chose as her running mate
Frederick Douglass, who later was said to remark, "I never heard of this,"
but he never formally requested that his name be removed from the ticket.

There were now three woman's rights organizations: the conservative
Boston AWSA, the NWSA under Anthony's sole control, and Woodhull's
Equal Rights Party, supported by Stanton and Hooker. The woman's rights
movement was hopelessly fragmented, a disaster that Isabella Beecher
Hooker failed to grasp. She wrote to Stanton,

> *Apollo Hall was a success* and through it the suffrage army moves in
> *three* columns instead of *two*—and each wing is a host. I have never
> realized the situation before and now I see the whole battlefield as
> plainly as though in the Heavens looking down upon it from the
> side of the Great-God Himself commanding the host. Do not
> smile at my enthusiasm. You know it is not *we* who have brought
> ourselves out of recent perils. . . . Though Victoria has been a heavy
> load . . . now by the absolutely deferential tone of the Press toward
> Apollo and by the red flags and Communistic mottoes there dis-
> played we must recognize the powerful aid the new party brings to
> Suffrage.

Isabella then wrote to Anthony praising Woodhull and asking if she was
not "overpowered by the sublimity of this hour." Anthony, feeling exhausted
and maligned, answered,

> *Yes, I am overpowered* with the sublimity of this hour—but no more
> so—*not* so much so—as to have been at the sublimity of every hour
> and day for the past *twenty years*. . . . But I am too much in the con-
> dition of tee-total collapse of heart and soul . . . to be able to see or
> say the word or work of the hour.

The following week Victoria Woodhull held a rally to ratify her nomination. She was introduced by Isabella, who sat next to her on the platform.

Using the pseudonym "Broadway," Isabella wrote about this event in the *Weekly*.

> Mrs. Woodhull, the nominee for the Presidency, passed into an ante-room, where her friends crowded to congratulate her. She was in ecstacy. . . . The ladies kissed her and embraced her, kissed each other and kissed her again. I never before saw so much kissing and hugging in public, nor, for that matter, in private either. Men were not afraid to pass hands round women who were not their wives, and women indulged in political osculation till they were tired.

Anthony wrote Stanton, "What a ridiculous letter that is that Mrs. Hooker has published. It is too bad this kissing and hugging and putting away old men and getting new ones to hug and kiss emblazoned in print constantly of *our leading* W.S. women—it's simply sickening—what can be Mrs. Hooker's object."

Susan B. Anthony had ample reason to distrust and dislike anyone or anything connected with Victoria Woodhull. In losing Stanton, Anthony had lost her other half. For almost a quarter of a century these two women had worked together, and the strength of the NWSA lay in this unity. Woodhull, in addition to being a blackmailer, had stolen away both her closest friend and the membership of her group, thereby jeopardizing the chances for enfranchisement. On Thursday, May 23, Anthony noted in her diary that she had stopped at the Rochester home of Mary Hallowell, an old friend, and had stayed for dinner with her, Amy Post, and a Mrs. Millis and her daughter. The evening was free of constraints, and the conversation revolved around Victoria and her sister Tennie C. Anthony was convinced that Woodhull would stop at nothing in order to force people to support her candidacy. She spoke of the "slips" against Phelps, Livermore, and Hanaford and told the others that Victoria was "resorting to blackmail intentionally and intended to succeed by that and other methods equally objectionable." What else was said—or allegedly said—that night was to have repercussions, for someone mentioned it to a Dr. Orvis who lived nearby.

The gossip spread with lightning speed. Fifteen days later, on the afternoon of June 7, Anthony arrived in Philadelphia and headed straight for the house of "my darling" Anna Dickinson. That night Anthony wrote in her diary, "Surprise found her home—not the old time greeting but cold, cold. She charges me with betraying her confidence—Livermore and Hanaford." Three days later, Anthony visited a friend and learned from him that Anna's sister Susan had told people that Anthony "*fabricated* terrible charges against T. C. [Tennessee Claflin]."

The entries from the next day, June 11, until June 22 and again from July 23 to July 28 were ripped from Anthony's diary and burned. However, correspondence with others during this period describes the nature of the charges she allegedly made. Martha Coffin Wright wrote to Anthony, "We do not believe the charge of Orvis that you made the public charge against Tennie Claflin that he asserts you did, as there was a law passed by our Legislature a year or two ago making the charge of unchastity an indictable offense. On that account, if no other, you would be careful." Adultery could bring a jail sentence.

In a burst of letter writing, Anthony denied that she had accused Tennie C. of adultery. To Isabella she wrote, "That letter of Dr. A. Orvis was a *perfect fabrication* of *course.* Mrs. Stanton gave me a similar one he had sent to Mrs. Woodhull. He's a *jack*—— you may supply the blank or not as you please. None but an *evil-doer* could report me thus but how *little faith* we have even *in those we know best.*" And five days later she wrote to Isabella again concerning Woodhull: "I shall welcome her work, every bit of it, for women's freedom—though I do not choose to follow her into a party with these *men.* I have never on paper or with tongue said to anyone aught else. I did not reply or explain that *Dr. Orvis'* letter from Rochester to you because I never dreamed of your counting it other than a *lie* as it was."

In a subsequent article in the *Weekly,* Victoria Woodhull stated that it had come to her attention that Anthony was assassinating the character of her sister Tennie and spreading rumors that Victoria was a blackmailer. She wrote, "The charges . . . as made by Miss Anthony . . . were either entirely without foundation or most outrageously perverted." Anthony again defended herself, writing that Woodhull had made her the "marplot." But, indicating that, in truth, she did speak out against the sisters, Anthony confided to her diary, "Well thanks to the good fates that somebody was enough to save us from that *swindle bound system*—it is too humiliating."

Perhaps Dickinson broke off her relationship with her dearest friend for fear that Woodhull might retaliate against her for Anthony's insults. Woodhull could destroy Anna's career. Later, when Dickinson was asked why she had abruptly terminated her relationship with Anthony, she replied that Susan had grown "too old"—hardly a convincing reason. In any case, for the next quarter of a century not one word passed between these two women.

There was no doubt that scandal swirled around Anna's head and that she was frightened by it. Several friends knew that she practiced free love, and she had confided to them the details of a sexual relationship with none other than that great abolitionist Wendell Phillips. Phillips, a married man, was Anna's "secret lover." Whitelaw Reid wrote her concerning Phillips, "By the way I have been hearing a precious mess about you." A letter from Isabella Beecher Hooker to her husband written at the same time indicates that knowledge of the Dickinson-Phillips affair was widespread. John Hooker's reply anticipates the devastating effect this revelation and other sexual scandals might have on the woman's movement.

> What you write us is shocking and overwhelming beyond expression. The matter of Anna D. was wholly new to me. I had heard a discreditable story about Phillips, but never a hint of her being the other party. It is horrible, I cannot conceive how she, at her ripe age, and with her good sense, and her comprehension of the whole case could submit herself to such a desecration.
>
> But it is very strange that it's got to get out—or get so generally known that, as you say, it has got to come out. I do not wonder that in her distress, she should have divulged it to one or two confidential friends but it is inconceivable that they should have told it to others. If they did they ought to be shot.
>
> But the case of H. [Henry] is more horrible in every way . . . it is greatly aggravated by the Woodhull matter mixing in with it. . . . When all this comes out—the H. story and that of Anna D. and Phillips, all woman suffragists, it will give that cause a heavy blow. . . . The Woodhull matter is a heavy load for it to carry and I do not wonder if all this superadded (and really illustrating Woodhullism) should create a reaction in the public mind that will send the struggle down to another generation and postpone its triumph for thirty years.

# CHAPTER TWENTY-SEVEN

# MRS. SATAN

Whoever is set up to be President of the United States is just set up to have his character torn off from his back in shreds and to be mauled, pummeled, and covered with dirt by every filthy paper all over the country. And no woman that was not willing to be dragged through every kennel, and slopped into every dirty pail of water like an old mop, would ever consent to run as a candidate. Why, it's an ordeal that kills a man. It killed General Harrison and it killed old Zach [Taylor]. And what sort of brazen tramp of a woman would it be that could stand it and come out of it without being killed?

S O COMMENTED Harriet Beecher Stowe when Victoria Woodhull announced her bid for the presidency. Horace Greeley might have heeded this advice as well, for the campaign of 1872 deteriorated into one of the most vicious in American history. The woman's rights advocates were divided among Grant, Greeley, and Woodhull. Anthony was enraged by the damage that Victoria Woodhull had done to her personal life and her cause. She wrote to Martha Coffin Wright, "*Victoria* and her *People's Party* seceded from us and we are left alone. She having shaken the very dust of us from off her feet. Next to Horace Greeley, she is the most taken off her feet by the honors conferred upon her. Horace is surely a second child, if he ever was anything else and Tilton's *fawning* around him is utterly disgusting." Moving forward with her remnant of the NWSA, Anthony and her group campaigned for Grant. "We must now all pull together to kill Greeley. . . . Let us hold up a looking glass before his eyes that will make him quake in his boots."

Beecher, too, supported the popular incumbent, President Grant. Tilton, seeing in Greeley his chance to redeem himself, dropped all other obligations to become Greeley's campaign manager. Since Tilton and

Beecher were once again politically opposed, Frank Moulton examined every speech by both men to make sure there would not be another confrontation to upset the peace they had vowed to uphold in the "tripartite agreement."

Greeley put Reid in charge of the *Tribune* and began a vigorous campaign, attacking the corrupt Grant administration. But soon Zach Chandler, chief of Grant's campaign committee, went to the railroad barons, stock manipulators, and promoters and warned them that if Greeley were elected he would put an end to the federal grants that netted them untold millions. Jay Cooke, who controlled the Northern Pacific Railroad stock syndicate, counted on federal aid. He'd given Greeley $20,000 worth of stock to promote his railroad, and now he felt this ungrateful editor had turned on him. Cooke promptly contributed $50,000 to Grant's campaign, and other powerful businessmen followed suit. Within weeks a realistic Greeley wrote, "The Grant folks are full of money and are using it with effect."

With business interests solidly behind Grant, Tilton and others advised Greeley to cultivate the Southern Democrats, who were reclaiming their states from the "carpetbag" administrations that had functioned mainly for their own profit. Tilton, who had said that Negro troops should be sent to the South as "terriers to watch such rats," now advocated the withdrawal of all federal troops, saying that their presence would only harden Southern hatred for the Negro. This man who had found Grant's Reconstruction policies "too soft" now abandoned all attempts at reform, writing,

> We believe that the anti-slavery battle has been fought out. Slavery is abolished, and the Thirteenth Amendment makes its re-enactment impossible. The negro has been invested with the right of suffrage, and the Fourteenth and Fifteenth Amendments make his disenfranchisement impossible. Legally the negro stands exactly where the white man does. Socially whatever stigma rests upon him is far more oppressive in the North than in the South.

Tilton, the former idealist, had become as self-serving as the times in which he was living. He turned his back on his old friends from abolition days. When Benjamin Butler tried to enlist his help to create a civil rights act that would contain a provision mandating integrated education, he refused to become involved. Similarly, Tilton declined when Frederick Douglass asked him to intervene in the case of James W. Smith, the first black cadet at West Point, who had endured three years of severe persecution only to be drummed out of the academy for supposedly failing a test—one given to no other cadet.

Tilton's barely veiled policy of placating the South in order to win Greeley's election soon angered Northern voters and especially newspapermen. The cartoonist Thomas Nast, for example, turned the powerful weapon of his pen on Horace Greeley in *Harper's Weekly*. In a savage parody of Greeley's presidential acceptance letter, in which he appealed for the North and the South to "clasp hands across the bloody chasm," Nast drew a series of cartoons, including pictures of Greeley shaking hands with a Confederate who had just shot a Union soldier, stretching out his hand to John Wilkes Booth across Lincoln's open grave, and assisting a Ku Klux Klan member who had just lynched a black man and stabbed a black mother and child. In the cartoon "What I Know About Bailing Out," Nast depicted Greeley clutching the bail that he'd put up in 1867 for the former president of the Confederacy, Jefferson Davis. Although Tilton had broken with Woodhull, the tar of free love stuck to him and his associates, and Nast depicted the straight-laced Greeley surrounded by embracing free lovers.

To a public always susceptible to the instantaneous vivid image, the politically inept Greeley came to be seen as a malevolent panderer to the South, a floundering old buffoon. But Susan B. Anthony, who not long before had said she wanted to "kill Greeley," now wrote that though working for the "Republican Party and all women . . . I shall not join with the Republicans . . . and the liberals . . . in hounding Greeley. . . . The fact that old pro-slavery men proposed to vote for him, no more makes him pro-slavery than that drunkards or rum-sellers vote for him makes him a friend and advocate of the liquor traffic. My sense of justice and truth is outraged by the *Harper's* cartoons."

With her break from Anthony, Anna Dickinson came more under the influence of Whitelaw Reid, who prevailed upon her to campaign for Greeley. Anna vacillated between Greeley and Grant. She deplored the excesses and corruption of the Grant administration, but she wanted proper payment to stump for Greeley. A courtship began: Tilton wrote her inviting her to spend the weekend with Greeley at his Chappaqua farm. But that same week, Grant offered her $20,000 to make six speeches for him. Finally Reid, realizing that Greeley needed a strong woman's rights speaker, offered Anna $10,000, to be delivered at some future date, to speak for Greeley. To further her career, Anna needed Reid's friendship and that of Greeley's *Tribune*. Under pressure, she agreed to Reid's proposal.

*The Whited Sepulchre. Greeley tries to cover a monument
to his infamy with his trademark white hat and coat,
in a Nast cartoon, 1872.*

Anna had begun her career as an abolitionist and she too had a difficult time justifying Greeley's friendship with the South. Ultimately, she defended her decision to support him by maintaining that a vindictive policy would embitter an entirely new postwar generation. When Dickinson finally spoke at Cooper Institute in New York, she accused Grant of putting "thieves" in the internal revenue service, the Post Office and "other departments of the government." She said that if he had disqualified those who gave him gifts, "the state of New York would be officerless." Grant, Anna alleged, was directly responsible for stealing millions of the people's money, "and the half not told!"

With Dickinson campaigning for Greeley, and Hooker campaigning for Woodhull's Equal Rights Party, Anthony found herself in the odd position of being allied with the Boston AWSA against her dearest friends and compatriots. The *Woman's Journal* stated of the NWSA, "We hope they have got rid of the 'Free Love' incubus which has done incalculable harm to the cause of woman suffrage. Women, like men, are known by the company they keep. The withdrawal of Mrs. Woodhull and her so-called 'radical reformers' will result we hope in bringing to the front of the New York society, women whose intellect and character command public respect." Lucy Stone wrote that she regarded the "Woodhull & Claflin tribe" as a "real curse."

Soon Henry Blackwell, Stone's wandering husband, added his advice:

> And now, dear Miss Anthony, let me give you a few words of counsel. You work with a somewhat different class of women from ours, and will have to exert an influence with some of them, or they will undo all I have done politically. . . . Don't let them try to drive, bully, or threaten the party. Women can *persuade* men, can reason with them, can appeal to their sense of *justice* and *chivalry*. They cannot scold them into compliance. . . . Above all keep the Victoria Woodhulls . . . at a distance. For God's sake do not let that destructive element come into your meetings.

Not only did Anthony and Blackwell alike shun Woodhull, but the newspapers too gave her scant coverage. "Isn't it amusing to see how the papers ignore the Equal Rights Party and candidate or the *Tribune* at least for I seldom see the *World* or other papers," observed Martha Coffin Wright. Victoria Woodhull and her associates felt that a deliberate campaign was being mounted to suppress her ideas. Greeley's *Tribune* decided not to report on Woodhull's political efforts, and the other newspapers followed suit.

Just as he had attacked Horace Greeley's credibility, Nast now demonized Victoria Woodhull for her demand for sexual equality. In *Harper's Weekly* he depicted her as Mrs. Satan. There she stood, a winged female devil, her countenance beautiful and sinister. A set of horns sprouted through her gleaming dark hair. She held a sign that read Be Saved By Free Love. Behind her stood an emaciated woman with two ragged children, and on her back she carried a disheveled man clutching a bottle of whiskey. The caption read, "Get thee behind me, Mrs. Satan."

*Thomas Nast demonizes Victoria Woodhull as Mrs. Satan.*

This was a mortal blow: Woodhull was no longer considered interesting or impassioned but was perceived as someone to be avoided. As quickly as her fame had come, so quickly did it vanish. In city after city her speaking engagements were canceled. Without Vanderbilt's support, the Wall Street firm of Woodhull, Claflin & Co. foundered. Victoria was nearly out of money and could not meet the rent on the Thirty-eighth Street house.

The lease was canceled. Down came the mirrors, the crystal chandeliers, the yards of velvet and damask, the Lawrence painting *Haying at Dorking,* the cherubs and smiling nymphs.

Once again, the Claflins were on the move. They rented a less expensive house on Twenty-third Street and supplemented their income by holding twice-monthly Psyche Club meetings where Spiritualism, free love, and utopian world government were discussed. At these meetings Utica openly solicited the attentions of men for money and, as in the old days, there were rumors that the upstairs rooms were used for sex. The newspapers soon carried the story of how Francisco de Martín, the chancellor to the counsel general of Spain in New York, spotted a girl of about fifteen standing quietly in the hall at one Psyche Club meeting. Seeing the tears streaming down her face, he approached her and said, "My child, this is no place for you. They're discussing things here which you shouldn't listen to." The girl, Rosa Burns, was so happy to find a sympathetic friend that she confided to de Martín that she was pregnant and had been abandoned.

Rosa was the daughter of Victoria's sister Polly Sparr and her first husband, Ross Burns, whom Polly had pursued so many years before, holding the body of their dead child in her arms. Burns had become lieutenant governor of Kansas and knew nothing of his daughter's whereabouts. De Martín determined to remove Rosa from the Claflins' home and with no objection from her mother took her to live at his house with his own daughter, whose name also was Rosa. Despite de Martín's attentions, Rosa Burns's baby was born dead. The following day Polly Sparr showed up, accused the Spanish official of being the baby's father, and demanded money from him. De Martín denied the accusation and said he would pay for the burial, but that was all.

Polly then went to the collector of the port and accused de Martín of smuggling. A case was brought against him but he was proved innocent. Not long after, he returned to his house one day to find that Polly had stolen all of his furniture. De Martín then wrote Ross Burns himself (since Rosa Burns was illiterate) telling him of all that had transpired, and Burns immediately sent for his daughter to come live with him in Kansas. Even with the best of care, Rosa died several months later from complications of childbirth. In her will, she left Rosa de Martín what little money she had. Polly Sparr sued to recover her daughter's money, but lost the case.

Scandal heaped upon scandal: In an effort to break his morphine addiction, Canning Woodhull's doctor cut his dose. As a result, he died. Utica, vowing to "take revenge on the family," rushed to the coroner's office and informed him that Dr. Woodhull had died "under suspicious circumstances." The coroner arrived at the house and claimed the body. Though an autopsy revealed no foul play, the newspapers carried the story along with playful references to the fact that Victoria Woodhull no longer had two husbands living in the same household. In the *Weekly* Victoria wrote that she had become the victim of her family's "insatiable vengeance."

As a result of this publicity, the family was ejected from the Twenty-third Street house. The Hoffman House, where they so splendidly began their career, now refused them. Again and again, they were denied lodging. Finally Polly, using the name of her former husband, Ross Burns, secured rooms at the Gilsey House, on the corner of Broadway and Twenty-ninth Street. Letters objecting to their presence soon began to arrive. When the manager asked the family to leave, Victoria thrust her hand into her purse and came up with a fistful of cash. "Here, here," she cried, "we are not paupers—what is wrong with our money?" And he relented.

Victoria appealed to Beecher:

My Dear Sir,

The social fight against me being now waged in this city is becoming rather hotter than I can well endure longer, standing unsupported and alone as I have until now. Within the past two weeks I have been shut out of hotel after hotel and am now, after having obtained a place in one, hunted down by a set of males and females who are determined that I shall not be permitted to live even, if they can prevent it.

Now I want your assistance. I want to be sustained in my position in the Gilsey House, from which I am ordered out and from which I do not wish to go—and all this simply because I am Victoria C. Woodhull, the advocate of social freedom. I have submitted to this persecution just so long as I can endure. . . . My business, my projects, in fact everything for which I live suffers from it and it must cease. Will you lend me your aid in this? . . .

Beecher turned the letter over to Moulton. "Will you answer this?" he asked. "Or will you see that she is to understand that I can do nothing! I shall not, at any and all hazards take a single step in that direction, and if it brings trouble—it must come."

Moulton told Victoria that no help from Beecher would be forthcoming, but he did so with regret and apprehension. He and his wife, Emma, had been intrigued by Victoria Woodhull, and Moulton could see the signs of her desperation. With an insight that few others possessed he would later observe, "I always knew what Woodhull really was—a proud, wounded, unlettered creature with some vigor of mind, the more vigorous for her ostracism. . . . We treated her with the courtesy the case required and by placing her under a higher motive than had generally been imputed to her, that of mercy and sacrifice, we had the scandal suppressed for a year and a half. . . . We abandoned her only when we found out that there was an adverse influence we could not overreach and that being the want and persecution she was to suffer."

A week after Victoria sent her letter to Beecher, four black lieutenants from the Spencer Grays called for their honorary chairman, Tennie C. Claflin, to take her to inspect a drill of their company. It was just the excuse the manager was waiting for. He told Tennie C., "If you go off with those niggers you need never come back here." Tennie, without answering, hopped into their carriage. When Victoria and Colonel Blood returned to the hotel later that evening they found Zulu Maud and Byron standing on the sidewalk surrounded by their luggage. At midnight they made their way to their newspaper office and hoisted Zulu over the transom. She unlocked the door, and they slept on the floor of the office. Even that did not last long, for the owner of the building raised the rent by $1,000 a year and asked for an entire year in advance. They did not have the money. *Woodhull & Claflin's Weekly* was forced to suspend publication. With no money, no newspaper, and few supporters, Woodhull's campaign was abandoned.

From the beginning the powerful men behind Victoria Woodhull believed that this campaign was, as Blood put it, "purely educational." Benjamin Butler and Stephen Pearl Andrews delighted in seeing their theories reach a large audience through this beautiful woman, and Colonel Blood wanted to justify his actions. Only Victoria believed that she could actually be president. She believed it irrevocably. Believed, as Joan of Arc, that what her spirit voices told her would come to pass. But with every passing day she became more bitter and desperate, sick with exhaustion, and uncomprehending of why the spirits were leading her down this thorny path. To make matters worse, the summer of 1872 was the hottest that Americans had yet endured. Three hundred people died of sunstroke in New York City in the month of August alone. Persecution and desperation walked hand in hand. Near summer's end, the executive committee of the International Workingmen's Association met in The Hague, and Karl Marx himself denounced Section 12—and Victoria Woodhull personally. He expelled them from the organization, and Vickie's labor support fell away.

Elizabeth Cady Stanton now reconsidered her position. Woodhull no longer had wealth and a constituency. Victoria's blackmail schemes no

*Zulu Maud Woodhull—*
*Victoria's loving and loyal daughter*

doubt offended Stanton's sensibilities and perhaps threatened her as well, for as Anthony was to observe, "Human nature is awfully weak and wanting." Lucretia Mott wrote, "Elizabeth . . . is disposed to be very cautious how she identifies herself in any way with her [Woodhull] now." Henry Blackwell and Lucy Stone, sensing a weakening in Stanton's support for Woodhull, wrote her that she had been mistaken in thinking that Woodhull's party was the road to enfranchisement and that if she allied her interests with theirs, together they might make more progress with Grant in securing the vote for women. Stanton in return wrote Blackwell and Stone placating letters, to which the blunt Anthony commented, "All in the world they want is just what she has given them over and over again this summer, an acknowledgment *from her* that she has been wrong and they immaculate in their management of affairs."

Evidently, Blackwell and Stone made an impression, for an article soon appeared in *Woman's Journal* that indicated Stanton's withdrawal and that of her group from the support of Woodhull.

The secret of the final rupture . . . is understood to be an attempt at certain blackmailing operations. . . . But the friendship must have come to an end, sooner or later, at any rate. There was something not unworthy of sympathy . . . in the tolerance of Mrs. Woodhull, Tennessee Claflin and that gang . . . for there was pecuniary aid promised and Miss Anthony and Mrs. Hooker and others felt so acutely the oppression under which they labor in being deprived of suffrage that they cannot help welcoming aid from any source. . . . They have recovered from the delusion. . . . The prospect is that most of the prominent ladies known as leaders will work for Grant in one way or another. . . . Greeley is "a radical gone to seed."

Woodhull immediately wrote Anthony about this article, saying that "the inference . . . was that either Stanton or Anthony had been the informant." She asked, "Are you willing it should be so recorded?" Anthony wrote Hooker, expressing contempt for Victoria and her supporters.

I have not and shall not reply—because it is merely a trap to get a letter from me to publish in their book and they don't get it—that is all!

So I suppose her long pent up store of slang and slander is now to be emptied into the public maw—If any of those *men have* ever been on their knees to her it was to little purpose—for her cry is that of the horse leech Give-Give!! If she does gather up every supposed and suspected weakness of every body and give them all in detail it will be a sickening heap.

The one group that still supported Woodhull was the National Association of Spiritualists. *The Word,* a Spiritualist publication, defended her.

If anything shows the inability of women to vote intelligently it would be the present . . . attitude of Lucy Stone and Susan B. Anthony. The Republican Party has done nothing worthy of the support of Woman Suffragists. It advocates war, military despotism and the perpetual spoilization of labor. We ask that when they meddle with reforms that they not always take the wrong side as Lucy Stone persistently does.

In September, Victoria Woodhull arrived in Boston for the National Association of Spiritualists convention. She had decided to resign as president of this organization, for she felt so drained and exhausted that she could "carry this load no longer." She mounted the platform determined to tell her supporters of this decision, but suddenly the familiar physical transformation took place: Her skin visibly paled, her eyes became as glazed and bright as azure marbles. "I was seized by one of those overwhelming gusts of inspiration which sometime come upon me." Sparing no one, she told all that she knew of the sexual behavior of Beecher and Mrs. Tilton, of Blackwell and Mrs. Patton, of Livermore and Hanaford, and on and on. Elizabeth Meriwether, the Memphis, Tennessee diarist who had so feared Negro emancipation, was a Spiritualist delegate to the convention. She wrote, "Mrs. Woodhull's speech poured out like a stream of flame. . . . Editors, teachers, preachers, she spared not. . . . When she finished off Beecher she came back to Boston and lifted some of its editors high in the air and scorched them with accusations. . . . Her fiery flame went on until she suddenly stopped and flashed from the platform and out at a side door just as swiftly as she had flashed in."

An immediate repercussion was that Abby Patton, at the behest of her husband, Ludlow, finally severed her relationship with Henry Blackwell. And Julia Ward Howe turned her pen on Victoria Woodhull in the *Woman's Journal,* calling her "a self-aggrandizing harlot" for destroying countless reputations with her "bogus revelations." In fact, Woodhull's revelations were so scorching that no newspaper dared print the particulars. The *World* came the closest, stating that Woodhull said that Mary Livermore and Phebe Hanaford were known to support free love practices. The *Boston Journal* noted only that she had made accusations against people of "impeccable reputation . . . and had sworn profanely." Woodhull replied, "I swore not profanely. I swore divinely."

The second week in October, Plymouth Church celebrated the twenty-fifth anniversary of Henry Ward Beecher's reign. A beaming Beecher watched as the Plymouth Church Sunday-school children paraded past his house and tossed bouquets of flowers at his feet. Henry Bowen spoke, and with great emotion recounted how he had brought the brilliant preacher from Indianapolis and persuaded him to take the pastorate of Plymouth Church. On the final day of the celebration, Beecher mounted the platform of Plymouth Church as his congregation swarmed about him. At his side stood the Reverend Richard Salter Storrs of the Church of the Pilgrims, who bitterly disapproved of Beecher's permissive doctrine, was jealous of his popularity, and opposed him politically. But Storrs delivered a florid congratulatory speech, after which Beecher embraced him and kissed him firmly on the cheek in front of the three thousand celebrants.

It was then that Woodhull, driven and hounded, announced, "I will make it hotter on earth for Henry Ward Beecher than Hell is below." If she was doomed to perish she would take this hypocrite down with her.

# CHAPTER TWENTY-EIGHT

# BURST LIKE
# A BOMBSHELL

W*oodhull & Claflin's Weekly* was closed, but Victoria scraped together the money and reactivated the presses. The world must know of the subterfuge and false propriety of those who professed to virtue. Victoria insisted that these hypocrites must be brought down. The spirits commanded it. This was the social revolution for which they had prepared her. Woodhull used a well-known quote that she attributed to Bismarck: "If an omelette has to be made, some eggs have to be broken." And she called this occasion, "Universal Washing Day."

One hundred thousand copies of *Woodhull & Claflin's Weekly,* dated November 2, 1872, were printed, obviously with the expectation that this publication would make enough money to replenish the Claflin family's empty coffers. One of the greatest scandals ever known was, as Victoria noted, about "to burst like a bombshell" on the public. "The Beecher-Tilton Scandal Case," as the exposé was called, appeared on the front page of the *Weekly,* couched in the form of an interview with Victoria Woodhull by an unnamed reporter. The reporter questioned her views and she answered, as she had on many other occasions, saying that "the marriage institution like slavery and monarchy and many other things which had been good or necessary in their day—are now in a general sense injurious instead of being beneficial to the community." To illustrate this, Woodhull provided the salacious details of Beecher's affair with Mrs. Tilton. She named Elizabeth Cady Stanton, Isabella Beecher Hooker, and Paulina Wright Davis as her sources and published letters from them substantiating the story. She also used this so-called interview to promulgate her free love doctrine.

*Reporter*—I confess, I cannot understand why you of all persons should have any fault to find with Mr. Beecher assuming everything to be true.

*Mrs. Woodhull*—I have no fault to find with him in any such sense as you mean, nor as that in which the world will condemn him. I have no doubt that he has done the very best he could do—under all the circumstances—with his demanding physical nature . . . passional starvation, enforced on such a nature, so richly endowed . . . is a horrid cruelty. Every great man of Mr. Beecher's type, has had in the past and will ever have, the need for and the right to the loving manifestations of many women.

Woodhull went on to say that free love was a necessity for Beecher, that it was from his strong "amative impulses" that he derived his preaching skills and magnetism. "Mr. Beecher is today, and after all that I have felt called upon to reveal of his life, as good, as pure and as noble a man as he ever was in the past, or as the world has held him to be, and Mrs. Tilton is still a pure, charming, cultured woman. It is then, the public opinion that is wrong and not the individuals." Woodhull emphasized that she did not condemn the practice of free love, for which she had the highest regard. Beecher's sin was not lechery but hypocrisy. She criticized him only "for failing to do what I do, to stand shoulder to shoulder with me and others who are endeavoring to hasten a social regeneration which he believes in."

The interview ended with a barely concealed threat of more revelations. Victoria told the imaginary reporter, "We have five hundred biographies of various persons in high circles of life, many of which persons are the present oracles of society. The facts of these biographies are similar to those presented in this article."

The *Weekly* was settling scores; Tennie C. too threatened blackmail through a letter that she alleged was written by "the Madam of a first-class house."

From the time that I opened my house, I have kept a sort of diary or record of the men who have visited it and entered in a business way the names and residences and some of the incidents of each visit of all the visitors at my establishment. What occurred to me was this. If you, in the prosecution of your blessed mission as a social reformer, have any need to see more behind the scenes and to understand the real state of New York society better, I will give you access to my two big books, or would even leave them with you in my absence. You will find in them the names of all classes—from doctors of divinity to counter-jumpers and runners for mercantile houses. Make what use of them you please.

Tennie indicated that she had accepted these books and that when the time came she might make use of them. Although several newspapers accused Tennie of writing this letter herself, it is probable that it came from her friend Annie Wood, who kept just such "big books." Madame Wood had a thriving business in prostitution as well as in assignation rooms such as the one she provided for Josie Mansfield and Ned Stokes. Annie was close to both Tennie and Victoria, and she herself admitted to receiving "profits" from Woodhull, Claflin & Co. Her "girls" no doubt also provided the sisters with a great deal of useful information.

The most inflammatory article in the November 2 issue, however, was one that appeared at Tennie's insistence—neither for revenge, nor for blackmail but for the sake of her conscience. Tennie explained that for three years this story had preyed upon her mind and that she must print it as a warning to her "sisters." Victoria agreed. "If this is a social revolution, we should start with a man like him." And so, on page 14 of the *Weekly,* in an article titled "Beginning of the Battle," the dastardly behavior of one Luther C. Challis was revealed. But what Victoria and Tennie C. had also unwittingly exposed was the world from which they had come, and in so doing they inadvertently stepped into the abyss.

The article began with Tennie's statement that she had lived among prostitutes and knew them well. She felt they were an unfairly reviled and persecuted class, put upon by policemen and courts and customers; persecuted by the very "whoremongers that may marry a pure woman, move in good society and be generally respected." She wrote, "The world shall know the wrongs these women suffer and the men who inflict them."

To illustrate her point she described an evening she and Vickie spent at New York's French Ball in 1869. The annual ball, organized by the Société des Bals d'Artistes, was the most scandalous and anticipated event of the demimonde. At houses of prostitution and in apartments maintained by wealthy men, women assembled risqué costumes. By far the most favored was the skimpy tutu of the ballerina and the revealing bodice of the bayadere and daughter of the regiment. Wigs and masks completed the ensembles and guaranteed anonymity.

The night of the ball, "three thousand of the best men and four thousand of the worst women" arrived at the imposing Academy of Music on the northeast corner of Fourteenth Street and Irving Place. By eleven, almost a thousand men and boys had congregated outside, where the police with their billy sticks beat back a narrow passage for the masqueraders as they alighted from their carriages. Unattended women were greeted by hoots, yells, and whistles. Tennie reported that she and Victoria arrived at midnight "closely dominoed," not having informed Colonel Blood of their intentions. They both wore shepherdess dresses from the court of Louis XV. Tennie C. carried a flower-entwined shepherdess crook. Satin masks concealed their faces.

A thousand gaslights in crystal chandeliers illuminated the seats and stage as they made their way through the crush to a private upstairs box, furnished with red velvet couches, gilt chairs, and heavy red damask curtains trimmed with gold cords. So many dancers crowded the floor that the bodies were compressed into a writhing mass. Leaning over the bronze rail, Tennie C. spotted Luther Challis, a Wall Street broker, and Charles Maxwell, an unusually handsome playboy from a wealthy family, who, having little money of his own, confessed that he "lived on the town." These men were accompanied by "two fresh-faced young schoolgirls perhaps fifteen or sixteen years of age." The party entered Woodhull's box, and Challis ordered wine. Though he and Maxwell drank little, the girls' glasses were constantly refilled. One of the young girls was so besotted that she sank onto the couch. Tennie C., aware of the danger the girl was in, knelt beside her and begged her to stop drinking. With this, Challis turned to Tennie and snapped, "Let them alone!"

By this time, the scene below was one of abandon. Although the women were in costume and masked, the majority of men were not. In the adjoining boxes men stood smoking their cigars and watching the crush of dancers below. Several gestured or shouted to their servants on the floor to pluck a half-naked woman from the crowd and bring her upstairs to their box. The dancing had become wild and orgiastic. According to an account in the *World,* published four days after the ball,

One of the women is caught up by the crowd and tossed bodily into a proscenium box, where she is dragged by half a dozen brutes in over the sill and furniture in such a manner as to disarrange as much as possible what small vestige of raiment there is on her. The feat awakens general merriment.

Presently the trick is repeated on the other side. A young woman, rather pretty and dressed in long skirts, is thrown up and falls back into the arms of the crowd, who turn her over, envelope her head in her own skirts, and again toss her up temporarily denuded. . . .

A heavier woman than the rest is thrown out of a box and falls heavily on the floor. She is picked up insensible by the police and carried out. There is not a whisper of shame in the crowd, it is now drunken with liquor and its own beastliness. It whirls in mad eddies round and round.

*The infamous French Ball of 1869, attended by "three thousand of the best men and four thousand of the worst women" in New York*

Tennie C. saw that Challis was standing behind one of the girls, his hands thrust into the bodice of her dress squeezing her breasts while she leaned against him as if she would fall if he moved away. A moment later, Maxwell announced that they were taking the girls up to "Molly's." Molly de Ford, like Annie Wood, was a client of Woodhull, Claflin & Co. and the madam of a "first-class" house of prostitution. Tennie, overwrought, begged the men not to take these girls to such a place. In reply, Maxwell for the first time removed his hat and with a sweeping gesture thanked her for her hospitality. Then they were gone.

Victoria glanced into the box to her right where a girl lay on the crimson velvet couch, her ballet skirts pulled up over her head while two men mounted her in full view of the public. The son of Mr. Mercier, the manager of the Academy, entered the box and asked them to stop. One of the men pressed a glass of champagne into his hand while the other pulled his hat down over his eyes.

Victoria and Tennie left shortly thereafter. On the dance floor a wild cancan had commenced. The article in the *World* said that this was "no longer a dance at all, but a series of indecent exposures, a tumultuous orgy in which one man is struck by an unknown assailant, and his cheek laid open with a sharp ring, his white vest and tie splashed with blood. . . . On the stairs and in the cloakrooms and through the narrow, tortuous passages leading to the stage dressing-rooms were vile tableaus of inflamed women and tipsy men, bandying brutality and obscenity." At a little past two o'clock the band played "Home Sweet Home," the gaslights were extinguished, and another French Ball drew to an end.

The fate of the two innocent schoolgirls troubled Tennie, perhaps because they reminded her of herself at that age. Both she and Victoria believed that if women cared to sell their bodies it was better than the slavery of marriage, but these were innocents who had no idea what they were doing. Within the week, Tennie persuaded her sister to visit the house of Molly de Ford. Here their worst fears were confirmed. The November 2, 1872, issue of *Woodhull & Claflin's Weekly* included some of the same details that appeared in the *World* in 1869. But Tennie's first-person account emphasized the plight of the schoolgirls involved. She wrote,

> You may be sure I followed those girls up and got the history of their connection with these men. They were seduced by them. . . . They were taken to a house . . . of prostitution, then they were robbed of their innocence by each of these scoundrels, Challis and "Smith," taking them to himself. And this scoundrel Challis, to prove that he had *seduced a maiden, carried for days on his finger, exhibiting in triumph, the red trophy of her virginity.* After three days these Lotharios exchanged beds and companions and when weary of this they brought their friends, to the number of one hundred and over, to debauch these young girls—mere children.

On October 26, a week prior to the publication date, issues of *Woodhull & Claflin's Weekly* were mailed to newspapers in the United States, Canada, and Great Britain. On October 28 a public sale began. Within three hours

*Anthony Comstock—*
*the obsessive crusader against vice*

scores of newsboys hawking the issue had lined up in Broad Street, blocking it for hundreds of feet. By nightfall the paper, which had a face price of 10 cents, was bringing $2.50 a copy. (In the next three days 150,000 new copies were printed and sold, some allegedly for $40.) On the evening of October 28, as the city reeled under this "heap of scandal," Henry Ward Beecher stood in the library of his Columbia Heights home with United States District Attorney Benjamin Tracy, his loyal parishioner and political ally, and Henry Bowen, who had signed the "tripartite agreement" of friendship earlier that year. Beecher took no visible role in what happened next, but at one o'clock in the morning, Tracy's secretary knocked on the door of the Brooklyn home of the commissioner in charge of obscenity and "impure literature" for the Young Men's Christian Association.

Anthony Comstock, five-feet-ten-inches tall and 210 pounds, his face framed in ginger-colored mutton-chop whiskers, was a fairly new arrival in Brooklyn. Thirteen months before, he had married Margaret Hamilton, a woman ten years his senior who he said reminded him of his mother. The Comstocks then moved from Connecticut to New York City, where he took a job as a dry goods salesman. After boarding in Williamsburg for two months he managed to buy a small house in Brooklyn for $500. But even as he worked as a salesman, sin was Comstock's obsession. For Comstock alcohol was evil, and he energetically harassed two local saloon keepers until one was driven out of business and the other died of a heart attack. But temperance never captured his imagination as much as the war against impure sex. In his adolescence Comstock had been a compulsive masturbator. His strict Calvinist upbringing convinced him that the profane images that accompanied such behavior led irrevocably to moral corruption. Comstock compared erotic feelings to electrical wires connected to the inner dynamite of obscene thoughts. Images of sexuality could cause a deadly explosion, destroying the soul.

Six months after his arrival in Brooklyn, Comstock scrawled a note to Robert R. McBurney, the director of the Young Men's Christian Association, which had been formed at the end of the war to provide the growing population of single young Christian men more wholesome pursuits than the city's gambling parlors, saloons, and brothels. Comstock's note was a desperate plea for help to eliminate the evils to which these men were exposed. The YMCA promptly hired Comstock to ferret out vice and pornography wherever it existed. He left his job as a salesman and began to pursue pornographers with such zeal that, with the aid of the police, as many as seven were arrested in a single day. After six months of employment, he was given $500 by McBurney as a token of appreciation. Comstock wrote in his diary, "God's hand was in this." But he wanted more. He longed to bring his crusade to the attention of the American public and to become known throughout the nation as a brave and famous warrior against sin—a paladin of purity.

Comstock was dressed in his nightshirt and cap when the one o'clock caller dispatched by Benjamin Tracy told him of the publication of "The Beecher-Tilton Scandal Case." He dressed quickly and went to Bowen's office at the *Independent*. At eight o'clock the following morning, Comstock dispatched three of Bowen's clerks to New York City to buy the *Weekly*, no matter what it cost, and to send it to certain persons by post. On November 2, armed with affidavits and postal receipts, Comstock proceeded to the office of District Attorney Noah Davis, another Beecher parishioner. Although it was a Sunday, Davis was waiting in his office and immediately issued a warrant to shut down *Woodhull & Claflin's Weekly* and to arrest Woodhull and Claflin for sending obscene material through the mail. The charge was based on a little-known postal law of 1865, which had never before been enforced.

Victoria and Tennie C. were intercepted in a carriage containing five hundred freshly printed copies of the *Weekly*. An overzealous arresting officer plopped himself on Tennie's lap and held her down as the sisters were carted off to the Ludlow Street jail, where they were immediately ushered into a side room. Five officials awaited them, three of whom were Plymouth Church parishioners. During the examination, one of these men blurted out that the sisters were accused not only of obscenity but also of "a gross libel on a reverend gentleman whose character it is well worth the while of the government of the United States to vindicate." Victoria insisted that they would say nothing until they obtained counsel, and therefore the sisters spent Sunday night in jail. On Monday, November 3, they were informed that their bail had been set at $8,000 each. Colonel Blood dipped into the profits from the *Weekly*'s sales, and they were released before nightfall.

The next morning they were rearrested and informed that the case had been moved to the jurisdiction of United States Commissioner Davenport. In a hearing that day, Davenport said that the charge of obscenity had nothing to do with the Beecher article but was based on a phrase used in the article about Luther Challis, "the red trophy of her virginity." "That came from the book of Deuteronomy," Victoria Woodhull interjected. "The tabloids are full of this, added Tennie. "Why don't you try the *World* and the *Sun*, not us?" At the end of the hearing Davenport admitted that "a case of this character was never contemplated" when the obscenity statute was written but added, "I am disposed to, and shall, hold the prisoners." With no further explanation they were returned to their cell.

On Election Day, Susan B. Anthony, accompanied by fourteen Rochester women, including three of her sisters, went to the polls and intimidated the officials into allowing them to vote. "I have been and gone and done it!! Positively *voted* the Republican ticket . . . ," Anthony noted with pride. Three weeks later a U.S. marshal knocked on the door of her home with an arrest warrant. Anthony knew she was a visible symbol to the women of the nation and demanded to be handcuffed before being taken away.

In a crowded courtroom, in front of the press of the nation, Susan B. Anthony was tried for the crime of voting. The case was brought before an all-male jury and, as a woman, Anthony was refused the opportunity to testify. Late in the day the judge reached into his pocket, drew out a decision he had written before he heard the case, and proceeded to read it to the court. He instructed the jury to find Anthony guilty and insisted that they do so. When the verdict was read, the judge asked, "Has the prisoner anything to say why sentence shall not be pronounced?"

"Yes, Your Honor . . . in your ordered verdict of guilty you have trampled underfoot every vital principle of our government. My natural rights, my civil rights, my political rights, are all alike ignored. . . ."

"The court must insist—the prisoner has been tried according to established forms of law . . . ," said the judge.

"Yes, Your Honor, but by forms of law all made by men, interpreted by men, administered by men, in favor of men, and against women. . . ."

"The sentence of the court is that you pay a fine of one hundred dollars and the costs of the prosecution."

". . . I shall never pay a dollar of your unjust penalty. . . . And I shall earnestly and persistently continue to urge all women to the practical recognition of the old revolutionary maxim that 'resistance to tyranny is obedience to God,' " declared Anthony.

Though Anthony had struck a blow for women, she violated the conventions of the day. Lucy Stone's group was unsympathetic. Anthony wrote to Isabella Beecher Hooker in exasperation, "Do you know, I have sometimes felt that our Boston friends . . . try to persuade themselves that my prosecution and verdict and sentence are a disgrace and that they shrink from affiliation with an adjudged criminal. I do hope you can feel out, why it is that you and Mrs. Stanton—the two greatest Woodhull sinners—are more respectable than I. Isn't it too sick."

On Election Day, as Ulysses S. Grant swept into office for a second term with almost a million-vote plurality, Victoria and Tennie were confined to their cell in the Ludlow Street jail. Victoria Woodhull received no votes for the presidency, at least none that were recorded. From her cell, she had written to Anthony,

> There is no time, now, to indulge in personal enmity. I have none toward anybody. . . . I fear they intend to crush out, in your person, the Constitutional Question of Woman's right to suffrage, as they are attempting, in my person, to establish a precedent for the suppression of recalcitrant Journals. . . . For my individual self, I have a pretty large fight of my own on hand, but . . . if you can, make use of me. Hoping to hear from you by return mail. . . .

Anthony did not reply.

Horace Greeley, having suffered a humiliating defeat, was broken in health and spirit. The week before the election, Mary Cheney Greeley lay dying at the end of a tortured life. Greeley left her bedside to write, "I have been so bitterly assailed that I hardly know whether I am running for the Presidency or the penitentiary." Mary Greeley died at four o'clock on the morning of October 30, 1872.

The day after the election, Greeley made the announcement that once again he would assume the editorship of the *Tribune*. But in his absence his great love—his newspaper—also had slipped away. While campaigning, the value of his stock had fallen from $10,000 to $6,000 a share. He had only six shares left of his original hundred and had borrowed heavily against them.

On Greeley's first day back, an editorial bitterly denouncing him appeared in his own paper. He wrote a rebuttal, but Whitelaw Reid refused to print it. Greeley was convinced that Reid had betrayed him and that there was a plot to be rid of him. He wrote to a friend, "I dread only the malignity with which I am hounded, and the possibility that it may ruin the *Tribune*. My enemies mean to kill that, if they would kill me instead I would thank them lovingly."

Greeley's instinct was correct. Although Reid was not directly conspiring against him, a syndicate was being formed to oust him from his own newspaper. Greeley wandered in despair about the *Tribune* offices, until, on November 12, he took to bed at the home of a friend, Alvin Johnson. There in the next few days, he wrote letter after letter disposing of his worldly goods. He wished to pay Elizabeth Cady Stanton's brother-in-law Dr. Edward Bayard the sum of $5,000. He wrote a rambling letter to remind Commodore Vanderbilt of the money he had given to Vanderbilt's epileptic son, Cornelius Jeremiah, and asked that the Commodore, upon Greeley's death, give an equivalent amount of money to his two daughters.

Reid prevailed upon Anna Dickinson to visit Greeley. "You will find him terribly broken," he commented. Greeley received her in a highly emotional state, brushing tears from his eyes. "Whitelaw tells me that since the speech you made on the twenty-fifth of October last, you have had over $14,000 of Lyceum engagements canceled," he said. "Is that true?" When she replied, "Yes," the grateful Greeley said, "Anna Dickinson, I think you are the most generous woman alive. . . . what you have done for me has cost you dear." Greeley was correct. The $10,000 she had been promised never materialized, and though the newspapers kept printing rumors of her impending engagement to Reid, her private letters indicate that he turned away from her the moment her popularity waned. Reid had persuaded her to support Greeley but joined the rest in deserting her once the election was lost.

The day after Anna's visit, Reid had Greeley committed to Dr. Choate's asylum in Pleasantville and took over as editor of the *Tribune,* explaining that Greeley was suffering from "nervous prostration." At the end of November, less than a month after the election, Greeley sank into a coma. He'd left instructions for his burial: "No Latin—no embellishments . . . Whitelaw will distribute locks of my hair." And as a final word, as if he knew all that was to come, he wrote, "Be kind to Tilton. He is foolish—but young."

Even in death, Greeley's wishes were not respected. His funeral was held at the Church of the Divine Paternity at Fifth Avenue and Forty-fourth Street. President Grant and Vice President Schuyler Colfax attended, as did the governors of four states. Whitelaw Reid and Theodore Tilton sat side by side listening to Henry Ward Beecher's effusive ovation. A public that had once excoriated Horace Greeley and heaped abuse on him now saw him as a hero. In death, the doddering fool became a subtle genius; the compromiser was now a conciliator.

Gabrielle and Ida Greeley, having lost both their parents, finally explored the basement of the house in Chappaqua. Here they found the trunks full of china, silver, and linen—the amenities that Mary Cheney Greeley had hidden from her husband during her lifetime. The comforts that Horace Greeley had always lacked were divided between the two daughters who had managed to survive the childhood neglect of their father and the abuse of their mother.

# CHAPTER TWENTY-NINE

# I CAN ENDURE
# NO LONGER

"CAN I HELP YOU?" Isabella wrote this single line on the day that the *Weekly* appeared. Henry answered,

> If you still believe in that woman you can not help me. If you think of her as I do you can perhaps, though I do not need much help. I tread falsehoods into the dirt from whence they spring and go on my way rejoicing. My people are thus far heroic and would give their lives for me. . . . I trust you give neither countenance nor credence to the abominable coinage that has been put afloat. The specks of truth are mere spangles upon a garment of falsehood. . . . Thank you for love and truth and silence, but think of the barbarity of dragging a poor, dear child of a woman into this slough.

Isabella was not reassured: she was tortured by the certainty that her brother not only was guilty but that he had, in all probability, incited the legal action against Woodhull. With her husband far away across the sea, she turned to her brothers Thomas and Edward Beecher for guidance. She wrote first to Thomas, a flinty preacher, "At last the blow has fallen," and enclosed Henry's letter with the following observation.

> Now, Tom, so far as I can see, it is he who has dragged the dear child into the slough and left her there and who is now sending another woman to prison who is innocent of all crime but a fanaticism for the truth as revealed to her, and I, by my silence, am consenting unto her death.
>
> Tom, can't you go to brother Edward at once . . . and when you have counseled together as brothers should, counsel me also, and come to me if you can. It looks as if he hoped to buy my silence

with my love. At present, of course, I shall keep silent, but truth is dearer than all things else and if he will not speak it in some way I cannot always stand as consenting to a lie. "God help us all."

If you can't come to me, send Edward. I am utterly alone, and my heart aches for that woman even as for my own flesh and blood. I do not understand her, but I know her to be pure and unselfish and absolutely driven by some power foreign to herself to these strange utterances, which are always in behalf of freedom, purity, truth—as she understands it—always to befriend the poor and outcast, and bring low only the proud, the hypocrites in high places.

Thomas Beecher replied,

Dear Belle,

To allow the devil himself to be crushed for speaking the truth is unspeakably cowardly and contemptible. I respect, as at present advised, Mrs. Woodhull while I abhor her philosophy. She only carries out Henry's philosophy against which I recorded my protest some years ago and parted lovingly and achingly from him saying, we cannot work together. . . . In my judgment Henry is following his slippery doctrines of expediency and in his cry of progress and the nobleness of human nature has sacrificed clear, exact, ideal integrity. . . . Of the two, Woodhull is my hero, and Henry my coward. . . .

But Thomas lacked his sister's bravery, and he refused to come forward or to involve Edward. He concluded his letter with, "Don't write to me. . . . You can't help Henry at present. . . . If Mr. and Mrs. Tilton are brought into court nothing will be revealed. Perjury for good reason is with advanced thinkers no sin."

John Hooker, then visiting in Florence, was unaware that the scandal had been printed in the *Weekly* and that Victoria and Tennie C. were in jail. He too advised Isabella to distance herself from Mrs. Woodhull.

It looks as if the exposure is near at hand. . . . Can you not let the report get out after the H. matter becomes public, without being exactly responsible for it, that you have kept up friendship with Mrs. W. in the hope of influencing her not to publish the story, you having learned its truth. . . . This will give the appearance of self-sacrifice to your affiliation with her and will explain your not com-

*The members of the Beecher family who became involved in the scandal*

ing abroad with me—a fact which has a very unwife-like look. I know that you will otherwise be regarded as holding Mrs. W.'s views, and that we shall be regarded as living in some discord, and probably (by many people) as practicing her principles.

Apparently no one was prepared to confirm Woodhull's story. Mrs. Fernando Jones, a prominent member of the Chicago NWSA, gave an interview to the *Mail* in which she declared that her good friend Elizabeth Cady

Stanton found Woodhull's allegations to be false. This was followed by an interview in the *Lewiston* (Maine) *Telegram,* reprinted in papers nationwide, in which Stanton was quoted as saying that Woodhull's story was "untrue in every particular." In fact, she had not denied the story, but had merely informed two clergymen from Lewiston that it was not she who had quoted Tilton as saying that Beecher was a "damned lecherous scoundrel." Unaware of this, Anthony, upon reading the Lewiston account, shot off a reproving letter to Stanton. Five days later, Stanton's answer arrived.

> Dear Susan,
>
> I had supposed you knew enough of the papers to trust a friend of twenty years' knowledge before *them.* I never made nor authorized the statement made in the Lewiston paper. . . . I have said many times since the *denouement* that if my testimony of what I did know would save Victoria from prison, I should feel compelled to give it.
>
> You do not monopolize, dear Susan, all the honor there is among womankind. I shall not run before I am sent, but when the time comes, I shall prove myself as true as you. No, no! I do not propose to shelter a man when a woman's liberty is at stake.

Though Anthony assumed a righteous position, when Isabella asked her to reveal what Mrs. Tilton had told her about the Beecher affair, she declined, writing that to do so would only injure Lib. "I feel the deepest sympathy . . . for poor, dear, trembling Mrs. Tilton. My heart bleeds for her every hour. I would fain take her in my arms, with her precious comforts— all she has on earth—her children—and hide her away from the wicked gaze of men."

The fact remained that still no one came to Woodhull's defense and thus Beecher was able to fend off the gossip-hungry press. On returning from a Sunday sermon, one reporter followed Beecher up the steps of his house brandishing a copy of the *Weekly,* and asked why Beecher had made no statement refuting Woodhull's charges. The preacher answered, "When a man is unlucky enough as he passes along on a sidewalk to be drenched by a torrent of dirty water thrown on him from some upper window by some careless or mischievous hand, the best he can do is go home, wipe himself, and say nothing."

"Of course, Mr. Beecher, the whole thing is a fraud from beginning to end," said the reporter.

"Entirely!" replied Beecher.

Anthony wrote Hooker,

*"Entirely."* Wouldn't you think if God ever did strike any one dead for telling a lie, He would have struck then? . . . For a cultivated man, at whose feet the whole world of men as well as of women sits in love and reverence, whose moral, intellectual, social resources are without limit—for such a man, so blest, so overflowing with *soul food*—for him to ask or accept the *body* of one or a dozen of his reverent and revering devotees, I tell you *he is the sinner—if it be a sin—and who shall say it is not*? My pen has faltered and staggered; it would not write you for these three days. . . .

Your brother will yet see his way out . . . and let us hope he will be able to prove himself above the willingness that others shall suffer for weakness and wickedness of his. . . . If he has no new theories, then he will surely be compelled to admit that he has failed to live or to preach those he has.

On November 23, Victoria Woodhull and Tennie C. Claflin were taken to the Tombs. This squat edifice on Centre Street, built to resemble the Temple of Karnak at Luxor, was the most dreaded of prisons. Open sewage pipes flowed past cells measuring only five by eight feet, some with ceilings so low that prisoners could not stand erect. Sometimes the vapors were so noxious that prisoners passed out. Victoria later said that the first night in the Tombs she had a vision of a fire sweeping toward the prison. She saw people screaming and bodies consumed by fire. She began crying hysterically and threatening to take her own life if she wasn't moved. On the day before Christmas, Victoria and Tennie C. were transferred back to the Ludlow Street jail. That evening a great fire swept Centre Street, but at the last minute a wind turned it away from the Tombs. Nearby, at the Fifth Avenue Laundry, seven scrub girls were reduced to ashes. The wooden roof of Barnum's circus caught fire, and all the wild animals that the circus had acquired over the years burned to death. Victoria speculated that the fire was arson, set by assassins who did not know she had been transferred.

From her prison cell, a despairing Victoria wrote Isabella that she was convinced that a campaign of suppression had been organized against her. Like Christ himself, she was being abandoned. She wrote that Mrs. Stanton knew all the facts and should come forward to deny the *Lewiston Telegram* story. Anthony too wrote to Gerrit Smith that Stanton should be the one to

*The Halls of Justice on Centre Street, known as "The Tombs,"*
*was New York's most dreaded prison.*

speak out. "It is she who should annul her Lewiston denial—while *that stands*—*for me* to speak *contrary to her* would place both of us in rather awkward positions before friends and the public."

Determined to set the record straight, but not wanting to be Henry's "first accuser," Isabella wrote an article under the pseudonym Justitia in the *Hartford Times,* asserting that as long before as the spring of 1871, Mrs. Stanton "had charged Mr. Beecher . . . with very much the same offense of which Mrs. Woodhull speaks." In an effort to induce Stanton to come forward, Isabella spoke freely of Stanton's confidences to her, including the fact that Elizabeth had always been in love with her brother-in-law, Edward Bayard. When Stanton learned that her most intimate secret had been revealed, she wrote to Isabella, "What did prompt you to betray all my confidences! . . . Do you not remember that consideration was in strict confidence. Who can we trust with anything. I begin to think our only safety is in living like oysters, each within a shell of secrecy without human sympathy." And a fortnight later,

I cannot tell you my surprise and sorrow in learning from four different sources how cruelly you are not only betraying my confidences but impeaching my integrity. What I would say I dare not put on paper. I considered that moonlight talk as sacred as if it had been with God himself.

I know the desperate effort that is being made to impeach in every possible way the integrity of Susan and myself, the two unswerving witnesses in the case on which turns the impending revolution. I cannot understand how you can so easily let all you do know of my head, heart, moral purpose and religious earnestness be outweighed by the designing words of an enemy and so cruelly expose the wounds I, in an unguarded moment, unveiled to you as never to mortal eye before. For although several friends know the material fact, to no one but you did I ever reveal the *steadfastness of my affection,* that instead of seeking solace elsewhere has gone out into my life work.

I have never yet put the least confidence in any woman that it was not betrayed, though I have sacredly guarded everything ever entrusted to my hearing. You have said many things to me that would not bear repeating that have never passed my lips. Be careful what you believe and report to Susan's and my detriment just now. Theodore Tilton, that prince of liars, is moving Heaven and earth to impeach our integrity. You have deeply wronged me already, I pray you go no further.

After the defeat of Greeley, Tilton's problems seemed to engulf him. He desperately wanted to recover his career and his reputation and therefore had as much invested in suppressing the scandal as Beecher did. Because Anthony and Stanton had been Lib's confidantes, Tilton tried to undermine them, writing that they were not above "twisting the truth for their own advantage" and that his wife "deeply regretted her association with them." She had always considered these "public women" dangerous, and he "wished he had listened to her."

Isabella chafed under these attacks and the abandonment of her "Darling Queen." She had worried that her brother might kill himself when the scandal was revealed, but now it had all come out and Henry was "going his merry way" while Victoria Woodhull occupied a jail cell. This injustice preyed upon her mind until, after a sleepless night, she awoke with a solution. Less than a year before, Victoria told Isabella that she would be a "heroine" if she could persuade Henry to admit he was a free lover. Now she knew what she must do: "It seems to me that God has been preparing me for this work and you [Henry] also for years and years," she wrote to her brother. There was "but one honorable way" to deal with the question and that was for Henry to admit he was a practicing free lover and expound his advanced social theories on the subject. Isabella believed that, with her brother at her side, she would lead "the grandest revolution in the world." Victoria Woodhull had foreseen this. Isabella revealed her plan to Henry:

> I will write you a sisterly letter, expressing my deep conviction that this whole subject needs the most earnest and chaste discussion . . . that I have observed for years that your reading and thinking has been profound on this and kindred subjects and now the time has come for you to give the world, through your own paper, the conclusions you have reached and the reasons therefore. If you choose I will then reply to each letter.
>
> I am sure that nearly all the thinking men and women are somewhere near you and will rally to your support if you are bold, frank, and absolutely truthful in stating your convictions. . . . My own conviction is that the one radical mistake you have made is in supposing that you are so much ahead of your time, and in daring to attempt to lead when you have anything to conceal. Do not, I pray you, deceive yourself with the hope that the love of your church, or any other love, human or divine, can compensate the loss of absolute truthfulness to your own moral convictions.

The unexpected letter was a major threat to a situation that Beecher had felt was finally in hand. The previous April, Isabella had sent him a similar request, but this letter was stronger and more final. After consulting with Frank Moulton, Beecher wrote his sister that a "*calm silence*" was the only course of action he wished to take and added, "I have no philosophy to unfold and no new theory of society."

But Isabella was not to be stopped. The day after Thanksgiving, she spent the afternoon communing with the spirits. That evening she read an interview with the political cartoonist Thomas Nast in the *Hartford Times*. When asked if he didn't think it a great undertaking to attack Mr. Greeley, Nast answered, "The people were fooled with Greeley, as they are fooled with Beecher, and he will tumble further than Greeley yet."

Isabella took it as a sign.

Dear Brother,

I can endure no longer. I must see you and persuade you to write a paper which I will read, going alone to your pulpit, and taking sole charge of the services. I shall leave here on 8 a.m. train Friday morning, and unless you meet me at Forty-second Street station I shall go to Mrs. Phelps' house, opposite Young Men's Christian Association where I shall hope to see you during the day. . . . I would prefer going to Mrs. Tilton's to anywhere else but I hesitate to ask her to receive me. I feel sure, however, that words from her should go into that paper and with her consent I could write as one commissioned from on high.

Do not fail me, I pray you. Meet me at noon on Friday as you hope to meet your own mother in Heaven. In her name I beseech you, and I will take no denial. Ever yours in love unspeakable.

Belle

Beecher burst into Moulton's study and handed him Isabella's letter. "This is a disaster!" he exclaimed. Moulton thought Beecher should go immediately to Elizabeth Phelps's house, speak kindly to his sister, and exhort her not to take this course. Beecher answered that his sister was "a dribbling old fool" and he would not deal with her. It was decided that Tilton should go instead and, so far as possible, shake Isabella's confidence in the truth of Woodhull's story. Then Edward Beecher arrived and reported that he had just visited Isabella and found her to be "wild and excited." She had threatened to come to Plymouth Church and proclaim from Henry's own pulpit that he was a free lover. Tilton and Beecher took the ferry to New York. Tilton headed for Mrs. Phelps's house while Beecher contacted his sister Harriet Beecher Stowe, who had come to the city for Greeley's memorial service. He told Harriet that Isabella was crazy and persuaded her to occupy the front pew at the Plymouth Church Sunday service in case Isabella entered the church and tried to force herself onto the pulpit.

When Tilton arrived at her home, Mrs. Phelps invited him to remain for dinner with Mrs. Hooker. After dinner, Isabella went upstairs, which gave Tilton the opportunity to question Elizabeth Phelps. She told him, "There is no doubt that Mrs. Hooker will bring Henry to the pillory or down from his pulpit." A moment later, Isabella returned and Tilton drew her into the parlor. Tilton would remember the conversation that followed, for, though he could hardly acknowledge as much, it was the moment he lost all honor.

"What have you to communicate to me?" he asked.

"You know very well, because you know what Henry has been doing," replied Isabella.

Sensing her hesitation, Tilton said, "Madam, confession is good for the soul. Speak plainly. You have nothing to fear from me."

"Very well. I am here to charge Henry Ward Beecher with adultery with Mrs. Theodore Tilton."

"Madam, I anticipated as much. I am here to charge you with adultery at the time you were in Washington with . . ." And he announced the name of a prominent senator.

Isabella seemed stunned. She stared at Tilton but said nothing.

"Where have you heard that Mr. Beecher is guilty?" asked Tilton.

"Don't be absurd. You know Victoria Woodhull and her sister are persecuted, imprisoned for telling the truth."

"If Mrs. Woodhull is the source of your information then I assure you that she is mine also. She has told me that you and the gentleman concerned have been criminally intimate."

As if Tilton's sword had finally penetrated, Isabella sank to the couch. Tilton left to the sound of her sobs. The following morning he reported to Moulton and Beecher in exact detail what had happened. When he'd finished, Beecher laughed, clapped his hands, and cried out, "Bravo!" But Moulton turned with a look of disgust on his face and left the room.

To make sure of the efficacy of Tilton's visit, Beecher himself appeared at Elizabeth Phelps's home the following day. When Mrs. Phelps inadvertently opened the door to the parlor she saw Isabella kneeling in front of Henry Ward Beecher as if imploring him for mercy. Within a fortnight, perhaps for insurance, a story appeared in the *Tribune* stating that Henry Ward Beecher and two other members of his family were so concerned that Mrs. Hooker had fallen under the Satanic influence of Victoria Woodhull that they had consulted Dr. Harold Butler about her mental condition. Dr. Butler gave his opinion that "Mrs. Hooker was laboring under a monomania superinduced by over-excitement" and that "Mrs. Woodhull had exercised a controlling influence over a too susceptible mind." The doctor then recommended that Isabella be temporarily confined to an asylum for the insane.

Isabella wrote Stanton that her own brother Henry was willing to have the world see her as insane and begged her to defend the truth. At last the floodgates opened. Stanton wrote to Isabella,

Victoria's story is exaggerated, rather higher-colored than I heard it but the main facts correspond with what Susan and I heard. I have not a shadow of a doubt of its truth. . . . The outrageous persecution of Mrs. Woodhull in our court shows money and power behind. . . . Your persecutions in another way are as grievous and I am not willing to withhold anything any longer that can help to make things easier for you either on paper or by word of mouth. We are in the midst of a great social battle that will end in the absolute freedom of women and when the victory is gained we shall know that it is worth all that we have suffered. I have been crucified in this matter as much as you. . . . This is the first thing I have committed to paper on this T [Tilton] and B [Beecher] matter so use it judiciously for your defense.

# WHAT HAVE WE DONE NOW?

A s THE year 1873 began, unemployment escalated in a weakening economy. After seven years of growth following the Civil War, seven years of decline had begun. The corruption and extravagance of William Marcy Tweed's political leadership of New York, which had been allowed to flourish in prosperous times, now came under scrutiny. With Thomas Nast's pen cutting like a scimitar, Tweed soon replaced Victoria Woodhull as the representative of the devil. But Tweed was hard to topple until a disgruntled employee, James O'Brien, came into possession of a copy of the Tweed Ring's books. In exchange for silence he asked the Boss to cancel a loan of $12,000 and give him some $50,000 more. O'Brien had picked a bad morning for blackmail. Tweed ordered his henchmen to toss him out into the street. O'Brien then went to several newspapers trying to sell the books, but, being the recipients of Tweed's patronage, they turned him down. Finally, wanting revenge more than money, he took the books to the incorruptible *New York Times.* Placing them on the desk, he said to the editor, "You have had a hard fight against the Boss," to which the editor replied, "Have still." O'Brien pushed the books forward. "I said you *have had* it."

The *Times's* exposé of the Tweed Ring revealed loot estimated at nearly $200 million. The chief scandal concerned the still incomplete courthouse, which so far had cost the taxpayers more than $17 million. The courthouse thermometers cost $7,500. Tweed's own printing company had received $187,000 for a single order of stationery. His own marble company had received $5 million. John H. Kaiser, the Tweed Ring's plumber, was paid $2 million. The plasterer Andrew Garvey got $3 million, and Tweed's friend James H. Ingersoll was paid $5 million for furniture and carpets. It was figured that Ingersoll could have covered half the island of Manhattan with high-grade Brussels carpeting for the money that had been spent and that Garvey could have applied his plaster six feet thick and used solid gold mesh for reinforcement. On January 2, 1873, Boss Tweed was arrested. After a protracted court battle, Tweed escaped to Spain only to be arrested a year later and shipped back to New York. The rigors of flight and imprisonment had ruined his health. He died in the spring of 1878 in the Ludlow Street jail.

In these hard economic times, the public sought retribution. Rumors circulated that powerful members of Congress, and even the vice president, had accepted at no cost stock and cash from "profits" in the Credit Mobilier, which had drained millions of dollars from the Union Pacific Railroad. A disgruntled congressman supplied newspapers with a list of these men, which he had surreptitiously taken from the office of Massachusetts Congressman Oakes Ames. The suspects denied the allegation. A government committee was formed to investigate the situation, but Republican businessmen exerted their influence to postpone the results of the inquiry until after the presidential election. On February 18, 1873, three months after Grant's reelection, the committee reported its findings to the House of Representatives. The investigation proved that Oakes Ames had kept careful records of payments to all the accused, a fact confirmed by deposits made to their personal accounts. Ames admitted his guilt. James Brooks of New York testified that Oakes Ames had given him free Credit Mobilier stock, but the others denied any involvement. The report stated that the investigating committee could not support the denials made by the congressmen. However, only Brooks and Ames, the two who had come forward with the truth, were found to be functioning from "corrupt motives." The committee recommended that they alone be expelled from Congress.

With the scandal of the Credit Mobilier, people began to look carefully into the financial structure of railroad bonds. By now the Northern Pacific was in deep trouble. With the monies expended to secure Grant's election and other expenses, Jay Cooke found that the Northern Pacific had overdrawn $1.6 million in one year while its previous overdrafts stood at an additional $5.5 million. Its bonds were selling at a heavy discount. Through political manipulation, when all other banks refused, Cooke was able to borrow $500,000 under favorable terms from the Freedmen's Savings and Trust Company, known as the Freedmen's Bank. This bank had been opened in 1865 to encourage the newly freed blacks to invest their money. The bank's advertisements proclaimed that Abraham Lincoln was their sponsor and read, "Cut off your vices—don't smoke—don't drink—don't buy lottery tickets. Put the money you save into the Freedmen's Savings Bank." In its first five years, blacks invested $3,299,201 in branches scattered

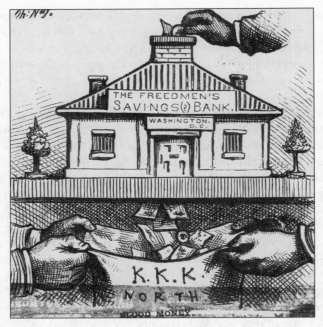

*The Freedmen's Savings and Trust Company made loans
to members of the Ku Klux Klan.*

across the country. Almost all of it came from small depositors—farmers and laborers—saving for a new life. Secretly, the reckless bank board freely squandered bank funds, making unsecured loans to friends, political cronies, and members of the Ku Klux Klan.

Although Cooke had not paid back a penny of the Freedmen's Bank loan, he tried to raise yet another $300,000 through a bond offering for the Northern Pacific. Suspicion mounted that these bonds, which had been promoted with so much publicity, were, in fact, nearly worthless. As a result, there were so few takers that the offering was withdrawn and pronounced a "resounding failure." Susan B. Anthony wrote a friend, "If the bond plan is a swindle I think it ought to be shown up in the daily papers. It is such a shame for poor, hardworking women and men to be juggleried out of their hard earnings."

ON NEW YEAR'S Day, the portly Anthony Comstock attended church services and resolved "to do something every day for Jesus." He had seen to it that the "indecent" Victoria Woodhull and her sister had been imprisoned for a month, but now they were free on $16,000 bail and awaiting trial. Comstock read that Victoria planned to deliver an address, far and wide, titled "Moral Cowardice and Modern Hypocrisy—The Naked Truth—Thirty Days in the Ludlow Street Jail." He feared this speech would severely criticize him.

Although Comstock was suffering from an ulcerated sore throat, he proceeded by train and sleigh to Greenwich, Connecticut, where he rented a Post Office box under the alias of J. Beardsley and sent a money order for six copies of the November 2 issue of *Woodhull & Claflin's Weekly*. He then went to Norwalk, Connecticut, and entered the same order in the name of a friend who lived there. A few days later, when he received notice from his friend that the papers had been delivered, although he was still ill, he repeated the trip, picked up the twelve newspapers, and secured new warrants for the arrest of Victoria and Tennie C. for sending obscene material across state lines. This time he added the name of Colonel Blood to the indictments.

Victoria planned to inaugurate her speech at Boston's Music Hall, but Harriet Beecher Stowe saw to it that it was canceled and no other hall was made available in that city. Harriet noted, "Those vile women 'jailbirds' had the impudence to undertake to advertise . . . a lecture. . . . It appears that lectures cannot be given without a license of the city government which was not to be forthcoming. The impudence of those witches is incredible!" Woodhull managed to get her lecture rescheduled for January 9, at Cooper Institute in New York City, where Mrs. Stowe could not stop her. Now her obstacle was Anthony Comstock, who alerted the police to arrest Victoria before she was able to deliver a speech that would undoubtedly damage him and his purity crusade.

Help now came from an unexpected source. Laura Cuppy Smith, a Woodhull supporter and a famous Spiritualist trance speaker, heard of the impending arrest through a friend on the police force and immediately rushed to warn Woodhull. Mrs. Smith had come to feel the hypocrisy of the present society through the pain she had experienced in her own life and had vowed to support women who wished to take a less traditional path. Widowed at twenty-two, Laura had one daughter, Peggy, to whom she devoted her life. When Peggy was sixteen, she confided to her mother that she was pregnant and that the lover who had promised to marry her had deserted her. "Well-meaning friends" advised an abortion and told Smith, "There is a way. Hide this thing from sight, send her on a journey. Destroy this evidence of youthful folly. All may yet be well." But Laura felt that abortion was a sin against God. She resolved, "No dark secret shall dog my child's footsteps through life, no lie on her lips. This child of my child shall live and has a right to life!"

Together mother and daughter "entered upon our future." Friends turned their backs, doors closed to them. When the grocer refused their money and would sell them no food, "a woman of questionable repute . . . opened her door to us." When the baby was born Mrs. Smith wrapped her in a blanket and, with her daughter at her side, paraded down the main street of the town, defying all those who had shunned them. "We walked the whole length of the street, running the gauntlet of curious eyes. The worst was over, the world could not wound us much after that. We had 'grasped the nettle,' it would sting us no more."

Smith spirited Victoria Woodhull away and hid her in Taylor's Hotel in Jersey City. Colonel Blood, unaware of the danger, took his usual morning walk down Broad Street. A policeman approached him and asked, "Are you not the publisher of *Woodhull & Claflin's Weekly*?" When Blood answered yes, he was arrested. When the police arrived at their newly rented house neither Victoria nor Tennie C. were to be found. The only occupant was a laundress doing the family wash. After the police left, she lifted her wash-tub and then the large barrel on which it rested. Concealed beneath was Tennie.

That evening marshals were posted at every doorway to Cooper Institute, poised to arrest Woodhull should she appear. Though people were informed there would be no lecture, many pushed inside and waited for something to happen. At eight o'clock, Laura Cuppy Smith appeared on-stage and announced that she would read Woodhull's speech. As she was about to begin, an elderly woman engulfed in a gray Quaker's cape and wearing a coal scuttle bonnet tottered down the aisle to a front seat. As Smith began, the Quaker lady limped up the stairway to the platform and walked halfway across the stage. Then with a sudden motion she flung her cape aside and tore off her bonnet. There stood Victoria Woodhull. "Comstock's defeated!" shouted Laura Cuppy Smith, and the audience cheered. The marshals dared not move. "I come into your presence from a cell in the American Bastille . . . indicted on the preposterous charge of sending obscene literature through the United States mail—a charge which the officers of the government will never dare bring to a trial."

Comstock, she avowed, was Beecher's tool. Officers had seized the *Weekly*'s type, destroyed its presses, purloined their private papers, and kept them from speaking to anyone. Public opinion had been turned against them. Victoria said that she had read in the *Tribune* that Comstock had vowed "to run me to the earth even if it took every hour of his life and every dollar of his fortune." If the "zealot Comstock" were allowed to prevail, "soon some woman may be arrested for adultery, for kissing her own baby boy." The case against her, she maintained, was concocted in a conspiracy between Comstock and Plymouth Church.

Woodhull asserted that the leaders of Plymouth Church, many of whom were involved in her prosecution, had said of the charges, "Whether they be true or not, we believe in *you* Henry Ward Beecher . . . church and congregation and the public . . . we accept *you.*" Woodhull spoke for an hour and a half. She concluded with, "Sexual freedom—the last right to be claimed for man in the long struggle for universal emancipation, the least understood and the most feared of all the freedoms, but destined to be the most beneficent of any—will burst upon the world." With that she dashed down the steps, ran to the back of the auditorium, threw her arms open in a gesture of crucifixion, and surrendered herself to the waiting officers.

On January 11, Victoria and Colonel Blood were brought forth for a hearing before the grand jury. During the examination Tennie, who had always stood by her sister, entered the room and surrendered herself to a deputy marshal. The sisters and Blood were to be represented by William F. Howe of the firm Howe & Hummel. Howe was a well-known defender of Wall Street confidence men, malcontented mistresses, and radicals. Like Jim Fisk and George Francis Train, he dressed in a flamboyant manner: plaid pants, a purple vest, a blue satin scarf set off by a diamond stickpin. His colleagues considered him effective with a jury but disreputable. Although Mr. Howe insisted that the particulars of the case and the exact charges be revealed, he was overruled. Bail was now raised to $21,000, and when it was forthcoming, the prisoners were released. Eleven days later they were re-arrested. "What have we done now?" Victoria asked the arresting officer, who seemed thoroughly confused. "I think this one is for libel," he answered.

By now, cell number eleven in the Ludlow Street jail had become a familiar place. On its floor was a rug that belonged in Victoria's house, and the rough cots were made up with her own linen. Laura Cuppy Smith organized a group of Spiritualists who wrote letters asking for monetary support. Many return envelopes contained small donations, usually from women. That Victoria and Tennie's circumstances were becoming desperate was evinced by a letter Victoria wrote to one Lafayette Beach, stating that she had found an empty envelope from him and asking what had been in it. In a note with many cross-outs she wrote, "We have had so many assisting us in our correspondence it has got somewhat mixed up, but please excuse it on account of our condition."

In February 1873, Comstock, seeking greater enforcement powers to implement his crusade against such "sins" as obscenity, pornography, birth control, and abortion, went to Washington to strengthen the postal law of 1865. In order to keep Victoria and Tennie in jail, he petitioned Congress to add weeklies to the list of publications that fell under this law. Comstock then asked Congress to declare it a crime to advertise contraceptive devices or sexually related materials or to sell them. To give any contraceptive information, even orally, was also to be banned. Furthermore, he urged that the law stipulate that the death of a fetus, or of a woman as a result of an abortion, be punishable by up to twenty years in prison. Benjamin Butler took home the proposed Comstock bill to study it for the House Judiciary Committee and concluded that it violated First Amendment rights.

Undaunted, on February 24 Anthony Comstock appeared before the committee. Setting a small, scuffed, brown leather suitcase on the table, he withdrew from it pornographic engravings and postcards, contraceptives, and devices to implement sexual pleasure—his own private collection. Taking each object, one by one, from the suitcase, he displayed them to the assembled congressmen and implored them in the name of all that was holy to expunge these obscenities. Perhaps his own guilt over his sinful sexual habits and thoughts made him emphasize that impressionable young men must be kept away from images and objects that could "stimulate masturbation." Comstock asked that he be appointed the government's special agent of the Post Office to enforce the law, which would grant him the power to carry a gun and make arrests. Comstock had influential backers among conservative religious members of Congress who believed as he did that abortion was a sin against God. He was also supported by such recent organizations as the Medico-Legal Society, which opposed abortionists and midwives in order to restrict the profession to the male medical establishment.

While waiting anxiously to see if his bill would pass, Comstock attended a presidential reception, but was dismayed by the ladies at the gathering and found them "caricatures of everything but what a modest lady ought to be. They were brazen—dressed extremely so silly—enameled faces and powdered hair—low dresses—hair almost ridiculous and altogether most extremely disgusting to every lover of pure, noble, modest woman. . . . They disgrace our land." Before dawn on Sunday, March 2, Anthony Comstock walked the deserted streets of Washington and prayed aloud for the passage of his bill. At three o'clock Sunday afternoon he was at his desk at the Young Men's Christian Association when a messenger informed him that the bill had been passed by the House, had moved on to the Senate, and had passed there also. The following morning, Ulysses S. Grant signed the act and Comstock was officially appointed by the postmaster general as the special postal agent for the government. As he dashed toward the White House—oblivious to everything but sin—to thank the president in person, he was surrounded by the sound of music and the beating of drums, by the marching of thousands down Pennsylvania Avenue. He had become caught up in Ulysses S. Grant's second inaugural procession. At twenty-nine, Anthony Comstock had become America's most powerful crusader for purity.

When he returned to New York he attended three hearings in which Victoria, Tennie, and Blood were examined. Then Comstock took the stand. Under Mr. Howe's vigorous cross-examination Comstock testified that the Challis article was "disgusting and obscene." However, when Howe read him chapter 22 of Deuteronomy containing the phrase "the token of the damsel's virginity"—which differed only slightly from what had been printed in the *Weekly*—he claimed it was not obscene. Mr. Howe pressed him, "Even if they say the same thing?" "Yes, even so," replied Anthony Comstock.

When Victoria Woodhull asked to testify in her own behalf, Judge Blatchford denied her petition on the grounds that she was a woman. Under this continued harassment, Victoria began to crack: She read in the *Eagle* that she was going to be sent to Sing Sing prison, and this rumor so unnerved her that she refused to eat for three days. A reporter from the *Sun* visited her in her cell and found her pale and listless. She confided to him that the previous evening she had been kneeling on the floor of her cell when she had been visited by Jesus Christ. She described how her cell "was lighted up with spirit-light and the power of Heaven overshadowed us, while a still small voice whispered comfort to our troubled souls. . . . I went before the throne of grace and asked that Jesus . . . come and show me the right and He said . . . 'in the fullness of time all hidden things shall be revealed and you shall be justified where now you stand condemned.' " She told the reporter that she had seen Jesus twice before, but never had she realized so clearly that his martyrdom was to be her own.

Shortly thereafter, Woodhull wrote an open letter to the *Herald* that was reprinted in newspapers throughout the country.

Cell 11, Ludlow Street Jail

Sick in body, sick in mind, sick at heart, I write these lines to ask if, because I am a woman, I am to have no justice, no fair play, no chance through the press to reach public opinion. . . . When has it ever been known in this land of so-called religious freedom and civil liberty, that pulpit, press and people tremble before a cowardly public opinion?

Is it not astonishing that all Christian law and civilization seemed to be scared out of their senses at having two poor women locked up in jail? Suppose, Mr. Editor, that some enemies of yours should throw you into a cell for publishing the Challis article . . . arrest your printers, prosecute your publisher, shut up your business office, close all avenues of press and lecture hall against your honorable defense? Would not every land ring with the outrage?

At this point Benjamin Butler stepped in to help by writing a letter to Woodhull that was published in the *Sun* and the *World,* stating that the statute under which the prisoners had initially been arrested had been "wholly misconstrued" and did not apply to the *Weekly.* "The statute was meant to cover, and does cover, sending that class of lithographs, prints, engravings, licentious books and other matters which are published by bad men for the purpose of the corruption of youth, through the United States mail. . . . If I were your counsel I should advise you to make no further defense but mere matter of law."

Mr. Howe argued Butler's point before Commissioner Davenport, who said that he tended to agree with Butler's premise and that ordinarily he would dismiss the charges, but he felt that the prisoners should remain under indictment until a grand jury made the final determination. Once again, the sisters were returned to their cell. A week later they were released on an aggregate of $60,000 bail, raised by selling the last of their possessions. Mr. Howe pointed out that Boss Tweed, who had been charged with looting the city of nearly $200 million, was released on bail of $51,000.

Anthony Comstock, afraid that the obscenity charge might be dismissed, leaving him with no case, visited Luther Challis and convinced him to sue Woodhull and Claflin for libel. On June 2, this case was called before Judge Noah Davis, a Plymouth Church deacon. Mr. Howe objected that Davis himself had instituted the obscenity proceedings against the defendants when he was district attorney. In the time that it took to shift the matter to another court a remarkable thing happened: Molly de Ford, at whose "house" Challis and Maxwell had debauched the two young women, supplied an affidavit confirming the *Weekly* account. Molly said that she was prepared to testify in court that every word was true. Molly must have known the great price she might have to pay for this declaration: Her "house" could be closed and her livelihood taken away. But Molly de Ford, the keeper of a brothel, told Victoria that this was a moral issue and that she was willing to take the consequences. Challis dropped the charges. Howe moved swiftly and petitioned the court to bring to trial a perjury case he had lodged against Charles Maxwell, alias "Smith," the man who had accompanied Challis on the evening of the French Ball and had testified that neither of them knew the two girls involved. The judge replied that he "had reasons satisfactory for not trying the case." Howe immediately accused the judge of being in collusion with Anthony Comstock and, by implication, Beecher. In the eyes of the public, if the Challis and Maxwell story could prove true, so could the Beecher-Tilton scandal.

Repeated arrests with no proven charges offended the American sense of fair play. Yet another person now came to Woodhull's defense: the flashy George Francis Train, the millionaire organizer of the Credit Mobilier who had campaigned with Anthony in Kansas and had financed *The Revolution.* Because Woodhull had been charged with obscenity for printing a phrase from the book of Deuteronomy, "red trophy of her virginity," Train published a short document called *The Train Ligue,* consisting of Old Testament verses dealing with nudity, murder, incest, and adultery. Then, hoping to make a test case, Train dared Comstock to arrest him for printing "disgusting slanders on Lot, Abraham, Solomon and David." Comstock responded, and Train was imprisoned in the Tombs without bail.

When he pleaded guilty to the obscenity charge, adding the words "based on extracts from the Bible," the plea was refused. The judge was none other than Plymouth Church's own Noah Davis, who had been disqualified in the Woodhull case for bringing the original action. Davis directed that the Train case be postponed. Train remained in the squalor of the Tombs for nearly five months. After that he was brought to trial, and Comstock recorded in his diary, "There was present the most disgusting set of Freelovers. The women, thin-faced, cross, sour-looking, each wearing a look of 'Well, I am boss'. . . . The men, unworthy the name of men, licentious looking, sneakish, mean, contemptible, making a true man blush to be seen near them. This is Free Love."

Judge Noah Davis persuaded Train's counsel to enter a plea of insanity by promising to dispose of the case by instructing the jury to bring in a not guilty verdict. After this was done, Davis, in what the *Sun* termed "a Plymouth Church betrayal," pronounced that since Train was insane, he must be committed to an asylum in Utica. Anthony Comstock broke into a broad grin, prompting the *Telegram* to comment, "Mr. Comstock, informer-general to the Young Men's Christian Association, looked quite triumphant at . . . the prospect of his victim being carried off to a dungeon in a lunatic asylum." Train drove away from the courtroom and boarded the first ship for England. Since he had been judged insane, the federal government impounded his fortune, including land worth approximately $20 million. He returned to America several years later, a pauper and a broken man. Some people said that having been pronounced insane, he became just that. He was known to sit for hours on a park bench feeding the pigeons crumbs of bread, and he would speak only to children.

In the face of this persecution of Woodhull and Claflin and their defenders, public sympathy increased. The Seymour, Indiana, *Times* wrote, "That these women have been shamefully persecuted admits of no doubt. . . . Perhaps no class of people are so thoroughly given over to licentiousness as the sleek and well-fed clergy, especially those of our cities." The *Hartford Times* commented that had the accusations against Beecher appeared in the *New York Times* there would have been no arrests. Even Woodhull's bitter enemies now defended her. Mary Livermore wrote in the *Woman's Journal* that both Woodhull and Susan B. Anthony were victims of a campaign to suppress women. And Martha Coffin Wright noted, "Her persecutors will gain nothing by the course they have pursued."

For the first time, Comstock and his obscenity crusade came under criticism. The *Brooklyn Eagle* stated, "The people of this country are living under a law more narrow and oppressive than any people with a written constitution ever lived under before." Other newspapers agreed. " 'Liberty of the Press,' is ours no longer, when, in the opinion of any single person, the contents of a paper are not exactly moral or high-toned and should therefore be suspended and its publisher imprisoned. The strong hand of the United States Government is felt too often in Commonwealths where the local laws are all sufficient," commented the Easton, Pennsylvania, *Weekly Argus*.

In a sporadic issue of the *Weekly* an editorial said, "From Maine to California we believe the new order of Protestant Jesuits called the YMCA is dubbed with the well merited title of the American Inquisition." However, Victoria commented that comparing Comstock to Torquemada was no more apt than "contrasting a living skunk with a dead lion." The *Weekly* also listed many of the books that Comstock sought to burn, works by such diverse authors as "Byron, Cervantes, Swedenborg, Goethe, Dante, Plutarch, Aeschylus, Shakespeare, Hugo, Spencer, Virgil," and, in the Bible, passages concerning "Moses, Ezekiel, Solomon, Isaiah, St. John. What book will be spared?" Victoria stated that portions of the November 2 issue had appeared in no fewer than thirty-five other publications and Comstock

*The seal of The New York Society for the
Suppression of Vice*

had neither attacked them nor banned their now illegal advertising concerning woman's complaints or medical advice. Why, she asked, did Comstock not deal with advertisements in respectable papers offering to buy and sell illegitimate newborn children? She quoted such advertisements, including "A beautiful boy, three months old, for adoption to a wealthy couple." And "Wanted for adoption, a little girl, two to three years of age, light hair and blue eyes preferred." "Here is a game worthy of your steel," she challenged.

Some members of the YMCA began to feel uneasy about the fanatical zeal of their purity crusader and wished to distance themselves from him. Thus the New York Society for the Suppression of Vice was formed as an offshoot of the YMCA and Comstock installed as its head. The seal of the society depicted on the right side a top-hatted man throwing books into a blazing bonfire, and on the left a marshal with a billy stick in his right hand pushing a man into a dungeon.

The battle against Victoria and her sister was Comstock's first crusade for the Lord, but in that year alone, according to Comstock's records, in his capacity as the government's postal agent he seized "134,000 pounds of obscene books, 194,000 lewd pictures, 60,300 rubber articles, and 5,500 indecent playing cards." He examined and burned each item. With a gun at his side, he arrested abortionists, confiscated radical publications, and destroyed the presses of "impure" publications. In the process, he acquired a long scar from his ear to his ginger mutton-chops when he was stabbed by a desperate book dealer whose stock he had seized and whom he had arrested three times.

Multiple arrests were one means Comstock used to pursue his victims. Victoria and her relatives were repeatedly arrested on a variety of charges brought by members of the Society for the Suppression of Vice and by two Plymouth Church parishioners. One such libel trial lasted ten days. In an effort to expose her to ridicule, Victoria was questioned extensively on her social theories. She was asked such questions as, "What would you advise if a wife deserted her husband to live with another man?" To which she answered, "If her will takes her away from a man, she surely ought to go. I hold that any man or woman, whether married or unmarried, who consorts for anything but love, is a prostitute." Among the witnesses who testified for Mrs. Woodhull was Laura Cuppy Smith, who said that she had stayed by Victoria's side throughout her prison arrests and that Mrs. Woodhull was "a lady, a woman, and a mother." During this testimony Victoria's daughter, twelve-year-old Zulu Maud, sat clasping her mother's hand, and when Mrs. Smith described the closeness between the two, Zulu reached up and kissed her mother's cheek. Later the child told a reporter from the *Sun* that every evening she sat next to her mother's empty chair and cried. The judge, one William Sutherland, openly favored the prosecution and called Woodhull's testimony "morally indecent." When the time came to instruct the jury, Judge Sutherland said that he felt there was no choice but to return a verdict of guilty. The jurymen retired to a room, where they debated the verdict throughout the night. The following morning at eleven o'clock they filed back into the courtroom and announced their verdict, reached after one hundred ballots: not guilty. Judge Sutherland cried out, "This is the most outrageous verdict ever recorded. It is shameful and infamous. . . . I am ashamed of the jury."

Victoria, Tennie, and Blood had won at last, but their financial resources were gone and the battle had taken its toll. When Victoria left the courtroom it was raining heavily. She stopped by the offices of the *Star* and asked them to insert a "card" protesting her unjust treatment in the courts. "They are trying to kill me," she remarked to a reporter. She returned to her boardinghouse and told Colonel Blood she felt ill. She took only a cup of tea for supper and climbed the stairs. Halfway up, Victoria collapsed. Colonel Blood scooped her up and carried her to bed, and Tennie ran for a doctor. When the doctor arrived, he held a looking glass in front of Vickie's mouth, but there was no condensation. He tickled her with a feather, but there was no reaction. Another doctor was summoned. This one pricked her with a pin. Again, no reaction. With her Claflin training to enlist the sympathy of the press, Tennie rushed to the offices of the *Sun* to inform reporters of what had happened. In the morning, newspaper headlines across the country proclaimed, "Victoria Woodhull—Dead."

# CHAPTER THIRTY-ONE

# A MONSTROUS CONSPIRACY

A s TENNIE sat sobbing next to her sister's bed, blood began to ooze from Victoria's mouth and Tennie heard the sound of shallow breathing. For four days Victoria lay in a coma, but on the fifth she spoke about the lawsuits and her concern about the future of the *Weekly*. On the sixth day she was fit enough to receive an unexpected visit from Henry Bowen.

Bowen was ushered into Woodhull's bedroom by an inebriated Utica, who, laughing hysterically, tripped over the doorstep, fell down, and had to be helped to her feet. Victoria was propped up in bed. Bowen told her that it had come to his attention that she had in her possession some letters from Mr. Beecher showing that the preacher's "beliefs on love were freer than his public statements on the subject." He told Victoria that those letters would be valuable to him "for my own vindication."

"I have asked no one to help vindicate me!" replied a contemptuous Victoria. "Eight months ago I began this fight and stood my ground without assistance. . . . You are all millionaires. You and the press have hounded me and blackguarded me as no woman has ever been hounded before. But I have touched bottom at last. I am on the incoming tide." After a time, however, Victoria did admit that she had several letters from Beecher and intimated that the correspondence "was not one of mere platonic affection." She informed Bowen that she was to be tried for obscenity the following week in a new suit and added cannily, "I will reserve what evidence I have until I see the outcome." The inference was clear: She would trade the incriminating letters for her freedom.

On the day of the trial, before the proceedings began, the judge said he had an important announcement to make to the jury. He declared that the statute on obscene literature did not apply to *Woodhull & Claflin's Weekly* because a modification to the statute to include the words "weekly" and "paper" had not been added until 1873, while the prosecution of this case had begun in 1872. Therefore, he instructed the jury to bring in a verdict of not guilty. The jury complied.

The following morning, Beecher wrote an open letter to the editor of the *Brooklyn Eagle*.

> I have just returned to the city to learn that application has been made to Miss Victoria Woodhull for letters of mine supposed to contain information respecting certain infamous stories against me. I have no objection to have the *Eagle* state in any way it deems fit that Mrs. Woodhull or any other person or persons who may have letters of mine in their possession have my cordial consent to publish them. . . . The stories and rumors which have for some time been circulated about me are untrue.

Bowen, having played his part, now wanted a reward, but there was none. He asked for yet another conference with Beecher, who is said to have replied, "There isn't force enough in Brooklyn to draw me into a private interview with Henry C. Bowen." When Bowen began to malign Beecher once again, Samuel Wilkeson lost all patience with him and released to the *Tribune* and the *New York Daily Graphic* the "tripartite agreement" in which all three parties had renounced their charges. He wrote, "It is high time that the torrent of slander against Henry Ward Beecher be arrested. . . . Mr. Bowen has of late repeatedly declared that he had never disavowed his charges against Mr. Beecher, but that he yet insisted on their truth. And now the public can understand the brave silence which the great preacher has kept under this protracted storm."

This was a disastrous miscalculation. People who had grown tired of the old rumors studied them anew. Why would three men sign a document to "repair and reinstate" their relationship no matter what wrong they had done one another? What had caused Beecher to state, "I deeply regret the causes for suspicion and estrangement"? And where were the letters "hereto annexed" that contained the "scandalous charges"?

After reading Beecher's letter in the *Eagle* and the newspaper account of the "tripartite agreement," Anthony wrote to Isabella, "Mrs. Stanton asked me what I think of the Plymouth pastor's denial. I think it flies straight in the face of assertions and confessions of the Brooklyn male trio [Tilton, Bowen, Beecher] to say nothing of [Woodhull's] allegations. I tell you when God shall take up His old plan of punishing *liars* there will be a good many people struck dead in Gotham and its suburbs."

Tilton added to the confusion. As the public began to speculate on Beecher's relationship with Mrs. Tilton, Theodore, hoping to put the blame on Beecher but still protect his wife's reputation, changed the accusation against Beecher from adultery to "attempted adultery," writing that Beecher had made "unhandsome advances" to his wife. He then forced the malleable Lib to write, "In July of 1870, prompted by my duty, I informed my husband that H. W. Beecher, my friend and pastor, had solicited me to become *a wife to him, together with all the relations which that term implies.*" Theodore delivered this "True Story" to a young journalist, Edward H. G. Clark of the *Troy Daily Press,* who had become interested in the case. But if Tilton thought that Clark would swallow his story whole, he was mistaken. Clark began an investigation of his own. He baited Paulina Wright Davis, who was then in Paris, by writing her a letter stating that Tilton had said she alone "stood responsible for the story."

In fact Mrs. Davis, who was suffering from tuberculosis, had removed herself from the fray. Her strength was failing. Her husband had taken her to Europe, away from the quarrels of the woman's movement. Because of her illness her family refused "utterly to let me get involved with this subject." Nevertheless, Paulina, who had not seen the November 2, 1872, issue of the *Weekly,* donned her chinchilla-trimmed blue velvet coat with matching hat, went to her banker's office, and asked him if he was holding any newspapers for her. Instead of answering directly, the stiff-collared banker told her, "The *Weekly* is unfit for a lady to read."

"Allow me to judge that for myself. If you have my property you cannot legally withhold it." With that, the banker reached into a small cubby and handed her the controversial issue of *Woodhull & Claflin's Weekly.*

Mrs. Davis then answered Edward Clark's letter, stating that she was not the sole source of information on the affair between Lib and the Reverend Beecher. She had heard the story well over a year before from Laura Curtis Bullard, to whom it had been confided by Tilton himself. She described her visit to Mrs. Tilton and Lib's confession and added, "It was even then almost common property." This letter was followed by one to Victoria Woodhull in which Mrs. Davis promised to return to America to defend her friend. Instead, she was sent to a sanitarium in Switzerland, lingered for a year and a half, and then died. Of what had happened to the woman's movement Paulina wrote, "I think our defeat is something like the Communists', the fight has been a brave one for freedom but too soon."

In May 1873, Clark printed a four-page, single-issue newspaper, *The Thunderbolt* (referring to Beecher's remark that Mrs. Tilton's confession "fell like a thunderbolt on me"). The eight-column headline read, "Beecher-

Bowen-Comstock Conspiracy. The Seal Broken at Last. The Account Horrible at Best. Not 'Obscenity,' but God's Truth." Clark was so opposed to Woodhull's radical politics and views on free love that he concluded that she ought to be "hanged" but felt "a monument to her memory [should be] erected at the foot of the gallows." With grudging admiration, Clark wrote that "a monstrous conspiracy" had been mounted against Woodhull to protect Beecher from "deserved shame." He documented how the arrest of Woodhull and Claflin had been engineered by Comstock and Bowen in the offices of the *Independent,* Bowen being "Mr. Beecher's chief 'supe' and conspirator in combining with that wretched Jesuit of Protestantism, Mr. Anthony J. Comstock, to violate American liberty." Clark declared,

> The special friends of Henry Ward Beecher—the skulkers of Plymouth Church and the Young Men's Christian Association—preferred to deflower the laws of their country and the freedom of its people by a gigantic performance of bigotry and chicanery. In the shadow of their false pretenses, the Woodhull slanders, however atrocious, have grown comparatively dim and insignificant.

Clark alleged that because Victoria and Tennie C. were blackmailers and free lovers, Anthony Comstock and members of Plymouth Church found them easy targets and asked, "What is blackmail compared to the great city dailies? How many times was the *World* blatant with threats at the Tammany Ring and then sopped into silence. Whitelaw Reid has lately elected himself editor and publisher of the *Tribune,* with half a million dollars behind him. Who owns the dog now that nosed Greeley into the grave?"

Clark asserted that powerful men had banded with Beecher to crush Victoria. He pointed out that Thomas Shearman, known as "Tearful Tommy" for his courtroom histrionics, was now advising Mr. Beecher. Shearman had been involved in many scandals, including the bribery of Tammany judges, and "covered the feculence of his career" by being superintendent of the Plymouth Church Sunday school. Plymouth Church, Clark concluded, was a social, political, and financial institution, and its parishioners could not afford to see their leader fall.

To counteract *The Thunderbolt,* Tilton now took his True Story to the Reverend Richard Salter Storrs, asking for his advice in this matter. When Tilton told Beecher of this he gasped, "Oh, Theodore, of all the men in world, I wish you had kept clear of Dr. Storrs!" By involving the church in this matter, Tilton had made a dangerous move, for Richard Salter Storrs

*The Reverend Richard Salter Storrs
called for a council of churches to
look into the scandal.*

*Storrs's Church of the Pilgrims on the corner of
Henry and Remsen Streets in Brooklyn*

was a man who deplored Beecher's laxity in eliminating the Articles of Faith, hated his appeal to the emotions, and envied his popularity. Storrs told Tilton that he would consider a church investigation of the matter. Beecher was devastated. He wrote Moulton that, "I have determined to make no more resistance. . . . I have a strong feeling upon me and it brings great peace with it, that I am spending my *last Sunday* and preaching my *last sermon.*"

In his suffering, Beecher turned to Frank Moulton's wife, Emma, who had been his parishioner since she was a child. According to her friends, Emma was an honest and retiring woman. Some thought her shy; in fact she was simply quiet. Emma had not approved when her husband had been drawn into this situation, but she felt that Frank had to carry through as mediator, for there was so much at stake—this scandal would bring disgrace on her close friend Lib and her poor innocent children. Beecher visited Emma Moulton and told her of his pain and regret. He spoke of his love and esteem for Mrs. Tilton, but as he grew more desperate he increasingly blamed Lib for his problems. He asked, "Why did she not tell me of the situation? It is to my great remorse and sorrow that she should ever have confessed to her husband." And why, he asked, did Theodore feel so "hard" toward him, since for over a year "he had condoned his wife's fault"? No longer was this Beecher's sin, but as Mrs. Morse had said of her daughter, it was "her sin." Emma was shocked by this injustice. She recalled that

He walked up and down the room in a very excited manner, with tears streaming down his cheeks and said that he thought it was very hard, after a life of usefulness, that he should be brought to this fearful end. . . . He sat down in a chair. . . . I stood behind him and put my hand on his shoulder. "I will always be your friend if you will only go down to the church and confess, because that is the only way out for you."

"You are always to me like a section of the Day of Judgment," he replied.

Then Emma said, "I have never heard you preach since I knew the truth that I haven't felt that I was standing by an open grave. I cannot express to you the anguish and the sorrow it has caused me to know what I have of your life. I believed in you since I was a girl—believed you were the only good man in this world. Now it has destroyed my faith in human nature. Now I don't believe in anybody."

As Beecher feared, Richard Salter Storrs saw his chance to seize power. A small group within Plymouth Church had brought an action to expel Theodore Tilton for his association with Victoria Woodhull although he had voluntarily retired from the church three years earlier. Beecher explained to Tilton that if he would simply appear before this committee, his name would quietly be removed from the rolls. But when Tilton appeared he found himself facing a hostile group that subjected him to a prolonged inquisition and then expelled him for "gross immoral behavior." Using this action as an excuse, Storrs called for a council of churches to review the case, maintaining that Plymouth Church had acted against "the purity of Congregational policy" and should be considered for disfellowship. Beecher was asked to appear before the council to "reaffirm the Articles of Faith and re-establish the administration of Christian and orderly discipline" at Plymouth Church. Beecher refused, maintaining that his church had the right to act independently in expelling Tilton, and the Plymouth Church rules of discipline were quickly amended to exempt him from going before a committee of his fellow ministers. Having at an early age lived through the heresy proceedings against his father, Lyman Beecher, Henry Ward knew how to come down on both sides of an issue. He declared his willingness for a council of churches to convene but said that Plymouth Church would not consent to it. "We can whisk the council down the wind," he told Moulton.

Tilton willingly appeared before the council at the Clinton Avenue Church, expecting the Reverend Storrs to vindicate him, but unexpectedly Storrs turned on Tilton, viciously attacking his character and prodding him to explain himself. Beecher nervously awaited the outcome, writing Moulton,

> My Dear Frank:
>     . . . I am indignant beyond expression. Storrs' course has been an unspeakable outrage. After his pretended sympathy and friendship for Theodore he has turned against him in the most venomous manner—and it is not sincere. His professions of faith and affection for me are hollow and faithless. They are merely *tactical.* His object is plain. He is determined to *force* a conflict and to use one of us to destroy the other if possible. . . . There are one or two reasons, empathetic, for *waiting* until the end of the Council before taking any action:
>     1. That the attack on Plymouth Church and the threats against Congregationalism were so violent that the public mind is likely to be absorbed in the ecclesiastical elements and not in the personal.

2. If Plymouth Church is *disfellowshipped* it will constitute a blow at me and the Church, far severer than at him.

3. That if Council does *not disfellowship,* then undoubtedly Storrs will go off into Presbyterianism, as he almost, without disguise, *threatened.* . . .

4. At any rate, while the fury rages in Council, it is not wise to make any move. . . . After the battle is over one can more exactly see what ought to be done. . . .

It was a wise course. In April, the Congregational Church Council disbanded, stating, "It is for Plymouth Church itself to vindicate its pastor." Within Plymouth Church the Beecher political contingent had now established a supremacy that Richard Salter Storrs's accusations of immorality could not erode. That fall, the liberal Republicans of Brooklyn nominated a candidate for Congress in a petition containing the signatures of ninety leading liberals, thirty-five of whom were members of Storrs's Church of the Pilgrims. Beecher and Benjamin Tracy promptly saw to it that a regular Republican candidate was nominated to run against Storrs's candidate, and their man won the election by 76 percent of the vote.

Immediately following the adjournment of the church council, Dr. Leonard Bacon, a powerful Connecticut clergyman who had been a lifelong friend of the Beecher family, delivered a lecture in New Haven before the students of Yale College. He told these young men, "I believe that the infamous women who have started this scandal have no basis for it. . . . Mr. Beecher would have done better to have let vengeance come on the heads of his slanderers." Bacon went on to say that Beecher's "magnanimity" and "generosity" were commendable and that both he and the council found Theodore Tilton to be "a knave and a dog."

The same week in the *Brooklyn Daily Union,* Tommy Shearman stated that the council should never have been called. "In regard to the scandal on Mr. Beecher, Tilton was out of his mind, off his balance, and did not act reasonably. He has received pecuniary favors from Mr. Beecher. As for Mrs. Tilton she has occasioned the whole trouble while in a half-crazed condition. She has mediumistic fits and while under the strange power that possessed her often spoke of the most incredible things. Mr. Tilton himself has acknowledged that other things she has told him in her mediumistic spiritual trances are false and impossible. Why should the scandal on Mr. Beecher be the only truth in her crazy words?"

Tilton realized that he and his entire family were to be sacrificed. He went to Beecher and begged him to set the record straight, but although

Beecher persuaded Shearman to write a short retraction saying that perhaps he had "confused Mrs. Tilton with Victoria Woodhull," he flatly refused to do any more. After that there was no controlling Tilton. He published an open letter to Leonard Bacon in the *Golden Age* in which he disavowed all the ameliorative measures he had previously taken and declared, "It was not I *but another man* who brought dishonor on the Christian name. And yet this other person, a clergyman, permitted his Church to brand me before the Council . . . as the sinner." Beecher, who had so stoutly maintained that this was an internal Plymouth Church matter that could not be judged by outsiders, was now forced by public pressure to declare a council within his own church. He chose for this council eight members of Plymouth Church who were all close and loyal friends, including Benjamin Tracy, who now controlled Brooklyn politics, and the ruthless Tommy Shearman. The prime organizer of the examining committee was none other than the young man whom Beecher had saved from Fort Lafayette prison, Joseph Howard, the son of his friend and substantial financial backer John Tasker Howard.

> Theodore, the Spirits say unto me, "Write and the truth shall make you free." . . . I told you a year ago that within six months you would fall away from me. "By all that's good, never!" you replied. Nevertheless the fall came. I told you that you were going to lead your friend to his grave. You thought it would be to the Presidential chair. He lies buried—the victim of the ill-starred movement led off by you.
>
> You became a champion of advanced freedom in your support of me and your name was on the lips and treasured in the heart of every radical in the world. You repudiated the course that has won this love, and neither radical nor conservative stands by you.
>
> And now I say, there is a single course of redemption left to you and for your own sake I pray you lead it. Accept the situation. Stand by principle and be not affrighted by public opinion. You have the most glorious opportunity ever vouchsafed to man. . . . Strike for the glorious and redeemed souls of the near future, and become their hero.

Not surprisingly, Victoria received no answer to her letter. She had risen from her sickbed much weakened. Newspapers across the country debated whether her near-death experience had been genuine or a publicity stunt. In her depleted state the Claflin influence became pervasive. No matter what evil her parents had done, Victoria and her sister Tennie clung to them. The emotionality of their childhood experience had created a unity that no betrayal could sever. Mama Roxy was allowed to move back in with the family. Money was a desperate concern. To supplement her meager lecture income Victoria went to old friends and acquaintances and begged or borrowed or threatened. Issues of the *Weekly* appeared sporadically as she could fund them. She began selling pictures of herself with a "Spirit Presence" standing behind her holding a crown above her head as if in an act of divine coronation. When the NWSA held its spring convention, Victoria was not invited to attend. At the convention *The Woodhull Memorial* was praised, but there was no mention of the woman herself. She was "deeply hurt."

The Claflins were still "cats and kits," attacking each other for no reason except their own inner rage at life. First Utica lodged a complaint that Victoria was maltreating her, and then their sister Margaret Ann lodged a complaint against Utica. Victoria responded in a letter to the *Sun*, "Utica Brooker in a drunken or insane rage, attacked Margaret Ann Miles with a heavy chair . . . for which Mrs. Miles had her arrested. It was, however, at my special solicitation that Mrs. Miles did not appear against Mrs. Brooker whose complaint is purely malicious and by her own avowal was made to affect the public against me."

Shortly thereafter, Victoria related how she was riding in a horse-car when she clearly heard Utica's voice calling out, "I'm all right now, Vickie." When she arrived at home Colonel Blood informed her that Utica had died. A reporter found Victoria weeping near the coffin of this jealous sister who had conspired to ruin her. "Dead at thirty-one," she said. "Do you wonder that I should feel desperately in earnest to reform the evils of our social life when I remember what I have suffered in my own family? Opposed and misunderstood by my parents and sisters. Compelled to bear an idiot child by a drunken husband, Oh, my God! And the world thinks me only ambitious of notoriety."

Rumors circulated that Utica had died of venereal disease. Victoria insisted on an autopsy and watched it being performed. She followed this with a newspaper interview stating that the results showed that Utica had been addicted to "narcotics and stimulants" and had died of Bright's disease. She informed readers that Utica's "uterus was without disease . . . as pure as that of a virgin."

With little money left, Victoria, so she said, compensated those who supported her in other ways. A young man named Benjamin Tucker, who later became a well-known editor, reported that he was among Victoria Woodhull's lovers and had accompanied her and Colonel Blood to the Spiritualist camp meeting at Silver Lake, Massachusetts, in the summer of 1873.

At the meeting Victoria was exhausted and in despair. When she stepped forward from the black night into the glow of the campfires, someone from the audience asked her to tell them exactly what it meant to live as a free lover. The inquisitor asked her if she was "ready in this connection to uncover individuals from Benjamin Butler on down." Then he asked if she had "prostituted herself—not for love or lust but for the power to carry on this glorious work." A torrent of words poured forth.

> I never had sexual intercourse with any man whom I am ashamed to stand side by side before the world with the act. I am not ashamed of any act of my life. At the time it was the best I knew. . . .
>
> And if I want sexual intercourse with one hundred men, I shall have it. . . . And this sexual intercourse business may as well be discussed now, and discussed until you are so familiar with your sexual organs that a reference to them will no longer make the blush mount to your face any more than a reference to any other part of your body. . . .
>
> Take this as coming from the wisest and best of Spirits . . . to whom for six years I have yielded a willing and appreciative obedience. I am commanded to declare unto you that in the despised problem of sexuality lies the key that shall serve to open the doors of materiality. . . .
>
> When I came out of prison I came out a beggar. I appealed to the Spiritualists, to the reformers of the country, to send in their money that I might send you my paper. But did you do it? No, you left me to starve in the streets. . . . I knew my paper had to live or I should assuredly be sent to Sing Sing. . . . I went to your bankers, presidents of railroads, gamblers, prostitutes, and got the money that has sent you the paper you have been reading and I do not think you are the worse for handling it. The Spirits . . . have entrusted me with a mission and I have done and shall do everything and anything that is necessary to accomplish it. I used whatever influence I had to get the money and that's my own business and none of yours. And if I devoted my body to my work and my soul to God, that is my business and not yours.

After this revelation she gestured with a sweep of her arm. "This is my lover, but when I cease to love him I will leave him." Observers were unsure whether she had gestured to Colonel Blood or to Benjamin Tucker.

*Chief Ogontz.*
*This medallion of the Sandusky chieftain hung in*
*the hallway of Jay Cooke's mansion.*

ON THE night of September 17, 1873, after a routine visit to Philadelphia, President Grant arrived at Ogontz, the palatial home of Jay Cooke. Ogontz had fifty-two rooms, including a conservatory and a full-scale theater. Its walls were decorated with frescoes. An Italian garden contained fountains and statuary. In the place of honor in the main hall stood a statue of Ogontz, the Indian chief for whom this palace was named. No one remarked that the genocide of the Indians had made possible the fortune that built this edifice.

Dinner was followed by brandy and Cooke's private brand of cigar. The two men sat quietly enjoying the evening's peace. The following morning, while they consumed a breakfast of kippers and eggs, the butler placed in front of Cooke a wire from his partner Harris C. Fahnestock in New York. As soon as President Grant left, Cooke rushed to his Philadelphia office. When he arrived he was told that Fahnestock had closed the New York branch. Just two hours later, the great doors of Philadelphia's Jay Cooke &

Co. on Third Street also swung shut, never to open again. Jay Cooke stood
behind them weeping. The Northern Pacific had failed.

The panic of 1873 had begun. Like a house of cards, one failure followed another. On September 18 railroad stocks plunged to half their previous value. The following day, the stock market closed and remained so for
ten days while the rout continued. By December, five thousand banks, brokerage houses, and businesses had failed.

By the new year it was estimated that one in every seven people in New
York City was unemployed. Thousands were on the verge of starvation, in
need of clothes and medical attention. A group of the unemployed in New
York banded together to appeal to the rich to help restore jobs. They
received police permission to parade down East Fourteenth Street to
Avenue B and into Tompkins Square, where they would hold a rally. The
day before the meeting, however, the police board rescinded its permission.
A throng of impoverished people, unaware of this decision, began pouring
through the gates of Tompkins Square. No sooner was the square filled
with men, women, and children than mounted police, with no warning or
provocation, charged in at a gallop, swinging clubs. In the melee that
ensued, people fell beneath the blows and were trampled to death by others
frantic to escape. Blood ran between the cobblestones of Tompkins Square.
The police board issued a statement that the incident was "unfortunate."
No official action was taken, and no policemen reprimanded.

All that bitter winter Victoria Woodhull, accompanied by Mama Roxy,
traversed the country lecturing night after night, seldom in the same place
twice. It was hard going, for now people had little money to spend on lectures. In towns where the halls were large, Victoria reduced her lecture fee
to 10 cents a head, of which she received approximately 4 cents after costs.
She ate little, slept less. Mama Roxy kept a careful watch, waiting for the
moment that she could reclaim her daughter for her own purposes.

Standing on makeshift platforms in icy halls, Victoria presented an
hour and a half lecture on free love, censorship, prostitution, social freedom, and sex education. She declared clearly and bluntly that children
must be taught about their own bodies and that the false modesty permeat-
ing society must be destroyed. She advocated teaching daughters about
menstruation. Reflecting on the environment in which she had been
spawned, she declared that she would rather see women living outside society, even as prostitutes, than enslaved by the present social conditions.

Every consideration of expediency demands that some one lead the
van in a relentless warfare against marriage. Marriage today . . . gilded

*Roxy Claflin, 1874*

over by priestcraft and law . . . is a license for sexual commerce to be carried on without regard to consent . . . the most consummate outrage on woman that was ever conceived. . . . The woman who sells her body promiscuously is no more a prostitute than she is who sells herself in marriage without love. . . . When I think of the indignities which women suffer in marriage, I cannot conceive how they are restrained from open rebellion.

My most bitter opponents among my own sex are the professional prostitutes who know I am going to break up their business, and the ignorant wives who read little and think less and who are in constant fear of losing their "Paw," over whom they have none except a legal control. . . . For my part I look beyond the ceremony and the law and observe the facts and if I find people living together in hate and disgust . . . I say they are prostituting their sexual functions and in the sight of the God of Nature are prostitutes. . . . Any theory of sexual intercourse for women, so long as they have no control over their maternal functions, is insanity.

The tone of Victoria's speeches now reflected her desperation. Her torments seemed to be bearing down on her with a crushing weight. She seemed close to the edge of some unknown precipice, caught up in visions. The suffering of all women had become her own.

Thousands of poor, weak, unresisting wives are yearly murdered, who stand in spirit-life looking down upon the sickly, half made-up children left behind, imploring humanity for the sake of honor and virtue to look into this matter, to look into it to the very bottom and bring out into the fair daylight all the blackened, sickening deformities that have so long been hidden by the screen of public opinion and a sham morality. . . . These suffering spirits are with me here. They are with me now.

As the spirits surrounded her, Victoria painted a picture of the hell in which she was living. "Repulsions, discontent and mutual torment haunt the household everywhere. Brothels . . . crowd the streets . . . passional starvation, enforced by law and a fractious public opinion . . . a galling domestic tyranny . . . sick and weary wives, and even husbands . . . overwrought, disgusted . . . in their utter incompetency to meet the legitimate demands of healthy natures. Couple with them ten thousand forms of domestic damnation and everybody crying, 'Peace! Peace!' when there is no peace."

# CHAPTER THIRTY-TWO

# HUMAN HYENAS

A WEEK before the church examination was scheduled to begin Benjamin Tracy visited Emma Moulton. He told her that unless she prevented her husband from producing documents damaging to Henry Ward Beecher, he would personally see to it that she would be ruined "socially, financially and in every way." Emma replied that Mr. Tracy was not welcome in her home. At the same time, Sam Wilkeson carried an offer to Theodore Tilton to leave the country with his family. It was too late. Tilton felt he had done no wrong, but was perceived as the villain. He vowed he would clear his name. Even if his judges were loyal to Beecher, he would vindicate himself through the press and public opinion. Thus, the Beecher-Tilton scandal was finally dragged into an open arena.

On July 10, 1874, Tilton appeared before the Plymouth Church Committee and detailed Henry Ward Beecher's adulterous relationship with his wife, supporting it with many of the letters and documents that had been held by Frank Moulton. On the morning after the first session, Mrs. Tilton was visited by Benjamin Tracy, who presented her with a statement prepared by Beecher.

> I cannot delay for an hour to defend the reputation of Mrs. Elizabeth R. Tilton, upon whose name, in connection with mine her husband has attempted to pour shame. One less deserving of such disgrace I never knew . . . she has had my sincere admiration and affection. I cherish for her a pure feeling, such as a gentleman might honorably offer to a Christian woman and which he might receive and reciprocate without moral scruple. I reject with indignation every imputation which reflects upon her honor or my own.

Lib Tilton, by now torn and destroyed, saw in Beecher's statement an expression of love and valor. Evidently it did not occur to her to question why this statement had been seen by no one except herself. Lib felt her hus-

band had betrayed her and their children for the sake of his own selfish
pride. The following morning, once and for all, she packed her bags and
told Theodore, "I will never take another step by your side. The end has
indeed come." Having won Mrs. Tilton's confidence, Beecher was careful
not to release his statement. It was found among Benjamin Tracy's papers
some years later.

Lib was received by Beecher's close friends, the Edward Ovingtons. The
next afternoon Benjamin Tracy visited her and found her so ready to defend
her beloved pastor that he rushed to Plymouth Church where the committee was meeting, "whereupon each of the gentlemen hurried to the hat
stand, grasped his hat and cane, and repaired to the residence of Mr. Ovington." This hand-picked committee asked no questions that might incrimi-
nate Beecher. It was clear from the start that they were looking for an
explanation that would justify a complete exoneration. In a five-hour examination before the delighted committee, Lib Tilton did her best to prove
Beecher innocent. But in the documents her husband had produced, in her
own hand, she had referred to a "dreadful secret" and "the sins" of which
she was guilty. This, followed by her confession, seemed almost impossible
to explain away. She began a stumbling attempt: The sin, she explained, was
that "I felt . . . I had done him [Theodore] wrong and that I had harmed
him in taking any one else in any way, although, on looking it over, I do not
think but that I should do it again, because it has been so much to my
soul. . . . I often said 'Theodore, if you had given to me what you give to
others, I daresay I should find in you what I find in Mr. Beecher.' . . . I do
not feel any great sin about it now."

Lib went on to say that her initial confession in which she admitted to
adultery was dictated to her by Theodore while she was in a weakened mental and physical state and was a lie. The subsequent letter, however, that she
had given to Beecher recanting her confession, was accurate. The third letter she gave her husband, in which she once again confessed to adultery, was
forced from her at midnight. The "dreadful secret," she explained, was to
know that her husband had forced her initial confession. She had told
Frank Moulton to burn all the correspondence, but he had betrayed her by
giving these documents back to her husband. Lib now referred to Frank
Moulton, whom once she had called "a saint" and "a friend indeed," as a
man not to be trusted.

In Beecher's interest, anyone who knew the truth of the story must be
discredited, but it was hard to explain away her once close association with
Susan B. Anthony and Elizabeth Cady Stanton. A fumbling Lib answered a

THE BEECHER MINSTRELS.

1. CHORUS: Mrs. Tilton.
2. BONES: Theodore Tilton.
3. FIRST FIDDLE: Counsellor Morris.
4. BANJO: Mrs. Cady Stanton.
5. MIDDLE MAN.: Frank Moulton, "Our Mutual Friend."
6. ACCORDEON: Miss Susan B. Anthony.
7. TROMBONE: General Ben Butler.
8. TAMBOURINE: Rev. Henry Ward Beecher.
9. ECCENTRIC VOCALIST: Miss Tennie C. Chaflin.

*The trial of the century: A cartoon of the primary players in this drama*

question concerning the allegation that she had told Anthony of her infidelity in the following manner, "I understand that Miss Anthony and another lady have both reported that I made confidantes of them, and I have, full of anguish of soul, many times talked freely to them and on one occasion Susan Anthony stayed all night and I talked with her."

This was followed by a sanitized version of the night spent barricaded with Susan in her bedroom. "I told her that Theodore could be so angry that I feared he would be really crazy. He charged me with infidelity with one and another and with Mr. Beecher particularly." In an effort to explain why she had confided in Anthony, Lib lied and said, "I was aroused to tell it by Mrs. Woodhull's being there." (In fact, Lib did not meet Victoria Woodhull until nine months after confiding in Anthony.) Lib told the committee that she was sure that it was Stanton and Anthony who had given Woodhull "a false view of what had transpired . . . and she printed it." She concluded her testimony by asserting that her husband "alone is responsible for this disruption of my family."

The following day Theodore Tilton came before the committee for a cross-examination that lasted almost three weeks. Under a barrage of questions and accusations he remained firm and asserted that he could prove conclusively that Henry Ward Beecher had engaged in "criminal commerce" with his wife. He was asked by a clever Benjamin Tracy how he could make this accusation and yet maintain that his wife was unblemished. "Have you not frequently asserted the purity of your wife?" asked Tracy, pressing the point.

"I have always had a strange technical use of words. . . . I have taken pains to say that she was a devoted Christian woman. . . . I have said that Elizabeth was a tender, delicate, kindly, Christian woman, which I think she is."

"Have not you stated that she was pure?"

"No."

In fact, Tilton skirted close to revealing the free love arrangement that had been practiced in his household. When asked whether he had alienated his wife because he was so free in his pursuit of other ladies, he answered, "If Elizabeth has been troubled concerning my attentions to any lady, take her testimony upon that subject." And later he repeated, "I say if Elizabeth's change of mind was due to the fact that I had loves and affections for other ladies, take her testimony for that fact. I will not deny her."

As to his so-called True Story that had changed the accusation of adultery to "unhandsome advances," Tilton said that he had written it to save his wife's reputation and "to put before the public a plausible answer to the Woodhull accusations that might explain them away." This line of questioning was followed by an extensive examination of Tilton's relationship with Victoria Woodhull. In his answers he tried to distance himself and his wife from her.

"Did Mrs. Tilton express her indignation at Mrs. Woodhull's being at your house the first time she had seen her?"

"I don't know. Oh no, Mrs. Woodhull had taken tea at our house."

"Mrs. Tilton always expressed her indignation at her being there, did she not?"

"Yes, she had a violent feeling against her. She had a woman's instinct that Mrs. Woodhull was not safe. . . . I wrote a biography about her. . . . Mrs. Tilton said she thought I would rue the day. She was far wiser than I was."

"Did she not discard Mrs. Woodhull's sentiments and denounce them?"

"Mrs. Woodhull had not then expressed her sentiments. . . . When I wrote the sketch of Mrs. Woodhull . . . her ideas were on Spiritualism and woman suffrage."

"Then you never succeeded in convincing your wife that it was necessary to placate Mrs. Woodhull?"

"No, Mrs. Tilton had a strong repugnance to Mrs. Woodhull and to two or three other public women—Mrs. Stanton and Susan Anthony. She would not permit them to come into the house, and some of her letters were very violent against them. She was frequently with them and took part in women's meetings, but then she took a violent antagonism to them after her troubles came on."

In this way, Theodore Tilton equated Victoria Woodhull with Susan B. Anthony and Elizabeth Cady Stanton, as if all three were identical in their views. The committee went even further than Tilton in its efforts to blacken the reputation of these women, implying that all three were free lovers. "Did you ever hear it stated or intimated that you had undue familiarities with those ladies at your house?"

"No, no," replied Tilton.

"I don't mean criminal familiarities, but undue familiarities such as visiting their room or appearing in their room before they were dressed?"

"No, I didn't. I cannot imagine any reason why anybody should."

"Don't you know that your wife's mind has been disturbed in regard to your associations with public women?"

"No sir. I have never associated with public women." Tilton's answer revealed that the term he himself had just used to describe Stanton, Anthony, and Woodhull had a double meaning.

"I don't mean prostitutes. I mean reformers," said his questioner.

"Oh yes, I said before, Elizabeth has been annoyed by my associations with persons out of the realm of religious orthodox ideas. I include Mrs. Stanton and Mrs. Anthony, beyond those persons Lucy Stone was one, she lived in Boston. Elizabeth was a reformer at one time, only now she cannot endure them." Tilton went on to admit that he felt his association with Mrs. Woodhull had been "foolish and wrong" and he "regretted it."

On the last day of Tilton's examination Joseph Howard asserted that Samuel Wilkeson had told him that Tilton had taken $5,000 from Henry Ward Beecher for his silence. Tilton replied, "If Mr. Wilkeson communicates the impression that I ever wanted money from Henry Ward Beecher it is false. I told him I would not take a penny of Mr. Beecher's money if I suffered from hunger or thirst." How then, Howard asked, was it that

Mr. Beecher's money had financed the *Golden Age*? "Mr. Moulton never informed me of that!" a shocked Tilton replied. This was followed by another startling question: Had not Mr. Frank Moulton threatened Henry Ward Beecher with a gun, forcing him to give up Mrs. Tilton's retraction of these heinous accusations? Again, Tilton said he knew nothing of this.

Frank Moulton did not wish to appear before the committee or to become involved in what he saw as a public airing of all he had hoped to keep private. Twice he was subpoenaed by the committee, and twice he refused to appear. With the third subpoena he was told by Tracy that his wife, Emma, would be drummed out of Plymouth Church and that he would be dismissed from his position at Woodruff & Robinson if he did not testify. On the night of August 5, Moulton appeared before the committee and said he had prepared a statement that he had read to both Mr. Tilton and Mr. Beecher. Defining himself "as the umpire and peacemaker for the last four years, with a conscientious regard for all the interests involved," he revealed much, but not all, of what had transpired.

He described his visit to Beecher when he had retrieved Mrs. Tilton's letter exonerating her preacher and said that he had been carrying a gun because he had come from an inspection of his company's warehouses and always did so during this procedure. That he should be accused of threatening Beecher was a bold lie that he was sure even Henry Ward Beecher would not confirm. In regard to the charge that Tilton had blackmailed Beecher into giving him the money for the *Golden Age,* Moulton declared, "Beecher never intimated to me that he thought there was any desire on Tilton's part to blackmail him. I had sole management of the money. Tilton knew nothing of its source."

By his second appearance, it was apparent that every statement Frank Moulton made was corroborated by an appropriate document. Whereas Theodore Tilton had been followed home every night by a horde of reporters and had given interviews on the day's proceedings while reclining on the now infamous red velvet chaise longue in his library, Moulton refused to talk to reporters but sent newspapers exact copies of all the evidence he presented. The impact was considerable. The *Graphic* stated, "Here are all the original documents that Beecher and his lawyers supposed were destroyed. Mr. Moulton's accompanying explanations are simple, self-consistent, and consistent with the facts that have been brought to light. Whatever their legal value may be, their moral effect is overwhelming." Whitelaw Reid wrote in the *Tribune* that although Moulton's documentation was "overwhelming . . . Those who believed in Mr. Beecher's innocence before will believe in it still."

During the examination of Tilton and Moulton, Henry Ward Beecher was secluded at his farm in Peekskill with his lawyer and strategist, Tommy Shearman. On a sweltering morning during the first week in August he came back to Brooklyn for his examination. The committee assembled in the library of Beecher's Columbia Heights home at eight o'clock in the morning. The fact that the committee had come to him signaled that this would be a friendly investigation. Beecher served broiled steak and lemonade for breakfast, after which he settled himself into a comfortable chair and read aloud a statement he had prepared, with the help of Shearman, denying Tilton's charges. He began with an analysis of his former protégé.

> Four years ago Theodore Tilton fell from one of the proudest editorial chairs in America . . . and in a few months thereafter became the associate and representative of Victoria Woodhull and the priest of her strange cause. By his follies he was bankrupt in reputation, in occupation, and in resources. . . . I can now see that he is and has been from the beginning a selfish and reckless schemer, pursuing a plan of mingled greed and hatred, and weaving about me a network of suspicions, misunderstandings, plots and lies. . . . It was hard to do anything for such a man. I might as well have tried to fill a sieve with water.

As his testimony began, Beecher recalled in a rose-colored haze of nostalgia his early days with the Tiltons. He pictured himself then as the paterfamilias of a beloved little family. "I was treated as a father or elder brother. Children were born; children died. They learned to love me and to frolic with me as if I were one of themselves. I have for Mrs. Tilton a true and honest regard. . . . I would as soon as misconceived the confidence of her little girls as the unstudied affection she showed me."

Beecher detailed how over the years his relationship with the Tiltons had deteriorated. The once-upstanding Theodore had turned away from religion, and over the years his infidelities and maltreatment of his wife had become so abominable that finally Beecher, as her pastor, with the counsel of his wife, Eunice, was forced to recommend a separation. He testified that in his opinion Tilton had almost ruined the *Independent,* "that great religious newspaper," with his radical views that "aroused a storm of indignation among representative Congregationalists."

In a clever combination of praise for the early days followed by accusations of duplicity in the latter days, Beecher also endeavored to undermine Frank Moulton: "In the first few months . . . he treated me as if he loved

me." But then, alleged Beecher, Moulton made him give up Lib Tilton's
retraction of her confession. According to the preacher's account, "Moulton
called at my house and came up into my bedroom." He said that Tilton had
destroyed his wife's first letter and demanded that Beecher give him the letter of retraction he had secured. "He was under great excitement. He made
no verbal threats, but he opened his overcoat and with some emphatic
remark showed a pistol, which afterwards he took out and laid on the bureau
near which he stood. I gave the paper to him and after a few moments' talk
he left."

Beecher said that Tilton had indeed tried to blackmail him and provided the following explanation.

> I did not at first look upon suggestions that I should contribute to
> Mr. Tilton's pecuniary wants as savoring of blackmail. This did not
> occur to me until I had paid perhaps $2,000. Afterwards I con-
> tributed at one time $5,000—I mortgaged the house I live in—
> then I felt very much dissatisfied about it. Finally, a square demand
> and a threat were made to me by confidential friends that if $5,000
> more was not paid, Tilton's charges would be laid before the pub-
> lic. This I saw at once was blackmail in its boldest form, and I never
> paid a cent of it.

Tommy Shearman had convinced Beecher that the only way to save
himself, his church, and his political influence was to renounce Mrs. Tilton.
His "angel incarnate" was about to be offered as the final sacrifice. When
asked why he had been so generous to the Tiltons, he replied with a clever
distortion of the facts.

> The family had well nigh been broken up and I had advised it. His
> wife had long been sick and broken in health and body and I, as I
> fully believed it, had been the cause of all this wreck by continuing
> that blind and heedless friendship which had beguiled her heart
> and had roused her husband into a fury of jealousy, although not
> caused by any intentional act of mine. Should I coldly defend
> myself? Should I pour indignation upon this lady? Should I hold
> her up to contempt as having thrust her affection upon me
> unsought?

Beecher's testimony revealed that he had used Tilton and Moulton to
distance himself from Victoria Woodhull but that they eventually came
under her spell.

One wing of the female suffrage party had got hold of the story in a distorted and exaggerated form and wanted it broadcast . . . and these difficulties were immensely increased by the affiliation of Mr. Tilton with the Woodhull clique. . . . It was delayed, ostensibly by Mr. Tilton's influence with Mrs. Woodhull, until November 1872. . . . She became the heroine of Mr. Moulton and Mr. Tilton. She was made welcome by both houses with the toleration, but not the cordial consent, of their wives. I heard the most extravagant eulogies upon her. She was represented as a genius, born and reared among rude influences, but only needed to be surrounded by refined society to show a noble and communing nature.

Of the efforts made to compel him to introduce Woodhull at Steinway Hall, he said that he had refused because "I understood that she was about to avow doctrines which I abhor." Tilton, he said, presided at the meeting "where Mrs. Woodhull gave vent as I understand, for the first time in public, to a full exposition of her free love doctrines."

Using the subject of free love as a springboard, the committee asked about Beecher's involvement with Anna Dickinson, Paulina Wright Davis, Stanton, and Anthony, all of whom knew about his alleged affair with Mrs. Tilton. He impugned them all. Beecher said that Woodhull and the woman's rights advocates who supported her were "the centre of loathsome scandals, organized, classified, and perpetuated with a greedy and unclean appetite for everything that was foul and vile. . . . It was inexpressibly disgusting to me and I would not associate with these women. Yet Mr. Tilton and Mr. Moulton had some strange theory concerning the management of this particular affair which made it necessary for them to maintain friendly relations with this group of human hyenas."

"Human hyenas!" As the newspapers printed Beecher's testimony, Stanton and Anthony were incredulous. The entire movement was drowning in a wave of recrimination. A *Herald* editorial was typical of the criticism:

Elizabeth Cady Stanton and the buzzards and creatures in her group are rapacious at this feast. From Mrs. Stanton's lips are the words and fruit of this new philosophy. We spurn it as an offense to human truth and all that is sweet and ennobling in modern life. As it now stands let us hear no more of this "reform" and we should like to hear no more of it for a generation. Mrs. Stanton has in one day undone all the good she ever achieved. Thirty years of agitation in favor of woman suffrage ends in the triumph of a flock of ravens to pick the carcass of Henry Ward Beecher and croak the doctrine of home, marriage, love, motherhood and religion.

Anthony still chose silence. She tried to forget about what was going on in Brooklyn and spent several evenings reading Nathaniel Hawthorne's *The Scarlet Letter.* When followed down the street by a reporter from the *Argus,* she told him, "During my whole public career I have never answered any personal newspaper allusions to myself, any scandal, charge, gossip or mean thing, not even the charge that I was drunk on the platform in New York last May. And now that I am fifty-five years of age I shall not commence." But an indignant Stanton was ready to tell the public all she knew. In an interview in the *Graphic* she spoke in vivid detail of the night that Anthony spent with Mrs. Tilton. When asked by the reporter, "You have no doubt in your mind but that Mrs. Tilton made a confession to Susan B. Anthony?" she replied, "Not in the slightest. Susan always speaks the truth." When the reporter said, "And that confession was of criminal intimacy with Henry Ward Beecher?" she answered, "Yes, criminal, as the word is generally understood." She said that Laura Curtis Bullard, Anna Dickinson, and others could confirm this report. When asked if, by corroborating Woodhull's story, was she not destroying the reputation of Mrs. Tilton, she answered, "I don't like to be represented by the press as striking a blow at a woman, but when it comes to the women of the suffrage movement and Mr. Beecher, I prefer to let him kick the beam, though he may take some one woman with him."

In several articles, Stanton outlined in precise detail the monetary and political implications of the scandal and repeated what Samuel Wilkeson had told her about how no matter what Beecher had done he must be supported for the sake of the money and power involved in the control of political patronage, the stock in Plymouth Church, and the investment in the *Christian Union* and *The Life of Jesus the Christ.*

When asked if she would appear before the committee, she answered, "No, not before *that* committee. . . . There is no stronger proof that the committee has a difficult case in sustaining Mr. Beecher than its understood determination to impeach the integrity of every witness against him. . . . I have no wish to give my testimony. I belong to a family of lawyers and I have great respect for the law."

"Mrs. Stanton, do you believe in the doctrine of free love as it is adopted by Mrs. Woodhull?" asked the reporter.

"No, I believe in law."

Susan B. Anthony was clearly annoyed by Stanton's public commentary. She wrote a friend, "Well, well, aren't they getting deeper and deeper into the bind there in Brooklyn and was there ever such a needless heedless foot splashed into the mud as that of E.C.S. and her boast that she belongs to a family of *lawyers*. Isn't it perfectly killing? Well, I do hope whoever else wants to plunge in they'll go *alone*."

Anthony resented the fact that Stanton had drawn her into the scandal in the *Graphic* interview, and she wrote and told her so. Stanton felt the entire woman's rights movement was now in mortal danger and answered,

> Offended Susan, come right down and pull my ears. I shall not attempt a defense. Of course I admit that I have made an awful blunder in not keeping silent so far as you were concerned on this terrible Beecher-Tilton scandal. The whole odium of this *scandalum magnatum* has, in some quarters, been rolled on our suffrage movement as unjustly as cunningly, hence I feel obliged just now to make extra efforts to keep our ship off the rocks. . . . This terrible onslaught on the suffrage movement has made me feel like writing for every daily paper . . . against this wholesale slaughter of womanhood. When Beecher falls, as he must, he will pull all he can down with him. But we must not let the cause of woman go down in the smash. It is innocent.

Beecher's cross-examination by his parishioners seemed more like an affirmation of all he had previously stated. In no case was he challenged. As witness after witness paraded before the committee, it became increasingly clear that its main purpose was to "impeach" anyone who did not assert Beecher's innocence. Samuel Wilkeson told the committee that Moulton and Tilton had tried to blackmail Beecher and that there was no way he could believe that Tilton did not know the source of the monies he received. Mrs. Tilton persuaded Bessie Turner to return from the West and in four hours before the committee she testified against Stanton, Anthony, and Theodore Tilton. She said that on two occasions, when Mrs. Tilton was away, Mr. Tilton "attempted my ruin." The first was when "Horace Greeley had been staying at the house. I had been sleeping and woke up . . . he [Mr. Tilton] must have lifted me out of my bed and put me in his. I asked what he was doing that for. He said that he was lonesome. I said that wasn't right and went back to my own room. . . . The second time he tried to get in bed with me. I got very indignant and as he would not leave my room, I went into another and locked the door after me."

*Bessie (Elizabeth) Turner testifies. Susan B. Anthony called her "half an idiot" for accusing Anthony of sexual improprieties.*

Bessie said that Theodore Tilton "seemed to think a great deal of Mrs. Stanton and Miss Anthony. I saw her sitting on his lap on one occasion when I was coming into the parlor and she jumped up pretty quick."

"Which one?" asked the questioner.

"Susan B. Anthony," Bessie replied.

"What was his conduct with Mrs. Stanton?"

"Well, I never saw him caressing her, but he used to be alone with her a great deal in his study. They used to play chess until two or three o'clock in the morning."

Although Anthony had vowed to say nothing, she could not resist responding to Bessie's testimony and told a *Tribune* reporter that Bessie Turner was "half an idiot . . . it is a shame to permit that girl to testify before a committee." And when asked if she sat on Tilton's knee, instead of denying it, she smiled and replied, "All the men have declared that Susan was so sour that she wouldn't get a husband and I thought I would show them I could sit on a young man's knee just like any foolish girl. I did not deny that I sat on Theodore's knee. Why should I not enjoy the opportunity to be womanly and loving, when I have been called an ogre all my life and everybody claims to know that I never had a chance to be married."

Susan's statement about Bessie's testimony constituted a rare breech of self-imposed silence, but her brother Colonel Daniel R. Anthony had no such inhibitions. In the *Leavenworth Times* he wrote an account, repeated in the *Chicago Tribune,* in which he said that he heard the scandal story from his sister more than a year earlier. He provided many details, among them: "Tilton accused his wife of adultery with Beecher and she replied with the accusation that he had procured an abortion for a young lady of Brooklyn whom he had seduced."

When asked about her brother's article, Anthony said, "Provided I did tell it to him, which I do not admit, if my brother and Mrs. Stanton have said what has been credited to them, it was a very ungracious thing of them to do. No one is able to repeat what another says . . . to attempt it is invariably to do injustice." And when pressed for a comment on the case, she responded,

> The time is coming when a woman will be answerable only to herself for her own deeds. In an abominable mixture of deceit, either of these men is ready to sacrifice Mrs. Tilton to save himself. The fact is, if a woman gives herself to a man either in marriage or out of marriage, he will trample her into the dirt to serve his own ends. Women sell themselves too cheap. They sacrifice themselves on the spot, and it does not matter whether the man has any brains or not. It is the creation over again. Old Adam said, "The woman tempted me and I did eat." Beecher says, "The woman tempted me and I did *not* eat." In both cases, she gets the blame.

In a more oblique way she wrote to her brother Daniel,

> Whatever comes to those closely united by marriage or by blood, the one lesson from recent developments in Brooklyn is that none of the parties ever should take in an outside person as confidant. If the twain can not themselves restore their oneness, none other can. If parents and children, brothers and sisters, can not adjust their own differences among themselves, it is in vain they look to friends outside. . . .
>
> Whether it be wealth, position, office or the society of one we love, if we have to steal it, though it may be sweet and seemingly real and lasting, the exposure of the illicit means of gaining it is sure to come, and then the thing itself turns to dross. When will the

children of men learn this fact, that nothing pays but that which is obtained fairly, openly and honestly?

Isabella Beecher Hooker cast the most doubt on her brother Henry's innocence. When a compilation of the testimony was published under the title *The Romance of Plymouth Church,* Isabella noted, "It is too bad but they are in sauce up to necks and have got to stay there and keep still or shall be deeper in." And later she scrawled in an unsent letter, "The case has gone out of our hands utterly and out of human hands it seems to me—the verdict will come from on high." The only course left to Henry Ward Beecher's defenders was to utterly destroy Isabella's credibility. Tommy Shearman went before the committee and testified of Isabella: "I know from a private and most reliable source that for a long time she was considered out of her head . . . insane . . . deluded. She was laboring under a hallucination . . . cultivated by her intimacy and strange relationship with Victoria Woodhull. She is well known to be weak minded and to prey upon her brother." He referred to the letter in which she addressed Victoria Woodhull as "My Darling Queen" and added a connotation to it that even her severest critic had not imagined, stating, "I cannot say it outright. The best way I can put it is that she [Isabella] had an *unnatural* affection for Mrs. Woodhull."

Isabella's own half-brother George Beecher ratified Shearman's testimony in an open letter to the *Eagle*: "She was devotedly attached to Mrs. Woodhull and has never withdrawn from her. The *strange fascination* which this woman possessed over her is evinced, among other things, by a letter she wrote commencing as follows, 'My Darling Queen'. . . . In an interview with our brother Edward, she seemed in a wild excited state of mind and Henry, to soothe and quiet her, refused to deny the stories." In fact, the appellation "Darling Queen" was fairly common parlance among women of the day. Anthony addressed Stanton as "My Darling Empress" and Stephen Pearl Andrews often called his wife, Esther, "Queen of the moral and social world."

In a society where women were frequently isolated from men, relationships among them often became unusually close. Anthony's feelings for other women, particularly Anna Dickinson, were infused with passion. It was not unusual for Anthony to sign a letter to another suffragist, "Your friend and lover." Frequently, she wrote of climbing into bed with one of "her girls" and spending the night. It was in just such a situation that Lib Tilton had confided in her. For women with the moral code of an Anthony or a Hooker, however, a lesbian relationship, with its active sexual implications, was out of the question, and Shearman's barely veiled accusation of such an attachment between Victoria and Isabella, backed by George Beecher, was entirely without foundation. Still, the effect was devastating.

Catharine Beecher joined in the attack, writing in the *Eagle* that her brother was "an honorable man . . . while on the other side are . . . half-crazy women." In a second newspaper article, Catharine maintained that she knew of a woman who, under pressure, confessed that she had been seduced when indeed it was all a fantasy. The most original defense came from Henry's brother, the Reverend William Beecher. "If Henry were in the habit of running after women . . . why should he choose an old, faded, married woman? There are plenty of young girls that he could have had if he had been so inclined. . . . It is easier for a preacher than anyone else, except perhaps a doctor, to take advantage of women."

The Hookers, once the social leaders of Nook Farm, were now considered pariahs. Mary Beecher Perkins and Harriet Beecher Stowe also broke off relations with their sister Isabella and barred her from their homes. Friends followed family. Mark Twain's sister-in-law Molly Clemens wrote of him, "Sam says Livy shall not cross Mrs. Hooker's threshold and if he talks to Mrs. H. [Hooker] he will tell her in plain words the reason." Under accusations of sexual perversity, betrayal, and insanity, Isabella could bear up no longer. She fled to Europe.

Although the press had been barred from the committee room, transcripts were leaked by one side or the other to the waiting reporters. The public was obsessed with the case, seemingly sensing that it had to do with issues larger than a simple seduction. It also provided summer's entertainment. At a performance of a play at Niblo's Theater, when a character asked, "What shall I do with these letters?" a member of the audience cried out, "Give them to Moulton."

On August 22, 1874, the church committee concluded its investigation by issuing a short statement that the Reverend Henry Ward Beecher had been exonerated. Two days later, the *Christian Union* carried excerpts from the committee report, which had concluded that Beecher was the victim of Tilton and Moulton's "vicious and revengeful designs." Mrs. Tilton was found guilty of plaguing the preacher with her "inordinate affection." Beecher himself was reprimanded only for having allowed his "great generosity" to blind him to the perfidy of these people.

Stanton was enraged, and wrote,

> What a holocaust of womanhood we have had in the investigation! . . . What statements and counter-statements they have

wrung from her [Mrs. Tilton's] unwilling lips. Then like a withered flower, *the Great Preacher* casts her aside and tells the world "she thrust her affection upon him unsought," the crowning perfidy in that bill of impeachment that blackens everyone who dared to hear or tell the most astounding scandal of the 19th century!

In common with the rest of the world, members of the National Woman Suffrage Association heard . . . the scandal as other men and women did and forsooth Mr. Beecher dubs them "human hyenas" and "free lovers," though his own sister, Isabella Beecher Hooker . . . one of their number . . . is presented as "insane," "deluded," "weak-minded."

If the secret history of this tragedy is ever brought to light, we shall have such revelations of diplomacy and hypocrisy in high places as to open the eyes of the people to the impossibility of securing justice for anyone when money can be used against him.

To those who take a surface view of the scandal, it is probably prurient, disgusting, nauseating. . . . This, to my mind, is an evidence, not of a depraved popular taste, but of a vital interest in the social problems that puzzle and perplex the best of us.

# CHAPTER THIRTY-THREE

# DANIEL IN THE LION'S DEN

T HE PUBLIC reading of the Plymouth Church committee report was merely pro forma, a demonstration of solidarity for Henry Ward Beecher. Emma Moulton felt her husband would be risking his life if he went to the church. "You will be Daniel in the lion's den," she warned him. "But Daniel defeated the lion," he answered. As he began walking toward his carriage, Emma ran after him, burst into tears, grabbed his arm, and implored him, "Oh Frank, if you must go, take me with you. Please Frank." Moulton turned and gently guided Emma back to the front door of 49 Remsen Street. A reporter from the *Argus,* who had been hiding behind a tree, recorded this scene and overheard Emma say to her husband as she reached the doorstep, "They are not Christians."

Plymouth Church was full. The *Times* estimated that more than three thousand, four hundred people were in attendance and the street was blocked with hundreds more. One hundred policemen tried to handle the crowd, which had poured through the doors and with high excitement flowed in a circular motion around the platform in the center of the church and scrambled into the balconies above. Some of the most impatient and agile shinnied up onto the window ledges. *Harper's Weekly* noted, "The Great White Church was like a hive, with the swarming bees hanging in clusters upon the outside." On the left-hand side directly underneath the preaching platform sat members of the press, forty strong, and closest to the door from which Henry Ward Beecher made his dramatic entrances sat two of the clerks from Woodruff & Robinson with an empty seat between them.

John Tasker Howard, his son Joseph, and Sam Wilkeson strode in together, the crowd parting before them like the Red Sea. Joe Howard was in high spirits and, turning to Wilkeson, remarked, "I see we have over three thousand voters here tonight to secure our great city of Brooklyn."

At eight-thirty, half an hour after the meeting was scheduled to commence, Joe Howard, wanting to delay no longer, assumed the platform and
began the meeting by calling for a prayer, after which the full report exonerating Henry Ward Beecher was formally entered into the proceedings,
and copies were passed from pew to pew.

As the report was circulating, Frank Moulton, who had been escorted by
Deacon Talmadge through Beecher's robing room and out a small door
under the choir loft, slipped unnoticed into the seat between his two clerks.
From the podium, Joe Howard declared, "Mr. Moderator, our report needs
no advocacy. It carries conviction with it by the irresistible sweep of its
logic. . . . The committee has taken into consideration everything they
should have taken and the report has proven to us the glorious character of
the work which has been accomplished . . . by our guiltless pastor . . . who
has passed through a trying ordeal instigated by reprehensible foes." As
Howard paused, a voice called out, "Question. Question."

All eyes turned toward Frank Moulton, and as they recognized him as
the questioner, slowly and steadily, a great sound arose in Beecher's church,
a steady hiss that permeated the entire room and resounded off the rafters.
"Question. Question!" repeated Moulton, his voice almost drowned out by
the hissing. Then someone shouted, "Put him out! Put the blackguard out!"

"Quiet. Quiet! No questions," Howard called out, and as the noise subsided he continued to read his speech in praise of Henry Ward Beecher,
ending with the words, "When the Reverend Beecher's vacation shall be
ended he shall come back to us refreshed in body and mind. Then, in this
place so true to him and to us, I trust he shall again appear to ornament the
pulpit he has so long adorned and as it never has been adorned before and
probably never will again."

With no time for reaction, Professor Rossiter Raymond—a member of
the committee, cousin of Henry Ward Beecher, and trained elocutionist—
began to speak. In a magisterial voice he read the report of the examining
committee, which point by point refuted the evidence against Beecher.
During this process Moulton sat quietly, furiously scribbling on a foolscap
pad braced upon his knee. Raymond asserted that Theodore Tilton, not
Beecher, was the one who had practiced "infidelity" and had exhibited "free
love proclivities." Why had Beecher not responded more promptly to the
accusations against him? "Mr. Beecher referred the men who had spoken to
him of this case to Francis Moulton, who poisoned their minds with infamous lies."

Moulton jumped to his feet. "You sir, are the liar!" he shouted. The
hissing began again, uncontrollable, menacing. The evening's moderator,

*The Plymouth Church report:*
*Frank Moulton objects to the vindication of Henry Ward Beecher.*

Deacon James Freeland, called out, "This meeting must come to order!"
No one listened. The cries of "Put him out!" resumed again and then men
began bobbing up from their seats and pushing their way down the aisles
toward Moulton. Sensing the danger, one of Moulton's clerks rushed to the
back of the church and frantically waved his arms in a signal to the police.

"Order!" yelled Freeland, and turning to Moulton he directed, "This
man will sit and hear." Moulton stood his ground, defying them all: "You
dare not put me out. You dare not!" Then the Reverend Halliday, who had
spoken the opening prayer, said imploringly, "Brethren, brethren, let this
man keep his seat." He was answered by cries throughout the church: "No!
No! No!" Moulton persevered, "Yes, I will whether you want me to or not."

Men were moving toward Moulton, and one voice louder than the rest
cried out, "Kill him! Kill him!" A dozen policemen rushed down the aisles
and surrounded the base of the preaching platform. Shaking their billy sticks,
they turned to stare down the audience. Samuel Wilkeson, a man adept at
handling people, stood, and in a clear, commanding voice instructed,
"Return to your seats, gentlemen. . . . In the name of Plymouth Church, I
request that this man shall be allowed to remain if he does not openly disturb
the meeting." There was a moment of silence, and then the men retreated.

Once again, Rossiter Raymond resumed. "One of these men charges
upon the other the seduction of his wife, and when he repudiates it, Mr.
Moulton who stands before you calls that a needless controversy." A voice

*The attack on Frank Moulton. A mob confronts*
*Moulton to berate him for opposing the report*
*upholding Beecher's innocence.*

from the audience yelled, "Hit him again!" and laughter filled the room. The atmosphere was more relaxed as the audience began to enjoy the performance. Raymond proceeded: "A word or two on the subject of Mr. Moulton and blackmail." "Give the blackmailer a shot," a heckler yelled, cupping his hands around his mouth. The merriment continued.

> We have been informed that a man cannot be blackmailed unless he knows it at the time. I don't think that is reasonable. People can be blackmailed by appealing to their finer feelings, and a man can be induced to give from generosity what threats could not extort from him. The question is purely and simply whether the parties who trafficked in this case against Mr. Beecher took any money. Tilton has confirmed as much. So far as this farce of Tilton not knowing where the money came from, we all know it went from Beecher's pocket to Moulton's pocket to Tilton's own pocket.

Moulton held himself in check, making notes on his pad. Finally, with a surge of mixed metaphors, Professor Raymond reached his conclusion. "The storm is almost over. . . . I know that in these deep waters Mr. Beecher has been sustained by everlasting arms. . . . We will stand beside him united by our church against all other churches, doctrines, and creeds. 'The foundation of God standeth sure, having this seal, and the Lord knoweth who are His.' "

A thunderous applause lasting a full four minutes engulfed the congregation, after which the Reverend Halliday called for a vote, asking all who pronounced Henry Ward Beecher innocent of the charges to stand. Thousands stood. Moulton remained seated. As if to emphasize the point, Joe Howard asked all those opposed to the adoption of the report to rise. Frank Moulton rose to his feet and remained standing, looking calmly around the church while on every side the derisive noise and epithets erupted once again. As they reached a crescendo, Howard said, "The resolutions to accept this report will now be voted upon: All in favor say 'Aye.' " "Aye" swept the church. "All opposed?" he asked. The lone voice of Frank Moulton rang out, "Nay."

"I wish to address the audience," Moulton called out in a clear voice, but was shouted down, and almost immediately the audience began singing the Doxology, which halted all discussion. Then the policemen surrounded the still standing figure of Moulton, and forming a human wedge, pushed their way to the small door from which he had entered. Moulton's progress was accompanied by cries of "Lay him out!" "Give it to him!" and many Plymouth Church parishioners raised fists or canes menacingly. At the last moment several men ran toward the line of police, trying to break through, but Moulton disappeared through the door.

On reaching the street, Moulton ran the gauntlet of yet another crowd. A woman dashed in front of him, stopped abruptly, and spat in his face. Another man struck him on the shoulder with his cane. The police, wielding their billy sticks, broke a path to Moulton's carriage. He leaped in, and the vehicle took off at top speed, a police captain from the second precinct perched precariously on the buckboard, an enraged crowd in hot pursuit. After three blocks the pursuers gave up and returned to the street in front of Plymouth Church, where they lingered in a state of high excitement for more than an hour and a half after the closing of the church doors.

When Moulton's carriage pulled up in front of his house, Emma dashed out the door and flung her arms about him. The following morning, as Emma left for the greengrocers, at the foot of her steps on a patch of lawn she saw a crude miniature black wooden coffin on which the name Francis D. P. Moulton had been scrawled in what appeared to be blood.

About the same time that Emma Moulton discovered this grisly relic on her lawn, Theodore Tilton presented himself at the Brooklyn City Court to file suit for "alienation of affection" against Henry Ward Beecher, asking $100,000 in damages.

ON THE day that the Plymouth Church committee report was read Victoria Woodhull delivered a lecture, "Tried as by Fire," in Des Moines, Iowa. She was still touring the country, trying to support the Claflin family, but the renegade glamour that attached itself to her had vanished in these depressed times. As she grew weaker the jackals attacked: Joseph Treat, a former associate and contributor to the *Weekly*, published a pamphlet purporting to support the philosophy of free love but deploring the methods used by Mrs. Woodhull, which he alleged had corrupted the movement. The *Treat Pamphlet* was a compendium of salacious gossip. Treat wrote that in the presence of Colonel Blood he had heard Victoria say that "it was right for a woman to prostitute herself when she could make $50 by it," and that she did so. Both sisters were "prostitutes" and had used this means "not only to carry on their paper but . . . to make money and enjoy life." Treat wrote that he had split with them on this issue because "prostitution can *never* be made the basis of reform. . . . Prostitutes should be brought out of their condition instead of being upheld as examples for the world to follow." He claimed that when Buck Claflin arrived in New York, he took Tennie C. to the brothels of Greene Street "and bade her get her living there." That was how both sisters had become so familiar with the life led in these places.

Treat wrote that Victoria and Tennie C. had sent their sisters Utica and Polly on assignations and that within Treat's hearing Colonel Blood had instructed Tennie to have assignations with several men and told her, "We must have money and you must get it for me." Tennie, Treat added, was addicted to gambling and had lost thousands of dollars "in a policy shop in the rear of Clute's brokerage office, 206 Broadway." She "was in the habit of telling young girls that she would find men who would love and support them." Psyche Club meetings at Woodhull's house were used to arrange assignations, and it was announced at every meeting that upstairs rooms were furnished and both ladies and gentlemen could stay the night. Treat's pamphlet sold more than forty thousand copies at 10 cents each.

Now when Victoria appeared on platforms, people came more to gape than to listen. But still she spoke, night after night, telling of her deepest feelings.

I am charged with seeking notoriety, but who among you would accept any notoriety and pay a tithe of its cost to me? Driven from my former beautiful home, reduced from affluence to want, my business broken up and destroyed, dragged from one jail to another . . . for telling the truth.

I have been smeared all over with the most opprobrious epithets, and the vilest names, am stigmatized as a *bawd* and a *blackmailer*. Now, until you are ready to accept my notoriety, with its conditions—to suffer what I have suffered and am yet to suffer—do not dare to impugn my motives. As to your approval or dissent, your applause or your curses, they have not a feather's weight with me. I am set apart for a high and sacred duty, and I shall perform it without fear or favor.

But she could not. She seemed to have lost her force. On returning home one night she stood in front of an oval mirror contemplating her image; then she took a shears, raised it, and with one swift, deliberate motion lopped off part of her long brown hair. Portraits from that time show a haunted, anxious face surrounded by ragged wisps of hair. She bore little resemblance to the charismatic, beautiful woman she had been. In a new lecture, "The Scarecrows of Sexual Freedom," she railed against enforced sexual intercourse, unwanted children, venereal disease. On a particularly cold night she stood before a Chicago audience and stared out at the crowd. "Can anyone tell me where I am?" she asked. Mama Roxy came onstage and led her daughter off.

MORE THAN six years after "A Day Memorable" had appeared in Mrs. Tilton's diary, on January 11, 1875, the civil trial of *Tilton v. Beecher* began. Ice in the East River prevented the ferries from operating, and the New York lawyers were unable to come to the Brooklyn courthouse. By the time the trial ended on July 2, the temperature in the courtroom had touched 98 degrees and one lawyer and two jurors had fainted. For 112 days the testimony was front-page news. Reporters were allowed in the courtroom, and every gesture, every glance of the principals was keenly observed. Tilton was said to sweat in cold weather. Beecher appeared "the center of beatific calm." The trial became an American obsession, a supershow, far transcending the question of innocence or guilt. Every day the courtroom was full; mobs flooded the street and jammed the corridors. One day an estimated three thousand people were turned away. Food vendors prowled the halls selling pretzels, sandwiches, and drinks. The nearby restaurants and saloons enjoyed an unexpected boom business. Tickets to the trial were sold on the black market at $10 apiece, and special seats were reserved for prominent members of the press, the famous, and the notorious. In the third week a lottery was instituted and the eight winners were allowed a seat in the courtroom.

Beecher's chief lawyer was none other than William Evarts, the Plymouth Church parishioner who had successfully defended President Andrew Johnson in the impeachment proceedings. He had never forgiven Theodore Tilton for being the first to suggest Johnson's impeachment and was glad to volunteer his services against him. Sentiment was clearly on Henry Ward Beecher's side. When he swept into the courtroom, flowers fell at his feet; his dropped handkerchief was seized upon so eagerly that the crowd tore it to shreds. When the time came for his testimony, he ascended the stand as if it were his pulpit. Every word he said was infused with high drama. In florid, romantic terms, he described his early relationship with the Tilton family. And sometimes, as he did in his sermons, he skated close to the edge of destruction. Looking over at his wife, Eunice, who followed his every word, once again he explained that if there was fault here it was Mrs. Tilton's, for she had developed a passion for him and had created this problem by not warning him that Theodore Tilton suspected him of being the object of her unwanted affections.

"Did you kiss Mrs. Tilton?" the prosecution's lawyer asked.

"Sometimes I did, and sometimes I did not."

"What prevented you upon the occasions when you did not?"

"It may be that the children were there then."

Beecher went on to relate the scene in which he said that as Mrs. Tilton sat on his knee he kissed her. Then he kissed Mr. Tilton, and then "I believe they kissed each other." George Templeton Strong, a diarist of the time, wrote,

> *February 20* . . . Tilton v. Beecher. The evidence begins to pinch Monsignor Beecher very hard. He is probably ruined by his utterly fatuous confidences and confessions. But Plymouth Church is a nest of "psychological phenomena," *vulgo vocato* lunatics, and its

*The Brooklyn City Court, January 11, 1875, during
the opening session of the* Tilton v. Beecher *civil trial*

*Henry Ward Beecher testifies. Public sympathy was on his side.*

chief Brahmin is as moonstruck as his devotees. Verily they are a peculiar people. They all call each other by their first names and perpetually kiss one another. The Rev. Beecher seduces Mrs. Tilton and then kisses her husband, and he seems to acquiesce in the osculation. . . . They all seem, on their own shewing, to have been behaving like bedlamites and to have been afflicted with both moral and mental insanity.

To prove Tilton's bad character, Evarts subpoenaed three former servants of "the notorious Mrs. Woodhull." All three testified that Mr. Tilton had been seen in Mrs. Woodhull's bedroom in the most intimate postures and that her house was without doubt a house of assignation. To rebut this testimony Tilton's lawyers called to the stand Stephen Pearl Andrews.

Andrews, whose philosophy of free love had brought on much of this trouble, clung to his theories with the fervor of a pedant. He said that Woodhull had run a salon not unlike that of Madame Roland during the French Revolution, and he reeled off a list of politicians and business leaders who had visited at her Murray Hill mansion. Next, Victoria Woodhull herself was called to testify. On May 12, 1875, Woodhull entered the Brooklyn city courtroom. She wore black, and her face was concealed by a veil. As soon as she was seated, Eunice Beecher stood, turned on her heel, and left the courtroom. When asked to produce all her correspondence with Theodore Tilton, she reached into a red Moroccan case, brought out a slim packet, and said sweetly, "I have reason to believe that some of my private letters are in the hands of the defense as well as the prosecution." Benjamin Tracy whispered in William Evarts's ear, after which he came forward and made a motion to dismiss Mrs. Woodhull without further testimony. The motion, unopposed, was granted. After Victoria Woodhull left the courtroom, Theodore Tilton once again stated that he deeply regretted his relationship with her. She had scarcely arrived home when a reporter brought her news of this. She commented, "I believe Mr. Tilton would make quite a man if he should live to grow up."

The public keenly anticipated new revelations from Francis De Pau Moulton. He was one of the last witnesses to testify but when he did there was no holding back. He released every document and every letter that had been entrusted to him. In the course of eleven days, Moulton tried to refute with documentation the accusations against Tilton and himself, and to establish Beecher's guilt. Most damning were Beecher's suicide threats, his writing repeatedly of having sinned, as well as the clandestine correspondence with Mrs. Tilton in which he declared his abiding love for her and told her exactly when she was "permitted" to write, which depended on when his wife was away. But most penetrating were Moulton's own insights into the individuals involved in this matter. Said Evarts, "You are criticized, Mr. Moulton, for bringing Mrs. Woodhull into your family. How do you reply to this?"

If I could tolerate Mr. Beecher in my family after what I knew of him, why not Mrs. Woodhull? . . . The scandal she published was wrung out of her by taunt and scorn and general persecution on Beecher's account. Besides, there was at her elbow old Stephen Pearl Andrews pushing her on to prove society falsely constructed. . . . She had reason to see from the class of people who called at her house that from the clergy to the press she was the object of both fear and desire.

"Did Mr. Beecher also fear his sister Mrs. Hooker, Mr. Moulton?"

He did. She was not a crazy woman but a bolder Beecher than he with equal appetite for the world. . . . Mr. Beecher's sister—the amiable, intelligent, enthusiastic, and clearheaded Mrs. Hooker, now happily, for her peace, abroad—who became the recipient of the knowledge of Beecher's guilt, has been placarded as insane because she advised him to make a clear and full confession in the interest of truth and justice, to rescue a woman from jail who Mrs. Hooker believed was incarcerated for having told simply the truth.

"Do you think the Beecher case, Mr. Moulton, will be of any harm to society?"

No, it has only brought down an impostor who could not be saved from the weakness of himself. We respected her [Mrs. Tilton] even after her fall because we had studied Beecher out and knew him to have a fine mind, a powerful animal nature, and between the two he got his power. He never could have preached the sermons he has, addressing the weakness of our flesh, but for the animality which drew him into libertinism and was followed by self-reproach. The fact is he has been sifted out of the little principle that he possessed, by the flattery of mankind. Everybody took care of him, paid his bills, wanted his society, and encouraged his self-

ishness. He has had bursts of emotion and tenderness, but they are
not reliable, and he was too mean to lose his fame.

Day after day the prematurely aged Eunice Beecher sat in the courtroom
listening to the evidence that characterized her as "a virago . . . cold . . . complaining . . . inhospitable." She heard how her husband had fled the "uncon-
genial atmosphere" of her home to find warmth and attention at Mrs.
Tilton's. And the press, observing her wizened countenance—pursed mouth,
wrinkled face, gray hair covered by a white lace mantle—ratified this opprobrium. Still she assumed the stand and testified that her husband was the
most noble of men, a victim of his own "kindness and sympathy." All the
Tiltons had taken advantage of her husband's goodwill: "It has been hard to
convince the dear, guiltless, simple-hearted man that such baseness and
treachery could exist . . . how weakly he has trusted . . . how fearfully he has
been muted or blackmailed." When Eunice finished her testimony, her husband rose from his seat, walked to the witness stand, and escorted his wife out
of the courtroom. She had become, after all, the perfect preacher's wife.

After Eunice Beecher testified, Mrs. Tilton stood and appealed to be
heard by the court. Since neither side wished to hear what she had to say,
her appeal was denied, but she released to the press the enigmatic statement
"I would like to tell the *whole* sad story *truthfully*—to acknowledge the frequent falsehoods wrung from me by compulsion."

By the end of the trial millions of words had been written about this
matter. Tilton's side had been represented by a dozen witnesses, a meager
showing. Beecher's case had been presented by ninety-five witnesses. The
summations took twenty-five days; the jury was sequestered for eight. As
the summer heat increased the jurors were assigned another room on the
cooler side of the courthouse. Reporters climbed the lampposts trying to
see what was going on inside. For lack of real news, they reported on the
most mundane of actions: which juror was asleep, what the jurors were eating. At eleven-thirty on the sweltering morning of July 2, 1875, the jurors
filed into the courtroom. After fifty-two ballots, there was still no agreement. On the first ballot the vote had been 8 to 4 against Tilton; on the last,
9 to 3. The judge declared a mistrial. The circus was over.

The economic depression had brought sterner times, and the gospel of
self-indulgence and sentimentality was losing its power. The *Times* noted,

There is only one good result which can possibly follow from this
exposure and trial. It may lead people in Brooklyn and elsewhere to
distrust the Gospel of Love and to allow no priests or ministers to

*Henry Ward Beecher and Eunice Beecher in the courtroom.*
*The press nicknamed the worn Mrs. Beecher "The Griffon."*

*Lib Tilton appeals to be heard. No one wanted to hear her explanation.*

come between husband and wife, or to interfere with family ties or sully family honor. Lastly it may induce them to return to the older and safer moorings which alone can prevent society from drifting into chaos. If this should be the fruit of the trial, a scandal which poisoned the air for six long months will not have been dragged to the light in vain.

# CHAPTER THIRTY-FOUR

# A METEOR'S DASH

LTHOUGH THE case ended in a mistrial, the Beecher forces clearly had triumphed. At their preacher's suggestion a Plymouth Church committee, nicknamed "the scandal bureau," was appointed specifically to quash further rumors. Most of the blame for the scandal fell on Henry Bowen. The *Eagle* pointed out that he was the Iago who had created the friction between Beecher and Tilton. Several members of Plymouth Church brought suit against Henry Bowen to recover the monies owed them, which had been forfeited through the bankruptcy of Jay Cooke & Co. Testimony given in the Brooklyn City Court showed that Bowen had used the *Independent* to promote Northern Pacific Railroad bonds while fully aware that they were nearly worthless, and that Tilton's opposition to this swindle was a factor in his dismissal. According to the *Eagle*, testimony also established that Bowen "was the link by which Wall Street was connected to the religious world." After several months the case was dismissed.

In December 1875, a Plymouth Church committee brought a formal action to dismiss both Emma Moulton and Henry Bowen from their rolls. Emma was dropped without a hearing, but Henry Bowen insisted on appearing before the committee. In his statement he branded Henry Ward Beecher "an adulterer, a perjurer, and a hypocrite." He vowed that he had done no wrong and would not willingly leave the church that he had founded. Bowen pointed out that this committee, like the first committee to investigate Mr. Beecher, was composed of partisan men, including Beecher's brother, his assistant pastor, his publisher, and his attorney. "This is no impartial court," he declared with some understatement. He concluded by saying, "I have been held up as a slanderer and a liar until my character has been blackened. . . . You have forced me into this trying and unwelcome position. . . . I now leave my case with you well understanding that you will continue to asperse my character and that I shall suffer. . . . So be it." Bowen was expelled by a unanimous vote.

In January 1876, the Plymouth Church Council organized a victory party of sorts in the form of a meeting to give its preacher a vote of support. Once again Plymouth Church was full. When the council commended Beecher for the way he had handled himself during the case, he stood upon the preaching platform, silent tears rolling down his cheeks. Then in a voice cracking with emotion he told his flock, "I have not been pursued as a lion is pursued. I have not been pursued even as wolves and foxes. I have been pursued as if I were a maggot in a rotten corpse."

Carried away, he provided as close an explanation for his behavior as one would ever hear. "When you shall find a heart to rebuke the twining morning glory or any other plant that holds on to that which is next to it . . . you may rebuke me for loving where I should not love. It is not my choice. It is my necessity. . . . And I have loved on the right and on the left, here and there, and it is my joy that today I am not ashamed of it, I am glad

*The final victory meeting at Plymouth Church.*
*Henry Ward Beecher's powers were undiminished.*

*Isabella Beecher Hooker. In her old age her
spirit communication sustained her.*

of it." No one seemed affected by the truth of his confession, only by the
emotion with which he presented it. In response, men and women alike
wept. Then the mercurial Beecher lashed out at the assemblage: "I do not
care for you or anybody else. . . . I do care and I don't—just as I happen to
feel. . . . I am tired of you. . . . I am tired of the world."

Although Henry Ward Beecher had emerged unscathed, other lives had
been destroyed. In her hotel room in Paris, during her self-imposed exile,
Isabella Beecher Hooker woke one morning from a deep sleep and mechanically began repeating to herself, "Thanks be unto God, the Father of our
Lord Jesus Christ, who giveth us the victory." She repeated this litany over
and over until the rhythmic flow of the chant induced "a deep and solemn
peace" that settled into her very soul. The thought occurred to her that
though she had been reviled, somewhere there was love, for "Love begets
love—love is God." Then miraculously, her mother, dead forty years,
appeared before her. Isabella had "drawn the veil" between herself and her
mother, but now and henceforth forever she would be nurtured by mother

love. She wrote, "From that time she has never left me, and such commu-
nion as we have had only the angels know, and He who is above all angels,
Jesus of Nazareth our brother, friend and Savior."

In the past, sometimes her visions had seemed "but a delusion and a
mockery," but now "the light of the eternities, past and future, shines into
my soul and all is peace and a great patience of waiting takes the place of all
unrest." For as Victoria Woodhull had predicted, past, present, and future
were as one.

As Moulton's documents had been revealed to the public, the feelings
of Nook Farm residents toward Isabella had softened. John Hooker wrote a
letter to Susan Howard in which he spoke of his wife's sorrow and how cruelly she had been dealt with. Finally, Susie Howard mustered the courage to
do what Isabella had asked her to do six years previously, to think for herself and come to her own conclusions. Despite the support her husband
and son, John Tasker and Joseph Howard, had given Beecher and the
attacks they had made on Isabella, she wrote a letter stating that, in her
opinion, Isabella was innocent of everything but telling the truth. She
wrote that all of Brooklyn knew of Lib Tilton's attachment to her preacher.
This letter along with John Hooker's was shown to Mark Twain. It convinced him and other residents of Nook Farm that Beecher had indeed
been guilty. He told his wife, Livy, that he would no longer forbid her to see
Isabella.

Harriet Beecher Stowe stubbornly continued to believe in her brother's
innocence, but she justified Isabella's behavior in a letter she wrote to their
sister Mary Perkins. She felt that "the Woodhull" had gained "an ascendancy" over "Belle" by showing her the apology Henry had written. (In
fact, Stanton had showed Isabella this letter.) She wrote that Woodhull,
Stanton, and Anthony had prevailed upon Henry that if he came out with
free love views there would be "an immediate rush to his standard of all the
emancipated." Perhaps confusing Woodhull and Anthony, Stowe blamed
the latter.

> In the letter which Belle sent to Henry when she urged this course
> was a postscript by S. B. Anthony saying in so many words, that the
> *needs* of a nature so large as his were evident and that the *only* sin he
> had committed was living in a false marriage and they hoped he
> would come out and confess that and show from his own experi-
> ence from Sunday to Sunday and from day to day the evil of the
> present system of marriage. I don't think they would have got Belle
> over, for she made strong resistance at first, if they had not pro-

duced a conviction on her mind that the only way to save her brother was to attack the laws of marriage.

When at last the scandal subsided, Isabella returned to Nook Farm, where she found solace and acceptance in the spirit world. She spent many hours in a spirit room she created from one of her upstairs bedrooms, communing with those who had "passed over." Frequently, Isabella sank into a trance, and the spirits spoke through her. On Sundays, she held meetings with Spiritualists, convinced that she was forming "the beginnings of the Church on Nook Farm which I have seen so distinctly in visions over and over again." On sunny days Isabella would climb out onto the tin roof below her spirit room window, open her silk parasol, and sit in the sun, waiting for the popping sounds that she interpreted as spirit messages.

Once the trial was over, Benjamin Tracy lodged libel suits against both Tilton and Moulton. The suits finally were dropped, but Tilton emerged bankrupt and the *Golden Age* was closed for lack of funds. In the winter of 1877, he moved to Paris, never to return. Mrs. Tilton was left with little money and four children to raise. She was rapidly going blind. Lucy Stone wrote of the case, "Of all the persons in the sad scene which has been passing before our eyes, Mrs. Tilton seems to me to be more wronged and injured than any other . . . carrying to the graves of her children the dead hopes of all her life. Driven to the wall in utter despair, endured for five miserable years, Elizabeth Tilton said what her tormentors required her to say." The only friends left to Mrs. Tilton were a small group of Spiritualists who called themselves The Christian Friends. They supported and sustained her emotionally and convinced her that she would never be at peace until she was no longer the instrument of others but became her own woman and lived in the light of truth. At their behest, she wrote a public letter to the *Times*.

A few weeks ago, after long months of mental anguish, I told . . . a few friends whom I bitterly deceived, that the charge brought by my husband, of adultery between myself and the Reverend Henry Ward Beecher, was true and that the lie I had lived so well the last four years had become intolerable to me. That statement I now solemnly re-affirm and leave the truth to God, to whom I also commit myself, my children, and all who must suffer.

With so many accusations and retractions and the interest of the public moving on to other events, this final confession engendered little interest. When Beecher was asked by a reporter to comment on the letter, he said that Mrs. Tilton was "an unbalanced clairvoyant" and asserted that Lib used to "grovel in the dust and roll in the gutter, even kissing the feet of those to whom she felt under obligation."

MAMA ROXY had brought Victoria back to New York, where they lived in a furnished flat in a brownstone on Eighteenth Street. Here they seemed to revert to their former living conditions. Mama or Tennie took the large pitcher from the washstand and walked to Third Avenue to have it filled with beer. Victoria was so weak that she remained in bed until it was nearly time to lecture, and then she roused and dressed herself. There was little call for her services.

One evening Tennie entered her sister's bedroom to find her kneeling on the floor, her palms pressed together in a gesture of supplication. "Oh, Tennie," she said. "I am afraid of dying. I don't know what will become of me." As she grew increasingly upset she confided to her sister that she no longer had the support that had sustained her all her life. Her beloved Demosthenes and Bonaparte and Josephine had deserted her. Her spirit voices were stilled. Like Joan of Arc, she had been abandoned. No longer was she on fire with the word of what the world could become. No longer could she be the savior of women. It was over.

Tennie, thinking that her sister's ailment was physical, took her to see a physician who diagnosed Victoria as suffering from "a female ailment amenable to surgery but aggravated by neglect." It was then that Mama Roxy moved to reclaim her daughter. In Victoria's weakened state her mother convinced her that the reason her beloved spirits had deserted her was that Colonel Blood was poisoning her in some undetectable way. Roxy also said Blood was possessed by the devil, whose presence blocked Victoria's spirit guides. Finally, Victoria agreed to go with her mother to see a group of monks who were said to be skilled in ridding one of evil spirits according to Catholic Church rituals. In the winter of 1875, Victoria Woodhull was "exorcised" by these monks. Roxy now was able to persuade her daughter to file for divorce from James H. Blood. Even though Victoria had no papers to prove she had remarried Blood, she nonetheless filed suit on charges of adultery. Colonel Blood never met the witness Victoria procured to testify that he had taken her to a house of prostitution, but he did not contest the suit. Later his only comment was, "The grandest woman in the world went back on me."

At the time that Victoria Woodhull was deserted by her spirits, Spiritualism itself was coming under attack. Margaretta Fox had converted to Catholicism, and although for some time professed not to believe in Spiritualism she had recently returned to the séance table to earn a living. Her sister Kate performed in London at séances, where she was often so hysterical and inebriated that she could make no contact with the spirit world.

The simple faith that had once brought comfort to women in their intolerable lives, and the promise of joy beyond, had become a highly profitable form of entertainment. Laura Cuppy Smith and her trance speaking had been the main event of the 1874 Spiritualist camp meeting at Silver Lake Grove, Plympton, Massachusetts, but the following year the meeting had become a carnival featuring a carousel, a singing midget, a Mrs. Suydam, who held fire in her hands, and a so-called Spiritualist who painted flowers while blindfolded.

The Foxes' eldest sister, Leah, was the first to produce a "full-form materialization" in which a spirit figure walked among those gathered at the séance table. Now spirits could not only speak but be seen. And soon, in the light of day, Spiritualists were seen as frauds. A document was discovered that instructed bogus mediums on how to produce the desired diaphanous and luminous effects when impersonating a ghost. A common recipe was also circulated: "One jar Balmain's Luminous Paint, half a pint of Demar varnish, one pint odourless benzine, and fifty drops lavender oil." Everywhere tricks began to be revealed—fraudulent ectoplasmic materializations, false trance messages, séances where instruments were used to produce eerie music and spirit messages. As Spiritualism weakened, the church condemned trance speakers, many of whom had replaced preachers as conduits for words from on high, while the male medical establishment attacked faith healers. In 1876, a medical report stated that the majority of women's diseases were caused by Spiritualism. Perhaps inevitably, adherents to Spiritualism now began to attack each other with accusations of occultism and personal aggrandizement.

The 1876 meeting of the loosely organized Association of Spiritualists was attended by only a few hundred people, and at the first session Victoria Woodhull resigned as president. Feeling that she had to defend herself, she told an *Argus* reporter,

It has been supposed in some quarters that because I resigned the presidency . . . I had become weak in the faith. . . . I wish at this time to publicly assert . . . though every professional medium in the country should be exposed, as most of them, apparently at least, are going to be, from their earliest childhood all of my sisters were mediums and were controlled, were subject to trances, to having visions, and to seeing spirits. This was before the commonly acknowledged advent of modern Spiritualism through the Fox girls at Rochester and was widely known in the country round about where we resided in Ohio.

Spiritualism had resisted organization, for it assumed that all human beings contained truth and power in their own souls. By the end of the decade other movements, Theosophy and Christian Science, drew the support of many former Spiritualists. On October 21, 1888, Margaretta Fox delivered what the press termed "a death blow" to Spiritualism by confessing that the rappings of the spirits had been produced by an abnormality of her big toe which sounded like "a muffled hammer." She reproduced the sounds to an astounded and disillusioned audience. Then Kate Fox confessed that at the Corinthian Hall demonstration in Rochester forty years earlier, she had arranged for a Dutch servant girl to rap from the cellar whenever she heard the sisters' voices calling upon the spirits. Margaret and Kate then wrote a book detailing their fraud. However, soon after, Margaret claimed that financial pressure had caused her to renounce the spirits, but she could not live with this lie. At her death in 1893 she was once again a practicing medium.

With the departure of her own sustaining spirits, Victoria became a pale replica of her earlier self. Stephen Pearl Andrews too was no longer Victoria's guide. Isabella Beecher Hooker had written her concerning Andrews, begging her "to shake off a serpent who is simply bringing you evil," and Victoria severed all connection with him. On her next tour she began her speeches by reading verses of Scripture. She devised a new lecture called "Breaking the Seals," which was, unbelievably for the woman she had been, a defense of the institution of marriage. In her desperation to secure an audience, she began to twist the meaning of free love into something mundane, respectable, and self-evident. In Kokomo, Indiana, she announced, "Free Love is the free love of God to the world. I have been traduced, vilified, and imprisoned for maintaining that right." In Boston she said, "God is love, and love is God. Who dares to tell me tonight that the love of God is not free. . . . Free Love is not what I asked for nor what I pleaded for. What I asked for was educated love."

Woodhull now lectured on purity, the sanctity of the body, and on "stirpiculture," a kind of eugenics advocating a scientific way of breeding to create superior human beings. Her lectures became murky, convoluted, pseudo-scientific. *Woodhull & Claflin's Weekly,* which appeared infrequently, also seemed to have lost its vigor and purpose. June 10, 1876, was the last issue, and in it Victoria Woodhull severed all connection with free love, stating that she had always advocated "the sanctity of marriage . . . I believe in the institution as a divine provision. . . . I do not believe in the loose system of divorces now so much in vogue."

As Victoria Woodhull vanished from the woman's rights platform she left behind her the wreckage of the movement. Women, had they stood together, might have found enfranchisement within their grasp. But the moral hypocrisy of domestic society that Woodhull clearly illuminated through her views on free love, marriage, and divorce had completely split an already divided movement. As Elizabeth Cady Stanton had predicted, the "scandalum magnatum" had been "rolled on our suffrage movement," and the chance of enfranchisement had "gone down in the smash." But Stanton, with a clearer view than most, realized as well that the work Victoria Woodhull had done on behalf of women would have a lasting effect no matter how she recanted her views or how quickly she became a mere footnote to women's history. In an interview in 1876, Stanton indignantly told a reporter who dismissed Woodhull's work,

Victoria Woodhull has done a work for woman that none of us could have done. She has faced and dared men to call her the names that make women shudder, while she chucked principle, like medicine, down their throats. She has risked and realized the sort of ignominy that would have paralyzed any of us who have longer been called strong-minded.

Leaping into the brambles that were too high for us to see over them, she broke a path into their close and thorny interstices with a steadfast faith that glorious principle would triumph at last over conspicuous ignominy, although her life might be sacrificed. And when, with a meteor's dash, she sank into a dismal swamp, we could not lift her out of the mire or buoy her through the deadly waters. She will be as famous as she had been infamous, made so by benighted or cowardly men and women. . . . In the annals of emancipation, the name . . . Victoria Woodhull will have its own high place as a deliverer.

The new world Victoria Woodhull had envisioned had not come about. The dream that a powerful nation would protect the rights of all its people was at best premature. Radical Reconstruction had failed. In the 1874 congressional election the Democrats had won in a landslide, and would remain in power for more than a decade. In Southern states, White Leagues were formed, openly dedicated to restoring white supremacy. The violence began again. During the 1876 presidential election campaign, blacks were prevented from voting by parades of white supremacists carrying rifles. Unlike the hooded Klan members, these men paraded in broad daylight. In Coahoma County, Mississippi, six black and three white men were killed, and yet President Grant failed to intervene.

A dubious Frederick Douglass, seeing the lack of interest in a real Reconstruction, asked a gathering of political leaders, "Do you mean to make good to us the promises in your Constitution?" The answer was soon to become obvious. The idealistic Douglass had been a pawn in the greedy profligacy of the postwar era. In March 1874, because of his prestige among his own people, he was invited to become president of the Freedmen's Bank, in which reposed the hopes of poor, hardworking black people who had literally invested their pennies to save for a better life. Douglass was so delighted with his job that he invested $10,000 of his own money in the bank. He was in office only three weeks, however, when by accident he came across a ledger that showed that the week he'd arrived the majority of the trustees of the bank had withdrawn their own money. Douglass investigated and found that the bank was insolvent. The trustees knew it and even the Senate Committee on Finance knew it. When the bank collapsed, Douglass was deluged with letters from people who had trusted and revered him. The best he could arrange was for them to receive 18 cents for every dollar they had invested. The Freedmen's Bank "has been the black man's cow but the white man's milk," noted a despondent Douglass.

Totally discouraged, Douglass began to see what others had already seen, the greed and corruption of the new America. "The moral atmosphere is more than tainted, it is rotten," he wrote. "Avarice, duplicity, falsehood, corruption, servility, fawning and trickery of all kinds, confront us at every turn." Of the shining hope of freedom for his people, Douglass wrote, "You say you have emancipated us. You have and I thank you for it. . . . But when you turned us loose, you gave us no acres. You turned us loose to the sky, to the storm, to the whirlwind, and, worst of all, you turned us loose to the wrath of our infuriated masters."

In 1877 all troops were removed from the South, leaving the blacks to fend for themselves. The federal government continued to make remarkable concessions to the railroad interests and land-hungry citizens. On the Great Plains, farmers and cattlemen were quickly disposing of the Indians.

*Frederick Douglass never gave up the fight for
equality. "Agitate, agitate, agitate," he instructed.*

Although Indian warfare would not end until the final massacre of the
Sioux at Wounded Knee in 1890, their world had vanished.

AT THE age of eighty-three, in January 1877, Commodore Cornelius Vanderbilt lay dying. The previous year, the Commodore had supervised the
laying of rails and the building of bridges that cut the running time of the
New York Central trains between New York and Chicago from fifty hours
to twenty-four. His obsession with speed had become the American obsession. Reporters were stationed across the street from 10 Washington Place
awaiting the death of this titan whose fortune was estimated at $110 mil-
lion, $5 million more than the United States had in its treasury. In his fail-
ing state he begged his wife, Frank, to call in Spiritualist healers to relieve
his pain, and as they came he said, "Why have I been deprived of this

so long? It is doing me so much good." He experienced visions of life after death and said he had no fear of "passing over" to where his mother awaited him.

At ten o'clock on the morning of January 4, thirty relatives gathered in the Commodore's bedroom. He requested the singing of a hymn, after which Frank read the Lord's Prayer. "That was a good prayer," the Commodore whispered. His eyes were like glass. One physician whispered to another that he was now sightless. The Commodore heard him, raised his hand, and with his own fingers pressed his eyelids shut. Ten minutes later he died.

Vanderbilt was survived by ten children; to his eight daughters he left modest bequests, the largest being a trust fund of $500,000. He left Cornelius Jeremiah, his epileptic son, only the income on a trust fund of $200,000. His entire residuary estate was left to his son William Henry. Cornelius Jeremiah and one of his sisters brought suit to invalidate the Commodore's will on the grounds that his long-held belief in the spirits and his rampant sexuality were signs of mental incompetency. Shortly thereafter, there was a knock at the door of the modest boardinghouse where Victoria and Tennie now lived. Their caller was William Henry Vanderbilt.

Laura Cuppy Smith, who was visiting at the time, later said that Mrs. Woodhull informed William Henry Vanderbilt that he had nothing to fear. Based on the correspondence Victoria possessed, there could be no doubt that his father had been brilliant and not unsound of mind, and she and Tennie were prepared to say so in open court. She would testify that the conversations with his dead mother had been beneficial to him, as had the advice she had given him while in her trances. Tennie interjected that the attentions paid to her were remarkable considering the Commodore's age, and was not virility considered a sign of health? Victoria also politely informed William Henry that she knew the details of how he had made the necessary arrangements to confine his mother, Sophia, to Dr. McDonald's insane asylum so that his father could pursue other women. She added that the Commodore had always appreciated his help in convincing physicians of Sophia's derangement.

A few weeks after William Henry's visit, Victoria was directed by the court to produce any correspondence she had with Commodore Vanderbilt; several of his servants had testified that from 1868 to 1872 they had carried numerous notes to her. However, Victoria replied by affidavit that she had none in her possession. During 1877, "The Great Vanderbilt Will Trial" made headlines across the nation, as all manner of Spiritualists—healers, clairvoyants, trance speakers, mediums—were subpoenaed. The testimony of the notorious sisters was eagerly awaited. But when they were summoned, Victoria and Tennessee were on a ship halfway to Southampton. Awaiting them in England was a cozy house at 8 Gilston Road, West Brompton, in the name of Mrs. Victoria Woodhull. Also awaiting them was a small fortune in Lloyd's Bank in London, enough for two gentlewomen to start a new life. Six months later, when she was comfortably settled, Victoria wrote William Henry Vanderbilt a short note requesting the return of "my box of letters concerning your father."

# CHAPTER THIRTY-FIVE

# THE LAST ENEMY

A S THE battle for Radical Reconstruction had been lost, so had the battle for woman's rights. Many of the women who had fought bravely found themselves disillusioned and disenfranchised. With the passing of time, the truth of what had gone wrong was gradually revealed, though few cared to see. In 1877, as Victoria and Tennessee sailed for England, Anna Dickinson's career was collapsing; her luster had tarnished. The previous year, she had written Whitelaw Reid saying that she was gravely ill, but was acting the part of Anne Boleyn, and a favorable mention in the *Tribune* would be of great service. He read the letter, wrote on the envelope "unanswered" and filed it away. That same year Whitelaw Reid chose a bride, the daughter of Darius Ogden Mills, a vastly wealthy banker who had made his money in California after the gold rush. Anna wrote, "I suspect Whitelaw is *actooally* engaged *this* time. I infer so from what I hear—also that the lady is rich and *humly.*"

Benjamin Butler remained fascinated by Anna, although with her waning fame, he saw her as a possible mistress but no longer as a wife. Soon after his wife died in 1876, Butler tried to persuade Anna to go with him to Atlantic City. She put him off and then canceled. He wrote, "I give it up. . . . I will have no more." But they stayed on friendly terms, and he continued to send Anna money until 1887, when he wrote her, enclosing a clipping from the *Graphic* stating that he had proposed marriage to her. An embarrassed Butler wrote that the article "pained" his daughter with the thought that he was trying "to fill her mother's place." He continued, "My lame and trembling hand bids me stop but I go on. . . . Will you therefore in the words that your own good sense will teach . . . write me a frank denial that I have tried to get another wife so far as you know. I must wish this could come from your pen."

Anna, undoubtedly realizing that this excuse was fabricated and that he thought her too low to marry, replied that Butler had made an "astounding and dastardly request." She reminded him that he had indeed proposed marriage to her and she would not disgrace herself by lying about the matter. After this, their correspondence became acrimonious. Butler wrote that he would send Anna no more money unless she wrote the letter denying his proposal. She answered,

> I want to see or hear from you *at once.* If I do not, *you* will see every letter you have written to me in print within the next month. This is neither blackmail nor the letter of a mad woman. You know what I was, I am. *You* know what *you* have written about many matters. . . . You may remember a letter written while your wife was dying. It will make good food for the public's palate. . . . I have endured all I am going to suffer. Enough *is* enough. Do you understand? I need some money. I need it immediately.

There is no record that Butler replied to this letter, and she never saw him again. At this time Anna suffered severe headaches. Her sister, Susan, said that she needed chloroform in order to sleep. On a frosty February day in 1891, Anna carried her press clippings into her bedroom and spread them across the floor until every inch of the rug was covered. Day after day she sat cross-legged, reading them obsessively. She allowed no one to enter, and Susan was obliged to leave Anna's meals on a tray outside the door. One evening Anna failed to return the tray. The next night was the same. On the third night, Susan entered the room to retrieve the trays, and Anna grasped her by the throat. For three days thereafter Anna ate nothing at all. Her sister then committed her to the state hospital for the insane in Danville, Pennsylvania.

Two months later Anna managed to write William Howe, Woodhull's former lawyer, of the intolerable conditions to which she was being subjected. He took her case and later arranged a press conference in which she professed her sanity and attacked the male establishment for suppressing her views and driving her to poverty. In a subsequent sanity hearing Anna recalled how Benjamin Butler had courted her and how Whitelaw Reid had persuaded her to speak for Greeley in 1872 but after the election had abandoned her. She said that Reid subsequently boasted that she had been his mistress and told many people that his shoes could be found outside her hotel room door at night. The truth, she said, was that he had proposed marriage to her, but she had rejected him because he was an epileptic who had inherited the disease from "the tainted blood of his father and the epileptic blood of his mother." He was forced to take powders "to make a man" of himself. The jury rendered a split verdict of 8 to 4 in favor of Anna's sanity.

In November 1895, Susan B. Anthony received a letter from someone long estranged.

> As I opened the envelope I said, "Why this looks like Anna Dickinson's writing & turning to the last page sure enough there it was, Anna E. Dickinson, the same dear old name.
>
> I'm awfully glad to know you still live and that I have a chance to tell you that my *motherly love*—my elderly sister's love has never abated for my *first Anna*—I have had several lovely *Anna* girls— "*nieces*" they call themselves now a day—since my *first Anna* but none of them ever has or ever can fill the niche in my heart that you did, my dear.

Anna lived to see the Lyceum lecture circuit replaced by movies and radio. At times this frail, white-haired old woman would visit the candy store in Goshen in the foothills of the Catskill Mountains and there would tell schoolchildren how she had known Lincoln and how she and a man named Theodore Tilton had been instrumental in securing for black men the right to vote. Anna died six days before her ninetieth birthday, on October 22, 1932, two weeks before Franklin D. Roosevelt was elected president.

IN 1890, after an eighteen-year separation, the warring women's groups were reunited as the National American Woman Suffrage Association, but their agenda had become conservative—"toothless," a newspaper called it. No longer did they deal with issues such as divorce and the exploitation of working-class women. Their ranks were filled, almost exclusively, with white, middle-class members. At their first convention Lucy Stone commented that her morning speech was "cheapened" by the knowledge that the people listening to her "did not care so much for us as if we had votes." By the fall of 1893, Stone was confined to her bed. On the evening of Wednesday, October 18, she signaled her daughter Alice Blackwell and whispered in her ear, "Make the world better." Then she died.

Elizabeth Cady Stanton never ceased fighting for the rights of women. Over the years she came to realize that the vote was only one element in securing woman's rights: "I feel that suffrage is but the vestibule of woman's emancipation!" A major effort of her later years was *The Woman's Bible*, wherein she reprinted passages from the Bible with her own commentary, emphasizing woman's strength and illustrating how this was a historical, not a sacred, document. *The Woman's Bible* created a controversy within the woman's movement, but it was a ripple compared to the tidal wave that Victoria Woodhull had caused and all that had followed.

Elizabeth Cady Stanton stayed on cordial terms with her brother-in-law Sam Wilkeson. In 1880, he brought suit against Henry Ward Beecher to recover the $10,000 that he'd advanced from his personal funds toward the publication of *The Life of Jesus the Christ*. The case was dismissed, but Wilkeson told Stanton that on the witness stand he'd said once again that "The Beecher-Tilton trial knocked 'The Life of Christ' higher than a kite" and it was "worth ten thousand dollars to see the expression on the faces of judge and jury."

Stanton was to see Victoria Woodhull one more time. In December 1882, she visited London but seldom left her hotel, for one of the most terrible fogs in British history had engulfed the city. Even during the day, she observed, "the gas was lighted in all the houses and streets, carriage lamps were burning, and other conveyances had flaming flambeaux." Early one evening "a heavily veiled lady" came to call, whereupon she "threw off her concealment and there stood Victoria Woodhull." Stanton wrote, "She has passed through great suffering. May the good angels watch and guard her. I will not condemn."

In February 1902, Stanton, then eighty-six, realized that the vote for women probably would not be achieved in her lifetime. She wrote in her diary, "Logically, our enfranchisement ought to have occurred in . . . Reconstruction days. And that was what I argued in the sixties. Our movement is belated and like all things too long postponed now gets on everybody's nerves." She died eight months later. The ever-organized Mrs. Stanton had instructed her daughter Margaret on the details of her funeral. "I should like to be in my ordinary dress, no crepe or black, no fripperies or fandangos of any sort, and some common sense women to conduct the services."

At the head of her coffin was placed the mahogany McClintock Spirit Table, recalling the time when the woman's movement had begun. The table, now the property of the Smithsonian Institution in Washington, is identified only as the table on which the original Woman's Declaration of Rights and Sentiments was written in 1848. There is no reference to the help of the spirits.

*Susan B. Anthony and Elizabeth Cady Stanton, c. 1898.*
*The fight for equality would last throughout their lives*
*and beyond.*

ONE BY one the old friends and enemies slipped away. On February 20, 1895, seventy-eight-year-old Frederick Douglass had accompanied the seventy-six-year-old Susan B. Anthony to a Washington woman suffrage meeting. That evening Douglass was relating the day's events to his wife when his heart failed. At the time of his death much that he had gained for his people had been lost. In his native Talbot County the only memorial to Douglass was a segregated schoolhouse.

Like Stanton, Susan B. Anthony would not live to see women vote, but when she was asked if they eventually would, she assured her listeners, "Failure is impossible." On March 13, 1906, Anthony followed her friend to the grave at the age of eighty-seven. In accordance with the Quaker custom, her house bore no symbols of mourning. In 1920, seventy-two years after the fight began, women at last were granted the vote. The amendment, the nineteenth to the Constitution, was named for Susan B. Anthony.

A few months after Anthony's death, Isabella Beecher Hooker, then eighty-six, died of a massive cerebral hemorrhage. She too had continued her work for woman's rights, serving as president of the Connecticut Woman Suffrage Association until 1905. Her reliance on spirit guidance, however, made many in the movement question her credibility. In later years she was to write, "I have been often ignored and never treated with the old time courtesy and appreciation of the value of my devoted service."

As a result of the Beecher-Tilton scandal, Isabella had become alienated from her daughter, Mary, who felt that her mother had endangered her father's health and well-being by supporting Victoria Woodhull. But after Mary died in 1884, Isabella erected a shrine to her, and they became reconciled. Isabella felt her daughter's love and approval and spoke with her spirit almost daily. Isabella cut herself off completely from the brothers who had conspired to destroy her. After a time, Harriet grudgingly reinstated her relationship with Isabella, but Catharine Beecher and Mary Perkins never forgave her for supporting Victoria Woodhull over their brother. However, once they had "passed over," Isabella said, these two sisters returned to her in friendship and forgave her. When John Hooker chastised his wife, Catharine's spirit took over her hand and in Catharine's own handwriting instructed John to be a more sympathetic husband. As the years passed, Isabella and John estimated that they had communicated with some 450 spirits, including Byron, Dickens, Beethoven, Haydn, and Harriet Beecher Stowe's son Fred, who had disappeared and when contacted, Isabella declared, was suffering from delirium tremens.

In the last decade of Henry Ward Beecher's life he enjoyed peace and prosperity as the acclaimed shepherd of his flock. In 1887, as Beecher lay dying, Isabella ventured to Brooklyn to see him, only to be turned away from his Columbia Heights home by Eunice. As he lay in his coffin in Plymouth Church, a veiled Isabella joined the end of a long line and filed past, thinking that she might see a sign of apology on the face of the brother she so loved. There was none. However, when she returned to her spirit room at Nook Farm, Henry's spirit appeared, and with tears streaming down his

face he knelt before her, as she had been forced to kneel before him, and
begged forgiveness.

IN 1883 Theodore Tilton rented a room on the Ile St.-Louis in Paris and
remained there for the next twenty-four years. He wrote poetry, a novel,
infrequent articles for French journals, nothing at all for American con-
sumption. Often he spent afternoons sipping Pernod and playing chess at
the Café de la Régence. When he died on May 25, 1907, his daughter Florence (Florry) issued a statement that no one in the family would attend the
funeral and that they had no plans to bring his body back to America.
Theodore Tilton's accomplishments vanished: Several histories confuse him
with the presidential candidate Samuel J. Tilden; others relate that Abraham Lincoln came to Brooklyn to ask the advice of Henry Ward Beecher,
not Tilton, and that Beecher's exile to England during the Civil War was
not attributable to his adulterous relationship with Mrs. Bowen, but to a
secret mission, assigned him by the president, to gain support for the
North.

Lib [Elizabeth] Richards Tilton preceded her husband to the grave by
ten years. From the time Lib issued her last letter admitting to adultery with
the Reverend Henry Ward Beecher, she wrote no more letters. She spent the
last decade of her life blind and a recluse, sustained only by the Spiritualist
group who believed in the final salvation of the soul through truth, atonement, and the sacrifice of Christ. Lib's Spiritualist belief in a glorious world
beyond, according to these friends, brought her peace in her final days.

ANTHONY COMSTOCK, whose battle to silence Victoria and Tennessee
launched his vindictive career, continued his purity crusade for almost
another half a century. In February 1878, a stocky, shabbily dressed man
presented himself at the basement office of Madame Restell's mansion at
1 East Fifty-second Street and asked for an abortion powder and later for a
contraceptive device for a woman who could support no more children.
Madame Restell asked the gentleman to return the following week. He did,
accompanied by two friends. When she gave him the contraceptive device
he revealed himself as Anthony Comstock, special agent of the Post Office
and the Society for the Suppression of Vice, and his friends as *World* and
*Tribune* reporters. He arrested her, and she was imprisoned in a cell in the
Tombs.

In her youth Ann Lohman, alias Madame Restell, had served a year on

*A rendering of Fifth Avenue, four years after the death
of the abortionist Madame Restell*

Blackwell's Island, and the bitter memory remained. She could not face another prison sentence. The night she was released on bail she was found in her marble bathroom with the frescoed ceiling, lying in the crimson water of her bathtub. She had so thoroughly slit her throat with an eight-inch ebony-handled carving knife that she severed the carotid artery and both jugular veins. When Comstock was told of her suicide he wrote in his diary, "A bloody ending to a bloody life."

As the Victorian era faded, Comstock became an object of ridicule. He was lampooned for his action against the Art Students League's use of nude models and for seeking to ban the Paul Chabas painting of a nude young bather, *September Morning,* which had received the medal of honor in the Paris Salon. In 1905, he sued George Bernard Shaw to prevent an American production of *Mrs. Warren's Profession*, and called him "this Irish smut dealer." Shaw in return coined the word "Comstockery" to connote buffoonery in censorship. A cartoon of the day represented Comstock as saying to a judge, "Your Honor, this woman gave birth to a naked child." Comstock's last campaign was against Margaret Sanger, the renowned birth control advocate. He sent her husband, William, to jail for thirty days for distributing her pamphlet "Family Limitation."

At seventy-four Comstock proudly recorded in his diary that he could fill a train sixty-one carriages long, sixty seats per carriage, with the sex-obsessed, immoral people he had brought to justice and that he had destroyed more than 160 tons of obscene material, including such "pornographic" books as *Fanny Hill* and the *Decameron*. Two years later, on September 21, 1915, Anthony Comstock died. The Comstock laws to keep America "pure" are still on the books and were lately revitalized by Congress in an attempt to police the Internet, but the Supreme Court, in a unanimous decision, found (as had Benjamin Butler one hundred twenty-four years earlier) that they were unconstitutional.


WHEN THE eminent British banker John Biddulph Martin first saw Victoria Woodhull, she was standing on the stage of St. James Hall in London delivering a quasi-religious, quasi-scientific lecture, "The Garden of Eden" (which she held to be the body itself). The moment he laid eyes on her, Martin determined to marry this extraordinarily vital woman, as if her force would invigorate his own pale life. It took six years to convince members of his family that Victoria was respectable. Antecedents—it had come down to that. Victoria invented them with no regard for truth. In a printed pamphlet she traced her family back to King Robert III of Scotland and King James of England. Her daughter, Zulu, was now Zula, and Roxy was now Anna. Her father was "an eminent barrister." Since the United States was far away, she found it easy to claim both Alexander Hamilton and George Washington as ancestors.

In an effort to escape her past, for several years she changed the spelling of her name, calling herself "Woodhall." And in an effort to impress British society with her leadership of the woman's movement, in 1879 she decided, although living in London, to run once again for president of the United States. Her campaign this time consisted mostly of publishing a supplement to the September issue of *The American Traveler* in London that showed her handsome face over the caption "Victoria C. Woodhall. Candidate for the Presidency of the United States." In the spring of 1892 she made a third mock run for the presidency, but plagued with scandalous revelations about her past, she never attempted another campaign.

By the time Victoria Woodhull married John Biddulph Martin in 1883, she had distanced herself from the woman she had been and abandoned everything that had once made her unique. Henry James (though he later denied it) was said to have written *The Siege of London* about Woodhull's efforts to launder her past in order to marry an affluent member of British society. His self-aggrandizing heroine, Nancy Headway, cleverly insinuates herself into a rich upper-class British family by convincing them that she is respectable. Nancy Headway says of herself, "I'm burying my past. You can't be delicate when you're trying to save your life. . . . I have done things I don't understand myself . . . but I've completely changed and I want to change everything."

In the pursuit of social acceptance Victoria started a conservative publication, *The Humanitarian,* and wrote, "During no part of my life did I favor Free Love even tacitly. . . . I regarded it with loathing when once I got a slight idea of its character and the deep infamy to which it led." She avowed that the *Weekly* had printed its most radical articles while she was "a thousand miles away." Woodhull denounced her former mentor, Stephen Pearl Andrews, declaring that this "high priest of debauchery—actually had the audacity and unblushing effrontery to affix Mrs. Woodhull's signature to his filthy effusions." She asserted that in 1856 Andrews had formed a club, subsequently closed by the police, where he taught free love principles to Elizabeth Phelps and Elizabeth Cady Stanton. Another article began, "Stephen Pearl Andrews! I impeach thee before the judgment bar . . . arch-blasphemer!"

Colonel James Blood too was sacrificed; she alleged in *The Humanitarian* that he had written articles without her knowledge and added that she was "near being the victim of slow poison" administered by him. After their divorce, for a time the impoverished Colonel James Blood had ventured out only at night because his clothes were so shabby he was ashamed to be seen in daylight. Eventually, he secured a clerkship on Governor's Island. After that he ran a bakery shop, a refreshment booth at Coney Island, a carnival show with exhibitions of mesmerism and clairvoyance. It was there that an African seer told him of a gold mine in West Africa. Blood sailed to Accra to find it. One hundred miles into the jungle he died of an unknown fever. The death date given was December 29, 1885, although by the time his body was recovered no one could tell exactly when he had died.

In the Martins' desperate attempt to establish Victoria's credibility, in 1893 they sued the trustees of the British Museum, in the first libel action brought against this institution, for housing two books on the Beecher-Tilton scandal. In a protracted trial, Victoria took the stand and with great hauteur eluded the lawyer's questions by garrulous vagueness. She said that she could not remember if she had ever performed on the stage, and she answered a question about free love by saying, "I never knew that love was anything but free."

The one thing she would not disavow, however, were her spirits. She said that Demosthenes and Bonaparte and Josephine had once been her advisers and announced dramatically, "There is an apparition appearing to me right now!" But she did come close to admitting how her spirits had deserted her. "I have been abandoned by those whom I would never abandon," she said plaintively. After all the melodramatics, the case was decided in favor of the British Museum, but the offending books were withdrawn.

In her quest for respectability, Victoria Woodhull Martin distanced herself from Isabella Beecher Hooker. Isabella wrote Victoria asking her to consult with her deceased mother, Harriet Porter Beecher, who she said possessed great wisdom. Victoria wrote back that she had indeed spoken with Isabella's dead mother and that she had told her that Victoria and Isabella should no longer work together in this world but surely would meet again on the "other side."

Still society shunned her. When they married, John Martin's friends stopped visiting 17 Hyde Park Gate, but the Martins' isolation only drew them closer. Slights became a way of life. Once at an Athletic Club dinner in London to which John Biddulph Martin, as president, was permitted to invite his wife and her sister, the wife of a member, a Mrs. Taylor, declared that these women were not "proper persons to be associated with." When Vickie and Tennie arrived they found themselves alone with Martin in the vast banquet room.

Unlike her sister, Tennessee cared little about what people thought of her and simply by retaining her lighthearted American enthusiasm she fared better than Victoria. In London in 1884 she met the vastly wealthy widower Francis Cook and told him that the spirit of his dead wife said he should marry her. And he did. At Doughty House, his mansion on the Thames, and at his marble castle at Montserrat, in Portugal, Tennessee entertained lavishly and invited everybody from the local gentry to the blacksmith. The British found Lady Cook, the Viscountess of Montserrat, witty and amusing. She lived in quiet security and died in 1923.

Mama Roxy came to live with Tennessee, and Buck moved into Victo-

*Tennessee Claflin as Lady Cook, the Viscountess Montserrat*

*Victoria Woodhull as Mrs. John Biddulph Martin,*
*a proper English matron*

ria's home at 17 Hyde Park Gate, where he died at age eighty-nine with his daughter at his side. Victoria was convinced that an anonymous letter to the London *Times* alleging that his death was the result of foul play was from her sister Polly Sparr. The Martins offered a reward if the identity of the writer was revealed. It never was.

Mrs. Martin was fifty-nine in 1897 when John Martin died, leaving her both his London residence and his country estate, along with a comfortable fortune of 171,779 pounds sterling ($831,410 in American dollars at that time). The dowager Martin spent more and more time at Bredon's Norton, becoming the virtual ruler of this small feudal kingdom beside the river Avon. At the Manor House, which one approached through an arch over which was chiseled the date 1585, she held court in a room arranged for her comfort. Sturdy oak chairs stood beside dark-green velvet sofas with Brussels lace antimacassars and several tables were covered with a profusion of trinkets: bottles, inlaid boxes, and photographs of the Martins with the few important personages they had managed to cultivate. One table was covered with pamphlets containing the history of the estate and Victoria's own bogus genealogy. Another was littered with literature on palmistry and astrology. A niche at the far end of the room was cordoned off with heavy green damask portieres behind which was a shrine to the goddess Nike. Mrs. Martin occasionally confided to visitors that in another life she herself had been Nike.

Victoria was a benevolent despot. She chose the local vicar, paid his salary, and provided a house for him. She established a flower show at Bredon, endowed a local elementary school, repaired rutted roads, and modernized the cottages of the tenant farmers, who for generations had lived without electricity or running water. A villager said that she was generous to the poor in a way that only someone who had been poor herself could be.

All her life Victoria Woodhull Martin had been intoxicated by ideas. Spiritualists, clairvoyants, fortune-tellers, trance speakers, astrologers, palmists, and assorted local gentry, including the Earl of Coventry, were eager to be invited for lunch and to stay for her "international country salon." Finally, Victoria achieved social acceptance of a sort: King Edward VII, when he was still Prince of Wales, visited Bredon's Norton, and on this occasion the dining room was decorated with Victoria's native American flag and the Union Jack intertwined.

After her eightieth year, when her heart began to fail, Mrs. Martin frequently retreated to Brighton for the sea air. No longer able to ride horseback, and her sex life behind her, she was still enamored of speed and insisted that she be driven at a breakneck pace about the countryside in her

Aston-Martin. No chauffeur had nerves steady enough to stay long in her employ. Victoria offered a substantial reward to the first man or woman to fly the Atlantic. In May 1927 Charles A. Lindbergh did just that, but by that time all Victoria's energies were concentrated on outwitting death.

To avoid germs she refused to shake hands or be kissed. Visitors were permitted to come no closer than six feet. She ordered her drinking water boiled. Long ago, when she still lived in the United States, she had told Theodore Tilton that she "would rather die than live—such was her infinite estimate of the other world over this." Her fervent belief in the afterlife had assuaged both grief and loss and inspired others. Then the spirits had been her "constant companions." Then she had prophesied, quoting Saint Paul, that, "The last enemy that shall be destroyed is death." Then she had not been afraid. Now she was.

Facing death, she seemed to regret her decision to negate all that she had been. One morning she arose from her bed and in her shaky hand wrote in large letters, "Sitting here today in this north room . . . dreary, smoky, foggy . . . I am thinking with all the bitterness of my woman's nature how my life has been warped and twisted out of shape in this environment until, as I catch a glimpse of my haggard face in the mirror opposite, I wonder whether I shall be able to pen the history of my turbulent existence." She never could.

Night after night she sat erect in a straight-backed wooden chair and defied death. At 2 a.m. on the morning of June 10, 1927, death visited her nonetheless. Victoria Woodhull left instructions that she be cremated and her ashes cast into the sea. She willed her fortune to Zulu, who never married, having devoted her life to her mother. Victoria requested that after her daughter's death whatever monies remained be donated to the Society for Psychical Research.

Sixty years earlier in Chicago, Victoria Woodhull had nursed a woman who received "extreme unction from her priest" and was "given up by the physicians." For ten days this gifted spiritual healer had stood over her patient day and night neither sleeping nor eating. At the end of that time the woman recovered and Victoria found that her own body, instead of being weary or exhausted, "was more fresh and bright" than it had ever been before. Her skin wore "an unearthly look of transparency." In that moment Victoria was struck by "the idea that the time will come when the living human body, instead of ending in death by disease and dissolution in the grave, will be gradually refined away until it is entirely sloughed off and the soul only remains."

Perhaps that is true of Victoria Woodhull. She was a woman before her

*Victoria Woodhull, 1874*

time in a world that was not ready to receive her. Her "soul," however, remains with us. A month before her death, she scrawled what might have been her epitaph:

> The deeper I delve for a sure footing, the higher I reach for light, the more convinced am I that only here and there do we find an instrument capable of responding to the hungry heart's desire for Truth. . . .
>
> On the retina of our brain the outline of Truth is revealed to those attuned to the music of the spheres. . . . Therefore, I feel well assured that whatever be the misrepresentations to which I may be subject, the events must be committed to time, who relentlessly unravels all distortions and rights all wrongs. . . . Whoever I am, whatever I have done, belongs to the spirits.

BTS

CT

ECS & SBA

EYM          *Eighty Years and* .

GAT          "Victoria C. Woodhull: A Biog
             Mrs. Woodhull," Theodore Tilton

HWB          Letters of Henry Ward Beecher

HWS          *History of Woman Suffrage,* Elizabeth Cady Stanton, Susan B. Anthony,
             and Matilda Joslyn Gage, eds.

IBH          Isabella Beecher Hooker Project, letters and papers

MCW          Martha Coffin Wright Correspondence

PCH          Transcript of the Plymouth Church Hearing of Henry Ward Beecher

TS           *The Terrible Siren: Victoria Woodhull (1838–1927),* Emanie Sachs

VCWM         Victoria Claflin Woodhull (Martin) Papers

WCW          *Woodhull & Claflin's Weekly*

# Notes

## Prologue  A Page of History

p.   3  "bright, glorious, young and strong spirit": Susan B. Anthony to Victoria Woodhull, February 4, 1871, *The Papers of Elizabeth Cady Stanton and Susan B. Anthony,* The Stanton and Anthony Project, ed. Ann D. Gordon and Patricia G. Holland (New Brunswick, NJ: Rutgers University) 110 reels, microfilm edition, Reel 15:387. Footnote citations taken from material originally at the University of Massachusetts supplied by Kathleen A. McDonough may differ from later *ECS & SBA,* the guide to the microfilm, Ann D. Gordon and Patricia G. Holland, eds., and Kathleen A. McDonough and Gail K. Malmgreen, assoc. eds., *The Papers of Elizabeth Cady Stanton and Susan B. Anthony, Guide and Index,* Vol. 1 (New Brunswick, NJ: Rutgers University. 110 Reels, microfilm edition, 1997). Whenever possible I have given both citations. Abbreviated as *ECS & SBA.*

"In the annals of emancipation": Elizabeth Cady Stanton interview on the subject of Victoria Woodhull, Tenafly, New Jersey (December 1875), printed in the Newark *Sunday Call* (January 2, 1876); *ECS & SBA,* Reel 18:510.

"I believe you were raised": Paulina Wright Davis to Victoria Woodhull, Providence, Rhode Island (February 4, 1871), Victoria Woodhull Papers, reprinted in *Woodhull & Claflin's Weekly* (May 13, 1871).

"Heaven sent": Isabella Beecher Hooker to Anna Savery, Hartford, Connecticut (November 12, 1871), Isabella Beecher Hooker Collection, Project #46 C3-12, the Harriet Beecher Stowe Center Library (formerly the Stowe-Day Foundation), Hartford, CT.

"If my political campaign": *Chicago Mail* (May 6, 1872); *New York World* (April 16, 1892); Victoria Claflin Woodhull (Martin) Papers, Southern Illinois University Special Collections, Morris Library, Carbondale.

"The statement that Mrs. Biddulph Martin": Lucy Stone statement issued May 11, 1892; reprinted in *Chicago Mail* (May 13, 1892).

"Knowing your love of *truth*": *ECS & SBA,* Reel 30.

5  "Mrs. Hooker, I am glad" and ff.: Interview between John Martin and Isabella Beecher Hooker at the Sherman House (May 1, 1892), typed May 13, 1892; *VCWM,* Reel 2: 37–40.

"Her dress was peculiar" and ff.: Ibid.

6  "Tennie and Her Vickie" and ff.: *Chicago Mail* (May 8, 1892), p. 1.

7  "It was so long ago": *Chicago Mail* (May 14, 1892).

"the look of pain and anguish": *VCWM;* Victoria Woodhull Autobiographical Sketch, London, 1895, p. 171.

## Chapter 1  Born Again in the Lamb's Blood

9  "a young Greek God": Paxton Hibben, *Henry Ward Beecher: An American Portrait* (New York: George Doran, 1927), p. 31; reprint, Press of the Readers Club, New York, 1942).

"We are connected": Ibid., p. 32.

"We will love and watch": Ibid., p. 39.

9 "demonstrating phrenology": Webster's dictionary defines phrenology as a study based on the now outdated theory that mental faculties and dispositions can be judged by observing the shape of the skull as a whole and different parts of its surface. The *Oxford English Dictionary* defines it as the branch of inquiry that deals with the shape and size of the cranium as supposed indicators of character and mental faculties.

"obliged to make the bed": Milton Rugoff, *The Beechers: An American Family in the Nineteenth Century* (New York: Harper & Row), pp. 260, 613. Taken from interview with Mrs. Henry Ward Beecher, *Ladies' Home Journal* (December 1891).

11 "a respectable woman": *History of Woman Suffrage*, 2 volumes, ed. Elizabeth Cady Stanton, Susan B. Anthony, and Matilda Joslyn Gage (Salem, NH: Ayer Publishers, 1985), Vol. 1, p. 335. Reprint from an original copy in the State Historical Society of the Wisconsin Library. Originally published by Fowler & Wells, 753 Broadway, 1882; also *Weld-Grimke Papers and Diaries,* Willard L. Clements Library, University of Michigan.

"lashed them with cowskin": William S. McFeely, *Frederick Douglass* (New York: W. W. Norton, 1991), p. 17.

13 "disrupt domestic harmony": "The Silent Feminist Revolution: Women and the Law (in New York State from Blackstone to the Beginnings of the American Woman's Rights Movement)," Margareth Rabkin, Ph.D. dissertation, State University of New York, Buffalo, 1975.

"the husband and wife are one": Sir William Blackstone, *The Great Commentaries on the Laws of England,* 1765–69.

14 "The royal blood of Germany": Emanie Sachs, *The Terrible Siren: Victoria Woodhull (1838–1929)* (New York: Harper & Bros., 1928; reprint, New York, Arno Press, 1978), p. 317; *VCWM,* Victoria Woodhull Autobiographical Sketch, 1895, London, p. 173.

"Nowhere": *Chicago Daily Mail* (May 9, 1892); also *TS,* p. 7.

"a real Hummel": *Chicago Daily Mail* (May 9, 1892).

15 "the holy mudder in Israel": *TS,* p. 12; also Johanna Johnston, *Mrs. Satan: The Incredible Saga of Victoria C. Woodhull* (New York: G. P. Putnam's Sons, 1967; London: Macmillan 1967), p. 17. A medium is a person who acts as a channel of communication between human beings and spirits. It is a passive ability. A psychic is sensitive to nonphysical forces but is in no way controlled by spirits. He or she receives information not available through the five senses, and thus uses what is known as the sixth sense. The words "psychic" and "medium" are not interchangeable.

16 "Religious love is": William Hepworth Dixon, *Spiritual Wives* (London: Hurst and Blackett, 1868), Vol. 2, p. 177.

"into a state of frenzy": Ibid., p. 28.

"After his departure": Ibid., p. 30.

"to praise the Lord": Ibid., p. 32.

17 "smote him on the face": Ibid.

"fiery hail": Ibid.

"Glory": Testimony of Frank Warner at civil trial in Chicago, *John Biddulph Martin v. John Dunlop,* excerpted in the *Chicago Mail* (May 9, 1892), p. 1.

"I am born again": Ibid.

## Chapter 2    A Child Without a Childhood

18 "Squalid vice": Stanley Weintraub, *Victoria: An Intimate Biography* (New York: Truman Talley Books, E. P. Dutton, 1987), p. 117. Excerpted from the journal of Queen Victoria (December 30, 1838).

19 "tormented and harried her children": Theodore Tilton, "Victoria C. Woodhull: A Biographical Sketch: Mr. Tilton's Account of Mrs. Woodhull," *Golden Age* (New York: 1874), tract 3, p. 6.

19 "She was worked like a slave" and ff.: *GAT*, p. 7. Of Buck Claflin's brutality, Tilton wrote:

> In a barrel of rain-water he kept a number of braided green withes made of willow or walnut twigs, and with these stinging weapons, never with an ordinary whip, he would cut the quivering flesh of the children till their tears and blood melted him into mercy. Sometimes he took a handsaw or a stick of firewood as the instrument of his savagery. Coming home after the children were in bed, on learning of some offence which they had committed, he has been known to waken them out of sleep, and to whip them till morning.

20 "He named this process animal magnetism": Mesmer wrote, "There exists a mutual influence between celestial bodies, the earth, and animated bodies. . . . This influence exhibits, particularly in the human body, properties analogous to those of a magnet. One can distinguish diverse and opposing poles which can be changed, diminished, and reinforced. . . . The property in an animal body which renders it susceptible to this influence . . . I have decided to call animal magnetism." Robert C. Fuller, *Mesmerism and the American Cure of Souls* (Philadelphia: University of Pennsylvania Press, 1982), pp. 4, 5.
"magnetized": Ibid., p. 10.

21 "The Marquis de Puységur": Full name is Amand Marie Jacques de Puységur.
"other eyes": *VCWM*, Reel 2, 1890, articles on the "Invisible World."
"the power of the soul": Fuller, *Mesmerism*, p. 11.
"sanctified": *GAT*, p. 5; also *VCWM*, Reel 2, undated.
"skills demonstrated by mesmerized subjects": Modern psychiatry (with the exception of the theories of Carl Jung) has repudiated or ignored this evidence of supernormal powers, providing explanations of suggestibility and the control exercised by the mesmerist.
"The sexual implications were obvious": A Boston mesmerist confessed that he had "telepathically" induced several young ladies to thrust their affections upon him. Ralph Waldo Emerson cringed at the idea that someone "should attempt to put me asleep by the concentration of his will without my leave" (Fuller, *Mesmerism*, p. 34), and Nathaniel Hawthorne warned his fiancée, who wanted to use mesmerism to cure her headaches, "My spirit is moved to talk to thee today about these magnetic miracles, and to beseech thee to take no part in them. . . . The sacredness of an individual is violated by it" (Ibid., p. 35).

22 "He succeeded in almost throwing me": Rugoff, *The Beechers*, p. 267.
"it would require": *Samuel F. B. Morse, His Letters and Journals*, Volumes 1 and 2, ed. Edward Lind Morse (Boston: Houghton Mifflin and New York: Riverside Press, 1914), p. 72.
"in Heaven": *The Banner of Light* (Boston, November 20, 1870).
"Catharine Beecher, the eldest child": Isabella often spells her sister's name "Catherine," but others spell it "Catharine," as she herself does in her books and writing.

23 "To American Mothers": Catharine E. Beecher, *A Treatise on Domestic Economy, For The Use of Young Ladies At Home, And At School* (Boston: Marsh, Capen, Lyon, and Webb, 1841).
"The physical and domestic education": Ibid., p. 38.

24 "her first spiritual vision": The details and circumstances were to change in Victoria Woodhull's written accounts of this incident—"I was four," "five," "a neighbor died," "a woman died," "Rachel Scribner, my nurse, died"—but the vision remained the same.
"felt herself gliding": *GAT*, p. 11; *VCWM*, Reel 3, p. 11.
"I saw the spirits descending": *GAT*, p. 11; *Boston Post* (October 20, 1876); *VCWM*, Reel 3.

25 "a child without a childhood": *GAT*, p. 4.
"a household drudge": Ibid., p. 7.

25 "She has been lifted": Ibid., p. 10.

"I often performed": Chapter in the unfinished autobiography of Victoria Woodhull, *VCWM*, Reel 1.

26 "ride around in their own carriages": Testimony of Roxanna Claflin in *Roxanna Claflin v. Col. James Blood*, May 11–May 21, 1871. Also, quoted in many newspapers, ex. *The World*, *Herald*, New York Public Library Scrapbook III.

"A red silk handkerchief": Chapter in the unfinished autobiography of Victoria Woodhull, *VCWM*, Reel 1.

"I saw not a booted foot": Ibid.

"pale white hands": *Boston Post* (October 20, 1876), reprinted in *The Banner of Light* (November 20, 1876).

"So shall sinners fall in Hell": Ibid.

"I am the Word" and ff.: Ibid.

27 "bleeding feet and haggard face": *GAT*, p. 6.

"There is a red glow" and ff.: *TS*, p. 14.

## Chapter 3    The Spiritual Telegraph

28 "Follow me" and ff: *TS*, p. 19.

"Now, do as I do" and ff.: Ibid.

29 "I did not think": Ruth Brandon, *The Spiritualists: The Passion for the Occult in the Nineteenth and Twentieth Centuries* (New York: Knopf, 1983), pp. 2, 3. E. W. Capron and H. D. Barron, *Spiritualism*, pp. 15, 16.

"I should love much": Frederick Douglass to Amy Post (April 11, 1848), Amy and Isaac Post Family Papers, University of Rochester Library, Department of Rare Books and Special Collections; Ann Braude, *Radical Spirits: Spiritualism and Women's Rights in Nineteenth-Century America* (Boston: Beacon, 1989), p. 11.

"moved by the spirit": Ida Husted Harper, *Life and Work of Susan B. Anthony* (Indianapolis: Bowen-Merrill, 1898), Vol. 1, p. 40. Taken from letters of Daniel B. Anthony.

"six-penny farm": Ibid., p. 48.

31 "Of what use is preaching": Katharine Anthony, *Susan B. Anthony: Her Personal History and Her Era* (Garden City, NY: Doubleday, 1954), p. 92. *ECS & SBA*, taken from letter, Daniel B. Anthony to Dear S. (Susan B. Anthony, 1849).

"the deep throbbing of": Braude, p. 14. Much of this account of spiritual phenomena is taken from Emma Hardinge, *Modern American Spiritualism: A Twenty Years' Record of the Communication Between Earth and the World of the Spirits*, 1869, and from Albert Cronise, *Beginnings of Modern Spiritualism in and Near Rochester* (Rochester, NY: Rochester Historical Society, 1925).

32 "automatic writing": There are numerous accounts of automatic writing in the letters and diaries of Spiritualists, including Isaac and Amy Post, Isabella Beecher Hooker, Paulina Wright Davis. Isaac Post, *Voices from the Spirit World, Being Communications from Many Spirits, by the hand of Isaac Post, Medium* (Rochester, NY: C. H. McDonell, 1852), p. 258. Andrew Jackson Davis also explains this phenomenon in *The Principles of Nature, Her Divine Revelations and a Voice to Mankind.* George Lawton, "The Drama of Life After Death: A Study of the Spiritualist Religion," *Dictionary of American Biography* (New York: Henry Holt and Company, 1932), p. 500.

"the God principles at work": Braude, p. 119.

33 "an unbroken chain" and ff.: Ibid., p. 13. Taken from Waterloo Friends, *Proceedings*, pp. 9, 20.

"Spiritual Telegraph": Hal D. Sears, *The Sex Radicals: Free Love in High Victorian America* (Lawrence, KS: Regent Press of Kansas, 1977), p. 13; Braude, p. 5.

"passed over": The common term used by Spiritualists to refer to those who had died and were now, they believed, residents of heaven or, as they called it, Summerland.

33 "Instead of the social existence" and ff.: Sears, p. 10.

34 "the Spirit World is derived" and ff.: Andrew Jackson Davis, *The Philosophy of Spiritual Intercourse* (New York: Fowler & Wells, 1851), p. 413.

"Charles Fourier": Born François Marie Charles Fourier but commonly called Charles Fourier.

"a common system of movement": Fuller, p. 5; Robert Darnton, *Mesmerism and the End of the Enlightenment in France* (Cambridge, MA: Harvard University Press, 1968), p. 143.

"incessant labor": Sears, p. 16. A complete account of this incident appears in John M. Spear, *Boston New Era* (June 29, 1854).

"living principle": Sears, p. 18.

"a crisis": Ibid.

"at precisely the time designated": Ibid.

"lofty electrical position": Ibid., p. 19.

"tore out the heart": Ibid.

35 "an awful foreboding": Letters of Louise Chandler Moulton, Library of Congress, Manuscript Division.

"in the depth of the night": John S. Hart, *The Female Prose Writers of America,* 1857, p. 533.

"rather than mourn": A typical spirit message read, "Gentle mother, your little Seraph boy is not *dead* but *liveth.* In his uncontaminated love, find comfort for the ills of life." See Braude, p. 40.

"Not in Church": Ibid., p. 24; Andrew Jackson Davis, *Philosophy of Spiritual Intercourse,* p. 96.

36 "are not gone": Braude, p. 55.

"In the funeral oration": Warren Felt Evans, *The New Age and Its Messenger* (Boston, 1864), p. 25.

## Chapter 4   My Long-Accumulating Discontent

38 "poured out . . . the torrent of": Elisabeth Griffith, *In Her Own Right: The Life of Elizabeth Cady Stanton* (New York: Oxford University Press, 1984), p. 51; Alma Lutz, *Created Equal: A Biography of Elizabeth Cady Stanton, 1815–1902* (New York: John Day, 1940), p. 48.

"convention to discuss": *ECS & SBA,* 6:708. Call to Woman's Rights Convention at Seneca Falls, NY, published in the *Seneca County Courier,* July 14, 1848. Authors: Elizabeth Cady Stanton, Lucretia Coffin Mott, Martha Coffin Pelham Wright, Mary Ann Wilson McClintock, and Jane C. Hunt.

"felt as helpless and": Griffith, p. 52; Lutz, *Created Equal,* p. 45; Mari Jo Buhle and Paul Buhle, eds., *The Concise History of Woman Suffrage: Selections from the Classic Work of Stanton, Anthony, Gage and Harper* (Urbana: University of Illinois Press, 1978), p. 92.

39 "We hold these truths": Elizabeth Cady Stanton, *Eighty Years and More: Reminiscences 1815–1897,* new introduction by Gail Parker (New York: Schocken Books, 1971), p. 149. Reprinted from the T. Fisher Unwin edition of 1898; Buhle and Buhle, p. 94.

"the first organized protest": *EYM,* p. 149.

"mental hunger": *Elizabeth Cady Stanton, as Revealed in Her Letters, Diary and Reminiscences,* 2 volumes, Theodore Stanton and Harriot Stanton Blatch, editors (New York: Arno & The New York Times, 1969), Vol. 1, p. 144. Originally published by Harper & Bros., NY, 1922.

"spiritlike": Christian Frederich Samuel Hahnemann, *Organon of Medicine,* translated by J. Kunzl et al. (London: Vic Gollancz, 1983), p. 269; Stanton and Blatch, p. 114.

"got up, bathed myself": Elizabeth Cady Stanton to Elizabeth Smith Miller, Seneca Falls, New York (February 10, 11, 13, 1851); *ECS & SBA,* 7:036–038; Stanton and Blatch, Vol. 2, pp. 26, 27.

39  "We know what not": Lutz, *Created Equal,* p. 160, taken from *The Revolution,* January 22, 1868.

41  "As an amusement": Ibid., p. 58, taken from the article "Women," January 1, 1850.
    "silent chamber of death": *EYM,* p. 20.
    "As he took no notice of me": Ibid.
    "I resolved . . . to be at the head": Ibid., p. 21.
    "prefers boys": Ibid.

42  "But I suffer not": Timothy 2:12; Lutz, *Created Equal,* p. 5.
    "I soon noticed that": *EYM,* p. 48.
    "I left him": Ibid., p. 49.

43  "To think that all in me": Griffith, p. 9.
    "streak of fire": Constance Mayfield Rourke, *Trumpets of Jubilee: Henry Ward Beecher, Harriet Beecher Stowe, Lyman Beecher, Horace Greeley, P. T. Barnum* (New York: Harcourt, Brace, 1927), p. 46.
    "I can see him now": *EYM,* p. 42.

44  "a monster of iniquity": Ibid., p. 41; Griffith, p. 21.
    "puzzling and harrowing": Griffith, p. 21.
    "I cannot understand what": *EYM,* p. 42.
    "Repent and believe" and ff.: Ibid., p. 43; Griffith, p. 21.
    "the nature of the delusion": *EYM,* p. 47.
    "the physical conditions": Ibid., p. 48.

45  "slowly through a beautiful grove": Ibid., p. 60.
    "dreaded the influence of Mr. Bayard": Griffith, p. 31.
    "in an unguarded moment" and ff.: Elizabeth Cady Stanton to Isabella Beecher Hooker, Tenafly, New Jersey (January 21, 1873); *ECS & SBA,* 16:968–973.

46  "RESOLVED—That it is the duty": "From the First Convention Ever Called to Discuss the Civil and Political Rights of Women," Seneca Falls, New York (July 19, 20, 1848), Woman's Rights Convention, *ECS & SBA,* 6:719.
    "Oh, Lizzie! If thou": Lutz, *Created Equal,* p. 46.
    "He stood there like an African Prince": Ibid., p. 39.
    "The ballot": Ibid., p. 47.
    "Our doctrine is that": July 28, 1848, *The North Star;* Philip S. Foner, *The Life and Writings of Frederick Douglass,* 5 volumes (New York: International Publishers, 1955), Vol. 1: Early Years, p. 321.

47  "foolish conduct": Griffith, p. 59.

48  "make the puddings and": *ECS & SBA,* microfilm edition, Reel 8.
    "Oh dear, dear! If the spirits": Susan B. Anthony to Elizabeth Cady Stanton (June 5, 1856); *ECS & SBA,* Reel 8:443; *Elizabeth Cady Stanton, Her Letters, Diary and Reminiscences,* pp. 65–66. This is an example of where Anthony's exact words were altered. Here it reads "right thing" in place of "rights," which appears in the original letter of June 5.
    "Gerrit Smith's daughter Elizabeth": Elizabeth Smith came for a visit. She was called Libby by her parents, but Lizzie by many of her friends. Elizabeth Smith married Charles Dudley Miller on October 18, 1843, at the age of twenty-one. Libby Smith would introduce "Bloomers." In the winter of 1850–1851 Elizabeth Smith Miller visited Elizabeth Cady Stanton and appeared on the streets of Seneca Falls wearing this costume. *Notable American Women 1607–1950: A Biographical Dictionary,* 3 volumes, ed. Edward T. James (Cambridge, MA: Belknap Press of Harvard University Press, 1971), Vol. 1, p. 180.
    "As to the rapping heard": George Willets to Isaac Post, October 23, 1848; Amy and Isaac Post Family Papers.

## Chapter 5   You Ugly Creature

50  "But where is the best fruit?" and ff.: *TS*, p. 16. Excerpted from *The Spiritualist* (November 4, 1870).

51  "The Wonderful Child": Sachs, p. 30.
"in my own home": *GAT*, p. 10.

52  "a woman before her time": Ibid., p. 14.
"All that I am": Martha Coffin Wright to Susan B. Anthony (April 6, 1871) *MCW*; from *ECS & SBA*, Reel 15:537–540.
"a majestic guardian": Rourke, p. 201.
"she would rise to": *GAT*, p. 11.
"I would talk to them": Ibid.; also in *Victoria Woodhull Prophesy, Boston Post* (October 20, 1876).
"gracious guests": *GAT*, p. 8; also in *Victoria Woodhull Prophesy, Boston Post* (October 20, 1876).
"My little puss": *GAT*, p. 13.
"not unwilling to be rid": Ibid., p. 14.
"My marriage was an escape": Ibid.

53  " 'New Age' Philosophy": Madeleine B. Stern, *The Pantarch: A Biography of Stephen Pearl Andrews*, p. 5. Stephen Pearl Andrews wrote, "I see now a new age beginning to appear."
"more troublesome than a crown": Sears, pp. 3, 4. Stern, excerpted from Josiah Warren, *Practical Applications of the Elementary Principles of "True Civilization,"* p. 21.
"the antithesis of enslaved love": Stephen Pearl Andrews, "Fragments," *New York Daily Tribune* (November 8, 1858), p. 3. Repeated in *Love, Marriage and Divorce and The Sovereignty of the Individual,* (A Discussion by) Henry James, Horace Greeley, and Stephen Pearl Andrews (New York: Stringer & Townsend, 1853).
"All sexual relations": Debate with Stephen Pearl Andrews, *New York Daily Tribune* (November 10, 1853).

55  "adultery": *New York Tribune* (November 10, 1858), repeated in *Love, Marriage and Divorce*, 1853.
"convinced beyond the shadow": Braude, p. 16. Excerpted from Hardinge, 1869, p. 71.
"Take your hands": William Harlan Hale, *Horace Greeley: Voice of the People* (New York: Harper & Bros., 1950), p. 123.
" 'dream boy' Pickie were soon communicating": Henry Luther Stoddard, *Horace Greeley: Printer, Editor, Crusader* (New York: G. P. Putnam's Sons, 1946), pp. 108, 119. Greeley recorded a typical spirit conversation with his dead son.

> Horace Greeley: "Pickie, tell the story of that last day that you were well—how you came up to my room where I was writing and kept trying to pull my pen from me—how about that?"
> Answer by rapping: "You put me out" (as was the fact . . .)
> Mary Greeley: "I do not see why you should bring up that disagreeable, melancholy reminiscence."
> Pickie: "No, mother it is *not* melancholy. I *disturbed* father."

Horace Greeley descriptions of "spirit rapping" seance and other rappings, New York Public Library, Manuscript Division.

56  "I am very lonely": Catherine Fox to John Fox (October 26, 1850), Catherine Fox to Amy Post (June 19, 1850), Catherine Fox to Amy Post (October, November 1850), Amy and Isaac Post Family Papers. Excerpted from Braude, p. 16.
"crazy for learning": Hale, p. 32. This description is attributed to Margaret Fuller.

57  "My wife is in bad health": Ibid., p. 34; documents in Horace Greeley Papers, New York Public Library; Horace Greeley Letters to Margaret Fuller, Harvard University Library.

57 "because her fire would not burn": Ibid.
"Mary is terribly ill": Ibid.
58 "Mrs. Greeley is in her usual bad health": Ibid.
"Mrs. Greeley's life is": Ibid., p. 120.
"Castle Doleful": Stoddard, p. 121.
"bad magnetism": Horace Greeley to Margaret Fuller (January 27, 1848), ibid., p. 114; Hale, p. 120.
59 "Castle Rackrent": Hale, p. 112.
"Catharine Beecher's *Treatise on Domestic Economy*": Chapter "On Washing," pp. 308–319; Chapter "On Whitening, Cleansing And Dyeing," pp. 327–336.
60 "a woolen ironing-blanket": Ibid., p. 324.
"inability to accomplish anything": Hale, p. 183.
"dirty food": Stoddard, p. 110.
"Your sore, sick father" and ff.: Horace Greeley, Papers; also in Hale, p. 116; Glyndon G. Van Deusen, *Horace Greeley, Nineteenth-Century Crusader* (Philadelphia: University of Pennsylvania Press, 1953), p. 153.
61 "while Mother often said": Hale, p. 119.
"Pickie regarded her": Ibid.
"I never saw a creature": Horace Greeley to Margaret Fuller (July 29, 1847), Harvard University Library; Stoddard, p. 111.
"A week after the funeral": Ibid.
"I had a pretty little sister": Pickie (dictated letter to his father, Horace Greeley) to be sent to Margaret Fuller, New York (August 14, 1849), Harvard University Library; Stoddard, p. 122.
"When I came home": Horace Greeley to Margaret Fuller (July 29, 1847), Harvard University Library; Hale, p. 119; Stoddard, p. 111.
"He is governed and restricted": Horace Greeley to Margaret Fuller (June 27, 1848), Harvard University Library; Stoddard, p. 116.
"the piano was sweetly played": Catherine Fox to Amy Post (November 1850), Amy and Isaac Post Family Papers; also Braude, p. 17.
62 "ring bells and move tables": Catherine Fox to Amy Post (October 30, 1850), Amy and Isaac Post Family Papers; also Braude, p. 17.
"How I hate her!": Catherine Fox to John Fox (October 26, 1850); Braude, p. 16.

## Chapter 6   True Wife

63 "walking unsteadily across": VCWM, Reel 1. Reprinted in *Victoria Woodhull Prophesy, Boston Post* (October 20, 1876).
"Did you marry that child": GAT, p. 14.
64 "mostly with his cups": Ibid.
"half-drunken husband": Ibid., p. 15.
"icicles clinging to her bed post": Ibid.
"the iron door": Ibid., p. 13.
"wrestling with God": Ibid., p. 15.
"true wife": Ibid., p. 16.
"the harlot to pack her trunk": Ibid.
65 "Go West, young men, and grow up with the country!": Rourke, p. 241, excerpted from *New York Daily Tribune*.
"Tied down the safety valve": Edwin P. Hoyt, *The Vanderbilts and Their Fortunes* (New York: Doubleday and Co., 1962), p. 119.
"cigar girl": GAT, p. 17.
"have somebody who can rough it": Ibid.

65 "It is no use": Ibid.
66 "I am meant for": *Victoria Woodhull Prophesy, Boston Post* (October 20, 1876).
   "Victoria, come home": *TS,* p. 25.
   "Come home!": Ibid.
   "thrown into such vivid": Ibid.
67 "send the spirits": Ibid.
   "A WONDERFUL CHILD!": Ibid., p. 30.
   "Miss Tennessee's Magnetic Life Elixir": Ibid., pp. 31–32.
   "It was a hard life": Testimony of Tennessee Claflin in *Roxanna Claflin v. Colonel James H. Blood* (May 15, 1871), Essex Market Police Court, New York City.
68 "Blue Book": Several such books are available in the Manuscript Division of the New York Public Library and in the collection of the American Psychical Society of New York.
   "through the power of her mind": A phrase used in such books as *Mind Cure in New England: From the Civil War to World War I,* by Gail Thain Parker (Hanover NH: University Press of New England, 1973) and Braude's *Radical Spirits.*
69 "Now we will sit up": Margaret Sanborn, *Mark Twain: The Bachelor Years: A Biography* (New York: Doubleday, 1990), pp. 380–381 ff.
   "I've done considerable": Mark Twain, *Huckleberry Finn* (Cleveland, OH: World Publishing Co., reprint 1947), p. 169.
   "thousands of women": Victoria Woodhull, *Tried as By Fire,* reprinted in *The Victoria Woodhull Reader,* pp. 6, 7, 8 ff.
70 "twisting and braiding": We have only Victoria's word that these phenomena took place. However, a new, twelve-year study at Princeton University headed by Professor Robert Jahn finds conclusively that such things occur. Tests on hundreds provided evidence of psychokinesis and the ability to transmit messages through the power of thought.
   "No. I will not permit": *GAT,* p. 21; also *TS,* p. 34.
   "servant girls": *Indianapolis Herald,* undated, preprinted in *Chicago Mail* (May 8, 1892), courtesy Chicago History Works, Oak Park, Illinois.
   "disorderly conduct": Ibid.
71 "Zulu Maud": One cannot know if Victoria named her daughter because at birth the baby resembled a member of that African tribe or if Victoria just liked the name. (There were so many unusual names in her family.) In all Woodhull's early writings and in documents, the child is referred to by her birth name, Zulu. However, after Victoria moved to England in 1877, for a time Zulu's name was changed to Zula.
   "staggering up the steps": *GAT,* p. 26.
   "Why should I any longer live": Ibid., p. 21.

## Chapter 7  Willfully Did Kill

72 "women in the fields": Katharine Anthony, p. 159.
73 "I cannot meet my Maker": Henry Bowen's statement, Plymouth Church Committee, December 1875, Beecher-Tilton trial, Scrapbook IV, Beecher-Tilton Correspondence, Lib Tilton Correspondence, Theodore Tilton Correspondence, Francis De Pau Moulton legal and personal Correspondence, Mrs. Morse Correspondence, newspaper articles, clippings, pamphlets, church and civil trial–related material, etc., from the offices of the *Independent.* Tucker-Sachs Correspondence, Scrapbooks I–VIII, New York Public Library, Manuscript Collection, New York.
75 "a failure": Hibben, p. 167.
76 "soul-food": A term used by Lib (Elizabeth) Tilton to Theodore Tilton (hereafter abbreviated as ET to TT), January 4, 1870, *BTS* II.
   "I sometimes feel": Henry Bowen to Theodore Tilton, June 16, 1863. Reprinted in the *Brooklyn Eagle,* January 21, 1875, *BTS* IV.

77 "cowardice and treason": Giraud Chester, *Embattled Maiden. The Life of Anna Dickinson* (New York: G. P. Putnam's Sons, 1951), p. 29.

"At Antietam in Sharpsburg": The battle of Antietam took place September 17, 1862. James M. McPherson, *Battle Cry of Freedom: The Civil War Era* (New York: Oxford University Press), 1988, p. 541.

"a human being cannot": Excerpt from the *London Spectator,* as cited in Kenneth M. Stampp, *The Era of Reconstruction, 1865–1877* (New York: Knopf, 1978, Vintage, 1965 reprint edition), p. 44.

78 "the most brutal mob": Elizabeth Cady Stanton to Mrs. Gerrit Smith, Johnstown, New York (July 20, 1863); *ECS & SBA*, Reel 10: 543–544; Stanton and Blatch, Vol. 2, p. 94. The house was at 75 W. 45th Street.

"Here's one of those": Ibid.

"Let's go in, fellows!": Ibid., p. 544; Stanton and Blatch, pp. 94–95.

"servants and the children": Ibid., pp. 543–544; Stanton and Blatch, p. 95.

"Colored Orphan Asylum": Ibid.; Stanton and Blatch, p. 94.

"three years of age": Mattie Griffith to Mary Estlin (July 27, 1863); Eric Foner, *Reconstruction: America's Unfinished Revolution, 1863–1877* (New York: Harper & Row, 1988), p. 33, footnote 58; excerpted from Estlin Papers, Dr. Williams' Library, London.

79 "weak" and ff.: *EYM,* p. 42; Henry B. Stanton, *Random Recollections* (Johnstown, NY: Blunck & Leaning, Printers, 1885), pp. 22, 23.

80 "For years before": *Victoria Woodhull Prophesy, Boston Post* (October 20, 1876); also in *Banner of Light, Original Essays, VCWM,* dated Boston, Saturday, November 20 (year obscured).

"When Lincoln was on his way": Ibid.

"American King of Cancers": Johnston, p. 32. Buck Claflin also claimed he could cure "all kinds of chronic diseases, fever sores, bone diseases, scrofula, piles, sore eyes in the worst stages, heart and liver complaints, female weaknesses, constipation, inflammatory rheumatism, asthma, neuralgia, sick headache, dropsy in the chest, and fits in various forms."

81 "cult of love": *Ottawa Free Trader* (April 4, 1863), courtesy of Chicago History Works.

"hobbled in on crutches": *The Romance of Plymouth Church, Plymouth Church and Its Pastor, or Henry Ward Beecher and His Accusers,* compiled by J.E.P. Doyle (Hartford, CT: Park Publishing, 1874), p. 440.

"There are only three cures": *VCWM,* Reel 3.

"Mrs. Rebecca Howe, recovering": *Ottawa Free Trader* (June 1, 1864).

"Miss Claflin is": Rebecca Howe letter printed in the *Ottawa Republican* (June 4, 1864); Sachs, p. 35.

82 "On the first day of November": Indictment issued June 1864, Ottawa, Illinois, La Salle County Courthouse, courtesy of Chicago History Works.

## Chapter 8    God Bless This Trinity

84 "I could never be": ET to TT (April 1, 1864).

85 "My friends, fellow citizens": *Brooklyn Eagle* (April 20, 1865), p. 5.

"brother soldiers": Ibid.; also in N. D. Hillis, *Lectures and Orations of Henry Ward Beecher* (New York: AMS Press, 1913, reprint 1970).

"Christ can save you": Leon Oliver, *The Great Sensation* (Chicago: Beverly Co., 1973), p. 210.

"What is orthodoxy?": Doyle, p. 413.

86 "I cannot think, only feel": ET to TT (February 7, 1869).

"Cool, fragrantly airy": *Brooklyn Eagle* (November 6, 1858), p. 8. Excerpted from pamphlet *Old Brooklyn Heights, The Brooklyn Savings Bank, 1827–1927.*

87  "most ideal woman": Theodore Tilton to Lib (Elizabeth) Tilton (hereafter abbreviated as TT to ET (January 14, 1867), *BTS.*
"fulfill his every need": Statement of Lib (Elizabeth) Tilton, Plymouth Church Hearing of Henry Ward Beecher (July 28, 1874) transcript, New York Public Library, New York Historical Association.

88  "a home": ET to TT (January 16, 1865), *BTS.*
"kind of ecstasy": ET to TT (December 28, 1866), *BTS.*

89  "Beecher's Bibles": Hibben, pp. 134, 148.
"to be sold by" and ff.: Hibben, p. 136.

90  "dazzled" and ff.: Statement of Theodore Tilton, Plymouth Church Hearing of Henry Ward Beecher (August 1, 1874).
"His mind was opening": Charles F. Marshall, *The True History of the Brooklyn Scandal* (Philadelphia: National Publishing Co., 1874), p. 256.

91  "At the birth of": Ibid., pp. 189–190; also in statement of Lib (Elizabeth) Tilton, Plymouth Church Hearing of Henry Ward Beecher (July 23, 1874).
"I had a very severe and prolonged sickness": Ibid. In a statement, Lib (Elizabeth) Tilton calls the doctor "Doctor Putnam."
"beautiful Mattie": Statement of Lib (Elizabeth) Tilton, Plymouth Church Hearing of Henry Ward Beecher (July 28, 1974).
"cold" and ff.: *Theodore Tilton v. Henry Ward Beecher,* civil trial, court testimony of Francis D. P. Moulton (February 11, 1875), New York Public Library Scrapbook VI; Marshall, p. 448.
"scolded and chided": Statement of Lib (Elizabeth) Tilton, Plymouth Church Hearing of Henry Ward Beecher (July 31, 1874); Marshall, p. 189.
"He spent a great deal": Lib (Elizabeth) Tilton Testimony, *PCH,* New York Public Library Scrapbook V; Altina L. Waller, *Reverend Beecher and Mrs. Tilton: Sex and Class in Victorian America* (Amherst: University of Massachusetts Press, 1982), p. 48; Marshall, p. 190.
"manias and frenzies": Statement of Theodore Tilton, Plymouth Church Hearing of Henry Ward Beecher (July 21, 1874); Marshall, p. 129; *Brooklyn Argus* (July 23, 1874), p. 1, New York Public Library Scrapbook V.

92  "make a name for himself": Statement of Lib (Elizabeth) Tilton, Plymouth Church Hearing of Henry Ward Beecher (July 31, 1874); New York Public Library Scrapbook V; Marshall, p. 193.
"And into whatsoever house": Marshall, p. 182.
"luxurious carelessness; the wallpaper was": *Brooklyn Eagle* (August 1, 1874).
"Alone I can do": Marshall, p. 191; statement of Lib (Elizabeth) Tilton, Plymouth Church Hearing of Henry Ward Beecher (July 23, 1874).

93  "small woman, without presence": *Theodore Tilton v. Henry Ward Beecher,* civil trial, court testimony of Francis D. P. Moulton (February 11, 18, 1875); New York Public Library Scrapbook VI.
"he had married her": Ibid.
"Here is Theodore": Ibid.

94  "going back to my own house": Hibben, p. 179.
"hell on earth": Robert Shaplen, *Free Love and Heavenly Sinners: The Story of the Great Henry Ward Beecher Scandal* (New York: Alfred A. Knopf, 1954), p. 38. Originally published in *The New Yorker* (June 5 and 12, 1954).
"the vainest, the most vapid": Hibben, p. 179; also Shaplen, p. 37.
"childlike in appearance": Marshall, p. 257. Statement of Henry Ward Beecher, Plymouth Church Hearing of Henry Ward Beecher, New York Public Library Scrapbook V.
"O Theodore, God might": Hibben, p. 178.
"I was almost in despair" and ff.: Statement of Henry Ward Beecher, Plymouth Church Hearing of Henry Ward Beecher, New York Public Library Scrapbook V; Hibben, p. 182.

95 "People have said that I": Ibid.

"tell whether a speech": Marshall, p. 159.

"I never felt a bit": Ibid., p. 197; statement of Lib (Elizabeth) Tilton, Plymouth Church Hearing of Henry Ward Beecher (July 28, 1874), *BTS*, Scrapbook V.

"I took my first walk": ET to TT (January 2, 1865), *BTS*.

"I am glad Mr. Beecher called": TT to ET (January 13, 1865), Cleveland, Ohio, *BTS*.

"a blessed Trinity": ET to TT (January 25, 1867), *BTS*.

"Tomorrow the whole nation": *Victoria Woodhull Prophesy, Boston Post* (October 20, 1876).

## Chapter 9 An Accident of Fate

96 "I had thought that states rights": Thursday, February 16, 1871, Lincoln Hall, Washington, before presenting the minority report on the Woodhull memorial. Buhle and Buhle, Vol. 1, p. 293.

"Reconstruction": Eric Foner, p. 5.

"soft peace": Stampp, p. 50.

"to unify the nation": Several historians posit that Benjamin Butler sought this Union Party nomination himself and therein lay the root of his antagonism toward Andrew Johnson.

"yet to be ratified": Indeed, Mississippi did not ratify this amendment until March 1995, 130 years later.

97 "temporary arrangements for the Freed People": Stampp, p. 46.

"Ile à Vache": (December 31, 1862); James M. McPherson, *The Negro's Civil War: How American Negroes Felt and Acted during the War for the Union* (Urbana and Chicago: University of Illinois Press, originally Pantheon Books, 1965), p. 96.

98 "The real trouble is": Stampp, p. 102.

"murderous and wasteful war": Ibid., p. 101.

"wretched treatment of black people": *Independent* (September 14, 1865, September 23, 1865), specifically attributed to Theodore Tilton in a sermon by Henry Ward Beecher, October 22, 1865, and in Theodore Tilton's letter to Lib Tilton, October 25, 1865.

"while the defeated South": *Independent* (September 23, 1865), p. 2.

"And may I not be": Henry Ward Beecher sermon (October 8, 1865), reprinted in the *Independent* (October 2, 1865).

99 "A Great Political Sermon": *New York Times* (October 24, 1865); also in the *New York Tribune* (October 26, 1865). Beecher wrote a letter to the *Tribune* stating that the sentence quoted from his sermon, "The laws and interests of the government and of ourselves will prove to no avail if they are hostile and unpleasant to the *white* people of the south," did not contain the word "hostile" and that he was "inaccurately reported." Therefore, I have removed "hostile" from the quote, but the sense is essentially the same.

"There is no such kindness" and ff.: *Independent,* byline Theodore Tilton (October 27, 1865).

"remote": Ibid.

"On the contrary" and ff.: Ibid.

"I have not seen Mr. Beecher": TT to ET (October 25, 1865), *BTS*.

"My friend, from my boyhood": Theodore Tilton to Henry Ward Beecher, Brooklyn (November 30, 1865).

100 "To demonstrate that there were": Theodore Tilton statement, *CT.*

"Woman's Influence in Politics": *Independent* (February 16, 1860).

"Well, old girl": Harper, Vol. 1, p. 234.

"re-examination of the Declaration": *Independent* (February 23, 1865).

"When Andrew Johnson began": *ECS & SBA*, Elizabeth Cady Stanton to Martha Coffin Wright (January 6, 1866); also cited in Stanton and Blatch, Vol. 2, p. 112.

101  "both classes of disenfranchised citizens?": Elizabeth Cady Stanton to Wendell Phillips, in the *National Antislavery Standard* (December 26, 1865).

"I have about made up my mind": *HWS,* Vol. 2, p. 168; also cited in Stanton and Blatch, Vol. 2, p. 106.

102  "While I could continue arguing": Wendell Phillips to Elizabeth Cady Stanton (February 18, 1866), *HWS,* Vol. 2, p. 152.

"We have fairly boosted the negro": Elizabeth Cady Stanton to Martha Coffin Wright (December 20, 1865), *ECS & SBA, 1865–66*; also cited in Stanton and Blatch, Vol. 2, p. 108. Gloria Steinem points out that until this time black and white women were allied in their fight for woman suffrage. Stanton's demand for enfranchisement based on the superior social position and education of white women adversely affected black women and their rights. Although limitations of space prohibit my dealing with this important issue, Steinem has written extensively on this subject.

"It mattered very little": Lib (Elizabeth) Tilton's statement to the Plymouth Church Committee, *PCH,* 1874; Marshall, p. 192.

"sick-bed" and ff.: Ibid., p. 197.

"I would give $500": Ibid., p. 198.

103  "You seldom meet a woman": Elizabeth Cady Stanton to Sara Jane Lippincott (May 30, 1873), *ECS & SBA, 1873.*

104  "a changed woman": ET to TT (February 7, 1869), *BTS.*

"dead to rights": Deposition of James Kerr reprinted in *Chicago Mail* (May 14, 1892), p. 2, courtesy of Chicago History Works.

"Not me. I'm just": Ibid.

"the most notorious woman": Ibid.

106  "Negro squatters were everywhere" and ff.: Elizabeth Avery Meriwether, *Recollections of 92 Years, 1824–1916* (Nashville: The Tennessee Historical Commission, 1958), p. 167.

107  "Blood saw Missouri": Missouri was ripped apart over the question of slavery. In Missouri there were 1,162 battles and skirmishes; only Virginia and Tennessee had more.

"on the spot": *GAT,* p. 24.

"wonderful cures": Handbill of Victoria Woodhull, *VCWM,* Box 2; also in *GAT,* p. 19.

"a debt of $3,700": *New York Times* (May 11, 1871) stated that the debt was "in excess of $5,000."

108  "Father, at times a Mephistopheles": *GAT,* p. 23.

109  "should earn all the money": Ibid., p. 7.

"Tennie has had ten men": Joseph Treat, M.D., *Beecher, Tilton, Woodhull, The Creation of Society: All Four of Them Exposed, and if Possible Reformed and Forgiven, in Dr. Treat's Celebrated Letter to Victoria C. Woodhull* (New York: Published by the author, 1874), p. 9.

"My God, have I got": Ibid.

"I was almost lost": Tennessee Claflin testimony at the trial *Roxanna Claflin v. Colonel James Harvey Blood,* Essex Market Police Court (May 15, 1871); *BTS,* Scrapbook II; *World* (May 17, 1871).

## Chapter 10   Draw Its Fangs

110  "This species of legislation": Eric Foner, p. 245.

"the rising young star of America": *Argus* (April 18, 1866); *BTS,* Scrapbook IV; *Independent* (February 29, 1866). Tilton's suggestion was endorsed by William Lloyd Garrison in editorials in the *Independent* the following month. In aligning himself with the Radical Republicans, Tilton wrote, "I shall endeavor to make and keep the *Independent* a member of Congress during the winter." Theodore Tilton to Thaddeus Stevens, Papers of Thaddeus Stevens, Library of Congress.

111 "I have argued constantly": Elizabeth Cady Stanton to Susan B. Anthony (August 11, 1865), *EYM*, Vol. 2, p. 105; *ECS & SBA*, 1865.

"even if it meant": Stampp, p. 116.

112 "to take control of the city": *Mass Violence in America: Memphis Riots and Massacres*, Facsimile Edition, House Report No. 101, U.S. 39th Congress, First Session (New York: Arno Press, 1969), p. 20.

"spontaneous": Ibid.

"One good result of the Memphis Riot": Meriwether, p. 91.

"They are the natural terriers": *Independent* (May 4, 1865).

113 "Mrs. President, this convention is" and ff.: *HWS*, Vol. 2, p. 155.

"According to the programme": Ibid., p. 154.

"You may . . . ask me" and ff.: Ibid., pp. 161, 162.

114 "There is neither Jew nor Greek" and ff.: Ibid.

"In the midst of" and ff.: Ibid., p. 167.

"I remember that": Ibid.

116 "praying for the enfranchisement": Harper, p. 323.

"I would rather cut off": Katharine Anthony, p. 193.

"What does ail Susan?" and ff.: Ibid.

"Oh, Susan" and ff.: Ibid.

"the most passionate affection": Ibid., p. 176.

117 "almost every day": Ibid., p. 177.

"her vim, her energy": Sanborn, p. 318.

"the possession of her soul": Katharine Anthony, p. 199.

118 "I must buy butter": Elizabeth Cady Stanton to Elizabeth Smith Miller (October 22, 1866); *ECS & SBA*, 1866; Stanton and Blatch, p. 115; Theodore Tilton, *Elizabeth Cady Stanton: Eminent Woman of the Age* (Hartford, CT: S. M. Batts & Co., 1869), p. 354; Griffith, p. 126.

"I only *scold* now": Susan B. Anthony to Antoinette Brown Blackwell (September 4, 1858), Griffith, p. 96.

"the people": Stampp, p. 114.

"much excited": Eric Foner, p. 276.

"the people of the South": Ibid.

"I say Thaddeus Stevens": Stampp, p. 133. Hans L. Trefousse, *Andrew Johnson: A Biography* (New York: W. W. Norton, 1989), p. 244. The Trefousse quote differs: "I say Thaddeus Stevens of Pennsylvania; I say Charles Sumner of Massachusetts; I say Wendell Phillips of Massachusetts."

"vulgar, vindictive and": Stampp, p. 114.

"The people have been witness": *Independent* (September 13, 1866); Trefousse, p. 266.

119 "If they [the Negroes] have": Henry Ward Beecher, *Patriotic Addresses*, p. 741; Rugoff, *The Beechers*, p. 395. The most detailed account of the so-called "Cleveland letter" affair appears in *Beecher to Special Committee of the Soldiers' and Sailors' Convention* (August 30, 1866), reprinted in *Theodore Tilton v. Henry Ward Beecher* (McDivitt Campbell and Company, 1875), pp. 476, 477, New York Public Library, Tucker-Sachs Collection.

"unqualified endorsement": *New York Times* (September 3, 1866).

"He has done more harm": *Independent* (September 6, 1866).

"During the first three": *Independent* (October 25, 1866); Hibben, p. 174.

"the worst candidate possible": Ibid.

"The spectacle at the": Ibid.

"full pardon": Louis M. Starr, *Bohemian Brigade: Civil War Newsmen in Action* (New York: Knopf, 1954), p. 316.

"the weeping bosom of his family": Hibben, p. 168.

## Chapter 11   A Dangerous Man

122   "with which to save": Philip S. Foner, *The Life and Writings of Frederick Douglass,* Vol. 4, pp. 21–22.

"in a manner which indicated" and ff.: Ibid., pp. 25, 241.

"The President no more expected . . . those damned sons of bitches" and ff.: Philip Ripley, private secretary to President Johnson, to Manton Marble (February 8, 1866), Marble Papers, Library of Congress; Trefousse, *Andrew Johnson,* p. 242.

123   "but not under such conditions": Buhle and Buhle, Vol. 2, p. 397.

"Gentlemen, with all respect" and ff.: *Life and Times of Frederick Douglass, Written by Himself,* ed. Rayford W. Logan (New York: Collier Books, 1962), pp. 397–399; ibid., Vol. 2, pp. 330, 331.

"Philadelphia Full of Miscegenists" and ff.: Stampp, p. 116; Frederick Douglass, *Life and Times of Frederick Douglass* (New York: Citadel Press, 1983), p. 386. Facsimile Edition.

"ashamed and afraid": Ibid., p. 397; Buhle and Buhle, Vol. 2, p. 331.

"I was the ugly": Ibid.

"He came to me in": Douglass, ibid., p. 398; Buhle and Buhle, ibid.

124   "A good many people here": Thaddeus Stevens to Dr. Kelley (May 5, 1870), Papers of Thaddeus Stevens, Stampp, p. 26.

"Miss Dickinson, Mr. Tilton and": Douglass, *Life and Times,* p. 405.

125   "By law December 18, 1866": In the South many former slaves knew nothing of the Thirteenth Amendment (submitted to Congress February 1, 1865, and ratified December 18, 1865), and their former masters kept them ignorant for a year, until the eve of December 18, 1866.

126   "I never thought that Abraham": TT to ET, Springfield, Illinois (December 20, 1866), *BTS.*

"The more I think of": TT to ET, Akron, Ohio (December 2, 1866), *BTS.*

" 'vile women' ": The concept of a "vile woman" used here and in the following chapters is explained in a letter, Isabella Beecher Hooker to Mary Livermore (March 15, 1871), *IBH.* Such a woman, commonly a prostitute or one of loose sexual behavior, was considered both seductive and dangerous. Examples of the day were contained in frequent sermons citing how Samson was shorn of his hair and destroyed by the "vile woman" Delilah, and in the accepted wisdom of the day that prostitutes who came to a bad end deserved their fate.

"Men and women who": TT to ET, on the cars, northern Indiana (December 7, 1866), *BTS.*

127   "rein and curb": Henry Ward Beecher, *Norwood: or Village Life in New England* (New York: J. B. Ford, 1868), p. 307.

"If love was proper": Second statement of Frank Moulton, civil trial, 1875, *BTS, CT.*

"I believe that I have": TT to ET (December 31, 1866), *Chicago Tribune,* New York Public Library Scrapbook IV.

"totally and thoroughly" and ff.: TT to ET, Altoona, Pennsylvania (November 26, 1866), *BTS.*

"falling into sin" and ff.: Lib (Elizabeth) Tilton statement to Plymouth Church Committee, 1875; also partially quoted in Marshall, p. 189.

128   "I live in profound wonder": ET to TT (January 11, 1867), *BTS.*

"No temptation or fascination": Ibid. (February 3, 1868).

"I am afraid!": Ibid. (February 20, 1867).

"I think any man": TT to ET (December 12, 1866), *BTS.*

"her sensuality" and ff.: Lib (Elizabeth) Tilton statement to Plymouth Church Committee, 1874.

128 "When Theodore said" and ff.: Ibid.
129 "I tried to give him a full accounting" and ff.: Ibid.
130 "Now that the *other* man": TT to ET (December 27, 1866), *BTS.*
"My espoused saint" and ff.: Ibid. (December 6, 1866).
"During the early part": ET to TT (January 14, 1867), *BTS.*
"My Own True Mate": ET to TT (December 28, 1866); *BTS.* In Rugoff, this letter appears in slightly different form. I chose the version from the Frank Moulton exhibit submitted to the courts in 1874.
131 "I like Mr. Beecher": TT to ET (December 30, 1866), Akron, Ohio, *BTS.* (Misdated in New York Public Library Scrapbook VI as December 2, 1866.)

### Chapter 12   Written in Fire

132 "This is a critical" and ff.: Elizabeth Cady Stanton to Martha Coffin Wright (June 27, 1867), Martha Coffin Wright correspondence, Sophia Smith Collection, Smith College. Abbreviated as *MCW;* Stanton and Blatch, p. 116; Lutz, pp. 140, 141; *HWS,* Vol. 2, p. 284.
133 "The ballot and the bullet": Another version of this appears in Harper, where it is stated as: "Certainly, Mr. Greeley, just as you fought in the late war—at the point of a goose quill." However, in the original letter Elizabeth Cady Stanton sent to Martha Coffin Wright (June 27, 1867) in Albany, New York, she writes, "Yes, we are ready to fight, sir, just as you did in the late war, by sending our substitutes." I used Stanton's own version.
"Mr. Chairman, I hold": Lutz, *Created Equal,* p. 141.
"Your committee does not": Ibid., p. 142.
"Prepare for a storm" and ff.: Elizabeth Cady Stanton to Emily Howland, New York (September 1, 1867), *ECS & SBA;* Stanton and Blatch, Vol. 2, pp. 116–118. The version that appears in Vol. 2 is abridged, and the text altered. I have used a longer and more detailed version.
"I saw the reporters" and ff.: Stanton and Blatch, Vol. 2, p. 117. In Lutz, p. 142, the conversation is as follows:
"You are so tenacious about your own name. Why did you not inscribe my wife's maiden, Mary Cheney Greeley, on the petition?"
"Because I wanted all the world to know that it was the wife of Horace Greeley who protested against her husband's report."
134 "Well, I understand the animus": *HWS,* Vol. 2, p. 287.
"I can not sign": Ibid., p. 317; also quoted in *The Elizabeth Cady Stanton-Susan B. Anthony Reader: Correspondence, Writings, Speeches,* ed. Ellen Carol DuBois (Boston: Northeastern University Press), 1981, p. 119.
"Would Horace Greeley": *ECS & SBA* (May 10, 1867), Reel 12:181.
"I am not alone": Elizabeth Cady Stanton to Susan B. Anthony, New York (August 22, 1864), *ECS & SBA;* Stanton and Blatch, Vol. 2, p. 100.
135 "Man has been molding": Address of Elizabeth Cady Stanton, AERA Convention (May 15, 1869), *ECS & SBA.*
"I wish you were a boy!": *EYM,* p. 23.
136 "This is the country": Elizabeth Cady Stanton to Henry Stanton from Kansas. In Lutz, *Created Equal,* p. 150. The letter reads "contracted" Eastern existence, but on microfilm I read the word as "constricted" and have used it accordingly.
137 "low-down nigger men" and ff.: Lutz, *Created Equal,* p. 151; Alice Stone Blackwell, *Lucy Stone, Pioneer of Woman's Rights* (Boston: Little, Brown, 1930), p. 212.
"a charlatan" and ff.: Griffith, p. 130.
"mortified and astonished beyond measure": Ibid.; Katharine Anthony, p. 217.
"Not one leading politician": Susan B. Anthony to Anna Dickinson, *ECS & SBA* Reel 12.

138 "All the old friends": *ECS & SBA* (January 1, 1868), Reel 12; Harper, p. 295.
"Not lack of brains" and ff.: Lutz, *Created Equal,* p. 153.
"Mr. Train . . . has some" and ff.: Elizabeth Cady Stanton to Martha Coffin Wright (January 8, 1868), *MCW;* repeated in Stanton and Blatch, Vol. 2, pp. 119–120; *The Revolution* (January 29, 1868); Griffith, p. 130.
"The old religious teachings": TT to ET (February 12, 1867), *BTS.*
"I have no ambition": TT to ET (December 2, 1866), *BTS.*
"I was struck with a little": TT to ET, Alton, Illinois (December 23, 1866), *BTS.*

139 "The *Banner of Light,* optimistically estimated": *Banner of Light* (January 18, 1868), New York Public Library, Manuscript Collection.
"How long have you" and ff.: Testimony of Colonel James H. Blood, *Roxanna Claflin v. James Blood,* Essex Market Police Court (May 15, 1871).

140 "By inspiration": *GAT,* p. 18.
"temporary sojourn": Ibid., p. 12.
"Your work is about to begin" and ff.: *Victoria Woodhull Prophesy, Boston Post* (October 20, 1876), fragmentary autobiography, Woodhull Reel 1, *VCWM.*

141 "Who are you?" and ff.: Ibid.

## Chapter 13  To Equal Account

143 "(now called Park Avenue)": Park Avenue was the name given in 1860 to Fourth Avenue between Thirty-fourth and Thirty-sixth Streets, but by 1868 the avenue was referred to as Park Avenue all the way up to Forty-second Street.

146 "Office Female Physician" and ff.: Clifford Browder, *The Wickedest Woman in New York: Madame Restell, The Abortionist* (Hamden, CT: Archon Books, 1988), pp. 117, 118.
"*The Revolution*": The following year Stanton and Anthony came under such criticism from the Sorosis Society and other groups housed in the Women's Bureau that they moved *The Revolution* to offices on Park Place.
"fit for an Empress's crown": *The Revolution* (December 31, 1868).

147 "Oh, you've come about" and ff.: *VCWM,* Box 1; Johnston, p. 42; from Woodhull's account, *Boston Post* (May 18, 1872).

148 "What do I care": Barbara Goldsmith, *Little Gloria . . . Happy at Last* (New York: Knopf, 1980), p. 77, from Allen Churchill, *The Splendor Seekers* (New York: Grosset & Dunlap, 1974), p. 82.
"Female physicians": Allan Keller, *Scandalous Lady: The Life and Times of Madame Restell, New York's Most Notorious Abortionist* (New York: Atheneum Encore Editions, 1981), p. 11; Browder, 1988, p. 73; James C. Mohr, *Abortion in America: The Origins and Evolution of National Policy, 1800–1900* (New York: Oxford, 1978), p. 197, illustrates these personal advertisements.
"quackery and charlatanry" and ff.: G. J. Barker-Benfield, *The Horrors of the Half-Known Life: Male Attitudes Toward Women and Sexuality in 19th-Century America* (New York: Harper & Row), 1976, p. 28; Mohr, pp. 92–96.
"heroic medicine": James Harvey Young, *The Medical Messiahs: A Social History of Health Quackery in Twentieth-Century America* (Princeton, NJ: Princeton University Press, 1967), p. 18, provides many sources for this and a specific description. Barker-Benfield, pp. 61–69, provides a concise explanation, titled "Midwives to Gynecologists," on how medical doctors tried to drive women from the practice of female medicine and childbirth.
"rest cure": This cure, identified with Dr. S. Weir Mitchell, is explained in Barker-Benfield, p. 130.
"recycled and taught" and ff.: Ibid., taken from the Reverend John Todd, "A Sermon Before the American Board of Commissioners for Foreign Missions," in Pittsburgh,

Pennsylvania, on October 5, 1869 (Boston: T. R. Marvin & Son, 1869), pp. 259–267, 277–279.

"Allied to the sexual organs": Barker-Benfield, p. 277, taken from "Our Children" by Augustus Kinsley Gardner, p. 20.

"over-exciting the sexual appetites": Barker-Benfield, p. 124.

149 "in close proximity to": Ibid., pp. 132, 270. A full explanation of the unnatural and contaminated nature of women's sexuality appears on pp. 229–307.

"as pretty as the dimple": Ibid., p. 132.

150 "According to the talk" and ff.: *The Diary of George Templeton Strong: Post-War Years 1835–1875,* ed. Allan Nevins and Milton Halsey Thomas (New York: MacMillan, 1952), Vol. 2, p. 42.

151 "The fashionable *demi-monde*": George Ellington, *The Women of New York, or the Underworld of the Great City* (New York: New York Book Company, 1869), p. 243. Reprinted by Arno Press, New York, 1971.

"There are many popular fallacies": "Tried as by Fire, or The True and The False, Socially. An Oration Delivered by Victoria C. Woodhull in All the Principal Cities and Towns of the Country During an Engagement of One Hundred and Fifty Consecutive Nights To Audiences Together Numbering A Quarter of a Million of People" in *The Victoria Woodhull Reader,* ed. Madeleine B. Stern (Weston, MA: M & S Press, 1974), Part 5: Sociology, p. 31.

153 "$3.00 to $10.00 a week": *WCW* (February 11, 1871).

"We are told that prostitution" and ff.: "Tried as by Fire; or, The True and The False, Socially." This speech, delivered on 150 consecutive nights, was first presented at the National Spiritualist Association convention in Boston September 1872. Stern, Part 5: Sociology, pp. 22, 23.

154 *A Gentleman's Guide* is available at the New York Historical Society Library (by appointment).

## Chapter 14   Consult the Spirits

157 "The old man is bound": The Vanderbilt Will Case Clippings, November 1877, New York Public Library, Room 315.

"I would never cross": Wayne Andrews, *The Vanderbilt Legend* (New York: Harcourt, Brace and Co., 1941), p. 8; Edwin P. Hoyt, *The Vanderbilts and Their Fortunes,* p. 177.

"lived nearly seventy-four years": *New York Tribune* (August 24, 1868).

158 "When I have to give up smoking": Wayne Andrews, p. 143.

"old boy" and ff.: Hoyt, p. 187.

"a thousand" and ff.: Treat, p. 9.

"Phebe Hand Van der Bilt": Although Victoria Woodhull was in touch with the commodore's mother, she had died fourteen years earlier, on January 22, 1854.

"After all, they're not Vanderbilts": Wayne Andrews, p. 30.

159 "Who the devil": Van Deusen, p. 423.

"If this printing press": W. A. Swanberg, *Jim Fisk: The Career of an Improbable Rascal* (New York: Charles Scribner's Sons, 1959), p. 41.

160 "going astray": *New York Herald* (November 25, 1871); Swanberg, p. 256; Ellington, pp. 37, 38.

161 "I want more": *New York Herald* (January 9, 1872), p. 1, in an account of the death of Jim Fisk.

162 "she obtained not only Fisk's money": *VCWM,* Box 3; *Argus* interview with Victoria Woodhull (December 18, 1872).

"It's bound to go up" and ff.: Commodore Vanderbilt to Susan A. King. Commodore Vanderbilt's remark, "Do as I do. Consult the spirits," was the seed from which this book grew. In the sections dealing with Commodore Vanderbilt I used material from my own *Little Gloria . . . Happy at Last*, which in turn was based on many sources, including biographies of Commodore Vanderbilt by Wayne Andrews, A. Croffut, and Edwin P. Hoyt and the court testimony of the so-called "Great Vanderbilt Will Contest," 1877.

163 "great luxury" and ff.: TT to ET, Newport, Rhode Island (August 23, 1866), *BTS*.

"I was not a happy woman": *Notable American Women 1607–1950*, Vol. 1, p. 444.

"Winslow's Soothing Syrup" is called "Dr. Winslow's Soothing Syrup" in Griffith, p. 133.

164 "Spiritual Wife": a full explanation of this philosophy appears in Dixon's *Spiritual Wives*.

"a great friendship": ET to TT (February 24, 1868), *BTS*.

"It is like the breath": Henry Ward Beecher, *Norwood*, p. 40.

"It would seem": Ibid., p. 171.

"My endeavor was entirely": Lib (Elizabeth) Tilton to Henry Ward Beecher; Doyle, p. 524; New York Public Library Scrapbook VII.

"I am hungry to see your children" and ff.: ET to TT (January 13, 1867), *BTS;* statement of Lib (Elizabeth) Tilton, *PCH.*

165 "You will be amused": ET to TT (March 13, 1868), *BTS*.

"a terrible wrestling" and ff.: TT to ET, Empire House, Akron, Ohio (January 10, 1870), *BTS*.

"a paroxysmal kiss": statement of Henry Ward Beecher, 1875, *CT.*

166 "I regard my": TT to ET, Crawfordsville, Indiana (February 9, 1868), *BTS*.

"Theodore, do you *know*": ET to TT (February 8, 1868), *BTS*.

"Innocence or guilt": TT to ET, on the cars from Independence to Cedar Rapids, Iowa (April 4, 1868), *BTS*.

"My brain has run wild": TT to ET, At Your Desk (April 6, 1868), *BTS*.

"Your last note reminded me": TT to ET, Washington (March 26, 1868), *BTS*.

167 "I have less faith": Ibid. (March 21, 1868).

168 "The country is going to the devil": This abbreviated account of the impeachment trial of President Andrew Johnson was drawn from many sources, including articles in the *Independent*, March 23, April 4 and 15, May 2 and 10, 1868; Eric Foner, pp. 333–337; Trefousse, *Andrew Johnson*, pp. 311–334; The Papers of Benjamin F. Butler, Library of Congress, Manuscript Division.

169 "Filled with sunshine": Harper, p. 200.

170 "Do you believe that" and ff.: Cross-examination testimony of Theodore Tilton civil trial, 1875, *CT.*

"A Day Memorable": October 10, 1868, diary entry (entered into evidence *CT,* 1875) quoted in many newspapers.

171 "The man who has been wallowing": Henry Ward Beecher's sermon, December 20, 1868; Rugoff, *The Beechers*, p. 476.

## Chapter 15 We Are Ready. We Are Prepared.

172 "Twenty-year-old Hester Vaughn": The case involving Hester Vaughn began on Friday, December 25, 1868. My account is drawn from articles in *The Revolution* over five days: January 21, 1869, January 28, 1869, February 18, 1869, May 12, 1869, November 12, 1869. All are from the Sophia Smith collection, Smith College. See also Kathleen Barry, *Susan B. Anthony: A Biography of a Singular Feminist* (New York: New York University Press, 1988), pp. 216–217; Lutz, *Created Equal*, pp. 162–163; Ellen Carol DuBois, *Feminism and Suffrage: The Emergence of an Independent Women's Movement in America 1848–1869* (Ithaca, NY: Cornell University Press, 1978), pp. 145–147, 179; *New York Tribune* and *New York Herald*.

In all contemporary accounts, including that of Anna Dickinson herself, the name of the doctor involved was Dr. Susan A. Smith. However, in Harper and in several other later accounts the doctor is referred to as Dr. Lozier. In the *ECS & SBA* microfilm index, the spelling of Vaughn is Vaughan. However, in all other accounts, including court records, the name is spelled as I have spelled it.

173 "the Queen of the Lyceum": Chester, p. 86.

174 "so I suppose thee'll": Ibid., p. 113.

"splendor on": Louis M. Starr, *Bohemian Brigade: Civil War Newsmen in Action* (New York: Knopf, 1954), p. 140.

"impending marriage to": Whitelaw Reid to Susan Dickinson (January 21, 1870), Papers of Anna E. Dickinson, Library of Congress, Microfilm Edition, 14:72.

175 "her love," "her darling," and "her chick a dee dee": these as well as other expressions of affection occur in such letters as Susan B. Anthony to Anna Dickinson, *ECS & SBA*, Reel 12 (July 12, 1867; February 15, 1868).

"My soul goes out": Susan B. Anthony to Anna Dickinson (January 15, 1868), *ECS & SBA*.

176 "I get two dollars" and ff.: Alma Lutz, *Susan B. Anthony: Rebel, Crusader, Humanitarian* (Boston: Beacon Press, 1959); Barry, pp. 211, 212; account in *The Revolution* by Elizabeth Cady Stanton (January 8, 1868), pp. 1–12, differs slightly from Barry's source. Stanton wrote,

> These are the prices paid to the lower classes who do the world's real work: for heavy cloth pantaloons, lined, finished and pressed shopwork, eighteen to twenty cents a pair; for linen coats with three pockets and six buttonholes, a dollar a dozen, eight cents each; for shirts, best quality, a dollar fifty a dozen; for shirts, second quality, retailing at two dollars each, a dollar twenty-five a dozen; for shirts, third quality, seventy-five cents a dozen; for fancy flannel shirts, lapel or breast, turned over collar, cuffs, gussets, buttonholes, six cents each. For jumpers (blue overshirts) ending at waist in a band with long sleeves, five cents a dozen.

"Women are starving today": *The Revolution*, April 22, 1869.

"The male element is": *The Revolution* (June 3, 1869); *HWS*, pp. 334–335. Stanton believed that women could not rely on the support of men. She wrote, "We must not trust any of you. All these men . . . have pushed us aside for years. . . . We are right in our present position. We demand in the reconstruction, suffrage for all the citizens of the Republic."

178 "We are now in the midst": Eleanor Flexner, *Century of Struggle: The Woman's Rights Movement in the United States* (Cambridge, MA: Belknap Press of Harvard University Press, 1959), p. 150; Lucy Stone to Olympia Brown (January 6, 1868).

"Omit my name": *The Revolution* (May 1, 1869; May 8, 1869).

"I have written to": Mary Livermore to Susan B. Anthony (April 4, 1869); Harper, Vol. I, p. 321; *HWS*, Vol. 2, p. 396.

179 "generous, sweet atmosphere will prevail": *HWS*, Vol. 2, p. 380. The rest of this account of the meeting is on pp. 380–392, 397–401. Elizabeth Cady Stanton's speech is on pp. 348–356; Frederick Douglass's speech appears on pp. 382, 383; Lucy Stone's speech appears on pp. 384–389. These scenes also appear in Harper, Vol. I, pp. 323–325 and Lutz, *Created Equal*, pp. 162–165. Stephen Foster was a farmer and is not to be confused with the famous composer of the same name, who died in 1864.

180 "The Republican party to-day congratulates": Stanton was primarily directing her protest against *male* domination rather than berating the Negro. Her sympathy for Negro women had been evident when she wrote, "The Negro's skin and the woman's sex are both [used as] *prima facie* evidence that they were intended to be in subjection to the white Saxon man." The battle to enfranchise black males before giving the vote to women hurt black women who had been included in the woman suffrage movement. It was at this point that Elizabeth Cady Stanton began arguing for the enfranchisement of "women of wealth and education," i.e., white women.

183 "This howl comes from": *HWS,* Vol 2, p. 390.

184 "I am unwilling": Ibid., p. 389.

"the Hutchinson family": For a short biography of this abolitionist family see *HWS,* Vol. 2, p. 398. Roseville, New Jersey, referred to as the residence of Abby Hutchinson Patton and her husband, is now part of Newark, New Jersey.

"grand and secret love" and ff.: Andrea Moore Kerr, *Lucy Stone: Speaking Out for Equality* (New Brunswick, NJ: Rutgers University Press, 1992), p. 144.

"I can say nothing" and ff.: Elizabeth Blackwell to Emily Blackwell (August 20, 1869), ibid.

"Mrs. P." and ff.: Emily Blackwell to Elizabeth Blackwell (September 14, 1869), ibid.

"butterfly streak": George Washington Blackwell to Elizabeth Blackwell (February 18, 1870), ibid., p. 149.

185 "I feel crushed": Lucy Stone to Antoinette Brown Blackwell (October 31, 1869), ibid., p. 145.

"The American Equal Rights Association": Harper, Vol. 1, p. 328; Barry, p. 150; Andrea Moore Kerr, p. 141.

186 "Having been drilled" and ff.: DuBois, *Feminism and Suffrage,* p. 191.

## Chapter 16   Soup for Three

187 "I have not authorized": This account of the attempt to corner the gold market is drawn from House Report no. 31, 41st Congress, Second Session, 1870, The Investigation into the Causes of the Gold Panic, Library of Congress. See also Swanberg, pp. 134–142; Maury Klein, *The Life and Legend of Jay Gould* (Baltimore: Johns Hopkins University Press, 1986), pp. 99–116. Victoria Woodhull's appearance and involvement is detailed in the *New York Sun* (October 1, 1869) and *TS,* pp. 49, 50.

191 "a ladies' drawing room": *New York Herald* (February 13, 1870).

"Simply to Thy Cross I Cling": *TS,* p. 49.

"Madame de Ford . . . profit" and ff.: *WCW* (February 3, 1873).

192 "All gentlemen will state their business": Ibid., p. 52.

193 "If I'd a married her" and ff.: Goldsmith, *Little Gloria,* p. 79, from Wayne Andrews, p. 145.

"Just wait until we" and ff.: *The Revolution* (March 10, 1870).

"If you wear that": *VWCM, New York Sun* (October 8, 1870).

194 "We assumed a gentleman" and ff.: *VWCM,* Box 3; also, *TS,* p. 63.

## Chapter 17   A Hard Place

196 "with their sorrows": *ECS & SBA* (June 27, 1870); Stanton and Blatch, p. 127.

"*Innocents Abroad*": Published in July 1869.

"measure up" and ff.: Isabella Beecher Hooker to John Hooker (June 27, 1852), *IBH.* The sources for this section on Isabella Beecher Hooker and other vital material were initially found in Jeanne Boydston, Mary Kelly, and Anne Margolis, *The Limits of Sisterhood: The Beecher Sisters on Women's Rights and Woman's Sphere* (Chapel Hill: University of North Carolina Press, 1988), pp. 80–111, which led me to the Harriet Beecher Stowe Center (formerly the Stowe-Day Foundation), in Hartford, Connecticut, and to the Isabella Beecher Hooker Project, containing heretofore unpublished letters and diaries of Isabella Beecher Hooker. Isabella Beecher Hooker is referred to as Belle, or as Bell, by family members; usually Belle is used.

197 "I do regret that": Isabella Beecher Hooker to John Hooker (August 30, 1859), *IBH.*

"I should enjoy reading": Isabella Beecher Hooker to John Hooker (February 21, 1847), *IBH.*

197 "At sixteen and a half": Isabella Beecher Hooker to Rachel Burton (January 25, 1859), *IBH*.

"Oh my *soul*" and ff.: Isabella Beecher Hooker to John Hooker (January 24, 1860), *IBH*.

"gently and persuasively": Journal entry, Isabella Beecher Hooker (March 17, 1852), *IBH*.

"She was frightened" and ff.: Ibid.

"If absolute power": Isabella Beecher Hooker to John Hooker (January 11, 1849), *IBH*.

"I would give an individual": Mrs. John Hooker, *Shall Women Vote? A Matrimonial Dialogue* (February 18, 1860), unpublished, *IBH*.

198 "A Mother's Letters to a Daughter": *Putnam's Magazine,* November-December 1868, *IBH*.

"Mrs. Stanton . . . is a noble woman": Isabella Beecher Hooker to Caroline M. Severance (August 27, 1869), *IBH; Lutz, Created Equal,* p. 182; Harper, p. 332.

"The True Story of Lady Byron's Life": *Atlantic Monthly* (October 1869); Rugoff, *The Beechers,* p. 526.

"revolting, obscene garbage": Rugoff, *The Beechers,* p. 526; *Independent* (August 26, 1869).

200 "worthy of a place" and ff.: Elizabeth Cady Stanton to Isabella Beecher Hooker (September 23, 1869), *ECS & SBA,* Reel 13.

"I did my best": (October 29, 1869), *ECS & SBA,* Reel 14; Lutz, *Created Equal,* pp. 182–183; Harper, Vol. 1, pp. 332, 325.

"injuriously and foolishly keeps" and ff.: Emily Blackwell to Elizabeth Blackwell (October 11, 1869), Andrea Moore Kerr, p. 145.

"underhanded": Boydston et al., p. 215.

"I *hope* that you": Lucy Stone to Elizabeth Cady Stanton (October 19, 1869), Andrea Moore Kerr, pp. 145–146.

201 "so dreadful an incubus": Lucy Stone to Antoinette Brown Blackwell (October 31, 1869), Andrea Moore Kerr, p. 146.

"hypocrites" and ff.: *The Revolution* (October 28, 1869); Andrea Moore Kerr, p. 146; Susan B. Anthony quoted in *New York Tribune* (November 25, 1869).

"So help me, Heaven!": *ECS & SBA,* Reel 14; Lutz, *Created Equal,* p. 184; Lutz, *Susan B. Anthony,* p. 172; Katharine Anthony, p. 238.

"rashness for courage": *New York Tribune* (November 25, 1869), *ECS & SBA,* Reel 14; Griffith, p. 139.

203 "At 5:30 in the afternoon" and ff.: This account of McFarland's assassination of Richardson is drawn from many sources. George Cooper, *Lost Love: A True Story of Passion, Murder, and Justice in Old New York* (New York: Pantheon Books, 1994) is a study in depth, but I have favored the court records of Daniel McFarland's trial as well as contemporaneous accounts appearing in the *New York Times,* the *New York Herald, The Revolution,* the *Argus,* the *Brooklyn Eagle,* etc., and most notably the *New York Times* of November 26, 27, 1869, December 6, 13, 1869, and May 7 (triple sheet), 11, 12, 13, 14, 15, 1870. This case was emblematic of the wildly divergent views of the marriage and divorce laws of the day and called into question rigid Victorian mores. Starr's *Bohemian Brigade* provided material on Richardson's career and the background. Harper, Vol. 1, pp. 351–355, covers the Apollo Hall protest.

"He would lock himself": Trial affidavit of Abby Sage McFarland.

"Lucia P. Calhoun": Calhoun was self-supporting and had a keen awareness that other members of her sex needed to earn money in a respectable way. At the end of the war, she began writing political articles for the *New York Tribune* along with notes on the glamorous activities of society. She was one of Hester Vaughn's most eloquent defenders.

204 "I am in need of a surgeon" and ff.: *New York Tribune, New York Sun,* and *New York Times* (November 26, 27, 28, 29, 30, 1869).

"Do you think I will live?" and ff.: *New York Times* (November 27, 1869), p. 2.

205 "Henry Ward Beecher marry him": *New York Times* (May 7, 1870), p. 2. When Beecher spoke at Richardson's funeral on December 22, criticism had already begun to mount. Beecher defended Richardson by comparing him to "a lion who in his strength and fastness is able to defend himself, but no sooner has the cruel arrow of the huntsman laid him low than he is set upon by every wild thing, every fly, every crawling worm."

"Consider, married men of New York!": *New York Tribune* (November 26, 1869). That the tide turned against Beecher was evident in the mounting criticism. Reverend J. M. Pullman of the Sixth Universalist Church on Thirty-fifth Street expressed the morality of the day when he wrote,

> Richardson the meddler was a social outlaw. If he got hurt in going where he should not, people, although they would not uphold the man who fired the shot, would agree that a man who cared for his home and believed in its purity should be allowed the natural justice of a revenging blow. It was that instinct that justified it. (*New York Times,* December 6, 1869, p. 8)

206 "I took every": *New York Times, New York Herald* (December 11, 1869); Marshall, pp. 561, 562.

"Once in a while" and ff.: Chester, p. 118.

"Marriage today is": Lutz, *Created Equal,* p. 190.

"Loose women" and ff.: *Woman's Journal,* 1870; Andrea Moore Kerr, pp. 156, 157.

207 "It is not good": Lucy Stone to Emily Blackwell (April 13, 1870), Andrea Moore Kerr, p. 151.

"has come to look upon" and ff.: Isabella Beecher Hooker to Susan Howard (January 2, 1870), *IBH.*

"Susie, you are in": Ibid.

208 "From what little I have": John Hooker to Isabella Beecher Hooker (January 5, 1870), *IBH;* Boydston et al., p. 293.

### Chapter 18    The Evangel

209 "wondrous dome a flood" and ff.: *New York Sun* (April 7, 1870).

"Modern Palace Beautiful": *New York Star* (April 15, 1870).

210 "Oh Doc, you poor fellow!": *Chicago Mail* (May 4, 1892), p. 1, col. 4; *VCWM,* Box 3, Victoria Woodhull.

"it costs us over": *New York Herald* (August 10, 1870); Johnston, p. 58.

"Your work is about to begin": *Boston Post* (October 20, 1876); see also *Banner of Light,* Boston (November 20, 1876).

"New Age" and ff.: Stern, *The Pantarch,* p. 5.

"a grand domestic revolution": Ibid., p. 82.

"Eclectic Medical College": Ibid., p. 99.

211 "the bereaved wife": Carol Farley Kessler, *Elizabeth Stuart Phelps* (Boston: Twayne Publishers, 1982), p. 31.

"heresy": Ibid., p. 33.

"The name of the gentleman was" and ff.: Chester, pp. 116, 117; Whitelaw Reid to Anna Dickinson (March 12, 1870), Papers of Anna E. Dickinson, 14:73.

212 "at night": *Washington, D.C., Daily Morning Chronicle,* interview with Victoria Woodhull (October 24, 1873), *VCWM,* Boston.

"an opportunity to feast" and ff.: Beecher-Tilton correspondence, newspaper articles, clippings, pamphlets, etc. from the offices of the *Independent.* Tucker-Sachs correspondence, Scrapbooks I–VIII, New York Public Library, Manuscript Division, Scrapbook V.

213 "edited in one world": *GAT,* 1871, p. 27.

214 "the ruler of the whole world": Isabella Beecher Hooker to Susan B. Anthony (March 11, 14, 1871), *ECS & SBA,* Reel 15; Boydston et al., p. 206.

"I am the evangel": The quote that appeared in *WCW* (November 2, 1872), p. 12, read, "I am the evangel—I am a savior if you would but see it. But I, too, come not to bring peace but a sword." This appears in slightly different form in Stern's *Victoria Woodhull Reader,* p. 13.

"beg at the pockets": Isabella Beecher Hooker interview with John B. Martin, Sherman House (May 1, 1892), *VCWM,* Reel 2.

215   "The Reverend May has adopted" and ff.: Buhle and Buhle, Vol. 2, p. 422.

"Like a shark" and ff.: Elizabeth Cady Stanton to Martha Coffin Wright, Tenafly, New Jersey (March 21, 1871), *ECS & SBA,* Reel 15; Stanton and Blatch, Vol. 2., p. 131.

"the husband's right" and ff.: Lutz, *Created Equal,* pp. 190, 191.

216   "I hate the whole doctrine": Lutz, *Susan B. Anthony,* p. 142.

"No, no," and ff.: *ECS & SBA,* Reel 15; Katharine Anthony, p. 239; Lutz, *Created Equal,* p. 175.

"I will form a new": Stone's account of reconciliation, National American Woman Suffrage Association Collection, Library of Congress; Andrea Moore Kerr, p. 151.

"grand times" and ff.: Elizabeth Cady Stanton to Martha Coffin Wright, *ECS & SBA,* Reel 15; Griffith, p. 145; Andrea Moore Kerr, p. 153.

217   "unconstitutional": Andrea Moore Kerr, p. 272.

"popular man": Buhle and Buhle, Vol. 2, p. 427.

"If Anna Dickinson will": *ECS & SBA,* Reel 14; Harper, Vol. 1, p. 361.

"was like signing my own death-warrant": (May 22, 1870), *ECS & SBA,* Reel 14; Harper, Vol. 1, p. 362.

"I feel a great calm": *ECS & SBA,* Reel 14; Anthony, pp. 244, 245; Harper, Vol. 1, p. 362.

"The Revolution is": Theodore Tilton to Anna Dickinson (June 1870), Anna Dickinson Papers, Letter no. 38.

218   "female demagogue" and ff.: William Lloyd Garrison to Theodore Tilton (April 5, 1870), Garrison Family Papers, Boston Public Library; Griffith, p. 119.

"stood firmly": *ECS & SBA,* Reel 23, quoted in Griffith, p. 142.

## Chapter 19   Your Child Is Not My Child

219   "One, two, three—jump,": Hibben, p. 200; *New York Tribune* (July 6, 1870), New York Public Library Scrapbook V.

220   "Beecher's boys.": Ibid. (December 21, 1869).

"desire" and ff.: Waller, p. 71.

"Lying in defense": Ibid., p. 81.

"second rate people": *Independent* (March 25, 1869).

"If we do not educate": *Independent* (December 2, 1869).

221   "There is no end" and ff.: Samuel Wilkeson to Jay Cooke (July 11, 1869; July 26, 1869); Ellis Paxson Oberholtzer, *Jay Cooke: Financier of the Civil War* (Philadelphia: George W. Jacobs, 1907), Vol. 2, pp. 120, 121.

"influencing the public": Hibben, p. 198.

222   "My friend, the time has come" and ff.: Marshall, p. 480.

"on this our glorious anniversary" and ff.: *New York Times* and *New York Herald* (July 8, 1870).

223   "I have come to tell you" and ff.: *PCH.* The alleged confession of Lib (Elizabeth) Tilton is drawn from Theodore Tilton's court testimony and his statement at the Plymouth Church hearing. It is repeated in Hibben, Marshall, and Doyle.

"affinity . . . to save her health": Lib (Elizabeth) Tilton's statement, *PCH;* Waller, p. 122; Marshall, p. 194.

"playfully reproached her" and ff.: Lib (Elizabeth) Tilton's statement, *PCH.*

224   "Henry Ward Beecher" and ff.: This account is drawn from *WCW* (November 2, 1872) and from *Victoria Woodhull's Complete and Detailed Version of the Beecher-Tilton Affair,* a pamphlet published by J. Bradley Adams, Washington, D.C., in Stern, *Victoria Wood-*

*hull Reader,* Section A, Sexual Relations, pp. 1–22. Elizabeth Cady Stanton corroborated this, saying that the story was "substantially true" but that she had not used the phrase "damned lecherous scoundrel."

226 "Mrs. Tilton told essentially the same": Elizabeth Cady Stanton to Isabella Beecher Hooker (November 3, 1873), *ECS & SBA,* Reel 16.

"a scoundrel" and ff.: This account is drawn from Theodore Tilton's civil court trial testimony (*CT*) and is repeated in Marshall, pp. 527–531, and in various newspapers of the day.

"Oh Theodore, Theodore! What shall I": ET to TT, written from Marietta, Ohio, to Brooklyn, New York (November 1870); *CT:* entered into evidence.

228 "So the harlot has returned!" and ff.: *CT;* Marshall, p. 536.

"Marriage without love": *Independent* (December 1, 1870).

"Women know their own wants": Blackwell, pp. 220, 221.

229 "the comfort of a paramour" and ff.: The following account is drawn from Tilton and Beecher's testimony in the civil trial, *CT.* It also appears in numerous newspapers and in Hibben, Marshall, and Doyle.

230 "all this torture" and ff.: Statement of Lib (Elizabeth) Tilton, *PCH.*

## Chapter 20  The Yawning Edge of Hell

232 "What is the meaning" and ff.: Testimony of Theodore Tilton, *CT,* also Theodore Tilton to Frank Moulton (February 7, 1871); Marshall, p. 260.

"If anybody in King's County" and ff.: *Independent* (September 26, 1870); Edwin W. Terry, *Theodore Tilton as Social Reformer, Radical Republican, Newspaper Editor, 1863–1872* (Ph.D. dissertation, St. John's University, 1971; University Microfilms International Dissertation Information Service, Ann Arbor, Michigan), p. 219.

"I understand what Mr. Tilton" and ff.: *BTS,* Scrapbook VI; *Brooklyn Eagle* (October 22, 1870).

233 "I will not mince words" and ff.: *Brooklyn Daily Union* (December 22, 1870).

"Then I surmise" and ff.: Testimony of Theodore Tilton (December 20, 1870), *CT.*

"In the nine years": Junius Henri Browne, *The Great Metropolis: A Mirror of New York* (Hartford, CT: American Publishing Co., 1870), p. 313.

234 "control federal patronage" and ff.: Waller, pp. 80, 86, 87; Harold Coffin Syrett, Ph.D., *The City of Brooklyn, 1865–1989: A Political History* (New York: Columbia University Press, 1944), p. 61.

235 "miscarriage" and ff.: Elizabeth Tilton to Laura Curtis Bullard (January 13, 1871), Doyle, p. 527.

"You infernal villain!": Letters of Mrs. Morse entered into evidence, *CT.* All the sources for the following events have been drawn largely from the testimony of Theodore Tilton, Henry Ward Beecher, Henry Bowen, and Frank Moulton during the civil trial found in Austin Abbot, *The Official Report of the Trial of Henry Ward Beecher With Notes and References* (New York: George W. Smith & Co., Law Booksellers and Publishers, 1875, 1876), 2 volumes, and in *BTS,* the New York Public Library Scrapbooks I–VIII, compiled in the offices of the *Independent.* They are repeated in Marshall, Doyle, Hibben, and Shaplen. All letters quoted were entered into evidence in the course of the trial.

239 "Dear Mr. Bowen, The understanding": December 21, 1870, made public when printed in the *New York Argus,* June 29, 1875, and later in transcripts of court testimony.

241 "Theodore, I am in a dream": Beecher was later to deny this wording but admitted that the news of Lib's confession "fell like a thunderbolt on me." See *CT* and Shaplen, p. 92.

245 "My Dear Friend Moulton": Full letter not entered in court trial but printed in its entirety in the *New York Times* (July 30, 1874).

## Chapter 21   The Woodhull Memorial

246 "I shall go to": Isabella Beecher Hooker to Susan B. Anthony (1870), *ECS & SBA,* Reel 14; Harper, p. 357. (Paxton Hibben incorrectly cites this as Susan B. Anthony to Isabella Beecher Hooker, p. 232.)

"Let us exalt Mrs. Hooker": Elizabeth Cady Stanton to Susan B. Anthony (December 1870), *ECS & SBA,* Reel 15.

"You know when I drop": Ibid., Reel 14.

"looked disgusted": Susan B. Anthony to Martha Coffin Wright (December 1870), *ESC & SBA,* Reel 14.

"I don't know": Isabella Beecher Hooker to Elizabeth Cady Stanton, *IBH;* Harper, p. 372.

247 "Mrs. Hooker's attitude": Susan B. Anthony to Elizabeth Cady Stanton (January 2, 1871), *ECS & SBA,* Reel 15; *MCW.*

As she had vowed, Elizabeth Cady Stanton did not attend the convention, although in *Frank Leslie's Illustrated* newspaper she is depicted as sitting directly behind Victoria Woodhull as Victoria presents the Woodhull Memorial. On May 24, 1873, this illustration was reprinted in *WCW,* still without correction.

"Miss Anthony, Congress has" and ff.: Isabella Beecher Hooker to Anna Savery, Hartford, Connecticut (November 12, 1871), *IBH.* Senator Pomeroy of Kansas was against linking Negro and woman suffrage, but since the Fifteenth Amendment had been added to the Constitution, he was now willing to help women.

248 "beautiful enough to win": Washington, D.C., *Daily Morning Chronicle* (December 19, 1870), *IBH.*

249 "It would ill become" and ff.: The writing of Victoria Woodhull (November, 1872), *WCW.* See also Stern, *Victoria Woodhull Reader,* Sociology, Part 2, p. 10.

250 "fire and freedom": Isabella Beecher Hooker to Anna Savery (November 21, 1871), *IBH;* Stern, *Victoria Woodhull Reader,* p. 112.

"All persons born": This and the quotations following it are drawn from the Memorial of Victoria C. Woodhull to the joint houses of Congress.

251 "The Heavenly Father": Isabella Beecher Hooker to Anna Savery, Hartford, Connecticut (November 12, 1871), *IBH.*

"a great vision": Victoria Woodhull to Isabella Beecher Hooker (August 8, 1871), *IBH;* *TS,* pp. 93, 94, 110; Marshall, pp. 333, 334.

"dead Congress": Isabella Beecher Hooker to Anna Savery (November 18, 1871), *IBH.*

"The Memorial of Victoria C. Woodhull": Isabella Beecher Hooker noted that franking privileges were "an immense advantage—we could not work without it. . . . We cannot begin to supply individual demand for tracts. These women are all so hungry." Isabella Beecher Hooker to Susan B. Anthony (March 11, 14, 1871), *IBH,* 44 D7, E14.

253 "In declaring that women": Elizabeth Cady Stanton to Victoria Woodhull (June 21, 1871), *ECS & SBA,* Reel 15.

"Bravo! My Dear Woodhull!": Susan B. Anthony to Victoria Woodhull (February 4, 1871), *ECS & SBA,* Reel 15.

"petitioner's prayer": Stern, *Victoria Woodhull Reader,* Vol. 2, p. 1.

"His [God's] own instrument": Isabella Beecher Hooker to Elizabeth Cady Stanton (May 12, 1872), *IBH,* 47 D9–E1; *ECS & SBA,* Reel 16.

"Burn this as soon as sent": Isabella Beecher Hooker to Victoria Woodhull, undated (written in 1872), *IBH,* 53 B10–13, also *VCWM,* dated 1872.

"her conviction": Isabella Beecher Hooker to Susan B. Anthony (March 11, 14, 1871), *IBH;* Boydston et al., p. 206.

"I have this moment read": Isabella Beecher Hooker to Victoria Woodhull, *IBH* (undated; February 16 given as approximate date); *VCWM.*

253 "did not dare": Isabella Beecher Hooker to Victoria Woodhull (February 4, 1889), *IBH*, 63 Bio–13.

"As I am about to speak": Victoria Woodhull to Isabella Beecher Hooker (November 22, 1872), *IBH;* Victoria Claflin Woodhull Correspondence, Butler Library, Columbia University, New York.

255 "It flowed out of my inner" and ff.: Isabella Beecher Hooker to John Hooker (February 4, 1889), *IBH.*

"a triumph": Elizabeth C. Stanton to Susan B. Anthony (January 31, 1871), *ECS & SBA,* Reel 15.

"Her hands are unclean": Susan B. Anthony to Laura DeForce Gordon (February 9, 1871), *ECS & SBA,* Reel 15.

"If I had time or space": Ibid.

256 "It is a great": Isabella Beecher Hooker to Elizabeth Cady Stanton (May 12, 1872), *IBH.*

"Dear Friend Susan": Isabella Beecher Hooker to Susan B. Anthony (May 11, 14, 1871), *IBH,* 44 D-7 E14.

"No one can be": Martha Coffin Wright to Susan B. Anthony (April 6, 1871), *MCW.*

"When we begin to search" and ff.: Susan B. Anthony to Isabella Beecher Hooker (March 21, 1871), *IBH.*

## Chapter 22   Silence, Time and Patience

258 "There came scarcely" and ff.: Paulina Wright Davis's account of her visit to the Tilton house as told to Victoria Woodhull, appearing in *Victoria C. Woodhull's Complete and Detailed Version of the Beecher-Tilton Affair,* Victoria C. Woodhull pamphlet (Washington, D.C.: J. Bradley Adams); *WCW* (November 2, 1872), pp. 9–13.

259 "I know of twelve persons": Letter of Mrs. "Judge" Morse to Henry Ward Beecher (January 27, 1871), entered in evidence, *CT,* reprinted in the *Daily Argus* (March 13, 1875); *BTS,* Scrapbook VII. The other sources for the quotes herein are Marshall, pp. 328–330, Hibben, pp. 228, 251, 269, 273.

"We have Plymouth Church": Isabella Beecher Hooker to Henry Ward Beecher, *IBH;* Marshall, p. 330; Hibben, p. 273.

260 "that the destruction of": Elizabeth Cady Stanton to Isabella Beecher Hooker, Tenafly, New Jersey (November 3, 1873), *IBH;* Hibben, p. 228.

"I have been the centre": Henry Ward Beecher to Frank Moulton (February 5, 1872), *CT;* Marshall, pp. 359–360.

"The church property is": *CT;* Hibben, p. 269.

"the lie" and ff.: Elizabeth Cady Stanton to Isabella Beecher Hooker (November 3, 1873), *IBH; ECS & SBA,* Reel 17.

261 "You are in trouble": Sam Wilkeson to Theodore Tilton (January 11, 1871); *Brooklyn Eagle* (May 20, 1875); *BTS,* Scrapbook VII; Hibben, p. 370.

"take back": Susan B. Anthony to Anna Dickinson (September 19, 1870), *ECS & SBA,* Reel 14.

262 "Can you help" and ff.: Mrs. "Judge" Morse to Henry Ward Beecher (January 27, 1871), *CT,* and *Daily Argus* (March 13, 1875); *BTS,* Scrapbook VII; Doyle, p. 320.

"When I saw you last": Henry Ward Beecher to Elizabeth Tilton (February 7, 1871), *CT;* Doyle, p. 524.

"Dear Friend and Sister": Lib (Elizabeth) Tilton to Laura Curtis Bullard (January 13, 1871), *CT;* Doyle, p. 527.

263 "Does you heart bound": Lib (Elizabeth) Tilton to Henry Ward Beecher (March 6, 1871), *CT; Daily Argus* (March 13, 1875); *BTS,* Scrapbook VII.

264 "as a talisman" and ff.: *GAT,* p. 20.

"My Dear, dear friend": Victoria Woodhull to Isabella Beecher Hooker (August 8, 1871), *IBH;* Marshall, p. 333.

265 "I could not ask": Rugoff, *The Beechers*, p. 46.

"No salvation!": Rourke, p. 50.

266 "As things are now" and ff.: Catharine Beecher's address on female suffrage delivered at the Boston Music Hall, 1870, *IBH;* Boydston et al., p. 232.

"Many intelligent and benevolent": Catharine Beecher, Appeal to American Women, *American Woman's Home,* pp. 463–468; Boydston et al., p. 257.

"just as much in love": Isabella Beecher Hooker to Catharine Beecher, *IBH,* Document 112.

267 "son, Henry, drowned": Isabella Beecher Hooker to Catharine Beecher, *IBH,* Document 112; Rugoff, p. 343.

"Why will you not speak" and ff.: Rourke, p. 131; Rugoff, *The Beechers,* p. 343.

"a reaction from the intense": Rugoff, *The Beechers,* p. 349.

"Mrs. Woodhull is": Isabella Beecher Hooker to Susan Howard (April 1871), *IBH.*

"Disastrous influences, the teachings": "Woman Suffrage and Woman's Profession," Catharine Beecher, p. 34; Boydston et al., p. 251.

269 "must come from a misunderstanding": *WCW* (November 2, 1872), reprinted April 1873. This account is solely Victoria Woodhull's. Catharine Beecher never gave the details of this interview, but thereafter referred to Victoria Woodhull variously as a "witch," "harlot," "free lover," and, later, "jailbird."

270 "Sister Catharine returned": (February 6, 1871), *IBH,* 115 E4–9; Harper, p. 379.

"bring her back to God": Harriet Beecher Stowe (and Mary Perkins) to John Hooker (March 2, 1871), *IBH.*

"Do you believe I" and ff.: Isabella Beecher Hooker to Harriet Beecher Stowe (March 16, 1871), *IBH;* also in *MCW.*

"Mrs. Woodhull's antecedents" and ff.: *ECS & SBA,* Reel 15; *New York Tribune* (January 28, 1872), Susan B. Anthony at Lincoln Hall Convention, January 1872.

"She and her five sisters": Martha Coffin Wright to (her daughter) Elizabeth Wright Osborne (March 16, 1871), *MCW.*

"Under all the curses": Victoria Woodhull to Isabella Beecher Hooker, *IBH,* 44 D-7 E14. In a letter to Susan B. Anthony (March 11, 14, 1871), Isabella Beecher Hooker encloses a copy of this letter from Victoria Woodhull. Isabella answers Victoria Woodhull's letter by writing, "In my observation all human souls are more or less lonely who have only human forces of sympathy and consolation" (*IBH,* 48 C4–10).

## Chapter 23  The Worst Gang

272 "that damn scoundrel Blood": This and quotes that follow are found in the court testimony of *Roxanna Claflin v. Colonel James Blood,* Essex Market Police Court (May 10, 15, 16, 1871), and accounts in the *New York Herald, New York Sun, New York World, New York Argus,* and *New York Times* (May 11–21, 1871), *BTS,* Scrapbook VII.

273 "They h'aint no friends of mine": Commodore Cornelius Vanderbilt, *New York Tribune* (May 21, 1871); *BTS,* Scrapbook VII.

"great trouble allowing Mrs. Woodhull": Susan B. Anthony to Martha Coffin Wright (March 31, 1871), *ECS & SBA,* Reel 15.

"to give her respectability": Johnston, p. 102.

"a small splinter of": *TS,* p. 77; Hibben, p. 233; excerpted from the *Philadelphia Press.*

274 "Why do I war": Apollo Hall speech (May 11, 12, 1871), *VCWM,* Box 2, reprinted in *WCW* (May 27, 1871), p. 9; *TS,* p. 87; Johnston, p. 103.

275 "Ridiculous string of resolutions": Martha Coffin Wright to Elizabeth Cady Stanton (May 27, 1871), *MCW.*

"Professor Purlo's hypotheses": Susan B. Anthony to Isabella Beecher Hooker (May 31, 1871), *IBH; ECS & SBA,* Reel 15.

279 "No subject discussed": *BTS, Independent* (May 28, 1871), Scrapbook VI; *TS,* p. 93.
"one who has two husbands": *BTS, New York Tribune* (May 20, 1871), Scrapbook VI; Boydston et al., p. 164.

280 "Mr. Greeley's home": *VCWM, WCW* (May 27, 1871).

281 "I would like to have": Sara Burger Stearns to Mrs. Griffing (June 20, 1871), *ECS & SBA,* Reel 15.
"I do not understand" and ff.: Isabella Beecher Hooker to Sara Burger Stearns of Minnesota, May 23, 1871 *IBH;* Boydston et al., p. 306.
"with a meaning of her own" and ff.: Isabella Beecher Hooker to Anna Savery (November 12, 18, 1871), *IBH.* Isabella explains her view of free love in a letter to Victoria Woodhull: "Lest you should misunderstand my position on the question of Social Freedom let me state it briefly here. Human law should not attempt to regulate marriage—this is a sacrament of Souls owing allegiance to God and their own consciences only. But the ideal marriage is between two only": Isabella Beecher Hooker to Victoria Woodhull (July 28, 1872), *IBH,* 48 C49.

282 "kept women": Susan B. Anthony to Isabella Beecher Hooker (April 22, 1871), *IBH.* See Isabella Beecher Hooker to Paulina Wright Davis (May 29, 1871). Also see Paulina Wright Davis to Victoria Woodhull, Providence, Rhode Island (May 1871).
"I will take by the hand": Oliver, p. 43; Susan B. Anthony to the *New York Tribune* (January 14, 1872).
"In regard to the": Harper, Vol. 1, p. 379; Lutz, *Created Equal,* p. 211; *TS,* p. 79.
"Mrs. Stanton whispered": Doyle, p. 57.

283 "were belching forth": Account of Victoria Woodhull as told to Allen Putnam, *Banner of Light* (November 20, 1875).
"communists . . . given the opportunity": *The Telegram* (October 28, 1871).
"a menace" and ff.: *New York World* (November 2, 1871).
"Come on, come on": *New York Tribune, Brooklyn Eagle* (May 28, 1871), *VCWM,* B3.

284 "a woman of the town": *Brooklyn Eagle* (May 28, 1871); *VCWM,* B3.
"Vickie, Colonel and Tennie included": *Brooklyn Eagle* (May 28, 1871); *TS,* p. 110.
"to lead the movement" and ff.: Blackwell, p. 223.

285 "What effort more than Herculean": Susan B. Anthony to Martha Coffin Wright (June 14, 1871), *ECS & SBA,* Reel 15.
"The division is so senseless": Martha Coffin Wright to William Lloyd Garrison II, her daughter Ellen's husband (May 15, 1871), *MCW.* Theodore Tilton concurred. See Terry pp. 160, 201.
"Without pretending to a perfect knowledge": National American Woman Suffrage Association Collection, Library of Congress, Washington, D.C.; *WCW* (June 8, 1871).
"This fresh howl": Susan B. Anthony to Martha Coffin Pelham Wright (May 20, 1871), *MCW.*

286 "Because I am a woman": *New York World* and *New York Times* (May 22, 1871); *TS,* pp. 96–97.

## Chapter 24   This Girl Is a Tramp

287 "Who do you mean" and ff.: *WCW* (November 2, 1872), pp. 9–13; *Victoria C. Woodhull's Complete and Detailed Version of the Beecher-Tilton Affair,* pamphlet; Stern, *Victoria Woodhull Reader,* Part A, Sexual Relations, 2, p. 12.
"some influence might be brought": Statement of Frank Moulton, *PCH,* abridged in Marshall, p. 562.
"Don't take any steps now" and ff.: The quotations are taken from various newspaper interviews with Victoria Woodhull, the November 2, 1872, issue of *WCW,* pp. 9–13, and Woodhull's speeches throughout the course of the scandal—November 2, 1872–June 30, 1875.

287  "Be kind to and sympathize": This quotation is repeated in the Woodhull speech, Stern, *Victoria Woodhull Reader*, Part A, Sexual Relations, 2, p. 30.

288  "unexpected modesty": Statement of Emma Moulton (May 23, 1875), *CT*, Vol. 2, p. 118.
"I want you to take a look": Ibid.
"a broad-minded, self-possessed woman": Ibid.
"life on the theory of human imperfection": Ibid.
"Such another family-circle": *GAT*, pp. 6–7.

289  "I must now let out a secret": *GAT*, pp. 8–9.
"If apples are wormy": *TS*, p. 120.
"Can anything but infatuation": Marianna Pelham Mott to Martha Coffin Wright, (September 24, 1871), *MCW*.

290  "A popular objection against Free Love": "Tried as by Fire," a speech by Victoria Woodhull, appears in Stern, *Victoria Woodhull Reader*, Part A, Sexual Relations, 5, p. 35.
"Mr. Tilton was my devoted lover": Doyle, p. 315; *Chicago Times* (June 4, 1874).
"Civilization is festering": *WCW* (June 3, 1871), received on May 22, 1871; Hibben, p. 272.

291  "My Dear Victoria, I have arranged": Theodore Tilton to Victoria Woodhull (June 5, 1871), *CT*, entered into evidence, exhibit UV 130.
"Marriage is the grave of love" and ff.: *WCW* (November 2, 1872), pp. 9–13; *Victoria C. Woodhull's Complete and Detailed Version of the Beecher-Tilton Affair*, Stern, *Victoria Woodhull Reader*, Part A, Sexual Relations, 2, p. 16.
"Why then do you not preach" and ff.: Ibid.
"held society to be upside down" and ff.: Frank Moulton's final statement, *CT*, reprinted from Abbot, Vol. 2, p. 343.
"a most indignant and rebuking letter": Isabella Beecher Hooker in a letter to Henry Ward Beecher (February 14, 1872) explains Woodhull's assertion of October 1871. Isabella, who frequently tried to influence Victoria Woodhull, had suggested that the Steinway Hall convention be restricted to women only. Woodhull, however, seemed impervious to Hooker's suggestions and wrote her that she had "carefully read" her letter and "I think it an *error* to exclude men from the hall. In doing that you pattern after the old custom. There should be nothing exclusive about it." Victoria Woodhull to Isabella Beecher Hooker (October 19, 1871), *IBH*, 142 D10-13.

292  "As to what Mrs. Woodhull means": Isabella Beecher Hooker to Anna Savery (November 12, 1871), *IBH*, 46 C3-12.
"A Lady of Connecticut": Sometimes even on the same page the spelling of Catharine changes to Catherine. Josephine Blatti of the Harriet Beecher Stowe Center informs me that the great preponderance of correspondence favors the *a*. I too have found this to be true. In this particular passage, for the reader's convenience I have used *a* even if *e* appears in the original letter.
"Every drop of Beecher blood": Reverend Phebe Hanaford to Isabella Beecher Hooker (September 13, 1871), *IBH*. In Boydston et al., p. 295, this letter is dated August 9, 1871.
"That private note of mine": Isabella Beecher Hooker to Anna Savery, Hartford, Connecticut (November 12, 1871), *IBH*, 46 C3–12.

293  "Mrs. Woodhull received me cordially": Whitelaw Reid to Charles W. Warner (October 13, 1871), *IBH*.

294  "I shall break all engagements": Whitelaw Reid to Anna Dickinson (March 24, 1871), Anna E. Dickinson Papers.
"I must and do always": Whitelaw Reid to Charles Dudley Warner (October 13, 1871), *IBH, VCWM*. "Demi-rep" was a common euphemism of the day for prostitute. Clearly Whitelaw Reid used this term as a snide reference to Victoria Woodhull.
"a snake and should be given": Johnston, p. 126. This quote is slightly altered in Rourke, p. 145. It reads, "The Woodhull is a snake and we should hit her with a shovel."

294 "My Wife and I": The complete title is *My Wife & I or Harry Henderson's History*. This work by Harriet Beecher Stowe was serialized in the *Christian Union*, 1870, 1871 (New York: J. B. Ford & Co., 1871; Boston: Houghton Mifflin, 1896).

"Mrs. Cerulean": Cerulean is defined in the *Oxford English Dictionary* as "sky-blue, the color of the cloudless sky, deep blue, azure."

296 "Dear Sir: For reasons in which" and ff.: Victoria Woodhull to Henry Ward Beecher (November 19, 1871), Marshall, p. 358. This encounter is detailed in *WCW* (November 2, 1872, pp. 9–13). Also in speeches of Victoria Woodhull, "Tried As By Fire," Stern, *Victoria Woodhull Reader*.

297 "Mr. Beecher, if I am compelled" and ff.: Testimony given by Stephen Pearl Andrews, Frank Moulton, and Theodore Tilton, letter entered into evidence March 3, 1875, *CT:* Abbot, Vol. 2, p. 60.

## Chapter 25   Yes! I Am a Free Lover!

298 "Victoria C. Woodhull": *TS*, p. 129; Johnston, p. 127. The Steinway speech, "The Principles of Social Freedom" (November 20, 1871) was reprinted in *WCW* (August 16, 1873), pp. 2–7, 11–15.

"I hope by God": *New York Tribune* (November 22, 1871). In *TS*, p. 129, the quote differs: "I hope, by gosh I haven't come here for nothing in all this rain."

"Your paper has never misrepresented": *New York Tribune* (November 22, 1871); *TS*, p. 129.

299 "There isn't one brave man" and ff.: *TS*, pp. 130–131; Marshall, p. 814; Frank Moulton statement reprinted in Abbot, Vol. 2, p. 346.

300 "The basis of society" and ff: All quotations that follow are from the speech "The Principles of Social Freedom" given by Victoria Woodhull November 20, 1871, reprinted in *WCW* (August 16, 1873), pp. 2–7, 11–15. Also excerpted in abridged form in Stern's *Victoria Woodhull Reader*, Part A, Sexual Relations, 1, pp. 17–26. I have also used accounts from the *New York Tribune, New York Sun, New York Times*. The various transcripts of this speech contain small but not substantive variations. I have, whenever possible, used the version that Woodhull herself printed. In this case, I used the pamphlet *A Speech on The Principles of Social Freedom* (New York: Woodhull, Claflin & Co., 1871). The subtitle reads: "To an audience of 3,000 people, to which hundreds found it impossible to obtain admission; which, in consideration of the dreuching [*sic*] rain of the evening, is the best evidence of what subject lies nearest the hearts of the people."

303 "Free Lover Lectures on Free Love": *Weekly Argus* (November 22, 1871).

"Died of Free Love . . . The Woman Suffrage Movement": *Lancaster Gazette* (November 25, 1871).

304 "It was not the printed speech": *New York Herald* (November 22, 1871).

"The free love panic" and ff.: Martha Coffin Wright to Elizabeth Cady Stanton (March 22, 1872), *MCW.*

"The Impending Revolution": This speech, delivered February 1, 1872, can be found in its entirety in Stern, *Victoria Woodhull Reader*, Section A, Part 3, and in the pamphlet "The Impending Revolution" (New York: Woodhull, Claflin & Co., 1872).

305 "there would be a riot": *Victoria Woodhull Prophesy*, "Honor to the Martyrs," *Boston Post* (October 20, 1876).

306 "Some people carp": Elizabeth Cady Stanton, *WCW* (December 18, 1871); *GAT* (December 9, 1871); Harper, Vol. 1, p. 379.

307 "It is only four years" and ff.: Swanberg, p. 250.

309 "I feel just as I used to" and ff.: Ibid., p. 275.

## Chapter 26  A Heavy Load

310 "Dear Mrs. Woodhull, Will you ask Demosthenes": Elizabeth Cady Stanton to Victoria Woodhull, Tenafly, New Jersey (December 29, 1871), *ECS & SBA,* Reel 15, pp. 852–857.
"Felicita": Also known as Felicité.

311 "I do not mean": Henry Ward Beecher to Frank Moulton, Brooklyn, New York (January 2, 1872), *CT.*
"I am ashamed": Frank Moulton to Henry Ward Beecher (February 5, 1872), *CT;* Marshall, p. 359.
"This whole affair [is]": Sam Wilkeson to Frank Moulton (April 2, 1872), *CT;* Marshall, p. 370.
"It seems a change": Henry Ward Beecher to Frank Moulton (February 5, 1872), *CT;* Hibben, p. 238; Marshall, p. 361. During the trial this letter became known as "The Ragged Edge" letter and the object of intense press scrutiny.

312 "The whole case has terminated": Theodore Tilton to Anna Dickinson (January 4, 1872), Anna E. Dickinson Papers, Reel 26.
"closing act": Sam Wilkeson to Frank Moulton (April 2, 1872); Marshall, p. 370.
" 'Grantism' became a synonym": Mark Twain commented in a manner that is easily applicable to today: "We will not hire a school teacher who does not know the alphabet . . . but when you come to our civil service we serenely fill great numbers of our minor public offices with ignoramuses. We put the vast business of a Custom House in the hands of a flathead who does not know a bill of lading from a transit of Venus. . . . Under our consular system we send creatures all over the world who speak no language but their own."

313 "You will be responsible": *VCWM; Boston Post* (October 20, 1876); *Banner of Light* (November 20, 1875).
"None but the liberals": (July 26, 1872), Harper, Vol. 1, p. 419.
"Baltimore Warned—Susan B. Anthony": *ECS & SBA,* scrapbooks; *New York World* (June 12, 1872), p. 1.
"the honest demands": Griffith, p. 153.

314 "Baltimore will not recognize": Susan B. Anthony to Martha Coffin Wright (June 13, 1872), *MCW.*
"Both parties were utterly corrupt": Martha Coffin Wright to her daughter Ellen Garrison (March 15, 1871), *MCW.*
"We have no element": Susan B. Anthony to Elizabeth Cady Stanton and Isabella Beecher Hooker, Leavenworth, Kansas (March 13, 1872), *IBH; ECS & SBA,* Reel 16; Lutz, *Created Equal* p. 217; Harper, Vol. 1, p. 413.
"Oh, if I were—" and ff.: Isabella Beecher Hooker to Olympia Brown (February 14, 1872), *IBH,* 47 B2-9.

315 "Mrs. Stanton told me precisely": Isabella Beecher Hooker to Henry Ward Beecher, Hartford, Connecticut (November 1, 1872), *IBH;* Doyle, pp. 506–507.
"The only reply I made": Hartford, Connecticut (November 1, 1872), *IBH;* Marshall, p. 330.
"My Dear Belle . . . I do not intend": Henry Ward Beecher to Isabella Beecher Hooker (April 25, 1872), *IBH.* Letter transcribed by Henry E. Burton, son-in-law of Mrs. Hooker, and a copy then sent to John Hooker on October 31, 1872.
"My mind flew back": Isabella Beecher Hooker to Henry Ward Beecher (April 25, 1872), *IBH;* Marshall, p. 334.

316 "We believe the time has come": Harper, Vol. 1, p. 413; Lutz, *Created Equal,* p. 218.
"I do not believe": Susan B. Anthony to Lillie Devereux Blake (May 14, 1872), *ECS & SBA,* Reel 16.
"millionairess" and ff.: This story appeared in *WCW* (March 18, 1871), pp. 5–6.

317 "the sexual liaisons and free love": Accounts of this blackmail scheme (which in one case included a death threat if the recipient of the letter did not pay up) are in the National American Woman Suffrage Association Collection, Reel 58; *TS*, pp. 164–165; Susan B. Anthony to Isabella Beecher Hooker (June 19, 24, 1872), *IBH*. Woodhull defended her use of blackmail, writing that for women, blackmail was "the only method of righting themselves" and a way to "avenge the oppressions of [their] sex," *WCW* (April 6, 1872).

"Phebe Hanaford": Mrs. Hanaford was living alone in New Haven while her husband, the Reverend Joseph Hanaford, remained in Reading, Connecticut, where he vowed to stay.

"practice what I preach": *WCW* (November 2, 1872), p. 13; *TS*, p. 95; Oliver, p. 300.

"Called on Mrs. Phelps": Diary entry of Susan B. Anthony (Monday, May 6, 1872), *ECS & SBA*, Reel 16.

"I concluded to shut the mouths": *WCW* (April 2, 1873), by Victoria Woodhull; Oliver, p. 299.

"My Dear Victoria, Driven to bay": Paulina Wright Davis to Victoria Woodhull, Oliver, p. 202.

318 "Narrow minded and domineering": Harper, Vol. 1, p. 414.

"claimed right to possess the meeting": Diary entry of Susan B. Anthony (Tuesday, May 7, 1872), *ECS & SBA*.

"There was never such a foolish *muddle*": Diary entry of Susan B. Anthony (Wednesday, May 8, 1872).

319 "Friday: National Convention—again small audience": Diary entry of Susan B. Anthony (Friday, May 10, 1872).

"Saturday: I was never so hurt": Diary entry of Susan B. Anthony (Saturday, May 11, 1872).

"I never before came so near": Diary entry of Susan B. Anthony (Friday, May 10, 1872), *ECS & SBA*.

"Woodhull paper comes freighted": Diary entry of Susan B. Anthony (Wednesday, May 22, 1872), *ECS & SBA*.

320 "At the Saturday Apollo Hall meeting": In her first speech to the convention, Victoria declared that her party would ensure that "the millions now paid into the pockets of wealth will remain in the pockets of industrial people. Instead of there being the *very rich* few and the *very poor* many, all will be rich enough to have all the comfort that wealth and enjoyment demand." She then advocated violence if no other method would secure an eight-hour workday and a fair wage. This speech may be found in Stern, *Victoria Woodhull Reader*, Political Theory, Part II, B, 9, pp. 11–14.

"*Apollo Hall was a success*": Isabella Beecher Hooker to Elizabeth Cady Stanton (May 12, 1872), *IBH*, 47 D9–E1. In this same letter Isabella writes, "I do wish that her Suffrage friends who think the cause was lost through the advocacy of Victoria and our advocacy of her would show us where the money and brains and unceasing energy of that paper would come from if she had not been moved to present the *Memorial* and follow it up with the prodigious outlays of the last year and a half. I verily believe she has sunk a hundred dollars in Woman Suffrage beside enduring loneliness of soul immeasurable—let us never forget this. Let us still look over her faults if she has them, remembering that she is human like ourselves."

"overpowered by the sublimity of this hour": Isabella Beecher Hooker to Susan B. Anthony (May 6, 1872), *IBH*.

"*Yes, I am overpowered*": Susan B. Anthony to Isabella Beecher Hooker (May 19, 1872), *IBH*.

321 "Mrs. Woodhull, The nominee": *Broadway's* article appeared in *WCW* (June 1, 1872), p. 10.

321 "What a ridiculous letter": Susan B. Anthony to Elizabeth Cady Stanton (June 1, 1872), *ECS & SBA*, Reel 14; Barry, p. 237.

"resorting to blackmail intentionally": *WCW* (November 2, 1872), p. 2.

"Surprise found her home": Diary entry of Susan B. Anthony (June 7, 1872), Ibid.

322 *"fabricated* terrible charges against T. C.": (Monday, June 10, 1872), ibid.

"We do not believe the charge": Martha Coffin Wright to Susan B. Anthony, Auburn, New York (May 20, 1872), *MCW.*

"That letter of Dr. A. Orvis": Susan B. Anthony to Isabella Beecher Hooker (June 19, 1872), Rochester, New York, *IBH.*

"I shall welcome her work": Susan B. Anthony to Isabella Beecher Hooker (June 24, 1872), *IBH.*

"The charges . . . as made": *WCW* (December 28, 1872).

"marplot" and ff.: Diary entry of Susan B. Anthony (May 29, 1872), *ECS & SBA.*

323 "By the way I have been hearing": Whitelaw Reid to Anna Dickinson (August 6, 1872), Anna E. Dickinson Papers, 14:1112; Chester, p. 130.

"What you write us is shocking": John Hooker to Isabella Beecher Hooker (October 31, 1872), *IBH.*

### Chapter 27   Mrs. Satan

324 "Whoever is set up to be President": Boydston et al., p. 284, excerpted from Stowe, *My Wife & I.*

"We must now all pull": Susan B. Anthony to Lillie Devereux Blake (May 17, 1872), *ECS & SBA.*

325 "The Grant folks": Hale, p. 345.

"terriers to watch such rats": *Independent* (May 4, 1865).

"We believe that the anti-slavery": *Golden Age* (June 15, 1872).

"a floundering old buffoon": Hale, p. 343.

326 "Republican Party and all women": Susan B. Anthony to Martha Coffin Wright (September 30, 1872), *ECS & SBA,* Reel 16:422.

328 "We hope they got rid": Lutz, *Created Equal,* pp. 220–221.

"Woodhull & Claflin tribe" and ff.: Leslie Wheeler, *Loving Warriors: Selected Letters of Lucy Stone and Henry B. Blackwell, 1853–1893* (New York: Dial Press, 1981), p. 236.

"And now, dear Miss Anthony": Henry Blackwell to Susan B. Anthony (September 7, 1872, copied by Martha Coffin Wright), *MCW.*

330 "Under suspicious circumstances": Isabella Beecher Hooker to Victoria Woodhull (April 10, 1872), *IBH,* 47 C12–D1. Isabella Beecher Hooker wrote a letter of condolence to Victoria in which she stated:

> I cannot always see truth just as you do, but I see that you love the truth and fol-
> low after it with all your soul—and that is just what I am trying to do. I feel that
> we are sisters—children of the same Father and bound to the same home—ever the
> kingdom of righteousness which is from on high.

331 "insatiable vengeance": *TS,* p. 154.

"My Dear Sir, The social fight": Victoria Woodhull to Henry Ward Beecher (June 3, 1872, sent by hand), *VCWM,* Box 3; *CT,* Vol. 2, Exhibit UU.

"Will you answer this?": Henry Ward Beecher to Frank Moulton (June 3, 1872); reprinted in the *New York Tribune* (November 8, 1872).

332 "I always knew what Woodhull": Frank Moulton's final statement, *CT,* Vol. 2, p. 239.

"only Victoria believed": Woodhull later described her feeling of hopelessness during this period. "The press suddenly divided between the other two great parties, refused all notice of our reformatory movement, and a series of pecuniary disasters . . . forced us into a desperate struggle for mere existence" *WCW* (November 2, 1872).

333 "Human nature is awfully weak and wanting": Susan B. Anthony to Isabella Beecher Hooker, Rochester, New York (August 7, 1872), *ECS & SBA*, Reel 16; Barry, p. 248.

"All in the world": Susan B. Anthony to Martha Coffin Wright (September 12, 1872), *MCW*.

334 "The secret of the final rupture": *Woman's Journal*, Boston, Chicago, and St. Louis (August 3, 1872). (Sent to subscribers July 27.)

"The inference . . . was that" and ff.: Victoria Woodhull to Susan B. Anthony (August 2, 1872), *VCWM*.

"I have not and shall not reply": Susan B. Anthony to Isabella Beecher Hooker, Rochester, New York (August 7, 1872), *IBH*, 47 D10–C2; Barry, p. 248.

"If anything shows the inability of women": *The Word* (September, 1872), New York Public Library, Manuscript Division.

335 "I was seized": *TS*, p. 154; *WCW* (December 28, 1872).

"Mrs. Woodhull's speech poured out": Elizabeth Avery Meriwether, *Memphis Appeal* (November 17, 1872); The Tennessee Historical Commission, Nashville, Tennessee, publishers of *Recollection of 92 Years; 1824–1916, The Diaries of Elizabeth A. Meriwether; TS*, p. 170.

"a self-aggrandizing": *Woman's Journal* (December 1872).

"I swore not profanely": *WCW* (December 28, 1872).

"The second week in October": Stoddard, p. 314.

336 "I will make it" and ff.: *WCW* (November 2, 1872).

## Chapter 28    Burst Like a Bombshell

337 "If an omelette has to be made": The Beecher-Tilton scandal and the story of Luther C. Challis and all the details in this account are drawn from *WCW* (November 2, 1872) and subsequent issues where these events are amplified and reiterated. The behavior of the people concerned is drawn from numerous contemporary newspaper accounts (see bibliography for a complete list of newspapers consulted).

338 "From the time that I opened my house": (alias) Mary Bowles to Tennie C. Claflin (December 16, 1871, and repeated August 19, 1873), *WCW*.

339 "three thousand of the best men": *New York World* (December 24, 1869); James D. McCabe Jr., *Lights and Shadows of New York Life; or, The Sights and Sensations of the Great City* (Philadelphia: National Publishing Co., 1872; New York: Farrar, Straus and Giroux, 1970), p. 604; Stern, *Victoria Woodhull Reader*, "Tried As By Fire or The True and The False Socially," Part A, Sexual Relations, 5.

340 "closely dominoed": The following quotations and events are drawn from reports in the *New York World* (December 24, 1872), *WCW* (November 2, 1872), and a subsequent interview in the *Argus* (November 19, 1872) as well as from testimony in the obscenity trials of Victoria Woodhull and Tennessee Claflin.

341 "Molly de Ford": In *TS* and McCabe, p. 604, the name is spelled Mollie, but in "Tried as by Fire, or The True and The False, Socially," Victoria Woodhull's speech, 1874, it is spelled Molly. See speech in Stern, *Victoria Woodhull Reader*, Part A, Sexual Relations, 5.

342 "On October 26": Although *WCW* is dated November 2, 1872, it was issued October 26, 1872.

344 "God's hand was in this": Heywood Broun and Margaret Leech, *Anthony Comstock: Roundsman of the Lord* (New York: Albert & Charles Boni, 1927), p. 91.

345 "a gross libel": Ibid., p. 103; "Tried as by Fire or, The True and The False, Socially," Stern, *Victoria Woodhull Reader*, Part A, Sexual Relations, 5.

"the red trophy of her virginity": The quotation is from Deuteronomy, Chapter XXII. Hibben, p. 285.

"The tabloids are full": Johnston, p. 169.

345 "a case of this character" and ff.: *WCW* (November 2, 1872); *New York World* (December 24, 1869); Johnston, p. 169; *TS*, p. 209; McCabe, p. 604. The prostitution quotations are from "Tried as by Fire," *Victoria Woodhull Reader*, Part A, Sexual Relations, 5, p. 31.

"I have been and gone and done it!!": This was perhaps Susan B. Anthony's most publicized moment and is recounted in Harper, Barry, Lutz, and other books and articles.

346 "Do you know, I have sometimes felt": Susan B. Anthony to Isabella Beecher Hooker (October 13, 1873), *IBH*.

"There is no time": Victoria Woodhull to Susan B. Anthony, New York (January 2, 1873), *ECS & SBA*.

347 "I have been so bitterly assailed": Stoddard, pp. 315–316.

"I dread only the malignity": Ibid., p. 319.

"You will find him" and ff.: Chester, pp. 141–142.

348 "No Latin—no embellishments": Hale, p. 352.

"Be kind to Tilton": Ibid.

### Chapter 29    I Can Endure No Longer

349 "If you still believe": Henry Ward Beecher to Isabella Beecher Hooker (October 28, 1872), *IBH*, original and copy by Henry E. Burton.

"At last the blow has fallen" and ff.: Isabella Beecher Hooker to Thomas Beecher (November 3, 1872), *IBH*.

350 "Dear Belle, To allow the devil": Thomas Beecher to Isabella Beecher Hooker (November 5, 1872), *IBH*.

"Don't write to me": Ibid.

352 "damned lecherous scoundrel": *Hartford Times* (November 25, 1872); the *Patriot* of Chariton, Iowa; Doyle, pp. 93–94. Elizabeth Cady Stanton to Isabella Beecher Hooker (November 19, 1872), *IBH*, 11:16, confirms the above. Stanton writes, "Only think of that item going the rounds of the papers that I said in Maine that I was convinced that Mrs. Woodhull's statements were false. I said no such thing, but . . . I should be ashamed to use such abominable language as she put in my mouth."

"Dear Susan, I had supposed you knew": Elizabeth Cady Stanton to Susan B. Anthony, *ECS & SBA*, Reel 16; Lutz, *Created Equal* p. 222.

"When a man is unlucky" and ff.: *New York Sun* (November 8, 1872), New York Public Library Scrapbook VII.

353 " 'Entirely.' Wouldn't you think if God": Susan B. Anthony to Isabella Beecher Hooker, Rochester, New York (November 16, 1872), *ECS & SBA*, Reel 16; "Mrs. Tilton's Story," *New York Tribune* (September 19, 1874), New York Public Library Scrapbook VII.

354 "It is she who should annul": Susan B. Anthony to Gerrit Smith (December 25, 1872), *ECS & SBA*, Reel 16.

"first accuser": Isabella Beecher Hooker to Mary Porter Chamberlin (November 4, 1874), *IBH*, 51 A2–9. Isabella's full explanation reads,

> I have always thought and do still think that the evidence before her, *she was fully justified in her action.* I told my brother the same and added as long as women were *slain by the mere breath of suspicion against their chastity,* I would never help to conceal the wrong doings of a man, though he were my own brother or son. I would not become his first accuser but when he was accused by trustworthy testimony I would not defend him and the higher his station and influence the less would I try to shield him.

"has charged Mr. Beecher": *IBH*, "Justitia" (November 25, 1872), *Hartford Times;* Doyle, pp. 92–97.

"What did prompt you to betray": Elizabeth Cady Stanton to Isabella Beecher Hooker, Willard Hotel Washington (November 19, 1872), *IBH*.

355 "I cannot tell you my surprise": Elizabeth Cady Stanton to Isabella Beecher Hooker (January 21, 1873), *IBH*. "Steadfastness of my affection"—emphasis added.
"twisting the truth for their own advantage": Theodore Tilton's "True Story" as given to Edward H. G. Clark. Reprinted in the *Thunderbolt*, Albany and Troy, New York, May 1873. Tilton made a similar statement in *CT*, Vol. 2, p. 339.

356 "It seems to me that God": Isabella Beecher Hooker to Henry Ward Beecher (November 1, 1872), *IBH;* Marshall, p. 331; Doyle, p. 587.
"but one honorable way": Ibid.
"I will write you a sisterly letter": Ibid.
"calm silence": Henry Ward Beecher to Isabella B. Hooker (November 9, 1872), *IBH,* original and copy by Henry E. Burton.

357 "Dear Brother, I can endure no longer": Isabella Beecher Hooker to Henry Ward Beecher (November 27, 1872), *IBH*.
"This is a disaster!" and ff.: *CT*, Vol. 2, pp. 745–748. This and quotes that follow concerning this incident are excerpted from the testimony of Frank Moulton.

358 "Victoria's story": Elizabeth Cady Stanton to Isabella Beecher Hooker (November 3, 1873), *IBH*.

## Chapter 30    What Have We Done Now

360 "You have had a hard fight" and ff.: Denis Tilden Lynch, *"Boss" Tweed: The Story of a Grim Generation* (New York: Boni and Liveright, 1927), p. 362.

361 "corrupt motives": This account is based on contemporary newspaper accounts of the Credit Mobilier Scandal and on information in Matthew Josephson, *The Robber Barons: The Great American Capitalists* (New York: Harcourt, Brace, 1934), pp. 164, 355.
"Cut off your vices": W.E.B. Du Bois, *Black Reconstruction in America 1860–1880: An Essay Toward a History of the Part Which Black Folk Played in the Attempt to Reconstruct Democracy in America* (New York: Russell & Russell, 1966), pp. 599–601.

362 "If the bond plan is a swindle": Susan B. Anthony to Lillie Devereux Blake (May 20, 1872), *ECS & SBA*, Reel 16.
"to do something every day for Jesus": See Broun and Leech, p. 116, and also Chapter 8, pp. 108–127, by Leech, for a full account of Comstock's repeated arrests of Victoria Woodhull and Tennessee Celeste Claflin.

363 "Those vile women jailbirds": Harriet Beecher Stowe to Hattie and Eliza Stowe (December 19, 1872), Harriet Beecher Stowe Center; Boydston et al., p. 288.
"Well-meaning friends" and ff.: Laura Cuppy Smith, "How One Woman Entered the Ranks of Social Reform: or, a Mother's Story," *WCW* (March 1, 1873), pp. 3,4,5.

364 "Are you not the publisher": *New York Sun* (January 10, 1872), New York Public Library Scrapbook IV.
"Comstock's defeated!": Laura Cuppy Smith quoted William Cullen Bryant, "The terrible syren has defeated you and charmed your cohorts and battalions to silence and inaction" *New York Evening Post* (January 9, 1873). At this time the tabloid newspapers were putting out extra sections to cover Woodhull's speech as well as Tweed's trial and the appeal of Edward Ned Stokes for Fisk's murder.
"I come into your presence" and ff.": *WCW* (January 25, 1873), pp. 3–8, 14, 15; Stern, *Victoria Woodhull Reader,* Part A, Sexuality, 3, "The Naked Truth; or the Situation Reviewed," pages unnumbered.

365 "to run her to the earth" and ff.: Excerpted from "The Naked Truth; or the Situation Reviewed" (January 9, 1873), Stern, *Victoria Woodhull Reader,* Part A, Sexual Relations, 3, pages unnumbered; *WCW* (January 25, 1873), pp. 3–7, 13–15.
"What have we done now?" and ff.: *TS*, p. 200.
"We have had so many": Victoria Woodhull to Lafayette Beech, Ludlow Street Jail, Cell 1, New York (December 2, 1872), collection of the author.

366 "caricatures of everything": Excerpted from Comstock's diary, February 25, 1873, as quoted in Broun and Leech, pp. 134–141. I have searched in vain for years for the original Comstock diaries. No institution or relative claims to know what has become of them. Although in 1927 Broun and Leech were permitted access to these diaries, and facsimile pages appear in their book, subsequent books and articles simply quote Broun and Leech but add no new information. The archives of the Young Men's Christian Association was the last place the diaries were said to exist. It is the opinion of several researchers and scholars that Anthony Comstock's diary entries concerning his compulsive masturbation were considered inappropriate in a purity crusader and were therefore destroyed by persons unknown.

367 "Disgusting and obscene" and ff.: This and the quotations that follow are drawn from the testimony of Anthony Comstock in the obscenity trials of Victoria Woodhull, Tennie C. Claflin, and Colonel James Blood, which took place January–March 1873, from the New York Public Library Scrapbook IV, as well as from contemporary newspaper accounts. An excellent summary of these proceedings appears in Broun and Leech, pp. 93–107, 114–127.

"was lighted up with spirit-light": *TS*, p. 234.

"Sick in body, sick in mind": *VCWM*, 3, Victoria Woodhull to the *New York Herald, TS*, p. 288.

368 "wholly misconstrued" and ff.: *New York Sun* and *New York World* (February 3, 1873); *TS*, p. 201.

369 "had reasons satisfactory": Ibid., p. 209.

"disgusting slanders on Lot": This account has been drawn from the *New York Times*, March 29, p. 2, April 1, p. 1, April 3, p. 2, April 4, p. 4, April 14, p. 4, April 19, p. 2, April 22, p. 4, April 23, p. 3, April, 24, p. 3, April 29, p. 3, April 30, p. 3, May 3, p. 3, May 7, p. 2, May 13, p. 3, May 17, p. 2, May 20, p. 2, May 21, p. 2, May 23, p. 2, May 30, p. 4, May 31, p. 4.; *WCW* April 12, 1873; "The Naked Truth; or the Situation Reviewed" in Stern, *Victoria Woodhull Reader,* Sociology, Part 3, pp. 26–27; *The Train Ligue;* Broun and Leech, Chapter 8; D.R.M. Bennett, *Anthony Comstock: His Career of Cruelty and Crime* (New York: Da Capo Press, 1971), pp. 1022–1023; George Francis Train *My Life in Many States and in Foreign Lands* (New York: D. Appleton and Company, 1902).

"There was present": Diary of Anthony Comstock (April 15, 1873), Broun and Leech, p. 112.

"a Plymouth Church betrayal": *VCWM, New York Sun,* May 23, 1873.

"Mr. Comstock, informer-general": *VCWM, New York Telegram* (May 20, 1873).

370 "That these women": *Indiana Times* (May 9, 1873).

"Her persecutors will gain": Martha Coffin Wright to her daughter Ellen Garrison (March 12, 1873), *MCW.*

"The people of this country": *Brooklyn Eagle* (November 7, 1873).

" 'Liberty of the Press' ": *Weekly Argus* of Easton, Pennsylvania, as excerpted in Broun and Leech, p. 124.

"contrasting a living skunk" and ff.: *WCW* (February 8, 1873).

371 "A beautiful boy" and ff.: *WCW* (February 15, 1873).

372 "What would you advise" and ff.: *VCWM,* New York Public Library, Scrapbook VI, trial testimony (January 16, 1874); *Brooklyn Eagle* (January 20, 1874).

"a lady, a woman, a mother": *VCWM,* New York Public Library Scrapbook VI, *Banner of Light* (November 1, 1873).

"This is the most outrageous verdict": *TS*, p. 227, trial testimony (March 12, 1874).

373 "Victoria Woodhull—Dead": *TS*, p. 210. This headline appeared in the *New York Sun, New York Daily Graphic, Cleveland Leader,* and various other publications.

## Chapter 31    A Monstrous Conspiracy

374 "for my own vindication" and ff.: Johnston, pp. 194–195.
"was not one of mere platonic affection": *Brooklyn Eagle*, New York Public Library Scrapbook V (June 22, 1873).
"I will reserve": *TS*, p. 214.

375 "I have just returned": Henry Ward Beecher to the editor of the *Brooklyn Eagle* (June 30, 1873), New York Public Library Scrapbook V.
"There isn't force enough": Doyle, p. 361.
"It is high time" and ff.: The tripartite agreement was signed by Tilton, Bowen, and Beecher on April 2, 1872. Wilkeson released it to the press on May 29, 1873, along with his statement concerning Bowen's treachery. Doyle, p. 362.
"Mrs. Stanton asked me": Susan B. Anthony to Isabella Beecher Hooker Rochester, New York (July 14, 1873), *ECS & SBA*, Reel 17:242.

376 "unhandsome advances": Theodore Tilton's "True Story" published in the *Thunderbolt*, Edward H. G. Clark, New York, Albany, and Troy: n.p., May 1873, Library of Congress; Marshall, p. 355.
"stood responsible for the story" and ff.: *IBH*. This account is derived from the letters of Paulina Wright Davis to Victoria Woodhull and Isabella Beecher Hooker, 1873, and from Elizabeth Cady Stanton's pseudonymous article under the nom de plume "Enquirer" in the *New York Daily Graphic* (July 24, 1874); Doyle, pp. 353–354.
"It was even then almost common property": "True Story," Clark, the *Thunderbolt*.
"I think our defeat": Paulina Wright Davis to Elizabeth Cady Stanton (July 20, 1872), *ECS & SBA*, Reel 16.

377 "ought to be hanged" and ff.: "True Story," Clark, the *Thunderbolt*.
"True Story": Johnston, p. 186.
"Oh, Theodore, of all the men": Ibid., p. 187.

379 "I have determined": Henry Ward Beecher to Frank Moulton (June 1, 1873); Marshall, p. 365.
"Why did she not tell me" and ff: Statement of Emma Moulton, *CT;* Rugoff, pp. 497–498.
"He walked up and down": Rugoff, *The Beechers*, pp. 497–498.

380 "We can whisk the council" and ff.: Henry Ward Beecher to Frank Moulton. These proceedings are thoroughly documented in Doyle, pp. 114–142 (Chapters V and VI).
"My Dear Frank:—I am indignant": Henry Ward Beecher to Frank Moulton (March 25, 1874); Marshall, pp. 367–368.

381 "I believe that the infamous women" and ff.: Dr. Bacon's speech and Tilton's reply are to be found in Marshall, pp. 40–42, 43–63.
"In regard to the scandal": *Brooklyn Union* (March 28, 1874), Thomas Shearman interview. Mr. Shearman was a founding partner of a law firm still in existence, Shearman and Stirling. Marshall, p. 48.
"confused Mrs. Tilton with Victoria Woodhull": Thomas Shearman to the *Brooklyn Union* (April 2, 1874); Marshall, p. 49.

382 "It was not I": Theodore Tilton to Reverend Leonard Bacon, D.D., Brooklyn (April 3, 1874).
"Theodore, the Spirits say unto me": Marshall, p. 60; Oliver, p. 197.

383 "deeply hurt": *TS*, p. 207.
"Mrs. Brooker in a drunken or insane rage": *TS*, p. 216.
"Dead at 31," and ff.: *WCW* (July 23, 1873); *TS*, p. 217; "Tried as by Fire," Stern, *Victoria Woodhull Reader*, Part A, Sexual Relations, 5, pp. 27, 28.

384 "ready in this connection" and ff.: The account of Benjamin Tucker, *TS*, p. 254.

384 "I never had sexual intercourse": *TS,* p. 254.
"This is my lover": *TS,* pp. 222–223.

386 "would hold a rally": This account of the Tompkins Square Rally of January 13, 1874, is taken from the *New York Times,* January 16, 18, 24, 1874.
"Every consideration of expediency" and ff.: "Tried as by Fire," Stern, *Victoria Woodhull Reader,* Part A, Sexual Relations, 5, pp. 6–8.

388 "Repulsions, discontent and mutual torment": Ibid., 5, pp. 9, 22; *TS,* p. 197.

## Chapter 32  Human Hyenas

389 "socially, financially and in every way": *CT,* Vol. 2, p. 528.
"I cannot delay": Henry Ward Beecher's statement to the *Brooklyn Daily Argus,* published July 22, 1874.

390 "I will never take": Marshall, p. 188; Shaplen, p. 187; *The Great Scandal: History of the Beecher-Tilton Case.* All the documents and letters (New York: The American News Company, 1874), TB transcript.
"dreadful secret" and ff.: *PCH.* All quotes and exhibits are contained in Marshall, the statement of Lib (Elizabeth) Tilton, pp. 181–188, Tilton's cross-examination, pp. 130–177, 189–214.

392 "criminal commerce" and ff: Theodore Tilton's statement and cross-examination before the Plymouth Church Committee, *PCH.* All quotes and exhibits are contained in Marshall, Theodore Tilton's "Sworn Statement," pp. 112–130, Theodore Tilton's cross-examination, pp. 130–177, 189–214.

394 "as the umpire and peacemaker" and ff.: Frank Moulton's testimony to the Plymouth Church Committee, *CT,* Vol. 1, pp. 307–390, with exhibits, Moulton's formal first statement, pp. 109–112, Moulton's second appearance and exhibits, pp. 227–240.

395 "Four years ago" and ff.: *PCH.* All in Marshall: the first statement of the Reverend Henry Ward Beecher, pp. 177–181, "Mr. Beecher's Defense," pp. 251–286, "Mr. Beecher's Cross Examination," pp. 286–307, "Final Attack," pp. 566, 603–609.

397 "Human hyenas!": *PCH;* Beecher "final attack," Marshall, p. 273.
"Elizabeth Cady Stanton and": The Friday *New York Herald* (July 31, 1874), supplement, New York Public Library Scrapbook VII.

398 "During my whole public career": *New York Argus,* correspondent, Rochester, New York (July 3, 1874), also in the fourth edition of the *New York Argus,* (August 2, 1874).
"You have no doubt" and ff.: Elizabeth Cady Stanton, *New York Daily Graphic* (August 6, 1874).

399 "Well, well, aren't they": Susan B. Anthony to Olympia Brown, Rochester, New York (August 6, 1874), *ECS & SBA,* Reel 18.
"Offended Susan, come right down": Elizabeth Cady Stanton to Susan B. Anthony, Tenafly, New Jersey (July 30, 1874), *ECS & SBA.*
"attempted my ruin" and ff.: *PCH.* Testimony of the Tilton's ward, Bessie Turner, Marshall, pp. 390–400; Anthony on lap, p. 393.

400 "half an idiot" and ff.: Statement made by Bessie Turner, Marshall, p. 393. Susan B. Anthony's answer and explanation, "All men have declared," appeared in the *Rochester Union* (August 24, 1874), p. 3.

401 "Tilton accused his wife": *Chicago Tribune* (October 13, 1874).
"Provided I did tell it": *ECS & SBA,* Reel 18.
"Whatever comes to those": Susan B. Anthony to Daniel R. Anthony (August 22, 1874), *ECS & SBA,* Reel 18; Katharine Anthony, p. 317; Harper, Vol. 1, p. 459.

402 "It is too bad": Isabella Beecher Hooker's comment on Doyle's *The Romance of Plymouth Church,* fragment of letter, *IBH,* 100 C11, 1874.

402 "The case has gone out": Fragment of letter, *IBH,* 100 C12, 1874.

"I know from a private" and ff.: *New York Daily Graphic* (August 21, 1874); Marshall, p. 387.

"She was devotedly attached": George H. Beecher's letter, Marshall, p. 43 (emphasis added).

403 "an honorable man": *Brooklyn Eagle* (September 25, 1874), New York Public Library Scrapbook VIII.

"If Henry were in the habit": Interview with Reverend William H. Beecher, *Chicago Post and Mail* (July 24, 1874), New York Public Library Scrapbook VIII.

"Sam says Livy shall not cross": Molly Clemens to her mother-in-law, Jane Clemens (November 26, 1872), Kenneth R. Andrews, *Nook Farm: Mark Twain's Hartford Circle* (Cambridge, MA: Harvard University Press, 1950), p. 39.

"What a holocaust of womanhood": New York Public Library Scrapbook VIII, *Chicago Tribune* (September 18, 1874), Lutz, *Created Equal,* pp. 226–227.

## Chapter 33  Daniel in the Lion's Den

405 "You will be Daniel" and ff.: This account of Friday evening, August 28, 1874, and all quotations contained therein are drawn from Marshall, "The Report of the Investigating Committee," pp. 405–433, "Scene at Plymouth Church," pp. 433–446, as well as from newspapers such as the *New York Argus* (August 30, 1874) and *New York Times* (August 30, September 4, 1874), and New York Public Library Scrapbook VIII.

410 "Tried as by Fire": "Tried as by Fire, or The True and The False, Socially," 1874, in Stern, *Victoria Woodhull Reader,* Part A, Sexual Relations, 5, pp. 1–44.

"published a pamphlet" and ff.: The Treat pamphlet, as it was commonly called, contains the quotations and accusations that follow. The proper name of the document is *Beecher, Tilton, Woodhull, The Creation of Society: All Four of Them Exposed, and if Possible Reformed and Forgiven, in Dr. Treat's Celebrated Letter to Victoria C. Woodhull,* by Joseph Treat, M.D. Treat's pamphlet, though never substantiated, has, I believe, framed the common perception that Victoria Woodhull and Tennessee C. Claflin were nothing more than self-aggrandizing prostitutes—clearly a misconception.

411 "I am charged with seeking": Doyle, p. 431.

"Can anyone tell me where I am?": *Chicago Mail* (January 2, 1875), New York Public Library Scrapbook VII.

"A Day Memorable" and ff.: The *Tilton v. Beecher* civil trial for alienation of affection was covered extensively in newspapers and later in books and compendiums of trial testimony. A full account of the testimony and exhibits can be found in Doyle, Marshall, and *CT.*

Literally millions of words were written on this trial, which touched a nerve in the American psyche of the day. So extensive was the coverage that one might compare it to that of the O. J. Simpson trial. There were, or course, no television cameras, but sketches of all the subjects and proceedings appeared in the newspapers daily. I counted twelve New York City newspapers on one day alone with virtually the same extensive coverage of this trial, which was then called "The Trial of the Century."

412 "I believe they kissed each other" and ff.: George Templeton Strong was also a well-known New York lawyer and the comptroller of Trinity Church. See *The Diary of George Templeton Strong: 1835–1875,* 4 volumes, edited by Allan Nevins and Milton Halsey Thomas (New York: The Macmillan Co., 1952), Vol. 4, p. 552. At another point, after a quarrel, Henry impetuously kissed Tilton on the lips, and later testimony indicated that Lib (Elizabeth) Tilton entered her bedroom and found Henry sitting on Theodore's knee. See Rugoff, *The Beechers,* p. 485.

414 "I believe Mr. Tilton": *TS*, p. 233.

416 "kindness and sympathy" and ff.: The testimony of Eunice Beecher, *CT*, Vol. 2, pp. 632–640. See "The Beecher Trial: A Review of the Evidence," *New York Times* (July 3, 1875), fifth edition.

"There is only one good result": "The Beecher Trial: A Review of the Evidence," *New York Times* (July 3, 1875), fifth edition.

## Chapter 34  A Meteor's Dash

419 "was the link": New York Public Library Scrapbook VIII, *Brooklyn Eagle* (October 13, 1875).

"an adulterer, a perjurer" and ff.: Shaplen, p. 263.

420 "I have not been pursued" and ff.: Rugoff, *The Beechers*, p. 500.

421 "I do not care for you": Ibid.

"Thanks be unto God" and ff.: Isabella Beecher Hooker diary (Thursday, May 11, 1876), Hartford, Connecticut, *IBH*, 1001 D4–9, 75.

"a deep and solemn peace": Ibid.

"Love begets love—love is God.": Isabella Beecher Hooker diary (Monday, September 18, 1876), *IBH*, 1002 D7–14, 75.

"drawn the veil" and ff.: Isabella Beecher Hooker diary, Hartford, Connecticut (August 8, 1876), *IBH*, pp. 84–88, the Connecticut Historical Society.

422 "From that time": Ibid.

"but a delusion and a mockery": Isabella Beecher Booker to Mr. Fishbough, Hartford, Connecticut (July 15, 1876), *IBH*, 1001 B8–75.

"the light of the eternities": Ibid.

"Susie Howard": Susan Howard wrote this letter February 5, 1875. Her letter and Mark Twain's reaction are detailed in Kenneth R. Andrews, *Nook Farm*, p. 40.

"an ascendancy" and ff.: Harriet Beecher Stowe to Mary Beecher Perkins (May 2, 1875), *IBH*.

"In the letter which Belle sent": Harriet Beecher Stowe to Mary Beecher Perkins (February 28, 1875), *IBH*.

"the beginnings of the Church": Rugoff, *The Beechers*, p. 584.

"Of all the persons": Lucy Stone in the *Woman's Journal* (August 29, 1874), Blackwell, p. 250.

"A few weeks ago": Lib (Elizabeth) Tilton to her lawyer, *New York Times* (April 13, 1878); Shaplen, p. 266.

424 "an unbalanced clairvoyant": Ibid., p. 267.

"a female ailment" and ff.: *TS*, p. 267.

"The grandest woman": (October 6, 1876), *VCWM*, Reel 1, Nos. 33–34.

425 "One jar Balmain's Luminous Paint": Ruth Brandon, *The Spiritualists: The Passion for the Occult in the Nineteenth and Twentieth Centuries* (New York: Knopf, 1983), pp. 100–101.

"It has been supposed": *New York Argus* (October 20, 1876).

426 "death blow": Howard Kerr, *Mediums, and Spirit-Rappers, and Roaring Radicals: Spiritualism in American Literature, 1850–1900* (Chicago: University of Illinois Press, 1972), p. 119.

"a muffled hammer": Brandon, p. 228.

"to shake off a serpent" and ff.: Isabella Beecher Hooker to Victoria Woodhull, *IBH*, circa 1876, uncatalogued.

"God is love and love is God": General correspondence, *VCWM*, Reel 1, Box 3, Folder 3, p. 1.

427 "scandalum magnatum" and ff.: Years later *The Nation* strongly corroborated this by observing that the woman's rights movement "received a severe blow from the figure cut by many of its leading supporters in the Tilton-Beecher scandal and by the adhesion to

Victoria Woodhull. . . . From this it can hardly be said ever to have recovered. It came to have in the eyes of the general public the air of being the first stage . . . of "free love." If it were not for the greater respectability of the Associations in Massachusetts . . . the movement would have kept itself alive here with great difficulty." *The Nation* (February 19, 1885), taken from Andrea Moore Kerr.

"Victoria Woodhull has done": Stanton's interview on Victoria Woodhull, Tenafly, New Jersey. Printed in the *Newark Sunday Call* (January 2, 1876), *ECS & SBA*, Reel 18.

428 "Do you mean to make good": Eric Foner, p. 567.

"The moral atmosphere is": Frederick Douglass to Gerrit Smith (September 24, 1874), Gerrit Smith Papers, Syracuse University; Philip S. Foner, *The Life and Writings of Frederick Douglass*, 534.

"You say you have emancipated us": Frederick Douglass, 1876. Dorothy Sterling, *The Troubles They Seen: Black People Tell the Story of Reconstruction* (Garden City, NY: Doubleday & Company, 1976). (This title later changed to *Nobody Knows the Trouble I Seen: The Story of Reconstruction in the Words of African Americans*.) A version that differs somewhat appears in Philip S. Foner, *The Life and Writings of Frederick Douglass*, p. 96.

429 "Why have I been deprived": Wayne Andrews, p. 176.

430 "That was a good prayer": Barbara Goldsmith, *Little Gloria . . . Happy at Last*, p. 80.

431 "my box of letters": *VCWM*, Reel 2, 79–80, Box 2.

## Chapter 35    The Last Enemy

432 "unanswered": Chester, p. 217.

"I suspect Whitelaw is *actooally* engaged": Chester, p. 216.

"I give it up": Benjamin Butler to Anna Dickinson, Atlantic City (July 22, 1878), Anna E. Dickinson Papers, 7:767.

"pained" and ff.: Benjamin Butler to Anna Dickinson, Boston (June 14, 1888), ibid., 7:805.

"astounding and dastardly request": 7:813. Butler's letter is undated but Anna gives a specific date when she writes to Butler, "your last letter to me—that of June 14, 1888 . . ."

433 "I want to see or hear": Anna Dickinson to Benjamin Butler (April 13, 1982), ibid. (A notation on the letter indicates that it is misdated and is actually from c. 1888.) 7:809.

"the tainted blood": Chester, pp. 267, 268.

"to make a man": Ibid., p. 268.

434 "As I opened the envelope": Susan B. Anthony to Anna Dickinson (November 5, 1895), Anna E. Dickinson Papers, 6:289.

"cheapened" and ff.: Andrea Moore Kerr, p. 236.

"not care so much": Ibid.

"Alice, make the world better!": Blackwell, p. 282.

435 "I feel that suffrage": Elizabeth Cady Stanton, Tenafly, New Jersey, in an interview on the subject of Victoria Woodhull (December 13, 1875), printed in the *Newark Sunday Call* (January 2, 1876); *ECS & SBA*, Reel 18:510.

"worth $10,000 to see the expression": Tenafly, New Jersey (December 1, 1880), Stanton and Blatch, Vol. 2, p. 180.

"the gas was lighted" and ff.: London (December 11, 1882), Vol. 2, p. 200.

"Logically, our enfranchisement": (February 20, 1902) Vol. 2, p. 363.

"I should like to be": Griffith, p. 218.

437 "Failure is impossible": Lynn Sherr, *Failure Is Impossible: Susan B. Anthony in Her Own Words* (New York: Times Books, 1995), p. 324.

"I have often been ignored": Isabella Beecher Hooker to Clara B. Colby (February 16, 1903), *IBH*. If Isabella's belief in the spirits called her credibility into question, she herself never doubted the validity of the spirits. In 1888, Isabella wrote her daughter Alice Hooker Day, "[N]early all the women I meet are more or less interested in some form of spiritual healing. It is simply amazing how the domain of the spirit is extending itself and what is before us in the near future no one can prognosticate." Isabella Beecher Hooker to Alice Hooker Day, 1888, *IBH*, 60 A5.

"passed over" and ff.: Isabella Beecher Hooker diary (Monday, September 18, 1876), *IBH*, 102 D7–14, p. 45.

439  "A bloody ending": Browder, p. 188.

440  "this Irish smut dealer": Broun and Leech, p. 230.

"Your Honor, this woman": *The Masses* (September 15, 1915), reproduced in Broun and Leech, p. 254.

"an eminent barrister": Victoria Woodhull autobiographical sketch, 1895, London, *VCWM*, Reel 3, no. 173; *New York World* (February 17, 1897).

441  "During no part of my life" and ff.: *VCWM*, Reel 3, no. 136; Johnston, p. 264.

"high priest of debauchery": Ibid., p. 267.

"Stephen Pearl Andrews!": Ibid.

"near being the victim": *The Humanitarian* (February 12, 1892).

442  "I never knew that love": *TS*, p. 368.

"There is an apparition" and ff.: Ibid., p. 369.

"other side": Isabella Beecher Hooker to Victoria Woodhull (September 14, 1906), *IBH*. So convinced was Isabella Beecher Hooker that her mother was guiding her that on September 14, 1906, she wrote Victoria Woodhull asking her to work with Isabella and with her deceased mother, Harriet Porter. Victoria Woodhull Martin, by then a conventional English matron, undoubtedly trying to maintain her reputation, wrote back that she had visited the spirit of Isabella's mother, who told her that they might work together in the heavenly realm but should avoid each other on earth. *VCWM*, Reel 2, Box 2.

445  "international country salon": *VCWM*, Reel 3; *New York World* (February 17, 1897).

446  "would rather die than live": *GAT*, p. 14.

"constant companions": Ibid., p. 8.

"the last enemy": Ibid., p. 33; *VCWM*, Reel 2, no. 85–88, taken from Victoria Woodhull Martin letter from London to the *Boston Globe*, circa 1888.

"Sitting here today": Victoria Woodhull fragmentary autobiography, 1895, London, *VCWM*, Reel 1, no. 1, 12.

"extreme unction from her priest" and ff.: *GAT*, p. 32, also in Victoria Woodhull Martin letter from London to the *Boston Globe*, circa 1888; *VCWM*, Boston Public Library Manuscript Collection.

"the idea that the time": Ibid., p. 33.

447  "The deeper I delve": *VCWM*, Reel 3, no. 45–48 and a duplicate no. 49–52, written by Victoria Woodhull Martin (July 1895).

# Bibliography

## Books

Abbot, Austin. *The Official Report of the Trial of Henry Ward Beecher with Notes and References.* 2 Volumes. New York: George W. Smith & Co., Law Booksellers and Publishers, 1875, 1876. Abbreviated as *CT*.

Abbott, Lyman, D.D. *Henry Ward Beecher, A Sketch of His Career: With Analyses of His Power as a Preacher, Lecturer, Orator, and Journalist, and Incidents and Reminiscences of His Life.* New York: Funk & Wagnalls, 1883.

———. *Henry Ward Beecher.* Boston: Riverside Press, 1903. Reprint Houghton Mifflin.

———. *Reminiscences.* Boston: Houghton Mifflin, 1915.

Abels, Jules. *Man On Fire: John Brown and the Cause of Liberty.* New York: Macmillan, 1971.

Allen, Frederick Lewis. *The Big Change.* New York: Harper & Brothers, 1952.

Alter, Robert, and Frank Kermode, eds. *The Literary Guide to the Bible.* Cambridge, MA: Belknap Press of Harvard University Press, 1987.

Andrews, Kenneth R. *Nook Farm: Mark Twain's Hartford Circle.* Cambridge, MA: Harvard University Press, 1950.

Andrews, Wayne. *The Vanderbilt Legend.* New York: Harcourt, Brace, 1941.

Anthony, Katharine. *Susan B. Anthony: Her Personal History and Her Era.* Garden City, NY: Doubleday, 1954.

Aries, Philippe. *Centuries of Childhood: A Social History of Family Life.* New York: Vantage Books, 1962.

Asbury, Herbert. *The Gangs of New York.* New York: Alfred A. Knopf, 1928.

———. *The Barbary Coast.* New York: Alfred A. Knopf, 1933.

*A Sense of History: The Best Writings From the Pages of American Heritage.* Introduction by Byron Dobell. New York: American Heritage Press, 1985.

Asimov, Isaac. *The Golden Door: The United States From 1865 to 1918.* Boston: Houghton Mifflin, 1977.

Atherton, Lewis. *Main Street on the Middle Border.* Bloomington: Indiana University Press, 1954.

Auerbach, Nina. *Woman and the Demon: The Life of a Victorian Myth.* Cambridge, MA: Harvard University Press, 1982.

Badeau, Adam. *Grant in Peace from Appomattox to Mount McGregor: A Personal Memoir.* Hartford, CT: Books for Libraries Press, 1887.

Barker-Benfield, G. J. *The Horrors of the Half-Known Life: Male Attitudes Toward Women and Sexuality in 19th Century America.* New York: Harper & Row, 1976.

Barkun, Michael. *Crucible of the Millennium: The Burned-Over District of New York in the 1840s.* Syracuse, NY: Syracuse University Press, 1986.

Barry, Kathleen. *Susan B. Anthony: A Biography of a Singular Feminist.* New York: New York University Press, 1988.

Beebe, Lucius. *The Big Spenders.* Garden City, NY: Doubleday, 1966.

Beecher, Catharine E. *A Treatise on Domestic Economy, For The Use of Young Ladies At Home, And At School.* Boston: Marsh, Capen, Lyon, and Webb, 1841.

Beecher, Catharine E., and Harriet Beecher Stowe. *The American Woman's Home Or, Principles of Domestic Science; Being A Guide To The Formation And Maintenance of Economical, Healthful, Beautiful And Christian Homes.* 4th ed. Hartford, CT: Stowe-Day Foundation, 1987.

Beecher, Henry Ward. *Norwood: or Village Life in New England.* New York: J. B. Ford, 1868.

————. *The Life of Jesus Christ.* 2 volumes. New York: J. B. Ford, 1871.

————. *The Original Plymouth Pulpit: Sermons of Henry Ward Beecher In Plymouth Church, Brooklyn.* [1868–1873]. From stenographic reports by T. J. Ellinwood. 10 volumes. New York: Fords, Howard & Hulbert, 1893.

————. *Autobiographical Reminiscences.* New York: F. A. Stokes, 1898.

————. *Plymouth Church.* New York Public Library Compilations. Printed sermons taken from 4 volumes.

Beecher, Lyman, D.D. *Autobiography, Correspondence, Etc. of Lyman Beecher, D.D.* Edited by Charles Beecher. Vol. 1, New York: Harper & Brothers, Franklin Square, 1864. Vol. 2, New York: Harper & Brothers, Franklin Square, 1865.

*Beecher-Tilton Investigation: The Scandal of the Age.* Philadelphia: Barclay & Co., 1874.

Beecher, Wm. C., and Rev. Samuel Scoville, assisted by Mrs. Henry Ward Beecher. *A Biography of Rev. Henry Ward Beecher.* New York: Charles L. Webster, 1888.

Benet, Stephen Vincent. *John Brown's Body.* New York: Holt, Rinehart and Winston, 1928.

Bennett, D.R.M. *Anthony Comstock: His Career of Cruelty and Crime.* New York: Da Capo Press, 1971.

Bentley, George R. *A History of the Freedmen's Bureau.* Philadelphia: University of Pennsylvania Press, 1955.

Berg, Barbara. *The Remembered Gate: Origins of American Feminism 1800–1860.* New York: Oxford University Press, 1978.

Bernstein, Iver. *The New York City Draft Riots: Their Significance for American Society and Politics in the Age of the Civil War.* New York: Oxford University Press, 1990.

Bernstein, Samuel. *The First International in America.* New York: Augustus M. Kelley, 1962.

Bigelow, John. *Retrospections of an Active Life.* Vol. 5. New York: Doubleday, Page, 1913.

Blackstone, Sir William. *The Great Commentaries on the Laws of England 1865–69.*

Blackwell, Alice Stone. *Lucy Stone, Pioneer of Woman's Rights.* Boston: Little, Brown, 1930.

Blanch, Lesley. *The Wilder Stories of Love.* New York: Simon and Schuster, 1954.

Blatch, Harriot Stanton, and Alma Lutz. *Challenging Years: The Memoirs of Harriot Stanton Blatch.* New York: G. P. Putnam's Sons, 1940.

Blight, David W. *Frederick Douglass' Civil War: Keeping Faith in Jubilee.* Baton Rouge: Louisiana State University Press, 1989.

Bloch, George. J., trans. *Mesmerism: A Translation of the Original Medical and Scientific Writings of F. A. Mesmer, M.D.* Los Angeles: William Kaufmann, 1980.

Blum, Stella, ed. *Ackermann's Costume Plates: Women's Fashions in England, 1818–1828.* New York: Dover Publications, 1978.

Boller, Paul F., Jr. *Presidential Campaigns.* New York: Oxford University Press, 1984.

Bontemps, Arna. *Free At Last: The Life of Frederick Douglass.* New York: Dodd, Mead, 1971.

Boydston, Jeanne, Mary Kelly, and Anne Margolis. *The Limits of Sisterhood: The Beecher Sisters on Woman's Rights and Woman's Sphere.* Chapel Hill: University of North Carolina Press, 1988.

Boyer, Paul S. *Purity in Print: The Vice-Society Movement and Book Censorship in America.* New York: Charles Scribner's Sons, 1968.

Brandon, Ruth. *The Spiritualists: The Passion for the Occult in the Nineteenth and Twentieth Centuries.* New York: Knopf, 1983.

Braude, Ann. *Radical Spirits: Spiritualism and Women's Rights in Nineteenth-Century America.* Boston: Beacon, 1989.

Bredvold, Louis I., ed. *Lord Byron: Don Juan and Other Satirical Poems.* New York: Odyssey Press, 1935.

Britten, William. *Art Magic; or mundane, sub-mundane and super-mundane spiritualism . . .* (1876) 1898 reprint.

Brockett, Linus P. *Men of Our Day.* Philadelphia: Ziegler & McCurdy, 1868.

Brockway, Beman. *Fifty Years in Journalism. Embracing Recollections and Personal Experiences with an Autobiography.* Watertown, NY: Daily Times Printing and Publishing House, 1891.

Brough, James. *The Vixens: A Biography of Victoria and Tennessee Claflin.* New York: Simon and Schuster, 1980.

Broun, Heywood, and Margaret Leech. *Anthony Comstock: Roundsman of the Lord.* New York: Albert & Charles Boni, 1927.

Browder, Clifford. *The Wickedest Woman in New York: Madame Restell, the Abortionist.* Hamden, CT: Archon Books, 1988.

Brown, Vinson. *Great Upon the Mountain.* New York: Macmillan, 1977.

Browne, Junius Henri. *The Great Metropolis: A Mirror of New York.* Hartford, CT: American Publishing Co., 1870.

Bruce, Robert V. *1877: Year of Violence.* Indianapolis: Bobbs-Merrill, 1959.

Buhle, Mari Jo. *Women and American Socialism, 1870–1920.* Urbana, Chicago, London: University of Illinois Press, 1981.

Buhle, Mari Jo, and Paul Buhle, eds. *The Concise History of Woman Suffrage: Selections from the Classic Work of Stanton, Anthony, Gage and Harper.* Urbana: University of Illinois Press, 1978.

Butler, Benjamin F. *Autobiography and Personal Reminiscences of Major-General Benjamin F. Butler; Butler's Book.* Boston, 1892.

Cadwallader, M. E. *Hydesville in History.* Chicago: Progressive Thinker Publishing House, 1917, 1922.

Callow, Alexander B., Jr. *The Tweed Ring.* New York: Oxford University Press, 1966.

Campbell, Joseph. *The Hero with a Thousand Faces.* Princeton, NJ: Princeton University Press, 1949.

Capers, Gerald M. *Occupied City: New Orleans Under the Federals 1862–1865.* Lexington, KY, 1865.

Carman, Harry J. *Social and Economic History of the United States.* Vol. 2, *The Rise of Industrialism 1820–1875.* New York: D. C. Heath, 1934.

Carter, Hodding. *The Angry Scar: The Story of Reconstruction.* Garden City, NY: Doubleday, 1959.

Carter, Paul. *The Spiritual Crisis of the Gilded Age.* DeKalb: Northern Illinois University Press, 1971.

Caskey, Marie. *Chariot of Fire: Religion and the Beecher Family.* New Haven, CT, and London: Yale University Press, 1978.

Catton, Bruce. *A Stillness at Appomattox.* New York: Washington Square Books, 1958.

Caverno, C. *The Brooklyn Council.* Chicago: Brewster & Bro., 1874.

Chester, Giraud. *Embattled Maiden. The Life of Anna Dickinson.* New York: G. P. Putnam's Sons, 1951.

Churchill, Allen. *The Splendor Seekers.* New York: Grosset & Dunlap, 1974.

Claflin, Tennessee, Lady Cook. *Essays on Social Topics.* London: Roxburghe Press, c. 1895.

Clark, Clifford E., Jr. *Henry Ward Beecher: Spokesman for a Middle-Class America.* Urbana: University of Illinois Press, 1978.

Cleveland, Cecilia. *The Story of a Summer, or Journal Leaves from Chappaqua.* New York: G. W. Carleton, 1874.

Clews, Henry. *Fifty Years in Wall Street.* New York: Irving Publishing, 1908.

Cohen, Daniel. *Curses, Hexes and Spells.* Philadelphia and New York: J. B. Lippencott, 1974.

Conant, Mrs. J. H. *Flashes of Light from the Past Spirit Land*. Boston: Colby & Rich.

Cooper, George. *Lost Love: A True Story of Passion, Murder, and Justice in Old New York*. New York: Pantheon Books, 1994.

Cox, La Wanda. *Lincoln and Black Freedom*. Chicago: University of Illinois Press, 1985.

Crabtree, Adam. *Animal Magnetism, Early Hypnotism, and Psychical Research 1766–1925*. White Plains, NY: Kraus International Publications, 1988.

————. *From Mesmer to Freud: Magnetic Sleep and the Roots of Psychological Healing*. New Haven, CT: Yale University Press, 1994.

Crichton, Michael. *Travels*. New York: Knopf, 1988.

Crimmins, John D. *Irish-American Historical Miscellany*. New York: The author, 1905.

Croffut, A. *The Vanderbilts and the Story of Their Fortune*. New York: Belford, Clarke, 1886.

Cronise, Adelbert. *The Beginnings of Modern Spiritualism in and Near Rochester*. Rochester, NY: Rochester Historical Society, 1925.

Cross, Barbara M., ed. *The Autobiography of Lyman Beecher*. 2 volumes. Cambridge, MA: Belknap Press of Harvard University Press, 1961.

Cross, Whitney R. *The Burned-over District: The Social and Intellectual History of Enthusiastic Religion in Western New York, 1800–1850*. New York: Harper & Row, 1950.

Danciger, Elizabeth. *Homeopathy: From Alchemy to Medicine*. Rochester, VT: Healing Arts Press, 1987, 1988.

Darewin, G. S. *Synopsis of the Lives of Victoria C. Woodhull (now Mrs. John Biddulph Martin) and Tennessee Claflin (now Lady Cook), The First Two Lady Bankers and Reformers of America*. London: 1891.

Darnton, Robert. *Mesmerism and the End of the "Enlightenment in France."* Cambridge, MA: Harvard University Press, 1968.

Davenport, Reuben Briggs. *The Death-Blow to Spiritualism: Being the True Story of the Fox Sisters. As Revealed by Authority of Margaret Fox Kane and Catherine Fox Jencken*. New York: G. W. Dillingham, 1897.

David, Deirdre. *Intellectual Women and Victorian Patriarchy: Harriet Martineau, Elizabeth Barrett Browning, George Eliot*. Ithaca, NY: Cornell University Press, 1987.

Davis, Andrew Jackson. *The Philosophy of Spiritual Intercourse*. New York: Fowler & Wells, 1851.

————. *The Principles of Nature, Her Divine Revelations and a Voice to Mankind*. (Trance lectures)

Davis, Burke. *Sherman's March*. New York: Random House, 1980.

DeLeon, David. *The American as Anarchist: Reflections on Indigenous Radicalism*. Baltimore: Johns Hopkins University Press, 1978.

DeMorgan, Sophia. *From Matter to Spirit*. (1863).

Depew, Chauncey M., L.L.D., United States senator from the state of New York, ed-in-chief; Nathan Haskell Dole, Caroline Ticknor, Thomas Charles Quinn, assoc. eds. *The Library of Oratory: Ancient and Modern with Critical Studies of the World's Great Orators by Eminent Essayists*. Vol. 15. New York: E. R. DuMont, 1896.

Dickerson, K. *The Philosophy of Mesmerism . . . 1842*.

Dijkstra, Bram. *Idols of Perversity*. New York: Oxford University Press, 1986.

Dingwall, Eric John, ed. *Abnormal Hypnotic Phenomena: A Survey of Nineteenth-Century Cases*. Vol. 4. United States of America, by Allan Angoff; Great Britain, by Eric J. Dingwall. London: J. & A. Churchill, 1967–68.

Ditzion, Stanley. *Marriage, Morals and Sex in America*. New York: Bookman Associates, 1953.

Dixon, William Hepworth. *Spiritual Wives*. 2 volumes. London: Hurst and Blackett, 1868.

Doctorow, E. L. *Ragtime*. New York: Random House, 1975.

Douglas, Ann. *The Feminization of American Culture*. New York: Knopf, 1977.

Douglass, Frederick. *Life and Times, Written by Himself*. Edited by Rayford W. Logan. New York: Collier Books, 1962. Facsimile edition, New York: Citadel Press, 1983.

————. *Narrative of The Life of Frederick Douglass, An American Slave*. Edited by Houston A. Baker Jr. New York: Penguin Group, 1986.

————. *My Bondage and My Freedom.* Edited by William L. Andrews. Urbana & Chicago: University of Illinois Press, 1987.

Doyle, J.E.P., compiler. *The Romance of Plymouth Church. Plymouth Church and Its Pastor, or Henry Ward Beecher and His Accusers.* Hartford, CT: Park Publishing Co., 1874.

Druesedow, Jean L. *In Style: Celebrating Fifty Years of the Costume Institute From Queen to Empress Victorian Dress 1837–1877.* New York: Metropolitan Museum of Art.

DuBois, Ellen Carol. *Feminism and Suffrage: The Emergence of an Independent Women's Movement in America 1848–1869.* Ithaca, NY: Cornell University Press, 1978.

————, ed. *The Elizabeth Cady Stanton-Susan B. Anthony Reader: Correspondence, Writings, Speeches.* Revised edition. Boston: Northeastern University Press, 1981.

Dursey, Leslie, and Janice Devine. *Fare Thee Well.* New York: Crown, 1964.

Edmiston, Susan, and Linda D. Cirino. *Literary New York: A History and Guide.* Boston: Houghton Mifflin, 1976.

Edmonds, I. G. *The Girls Who Talked to Ghosts: The Story of Katie and Margaretta Fox.* New York: Holt, Rinehart and Winston, 1979.

Edwards, Stewart, ed. *The Communards of Paris, 1871.* Ithaca, NY: Cornell University Press, 1973.

Eliade, Mircea. *The Sacred and the Profane: The Nature of Religion.* New York: Harcourt Brace Jovanovich, 1959.

Ellington, George. *The Women of New York, or the Underworld of the Great City.* New York: New York Book Company, 1869. Reprint, New York: Arno Press, 1971.

Ellis, Dr. John B. *Free Love and Its Votaries.* New York, 1870.

Evans, Warren Felt. *The New Age and Its Messenger.* Boston, 1864.

Everdell, William R., and Malcolm Mackay. *Rowboats to Rapid Transit: A History of Brooklyn Heights.* New York: Brooklyn Heights Association, 1973.

Ewing, Elizabeth. *Underwear: A History.* New York: Theatre Arts Books, 1972.

Farren, David. *Living with Magic.* New York: Simon and Schuster, 1974.

Feaver, William. *Masters of Caricature.* New York: Knopf, 1981.

Firestone, Shulamith. *The Dialectic of Sex.* New York: William Morrow, 1970.

Flexner, Eleanor. *Century of Struggle: The Woman's Rights Movement in the United States.* Cambridge, MA: Belknap Press of Harvard University Press, 1959.

Foner, Eric. *Reconstruction: America's Unfinished Revolution, 1863–1877.* New York: Harper & Row, 1988.

Foner, Eric, and Olivia Mahoney. *A House Divided: America in the Age of Lincoln.* Chicago: Chicago Historical Society in association with W. W. Norton & Company, 1990.

Foner, Philip S. *The Life and Writings of Frederick Douglass.* Volume 4: *Reconstruction and After.* New York: International Publishers, 1955.

————. *Frederick Douglass.* New York: Citadel Press and International Publishers, 1964.

Fowler, Orson S. *Phrenology Proved, Illustrated and Applied.* Philadelphia: Fowler and Brevoort, 1836.

————. *The Great Brooklyn Romance: All the Documents in the Famous Beecher-Tilton Case.* Unabridged. New York: J. H. Paxon, 1874. Abbreviated as *CT.*

Franklin, Allan. *The Trail of the Tiger: 1789–1928.* New York: Allan Franklin, 1928.

Fuller, Robert C. *Mesmerism and the American Cure of Souls.* Philadelphia: University of Pennsylvania Press, 1982.

Fuller, Robert H. *Jubilee Jim: The Life of Col. James Fisk, Jr.* New York: Macmillan, 1928.

Garrison, Wendell Phillips, and Francis Jackson Garrison. *William Lloyd Garrison, 1805–1879; the Story of His Life as Told by His Children.* Vol. 4. Boston: Houghton Mifflin, 1889.

Gauld, Alan. *A History of Hypnotism.* Cambridge, UK: Cambridge University Press, 1992.

Gay, Peter. *The Bourgeois Experience, Victoria to Freud.* Vol. 1, *Education of the Senses.* New York: Oxford University Press, 1984.

————. *The Bourgeois Experience, Victoria to Freud.* Vol. 2, *The Tender Passion.* New York: Oxford University Press, 1986.

Geller, Uri, and Guy Lyon Playfair. *The Geller Effect.* Grafton Books, 1988.

Goethe, Johann Wolfgang von. *Elective Affinities.* Translated and with an introduction by Victoria Woodhull. Boston: D. W. Niles, 1872. See also the edition translated and with an introduction by R. J. Hollingdale, New York: Penguin, 1983. Originally published in 1809 as *Die Wahlverwandtschaften.*

Goldsmith, Barbara. *Little Gloria . . . Happy at Last.* New York: Knopf, 1980.

Goldsmith, Margaret. *Franz Anton Mesmer: A History of Mesmerism.* Garden City, NY: Doubleday, Doran, 1934.

Goldstone, Harmon H., and Martha Dalrymple. *History Preserved: A Guide to New York City Landmarks and Historic Districts.* New York: Simon and Schuster, 1974.

Gordon, John Steele. *The Scarlet Woman of Wall Street: Jay Gould, Jim Fisk, Cornelius Vanderbilt, the Erie Railway Wars, and the Birth of Wall Street.* New York: Weidenfeld & Nicolson, 1988.

Gordon, Ann D. and Patricia G. Holland, eds. *The Papers of Elizabeth Cady Stanton and Susan B. Anthony, Guide and Index,* Vol. 1. New Brunswick, NJ: Rutgers University, 1997.

Gordon, Linda. *Woman's Body, Woman's Right: A Social History of Birth Control in America.* New York: Grossman, 1976.

Grafton, John. *New York in the Nineteenth Century: 317 Engravings from Harper's Weekly and Other Contemporary Sources.* 2nd ed. New York: Dover, 1980.

Gray, Eden. *A Complete Guide to the Tarot.* New York: Bantam Books, 1972.

*The Great Scandal: History of the Beecher-Tilton Case.* All the documents and letters. New York: American News Company, 1874. Abbreviated as *CT.*

Green, Harvey. *The Light of the Home: An Intimate View of the Lives of Women in Victorian America.* New York: Pantheon Books, 1983.

Gregory, William. *Animal Magnetism: or, Mesmerism and its Phenomena.* 5th ed. London: Nichols & Co., 1909.

Griffith, Elisabeth. *In Her Own Right: The Life of Elizabeth Cady Stanton.* New York: Oxford University Press, 1984.

Gruber, Dorothy Whitney. *The Chappaqua Life of Horace Greeley: An Illustrated History of His Farm, His Family and His Houses.* New Castle, NY: Chappaqua Historical Society, 1974.

Hacker, Louis M., and Benjamin B. Kendrick. *The United States Since 1865.* New York: F. S. Crofts & Co., 1933.

Hahnemann, Christian Frederick Samuel. *Organon of Medicine.* Translated by J. Kunzl et al. London: Vic Gollancz, 1983.

Haight, Gordon. *George Eliot: A Biography.* Oxford University Press, 1968.

Hale, William Harlan. *Horace Greeley: Voice of the People.* New York: Harper & Bros., 1950.

Handford, Thomas W. *Beecher: Christian Philosopher, Pulpit Orator, Patriot and Philanthropist.* New York: Belford, Clark, 1887.

Harding, Vincent. *There Is a River: The Black Struggle for Freedom in America.* New York: Vintage Books, 1983.

Hardinge, Emma. *Modern American Spiritualism: A Twenty Years' Record of the Communication Between Earth and the World of the Spirits.* 1869.

Harlow, Alvin F. *Old Waybills: The Romance of the Express Companies.* New York: D. Appleton-Century, 1934.

Harnsberger, John Lewis. *Jay Cooke and Minnesota: The Formative Years of the Northern Pacific Railroad 1868–1873.* New York: Arno Press, 1981.

Harper, Ida Husted. *The Life and Work of Susan B. Anthony.* Volumes 1 and 2. Indianapolis, IN: Bowen-Merrill, 1898.

Hart, John S. *The Female Prose Writers of America,* 1857.

Haskell, Molly. *From Reverence to Rape.* Canada: Holt, Reinhart and Winston of Canada Ltd., 1973, 1974.

Hawthorne, Nathaniel. *The Scarlet Letter.* 2nd ed. New York and Boston: Thomas Y. Crowell, 1850.

Hay, John. *Lincoln and the Civil War in the Diaries and Letters of John Hay.* Edited by Tyler Dennett. New York: Dodd, Mead, 1939.

Hays, Elinor Rice. *Morning Star: A Biography of Lucy Stone, 1818–1893.* New York: Harcourt, Brace & World, 1961.

Heininger, Mary Lynn Stevens, Karin Calvert, Barbara Finkelstein, Kathy Vandell, Anne Scott MacLeod, and Harvey Green. *A Century of Childhood 1820–1920.* Rochester, NY: Margaret Woodbury Strong Museum, 1984.

Henretta, James. *The Evolution of American Society 1700–1815.* Lexington, MA, 1973.

Hibben, Paxton. *Henry Ward Beecher: An American Portrait.* New York: George H. Doran, 1927. Reprint, Press of the Readers Club, New York, 1942.

Hibbert, Albert. *Smith Wigglesworth: The Secret of His Power.* Tulsa, OK: Harrison House, 1982.

Hillis, N.D. *Lectures and Orations of Henry Ward Beecher.* New York: AMS Press, 1913. Reprint, 1970.

Himmelfarb, Gertrude. *Marriage and Morals Among the Victorians.* New York: Knopf, 1986.

Hobson, Barbara Miel. *Uneasy Virtue: The Politics of Prostitution and the American Reform Tradition.* Chicago: University of Chicago Press, 1990.

Holbrook, Stewart H. *The Age of the Moguls.* Garden City, NY: Doubleday, 1953.

———. *The Story of American Railroads.* New York: Crown, 1947.

Hole, Judith, and Ellen Levine. *Rebirth of Feminism.* New York: Quadrangle Books, 1971.

*Holy Bible, The: Containing the Old and New Testaments and Commonly Known as the King James Version.* New York: American Bible Society, 1816.

Holzman, Robert S. *Stormy Ben Butler.* New York: Macmillan, 1954.

Howard, Joseph, Jr. *Life of Henry Ward Beecher, The Eminent Pulpit and Platform Orator.* Philadelphia: Hubbard Brothers, 1887.

Howard, Robert West. *The Great Iron Trail: The Story of the First Trans-Continental Railroad.* New York: G. P. Putnam's Sons, 1962.

Hoyt, Edwin P. *The Vanderbilts and Their Fortunes.* Garden City, NY: Doubleday, 1962.

Huggins, Nathan Irvin. *Slave and Citizen: The Life of Frederick Douglass.* Edited by Oscar Handlin. Boston: Little, Brown, 1980.

Hungerford, Edward. *Men of Erie.* New York: Random House, 1946.

*Instructive and Amusing: An Essay on Toys, Games and Education in New England.* Volume 123, No. 2. Essex Institute, April 1987.

Jahn, Robert G., and Brenda J. Dunne. *Margins of Reality: The Role of Consciousness in the Physical World.* New York: Harcourt Brace Jovanovich, 1987.

James, Henry. *Siege of London.* London: Macmillan, 1883.

———. *The Great Short Novels of Henry James: The Siege of London.* New York: Dial Press, 1944; New York: Penguin, 1983. (*The Siege of London* first appeared in *Cornbill Magazine,* January–February 1883).

James, Henry, Horace Greeley, and Stephen Pearl Andrews (A Discussion by). *Love, Marriage and Divorce, and the Sovereignty of the Individual.* New York: Stringer & Townsend, 1853.

Johnston, Johanna. *Mrs. Satan: The Incredible Saga of Victoria C. Woodhull.* New York: G. P. Putnam's Sons, 1967; London: Macmillan, 1967.

Jones, Willoughby. *The Life of James Fisk, Jr.* Philadelphia, Chicago: Union Publishing Co., 1872.

Jordan, Robert Paul. *The Civil War.* New York: National Geographic Society, 1969.

Josephson, Matthew. *The Robber Barons: The Great American Capitalists.* New York: Harcourt, Brace and Company, 1934.

Keller, Allan. *Scandalous Lady: The Life and Times of Madame Restell, New York's Most Notorious Abortionist.* New York: Atheneum, 1981.

Keller, Morton. *The Art & Politics of Thomas Nast.* New York: Oxford University Press, 1968.

Kenner, Hugh. *Magic and Spells.* Bennington, VT: Bennington Chapbooks in Literature, 1987.

Kerr, Andrea Moore. *Lucy Stone: Speaking Out for Equality.* New Brunswick, NJ: Rutgers University Press, 1992.

Kerr, Howard. *Mediums, and Spirit-Rappers, and Roaring Radicals: Spiritualism in American Literature, 1850–1900.* Chicago: University of Illinois Press, 1972.

Kerr, Howard, and Charles L. Crow, eds. *The Occult in America: New Historical Perspectives.* Chicago: University of Illinois Press, 1983.

Kessler, Carol Farley. *Elizabeth Stuart Phelps.* Boston: Twayne Publishers, 1982.

Klein, Maury. *The Life and Legend of Jay Gould.* Baltimore: Johns Hopkins University Press, 1986.

Kneeland, George Jackson. *Commercialized Prostitution in New York City.* Montclair, NJ: Patterson Smith, 1969.

Koch, Freda Postle. *Civil War Heroines: The Coggeshall Ladies.* Columbus, OH: PoKo Press, 1992.

Kouwenhoven, John A. *The Columbia Historical Portrait of New York (1857–1900).* New York: Harper & Row, 1972.

Kugler, Israel. *From Ladies to Women. The Organized Struggle for Woman's Rights in the Reconstruction Era.* Contributions in Women's Studies, Number 77. New York, Westport, CT; London: Greenwood Press, 1987.

Lancaster, Clay. *Old Brooklyn Heights: New York's First Suburb.* 2nd ed. New York: Dover, 1979.

Lane, Wheaton J. *Commodore Vanderbilt: An Epic of the Steam Age.* New York: Knopf, 1942.

Larson, Henrietta. *Jay Cooke: Private Banker.* New York: Greenwood Press, 1968.

Latham, Jean. *Victoriana: A Guide for Collectors.* New York: Stein & Day, 1971.

Latimer, Margaret, ed. *Brooklyn Almanac: Illustrations/Facts/Figures/People/Buildings/Books.* New York: Brooklyn Rediscovery, Brooklyn Educational & Cultural Alliance, 1984.

Lawton, George. *The Drama of Life After Death: A Study of the Spiritualist Religion.* New York: Henry Holt, 1932.

Leach, William. *True Love and Perfect Union: The Feminist Reform of Sex and Society.* New York: Basic Books, 1980.

Levine, George, and William Madden. *The Art of Victorian Prose.* New York: Oxford University Press, 1968.

Lindsay, Gordon. *The Chaos of the Psychics.* Dallas: Christ for the Nations, 1978.

———. *Astrology, Reincarnation, Flying Saucer Men, Edgar Cayce, Psychics.* Sorcery In America Series, Volume 2. Dallas: Christ for the Nations, 1982.

———. *Spiritualism, Telepathy, ESP, Ouija Board, Hypnotism.* Sorcery In America Series, Volume 1. Dallas: Christ for the Nations, 1985.

———. *Jeane Dixon—Prophetess or Psychic Medium.* Dallas: Christ for the Nations, 1987.

Longford, Elizabeth. *Queen Victoria: Born to Succeed.* New York: Harper & Row, 1964.

———. *Byron.* London: Cox & Wyman, 1976.

Lundberg, Ferdinand. *America's 60 Families.* New York: Vanguard Press, 1937.

Lutz, Alma. *Created Equal: A Biography of Elizabeth Cady Stanton 1815–1902.* New York: John Day, 1940.

———. *Susan B. Anthony: Rebel, Crusader, Humanitarian.* Boston: Beacon, 1959.

Lynch, Denis Tilden. *"Boss" Tweed: The Story of a Grim Generation.* New York: Boni and Liveright, 1927.

Mabee, Carleton. *The American Leonardo. A Life of Samuel F.B. Morse.* New York: Knopf, 1943.

Maddow, Ben. *A Sunday Between Wars: The Course of American Life 1865–1917.* New York: W. W. Norton, 1979.

Maher, James T. *The Twilight of Splendor.* New York: Little, Brown, 1976.

Mandelbaum, Seymour J. *Boss Tweed's New York.* New York: John Wiley & Sons, 1965.

Marberry, M. M. *Vicky: A Biography of Victoria C. Woodhull.* New York: Funk & Wagnalls, 1967.

Markun, Leo. *Mrs. Grundy: A History of Four Centuries of Morals Intended to Illuminate Present Problems in Great Britain and the United States.* New York: D. Appleton, 1930.

*Marriage: For & Against.* Introduction by Harold H. Hart. New York: Hart Publishing Co., 1972.

Marshall, Charles F. *The True History of the Brooklyn Scandal.* Philadelphia: National Publishing Company, 1874.

Martin, Edward Winslow. *The Secrets of the Great City: A Work Descriptive of the Virtues and the Vices, the Mysteries, Miseries and Crimes of New York City.* Philadelphia: Jones Brothers & Co., 1868.

Martin, Victoria (Claflin) Woodhull. *A Fragmentary Record of Public Work Done in America. 1871–1877.* London: Self-published, 1877.

———. *Stirpiculture: or, The Scientific Propagation of the Human Race.* London: Self-published, 1888.

Martin, Waldo E., Jr. *The Mind of Frederick Douglass.* Chapel Hill: University of North Carolina Press, 1984.

*Mass Violence in America: Memphis Riots and Massacres.* New York: Arno Press, 1969. Facsimile edition, House Report No. 101, U.S. 39th Congress, First Session.

McCabe, James D., Jr. *Lights and Shadows of New York Life; or, The Sights and Sensations of the Great City.* Philadelphia: National Publishing Co., 1872. Facsimile edition, New York: Farrar, Straus and Giroux, 1970.

McCaffrey, Lawrence. *The Irish Diaspora in America.* Bloomington: Indiana University Press, 1976.

McCaughey, Elizabeth P. *Government By Choice: Inventing the United States Constitution.* New York: New York Historical Society and Basic Books, 1987.

McClinton, Katherine Morrison. *Antiques of American Childhood.* New York: Bramhall House.

McFeely, William S. *Grant: A Biography.* New York: W. W. Norton, 1982.

———. *Frederick Douglass.* New York: W. W. Norton, 1991.

McLoughlin, William G. *The Meaning of Henry Ward Beecher: An Essay in the Shifting Values of Mid-Victorian America.* New York: Knopf, 1970.

McPherson, James M. *The Negro's Civil War: How American Negroes Felt and Acted during the War for the Union.* Urbana and Chicago: University of Illinois Press, originally Pantheon Books, 1965.

———. *Battle Cry of Freedom: The Civil War Era.* New York: Oxford University Press, 1988.

Meade, Marion. *Free Woman: The Life and Times of Victoria Woodhull.* New York: Knopf, 1976.

Ment, David. *The Shaping of a City: A Brief History of Brooklyn.* New York: Brooklyn Rediscovery, Brooklyn Educational & Cultural Alliance, 1979.

Meriwether, Elizabeth Avery. *Recollections of 92 Years, 1824–1916.* Nashville: Tennessee Historical Commission, 1958.

Milbauer, Barbara. *The Law Giveth.* New York: McGraw-Hill, 1984.

Mill, John Stuart. *The Subjection of Women.* Introduction by Wendell Robert Carr. Cambridge, MA: MIT Press, 1970.

Minnigerode, Meade. *Certain Rich Men.* Freeport, NY: Books for Libraries Press, 1927. Reprint, 1970.

Mohr, James C. *Abortion in America: The Origins and Evolution of National Policy, 1800–1900.* New York: Oxford University Press, 1978.

Moore, R. Laurence. *In Search of White Crows: Spiritualism, Parapsychology, and American Culture.* New York: Oxford University Press, 1977.

Morris, Lloyd. *Incredible New York: High Life and Low Life of the Last Hundred Years.* New York: Random House, 1951.

Morse, Edward Lind, ed. *Samuel F.B. Morse: His Letters and Journals.* Volumes 1 and 2. Boston: Houghton Mifflin; New York: The Riverside Press, 1914.

Mumford, Lewis. *Sticks and Stones.* New York: Dover, 1955.

Nash, Howard P., Jr. *Stormy Petrel: The Life and Times of General Benjamin F. Butler, 1818–1893.* Rutherford, NJ: Fairleigh Dickinson University Press, 1969.

Nast, Thomas. *Thomas Nast, Cartoons and Illustrations.* New York: Dover, 1974.

Nevins, Allan. *A History of American Life in Twelve Volumes.* Edited by Arthur M. Schlesinger and Dixon Ryan Fox. New York: Macmillan, 1927.

Nevins, Allan, and Milton Halsey Thomas, eds. *The Diary of George Templeton Strong: Post-War Years 1865–1875.* New York: Macmillan, 1952.

Nevins, Deborah, ed. *Grand Central Terminal: A City Within the City.* New York: Municipal Art Society of New York, 1982.

Newman, Richard. *Words Like Freedom: Afro-American Books and Manuscripts in the Henry W. and Albert A. Berg Collection of English and American Literature.* New York Public Library, 1989.

Northrup, Flora. *Record of a Century, 1834–1934.* New York: American Female Guardian Society, 1934.

*Notable American Women 1607–1950: A Biographical Dictionary.* 3 volumes. Edited by Edward T. James. Prepared under the auspices of Radcliffe College. Cambridge, MA: Belknap Press of Harvard University Press, 1971.

Noyes, Alexander Dana. *Forty Years of American Finance: A Short Financial History of the Government and People of the United States Since the Civil War, 1865–1907* (the second and extended edition of "Thirty Years of American Finance"). New York: G. P. Putnam's Sons, the Knickerbocker Press, 1898, 1909.

Oates, Stephen B. *To Purge This Land With Blood: A Biography of John Brown.* 2nd ed. Amherst: University of Massachusetts Press, 1984.

Oberholtzer, Ellis Paxson, Ph.D. *Jay Cooke: Financier of the Civil War.* 2 volumes. Philadelphia: George W. Jacobs, 1907.

Offit, Avodah, M.D. *The Sexual Self.* J. B. Lippencott, 1977.

*Old Brooklyn Heights: 1827–1927.* To Commemorate the One Hundreth Anniversary of the Founding of The Brooklyn Savings Bank, 1827–1927.

Oliver, Leon. *The Great Sensation.* Chicago: Beverly Co., 1973.

Pagels, Elaine. *Adam, Eve and the Serpent.* New York: Random House, 1988.

Papachristou, Judith. *Women Together: A History in Documents of the Women's Movement in the United States.* New York: Knopf, 1976.

Parker, Gail Thain. *Mind Cure in New England: From the Civil War to World War I.* Hanover, NH: University Press of New England, 1973.

Patterson, Jerry E. *The City of New York.* New York: Harry N. Abrams, 1978.

Peterson, Merrill D. *Lincoln in American Memory.* New York: Oxford University Press, 1994.

Phelps, Elizabeth Stuart (Ward). *The Story of Avis.* Boston: James R. Osgood & Co., 1877.

———. *Our Famous Women: An Authorized Record of Their Lives and Deeds.* 1883. Reprint, Freeport, NY: Books for Libraries Press, 1975.

Pike, E. Royston. *Golden Times (Human Documents of the Victorian Age).* New York: Frederick A. Praeger, 1967.

Pivar, David J. *Purity Crusade: Sexual Morality and Social Control, 1868–1900.* Westport, CT: Greenwood Press, 1973.

Post, Isaac. *Voices from the Spirit World, being Communications from Many Spirits, by the Hand of Isaac Post, Medium.* Rochester, NY: C. H. McDonell, 1852.

Potter, George W. *To the Golden Door.* Boston: Little, Brown, 1960.

Potts, E. Daniel, and Annette Potts, eds. *A Yankee Merchant in Goldrush Australia: The Letters of George Francis Train 1853–55.* Melbourne: William Heinemann, 1970.

Preston, Dickson J. *Young Frederick Douglass: The Maryland Years.* Baltimore: Johns Hopkins University Press, 1980.

Pullen, C. H. *The Fight at Dame Europa's School.* Illustrated by Thomas Nast. New York: F. B. Felt, 1871.

———. *Miss Columbia's Public School or Will it Blow Over?* Illustrated by Thomas Nast. New York: F. B. Felt, 1871.

Putnam, Allen. *Mrs. J. H. Conant: The World's Medium of the Nineteenth Century.* Boston: William W. & Co., 1873.

Quarles, Benjamin. *The Negro in the Civil War.* Boston: Little, Brown, 1953.

Rabinowitz, Richard. *The Spiritual Self in Everyday Life: The Transformation of Personal Religious Experience in Nineteenth-Century New England.* Boston: Northeastern University Press, 1989.

Rable, George C. *Civil Wars: Women and the Crisis of Southern Nationalism.* Chicago: University of Illinois Press, 1989.

Raleigh, Dr. A. S. *Metaphysical Healing.* Volume 1. San Francisco: Hermetic Publishing Co., 1916.

———. *Scientifica Hermetica.* San Francisco: Hermetic Publishing Co., 1916.

Randolph, P. B. *The New Mola!: The Secret of Mediumship! A Handbook of White Magic, Magnetism and Clairvoyance.* 1873.

Reade, Charles. *Griffith Gaunt or Jealousy.* London: Chapman and Hall, 1866.

Reed, Henry Hope, and Sophia Duckworth. *Central Park: A History and Guide.* New York: Clarkson N. Potter, 1972.

Reynolds, David S. *Beneath the American Renaissance.* New York: Knopf, 1988.

Reynolds, Moira Davison. *Nine American Women of the Nineteenth Century: Leaders into the Twentieth.* Jefferson, NC: McFarland, 1988.

Richmond, Rev. J. F. *New York and Its Institutions.* New York: E. B. Treat, 1872.

Rose, Phyllis. *Parallel Lives: Five Victorian Marriages.* New York: Knopf, 1984.

Rourke, Constance Mayfield. *Trumpets of Jubilee: Henry Ward Beecher, Harriet Beecher Stowe, Lyman Beecher, Horace Greeley, P.T. Barnum.* New York: Harcourt, Brace, 1927.

Rugoff, Milton. *Prudery & Passion: Sexuality in Victorian America.* New York: Putnam, 1971.

———. *The Beechers: An American Family in the Nineteenth Century.* New York: Harper & Row, 1981.

———. *America's Gilded Age: Intimate Portraits from an Era of Extravagance and Change, 1850–1890.* New York: Henry Holt, 1989.

Russell, Sharman Apt. *Frederick Douglass.* New York: Chelsea House Publishers, 1988.

Russet, Cynthia Eagol. *Sexual Science: The Victorian Construction of Womanhood.* Cambridge, MA: Harvard University Press, 1989.

Ryan, Mary P. *Women in Public: Between Banners and Ballots, 1825–1880.* Baltimore: Johns Hopkins University Press, 1990.

Sachs, Emanie. *The Terrible Siren: Victoria Woodhull (1838–1927).* New York: Harper & Brothers, 1928. Reprint, New York, Arno Press, 1978. Abbreviated as *TS.*

Sanborn, Margaret. *Mark Twain: The Bachelor Years: A Biography.* New York: Doubleday, 1990.

Schickel, Richard. *Intimate Strangers: The Culture of Celebrity.* Garden City, NY: Doubleday, 1985.

Schulze, Suzanne. *Horace Greeley: A Bio-Bibliography.* New York: Greenwood Press, 1992.

Sears, Hal D. *The Sex Radicals: Free Love in High Victorian America.* Lawrence, KS: Regent Press of Kansas, 1977.

Seely, Lida. *Mrs. Seely's Cook Book.* New York, London: Macmillan, 1902.

Seitz, Don Carlos. *Uncommon Americans: Pencil Portraits of Men and Women Who Have Broken the Rules.* Indianapolis: Bobbs-Merrill, 1925.

———. *Horace Greeley: Founder of the New York Tribune.* Indianapolis: Bobbs-Merrill, 1926.

———. *The Dreadful Decade: Detailing Some Phases in the History of the United States from Reconstruction to Resumption, 1869–1879.* Indianapolis: Bobbs-Merrill, 1926.

Shaplen, Robert. *Free Love and Heavenly Sinners: The Story of the Great Henry Ward Beecher Scandal.* New York: Knopf, 1954. Originally published in *The New Yorker,* June 5 and 12, 1954.

Sherr, Lynn. *Failure Is Impossible: Susan B. Anthony in Her Own Words*. New York: Times Books, 1995.

Showalter, Elaine. *The Female Malady: Women, Madness, and English Culture 1830–1980*. New York: Pantheon Books, 1985.

Silver, Nathan. *Lost in New York*. New York: Schocken Books, 1971.

Simon, John Y., ed. *The Personal Memoirs of Julia Dent Grant*. New York: G. P. Putnam's Sons, 1975.

Sinclair, Andrew. *The Better Half: The Emancipation of the American Woman*. New York: Harper & Row, 1965.

Sklar, Kathryn Kish. *Catharine Beecher: A Study in American Domesticity*. New Haven & London: Yale University Press, 1973.

Sloane, Florence Adele. *Maverick in Mauve*. Garden City, NY: Doubleday, 1983.

Smith, Gene. *Lee & Grant*. New York: McGraw-Hill, 1984.

Smith, Matthew Hale. *Sunshine and Shadow in New York*. Hartford, CT: J. B. Burr, 1868.

———. *Twenty Years among the Bulls and Bears of Wall Street*. Hartford, CT: J. B. Burr, 1870.

Smith, Page. *The Rise of Industrial America*, Volume 6. New York: McGraw-Hill, 1984.

Smith, Thomas E. V. *The City of New York: In the Year of Washington's Inauguration 1789*. New York: Trow's Publishing and Bookbinding Co., 1889.

Smith-Rosenberg, Carroll. *Disorderly Conduct: Visions of Gender in Victorian America*. New York: Knopf, 1985.

Squire, Geoffrey. *Dress and Society 1560–1570*. New York: Viking, 1974.

Stampp, Kenneth M. *The Era of Reconstruction, 1865–1877*. New York: Knopf, 1965, Vintage Books, 1978 Reprint Edition.

Stansell, Christine. *City of Women: Sex and Class in New York 1789–1860*. New York: Knopf, 1986.

Stanton, Elizabeth Cady. *Eighty Years and More: Reminiscences 1815–1897*. New York: Schocken Books, 1971. Reprinted from the T. Fisher Unwin edition of 1898. Abbreviated as *EYM*.

Stanton, Elizabeth Cady, Susan B. Anthony, and Matilda Joslyn Gage, eds. *History of Woman Suffrage*. Volumes 1 and 2 of 6 volumes. Salem, NH: Ayer Publishers. Reprint edition 1985 from an original copy in State Historical Society of the Wisconsin Library. Originally published by Fowler & Wells, New York, 1882. Abbreviated as *HWS*.

Stanton, Henry B. *Random Recollections*. Johnstown, NY: Blunck & Leaning, Printers, 1885.

Stanton, Theodore, and Harriot Stanton Blatch, eds. *Elizabeth Cady Stanton, As Revealed in Her Letters, Diary and Reminiscences*. 2 volumes. New York: Arno and the *New York Times*, 1969. Originally published by Harper & Bros., New York, 1922.

Starr, Louis M. *Bohemian Brigade: Civil War Newsmen in Action*. New York: Knopf, 1954.

Stein, Dorothy. *Ada: A Life and a Legacy*. Cambridge, MA: MIT Press, 1985.

Sterling, Dorothy, ed. *The Troubles They Seen: Black People Tell the Story of Reconstruction*. Renamed *Nobody Knows The Trouble I Seen: The Story of Reconstruction in the Words of African Americans*. Garden City, NY: Doubleday, 1976.

Stern, Madeleine B. *We the Women: Career First of Nineteenth-Century America*. New York: Schulte Publishing Company, 1963.

———. *The Pantarch: A Biography of Stephen Pearl Andrews*. Austin: University of Texas Press, 1968.

———. *Heads and Headlines: The Phrenological Fowlers*. Norman: University of Oklahoma Press, 1971.

———, ed. *The Victoria Woodhull Reader*. Weston, MA: M & S Press, 1974.

Stiles, Henry R. *A History of the City of Brooklyn: Including the Old Town and Village of Brooklyn, the Town of Bushwick, and the Village and City of Williamsburgh*. 3 volumes. Brooklyn: Published by subscription. Volume 1, 1867; Volume 2, 1869; Volume 3, 1870.

———. *The Civil, Political, Professional and Ecclesiastical History and Commercial and Industrial Record of the County of Kings and the City of Brooklyn, New York, 1683–1884*. 2 volumes. New York: W. W. Munsell & Co., 1884.

Stoddard, Henry Luther. *Horace Greeley: Printer, Editor, Crusader.* New York: G. P. Putnam's Sons, 1946.

Stoehr, Taylor. *Free Love in America: A Documentary History.* New York: AMS Press, 1979.

Storrs, Richard S. *The Church of the Pilgrims, Brooklyn, New York: Its Character and Work, with the Changes around It, during Forty Years of Pastoral Service.* New York: A. S. Barnes, 1886.

Stowe, Harriet Beecher. *Lady Byron Vindicated.* Boston: Fields Osgood & Co., 1870.

————. *My Wife & I or Harry Henderson's History.* New York: J. B. Ford, 1871. Boston: Houghton Mifflin, 1896. Serialized in the *Christian Union,* 1870, 1871.

Strasser, Susan. *Never Done: A History of American Housework.* New York: Pantheon Books, 1982.

Strong, George Templeton. *The Diary of George Templeton Strong: 1835–1875.* 4 volumes. Edited by Allan Nevins and Milton Halsey Thomas. New York: Macmillan, 1952.

Sutherland, Daniel E. *Americans and Their Servants.* Baton Rouge: Louisiana State University Press, 1981.

Swanberg, W. A. *Jim Fisk: The Career of an Improbable Rascal.* New York: Charles Scribner's Sons, 1959.

Syrett, Harold Coffin, Ph.D. *The City of Brooklyn, 1865–1989: A Political History.* New York: Columbia University Press, 1944.

Talese, Gay. *Thy Neighbor's Wife.* New York: Dell, 1981.

Taylor, W. G. Langworthy. *Katie Fox: Epochmaking Medium and the Making of the Fox-Taylor Record.* New York: G. P. Putnam's Sons, 1933.

Teltscher, Harry O. *Handwriting, A Revelation of Self: A Source Book of Psychographology.* Alexandria, VA: Red Dragon Press, Hawthorn Books, 1971.

*Theodore Tilton v. Henry Ward Beecher: Action for Criminal Conduct Tried in the City Court of Brooklyn, Chief Justice Joseph Neilson, Presiding. Verbatim Report by the Official Stenographer.* 3 volumes. New York: McDivitt, Campbell & Co., Law Publishers, 1875.

Thomas, George M. *Revivalism and Cultural Change: Christianity, Nation Building, and the Market in the Nineteenth-Century United States.* Chicago: University of Chicago Press, 1989.

Thurston, Carol. *The Romance Revolution.* Chicago: University of Chicago Press, 1987.

Tilton, Theodore. *The True Church.* Philadelphia: J. P. Lippincott, 1867.

————. *Sanctorum.* New York: Sheldon, 1870.

————. *Tempest-Tossed: A Romance.* New York: Sheldon, 1874.

Tozer, Jane, and Sarah Levitt. *Fabric of Society: A Century of People and Their Clothes 1770–1870.* Wales: Laura Ashley Ltd., 1983.

Tracy, Benjamin F. *The Case of Henry Ward Beecher: Opening Address of Counsel for the Defendant.* New York: G. W. Smith, 1875.

Trager, James, ed. *The People's Chronology: A Year-by-Year Record of Human Events from Prehistory to the Present.* New York: Holt, Rinehart and Winston, 1979.

Train, George Francis. *The Great Epigram Campaign of Kansas: Championship of Women.* Leavenworth, KS: Prescott & Hume, 1867.

————. *My Life in Many States and in Foreign Lands.* New York: D. Appleton, 1902.

————. *Young America in Wall Street.* New York: Greenwood Press, 1968. Originally published in 1857, Derby and Jackson.

————. *Yankee Merchant in Gold Rush Australia.* Melbourne: William Heinemann, 1970.

Trefousse, Hans L. *Ben Butler: The South Called Him BEAST!* New York: Twayne Publishers, 1957.

————. *Andrew Johnson: A Biography.* New York: W. W. Norton, 1989.

Trumbull, Charles Gallaudet. *Anthony Comstock, Fighter: Some Impressions of a Lifetime of Adventure in Conflict with the Powers of Evil.* 2nd ed. New York: Fleming H. Revell, 1913.

Truth, Sojourner. *Narrative of Sojourner Truth.* Edited by Olive Gilbert. Battle Creek, MI, 1878.

Tuchman, Barbara W. *The Proud Tower: A Portrait of the World Before the War: 1890–1914.* New York: Macmillan, 1966.

Twain, Mark. *Huckleberry Finn.* Cleveland: World Publishing Co. Reprint, 1947.

*Uncontradicted Testimony in the Beecher Cases, Compiled From the Official Records.* New York: D. Appleton, 1876.

Underhill, Lois Beachy. *The Woman Who Ran for President: The Many Lives of Victoria Woodhull.* Bridgehampton, NY: Bridge Works Publishing Co., 1995.

Vandal, Gilles. *The New Orleans Riot of 1866: Anatomy of a Tragedy.* Lafayette: Center for Louisiana Studies, University of Southwestern Louisiana, 1983.

Van Deusen, Glyndon G. *Horace Greeley, Nineteenth Century Crusader.* Philadelphia: University of Pennsylvania Press, 1953.

Vickers, Hugo. *Gladys, Duchess of Marlborough.* New York: Holt, Rinehart and Winston, 1979.

Vidal, Gore. *1876: A Novel.* New York: Random House, 1976.

———. *Lincoln.* New York: Random House, 1984.

Vidal, Gore, V. S. Pritchett, David Cante, Bruce Chatwin, Peter Conrad, Edward Jay Epstein. *Great American Families.* New York: W. W. Norton, 1977.

Vinson, John Chalmers. *Thomas Nast, Political Cartoonist.* Athens: University of Georgia Press, 1967.

Vithoulkas, George. *Homeopathy: Medicine of the New Man.* New York: Prentice Hall, 1979.

Wallace, Irving. *The Nympho and Other Maniacs.* London: Cassell, 1971.

Waller, Altina L. *Reverend Beecher and Mrs. Tilton: Sex and Class in Victorian America.* Amherst: University of Massachusetts Press, 1982.

Warren, John H. *The Rise of Urban America: Thirty Years of Battle with Crime.* New York: Arno Press, 1970.

Warren, Josiah. *Practical Applications of the Elementary Principles of "True Civilization."*

Washington, Booker T. *Frederick Douglass.* 1906. Reprint, New York: Argosy-Antiquarian Ltd., 1969.

Wecter, Dixon. *The Saga of American Society.* New York: Charles Scribner's Sons, 1937.

Weideger, Paula. *Menstruation and Menopause: The Physiology and Psychology, The Myth and the Reality.* New York: Knopf, 1976.

Weintraub, Stanley. *Victoria: An Intimate Biography.* New York: Truman Talley Books, E. P. Dutton, 1987.

Werner, M. R. *Tammany Hall.* Garden City: Doubleday, Doran, 1928.

West, Richard S., Jr. *Lincoln's Scapegoat General: A Life of Benjamin F. Butler, 1818–1893.* Boston: Houghton Mifflin, 1965.

*Westminster Study Edition of The Holy Bible: Containing Old And New Testaments in the Authorized (King James) Version.* Philadelphia: Westminster Press.

Wheeler, Leslie. *Loving Warriors: Selected Letters of Lucy Stone and Henry B. Blackwell, 1853–1893.* New York: Dial, 1981.

Wheeler, T. C., ed. *The Immigrant Experience.* New York: Dial, 1971.

White, Howard A. *The Freedmen's Bureau in Louisiana.* Baton Rouge: Louisiana State University Press, 1970.

Wilson, Edmund. *Patriotic Gore: Studies in the Literature of the American Civil War.* Boston: Northeastern University Press, 1984.

Wingate, Charles. *How the Times Broke the Tweed Ring.* New York: Kilbourne Tompkins, 1875.

Woodhull, Victoria Claflin. *The Origin, Tendencies and Principles of Government: A Review of the Rise and Fall of Nations from Early Historic Time to the Present: with Special Consideration Regarding the Future of the United States as the Representative Government of the World.* New York: Woodhull & Claflin Co., 1871 (probably ghostwritten by Stephen Pearl Andrews).

Woodhull, Victoria Claflin (Mrs. John Biddulph Martin), and Tennessee C. Claflin (Lady Cook). *The Human Body, the Temple of God: or The Philosophy of Sociology.* London: Published by the authors, 1890. (Includes Woodhull's announcement for president, her memorial to Congress, the majority and minority committee reports, her major suffrage speeches.)

Young, G. M. *Victorian England.* New York: Oxford University Press, 1936.

Young, James Harvey. *The Medical Messiahs: A Social History of Health Quackery in Twentieth-Century America.* Princeton, NJ: Princeton University Press, 1967.

Younger, William Lee. *Old Brooklyn In Early Photographs 1865–1929.* New York: Dover, 1978.


## Magazine and Journal Articles

Andrist, Ralph K. "Paladin of Purity." *American Heritage,* October 1973.

Hoff-Wilson, Joan. "The Unfinished Revolution: Changing Legal Status of U.S. Women." *Signs: Journal of Women in Culture and Society* 13, no. 1 (1987):

Holmes, Jack. "The Underlying Causes of the Memphis Riot of 1866." *Tennessee Historical Quarterly* 17 (1958).

Johnson, Howard P. "New Orleans Under General Butler." *Louisiana Historical Quarterly* 24, (1941)

Lovett, Bobby L. "Memphis Riots: White Reaction to Blacks in Memphis, May 1865–July 1866." *Tennessee Historical Quarterly* 9–33.

McPherson, James M. "Grant or Greeley? The Abolitionist Dilemma in the Election of 1872." *American Historical Review* 71 (October 1965): 43–61.

Mott, Franz L. *"Woodhull & Claflin's Weekly." A History of American Magazines* 3 (1938): 443–453.

*The Northeast Ohio Quarterly: A Journal of History and Civilization* 44, no. 4 (fall 1972): 85–99.

*Report of the Mysterious Noises, heard in the House of Mr. John D. Fox, in Hydesville, Acadia, Wayne Co. Authenticated by the Certificates and Confirmed by the Statements of Citizens of that Place and Vicinity.* Undated, New York Public Library, Manuscript Collection.

Riddleberger, Patrick W. "The Radicals' Abandonment of the Negro During Reconstruction." *The Journal of Negro History* 45, no. 2 (April 1960): 88–102.

Ryan, Gilbert James. "The Memphis Riots of 1866: Terror in a Black Community During Reconstruction." *The Journal of Negro History* 62, no. 3 (July 1977): 243–257.

Seitz, Don. "Horace Greeley and His Wife." *McNaught's Monthly* 4, no. 2 (August 1925): 40–42.

Smith-Rosenberg, Carol. "The Female World of Love and Ritual: Relations between Women in Nineteenth Century America." *Signs* 1, no. 1 (autumn 1975): 1–29.

———. "The Hysterical Women: Sex Roles and Role Conflict in Nineteenth-Century America." *Social Research* 39, no. 4 (winter 1972): 652–678.

Strong, Byron. "Toward a History of the Experiential Family: Sex and Incest in the Nineteenth-Century Family." *Journal of Marriage and the Family* 35 (August 1973): 457–466.

Waller, Altina L. "Community, Class and Race in the Memphis Riot of 1866." *Journal of Social History* (winter 1984): 233–243.


## Pamphlets, Articles, Theses

Andrews, Stephen Pearl, Henry James, and Horace Greeley. *Love, Marriage and Divorce: A Discussion.* New York: Stringer and Townsend, 1853.

Basch, Norma. *Invisible Women: The Legal Fiction of Marital Unity in Nineteenth-Century America.*

Beecher, Henry Ward. "An Address Delivered Before the Long Island Historical Society," Brooklyn. March 8, 1897.

———. *Beecher to Special Committee of the Soldiers' and Sailors' Convention, August 30, 1866.* New York Public Library Tucker-Sachs Collection.

———. *Patriotic Addresses.* New York Public Library, Manuscript Collection.

Benson, Eugene. "New York Journalists—Theodore Tilton." *Galaxy* 8 (September 1869):355–359.

Boucher, Francois. *20,000 Years of Fashion: The History of Costume and Personal Adornment.* New York: Harry N. Abrams.

*The Beecher Trial: A Review of the Evidence.* Reprinted from the *New York Times,* July 3, 1875, with some revision and additions. New York, 1875.

*Catalogue of Games and Amusements 1869–70.* Springfield, MA: Milton Bradley & Company.

Chused, Richard H. *Late Nineteenth-Century Married Women's Property Law: Reception of the Early Married Women's Property Acts by Courts and Legislatures.*

Clark, Edward H. G. *The Thunderbolt.* New York, Albany, and Troy: n.p., May 1873. Library of Congress.

Court of Appeals. Theodore Tilton, respondent, v. Henry Ward Beecher, appellant. Appellant's points. Statement. Brooklyn, NY, 1874.

Davis, Paulina Wright. *A History of the National Woman's Rights Movement for Twenty Years, with the Proceedings of the Decade Meeting held at Apollo Hall, October 20, 1870, from 1850 to 1870, with an Appendix Containing the History of the Movement during the winter of 1871, in the National Capitol.* New York: Journeymen Printers' Cooperative Association, 1871. Also, New York: Kraus, reprint, 1971.

Du Bois, W.E.B. *Black Reconstruction in America 1860–1880: An Essay Toward a History of the Part Which Black Folk Played in the Attempt to Reconstruct Democracy in America.* New York: Russell & Russell, 1966.

Farnam, Elsie Anne. *Isabella Beecher Hooker as Reformer: The Vote for Women or a Quest for Personal Power?* New York University, 1967. (A thesis submitted in partial fulfillment of the requirements for the degree of Master of Arts at the University of Connecticut, 1970.)

Gerteis, Louis S. *From Contraband to Freedman: Federal Policy Toward Southern Blacks 1861–65.* Westport, CT, 1973.

Grisaffi, Philip E. *Beecher-Tilton Investigation of 1874.* Brooklyn Historical Studies, Spring 1878.

Holmes, Jack D. L. *The Effects of the Memphis Race Riot, 1866.* West Tennessee Historical Society, XII.

*Old Brooklyn Heights.* The Brooklyn Savings Bank, 1827–1927.

Rabkin, Margareth. *The Silent Feminist Revolution: Women and the Law (in New York State from Blackstone to the Beginnings of the American Woman's Rights Movement).* Ph.D. dissertation, State University of New York, Buffalo, 1975.

Sachs, Albie, and Joan Hoff Wilson. *Sexism and the Law: A Study of Male Beliefs and Legal Bias in Britain and the United States.* Law in Society Series, edited by C. M. Campbell and P.N.P. Wiles.

*Star and Planet Locator.* Edmund Scientific Company, 1966.

Terry, Edwin W. *Theodore Tilton as Social Reformer, Radical Republican, Newspaper Editor, 1863–1872.* Ph.D. dissertation, St. John's University, 1971; University Microfilms International Dissertation Information Service, Ann Arbor, MI.

Tilton, Theodore. *Elizabeth Cady Stanton: Eminent Woman of the Age.* Hartford, CT: S. M. Batts, 1869.

———. "Victoria C. Woodhull: A Biographical Sketch: Mr. Tilton's Account of Mrs. Woodhull." *Golden Age,* New York, 1871, tract 3. Abbreviated as *GAT.*

Tilton, Theodore, et al. *The Enfranchisement of Women.* March 14, 1870, proof copy, New York Public Library.

Treat, Joseph, M.D. *Beecher, Tilton, Woodhull, The Creation of Society: All Four of Them Exposed, and if Possible Reformed and Forgiven, in Dr. Treat's Celebrated Letter to Victoria C. Woodhull.* Published by the author. New York, 1874.

*U.S. Report of the Select Committee on the Memphis Riots and Massacres.* 39th Congress, First Session, Report No. 101. Washington, 1866.

Woodhull, Victoria Claflin. "Tendencies of the Government." *New York Herald,* April 16, 25; May 2, 9, 16, 27; June 4, 19; July 4, 11, 1870.

———. *Victoria C. Woodhull's Complete and Detailed Version of the Beecher-Tilton Affair.* Washington, D.C.: J. Bradley Adams, 1876.

## Newspapers

| | |
|---|---|
| Banner of Light | Louisville *Courier Journal* |
| Boston *Globe* | *Memphis Argus* |
| Boston *Journal* | Memphis *Daily Avalanche* |
| Boston *Post* | Memphis *Post* |
| Brooklyn *Daily Argus* | New Orleans *Daily Picayune* |
| Brooklyn *Daily Eagle* | New Orleans *Tribune* |
| Brooklyn *Daily Union* | *Newark Sunday Call* |
| Brooklyn *Eagle* (Sunday) | *New York Argus* |
| Brooklyn *Review* | *New York Daily Graphic* |
| Brooklyn *Sunday Press* | New York *Evening Post* |
| Brooklyn *Union* | *New York Herald* |
| Burlington *Free Press* | *New York Observer* |
| *Chicago Mail* | New York *Telegram* |
| *Chicago Post and Mail* | New York *Star* |
| *Chicago Times* | *New York Sun* |
| *Chicago Tribune* | *New York Times* |
| *Christian Union* | *New York Tribune* |
| *Cincinnati Enquirer* | *New York World* |
| *Cincinnati Gazette* | *North Star* |
| *Cleveland Leader* | *Ottawa Free Trader* |
| *Daily Morning Chronicle* | *Ottawa Republican* |
| *Daily Patriot* | *Philadelphia Press* |
| *Frank Leslie's Illustrated* | *Rochester Democrat* |
| *Golden Age* | *Seneca County Courier* |
| *Hartford Courant* | Seymour *Times* |
| Hartford *Evening Post* | *Springfield Republican* |
| *Hartford Times* | St. *Louis Times* |
| *Independent* | *Sunday Press* |
| *Indiana Times* | *Thunderbolt* |
| *Lancaster Gazette* | Toledo *Sun* |
| *Leavenworth Times* | *Train Ligue* |
| *Lewiston Telegram* | *Troy Daily Press* |
| *Liberator* | *Weekly Argus* |

## Publications

| | |
|---|---|
| *American Heritage* | *The New Yorker* |
| *The Arrow* | *Omni* |
| *Atlantic Monthly* | *Putnam's Magazine* |
| *Bonner's Weekly* | *The Revolution*—entire run, Jan. 8, 1868–May |
| *Harper's Weekly* | 1870. Sophia Smith Collection, Smith |
| *The Humanitarian* | College (bound edition). |
| *Ladies Home Journal* | Syracuse University *Connections*, April 1990 |
| *Macmillan's Magazine* | *Woman's Journal* |
| *The Masses* | *The Word* |
| *The Nation* | |

## Library and Archive Collections

*A Gentleman's Guide.* New York Historical Society, New York.
The American Society for Psychical Research, Inc., New York.

Beecher-Tilton Correspondence and trial, Lib Tilton Correspondence, Theodore Tilton Correspondence, Francis De Pau Moulton Correspondence, Mrs. Morse Correspondence, newspaper articles, clippings, pamphlets, church and civil trial–related material, etc., from the offices of the *Independent*. Tucker-Sachs Correspondence, Scrapbooks I–VIII, New York Public Library, Manuscript Collection. Abbreviated as *BTS*.

Colonel James H. Blood Correspondence. New York Historical Society.

The Boston Public Library.

Butler, Benjamin F., The Papers of. Library of Congress, Manuscript Division, Washington, D.C. Ref: Impeachment Trial.

Butler, Benjamin F., The Papers of. Massachusetts Historical Society, Boston Public Library.

Columbia University, Rare Book Room, New York.

Davis, Paulina Wright, The Papers of. Alma Lutz Collection, Vassar College Library, Poughkeepsie, NY.

Dickinson, Anna E., The Papers of. Library of Congress, Manuscript Division, Washington, D.C. 25 reels, 10,000 items.

Garrison Family Papers, Garrison Collection, Sophia Smith Collection, Smith College Library. Also in Boston Public Library.

Horace Greeley Papers. New York Public Library.

Isabella Beecher Hooker Project. Letters and Papers of Isabella Beecher Hooker now at Harriet Beecher Stowe Center, Hartford, CT (formerly Stowe-Day Foundation). Material was at University of Massachusetts until 1990 and at the Connecticut Historical Society, Isabella Beecher Hooker (Mrs. John, 1822–1907, correspondence and papers); 1871–1903 Reel 80009. Abbreviated as *IBH*. Footnote citations are often taken from material at the University of Massachusetts and the Connecticut Historical Society supplied by Kathleen A. McDonough and may differ from later *ECS & SBA*, the guide to the microfilm, Ann D. Gordon and Patricia G. Holland, eds., and Kathleen A. McDonough and Gail K. Malmgreen, assoc. eds., *The Papers of Elizabeth Cady Stanton and Susan B. Anthony, Guide and Index*, Vol. 1 (New Brunswick, NJ: Rutgers University. 110 Reels, microfilm edition, 1997). Whenever possible I have given both citations. Abbreviated as *ECS & SBA*.

"Investigation into the Causes of the Gold Panic." House Report No. 31, 41st Congress, Second Session, 1870. Library of Congress, Washington, D.C.

Moulton, Louise Chandler, Letters of. Library of Congress, Manuscript Division, Washington, D.C.

National American Woman Suffrage Association Collection. Library of Congress, Washington, D.C.

New York Historical Association.

New York Public Library, Manuscript Collection. Scrapbooks I-VIII, newspapers, bound court records, etc. All made available in the Frederick Lewis Allen Room.

New York University, Bobst Library, New York.

Plymouth Church Hearing of Henry Ward Beecher (July 28, 1874) transcript, New York Public Library, New York Historical Association.

Post, Amy, and Isaac Post, Family Papers of. University of Rochester Library, Department of Rare Books and Special Collections, Rochester, NY.

Whitelaw Reid Collection. Library of Congress, Washington, D.C.

Reid, Whitelaw, Letters of. New York Society Library.

Schlesinger Library, Radcliffe College, Cambridge, MA.

Smith, Gerrit, The Papers of. Syracuse University, Syracuse, NY.

Smith, Sophia, Collection. Smith College, Northampton, MA.

Stanton, Elizabeth Cady, and Susan B. Anthony, Papers of. University of Massachusetts, Amherst.

Stanton, Elizabeth Cady, and Susan B. Anthony, Papers of. The Stanton and Anthony Project. Ann D. Gordon and Patricia G. Holland, editors. New Brunswick, NJ: Rutgers University. 110 reels (including 7 reels Susan B. Anthony Scrapbooks and Diaries 1848–1900), microfilm edition. *Woodhull & Claflin's Weekly,* v. 1–3, Reel 4798. Abbreviated as *ECS & SBA.*

Elizabeth Cady Stanton Correspondence. New York Public Library, Manuscript Collection.

Stevens, Thaddeus, The Papers of. Library of Congress, Washington, D.C.

Transcript of the Plymouth Church Hearing of Henry Ward Beecher. New York Public Library, New York Historical Association. Abbreviated as *PCH.*

Vanderbilt Will Case Clippings, November 1877. New York Public Library, Room 315.

Weld-Crimke, Papers and Diaries. Willard L. Clements Library, University of Michigan.

Victoria Claflin Woodhull Correspondence. Butler Library, Columbia University, New York.

Victoria Claflin Woodhull Correspondence. Manuscript Collection, Historical Society of Pennsylvania, Philadelphia.

Victoria Claflin Woodhull Correspondence. Alma Lutz Collection, Vassar College Library, Poughkeepsie, NY.

Victoria Claflin Woodhull (Martin) Correspondence. New York Historical Society.

Victoria Claflin Woodhull (Martin) Papers. Boston Public Library, Manuscript Collection.

Victoria Claflin Woodhull (Martin) Papers. Southern Illinois University Special Collections, Morris Library, Carbondale, IL. Abbreviated as *VCWM.*

*Woodhull & Claflin's Weekly.* Reel 1, Vol. 1–3, May 14, 1870–Nov. 18, 1871. Reel 2, Vol. 4–7, Nov. 18, 1871–May 30, 1874. Reel 3, Vol. 8–12, June 6, 1874–June 10, 1876. Abbreviated as *WCW.*

Martha Coffin Wright Correspondence. Sophia Smith Collection, Smith College Library; 1,500 letters in William Lloyd Garrison Papers, Smith College, Northampton, MA. Abbreviated as *MCW.*

# *Acknowledgments*

IT HAS TAKEN ME over a decade to research and write this book. When I started out, I thought I would write a biography of Victoria Woodhull but as I researched further, I realized that her life and the age in which she lived were inextricably intertwined. This combination led me to many sources and many people whom I wish to acknowledge, for without them I could not have written the book that I did. Vartan Gregorian, the late Timothy Healy, and Paul LeClerc—all presidents of the New York Public Library—gave me access to material that I studied in the Frederick Lewis Allen Room of that institution, where much of this book was written. John Baker, Duane Watson, and Wayne Furman found rare materials (including eight scrapbooks compiled in the offices of the *Independent*). Mark Piel of the New York Society Library not only researched the answers to countless questions but requested books and papers from libraries the world over. Carlton Rochell provided access to research materials at the Bobst Library of New York University.

It was particularly difficult to penetrate the Victorian propriety that prevented me from seeing more than the prissy cardboard characters depicted in the books of the era. For that I needed primary sources: diaries, letters, newspaper accounts, advertisements, records of woman's rights meetings, church records, court transcripts, etc. I found an extraordinary group of people who helped me to find these documents and I feel that this infused life into my subjects.

Ann D. Gordon of the Elizabeth Cady Stanton and Susan B. Anthony Project worked with me, first at the University of Massachusetts with her colleague Patricia G. Holland, and then at Rutgers University. Kathleen McDonough was invaluable in finding Stanton and Anthony papers and the never-published diaries and letters of Isabella Beecher Hooker. Jo Blatti and Susan Zack at the Harriet Beecher Stowe Center (formerly the Stowe-Day Foundation) provided expertise and advice concerning the Beecher family.

Lynn Sherr gave me insight into the life of Susan B. Anthony, as well as the mixed blessing of a projector and 110 reels of microfilm from the Stanton and Anthony Project, which kept me researching nights as well as days. John B. Jentz of History Works, Inc., located the manslaughter indictment against Tennessee Celeste Claflin and affidavits covering the case. Karen Sturges meticulously researched Martha Coffin Wright, Lucretia Mott, and other members of the suffrage and Spiritualist movements. Edith Mayo, curator of Women's History at the Smithsonian, supplied the history of the McClintock table. Patrice Keane of the American Society for Psychical Research, Inc., as well as Maria Janis, provided both historical and present-day accounts of psychic powers.

My first researcher, Christopher Stevens, began the search for material well over a decade ago. Linda Amster has, over the years, continued that search and lent friendship and support. Vanessa Stark's computer knowledge, patience, and goodwill are appreciated. Elizabeth Newell, followed by Diana Stagner, have dealt with innumerable drafts of my manuscript, assisted me personally, and cheered me on. Joanne Arestou, Cinda Siler, Elizabeth Drorbaugh, Martin Timins, Elizabeth Berne, and Susan Carroll all contributed to the technical production of this book.

Several experts enriched the manuscript in its final stages, but I would particularly like to thank Sean Wilentz of Princeton University and Nicole Bisel, an expert on Anthony Comstock, of Northwestern University. Gloria Steinem provided innumerable insights into how Victoria's life resonates for women both in the past and present. The psychic and author Mary T. Browne explained Victoria and Tennie's powers in light of her own experience.

At Knopf, I thank Victoria Wilson, an editor with an incomparable eye who always believed in this book, as well as Sonny Mehta, Jane Friedman, Bob Gottlieb, Katherine Hourigan, Lee Buttala, Karen Deaver, and Carol Devine Carson. I also wish to thank Lynn Nesbit, Morton Janklow, Yves-André Istel, Jane Hitchcock, Jim Hoagland, Wayne Lawson, and Bernard Lewis.

Finally, my gratitude and admiration to the person who should have had first billing, Jason Epstein. You drove me back to the desk when I nearly abandoned this project and subsequently read successive drafts, demonstrating both your friendship and prodigious editorial skills. Yes, I know you would tell me to cut the word "prodigious."

# Index

Page numbers in *italics* indicate illustrations.

abolitionism, 11, 29, 31, 45, 89–90
abortion, 148, 235, 363, 366
American Equal Rights Association (AERA),
    101–2, 113, 116, 137, 165, 176, 177–8, 214,
    217
    New York convention (1869), 178–85
American Labor Reform League, 264–5
American Woman Suffrage Association
    (AWSA), 214, 282
    attacks on Woodhull, 255, 284–5
    AWSA-NWSA reconciliation effort, 217
    Cleveland convention (1869), 200–1
    dominant woman's organization, emer-
        gence as, 217–18
    formation of, 200
    New York convention (1870), 217
    New York convention (1871), 272, 275
Ames, Oakes, 361
Anderson, General Robert, 72, 84
Andrews, Esther, 210–11, 272
Andrews, Stephen Pearl, 53–4, *54*, 210, 212,
    264–5, 272, 273, 274, 276, 292, 296, 300,
    304, 305, 332, 414, 415, 426, 441
animal magnetism, 20, 21
Anthony, Daniel, 29, 31, 47
Anthony, Colonel Daniel R., 401
Anthony, Lucy, 47
Anthony, Mary, 47
Anthony, Susan B., xi, xiii, 3, 4, 31, *47*, 100,
    102, 115, 146, 164, 165, 169, 198, 224, 261,
    270, 275, 282, 362, *391*, 436, *436*
    American Equal Rights Association,
        179–80, 182, 183
    American Woman Suffrage Association,
        201, 217, 285
    appearance of, 47–8
    arrest and trial for voting, 345–6
    Beecher-Lib Tilton relationship, 225–6
    Beecher-Tilton scandal, 282, 352, 353, 375;
        Plymouth Church Committee investiga-
        tion, 390–1, 393, 397, 398, 399, 400–2
    Civil War, 73
    death of, 437

Democratic National Convention of 1868,
    168
diary of, 319–20, *319*, 322
Dickinson's relationship with, 116, 117, 175,
    321–2, 434
enfranchisement of blacks and women
    simultaneously, 112, 113, 116, 134
Fifteenth Amendment, 134
Fourteenth Amendment, 111
free love, 183
Kansas State Constitution, proposed
    amendment of, 136, 137–8
lecturing career, 173
National Woman Suffrage Association,
    185–6, 216, 246, 247, 273, 311, 318–20
New York State Constitution, proposed
    amendment of, 132–4
presidential election of 1872, 313, 314, 316,
    318, 324, 326, 328, 333, 334, 345
remarriage issue, 216
*The Revolution,* 218
sexual views, 118
Sixteenth Amendment for woman suf-
    frage, proposed, 247
slandering of Tennessee Claflin, alleged,
    321–2
Stanton's partnership with, 47–8
Vaughn infanticide case, 175
women, relationships with, 402
*Woodhull Memorial* presentation, 247–8,
    249, 251
Woodhull's first meeting with, 193
Woodhull's presidential candidacy, 318–20,
    321, 334
Woodhull's relationship with, 252–3, 256–7
Workingwomen's Association, 176–7
Anti-Slavery Society, 101, 112–13
Association of Spiritualists, 425
automatic writing, 32

Bacon, Leonard, 381, 382
Bartels, John, 106

Bartlett, William A., 205
Bayard, Edward, 39, 42, 43, 44–5, 347
Bayard, Henry, 42
Bayard, Tryphena Cady, 39, 42, 43, 44
Beach, Lafayette, 365
Beauregard, Brigadier General Pierre G. T., 72
Beecher, Catharine, xiii, 23, 127, 198, 207,
    216, 219, 255, 351, 437
  Beecher-Tilton scandal, 269–70, 403
  domestic economy, work on, 22–4, 59–60
  early years, 265–6
  woman's rights, approach to, 265, 266
  Woodhull's relationship with, 266–7,
    269–70, 292
Beecher, Charles, 35
Beecher, Edward, 119, 128, 219, 349, 350, 357
Beecher, Eunice Bullard, 10, 11, 12, 88, 261,
    412, 414, 417, 437
  married life, 9, 94
  Tiltons' separation, 229–30
Beecher, George, 402
Beecher, Harriet Porter, 442
Beecher, Henry Ward, xiv, 5, 10, 12, 101, 146,
    178, 198, 200, 205, 214, 243, 249, 255,
    294, 348, 351, 391, 413, 417
  acquisitiveness of, 90
  American Woman Suffrage Association,
    200, 217
  antislavery efforts, 89–90
  Bowen's relationship with, 73, 75, 76, 219,
    222–23, 238–40
  Christ, book on, 164, 311, 435
  civil rights issue, 98–9, 118–19
  "Cleveland Letter," 118–19
  death of, 437–8
  dismissal from Plymouth Church, threat
    of, 120–1
  early years, 9
  England, tour of, 75, 76, 85
  father's heresy trial, 8–9
  fiction writing, 93, 94–5, 164
  Fort Sumter excursion, 84–5, 95
  Friday-night meetings, 240
  Gospel of Love, 36, 85–6
  Grant, support for, 170, 324
  Howard family and, 120
  Indianapolis pastorate, 9, 11
  lavish lifestyle, 86
  Lincoln, attitude toward, 75, 94
  love, capacity for, 9
  married life, 9, 94
  McFarland-Richardson case, 205–6
  mesmerism and, 22
  newspaper editorship, 219
  newspaper writings, 88, 89
  Northern Pacific Railroad and, 221
  permissive doctrine, 13
  Plymouth Church twenty-fifth anniver-
    sary, 335–6
  political power, 219–20, 222–3, 381
  portrait of, 94
  revivalism and, 11, 13
  seduction of parishioners, 73, 75
  sexual views, 127
  showmanship of, 85
  Theodore Tilton's relationship with, 75, 76,
    88, 89, 90, 94, 224; deterioration of,
    99–100, 112, 113, 114–15, 119
  Tiltons' separation, 228–30
  Wilkeson's suit against, 435
  *Woman's Journal,* 207
  woman's rights advocacy, 100, 113–14
  Woodhull's "Principles of Social Freedom"
    speech, 296–7, 298–9
  Woodhull's relationship with, 290–1,
    296–7, 331, 336
  writing room of, 171
  *see also* Beecher-Lib Tilton relationship;
    Beecher-Tilton scandal; Plymouth
    Church Committee investigation
Beecher, Lyman, 8–9, 36, 43, 265–6
Beecher, Roxanna Foote, 9, 36
Beecher, Thomas, 349–50, 351
Beecher, William, 219, 351, 403
Beecher home in Brooklyn, 87
"Beecher's Bibles," 89
Beecher-Lib Tilton relationship
  Beecher's final comments on Tilton, 424
  Beecher's preaching and, 88
  Beecher's salutory effect on Tilton, 95
  Beecher's writings and, 95, 164–5
  clandestine correspondence, 263
  first meetings, 94
  sexual relationship, 128, 165–6, 223, 244
  Tilton's account of, 225–6
  Tilton's honorable intentions, 100
  Tilton's love for Beecher, 130–1
  Tilton's pregnancy, 223, 224, 225, 229, 230,
    235
  Theodore Tilton's assessment of, 169–70
  Theodore Tilton's concern about, 128–30
Beecher-Tilton scandal, xii, 5–6, 282
  aftermath of, 419–24
  Beecher-Bowen alliance, 238–40
  Beecher's apology to Theodore Tilton, 245,
    259
  Beecher's blaming Lib Tilton for, 379
  Beecher's consideration of suicide, 314–16
  Beecher's denial of wrongdoing, 352–3
  Beecher's letters and, 374–5
  Beecher's statement of devotion to Lib
    Tilton, 389–90

Beecher's victory speech, 420–1
Catharine Beecher's learning of, 269–70
Bowen blamed for, 419
bribing of Bowen and Theodore Tilton, 312
cartoon about, *391*
civil trial, 410, 411–12, *413*, 414–16, *417*, 418
Congregational Church Council hearings, 380–1
financial issues, 259–61
Hooker's involvement in, 349–51, 353–9
Moulton's mediation efforts, 261–3
"scandal bureau" to quash rumors, 419
Storrs's involvement in, 377, 379
*Thunderbolt* exposé, 376–7
Lib Tilton's confession of adultery, 237, 240–4, 390
Lib Tilton's rejection by community, 258
Theodore Tilton's anger and depression, 223–5, 226, 258–9, 311–12, 381–2
"tripartite agreement" between Bowen, Beecher, and Theodore Tilton, 312, 325, 375
ultimatum to Beecher from Bowen and Theodore Tilton, 236–8
Woodhull's learning of, 258
Woodhull's public statements on, 335
Woodhull's silence, efforts to obtain, 287–8
Woodhull's vow to destroy Beecher, 336
Woodhull's writings on, 286, 337–8
*see also* Plymouth Church Committee investigation
Bingham, John A., 249
"Black Codes," 98, 111
black enfranchisement
AERA position on, 180–2
Fifteenth Amendment and, 125, 134
Johnson's opposition, 122
Kansas State Constitution, proposed amendment of, 135–8
Loyalist convention and, 123–5
woman suffrage and, 100–2, 112–13, 115–16, 134
Black Friday gold market collapse, 187–90, *190*, 307
blacks
Beecher's "Cleveland Letter" on, 118–19
civil rights legislation, 98–9, 110–11, 325–6
draft riots and, 78, *79*
emigration programs, 97–8
Freedmen's Bank and, 361–2, 428
repression following Reconstruction, 428
violence against, 111–12, 118, 428
*see also* black enfranchisement; slavery
Blackstone, Sir William, 13, 41
Blackwell, Alice, 434

Blackwell, Elizabeth, 184
Blackwell, Emily, 184, 200, 206
Blackwell, Henry, 123, 180, 182, 201, *202*, 313, 328, 333
Patton's affair with, 184–5, 200, 335
Blatchford, Judge, 367
Blood, George, 149, 191
Blood, Colonel James Harvey, xii, 106–7, *108*, 149, 189, 191, 209, 210, 211, 212, 213–14, 248, 332, 345, 363, 364, 372, 383, 410, 441
Roxy Claflin's suit against, 275–9, 283–4
marriage to Woodhull, 106, 107, 109, 139–40, 276–7, 424
Bloomer, Amelia, 282
bloomers, 48, 194
Bonner, Robert, 88, 93
Booth, John Wilkes, 95
Boutwell, George, 188, 189
Bowen, Henry, *76*, 84, 85, 88, 89, 90, 91, 312, 335, 343
Beecher's dismissal from Plymouth Church, move for, 120
Beecher's relationship with, 73, 75, 76, 219, 222–23, 238–40
Beecher-Tilton scandal, 236–40, 312, 374–5, 419
criticism of Woodhull, 279
expulsion from Plymouth Church, 419
Northern Pacific Railroad, 239, 419
political power, 121, 220–3, 232–5
Theodore Tilton's relationship with, 75, 220–1, 232–4, 235–6, 239–40
wealth accumulation, 75–6
Bowen, Henry, Jr., 120
Bowen, Henry A., 221–2
Bowen, Lucy, 73, 75, 89
Brady, Mathew, *260*
Bredon's Norton estate, 445
British Museum, 442
Brooker, Utica, *see* Claflin, Utica
Brooklyn, 86, 220
*Brooklyn Daily Union*, 219, 221–2, 232, 233–4
Brooks, James, 361
Brown, Benjamin Gratz, 313
Brown, Maria, 16
Buckhout, Isaac C., 143
Bullard, Laura Curtis, 103, 228, 261, 317, 376, 398
Lib Tilton's friendship with, 224, 262–3
Theodore Tilton's affair with, 163–4, 165, 218
Burned-Over District, 11
Burns, Rosa, 209, 330
Burns, Ross, 50, 330
Bush, Abigail, 47

Butler, Benjamin, 94, 96, *97*, 110, 111, 123, *169*, 251, 253, 254, 325, 332, *391*
  Dickinson's relationship with, 174, 211, 432–3
  Johnson's impeachment proceedings, 167, 168
  purity campaign and, 366
  Woodhull-Claflin obscenity case, 368
  *Woodhull Memorial* presentation, 247, 248, 249
  Woodhull's relationship with, 211–12
Butler, Blanche, 174
Butler, Harold, 358
Butler, Sarah, 174
Butterfield, Daniel, 187, 189, 190
Byron, Lord and Lady, 198

Cady, Daniel, 41, 42, 43, 44, 45, 46
Cady, Margaret, 41–3, 44
Calhoun, Lucia P., 203
California gold rush, 65
Calvinism, 8, 13, 43, 44, 266
Campbell, Flora, 42
Central Pacific Railroad, 162
Chabas, Paul, 439
Challis, Luther C., 368, 369
  Tennessee Claflin's article about, 339–42
Chandler, Zach, 325
Chapin, William O., 188
Chase, Salmon P., 79
Cheever, George B., 206
*Chicago Mail,* 6–7
child preachers, 26
Christian Friends, 423
Christian Science, 426
*Christian Union,* 219
Church of the Pilgrims, *378*
civil rights legislation, 98–9, 110–11, 325–6
Civil War, 72, 76–7, 82–3
  draft riots, 78, *79*
  women's involvement in, 72–3
Claflin, Carrington, 14–15
Claflin, Delia, 16
Claflin, Hebern, 16, 21, 80, 104
Claflin, Maldon, 16, 19
Claflin, Margaret Ann (later Miles), 15, 16, 50, 80, 108, 209, 383
Claflin, Odessa, 16
Claflin, Polly (later Sparr), 16, 50, 80, 108, 209, 276, 278, 330, 331, 445
Claflin, Reuben Buckman (Buck), 6, *20*, 26, 50, 52, 109, 149–50, 156, 209–10, 273, 279, 442, 445
  appearance of, 15
  arson by, 27

blackmailing by, 107–8
early years, 14–15
as father, 19
married life, 15, 16
"medical" career, 80, 81–2
sexual abuse of Woodhull, 51–2
Spiritualist road show, 51, 67–8
Woodhull's conception, 17
Claflin, Robert, 19
Claflin, Roxanna Hummel (Roxy), xii, 6, *20*, 26, 52, 64, 67, 70, 80, 109, 209, 272–3, 383, 386, *387*, 411, 424, 442
  appearance of, 14
  Blood, suit against, 275–9, 283–4
  early years, 13–14
  married life, 15, 16
  as mother, 19
  revivalism, enthusiasm for, 8, 13, 17
  Spiritualist powers, 15–16, 19, 21, 25–6
  Woodhull's conception, 17
Claflin, Tennessee Celeste (Tennie C.), 3, 7, 66, *103*, *192*, *195*, 283, 298, 299, 305, *391*, 410, 424, *443*
  Anthony's alleged slandering of, 321–2
  appearance of, 4, 80–1
  birth of, 18
  blackmailing by, 104, 338–9
  childhood of, 18–19, 21, 26
  Roxy Claflin's suit against Blood, 277–9, 283–4
  death of, 442
  Delmonico's incident, 194–5
  England, move to, 431
  escape from Claflin family, 109
  manslaughter charge against, 82
  marriage to Bartels, 106
  marriage to Cook, 442
  men's clothing, preference for, 193–4
  New York City, move to, 142, 146–7
  prostitution by, 81, 108–9
  prostitution medications business, 149–50
  revelation of French Ball of 1869, 339–42
  Spencer Grays and, 332
  Spiritualist powers, 21, 50–1, 80, 81–2, 95
  Spiritualist road show, 51, 67–8, 104, 106
  Vanderbilt's relationship with, 156, 157–8, 192–3, 273
  Vanderbilt Will Trial, 430–1
  wealth accumulation, 162, 430–1
  *Woodhull Memorial* presentation, 249, 251
  Woodhull's near-death experience, 372–3, 374
  *see also* Woodhull, Claflin & Co.; *Woodhull & Claflin's Weekly*; Woodhull-Claflin obscenity case

Claflin, Utica (later Brooker), 18, 51, 80, 108, 109, 158, 209, 283, 284, 330–1, 374
appearance of, 80–1
death of, 383
Woodhull's "Principles of Social Freedom" speech, 299, 300, 301, 302, 303
Clark, Edward H. G., 376–7
Clark, Mary Louise and Horace, 157
Clemens, Molly, 403
*Cleveland Leader,* 279
clitoridectomies, 149
clothing, politics of, 193–4
Cogswell, Anna, 65, 66
Colfax, Schuyler, 174, 348
Colored Orphan Asylum, 78, *79*
communism, 283
*Communist Manifesto* (Marx and Engels), 305
Comstock, Anthony, *343*
background, 343–4
New York Society for the Suppression of Vice, 371
purity campaign, 344, 366–7, 369–70, 371–2, 438–40
Woodhull-Claflin obscenity case, 344, 362–3, 364–5, 367, 368, 370–1
Comstock, Margaret Hamilton, 343
Congress, U.S., 33
civil rights legislation, 110
corruption in, 361
Johnson's impeachment, 166–8
mesmerism and, 22
purity campaign, 366–7, 440
Stanton's candidacy for, 117–18
woman suffrage issue, 247, 248–51, 253
*Woodhull Memorial* presentation, *xii,* 5, 247, 248–51
Connecticut Woman Suffrage Association, 198
Constitution, U.S., 250
*see also* specific amendments
contraceptives, 366
Cook, Francis, 442
Cooke, Jay, 164, 219, 221, 325, 361, 362, 385–6
Cooper, Peter, 146
Corbin, Abel Rathbone, 187, 188, 190
Corbin, Jenny Grant, 187, 188
Credit Mobilier company, 136, 361
Curtis, Frank, 163

Davenport, U.S. Commissioner, 345, 368
Davis, Andrew, 35
Davis, Jefferson, 326
Davis, Noah, 344, 368, 369

Davis, Paulina Wright, 3, 48, 103, 163, 198, 199, 258, 274, 317–18, 337, 376, 397
Davis, Thomas, 163
Declaration of Rights and Sentiments, 38–9
Deere, John, 11
de Ford, Molly, 191, 342, 343, 368–9
Delmonico, Lorenzo, 194
Delmonico's restaurant, 194–5
Democratic National Convention of 1868, 168
Dickinson, Anna, *117,* 123, 124–5, 137, 146, 288, 312, 397, 398
Anthony's relationship with, 116, 117, 175, 321–2, 434
Butler's relationship with, 174, 211, 432–3
collapse of her career, 347, 432
death of, 434
insanity case, 433–4
launching of her career, 77
McFarland-Richardson case, 206
Phillips's relationship with, 116–17, 174, 322–3
popularity of, 173
presidential election of 1872, 326–8
Reid's relationship with, 174, 211, 293–4, 323, 326, 432, 433–4
*The Revolution,* 218
Vaughn infanticide case, 173, 174–5
Dickinson, Edwin, 174
Dickinson, Susan, 174, 433
divorce laws, 204, 206, 207, 216, 228
domestic economy, 22–4, 59–60
Douglass, Frederick, 29, 77, 101–2, *124,* 178, 181–2, 325, *429*
black enfranchisement, 122, 123–5
death of, 436
Freedmen's Bank and, 428
Johnson, meeting with, 122
presidential election of 1872, 320
woman suffrage, support for, 46
draft riots, 78, *79*
Duesler, William, 28–9
Dunlop, Joseph R., 6–7

Edward VII, king of England, 445
electricity, 32
Ellington, George, 151, 160
Emancipation Proclamation, 77–8
Emerson, Ralph Waldo, 33, 56
Engels, Friedrich, 305
Equal Rights Party, 314, 316, 318–21, 328
Erie Railway Company, 159, 307
Evans, Warren Felt, 36
Evarts, William, 168, 412, 414, 415, 416

Fahnestock, Harris C., 385
Fifteenth Amendment, 125, 134, 182, 186, 250
Finney, Charles Grandison, 43, 44
Fish, Leah Fox, 29, *30,* 31–3, 425
Fish, Lizzie, 31
Fisher, Alexander, 265
Fisk, Jim, 159, 160, 161–2, *161,* 191
    gold market collapse of 1869, 187, 188–90
    murder of, 307, *308,* 309
Fisk, Lucy, 307
Fondolaik, Constantine, 9
Foster, Stephen, 179–80
Fourier, Charles, 34
Fourteenth Amendment, 110–11, 115, 250
Fowler, W. A., 233, 234
Fox, Catherine (Kate), 28, 29, *30,* 31, 55–6, 62,
    425, 426
Fox, David, 56
Fox, John, 28
Fox, Margaret, 28
Fox, Margaretta (Maggie), 28, 29, *30,* 32–3,
    425, 426
Franklin, Benjamin, 32
Freedmen's Bank, 361–2, *362,* 428
Freedmen's Bureau, 110, 112
Freeland, James, 407
free love
    American Equal Rights Association and,
        182–4
    McFarland-Richardson case and, 206–8
    multiple meanings of, 183
    NWSA's endorsement of, 274–5
    Spiritualism and, 34
    tenets of, 208
    Theodore Tilton's advocacy of, 228
    utopianism and, 53–4
    woman's rights movement and, 208
    Woodhull's advocacy of, 139, 149, 290, 296,
        298–304, 337–8, 383–4, 426, 427, 441
    Woodhull's denial of, 426, 427, 441
French Ball of 1869, 339–42, *341*
Frothingham. O. B., 179
Fuller, Margaret, 57, 61


Gardner, Augustus Kinsley, 149
Garrison, Ellen, 314
Garrison, Fanny, *215*
Garrison, William Lloyd, 29, 77, 110, 137,
    214, *215,* 218
Garvey, Andrew, 360, 361
*Gates Ajar, The* (Phelps), 211
Geary, John W., 175–6
*Gentleman's Guide, A,* 150, 154
Godkin, E. L., 313
*Golden Age,* 261, 288, 311, 382, 394, 423

gold market collapse of 1869, 187–90, *190,* 307
gold rush of 1849, 65
Gordon, Laura De Force, 211, 255
Gospel of Love, 36, 85–6
Gould, Jay, 159, 187, 188, 189, 190
Graham, Sylvester, 55, 56
Grand Central Station, 143
Grant, Julia Dent, 187, 188, 190, 252
Grant, Ulysses S., 82–3, 168, 170, 219, 220,
    221–2, 232, 348, 367, 385, 428
    gold market collapse of 1869, 187–8, 189,
        190
    presidential election of 1872, 312, 313, 324,
        325, 326, 346
    Woodhull's meeting with, 252
Great Awakening, 11
Greeley, Arthur (Pickie), 55, 60–2
Greeley, Dotty, 61
Greeley, Gabrielle, 94, 132, *280,* 348
Greeley, Horace, 53, *57,* 65, 94, 119, 157, 159,
    185, 201, *280,* 293
    death of, 347–8
    eccentricities of, 58
    family's conspiracy against, 132
    Kansas State Constitution, proposed
        amendment of, 136
    married life, 56–62
    McFarland-Richardson case, 205
    Nast's cartoons about, 326, *327*
    newspaper career, 56, 58, 347
    New York State Constitution, proposed
        amendment of, 132–4
    Northern Pacific Railroad and, 221
    presidential election of 1872, 313, 324, 325,
        326, 346
    sexual relations, views on, 53–5
    Spiritualism, involvement in, 55
    Tiltons' relationship with, 93–4
    Woodhull's conflict with, 279–81
Greeley, Ida, 62, 94, 132, *280,* 348
Greeley, Mary Cheney, *57,* 93, 168, *280*
    death of, 346–7
    early years, 56
    married life, 56–62
    as mother, 60, 61–2
    New York State Constitution, proposed
        amendment of, 132, 133
    Spiritualism, involvement in, 55–6, 58–9,
        62
    woman's rights advocacy, 132
Greenwood Cemetery, 231, *231,* 259
Grimké, Angelina, 11


Hahnemann, Samuel, 39
Haiti, 97

Halliday, Reverend, 407, 409
Hallowell, Mary, 321
Hanaford, Phebe, 282, 293, 317, 335
Hare, Robert, *36*
Harper, Ida Husted, xiii
Hatcher, Rachael, 112
Hayden, William, 36
Hicks, Elias, 29
homeopathic medicine, 39, 41, 148
Homer, Ohio, 18
Hooker, Isabella Beecher, 3, 4–6, 45, 196, *199*,
   *252*, 264, 271, 291, 294, 311, 322, 323, 334,
   *337*, 346, *351*, *421*, 426
   adultery charge against, 358
   Beecher-Tilton scandal, 5–6, 314–16,
      349–51, 353–9, 375; Plymouth Church
      Committee investigation, 402–3
   death of, 437
   defaming of, 402–3
   defense of Woodhull, 265, 266–7, 270, 281,
      292, 293
   education of, 197
   fictional portrayal of, 294–6
   free love issue, 207
   insanity diagnosis, 358
   later years, 437–8
   lecturing career, 254–5
   married life, 196–7
   as mother, 197
   Moulton's defense of, 415
   National Woman Suffrage Association,
      198, 200, 246–7
   rehabilitation of her reputation, 422–3
   Spiritualism, involvement in, 314, 421–2,
      423, 437–8
   woman's rights advocacy, 197–8
   *Woodhull Memorial* presentation, 5, 247,
      249, 250, 251
   Woodhull's presidential candidacy, 314,
      320–1
   Woodhull's relationship with, 251, 253–7,
      442
Hooker, John, 196, 198, *199*, 208, 254, 270,
   316, 323, 350–1, 422, 437
Hooker, General Joseph, 77
Hooker, Mary, 197, 437
Hooker, Ned, 198
Howard, Flavilla, 16–17
Howard, John Tasker, 89, 120, 164, 219, 222,
   239, 405
Howard, Joseph, 120, 207–8, 382, 393–4, 405,
   406, 409
Howard, Susan, 207, 422
Howe, Julia Ward, 289, 335
Howe, Rebecca, 81–2
Howe, William F., 365, 367, 368, 369, 433

*Huckleberry Finn* (Twain), 69
Hughes, John, 145
*Humanitarian, The,* 441
Hummel, Captain Jake, 14
Hunt, Jane, 38

"Impending Revolution, The" (Woodhull),
   304–5
*Independent,* 73, 75, 88, 90, 91, 98, 138, 221–2,
   233–4, 279, 419
Indians, 428–9
infanticide, 148
   Vaughn case, 172–3, 174–6
Ingersoll, James H., 360
International Workingmen's Association, 273,
   283, 304, 305, 306, 332
Internet, 440

James, Henry, 441
Johnson, Alvin, 347
Johnson, Andrew, 95, 96, 118, 121
   black enfranchisement, 122
   civil rights policy, 98–9, 110
   Fourteenth Amendment, 111
   impeachment of, 110, 166–8
Jones, Mrs. Fernando, 351–2
Julian, George W., 98, 176, 247, 248, 251

Kaiser, John H., 360
Kansas State Constitution, proposed amend-
   ment of, 135–8
Kerr, James, 104
Ku Klux Klan, 111, 362

Langdon, Olivia, 68–9, 196
laudanum, 150
Lawlor, Frank, 66, 159–60
Ledwith, Judge, 275, 277, 278
Lee, Robert E., 82–3
lesbian relationships, 402–3
liberal Republicans, 312–13
*Life of Jesus Christ, The* (H. W. Beecher), 164,
   311, 435
Lincoln, Abraham, 72, 75, 77–8, 80, 82, 94,
   95, 96, 97, 126, *268*
Lincoln, Mary, 16–17
Lincoln, Mary Todd, 78
Lincoln, Robert, 78
Lind, Jenny, 55
Lindbergh, Charles A., 446
Livermore, Mary, *73*, 178, 183, 185, 194, 255,
   257, 275, 282, 284, 317, 335, 370

Livermore, Mary, (*continued*)
  Civil War work, 72–3
  *Woman's Journal,* 207
Livingston, Colonel James, 42
Lohman, Ann (Madame Restell), 145, *145,*
  146, 235, 438–9
Lohman, Charles, 145–6
Loughridge, William, 253
*Love, Marriage, and Divorce, and the Sover-
  eignty of the Individual* (Andrews), 54
Lovejoy, Elijah, 11
Lovett, Simon, 16
Loyalist convention (1866), 122–5
Lyceum lecture circuit, 173

magnetic healing, 20, 68–9, 158
Mansfield, Josie, 66, 159–61, *161,* 162, 189, 191,
  307, 309
Martín, Francisco de, 330
Martin, John Biddulph, 3, 4–7, 440, 441, 442,
  445
Martín, Rosa de, 330
Marx, Karl, 7, 210, 305, 306, 332
Maxwell, Charles, 340, 341, 369
May, Samuel, 214–15
Maynard, Nettie Colburn, 78
McBurney, Robert R., 344
McClellan, General George B., 77
McClintock, Mary Ann, 31, 38, 46
McClintock, Thomas, 31
McFarland, Abby Sage, xv, 203–5, *205*
McFarland, Daniel, 203–5, 216
McFarland-Richardson case, xii, xv, *205*
  deathbed marriage and aftermath, 205–8
  murder of Richardson, 203–5
  trial of McFarland, 216
  Woodhull's comments on, 302
medical practice, 39, 41, 57, 148–9, 210–11, 425
Medico-Legal Society, 366
*Memorial of Victoria C. Woodhull, The, see*
  *Woodhull Memorial*
Memphis, 104, 106, 111–12
Meriwether, Elizabeth, 106, 112, 335
Mesmer, Franz Anton, 19–20
mesmerism, 19–22
Midnight Mission for the Rescue of Fallen
  Women, 150
Miles, Enos, 50
Miles, Margaret Ann, *see* Claflin, Margaret
  Ann
Miller, Elizabeth Smith (Libby), 48, 194
Mills, Darius Ogden, 432
Mitchell, Lucy, 242
Modern Times community, 53
Morrill, Lot M., 110

Morris, District Attorney, 220
Morse, Mrs. (Lib Tilton's mother), 90, 91,
  226–7, 228–30, 235, 259, 261–2
Morse, Nathaniel B., 90, 91, 226
Morse, Samuel F. B., 22
Morton, Colonel, 234
"Mother's Letters to a Daughter on Woman
  Suffrage, A" (Hooker), 198
Mott, James, 47
Mott, Lucretia Coffin, 38, *40,* 46, 52, 179,
  256, 273, 274, 333
Mott, Marianna, 289
Moulton, Emma, 93, 235, 288, 331, 379, 389,
  394, 405, 409–10, 419
Moulton, Francis De Pau (Frank), 92–3, 94,
  127, *238,* 287, 288, 291, 298, 299, 311, 325,
  331–2, 356, *391, 407, 408*
  Beecher-Tilton scandal, 237, 240, 241,
    243–4, 245, 259, 312, 357, 358, 379, 390;
    civil trial, 414–16; mediation effort,
    261–3; Plymouth Church Committee
    investigation, 394, 395–6, 405, 406–10
  married life, 93
  mob attack on, *408,* 409–10
  professional life, 93
Moulton, Louise Chandler, 34–5
*Mrs. Warren's Profession* (Shaw), 440
mulatto women, 154
"My Wife and I" (Stowe), 294–6, *295*

Nast, Thomas, 170, *233, 326, 327,* 328, *329,*
  356, 360
National American Woman Suffrage Associa-
  tion (NAWSA), 3, 4, 434
National Association of Spiritualists, 334–5
National Woman Suffrage Association
  (NWSA), 198, 201, 216, 383
  AERA branches, absorption of, 217
  AWSA-NWSA reconciliation effort, 216
  formation of, 185–6
  goals of, 186
  Hartford convention (1869), 198, 200
  McFarland-Richardson case, 206
  New York convention (1870), 217
  New York convention (1871), 272, 273–5
  New York convention (1872), 314, 316,
    318–20
  presidential election of 1872, 324
  Theodore Tilton's election as president of,
    217
  Washington convention (1870), 214–15
  Washington convention (1871), 246–7, 248
  Washington convention (1872), 310–11
  Woodhull's presidential candidacy, 316, 318
neurasthenia, 148

*New Age and Its Messenger, The* (Evans), 36
New Motor machine, 34
Newton, Jarvis Rogers, 69
New York City, 56
    Broadway, *147*
    development of uptown, 143, 145–6
    draft riots, 78, *79*
    Fifth Avenue, *439*
    fire of 1872, 353
    pollution problem, 142
    poverty and wealth, 142–3, 146
    prostitution in, 150–1
    Reservoir at Forty-second Street and Fifth
        Avenue, 143, *144*
    Tombs, the (prison), 353, *354*
    Tweed Ring, 360–1
    unemployment demonstration of 1874, 386
*New Yorker, The,* 56
New York Free Love League, 53
*New York Observer,* 87
New York Society for the Suppression of
    Vice, 371, *371*
New York State Constitution, proposed
    amendment of, 115–16, 132–4
*New York Times,* 360
*New York Tribune,* 53, 58, 134, 279, 328, 347,
    348
Northern Pacific Railroad, 221, 239, 312, 325,
    361, 362, 385–6, 419
*Norwood* (H. W. Beecher), 93, 94–5, 127,
    164
Noyes, John Humphrey, 16, 53


O'Brien, James, 360
obscenity issue, *see* purity campaign; Wood-
    hull-Claflin obscenity case
Ogontz, Chief, 385, *385*
Ogontz estate, 385
Ormsby, Mary Frost, 4
Orvis, Dr. A., 321–2
Ovington, Edward, 390


Page, William, 94
panic of 1873, 385–6
Pantarchy, 210
Paris Commune, 264, 283, *284,* 305
Paris Commune memorial parade, 305–6
Patton, Abby Hutchinson, 184–5, 200, 335
Patton, Ludlow, 184, 335
Pendergast family, 112
People's Party, *see* Equal Rights Party
Perkins, Mary Beecher, 255, 270, 403, 422,
    437
Perley, D. W., 66

Phelps, Elizabeth Stuart, 211, 316–17, 357, 358
Phillips, Wendell, 11, 29, 94, 98, 101, 102, 110,
    111, 113, 115–16, *115,* 118, 214, 215
    Dickinson's relationship with, 116–17, 174,
        322–3
phrenology, 9
Pitman, Isaac, 53
planchettes, 35
Plymouth Church, *74,* 85, 220, *420*
    admission requirements, 220
    Beecher's dismissal, consideration of, 120–1
    Beecher's twenty-fifth anniversary with,
        335–6
    Bowen's expulsion, 419
    Civil War and, 73
    Friday-night meetings, 240
    Theodore Tilton's expulsion, 380
    victory party for Beecher, 420–21
    Woodhull-Claflin obscenity case, 365
Plymouth Church Committee investigation,
    382
    Beecher's exoneration, 403–4
    Beecher's testimony, 395–7, 399
    coercion of Beecher's accusers, 389
    congregation's vote, 409
    defaming of Hooker, 402–3
    Moulton's testimony, 394
    press coverage, 394, 397–8, 403
    public interest in, 403
    purpose of, 399
    report of the committee, 405–10, *407*
    Stanton's and Anthony's responses to
        charges, 397–9, 400–2
    Lib Tilton's testimony, 390–2
    Theodore Tilton's testimony, 389, 392–4
    Turner's testimony, 399–400
Pomeroy, Samuel C., 176, 247
Porter, General Horace, 187, 188
Post, Amy, 29, *30,* 31, 32, 46–7, 56, 62, 321
Post, Isaac, 29, 32, 48
presidential election of 1872
    Anthony's voting, 345
    campaigning, 324–8
    major party candidates, 312–14
    results, 346
    Woodhull's candidacy, 212, *213,* 265, 272,
        314, 316–21, 324, 328, 332–5, 346
"Principles of Social Freedom, The" (Wood-
    hull), 291, 296–7, 298–304
property rights, 163
prostitution, *152*
    Claflins' prostitution business, 81, 104,
        108–9
    "common wisdom" about prostitutes, 151–2
    drug use and, 150
    finances of, 152–3

prostitution (*continued*)
high finance and, 159, 162
in New York City, 150–1
medications for prostitutes, 150
Southern women's involvement in, 150–1, 154
*Woodhull & Claflin's Weekly* articles on, 265
Woodhull's involvement in, 66, 70, 81
Wood's establishment, 154–5
Psyche Club, 330, 410
purity campaign, 344, 366–7, 369–70, 371–2, 438–40
*see also* Woodhull-Claflin obscenity case
Puységur, Marquis de, 21

Quakerism, 29, 33

radical Republicans, 96, 98, 110, 167
railroad industry, 136, 143, 178, *179*, 361–2, 385–6, 428
Raymond, Rossiter, 406, 407–9
Reconstruction, 96, 98–9
Reform Labor League, 304
Reid, Whitelaw, 174, *175*, 204, 211, 293–4, 312, 313, 323, 325, 326, 347, 348, 377, 394, 432, 433–4
remarriage issue, 216
Republican Party, 220
liberal Republicans, 312–13
radical Republicans, 96, 98, 110, 167
Restell, Madame, *see* Lohman, Ann
revivalism, 8
Beecher's involvement in, 11, 13
Roxy Claflin's enthusiasm for, 8, 13, 17
ritualistic transformation for participants, 17
sexuality of, 16–17
Stanton's interest in, 43–4
*Revolution, The,* 146, 165, 175, 176, 177, 218, 261
Reymert, John, 277, 278
Richards, Joseph, 88
Richardson, Albert, 203, 204–5, *205*
Riddle, Albert Gallatin, 251
Rochester, N.Y., 29
Rochester convention (1848), 46–7
Rose, Ernestine, 185
Rossel, Louis-Nathaniel, 305
Ruffin, James L., 104

*St. Louis Times,* 279
Saint Patrick's Cathedral, 145
Sand, George, 213

Sanger, Margaret, 440
Sanger, William, 440
Savery, Anna, 292
Schurz, Carl, 283
Scott, Rose, 21
Scott, W. A., 206
Scribner family, 22, 24
seamstress profession, 176–7
séances, 35, *59*, 62
Seneca Falls convention (1848), 38–9, 46
sexual relations
Anthony's views on, 118
Beecher's views on, 127
Greeley's views on, 53–5
sexual repression of women, 148–9
Theodore Tilton's views on, 126–8, 228
*see also* free love
Seymour, Horatio, 168, 170
"Shall Women Vote? A Matrimonial Dialogue" (Hooker), 197–8
Shaw, George Bernard, 439–40
Shearman, Thomas, 377, 381, 382, 395, 396, 402
*Siege of London, The* (James), 441
slavery, 11, 72
abolitionism, 11, 29, 31, 45, 89–90
Emancipation Proclamation, 77–8
ending of, 96–7, 125
sexual relations between masters and slaves, 154
Smith, Gerrit, 45, 134, 353
Smith, James W., 325–6
Smith, Laura Cuppy, 363–4, 365, 372, 425, 430
Smith, Peggy, 363–4
Smith, Susan A., 172, 173
Snook, John B., 143
Snyder, John, 14, 15
Snyder, Simon, 14
Sparr, Benjamin, 272, 273, 277–8, 284
Sparr, Polly Claflin, *see* Claflin, Polly
Spear, John Murray, 34, 53
Spencer Grays military unit, 332
spiritscope, *36*
Spiritualism, xi, 27
automatic writing, 32
Claflin family's road show, 51, 67–8, 104, 106
Roxy Claflin's powers, 15–16, 19, 21, 25–6
Tennessee Claflin's powers, 21, 50–1, 80, 81–2, 95
death's prevalence and, 35
decline of, 425–6
Emancipation Proclamation and, 78
fraud, public tests for, 32–3
fraudulent practices, 68, 425, 426

free love and, 34
Greeleys' involvement in, 55–6, 58–9, 62
Hooker's involvement in, 314, 421–2, 423, 437–8
machinery of, 34, *36*
magnetic healing, 20, 68–9, 158
mediumship and clairvoyance, 31, 35
mesmerism, 19–22
number of adherents, 78, 139
post-war popularity, 139
rappings by spirits, 28–9, 31
religious leaders and, 36
séances, 35, *59*, 62
social context of Spiritualism's rise, 33
Stowe's involvement in, 22, 267
Swedenborg and, 33–4
tables as catalysts to transmit thoughts of spirits, 31
Lib Tilton's involvement in, 168–9
Theodore Tilton's involvement in, 138–9
unbroken chain of communication, 33
Vanderbilt's involvement in, 143, 156
woman's rights movement and, xiii–xiv, 48–9
women's attraction to, 34–7
Woodhull's powers, xiv, 7, 21, 24–5, 26, 51–2, 63, 66–7, 68, 69–70, 140–1, 158, 159, 213–14, 254, 289, 305–6, 367, 424, 425–6, 442
Stanton, Daniel (Neil), 78, 79
Stanton, Edwin M., 167
Stanton, Elizabeth Cady, xi, 3, *40*, 55, 79–80, 94, 100, 102, 115, 146, 198, 224, 226, 337, *391, 436*
American Equal Rights Association, 178, 179–81, 185
American Woman Suffrage Association, 201
Anthony's partnership with, 47–8
Bayard's relationship with, 44–5
Beecher-Tilton scandal, 259, 260, 282, 351–2, 354–5, 358–9, 375; Plymouth Church Committee investigation, 390–1, 393, 397–9, 403–4
clothing issue, 194
congressional candidacy, 117–18
death of, 435
Declaration of Rights and Sentiments, 38–9
defense of Woodhull, 282, 306–7
divorce laws, 206, 216
draft riots, 78
early years, 41–3
education of, 43
enfranchisement of blacks and women simultaneously, 100–1, 102, 116, 134

Fifteenth Amendment, 134
Fourteenth Amendment, 111
free love issue, 206, 207–8
homeopathic medicine, 39, 41
Kansas State Constitution, proposed amendment of, 136, 137
later years, 434–5
lecturing career, 173
married life, 39, 45, 136, 196
National Woman Suffrage Association, 185–6, 200, 214–15, 217, 246–7, 272, 273, 311, 318
newspaper career, 177
New York State Constitution, proposed amendment of, 132–4
oppression, sense of, 39, 41, 42, 43, 134–5
presidential election of 1872, 313–14, 316, 318, 332–4
racism of, 102, 134, 180–1
radicalism of, 177–8
revivalism, interest in, 43–4
ridicule and reproach directed at, 218
Rochester convention (1848), 47
Seneca Falls convention (1848), 38–9, 46
Spiritualism and, 48
suffrage resolution, 46
Train, attitude toward, 138
Vaughn infanticide case, 175–6
Woodhull's lasting effect on woman's rights movement, 427
Woodhull's presidential candidacy, 314, 316, 318, 320, 321, 332–4
Woodhull's relationship with, 252–3, 435
Woodhull's Spiritualism, use of, 310
Stanton, Henry, 39, 45, 46, 78, 79, 136, 186, 196
Stanton, Margaret, 435
Stearns, Sara Burger, 281
Stevens, Thaddeus, 110, 111, 118, 123, 124, 168
stirpiculture, 426–7
Stokes, Edward Stiles (Ned), xii, 161–2, 307, *308, 309*
Stone, Lucy, 4, 48, 72, 123, 137, 163, 178, 183–4, *202*, 228, 328, 333, 346, 393, 423, 434
American Woman Suffrage Association, 200–1
AWSA-NWSA reconciliation effort, 217
free love, 206–7
husband's extramarital affair, 184–5, 200, 335
*Woman's Journal*, 207
Storrs, Richard Salter, 89, 336, 377, *378*, 379, 380, 381
Stout, Joseph, 82
Stowe, Calvin, 196, 267, *268*

Stowe, Fred, 437
Stowe, Harriet Beecher, 196, 197, 219, 255–6,
    265, 266, *268*, 324, *351*, 357, 363, 403, 437
  Byron book, 198
  defense of Hooker, 422–3
  satire on Woodhull, 294–6
  Spiritualism, involvement in, 22, 267
  *Woman's Journal,* 207
  Woodhull, attitude toward, 267, 270
Stowe, Henry, 267
Strong, George Templeton, 150–1, 412, 414
Sumner, Charles, 251
Supreme Court, U.S., 440
Sutherland, William, 372
Swedenborg, Emanuel, 33–4

Tappan, Lewis, 89
telegraph, 22, 33
Theosophy, 426
Thirteenth Amendment, 96–97, 98
*Thunderbolt,* 376–7
Tilton, Alice, 92, 165
Tilton, Elizabeth Richards (Lib), 77, 84, 86,
    *89*, 99, 126, *129*, 138, 178–9, 186, *243*, *391*,
    *417*
  AWSA-NWSA reconciliation effort, 217
  birthing experiences, 91
  Bullard's friendship with, 224, 262–3
  isolation period, 230–1
  married life, 86–7, 88, 90–3, 127–8, 130–1,
    165–6, 169, 224
  post-scandal life, 423–4, 438
  religious fervor, 91
  separation from Theodore, 226–30, 390
  son's death, 37
  Spiritualism, involvement in, 168–9
  woman's rights advocacy, 102–4, 165
  Woodhull's relationship with, 287
  *see also* Beecher-Lib Tilton relationship;
    Beecher-Tilton scandal; Plymouth
    Church Committee investigation
Tilton, Florry, 77, 92, 438
Tilton, Matilda, 91
Tilton, Paul, 37, 165, 168–9
Tilton, Ralph, 223, 263
Tilton, Theodore, 52, 84, *89*, 115, 118, *129*, 201,
    291, 317, 348, *391*, 446
  acquisitiveness of, 92
  anti-corruption efforts, 233
  AWSA-NWSA reconciliation effort, 217
  Beecher's relationship with, 75, 76, 88, 89,
    90, 94, 224; deterioration of, 99–100,
    112, 113, 114–15, 119
  Beecher-Lib Tilton relationship: assess-
    ment of, 169–70; concern about, 128–30

biography of Woodhull, 19, 25, 140,
    288–90
black enfranchisement, 112, 116, 122–5
Bowen's relationship with, 75, 220–1,
    232–4, 235–6, 239–40
Bullard's affair with, 163–4, 165, 218
civil rights legislation, 98, 99, 325–6
enfranchisement of blacks and women
    simultaneously, 101
expulsion from Plymouth Church, 380
Grant, criticism of, 220–1, 232
Johnson's impeachment, 110, 167, 168
Kansas State Constitution, proposed
    amendment of, 136
Lincoln and, 77
Loyalist convention, 122, 123–5
married life, 86–7, 88, 90–3, 127–8, 130–1,
    165–6, 169, 224
National Woman Suffrage Association,
    217
newspaper career, 87–8, 90, 91, 138, 219,
    232–4, 239–40, 261
Northern Pacific Railroad and, 221
post-scandal life, 423, 438
presidential election of 1872, 312–13,
    324–6
questioning of his beliefs, 125–6, 138
*The Revolution,* 217
separation from Lib, 226–30, 390
sexual views, 126–8, 228
Spiritualism, involvement in, 138–9
Woodhull's "Principles of Social Freedom"
    speech, 298–9, 303, 304
Woodhull's relationship with, 287–90,
    312–13, 414
*see also* Beecher-Tilton scandal; Plymouth
    Church Committee investigation
Tilton home in Brooklyn, 92
*Tilton v. Beecher* civil trial, 410, 411–12, *413*,
    414–16, *417*, 418
Tombs, the (prison), 353, *354*
Townsend, Steven, 276–7, 278
Tracy, Benjamin, 220, 234, 240, 343, 381, 382,
    389, 390, 392, 394, 414, 423
Train, George Francis, 136–7, *137*, 138, 178,
    179
  obscenity case against, 369–70
*Train Ligue, The,* 369
Treat, Joseph, 410
*Treatise on Domestic Economy* (Catharine
    Beecher), 22–4, 59–60
"True Story of Lady Byron's Life, The"
    (Stowe), 198
Truman, Achsah, 284
Tucker, Benjamin, 383, 384
Tufts, Mrs. (medium), 156

Turner, Elizabeth (Bessie), 229, 235, 241, 261, 399–400, *400*
Twain, Mark, 69, 117, 196, 403, 422
Tweed, William Marcy, 147–8, 161, *233,* 360–1

*Uncle Tom's Cabin* (Stowe), 197
Underground Railroad, 29
Union Pacific Railroad, 136, 361
utopianism, 53–4, 210

Vanderbilt, Commodore Cornelius, xi, *144,* 148, 309, 347
  California gold rush and, 65
  Tennessee Claflin's relationship with, 156, 157–8, 192–3, 273
  death of, 429–30
  gold market collapse of 1869, 188, 189, 190
  married life, 156–7
  railroad interests, 143, 159, 162
  sexual appetite, 156, 157
  Spiritualism, involvement in, 143, 156
  Woodhull, Claflin & Co., 190, 191, 192
  Woodhull's attack on, 304–5
  Woodhull's relationship with, 156, 157–9, 162, 273
Vanderbilt, Cornelius Jeremiah, 158–9, 430
Vanderbilt, Frank Crawford, 193, 429, 430
Van der Bilt, Phebe Hand, 157, 158
Vanderbilt, Sophia, 157, 430
Vanderbilt, William Henry, 143, 157, 158, 192, 304, 430, 431
Vanderbilt Will Trial, 430–1
Vaughn, Hester, xii, xiv–xv, 172–3, 174–6
venereal disease, 149
Verne, Jules, 136
*Voices from the Spirit World* (Post), 32

Warner, Charles Dudley, 196
Warren, Josiah, 53
Warren, Richard, 66
Waterloo Congregational Friends, 29, 33, 38
Webster, Erastus D., 232–3, 234
*Weekly Argus,* 370
Western, Lucy, 114
White Leagues, 428
Wilkeson, Samuel, 164, 219, 221, 239, 259–61, *260,* 311, 312, 375, 389, 393, 398, 399, 405, 407, 435
Willets, George, 48
*Woman's Bible, The* (Stanton), 435
"Woman's Influence in Politics" (H. W. Beecher), 100
*Woman's Journal,* 207, 255, 328, 334

Woman's Property Act, 163
woman's rights movement, xi
  clothing issue, 194
  Declaration of Rights and Sentiments, 38–9
  divisions within, 177–8, 185–6, 216–18, 427
  1850s convention, *135*
  free love and, 208
  property rights, 163
  Rochester convention (1848), 46–7
  Seneca Falls convention (1848), 38–9, 46
  Spiritualism and, xiii–xiv, 48–9
  Stanton-Anthony partnership, 47–8
  Stanton's post-mortem on, 435
  Lib Tilton's involvement in, 102–4, 165
  Woodhull's lasting effect, 427
  *see also* American Equal Rights Association; woman suffrage
Woman's Rights Society, 101, 112–13
woman suffrage
  AERA's position on, 180–2
  Beecher's support, 100
  black enfranchisement and, 100–2, 112–13, 115–16, 134
  congressional consideration of, 247, 248–51, 253
  constitutional defense of, 250
  Democratic National Convention of 1868 and, 168
  failure in nineteenth century, 282–3
  Fifteenth Amendment and, 134
  Kansas State Constitution, proposed amendment of, 135–8
  New York State Constitution, proposed amendment of, 115–16, 132–4
  presidential election of 1872 and, 313–14
  Sixteenth Amendment proposal, 247, 248
  Stanton's resolution on, 46
  success in 1920, 437
  *Woodhull Memorial,* 247–51
  *see also* American Woman Suffrage Association; National Woman Suffrage Association
*Woman Suffrage and Woman's Profession* (Catharine Beecher), 265
women of fashion, 160
Women's Bureau, 185
women's position in society, 12–13, 22–4, 42, 148–9
Wood, Annie, 146, 159, 160, 307, 309, 339
  prostitution business, 154–5
Woodford, General Stewart L., 222
Woodhull, Byron, 64, 70, 80, 209, 332
Woodhull, Canning (Doc), 52, 63–5, 70, 71, 80, 210, 277, 330–1

Woodhull, Claflin & Co., 162, 329
   establishment of, 190–1
   success of, 191–2
Woodhull, Victoria Claflin, *ii*, xi, *xii*, xv, *105*,
      *192, 329, 444, 447*
   acting career, 65–6
   Anthony's first meeting with, 193
   Anthony's relationship with, 252–3, 256–7
   appearance of, 3–4, 24, 80–1
   Catharine Beecher's relationship with,
      266–7, 269–70, 292
   H. W. Beecher's relationship with, 290–1,
      296–7, 331, 336
   Beecher-Tilton scandal, 258, 286, 287–8,
      314–15, 335, 336, 337–8, 374–5; civil trial,
      414; Plymouth Church Committee
      investigation, 392–3, 396–7
   biography of, 19, 25, 140, 288–90
   birth of, 18
   blackmailing of suffrage figures, 316–18, 321
   Butler's relationship with, 211–12
   childhood of, 18–19, 21, 22, 24–7
   "cigar girl" experience, 65
   Roxy Claflin's suit against Blood, 276
   conception of, 17
   death of, 446
   Delmonico's incident, 194–5
   England, move to, 431
   entitlement, feeling of, 26
   exorcism of, 424
   fictional portrayals of, 294–6, 441
   financial downfall, 329–30, 382–3
   free love, advocacy of, 139, 149, 290, 296,
      298–304, 337–8, 383–4, 426, 427, 441
   gold market collapse of 1869, 188, 189, 190
   Grant's meeting with, 252
   Greeley's conflict with, 279–81
   Hooker's relationship with, 251, 253–7, 442
   hostessing by, 211
   *The Humanitarian*, 441
   intelligence of, 26
   Jesus Christ, identification with, 367
   labor groups, alliance with, 264–5, 273,
      304–6, 332
   lasting effect on woman's rights movement,
      427
   later years, 445–7
   lecturing career, 254, 255, 273–4, 288, 296,
      298–305, 363–5, 386–8, 410, 411, 426–7
   manufactured background, 270–1, 440–2
   marriage to Blood, 106, 107, 109, 139–40,
      276–7, 424
   marriage to Martin, 440, 441, 442, 445
   marriage to Woodhull, 52, 63–5, 70–1, 80
   McFarland-Richardson case, 302
   men's clothing, preference for, 194

   as mother, 64, 70–1
   Moulton's defense of, 415
   "Mrs. Satan" cartoon, 328, *329*
   National Woman Suffrage Association,
      272, 273–4
   near-death experience, 372–3, 374, 382
   New York City, move to, 140–1, 142, 146–7
   Paris Commune memorial parade, 305–6
   Paris Commune uprising, 283
   persecution of, 255–6, 279–82, 284–6,
      292–6, 328–9, 331–2, 410
   political writings, 213–14
   power to alleviate burdens of women,
      263–4
   preaching career, 26–7
   presidential candidacy of 1872, 212, *213*,
      265, 272, 314, 316–21, 324, 328, 332–5,
      346
   presidential candidacy of 1892, 3–7, 440–1
   prostitution business, analysis of, 151–3
   prostitution by, 66, 70, 81
   prostitution medications business, 149–50
   "ruler of the whole world" self-image, 214,
      254
   sexual abuse by father, 51–2
   Spiritualist powers, xiv, 7, 21, 26, 51–2, 63,
      66–7, 68, 69–70, 140–1, 158, 159, 213–14,
      254, 289, 305–6, 310, 367, 424, 425–6,
      442; first spiritual vision, 24–5
   Spiritualist road show, 51, 68, 104, 106
   Stanton's relationship with, 252–3, 435
   Lib Tilton's relationship with, 287
   Theodore Tilton's relationship with,
      287–90, 312–13, 414
   Vanderbilt, attack on, 304–5
   Vanderbilt's relationship with, 156, 157–9,
      162, 273
   Vanderbilt Will Trial, 430–1
   wealth accumulation, 162, 188, 189, 190,
      430–1, 445
   white rose trademark, 3
   woman's rights mission, beginning of, 210
   as women's confidante, 69, 104
   *Woodhull Memorial* presentation, *xii*, 5,
      247, 248–51
   *see also* Woodhull, Claflin & Co.; *Woodhull
      & Claflin's Weekly*; Woodhull-Claflin
      obscenity case
Woodhull, Zulu Maud, 70–1, 80, 209, 332,
      *333*, 372, 446
*Woodhull & Claflin's Weekly*, 212–14, *213*, 248,
      279, 285, 290, 305, 332, 363, 383
   Beecher-Tilton scandal, article on, 337–8
   closing of, 427
   "French Ball" article, 339–42
   Woodhull's active involvement, 265

Woodhull-Claflin house in New York, 209
Woodhull-Claflin obscenity case
  acquittal of Woodhull and Claflin, 372,
    374–5
  arrests of Woodhull and Claflin, 344–5,
    362–3, 364, 365, 372
  articles on Beecher and Challis, 337–43
  Butler's intervention, 368
  exposure as conspiracy against Woodhull,
    377
  hearings, 365, 367, 368, 372
  hypocrisy of Comstock's actions, 370–1
  imprisonment of Woodhull and Claflin,
    353, 365
  libel actions, 368–9, 372

  Plymouth Church's role, 365
  public opinion on, 370
  toll on Woodhull, 367–8, 372
  Train's intervention, 369–70
  Woodhull's speech about, 363–5
*Woodhull Memorial,* xii, 5, 247–51, 383
Workingwomen's Association, 175, 176–7
Worth, Oliver, 234
Wright, Eliza, 271
Wright, Martha Coffin, 38, *40,* 52, 256, 270–1,
  275, 285, 304, 314, 322, 324, 328, 370

Young Men's Christian Association (YMCA),
  344, 370, 371

# ILLUSTRATION CREDITS

Barbara Goldsmith, author of *Little Gloria . . . Happy at Last* and *Johnson v. Johnson*, is a social historian. A trustee of the New York Public Library, she lives in New York City.